Ronnie Peterson

A photographic portrait

Bengt-Ronnie Peterson was born on 14 February 1944 in Örebro, Sweden. A professional racing driver almost all his adult life, he enjoyed tennis, badminton, squash and occasionally golf, and was a collector of tropical fish. He was married to Barbro, and they had a daughter, Nina. He died on 11 September 1978 in Milan, Italy.

First published in September 2008

A catalogue record for this book is available from the British Library

ISBN 978 1 84425 548 1

Library of Congress control no 2008922585

Published by Haynes Publishing,
Sparkford, Yeovil, Somerset BA22 7JJ, UK
Tel: 01963 442030 Fax: 01963 440001
Int. tel: +44 1963 442030 Int. fax: +44 1963 440001
E-mail: sales@haynes.co.uk
Website: www.haynes.co.uk

Haynes North America Inc.
861 Lawrence Drive, Newbury Park,
California 91320, USA

All pictures in this book are courtesy of LAT Photographic, with the exception of those on pages 18–23 (Tommy Peterson Collection) and page 175 (Michael Keppel/GP Library).

The publisher wishes to thank all at LAT for their collaboration on this book, and in particular Peter Higham, Kathy Ager, Tim Wright, Kevin Wood, Stephen Carpenter, Matt Smith and Emma Champion. In addition Quentin Spurring wishes to thank Tommy Peterson, Mark Burgess (editor of *Karting* magazine), and Joakim Thedin and Michael Olsson of the Ronnie Peterson Museum in Örebro.

Design and layout by Richard Parsons

Printed and bound in Great Britain by
J. H. Haynes & Co. Ltd

CONTENTS PAGE Quintessential Ronnie. Opposite-locking the JPS Lotus 72 on home ground at Anderstorp on his way to second place in the 1973 Swedish Grand Prix.

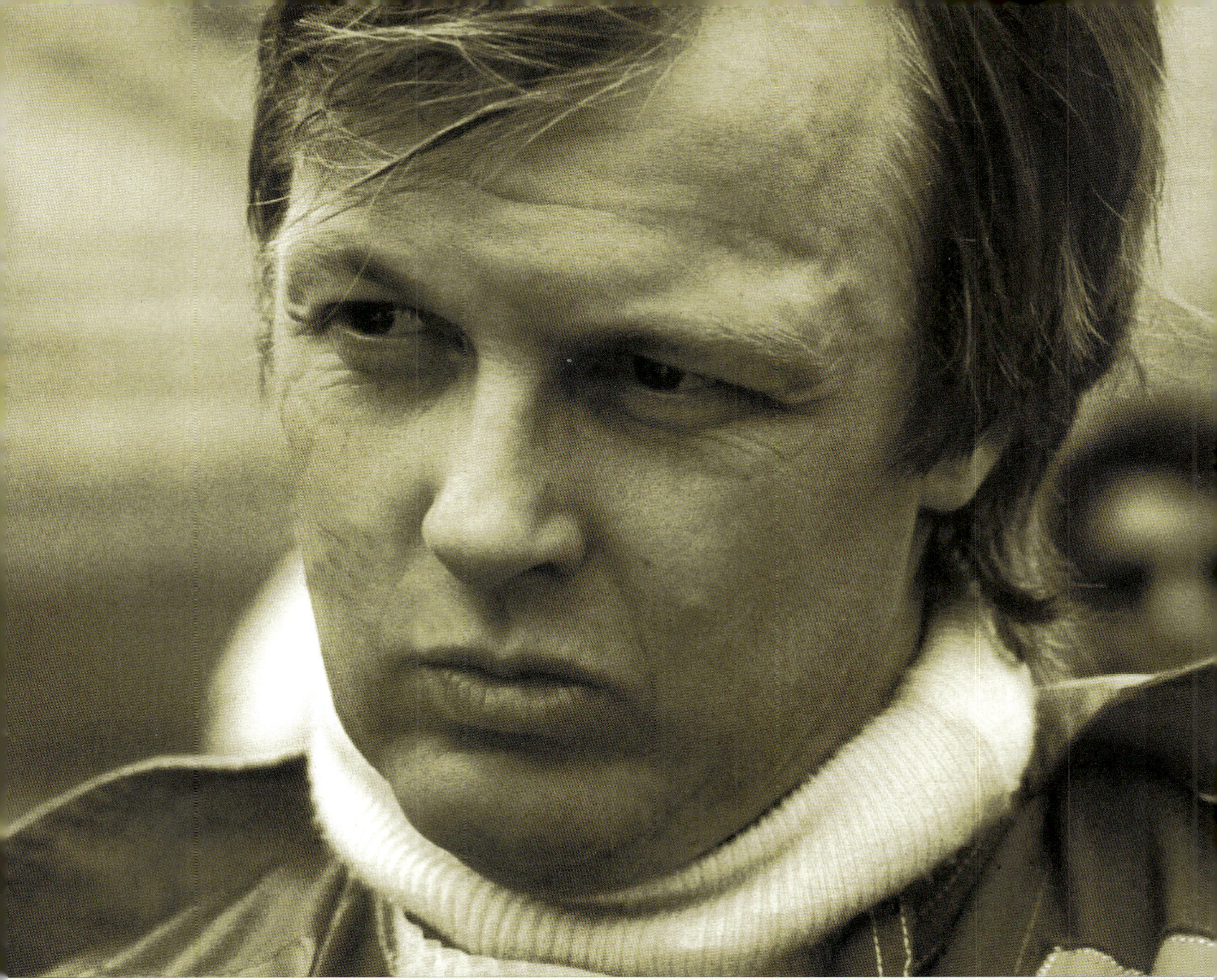

Ronnie Peterson

A photographic portrait

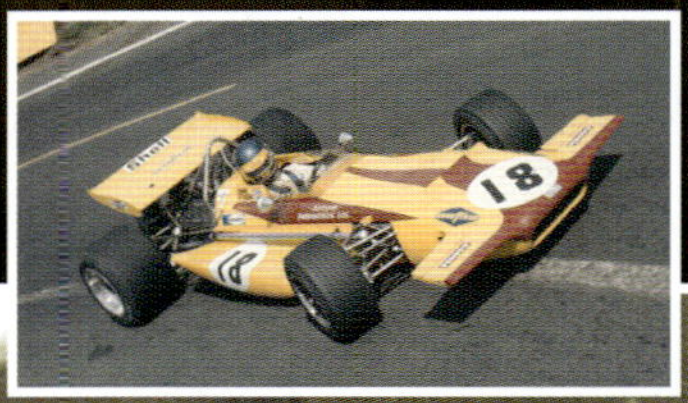

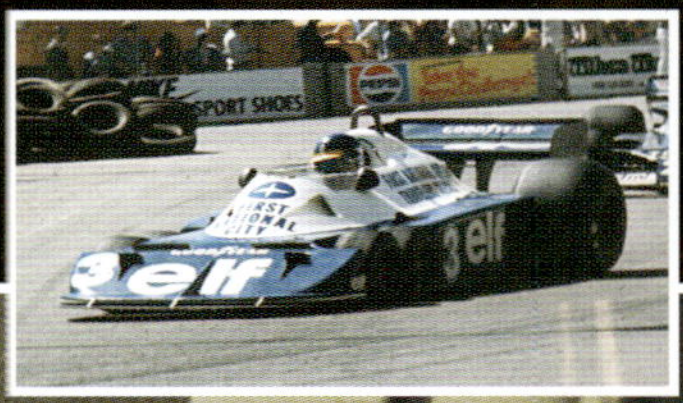

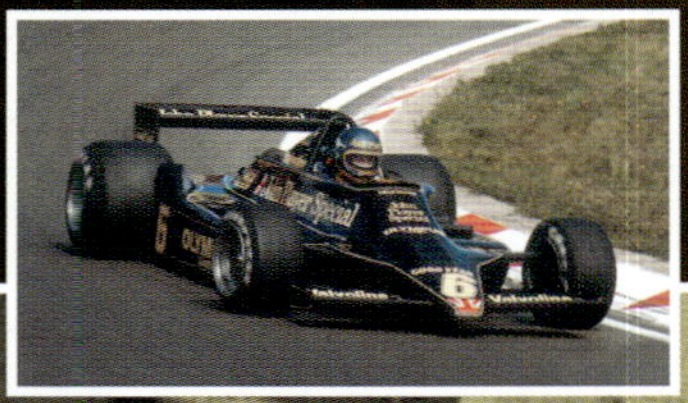

Photographs by **LAT** • Photo commentary by **Quentin Spurring** • Reminiscences by **Alan Henry**

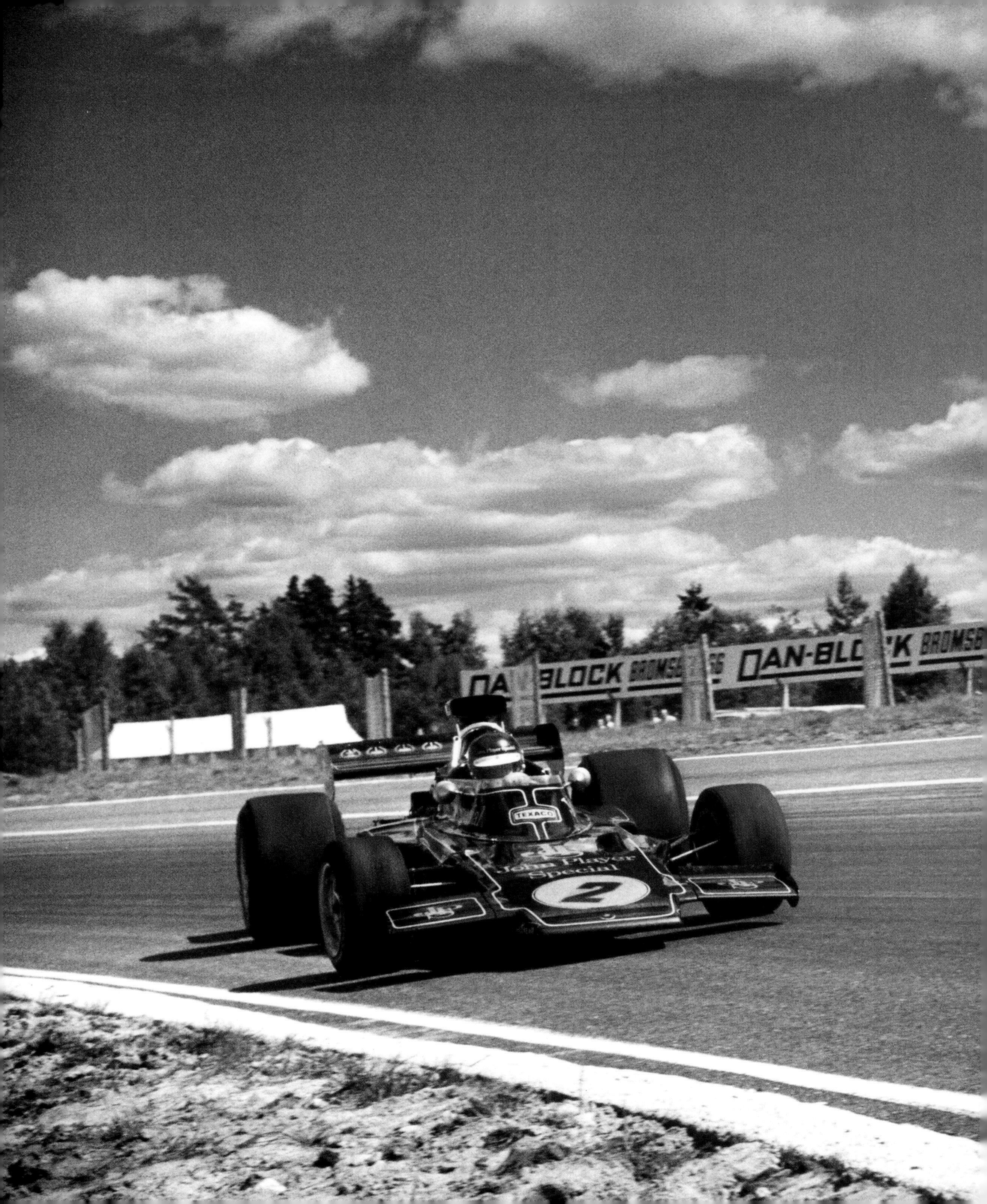
DAN-BLOCK
TEXACO
John Player Special
2

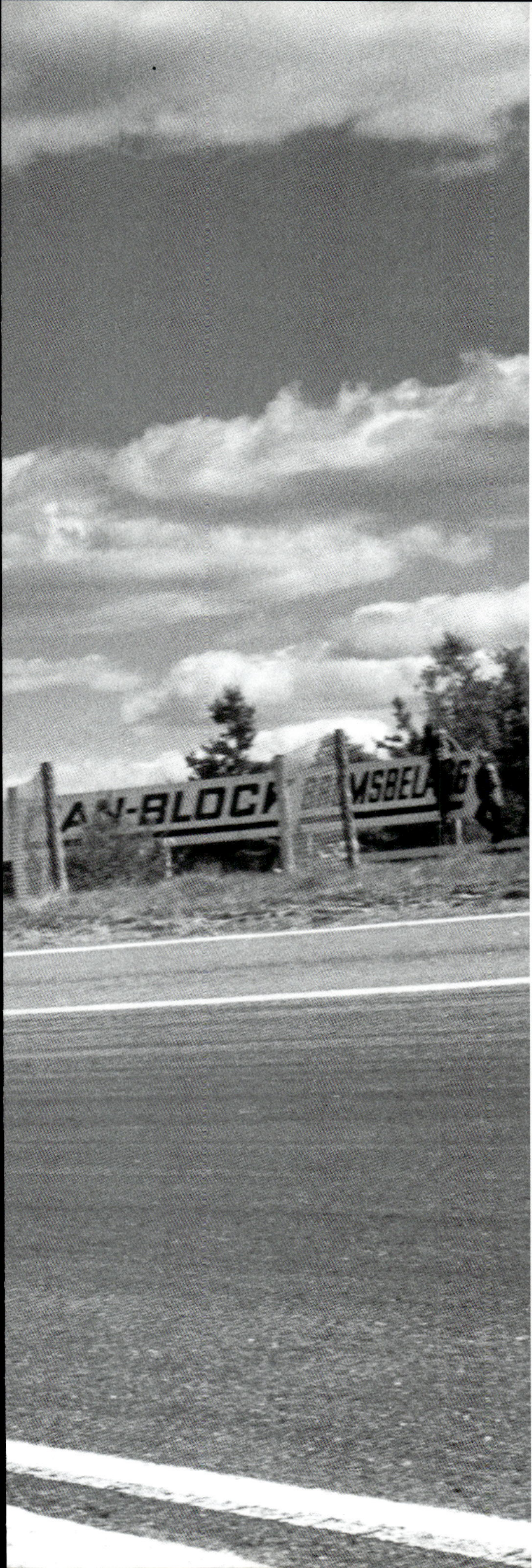

CONTENTS

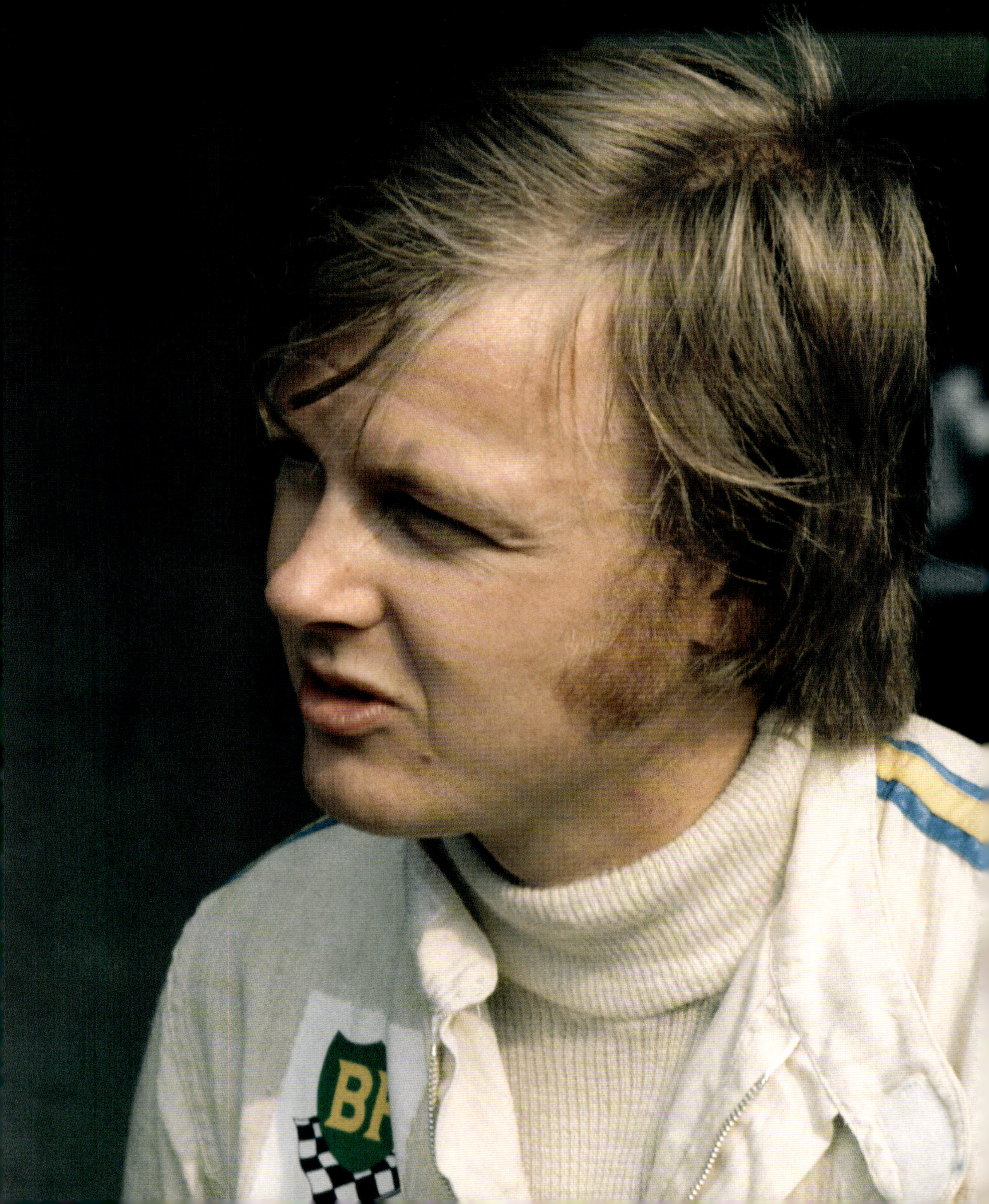

Ronnie Peterson

BY ALAN HENRY

Ronnie Peterson was more than a towering F1 talent. In so many ways he defined an era of motorsport history, a time when the sport's structures were clearly defined and the path to the top – through F3 and then via F2 into F1 – was formally and clearly delineated.

You just knew that if a bright young hopeful beat an established driver in F2 then that new boy was going to travel all the way to stardom. So it was with Ronnie, who became one of my closest friends in the F1 business – probably my closest after his sometime team-mate Niki Lauda – through to the day he died in tragically unnecessary circumstances at Monza 30 years ago.

Yet there was an overwhelming streak of normality to this brilliant driver. It wasn't a case of being a tax exile with a private jet to carry him to the races. Jackie Stewart and Mario Andretti apart, there were almost no multi-millionaires on the starting grid. Ronnie and his wife Barbro travelled to the distant Grands Prix on commercial airliners, even rubbing shoulders with members of the fourth estate, and often drove to races in Europe.

Home for much of his time in F1 was a neat, modern and unremarkable detached house on the fringes of Maidenhead. On one occasion I visited him and he came to pick me up at the railway station. His big blue Mercedes S-class saloon swept into the station car park amidst a shriek of tortured tyres. But nobody gave him a second glance. There must be times when Lewis Hamilton craves such anonymity. F1 had become big business by the 1970s but nothing approaching the sort of levels reached after the sport started its dash for growth in the '80s.

Later in the '70s, a year or two before his death, Ronnie and Barbro moved to an elegant country house in the nearby village of Cookham Dean. It was spacious and tasteful, the sort of home in which you might expect a successful surgeon or stockbroker to be living today. By 1978 F1 drivers were still sufficiently connected with normality that they lived on a street like anybody else. And it was from this home in rural Buckinghamshire that he departed for that fated trip to his final race.

I still find it hard to believe that more than a generation has passed since that horrifying startline shunt at Monza left this fine man with legs so badly shattered that, within hours, a bone marrow embolism escaped into his bloodstream and killed him. It will come as no surprise, I'm sure, that I can still remember the precise place in the paddock where I last chatted with him.

"Morning, Albatross," he said cheerfully. He'd called me that ever since the March F2 lads had introduced him and Niki Lauda to the zany, off-beat humour of *Monty Python's Flying Circus* during his European Trophy-winning '71 season. Looking back, it's lost in the mists of time quite how we got it across to a baker's boy from rural Sweden and a well-heeled banker's son from Vienna that shouting "Stormy Petrel on a stick" or "What flavour is it? It's bleedin' seabird flavour" was so uproariously amusing. But both Ronnie and Niki joined in and laughed politely. They must have thought we were crazy.

From a purely personal perspective, that dark afternoon at Monza marked the end of an odyssey that had begun on a bright, breezy and very cold day at Silverstone in late January 1970. The occasion was the launch of the March 701 and there was a media scrum the like of which you've rarely seen, even in today's high-profile world of intensely televised international sport.

From one pit, reigning World Champion Jackie Stewart, wearing an unusual helicopter pilot's helmet with tinted

OPPOSITE The Formula 1 'rookie', in 1970. Commercial pressures meant that Ronnie was unexpectedly omitted from the March factory team and had to undertake his maiden Grand Prix season with a low-budget privateer.

OPPOSITE Free of over-confident engineering adventures at March, Ronnie was happily installed at John Player Team Lotus in 1973. That year he secured his maiden Grand Prix victory at Paul Ricard, and three more by season's end.

vizor, was having his first run in the Tyrrell team's dark blue 701. Further along, Chris Amon was getting to grips with the power and punch of a Cosworth DFV for the first time in his career, having turned his back on the Ferrari team the previous year after three largely fruitless seasons.

At the epicentre of all this activity were March directors Max Mosley and Robin Herd, both masters of the polished sales spiel, who spent their day 'bigging up' this latest commercial venture in their uniquely compelling style.

Mingling in this crowd of racing personalities was a tall, blond and curiously youthful-looking Swede wearing an ankle-length fur coat complete with astrakhan collar. Both his wrists bore horrifying scarlet burns, the legacy of a frightening accident at the wheel of the prototype F3 March 693 the previous year at Montlhéry, near Paris.

"Looking back, it's lost in the mists of time quite how we got it across to a baker's boy from rural Sweden that shouting 'Stormy Petrel on a stick' or 'What flavour is it? It's bleedin' seabird flavour' was so uproariously amusing."

His name was Ronnie Peterson and he looked much younger than his 27 years. This was the first time I had met Ronnie and never could I have imagined just what a friend this self-effacing character would become or how his death would have such a profound effect on me, an effect that lingers still to this day, nearly 30 years later.

Bengt-Ronnie Peterson was the son of a provincial Swedish baker, an unlikely background, you might think, for one of the most exciting talents ever to practise the art of opposite-lock motoring in the cockpit of an F1 car. Outwardly he was a mild-mannered fellow who projected a cautiously unruffled charm. But when the vizor on that helmet snapped down, Peterson was transformed into a dazzlingly spectacular automotive acrobat.

F3 in the mid-1960s was probably the most effective ever cauldron in which to forge a generation of future Grand Prix stars. The high-revving 1-litre Cosworth engines were tricky to keep 'on the cam' and the absence of wings – still well over the horizon in the future as far as this cut-throat junior formula was concerned – meant that the drivers had to learn how to juggle tyre pressures and rollbar settings in a bid to squeeze the last ounce of speed from their machines. Life was less technical, but driver skill was arguably more at a premium.

At this early stage in his career, the British F3 brigade hadn't heard much about Ronnie Peterson apart from odd snatches of conversation about a young Swede who was "amazingly quick" from those UK-based competitors who struck out into Scandinavia in a bid to gain a taste of F3 success away from the main championship contests.

Yet the cut-and-thrust of F3 would deliver the defining moment of Ronnie's emergent career. Now equipped with one of the legendary, short-wheelbase, kart-derived Tecno F3 cars, he journeyed to Monaco in 1969 to compete in the prestigious Monaco Grand Prix supporting race. Added piquancy was given to the battle by the fact that Ronnie would be going head-to-head with his arch-rival Reine Wisell, who was driving the works Chevron.

They both won their respective heats, and the final, from the first corner, was Ronnie versus Reine in one of the most frantic confrontations ever seen through those sunlit streets. They touched wheels and grazed barriers all round the Monaco track, but it was Reine who blinked first, sliding up the escape road at the chicane. Ronnie was home and dry as the clear winner.

Nearly 30 years after Ronnie's death I was seeking shade from the oppressively humid heat which blanketed the paddock at Sepang, home of the Malaysian Grand Prix, when McLaren boss Ron Dennis beckoned me towards a figure sitting at one of the other tables. It was Reine Wisell, and we soon settled down to debate the ins and outs of that Monaco F3 event – let it be whispered – some 39 years earlier.

"Ronnie had the edge, no question," said Reine wistfully, "and once I'd gone up that escape road there was just no chance of my getting back on terms with him." Then he added, with a twinkle in his eyes, "Even now, I do think the marshals held me for a long time before waving me back into the race. Probably because Jean-Pierre Jabouille was coming up fast in third place driving an Alpine-Renault!"

Alan Rees was watching and vowed to approach Ronnie at the following weekend's Spring Bank Holiday International at Crystal Palace, that parkland circuit in south London which always seemed to engender an attractive garden party atmosphere at its meetings. Ronnie took second place to Tim Schenken's Brabham, outfumbled by a backmarker in the sprint to the chequered flag.

Rees then made his move, but was not at all surprised to find that he was second in the queue. The works Tecno team had signed Ronnie to drive one of their F2 cars in the prestigious Monza Lottery Grand Prix and Ronnie's sense of propriety told him that he should wait until he'd completed that event before talking to Rees any further.

He duly finished seventh in that lurid, flat-out blind, only losing a possible debut F2 victory when he touched

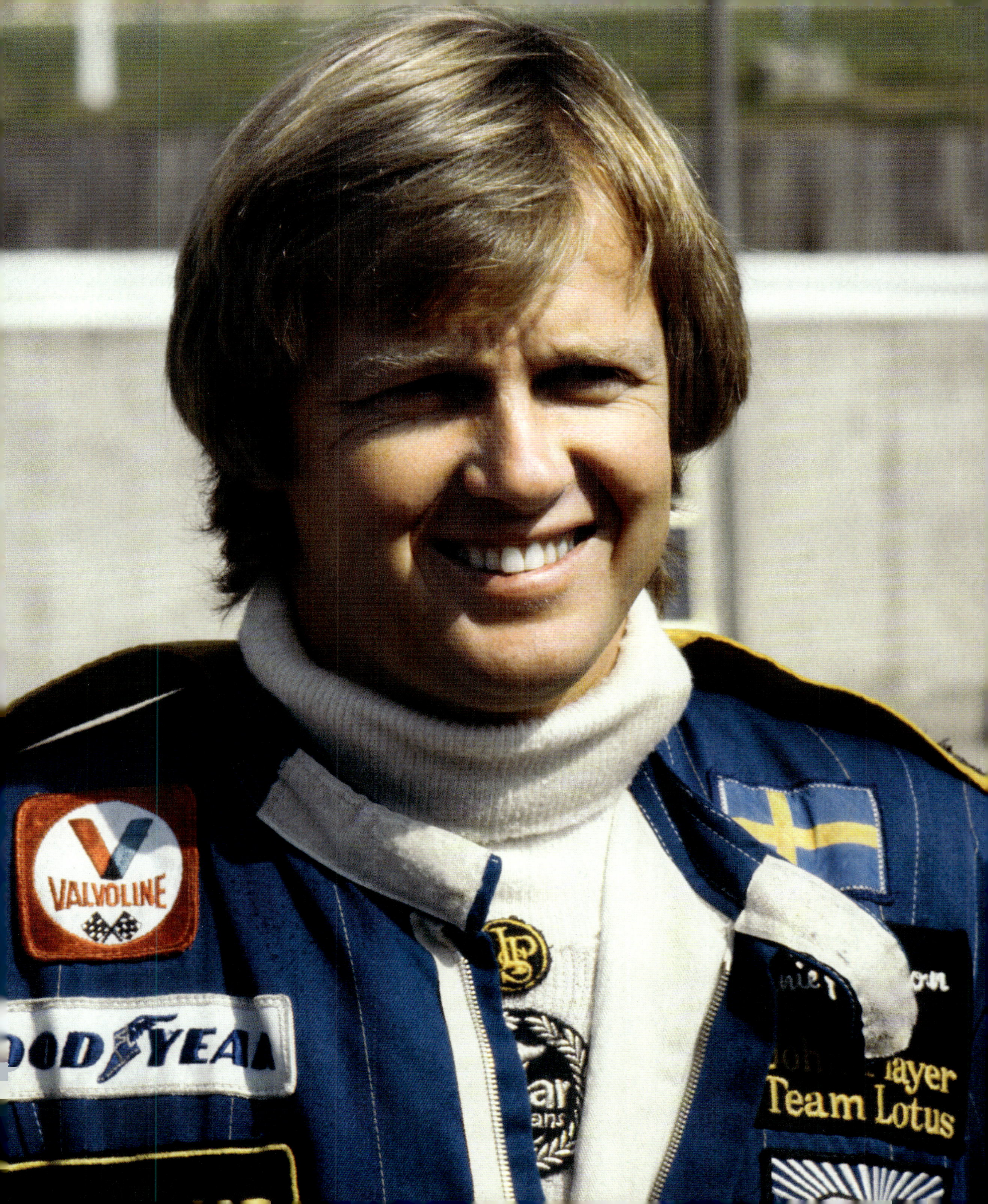
VALVOLINE
Team Lotus

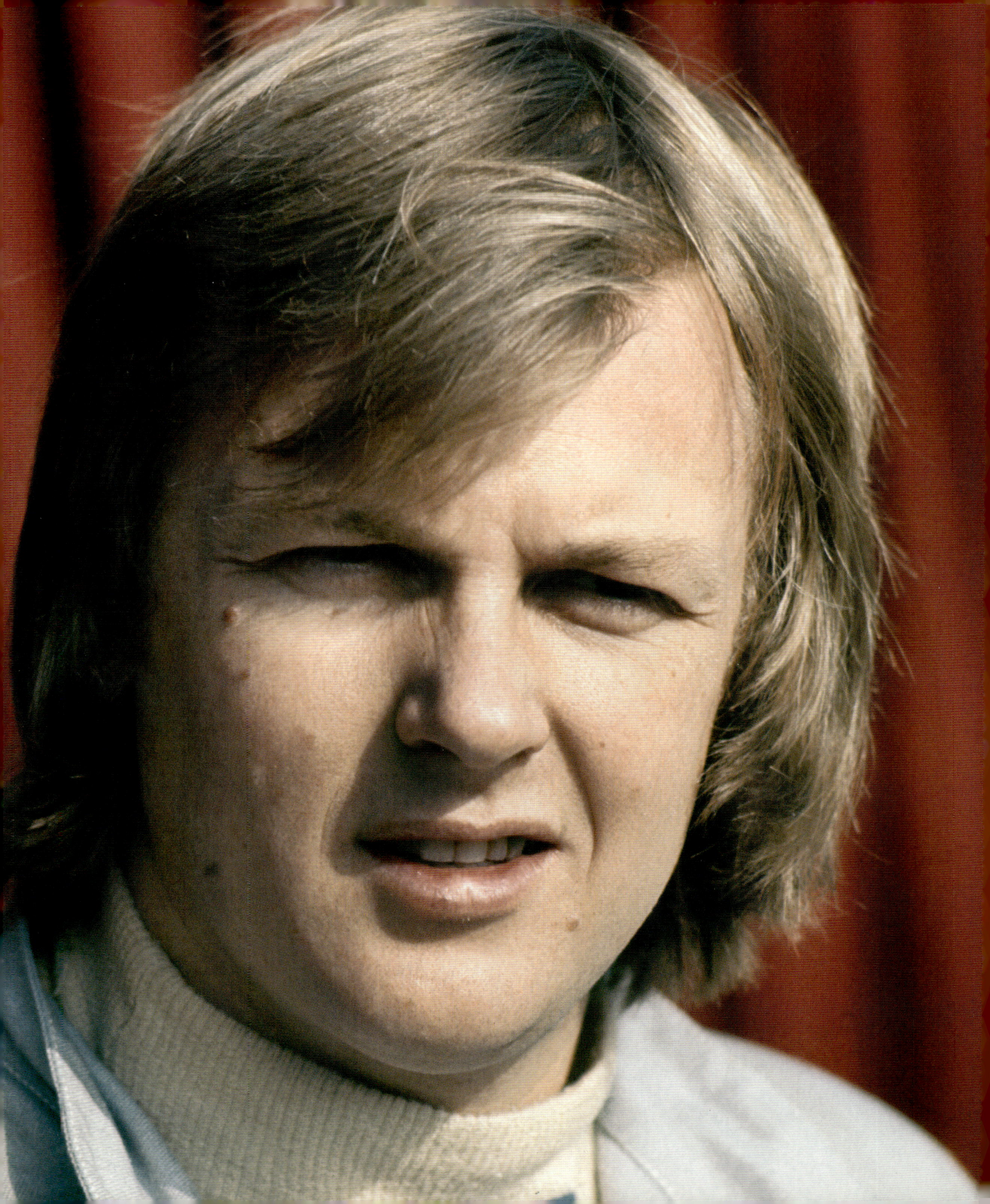

the guard rail at the 140mph Lesmo right-hander, wisely coming into the pits to check a bent steering arm. But it was another straw in the wind to signal that the blond boy from Orebro had real talent. World-class talent.

Yet the final piece of the mosaic was still to be put in place. For the Albi F2 international in south-west France in early September, Winkelmann Racing fielded a third car for Peterson, this being the Lotus 59 previously driven by future FIA president Max Mosley that had lain vacant since its driver retired from racing following a spill at the Nürburgring earlier in the year. Ronnie finished fifth, but it was his performance in practice that really marked him out as something special in Rees's eyes.

"I simply couldn't believe it," Rees recalled. "Ronnie happened to go out of the pits during a rain shower in practice and came up on to the tail of Jackie Stewart's Matra and kept up with him for five laps on a soaking track. You could see Stewart glancing in his mirrors, trying to work out who was chasing him. He could see it was one of our Lotuses, but it wasn't Graham Hill or Jochen Rindt driving it. That's a real test of a driver, the wet, and Stewart had to come into the pits to finally get rid of him. I was one hundred per cent sure that Ronnie would win Grands Prix on the strength of those five laps. It wasn't speculation, it was obvious."

In a sense, this was the whole point about Peterson. He only knew one way to drive a racing car and that was flat-out. He came into F1 on a three-year contract with the emergent March team at the start of the 1970 season, spending his first year at the wheel of a private March 701 before being promoted to the works team for 1971.

On the whole, Ronnie's first season in F1 was a modest affair, but then even stars like Jackie Stewart and Chris Amon, driving respectively for Ken Tyrrell and the factory team, found that the March 701 was a bit canine in nature. When designer Robin Herd suggested a wager whereby if Stewart lost a golf match between them, then the Scot would race the March rather than his Tyrrell 001 in the 1970 Canadian Grand Prix, Jackie replied "Robin, never has anyone had such an incentive not to lose a golf match before." They played the game to its conclusion. Jackie finished one-up and raced the Tyrrell.

So Peterson didn't do badly by comparison. In the French Grand Prix at Clermont-Ferrand he qualified the March 701 alongside Pedro Rodriguez in the BRM P153 on the fifth row of the starting grid and ran in the middle of the field until his car's transmission packed up. Next stop was the British Grand Prix at Brands Hatch, a race in which a pit stop dropped him to ninth, just one place behind Lotus debutant Emerson Fittipaldi in his Lotus 49C.

The March 701 may be remembered as one of the real 'instant' F1 cars, but one man who was less than convinced was German F2 driver Hubert Hahne, who succumbed to Max Mosley's legendary 'silver-tongued' sales pitch. Hahne duly rolled up to the March factory, handed over the appropriate wad of deutschmarks and drove off with his shiny silver 701 in the general direction of Hockenheim, the venue for that year's German Grand Prix. Unsurprisingly, Hahne failed to qualify and immediately jumped to the conclusion that he'd been sold a dud.

In an effort to ram home his sense of dissatisfaction to Mosley and the March directors, Hahne took legal action that saw the works March transporter briefly impounded at the Belgian frontier on the return trip from Hockenheim. But Ronnie came riding to the rescue. In a staged shoot-out at Silverstone, he set a competitive time driving one of the works 701s – and then matched it at the wheel of Hahne's car. The German driver immediately announced his retirement.

"On one occasion I visited him and he came to pick me up at the railway station. His big blue Mercedes S-class saloon swept into the station car park amidst a shriek of tortured tyres. But nobody gave him a second glance. There must be times when Lewis Hamilton craves such anonymity."

I first came across Ronnie in racing action in the spring of 1970 when *Motoring News* gave me a weekend away from my day job as a bank clerk to pay me the handsome sum of £25 to cover a Formula Ford race supporting the F2 race at Zolder. Twenty-four hours after being berated by my manager at Barclays Bank International, a stone's throw away from Liverpool Street station in the City, I was enveloped in dust and reverberating exhausts in the confined Zolder pit lane, rubbing shoulders with Ronnie, Derek Bell and John Watson.

This was my personal Epiphany on the Road to Damascus; there was no way I was going to stay at the bank if there was a chance of getting involved in motor racing. Two months after watching Ronnie manhandling his Malcolm Guthrie Racing March 702 round the Zolder track I would join the staff of *Motoring News*.

Guthrie – now Sir Malcolm – was a keen amateur who helped fund the March F2 team and drove the second car alongside Ronnie. His father, Sir Giles, had been chairman

OPPOSITE Ronnie was the *de facto* team leader at Lotus in 1974, and won three Grands Prix. But the team's performance was compromised in trying to develop an overly complex new car, and its finishing record was woeful.

OPPOSITE Ronnie was at the peak of his formidable powers in 1975, but Team Lotus let him down. He had to endure an entire season with a car designed six years before, and could score championship points on only three occasions.

Max Mosley on the March period: "He was the only driver I ever met who appreciated just what a risk we were taking offering him a three-year contract. We paid him £2,000 in 1970, £5,000 in 1971 and £10,000 in 1972. He was totally loyal and would never have dreamed of breaking that commitment."

of BOAC. Malcolm used to affectionately refer to Ronnie as 'yer actual ace', usually after he'd walked back to the pits brushing the debris out of his hair following his latest shunt in the difficult-to-drive 702. Years later Malcolm told me wistfully: "Ronnie was a lovely guy and, hell, things were so much simpler then. We just went out and went racing. It all seemed so straightforward."

In 1971 Ronnie showcased his strength in depth with a string of five Grand Prix second places that made him World Championship runner-up behind Jackie Stewart. More importantly, this was brilliantly underscored by victory in the European F2 Trophy series. His sheer speed at the wheel of the March 712M was baffling to behold. There were several such cars contesting the championship, but Ronnie wrapped his around his little finger like a kart. It literally danced around the circuits of Europe, carrying its intrepid young driver to his greatest success as an aspiring star.

All of us in the close-knit F2 community regarded Ronnie as being let out of our sight on licence on alternative Sundays to compete in Grands Prix. He was ours and we didn't like sharing him with the snooty F1 brigade. And Ronnie seemed to understand that, even identify with it. He and his long-time girlfriend Barbro Edvardsson were our pitlane royalty and we jealously guarded our friendships with them both.

By now he was clearly ready to win Grands Prix, but not until he switched to Lotus in 1973 would he be in the right place at the right time.

Throughout his three-year F1 contract with the March team, Peterson remained touchingly loyal to the company's founders, even allowing for the fact that Mosley's legal aptitude meant that the documents binding the drivers to the team were extremely difficult to challenge. Not that any such constraints prevented Colin Chapman from attempting repeatedly to lure Peterson away from the team that gave him his F1 chance.

Mosley was impressed with his loyalty. "He was the only driver I ever met who appreciated just what a risk we were taking offering him a three-year contract," he said. "We paid him £2,000 in 1970, £5,000 in 1971 and £10,000 in 1972. He was totally loyal and would never have dreamed of breaking that commitment."

Yet when that contract expired, the lure of Lotus proved irresistible. Highly motivated, Ronnie could see that a very real possibility of challenging for the World Championship was now beckoning. Even though moving to Lotus was calculated to put sitting tenant Emerson Fittipaldi's nose out of joint – he was the reigning title holder, after all – Ronnie grabbed the chance.

For his part, Emerson reacted diplomatically. He knew about the approaches that were being made towards Ronnie during the summer of '72 and fully appreciated the threat to his personal supremacy that they represented. But Emerson and Ronnie were close friends and remained so through to the end of the Swedish driver's life.

Fittipaldi won three races in 1973, Peterson four. But the two Lotus pace-setters spent much of the year inevitably taking championship points off each other. It allowed Jackie Stewart to dodge through to take his third World Championship title, although the possibility of Fittipaldi retaining his crown remained on the cards right up to the Italian Grand Prix at Monza.

In 1974 Emerson switched to McLaren and won a second World Championship. But for Ronnie, who had been so used to taking Emerson's chassis settings in the final moments of practice and qualifying faster than his colleague, Ronnie found himself battling to get the best out of the now-ageing Lotus 72 and the fact that they won three races that season was more down to the blond boy's lightning reflexes and seat-of-the-pants talent.

Watching at the Nürburgring in '74, you could see that Ronnie still had the spark as he threw himself into a four-way fight with Jacky Ickx in the other Lotus, Mike Hailwood's McLaren and local hero Jochen Mass. After 11 laps Mass's superb drive in front of his home crowd came to an end when the engine in his Surtees TS16 suddenly failed. That left the two Lotus drivers fighting it out with Mike the Bike.

Disastrously, Mike's McLaren landed slightly askew after leaping over the crest at Pflanzgarten. It speared right into the guard rail with a ferocious impact that left Hailwood with a badly broken ankle and out of racing for the rest of the season. In fact, Mike the Bike never raced again on four wheels through to his tragic death in 1981.

After the race, Ickx left the circuit without saying a word to Peterson. Both men had passed the accident at reduced speed while track workers struggled to release Hailwood

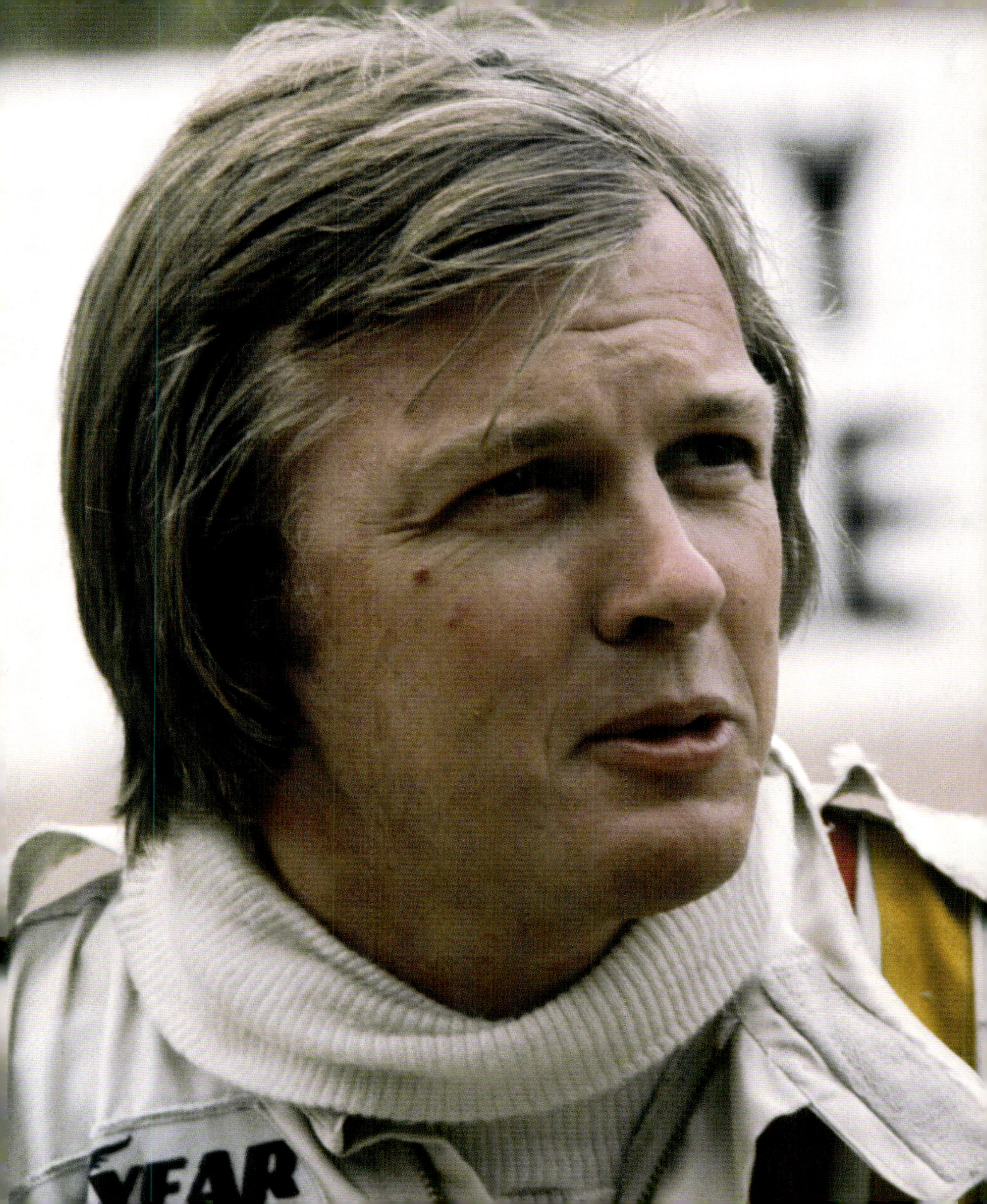

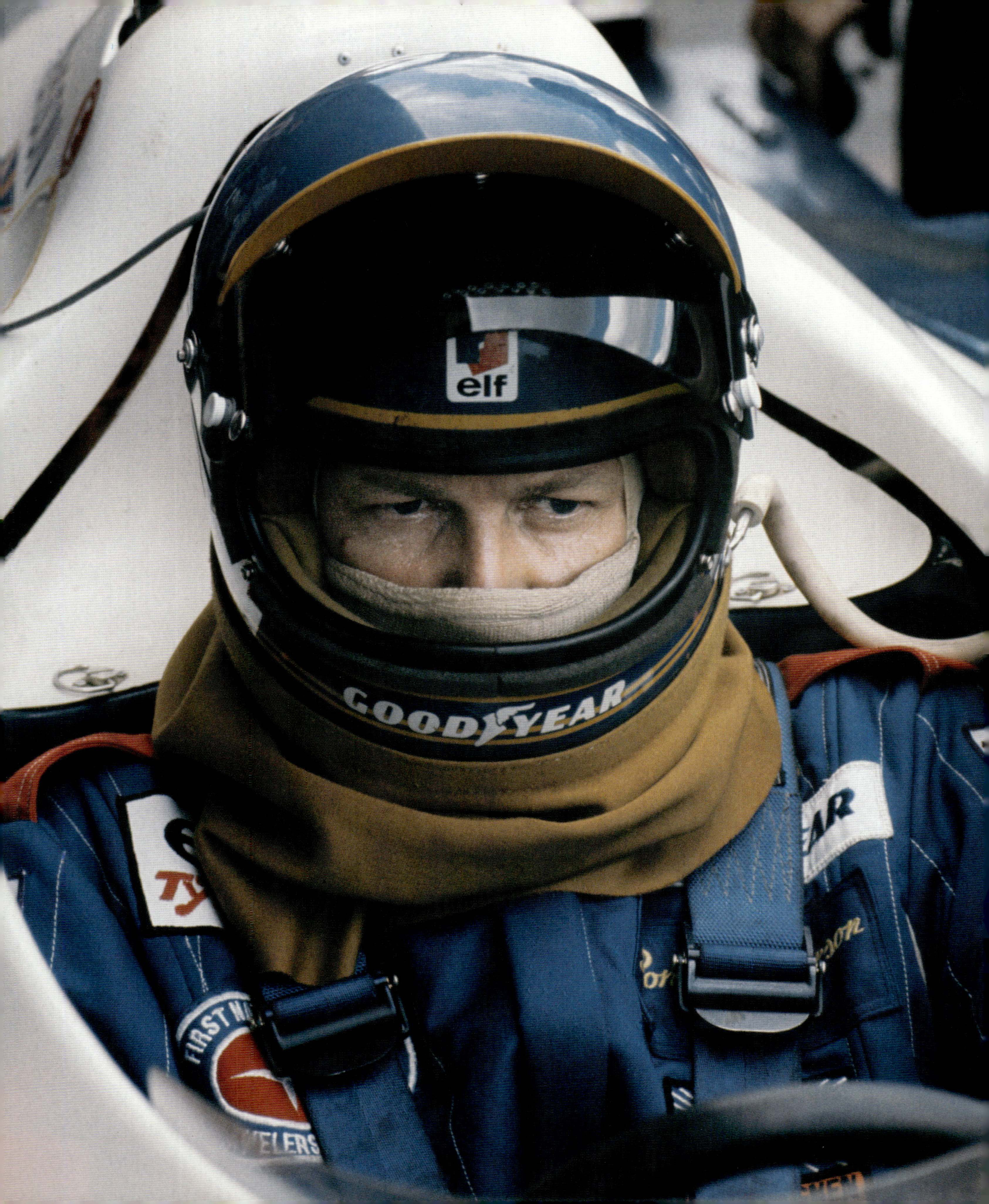
elf
GOODYEAR

from the wreckage, but Ickx had perhaps backed off just a touch more. Ronnie surged up alongside the Belgian for fourth place. Ickx said nothing, but privately felt that Ronnie had taken unfair advantage of the situation in order that he could claim third place.

This led to suggestions – admittedly only from the sport's wilder fringe – that Ronnie had been driving erratically in the heat of their four-way battle, and that Mike's injuries were somehow the by-product of the Swede's recklessness.

When I mentioned this to Hailwood, he sprang to Ronnie's defence. "No, not at all," he insisted in an interview a year after the accident. "I just can't imagine that anybody could say such terrible thing about that lovely guy. There was absolutely no way that Ronnie drove improperly. He never put a wheel wrong that I could remember."

Meanwhile, Ronnie was finding that his personal relationship with Colin Chapman was becoming increasingly fraught as the Lotus team dropped from the competitive high wire. At the 1975 British Grand Prix Chapman objected to Ronnie's plans to be involved in the launch of his biography – written by the writer and published by Haynes.

"I take exception to being told what I can or cannot do with regard to my non-race driving activities by you or Team Lotus personnel," he wrote to Chapman on 12 June 1975. He also complained that during the previous 14 months he had suffered "a total of 11 semi or total brake failures" and rounded off this missive by pointing out that his contractual payments were late. He was clearly looking for a way out of his contract.

Tim Schenken, who drove with Ronnie in the Ferrari sports car team throughout 1972, echoed Hailwood's sentiments more than half a lifetime later. One of the handful of surviving 'old guard' from Peterson's early days in F3 and F2, the genial Australian recalls his old friend with genuine pleasure and affection.

"Ronnie was a lovely guy who never changed in the slightest from the moment I first met him during our F3 days through to the time he died, by which time he was a World Championship contender," recalled Schenken, now Clerk of the Course for the Australian Grand Prix.

Still as fit and trim as he was when he partnered Peterson in the Ferrari sports car racing line-up 36 years ago, Schenken confesses that just talking about Ronnie brings a lump to his throat. "I must be getting old and sentimental, but Ronnie was totally uncomplicated with a really gentle side to his character.

"I first met him at Brands Hatch when we were racing in F3 back in 1969. I used to guard all the details of my car's technical set-up really closely, particularly the gear ratios, but when Ronnie innocently inquired 'can you help me with the gear ratios?' all my previous rules went out of the window and I offered him all the help he needed."

In 1976 Ronnie's biggest problem would be the challenge of trying to make up for the deficient machinery he now found himself saddled with. Lotus increasingly looked lost as they developed their 'all-adjustable' Type 77s at the start of 1976, so Ronnie was again stuck in an uncompetitive machine, looking for a way out.

Max Mosley did a deal for him to switch back to a third works March 761 in time for the second round of the title chase, the South African Grand Prix at Kyalami. The feeling was that the March would be more to Ronnie's taste, more user-friendly and easier to set up. He would still need a little bit of luck to nail down another Grand Prix win and a mid-race rain shower at Monza – which Ronnie freely confessed he hardly noticed – helped him clinch his third victory at the famous Italian track. Overall, though, the car's reliability wasn't good enough and prompted Peterson to make the cataclysmic decision to sign for Tyrrell for 1977.

Max Mosley on the Tyrrell period: "In my heart I just couldn't see him getting the best out of the six-wheeler. It was just far too complicated for Ronnie…I tried to persuade him that the Tyrrell wouldn't be his cup of tea but he'd set his stall on leaving and we were not able to change his mind."

"I didn't have any regrets about leaving March at the time, not even after that Monza win," said Ronnie. "I really couldn't see an end to the problems with the 761, or indeed a sign that the team might finally get on and do things properly. When I signed for them, it was agreed that we would do a lot of testing, but in the end we didn't."

He added wistfully; "Trying to run three or four cars was just too much and we had a lot of reliability problems, mainly connected with the front brakes and tyre wear problems." Yet Mosley could see that the overweight six-wheeled Tyrrell P34 would spell nothing but trouble and spent a long time trying to talk Ronnie out of it.

"In my heart I just couldn't see him getting the best out of the six-wheeler," Mosley said. "It was just far too complicated for Ronnie. I always believed that if he was going to have a chance of the championship then he would either have to be joint number one with the man

OPPOSITE The strain of a deeply frustrating 1977 Formula 1 programme with Elf Team Tyrrell shows in Ronnie's eyes. Overweight and lacking tyre development, the unique six-wheel Project 34 was no longer competitive.

OPPOSITE In 1978, Ronnie was back in a competitive car at last. Seven podiums, including victories at Kyalami and on the Osterreichring, made him entirely comfortable with his decision to return to John Player Team Lotus.

who was going to set up the car, or would have to be given a car which was relatively straightforward to adjust."

Mosley acknowledged that Peterson gave plenty of worthwhile feedback during his second time round at March, "although he wasn't in the same street as a Fittipaldi, Lauda or Andretti in that respect. I tried to persuade him that the Tyrrell wouldn't be his cup of tea – and I think he believed me – but he'd set his stall on leaving and we were not able to change his mind."

Mosley was right. The over-complex Maurice Phillippe-designed six-wheeler P34 wasn't sufficiently competitive and Ronnie had a troubled year. Inwardly he retained his confidence, but it became clear that he was frustrated and out of step with the Tyrrell squad. The best the car could deliver him was a lucky season-best third in the Belgian Grand Prix.

Observing his relationship with Ken Tyrrell was akin to watching an irascible headmaster trying to come to terms with a petulant child. Long before the end of the season it had become abundantly clear that this was no marriage made in heaven. Long before the end of the year, Ronnie was casting his net wide, looking for a fresh opportunity. Amazingly, this came from the most unlikely direction of all. Lotus.

"Observing his relationship with Ken Tyrrell was akin to watching an irascible headmaster trying to come to terms with a petulant child."

Determined to prove he was still a potential World Championship contender, Ronnie gambled on rejoining Colin Chapman's operation in 1978 – but accepting number two status to Mario Andretti. Ronnie freely acknowledged that the American driver's great talent at test and development work was responsible for making the new ground-effect Lotus 79 a race-winning tool.

It didn't take long for the old Peterson to re-emerge – fast, focused and fitter than he had been at any stage previously in his career. He was honourable enough to abide by his agreement to defer to Andretti, but by the same token he would make Mario work as hard as he could for every ounce of his well-deserved success.

He worked hard to get fitter. Together with his close pal, saloon car racer David Brodie, he began submitting himself to regular, extended runs through the country lanes close to his home. "When he put his mind to it, Ronnie could be amazingly single-minded," said Brodie. "He knew what a big opportunity this was and certainly was not about to waste it."

As the rest of the season unfolded, Peterson began to walk tall again. He became more relaxed as his confidence was re-confirmed. Most of the time he played second fiddle to Mario in efficiently dutiful style, only at Brands Hatch and Hockenheim deliberately rattling the American driver's cage.

At the German track Peterson towed past Andretti on the opening lap, but only after Mario made a slight slip, sliding wide on to the dirt on the exit from one of the chicanes. A few laps later he slipstreamed back ahead of his team-mate and raced away to win, helped in the closing stages by a gearbox failure on Peterson's car that left the other Lotus parked at the side of the circuit long before the chequered flag was waved at the startline.

Mathematically, this was a particularly good day for Andretti. He now had an 18-point championship lead over Peterson, but he threw half of it away by spinning into the barrier on the first lap on the Osterreichring, removing his Lotus 79's rear wing after Carlos Reutemann's Ferrari moved over on him and put his left-hand wheels on the damp grass as a result. The race was briefly red-flagged as the rain intensified, but it was restarted shortly afterwards, allowing Ronnie an unchallenged flag-to-flag victory – his last-ever F1 success.

At Zandvoort, things were back to usual for the Lotus twins with Peterson following steadily in Mario's wheel tracks, staying close to the rear of his team-mate's car even when it developed a slight fire in its engine bay – caused by a cracked exhaust – during the closing stages of the race.

Then came Monza and the brutal severing of the story line. And for the author, the end of the warm friendship of a man who, it always struck me, radiated genuine iconic status. It all started unravelling on race morning, from the moment Ronnie badly damaged his Lotus 79 when a rear brake failed and caused him to fly off the road, through to his arrival, desperately injured with smashed legs, at a Milan hospital later that afternoon.

Forced to take over the old Lotus 78 for the race, he was pitched head-on into a guard rail as the pack accelerated hard towards the first corner. The Lotus briefly erupted in flame, but thanks to the bravery of James Hunt, Patrick Depailler and Clay Regazzoni, Peterson was quickly released from the wreck.

The race was restarted over an hour later and Mario finished the day World Champion. For him, the job was done. Yet that golden moment would be tarnished forever in his mind with the news in the small hours of the next morning that Ronnie had unexpectedly died.

He was a fine man and I miss him still.

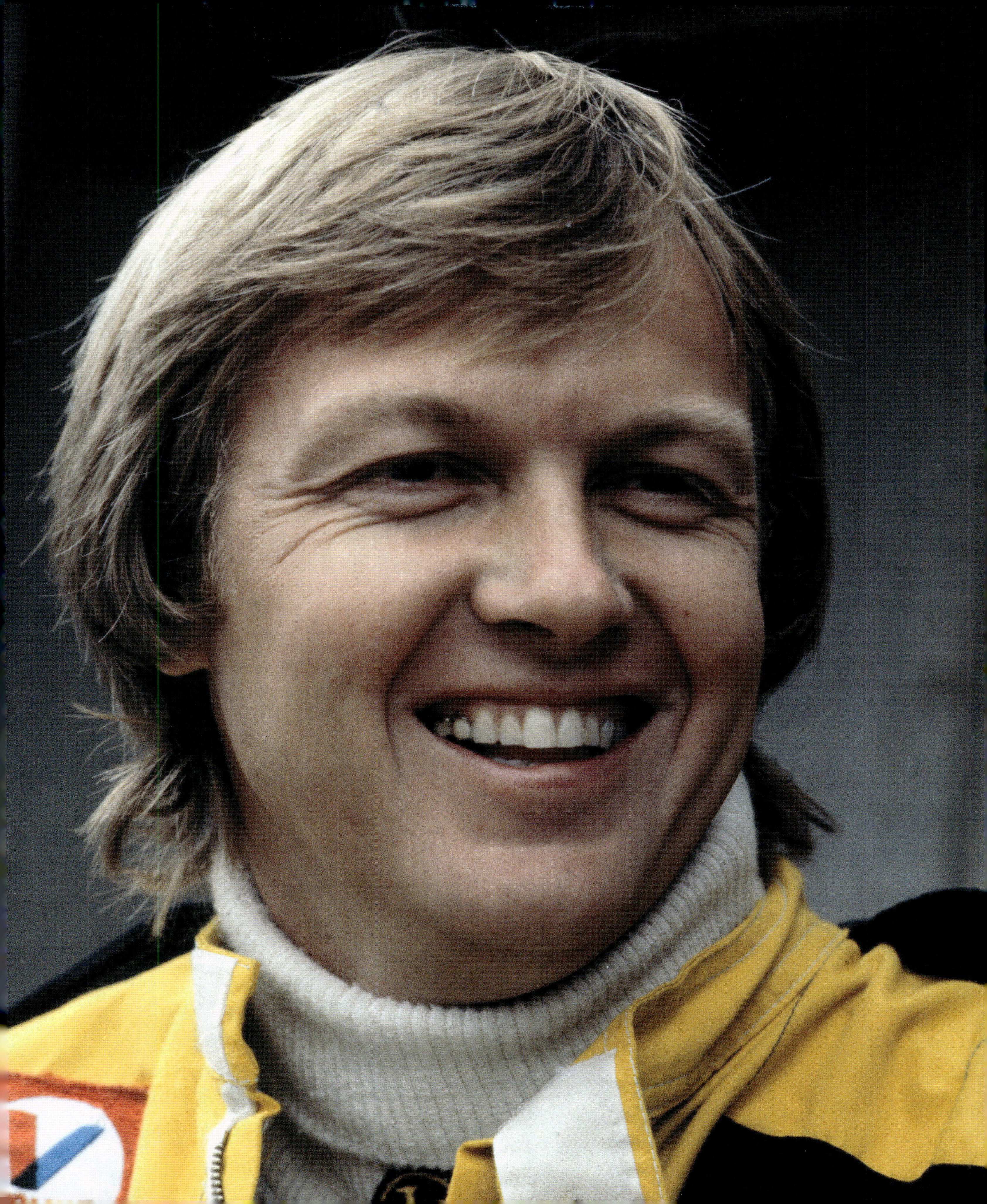

1962 – 1966

THE FIRST GRADUATE FROM KART RACING

BY QUENTIN SPURRING

Ronnie Peterson was caught up as a boy with his father's fascination with all things mechanical. Bengt Peterson was a baker, but not by choice. He was about to complete an engineering course when the death of his mother in 1945 caused him to quit his studies and, with his wife, May-Britt, and their baby son, take over the family bakery business in Örebro.

Bengt had been hooked by motorsport in his early teens, and had competed in ice and speedway racing on a Puch 250 motorcycle. Car racing was almost non-existent in post-war Sweden, but there was a handful of stadium venues. In 1947, Bengt got together with a fellow bike competitor, Sven Andersson, to build a front-drive single-seater based on the American 'Midget' concept. An acronym of their given names, the first Svebe was powered by a two-stroke, 800cc engine recovered from a burned out DKW automobile. Three-year-old Bengt-Ronnie was taken to the races.

In 1948, Bengt and Sven built two Mk2 versions of the Svebe, with 500cc JAP motorcycle engines of the type that was changing the face of motorsport in post-war England. They sold these cars at the end of the season and used the money to build two lightweight, Mk3 Svebes with which they were very successful in oval racing in 1949. Although Bengt quit racing shortly afterwards, Sven continued to build and race Svebes for many years. The next of the cars complied with the first FIA Formula 3 regulations in 1950, and Sven remained a close friend of the Peterson family.

In 1952, Bengt cobbled together a toy vehicle for eight-year-old Ronnie and his younger brother, Tommy. Resembling a miniature tractor, the 'Tractorn' was powered by a 50cc moped engine and had a top speed of almost 10mph. This rugged device saw extensive use on Ronnie's maternal grandparents' farm in Kumlabyn, outside Örebro, where Ronnie arranged races with his friends. It got a new, 118cc Husqvarna motor in 1954, and could then achieve more than 25mph.

The 'Tractorn' was supplemented by a 50cc Puch moped for 15-year-old Ronnie in 1959, when he competed in his first race, an endurance scramble in his home town. Ronnie was never a keen student and he left school at 16, in 1960, to take a job as a mechanic in the local Renault dealership. Shortly afterwards, he went as a spectator to the opening of Sweden's first permanent kart racing track, in Laxå – and resolved to build himself a kart.

Bengt was quick to offer his help in this project. He made a lightweight chassis from ejection seat frames from wrecked aircraft, and fitted it with a two-stroke, 194cc Ardie motorcycle engine. Bengt named the device 'Robardie' – another acronym, for Ronnie, Bengt and the German-made motor. Ronnie tried it out in February 1962, first on a frozen lake, then on a track at Höör in the south of Sweden.

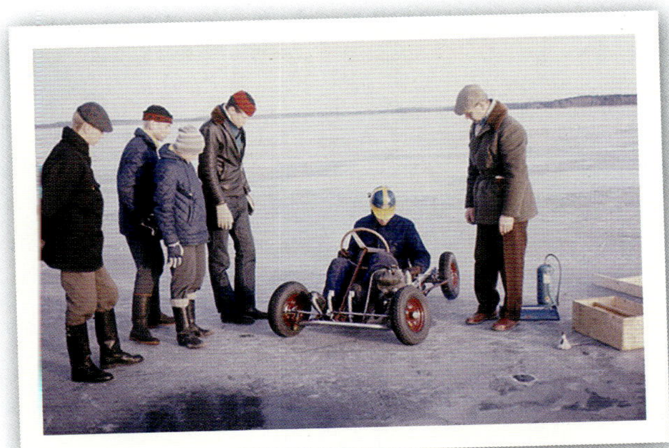

RIGHT The very first test of the original Robardie kart built by Bengt Peterson, Ronnie's father (at right), on a frozen Lake Hjälmaren near home on New Year's Day 1962. Tommy, Ronnie's younger brother, is standing immediately to the left of the kart, with some family friends. Note the barrow wheels... *(Photo courtesy of Tommy Peterson Collection)*

No one knew it at the time, but the Mk1 Robardie was the start of something very big. It was only three years since the first US-built karts had been demonstrated in Europe, where the sport was starting to take hold. The first karting World Championship was still two years away. But Ronnie would become the very first driver to make it to Formula 1 having originally honed his car control skills in karting.

He entered his first race in May 1962, at Laxå, finishing seventh. Next time out, he won a Class D invitation race at Höör, and was fourth overall in the main event. He continued to show competitive ability and, from 10 starts, he had two wins, two podiums and four fourths during this début season, the highlight a fourth in the national championship event at Laxå, second in Class D behind Inge Nilsson.

For the 1963 season, Bengt bought Nilsson's Bultaco motor and installed it in a new, more sophisticated Robardie chassis. Thus equipped, Ronnie startled his family with his natural ability and flair. He entered 12 races and landed victories in eight of them, with two second places. The season closed with the Swedish championship event at Kilafors, and this time Ronnie won the Class D title.

Bengt built up two new karts for 1964, and the Peterson family began to spread its wings. Over a busy season of 25 meetings, Ronnie contested Class D again with the Bultaco motor, and Class A (the International category) with a Parilla. The schedule included his first events outside Sweden. Three European championship contests set him against the cream of European karting – and he was almost immediately competitive.

He was the only Swedish competitor in Munich,

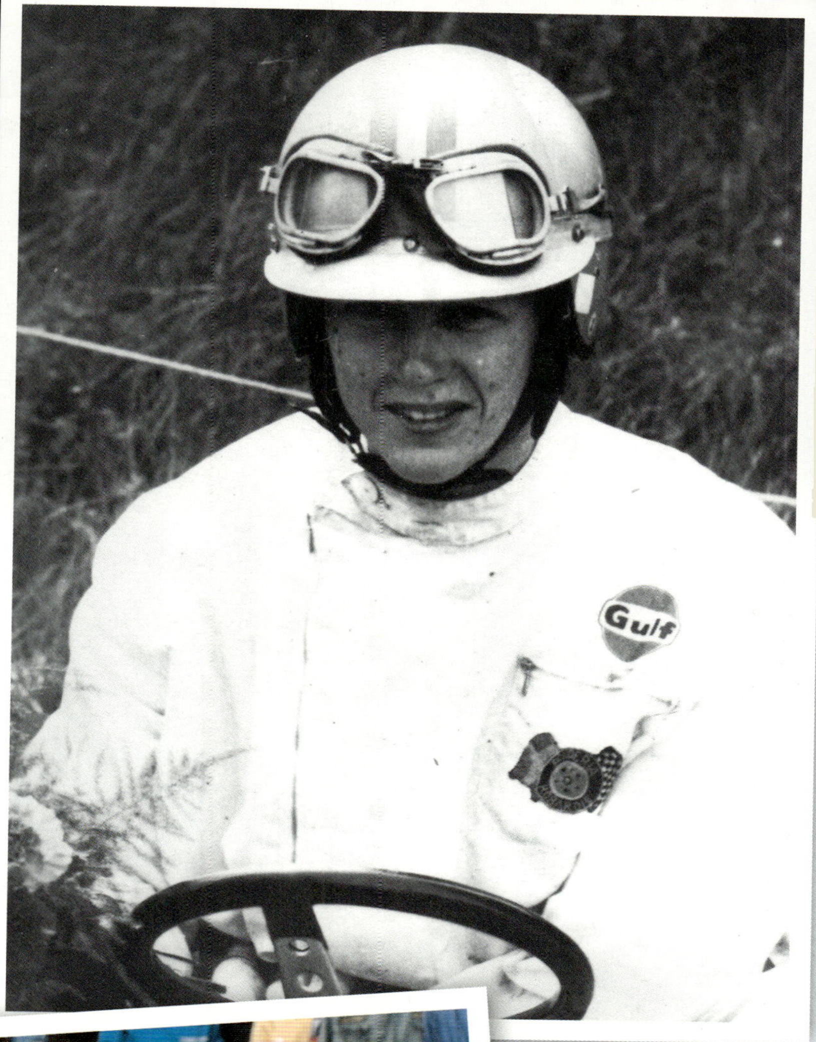

ABOVE Young Bengt-Ronnie, aboard his home-made kart, has no idea that he will one day be a Grand Prix winner. *(Photo courtesy of Tommy Peterson Collection)*

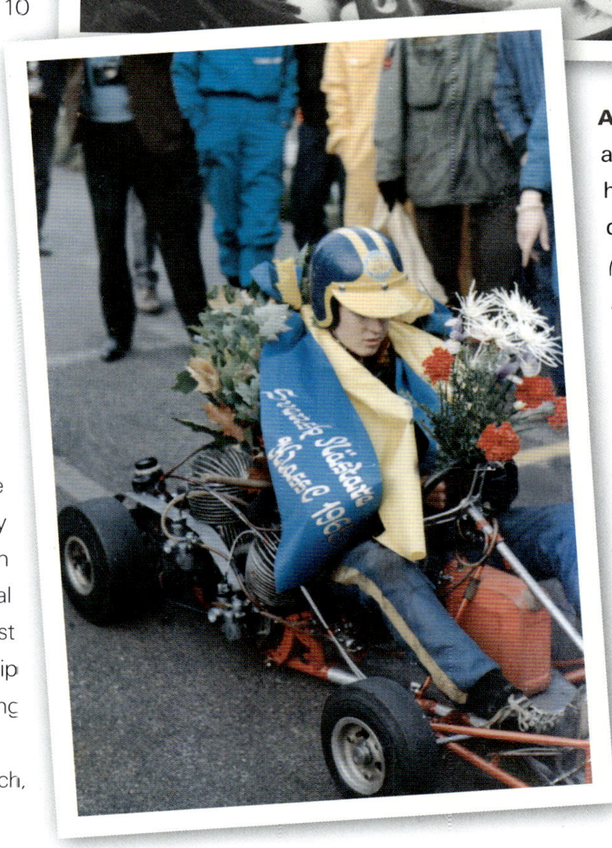

LEFT Ronnie on the twin-engined Robardie Class C kart after winning the Nordic regional and Swedish national championship event at Malmö in October 1965. *(Photo courtesy of Tommy Peterson Collection)*

RIGHT Chatting up Suzy Raganelli, Italy's sensational 1966 World Champion aboard her Tecno-Parilla. Ronnie had many hard-fought battles with 'La Suzy', who was a skilful and notoriously wily competitor. Making the most of her weight advantage, she beat him often, and the two became firm friends. *(Photo courtesy of Tommy Peterson Collection)*

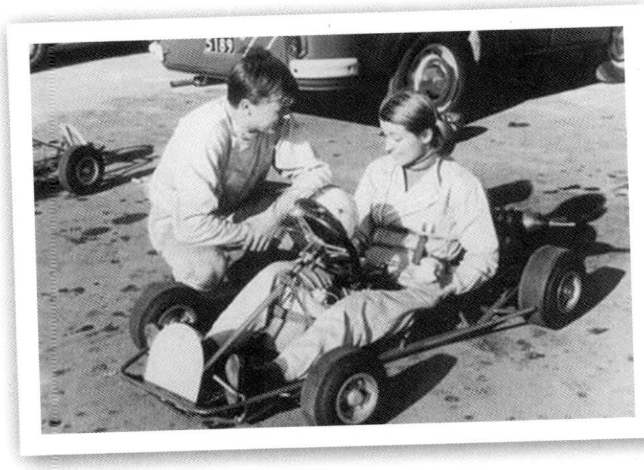

Germany, but failed to finish. However, he startled the kart racing community at Leidschendam, in the Netherlands, when he narrowly lost a duel with Italian ace Guido Sala for second place in the final, behind Dirk van Staalduinen. He did it again at the French venue at Villacoublay, near Paris, by outqualifying the entire field, but again registered a DNF. Here was international confirmation of an exceptional talent.

In August, Ronnie won all three heats to clinch the Class D Nordic championship at Älmhult, Sweden, and he followed with the Swedish Class A title. From a total of 40 race starts in 1964, he won his class on 23 occasions, and scored seven second places.

Ronnie quit his job as a Renault mechanic and started work as a lift technician in Örebro, investing his wages and almost all his spare time in karting. He continued to win regularly in Sweden, but the Peterson family travelled all over Europe during the summer of 1965. Ronnie rewarded them with yet more success, racing new Robardie karts in three classes: A and C with Parilla motors, D with Bultaco.

He was again chosen to represent his homeland in the European Championship for Teams, held for the 100cc Class A karts over three events in Switzerland, Holland and France. On a track laid out in the main square in Vevey in April, Ronnie finished third in the final, behind Italians Oscar Constantini (BR-Parilla) and 19-year-old débutante Suzy Raganelli (BM-Parilla). Constantini had finished third in the inaugural World Championship the previous season, and among those beaten by Ronnie was the sport's first champion, Guido Sala. On the 'kartodrome' at Leidschendam in June, however, the Milanese former motorcycle racer qualified his Tecno fastest and dominated the final, pursued by a bevy of Belgians. Ronnie had a DNF and was classified 18th.

After a string of victories back home, Ronnie went to the second ever karting World Championship. The new sport had really taken off in Italy and, like the inaugural such meeting the previous year, the event was held on the 1000yd Pista d'Oro track in Rome – this time under steady rain. Each driver contested three heats to qualify on

RIGHT Ronnie leads double World Champion Guido Sala during the big Coupe Internationale invitation race in Monaco in June 1966. He won one of the heats but did not finish the event. The final was led all the way by Sala, but the Italian was later disqualified when his engine was found to be illegal, on five counts. The win was awarded to British driver Richard Newton. *(Photo courtesy of Tommy Peterson Collection)*

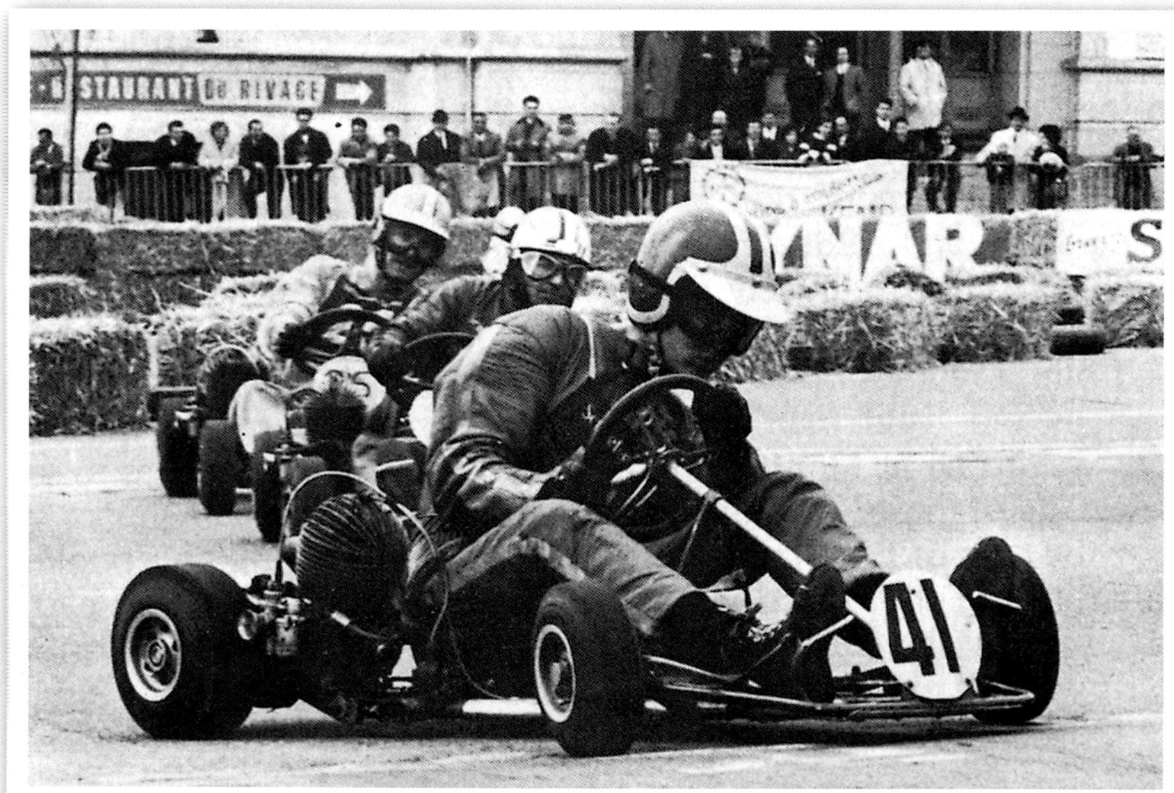

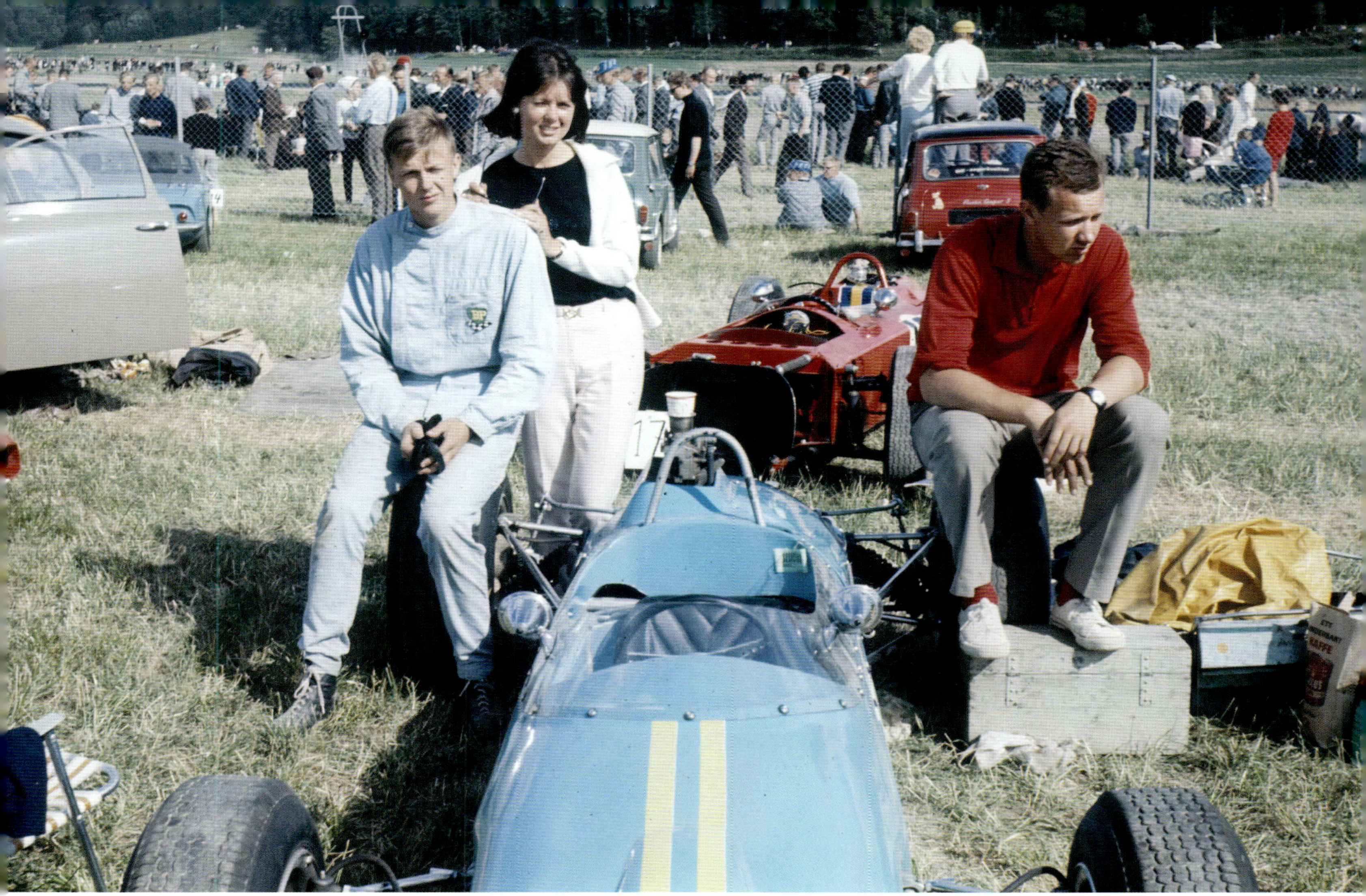

a points system for three finals. Ronnie's day was beset by mechanical problems, but he won a heat before failing to finish another. This meant that he had to finish in the first two in a 'recupero' race to qualify for the finals, which he did, with Staalduinen second. The two lined up at the back of the first final which, after Werner Ihle had spun away the lead, was won by Oscar Sala from Falco Graf and Guido Sala. Ihle won the second final, with Ronnie second and the defending champion again third. All Sala had to do to clinch back-to-back championships was to finish second to Ihle in the third final. Dutchman Toine Hezemans was classified third, and Ronnie 14th.

The finale of the European series was run the following weekend at Villacoublay. Ronnie qualified second fastest of 40 competitors, behind Guido Sala, but utterly dominated the event thereafter. He beat Sala into second place in all three heats they contested. When the new World Champion was stopped by oiled sparkplugs, Ronnie won the final as he liked, from Ihle and Mickey Allen. The result lifted the Swedish team into third place in the championship, behind Italy and Britain. It also lifted Ronnie's morale because it proved what he had known all along – that he was as good as the best.

Two weeks later, back home at Malmö, he won the Nordic regional and Swedish national Class C championships. In Class D, he again landed the Nordic title, and was the runner-up in the Swedish event. The 1965 season had contributed a further 21 kart wins for Ronnie, from 32 starts.

By this time, however, his mind was on greater things. He was now 21, and wanted to move on from karting. Sven Andersson had designed a more modern Svebe single-seater, based closely on the spaceframe Brabham BT15. This was the most popular contemporary Formula 3 customer car, and one was taking Picko Troberg to that season's Swedish national title. Sven wanted Bengt to build the Svebe, and Ronnie to race it.

To get a competition licence allowing him to compete in Formula 3, Ronnie was sent with his father's diesel Mercedes-Benz road car to the racing school at the Karlskoga circuit. His tutor was 25-year-old Reine Wisell, himself an aspiring race driver. Wisell had had three

ABOVE Encouraged by his current girlfriend and brother Tommy, Ronnie prepares for his very first motor race, a non-championship Formula 3 event during the Bengtsforloppet meeting on the Dalslandring circuit in July 1966. The Svebe was a Brabham BT15 copy, liveried in the blue-and-yellow style of Sweden that Ronnie always used on his helmets. *(Photo courtesy of Tommy Peterson Collection)*

seasons in saloon car racing and was now running a Cooper in Formula 3. He was such a good teacher that, at the end of the day, Ronnie won a race for pupils in the school's single-seaters. It was a momentous meeting: the two blond Swedes would soon be the men to beat in European Formula 3 racing, and would compete together for many years thereafter.

While the Svebe was under build, Ronnie cut back his karting programme for the 1966 season, contesting only Class A with another home-built Robardie-Parilla – but resolving, nonetheless, to have a serious crack at winning at the summit level of the sport. The 1966 European Championship was contested by nine nations, this time over four meetings in Switzerland, Italy, Belgium and France. In the first event, in May at Vevey, he qualified fastest, edging out the very quick and artful Suzy Raganelli. Ronnie won both his heats but the lightweight Italian girl beat him into second place in the final.

Early that June, Ronnie raced for the first time in Monaco. The week after the Formula 1 meeting in the principality, the Coupe Internationale Monaco was contested by a dozen national teams on a track laid out on the harbourfront, using the start-finish straight of the Grand Prix circuit with a right-hand hairpin at Ste Devote taking the karts onto the seafront, round the swimming pool and along to Rascasse. That weekend, the circuit from Portier through the tunnel and towards Tabac was also closed, for the filming of John Frankenheimer's 'Grand Prix' movie. Ronnie again beat Guido Sala to win his first heat, but mechanical problems intervened.

Ronnie went straight from Monaco to Lissone, near Monza, for the next European Championship event, and again qualified fastest. He won his first heat, finished second to Oscar Sala in the second heat, and collided with Sala in the third. However, he came through to win the final, from Tecno team-mates Giulio Pernigotti and Raganelli, with Allen fourth. Three weeks later, when it rained heavily at Coo, Belgium, the Italian team rested Raganelli. Ronnie finished fourth, first and fourth again in his heats. In the final, he was beaten into second place by local driver Franz Coolens, but gained his revenge on Pernigotti, who was third.

The following Sunday, 3 July 1966, Ronnie made his single-seater racing début in a club event on the Dalslandsring circuit, finishing a promising third behind Brabhams driven by Ulf Svensson and Jan Heggov. During August, he did three International-status events with the new Svebe, the first two in Denmark. In a race again dominated by Brabhams, led by Trevor Blokdyk and Picko Troberg, he finished seventh on the Djurslandring. He went on to Roskilde – to face the cream of the European Formula 3 teams, which were *en route* to the Kanonloppet, the biggest event of the season at Karlskoga, where they would contest a support race on the Formula 2 bill. Kurt Ahrens's Brabham claimed pole position, and Ronnie's new friend, Reine Wisell, won his heat with another Brabham. In the final, the top seven places were filled by Brabhams, led by Chris Irwin's Chequered Flag entry. Ronnie's Svebe was classified 21st.

When Irwin won again at Karlskoga the following weekend, with Piers Courage second, Ronnie was off the pace once more, finishing 15th. The one-off Svebe was clearly inferior to the Brabham BT15 on which it had been based, let alone the new BT18. A deal was struck to replace it with Ahrens's BT18, which had finished fifth in the Kanonloppet, as it had in Monaco.

Before he had a chance to race the family's new acquisition, Ronnie had karting appointments at the World Championship, and at the finale of the European series. Ronnie's performances with his one-off Robardie had been dismaying Tecno, the Pederzani brothers' Bologna company that had produced its first karts in 1961, and now had them in series production. Tecno, which was itself embarking on a long journey that would culminate in Formula 1, had won the World titles in 1964–65 and had the biggest representation in the 1966 event in Copenhagen, Denmark. Having proved he could beat the Italians, Ronnie had high hopes, but he was unlucky.

Again, the 42 drivers each had to do three qualifying heats, and the fastest 20 went on to three finals, over 20, 30 and then 50 laps. Raganelli qualified fastest with Ronnie sixth, feeling his engine down on power. In trying to compensate, Ronnie spun away the lead in two of his heats. Meanwhile Raganelli won all three of her heats, and then all three finals – thus humbling 41 young men and emphatically confirming her status as the fastest kart racer of the season. Ronnie came from the back to finish seventh in the first final, third in the second and fourth in the third. In the aggregate results, he was placed third behind his compatriot, Leif Engstrom, who was racing a Tecno-Parilla similar to Raganelli's. Later Ronnie and Bengt discovered a holed carburettor float chamber. Of the stars of the previous season, Ihle was fourth, Hezemans fifth, Pernigotti sixth and Sala, twice the World Champion, ninth. The elite field also included Finland's 17-year-old

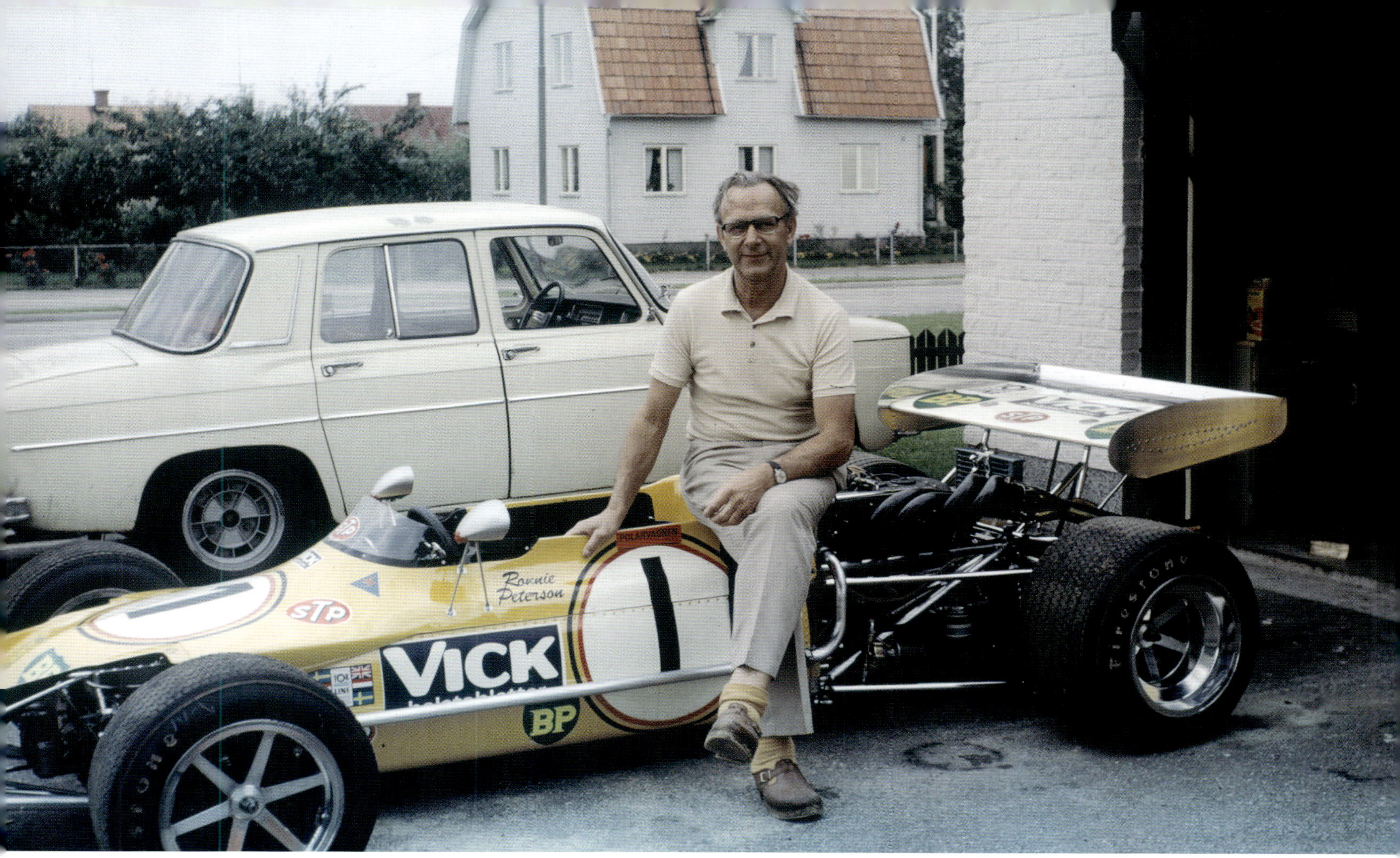

Keke Rosberg and François Goldstein, the Belgian who would go on to win five World Championships.

Ronnie then contested the European finale in Paris, the format of which specified three heats and a final. He took a revenge over Raganelli by beating her into second place in the first heat, only to lose time in dislodging a straw bale while leading the second heat, and in tangling with his rival in the first corner of the third. Lacking the physical strength to push-start her Tecno, she had to retire. Ronnie had to start the final in 13th place but came in fourth, behind Staalduinen, Goldstein and Engstrom. Ronnie's last kart season was completed with 13 starts that yielded just six more wins.

The Sunday following his return from France, Ronnie raced the Brabham for the first time, in the final round of the Swedish Formula 3 series at Karlskoga. Being substantially taller than Ahrens, he had taken the precaution of fitting a higher rollover bar. This was a wise move. A driver just in front of him aborted an overtaking attempt and swung back into his path, clipping his front wheel. The Brabham was launched airborne, careened off the circuit and ended up in some trees, upside down. Ronnie was very lucky to escape injury.

He was not deterred. He put the accident down to inexperience, and remained convinced of his ability. The Brabham was trailered home for repairs behind the family's VW camper van, and they prepared for Ronnie's first full season of single-seater racing in 1967.

By now, Ronnie had become very friendly with Suzy Raganelli. For the 1967 season, he got his father to customise a Robardie for her – the very first kart with a self-starter. Raganelli successfully ran this alongside her Tecno and Ronnie took her on in a World Championship qualifying event at Vevey. This was Ronnie's last karting International. He qualified third behind 'La Suzy' and Tomas Nilsson, but blew an engine while dicing with his compatriot for the lead of the first heat. He was chasing Raganelli in the second heat but was passed by Allen and Goldstein, to finish fourth. In the final, he was racing these three when he hit a strawbale. He was spectating when Raganelli won.

In subsequent seasons, Bengt's Robardies were winning races in other hands. Thus equipped, Tomas Nilsson won the World Championship in 1968, and François Goldstein in 1969–70. But Ronnie Peterson had moved on.

ABOVE Bengt Peterson, Ronnie's father, at home in Örebro with the March 712M in which Ronnie trounced all opposition in the 1971 European F2 Trophy series. *(Photo courtesy of Tommy Peterson Collection)*

1967–1969

THE YOUNG MAN TO BEAT IN FORMULA 3

Ronnie Peterson's race driving career began with three seasons in Formula 3, in 1967 with his second-hand Brabham, then with state-of-the-art Tecnos that delivered consecutive Swedish national championships in 1968 and 1969. The Italian cars brought him 27 victories in those two seasons, including eight in Internationals. These were the halcyon days of the super-competitive 1-litre formula, featuring so many cars that event formats of heats and finals were normal, and contested by future stars such as Brambilla, Cevert, Depailler, Fittipaldi, Hunt, Laffite, Schenken and Wisell. Ronnie could beat them all. Stunning victories in 1969 at Monaco and Monza put him firmly in the spotlight, and he had twice raced in Formula 2 when he was signed up by the new March company with promises of a future bright.

RIGHT Ronnie raises an arm in triumph at the crowning moment of his Formula 3 career, in Monaco in 1969. He fought a breathless battle with his friend and compatriot, Reine Wisell, the two side-by-side often, touching wheels and brushing the barriers. With two laps remaining, Reine's works Chevron was in the escape road, its brakes shot, and Ronnie could cruise his Tecno to the chequer.

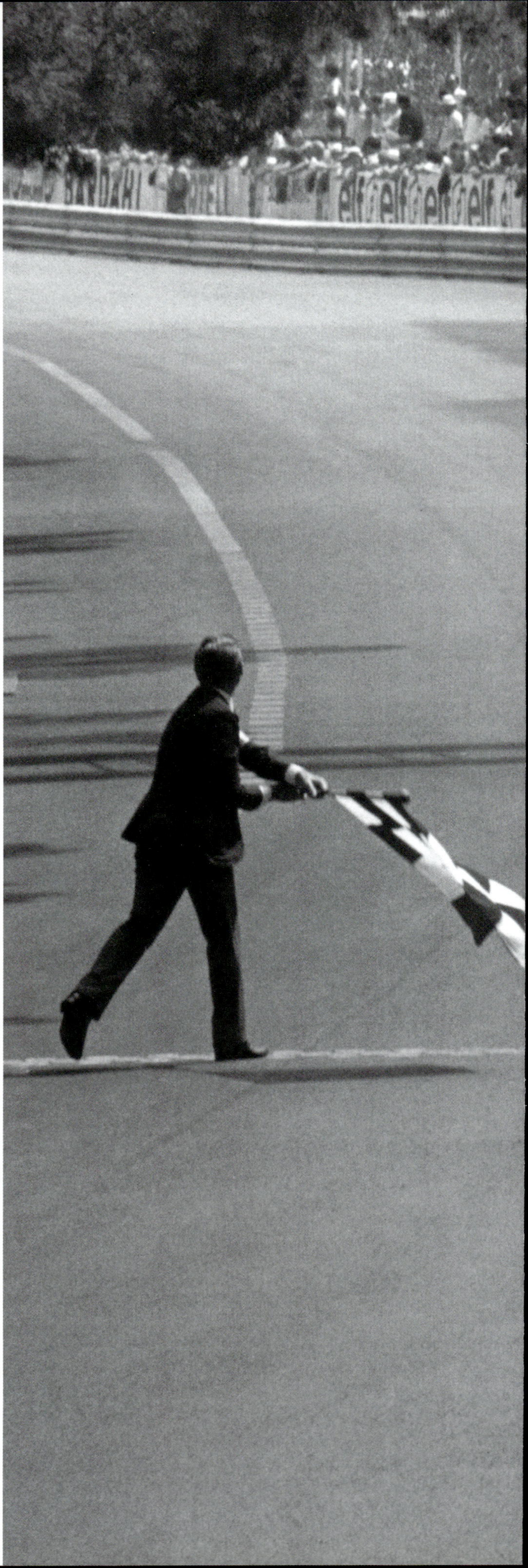

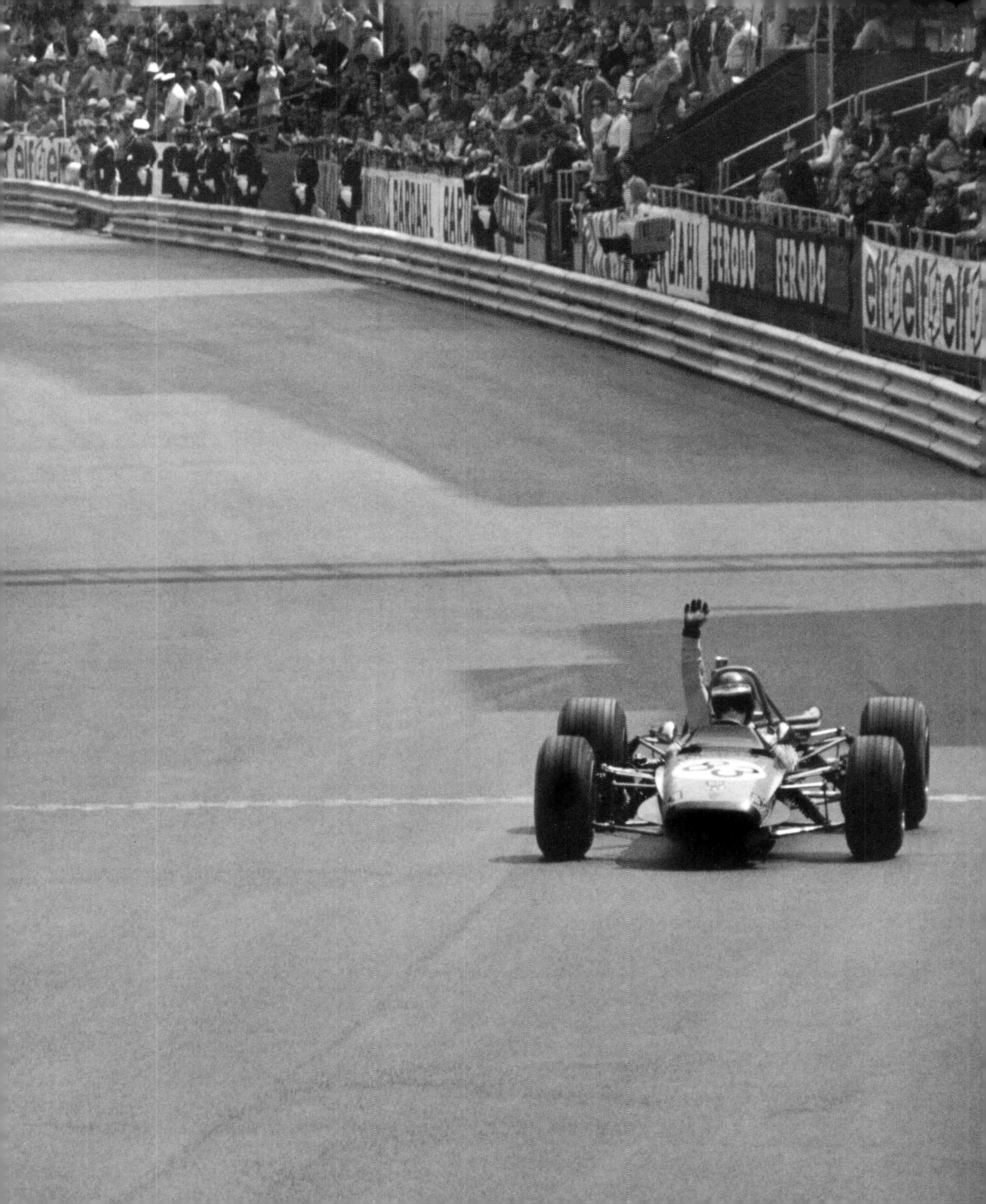
BARDAHL
FERODO
FERODO
elf elf elf

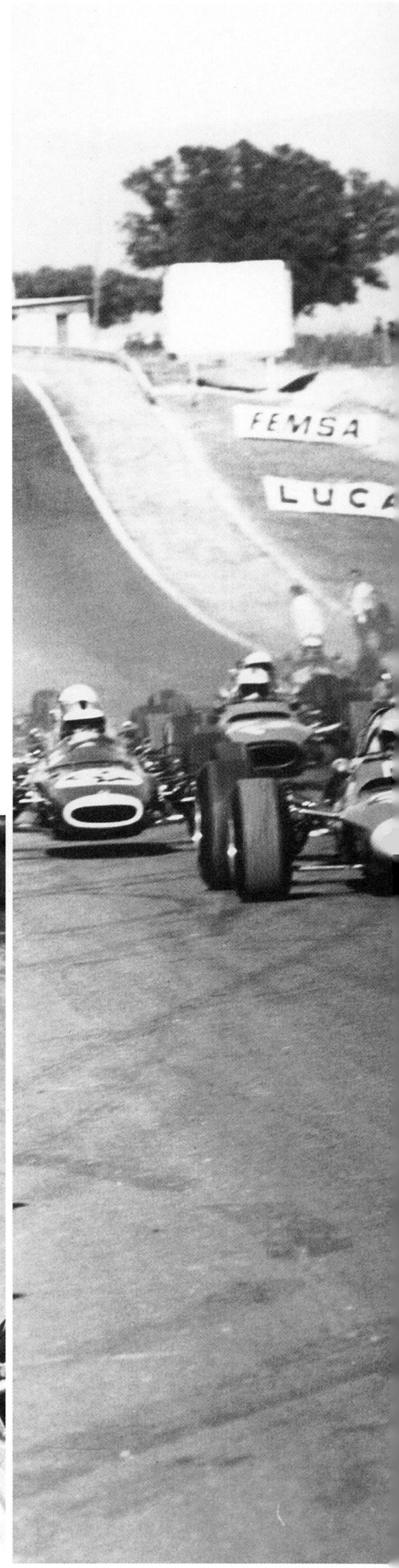

RIGHT Repaired by Bengt Peterson after its crash at the end of the 1966 season, the chassis of the ex-Kurt Ahrens Brabham ET18 remained slightly twisted, but it gave Ronnie a foundation in his first full single-seater season in 1967. He used it for 15 races in Scandinavia and for ventures further afield to Portugal, France, Germany and Britain, with mechanic Bo Hallqvist and troupes of fellow Swedish competitors. None of these events delivered a result, but he achieved 12 finishes in the top four nearer to home, including some in a Swedish championship that was hotly contested by Ulf Svensson, Lasse Lindberg and Ahrens with new Brabham BT21s, Reine Wisell with his BT18, and Freddy Kottulinsky with a Lotus. Ronnie's best results came in August in a club meeting at Knutsdorp, when he landed his maiden F3 victory in a heat, and finished a close second in the final between Wisell, newly crowned as the Swedish Champion, and Kottulinsky, the outgoing champion. At season's end, he contested the Spanish Grand Prix support race at Jarama. As Svensson makes a strong start in the second heat here, Ronnie's striped Brabham gets off the line alongside the Matras of Jean-Pierre Jaussaud and Patrick Guénard. Ronnie was an early retirement, but watched with interest as a strong field was humiliated in the final by Clay Regazzoni in the impressive new Tecno, with Wisell an outpaced second.

BELOW Ronnie looks on as his friend and Formula 3 rival Lasse Lindstrom tries the cockpit of the 1968 Tecno at the factory in Bologna. The Italian company had been formed in 1961 by Luciano and Gianfranco Pederzani to make karts. Three years later, Tecno had built a 250cc Ducati powered single-seater for Formula 4, a now defunct stepping-stone between karting and Formula 3. The Pederzani brothers produced their first Formula 3 car in 1966 and their 1967 model delivered their maiden international success when Clay Regazzoni won at Jarama that November. Suddenly the Tecno was the chassis to have, and Ronnie and Reine Wisell put down deposits on cars for 1968 – two of no fewer than 50 orders that winter.

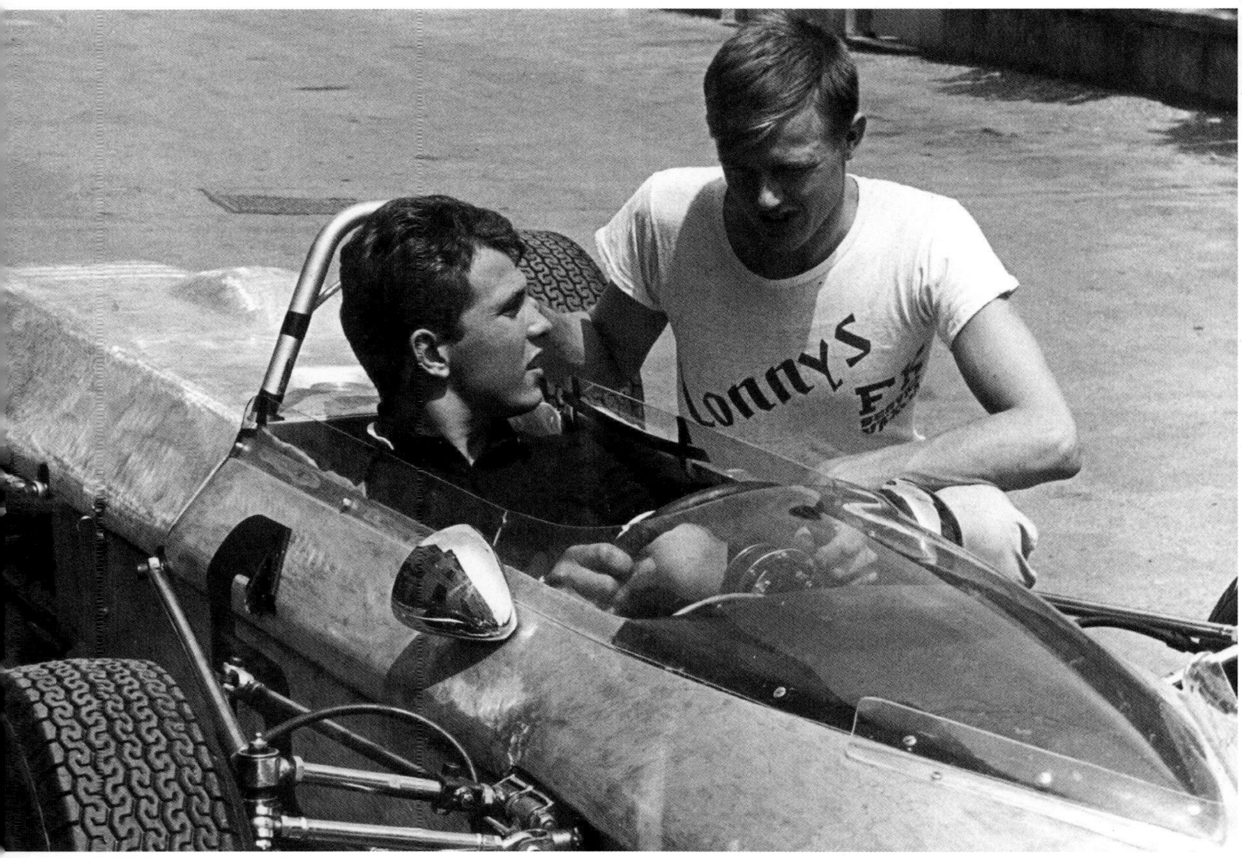

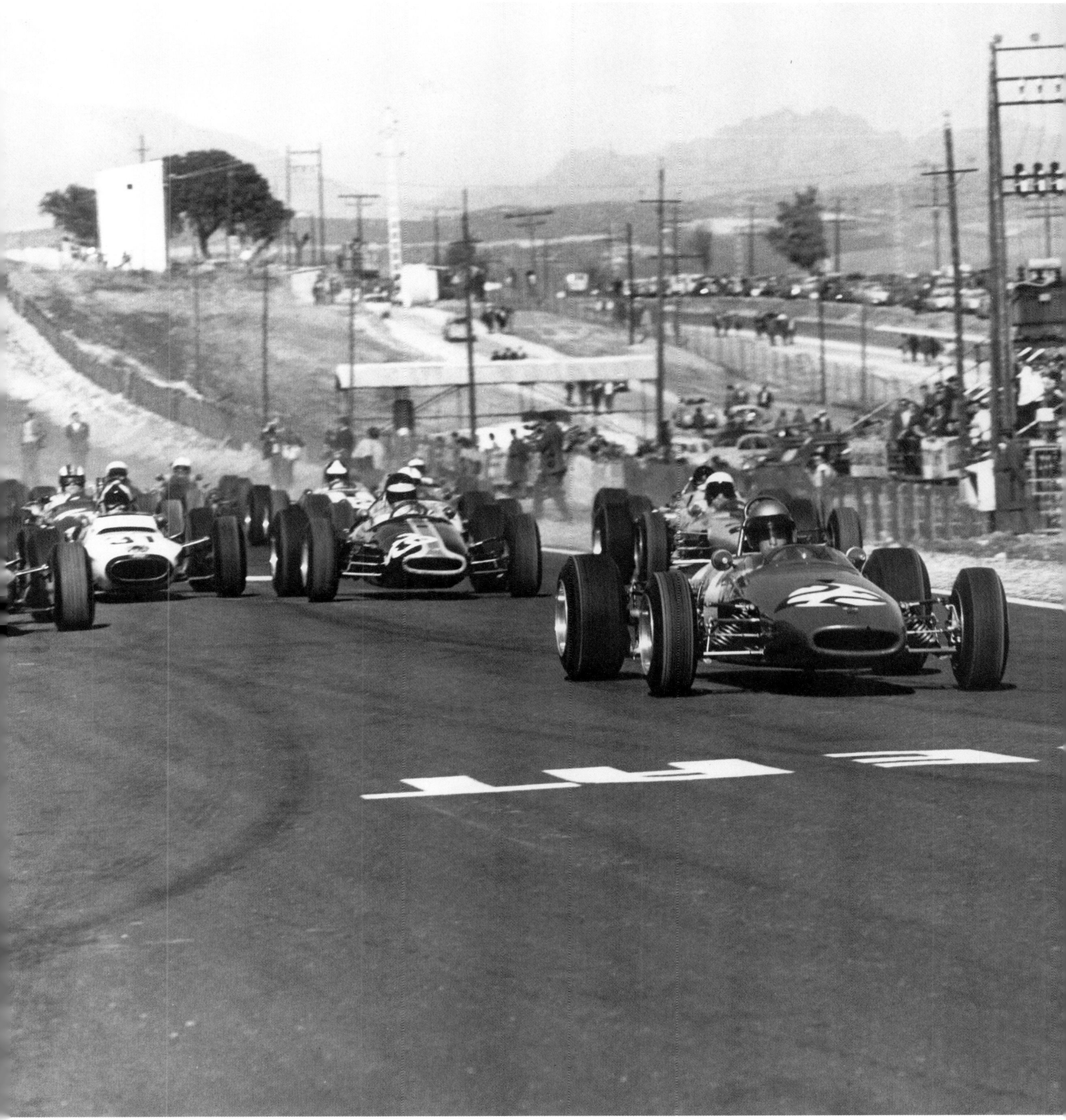

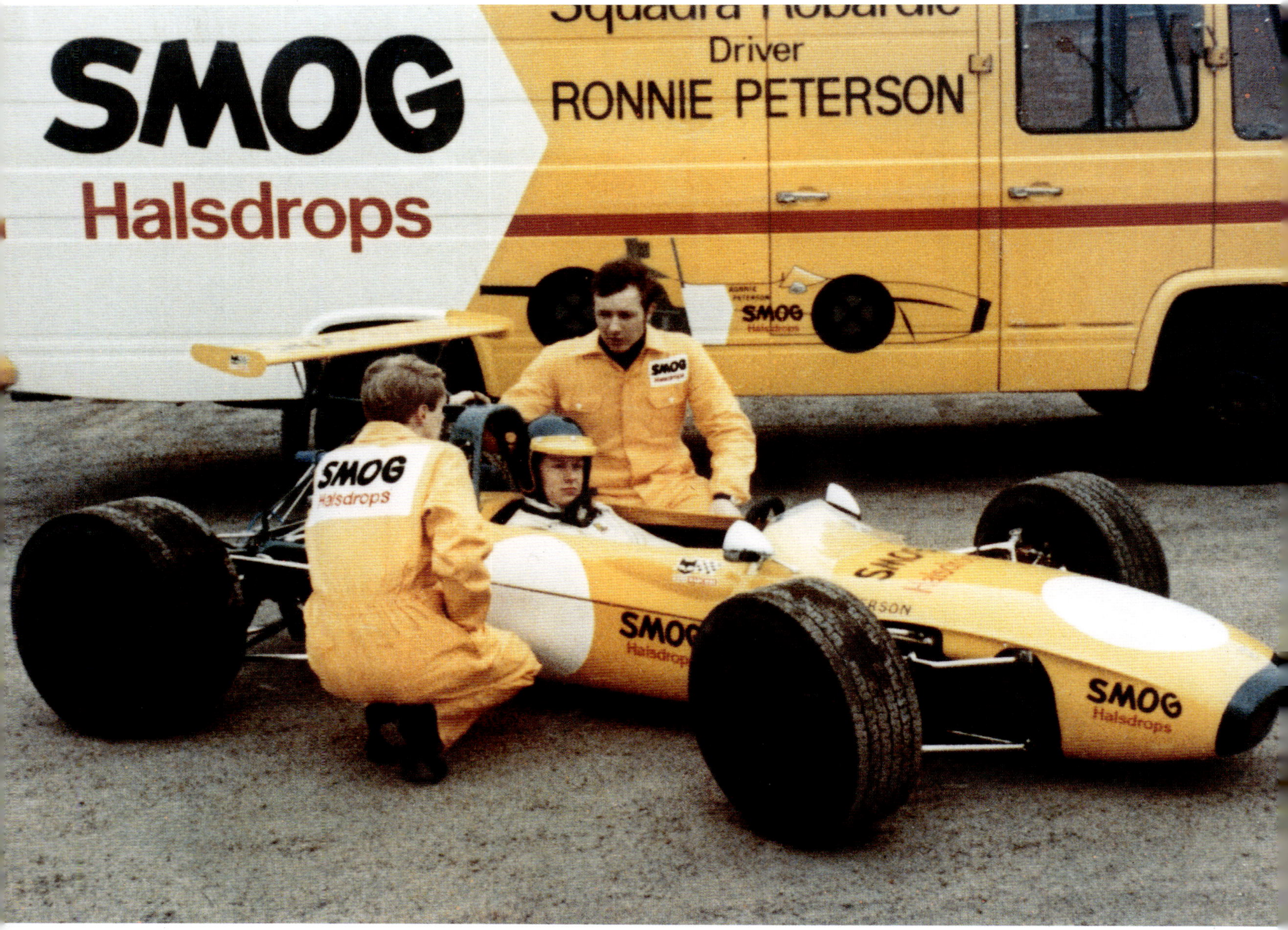

ABOVE Ronnie about to embark on his 1968 Formula 3 season with the 'Squadra Robardie' Tecno. Ronnie was granted a year's 'sabbatical' by the lift installation company that employed him so as to have a serious crack at Formula 3. At season's end, he told his boss that he would not be coming back. This was the start of Ronnie's enduring sponsorship relationship with the Swedish division of Vicks, promoting its 'Smog' brand of throat lozenges.

RIGHT Ronnie's new Tecno at the head of the field before its first event, the support race for the third Formula 2 Gran Premio de Barcelona on the Montjuic parkland circuit at the end of March 1968. He qualified fourth behind Mike Walker (McLaren M4A), Jean-Pierre Jabouille (Matra MS5) and Charles Lucas (Titan Mk3), but his new racing programme started badly. A stone punctured a tyre on the first lap of his heat and the Tecno was pitched violently through a fence, missing a tree by inches. In contrast, Reine Wisell's relationship with Tecno began with a comfortable victory in the final. The Italian company won 32 of 65 events in Europe in 1968, when the 1-litre Formula 3 was at its zenith, and the two blond Swedes contributed 23 of them.

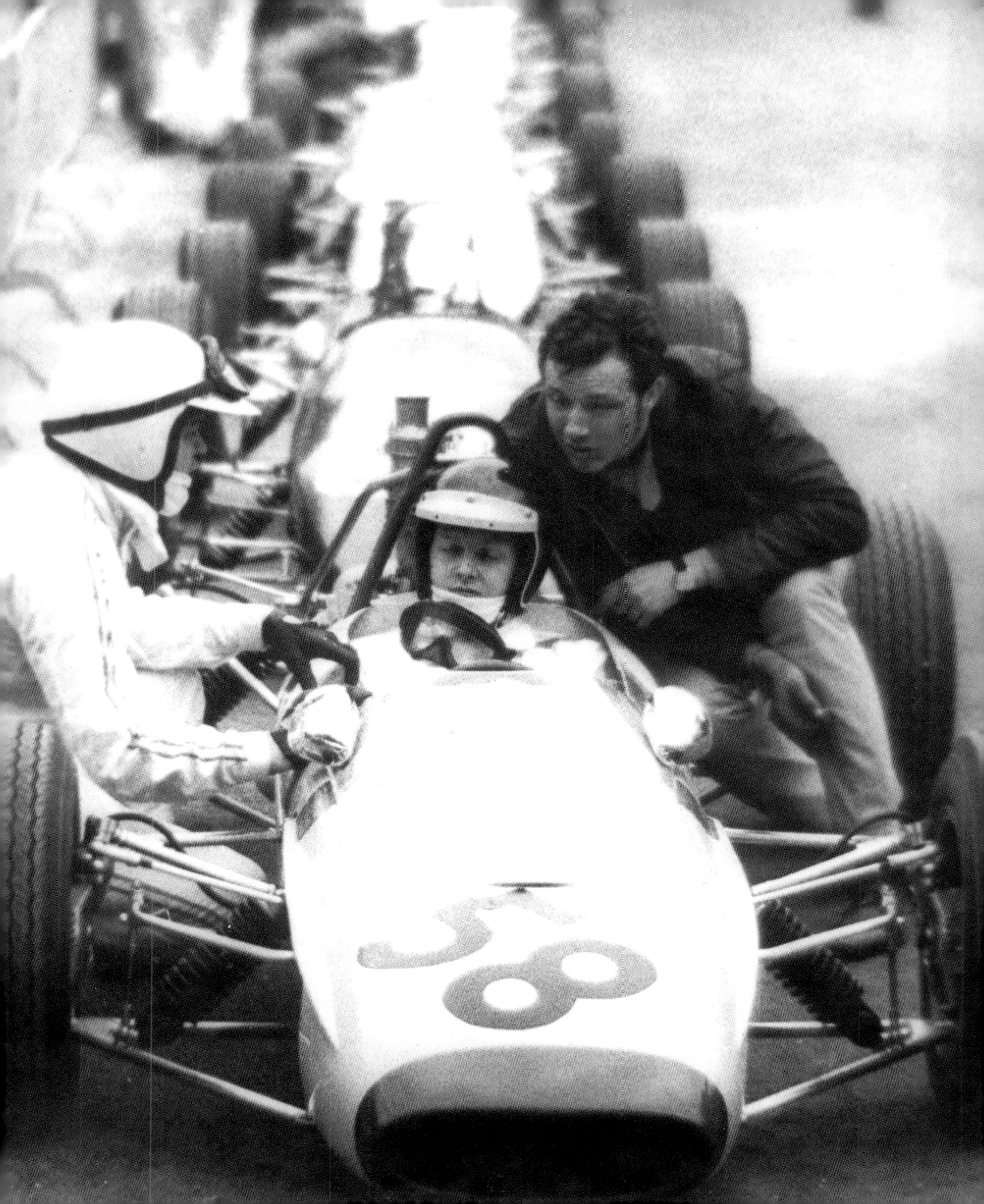

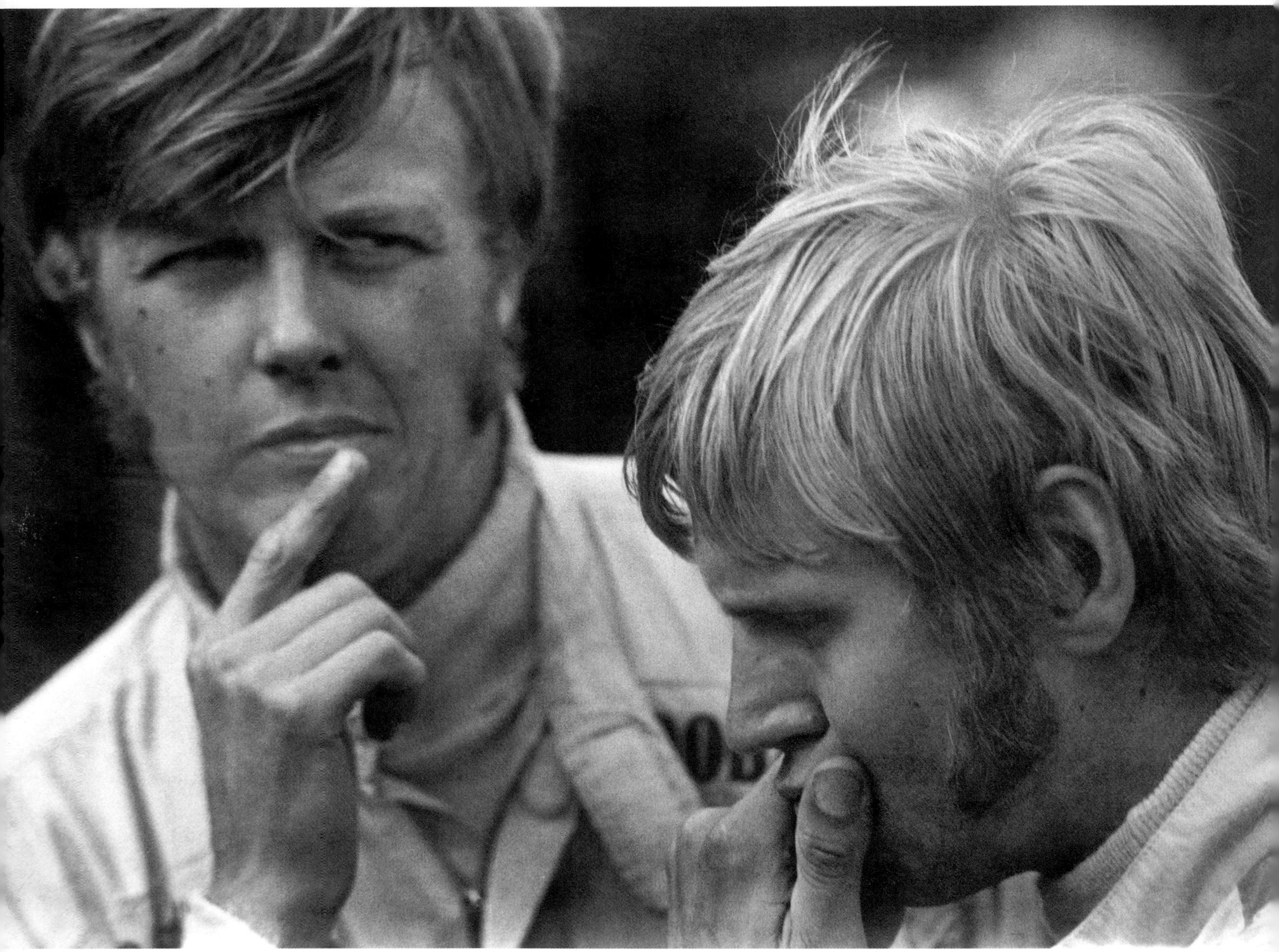

ABOVE Compatriots, friends, rivals... A week after Barcelona, at Monza, Ronnie finished second in his heat to Clay Regazzoni's works Tecno, and edged out Reine for fourth place in the final behind Jean-Pierre Jaussaud in another Tecno, Regazzoni and Ulf Svensson in his Brabham. These two then vied with each other to be Sweden's brightest young prospect. Although Reine did not seriously defend his 1967 national Formula 3 title, they met frequently in internationals in both 1968 and in 1969, when Wisell had the works Chevron deal. They often travelled together and had a lot of fun while not discouraging stories in the Swedish media of mutual antipathy.

RIGHT Ronnie began his domestic 1968 season by inflicting heavy defeats on Brabham driver Ulf Svensson in two club races before they contested the opening round of the Swedish championship. He was outqualified at a very cold Karlskoga by Reine Wisell, and hampered in the race (won by Ingvar Petterson's Brabham) by an iced-up fuel system – but he was not beaten in his national championship again. Here he has just won a non-championship race on the Djurslandring that July in Denmark.

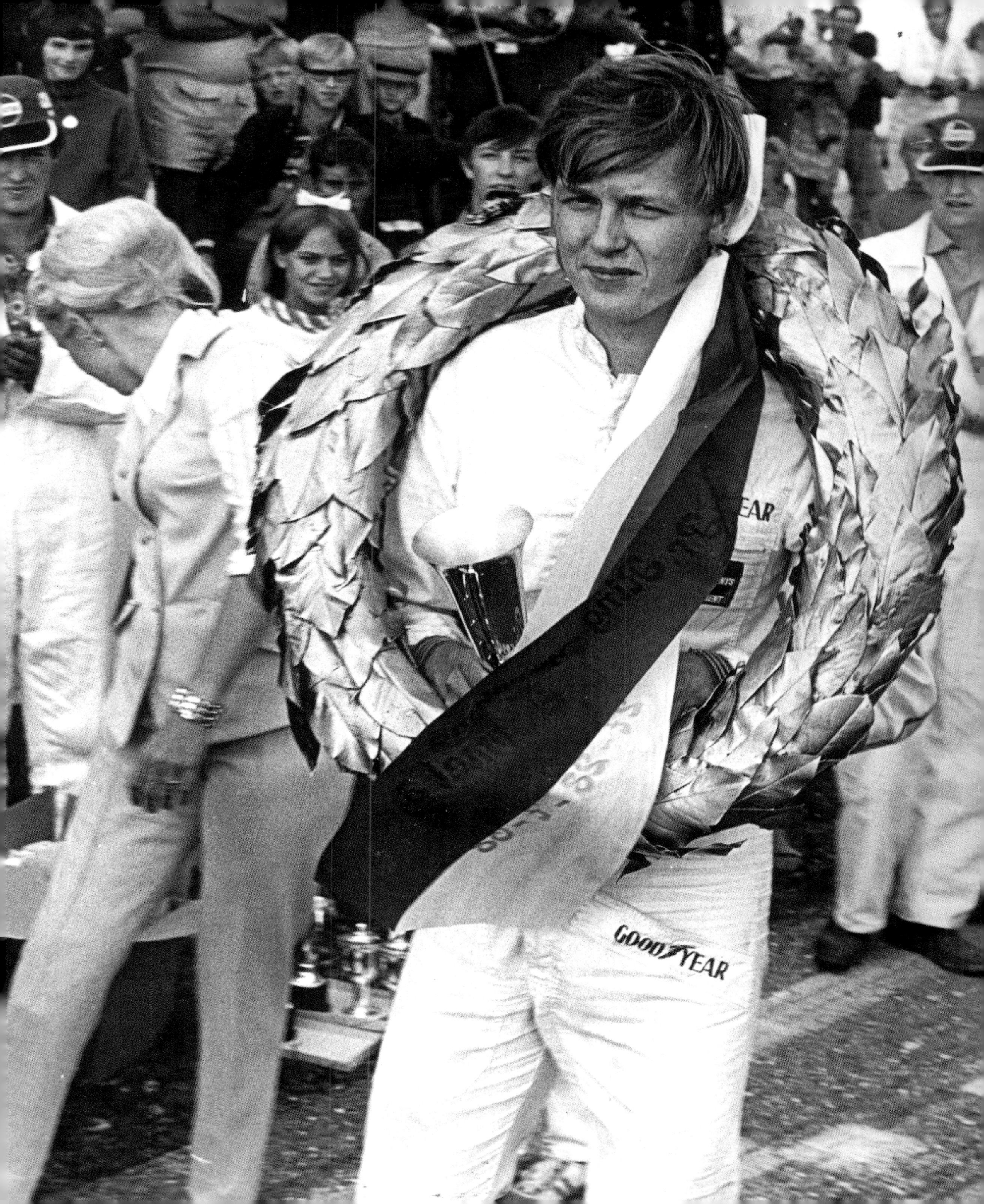
GOODYEAR

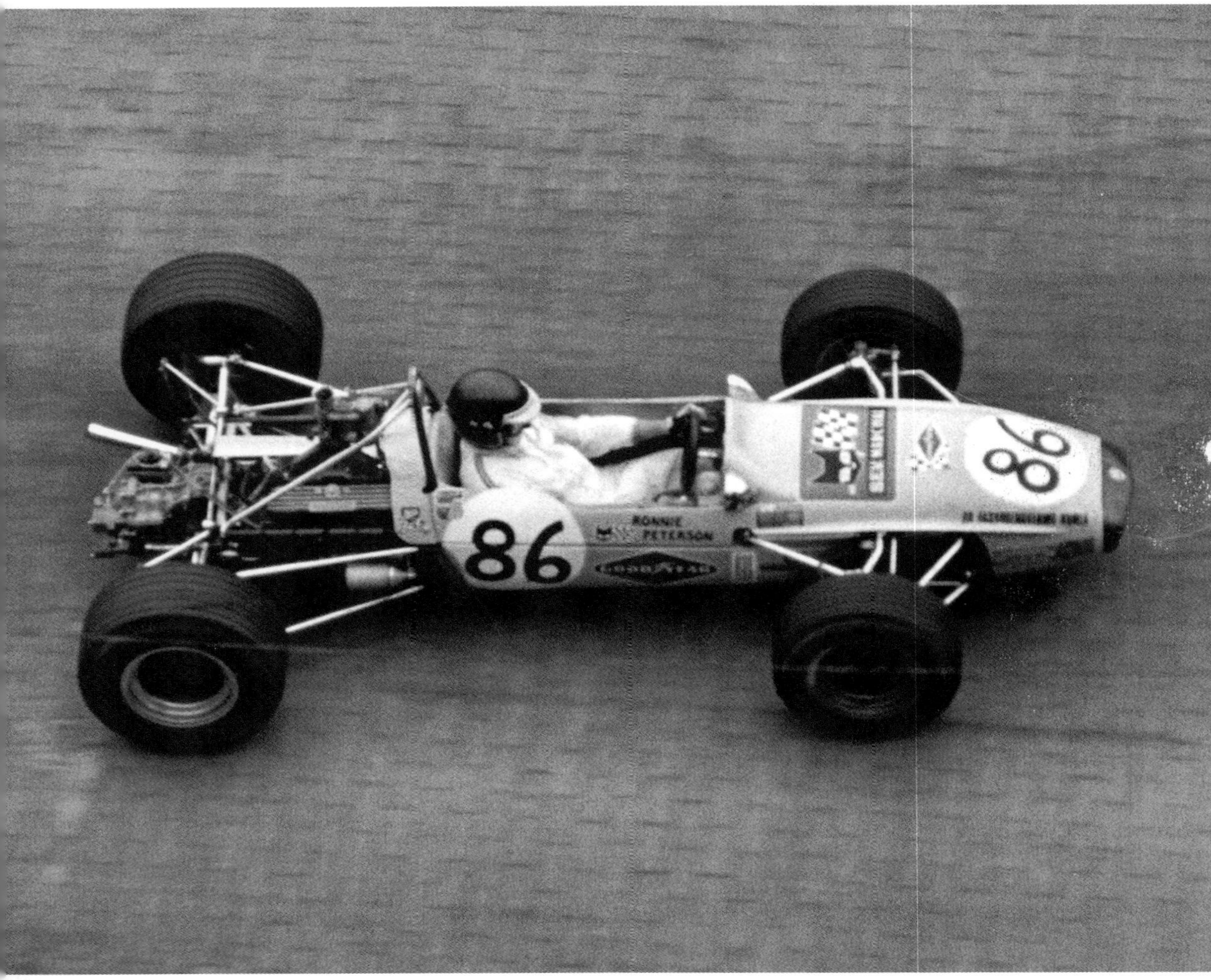

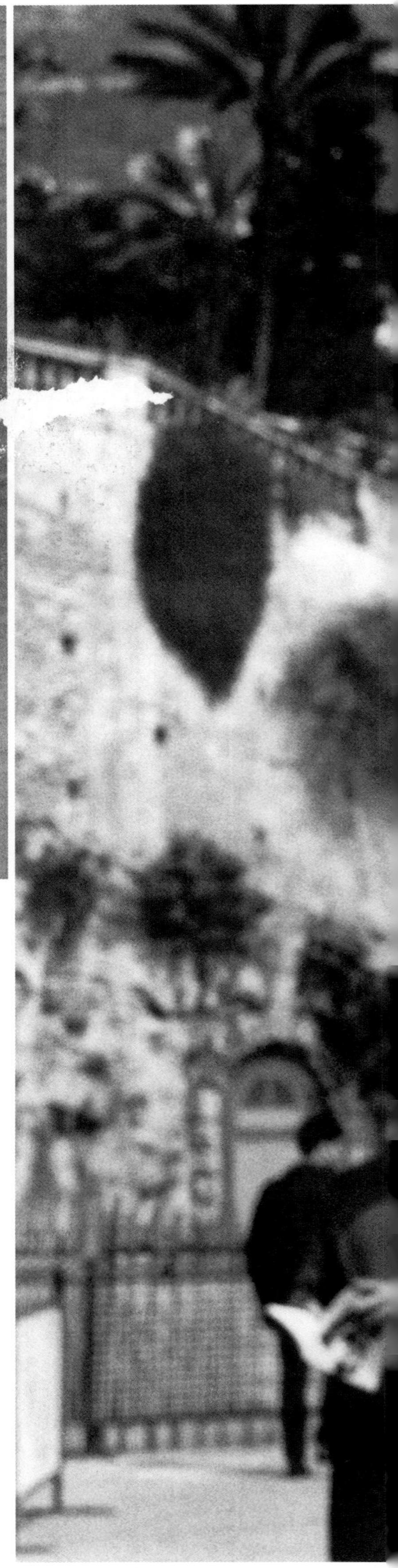

ABOVE Ronnie's first Formula 3 race in Monaco resulted in third place in his heat behind Jean-Pierre Jaussaud's Ecurie Arnold Tecno and Patrick Depailler's works Alpine-Renault. Jaussaud easily won the final with Peter Gethin second in Frank Lythgoe's Brabham, and Ronnie third again with his hands full with François Cevert in another Tecno. A disappointed Ronnie went straight from Monaco to Hockenheim, where he won the Hessenpreis international against less competitive opposition. Ronnie's 12 Formula 3 victories from 26 starts in 1968 marked him as a rising star on the international stage, because they included three outside Scandinavia, at Hockenheim (twice) and Monza.

RIGHT Ronnie ready to make his bid for the big time, at Monaco in May 1969 for his second Formula 3 race there. All 11 previous winners of the 'junior' race in the principality had subsequently graduated to Grand Prix racing, so he hoped that a victory in the season's most hotly contested Formula 3 race would issue his ticket to Formula 1. It did – and would continue to do the job for other young drivers for the next 16 years.

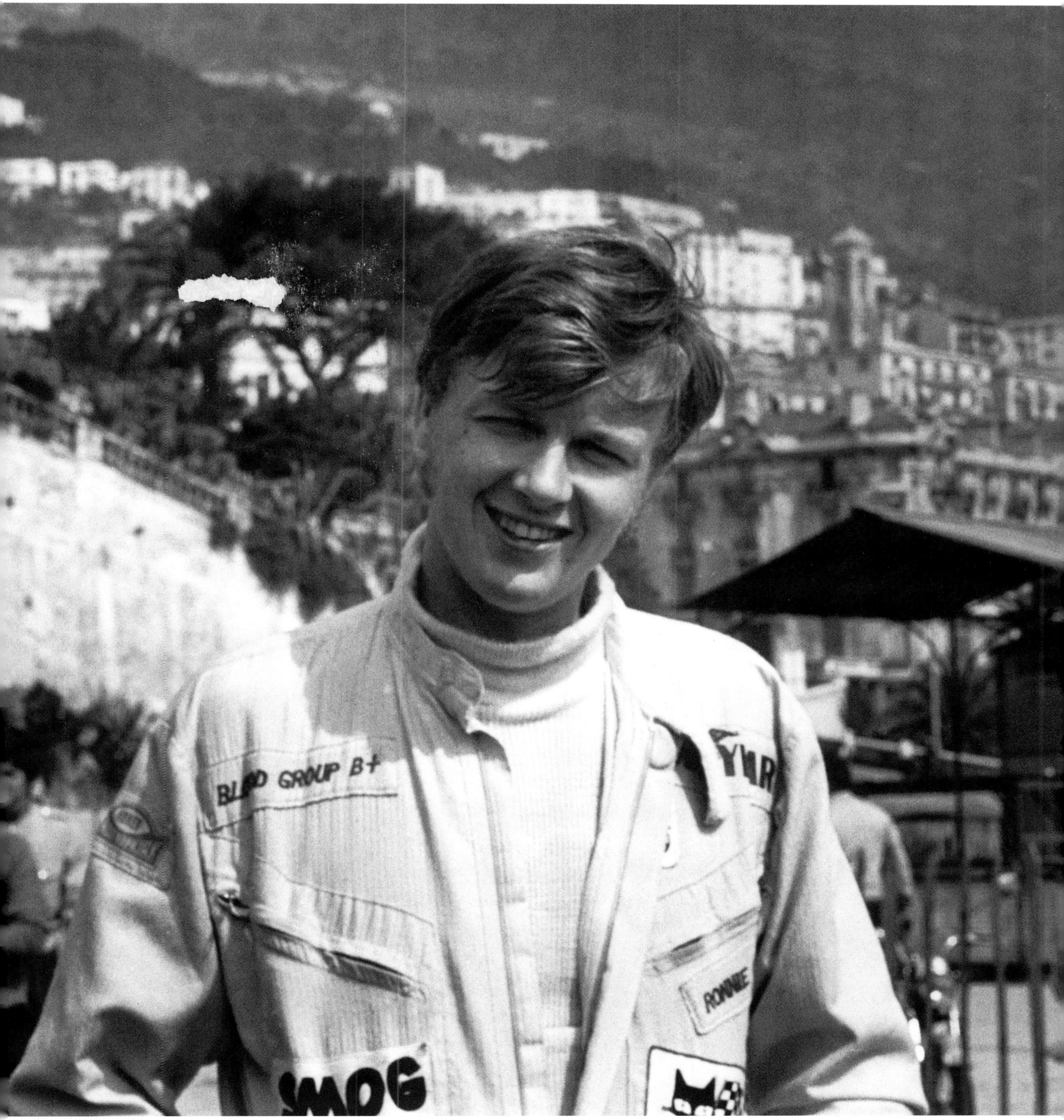
GROUP B+
RONNIE
SMOG

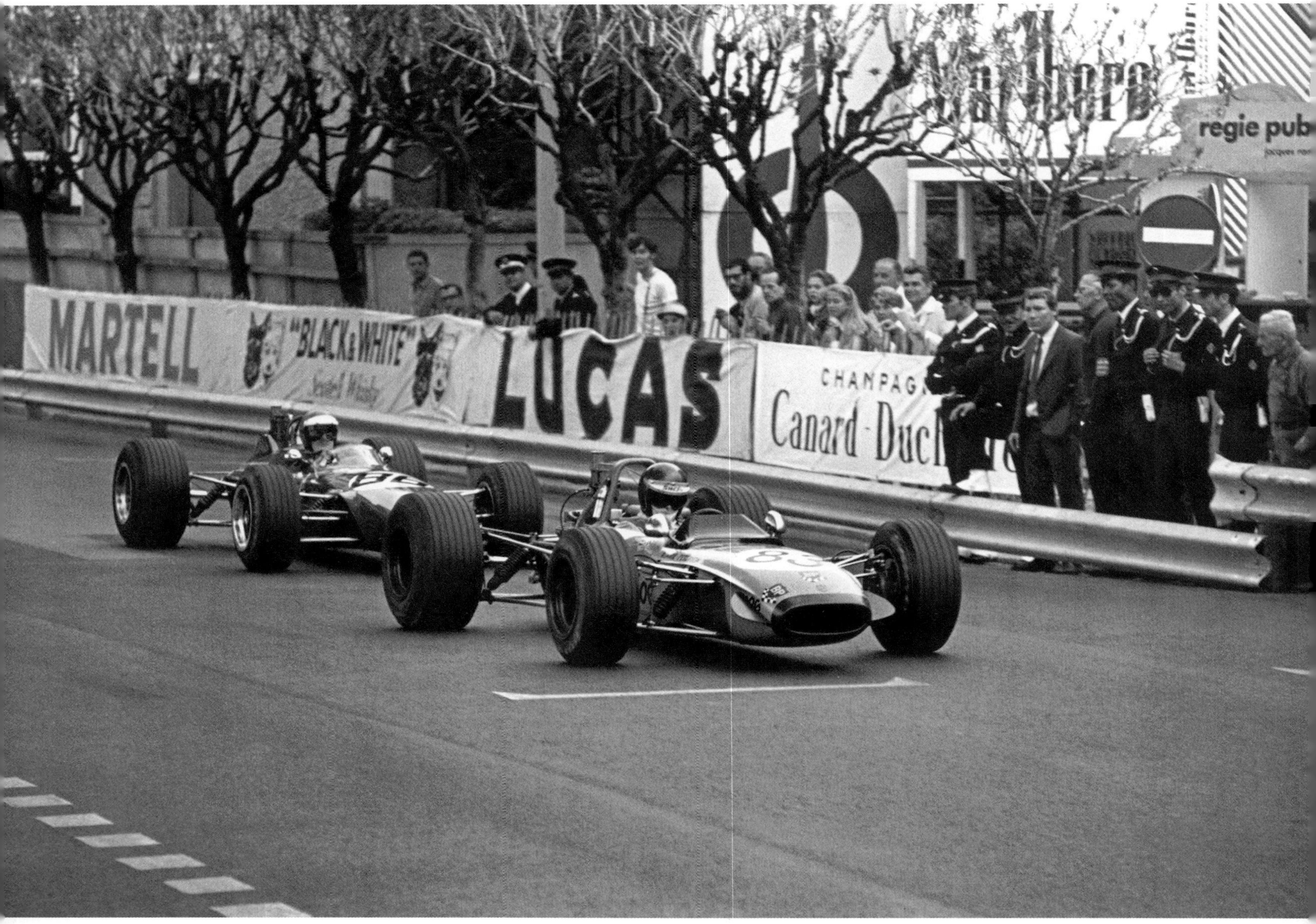

ABOVE Equipped with the works Novamotor engine, and now enjoying extended works status with Tecno, Ronnie qualified fastest at Monaco with a time almost 2sec under the lap record. He and Reine Wisell, now driving the works Chevron B15, each won a 16-lap heat. In the 23-lap final, they produced one of the most famous Formula 3 duels of all time. It endured for 21 spectacular laps. At that point Wisell, leading narrowly but with ruined brakes, skittered up the escape road at the chicane. Ronnie's Tecno ran out the winner by 8.5sec. The battle had taken the Swedish drivers so far from the opposition that Wisell was able to retrieve second place, still ahead of the works Alpine-Renaults of Jean-Pierre Jabouille and Patrick Depailler, which were split in fourth place by Tim Schenken's Sports Motors entered works Brabham.

RIGHT Ronnie after his victory in the epic 1969 Monaco Formula 3 event. He had arrived in the principality undefeated in six races, and highlighted his season on this never-to-be-forgotten day by emerging triumphant from his torrid battle with Reine Wisell. The performance grabbed the attention of onlookers from the Formula 1 community and particularly Alan Rees, who was plotting the new March Engineering company with his partners.

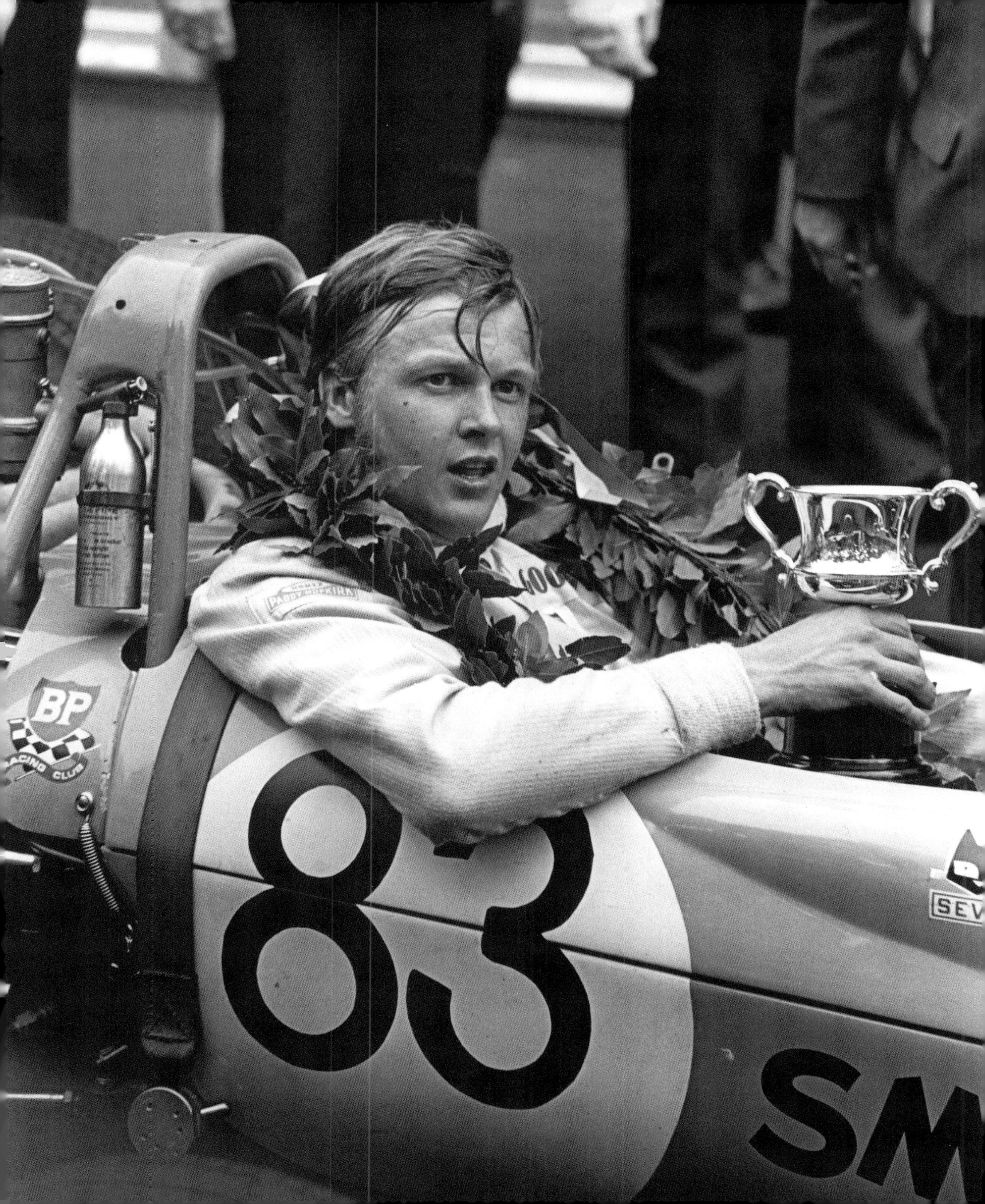
BP
RACING CLUB
83

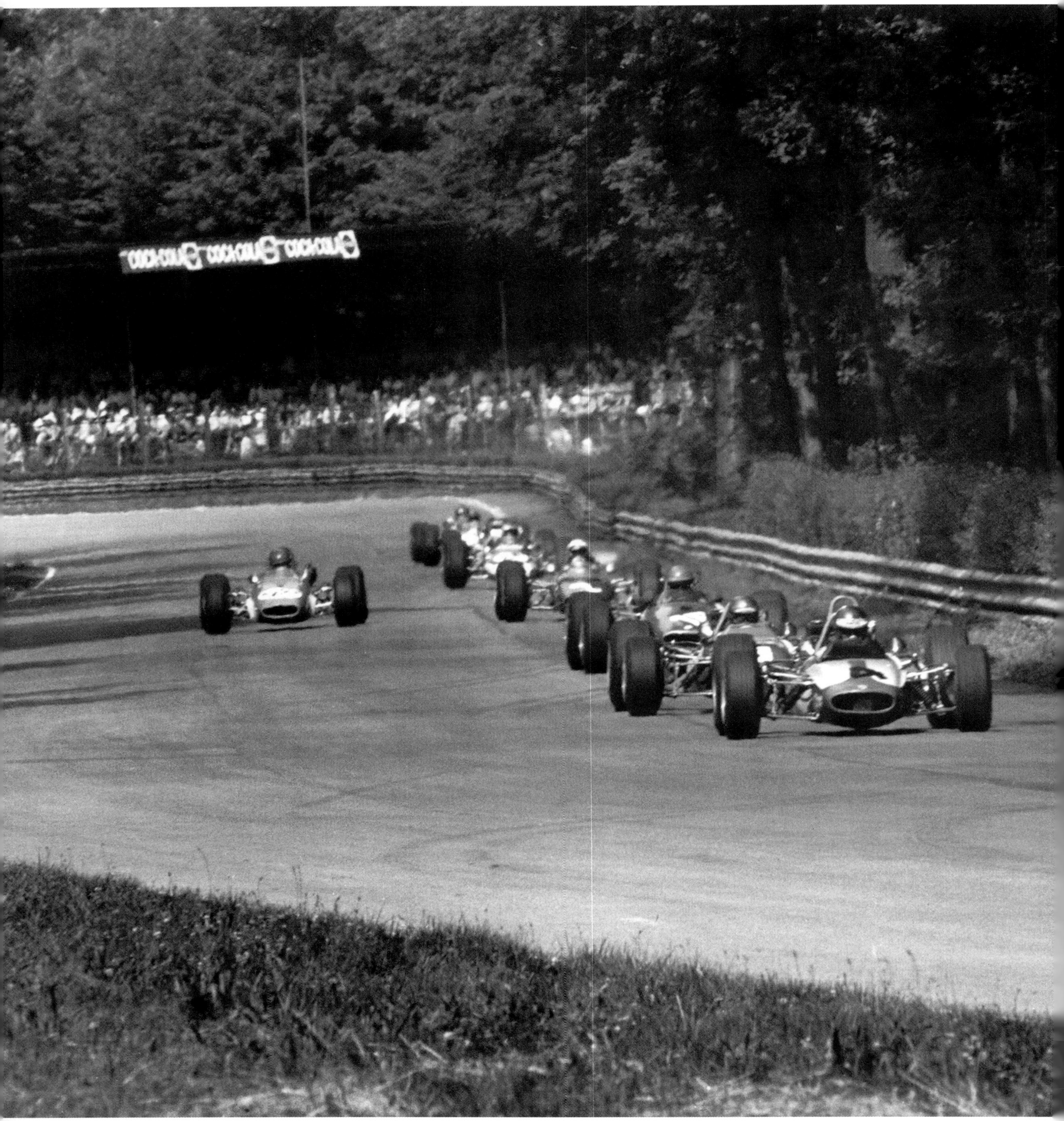

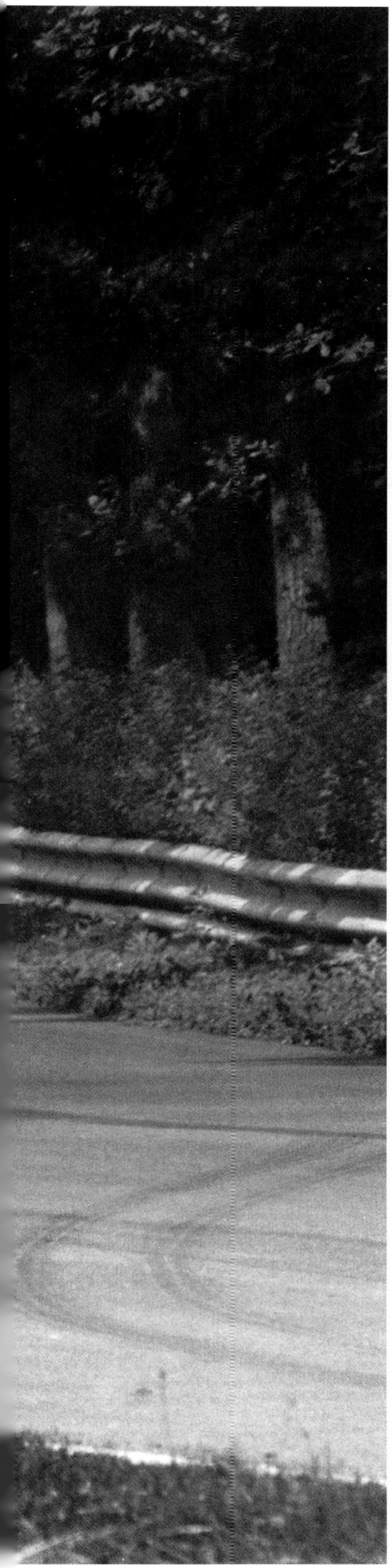

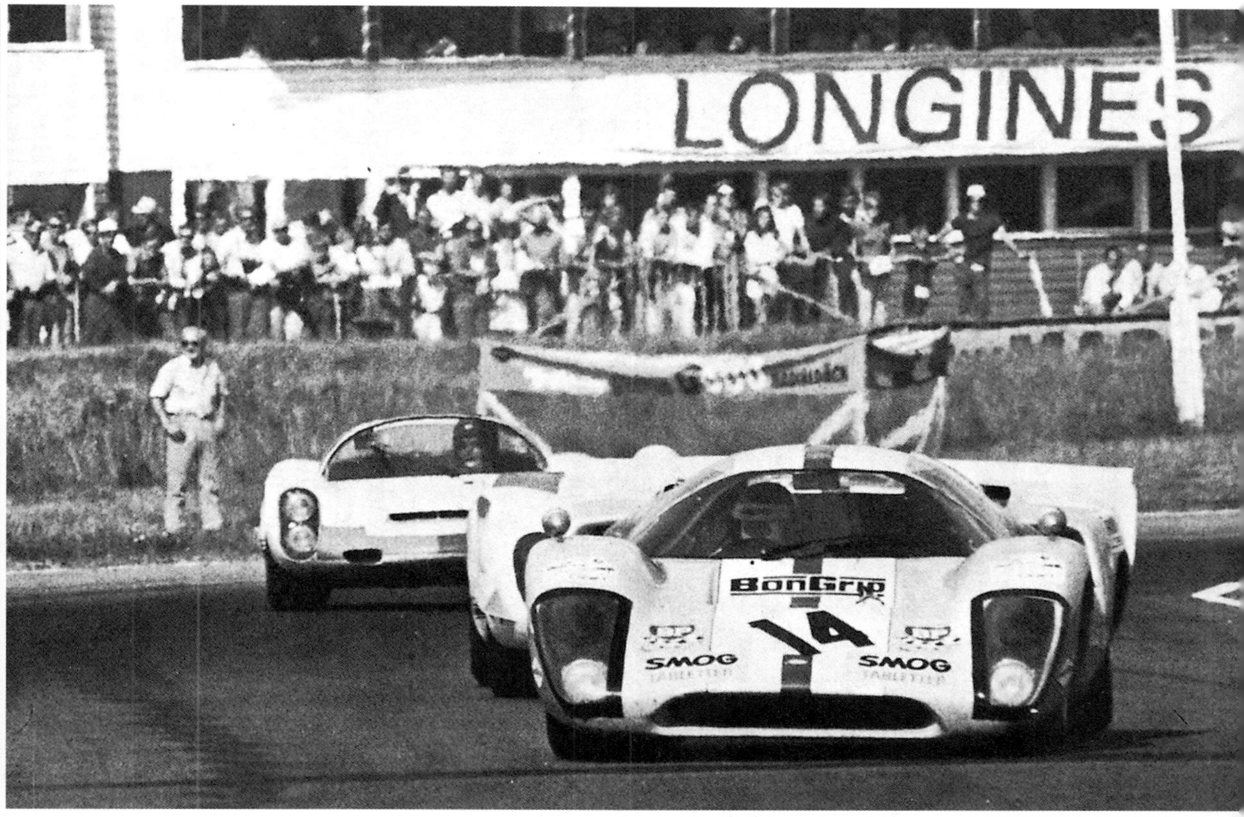

LEFT Five weeks after Monaco, having also won two big Formula 3 events for Tecno at Monza, Ronnie was taken back to the Autodromo Nazionale at the expense of the Italian company. He was invited to drive a third works car alongside François Cevert and Nanni Galli in the Gran Premio di Lotteria, the popular annual non-championship Formula 2 race. He qualified 13th but was engaged from the start in one of the track's notorious slipstream battles. Here he has actually hit the front of the race-leading group, comprising Brabham drivers Peter Westbury, Malcolm Guthrie, Graham Birrell and Rob Widdows, Derek Bell and Vittorio Brambilla in works Ferrari Dinos, Cevert, and Jonathan Williams (De Tomaso). Ronnie was still in the bunch on the 27th of 45 laps when he clipped a barrier in the Lesmos at 140mph, and pitted to check for damage. He continued and finished seventh. This unremittingly hectic race was won by Widdows in Bob Gerard's Brabham – at left in the picture, having pulled out of Bell's tow. Three months after this impressive Formula 2 début, Ronnie scored his final (and one of his finest) Formula 3 victories at the same venue.

ABOVE Ronnie had his first taste of real power in the summer of 1969 with three outings in Chevrolet V8 powered Lola T70 sportscars. Picko Troberg offered him a drive at Magny-Cours, where Ronnie won his Formula 3 heat but was narrowly beaten in the final by François Mazet in another Tecno. He consoled himself with victory in the sportscar race, over Barrie Smith's Chevron B8 and Jean-Pierre Jaussaud's Alfa Romeo T33. Ronnie raced Troberg's car again in the event that inaugurated the new Osterreichring circuit in July, but crashed, leaving Andrea de Adamich to win for Alfa Romeo from Jo Bonnier in another Mk3B. The following month, Ronnie was in Karlskoga for the big European Formula 3 Challenge event when Bonnier arrived, bruised after crashing his Formula 1 Lotus 49 two days before in qualifying for the Oulton Park Gold Cup. Bonnier asked Ronnie to race his Lola. This time, Ronnie led the sportscar race in style (pictured) until a misfire dropped him behind Brian Redman in Sid Taylor's Lola and David Piper in a Porsche 908. Then he won the Formula 3 race, defeating Tim Schenken (Brabham) and clinching the challenge trophy for Sweden.

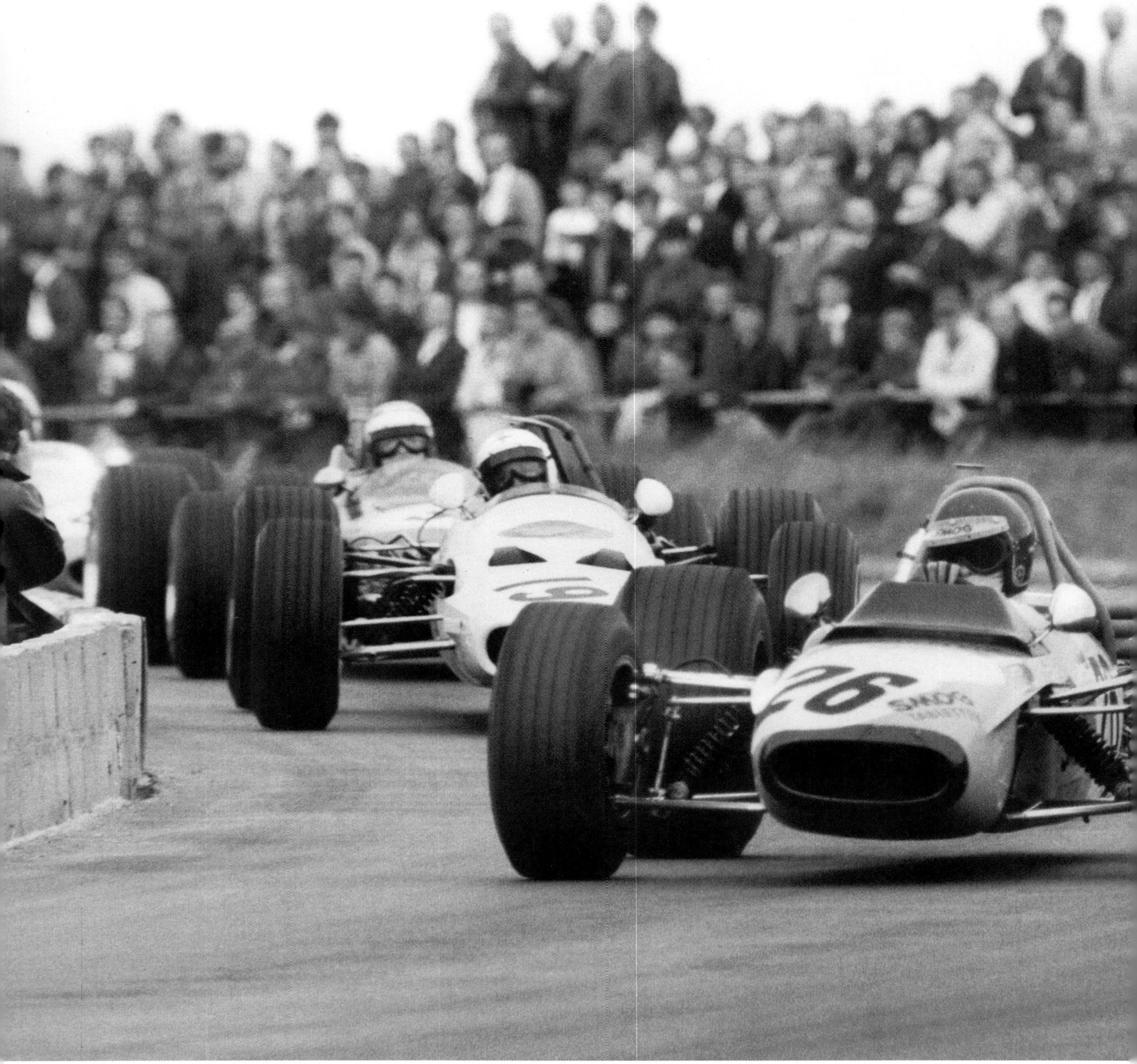

LEFT The second most important event of the Formula 3 season was the British Grand Prix support race, in which Ronnie is pictured leading Tetsu Ikusawa in Mike Spence's Lotus 59 and Reine Wisell in Derek Bennett's works Chevron B15, at the head of a seven-car scrap for the lead. As usual in these slipstreaming races at Silverstone for wingless 1-litre 'screamer' F3 cars, the front-runners all slowed on the last lap to avoid leading at the end of the Hangar Straight. Alan Rollinson was the first to attempt a breakaway with Goodwin Racing's Chevron, and he held on to win narrowly from Ikusawa, Peterson and Wisell. This was a rare blip in Ronnie's 1969 season, in which he successfully defended his Swedish title and secured 15 wins from 19 starts.

BELOW As the standout Formula 3 driver of the season, Ronnie was wooed by the promoters of the 56-car Guards International at Brands Hatch in the late summer of 1969. He accepted, although he had a commitment to a Swedish race at Knutsdorp the day before. When arrangements to fly his Tecno into England overnight fell through, the organisers found a ride for him in a Lotus 59 that was surplus to the requirements of Mike Warner's Lotus Components team. Ronnie left home without his passport and the consequent delay meant he had little sleep, but he got to grips with the unfamiliar Lotus as his heat progressed. He finished it in second place behind a similar car driven by Emerson Fittipaldi, in the Brazilian's first International. Here in the final, Ronnie leads Mo Nunn's works Lotus and François Mazet's Tecno, which will shortly hit Ronnie from behind. Reine Wisell won with the works Chevron in a virtual dead-heat with Tim Schenken in the works Brabham, with Fittipaldi not far behind in Jim Russell's Lotus. After a delay, Ronnie continued to finish an unlucky 13th.

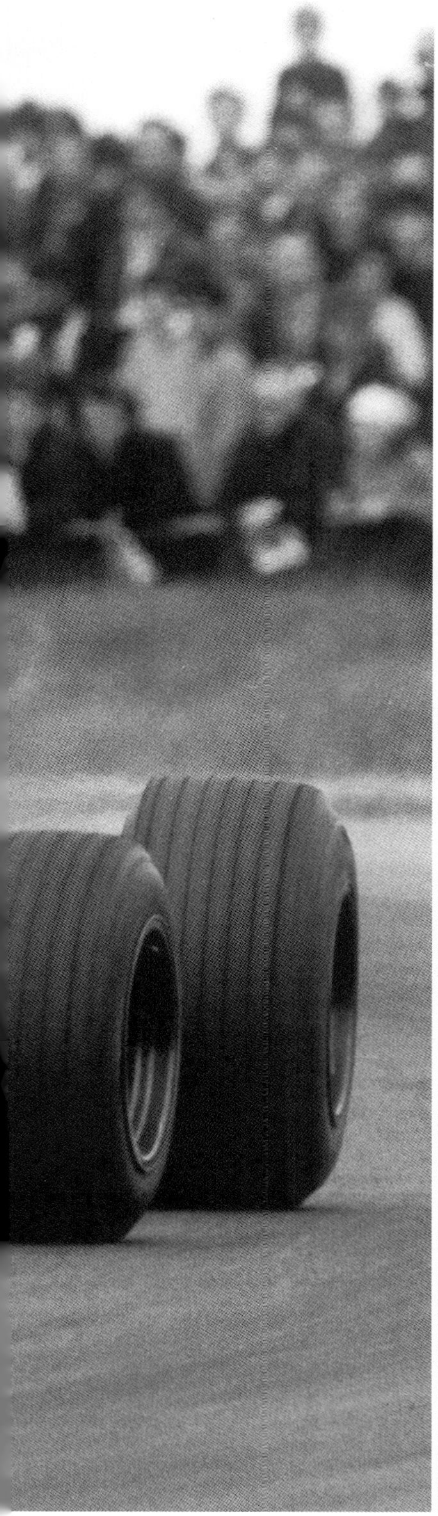

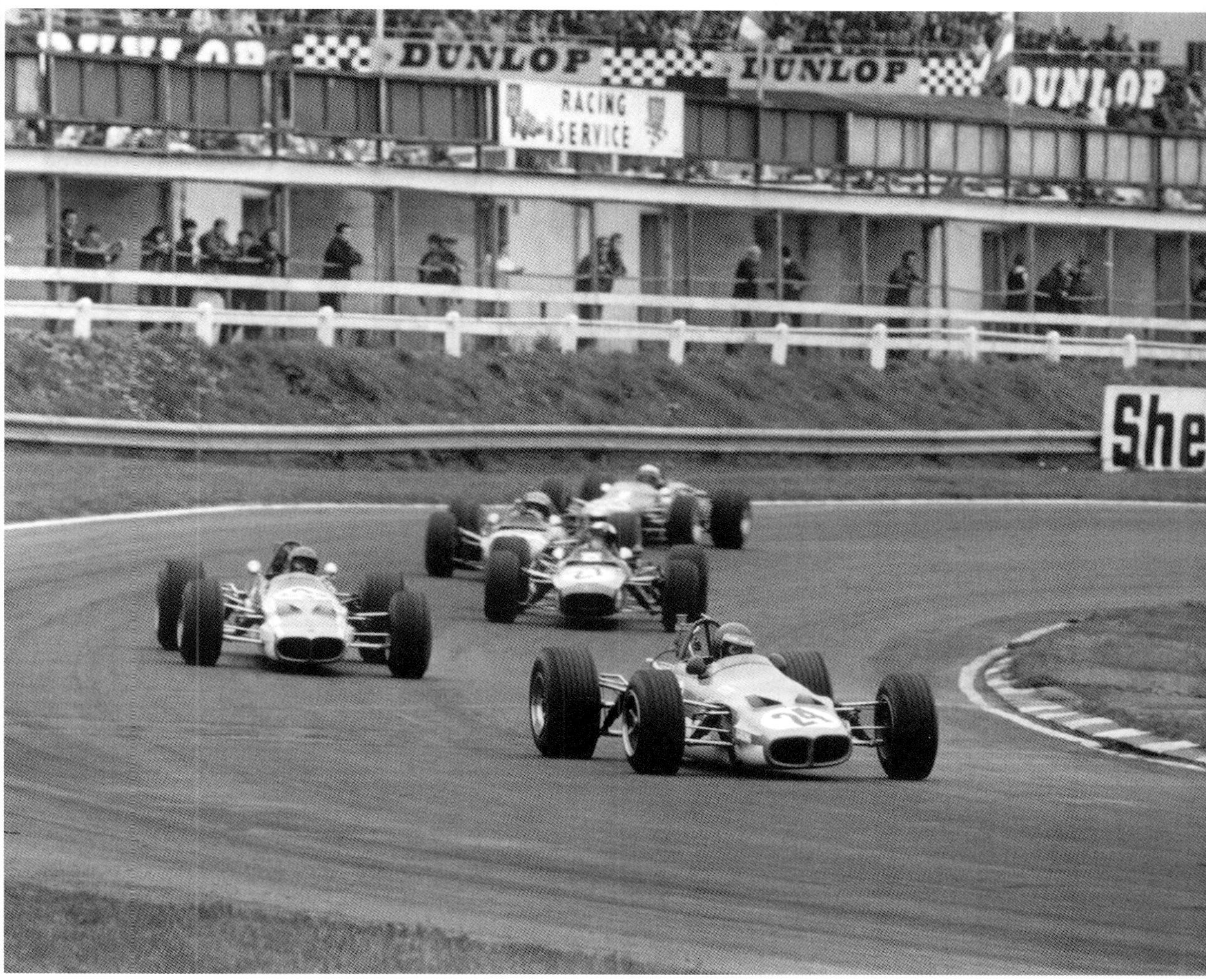

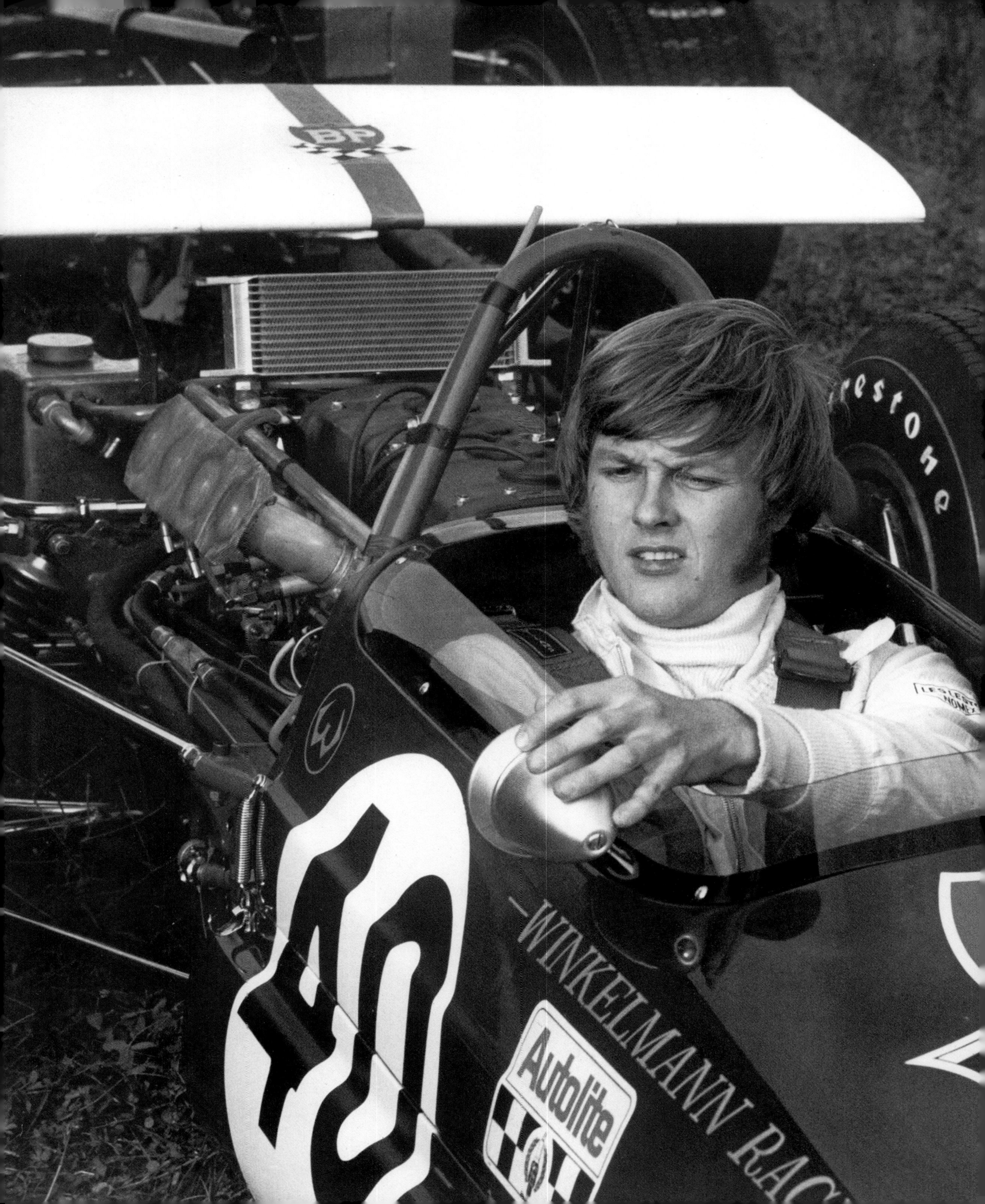
BP
WINKELMANN
Autolite

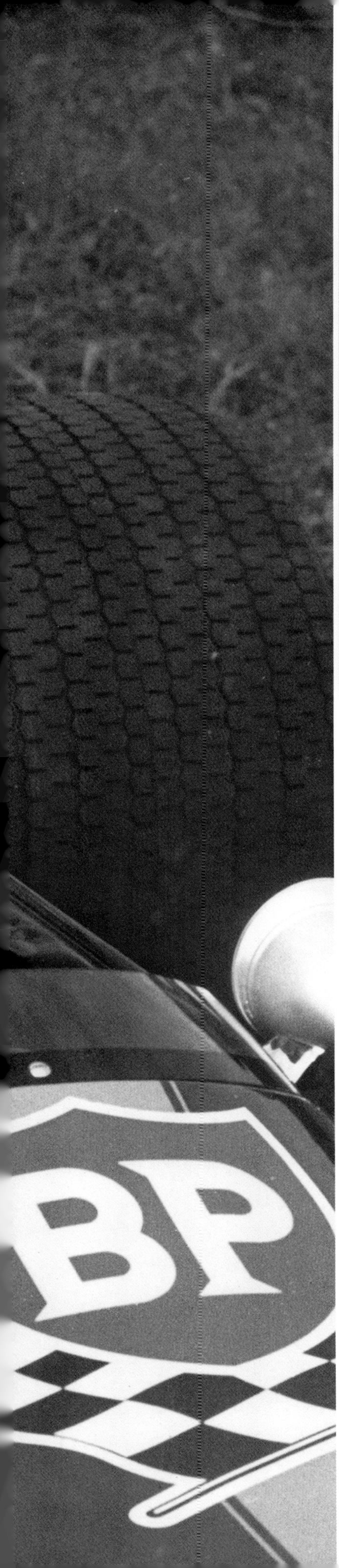

LEFT Straight after winning at Monaco, Ronnie was invited for another Formula 2 outing at Albi in late September, to race a third Lotus 59B for Roy Winkelmann Racing alongside Jochen Rindt and Graham Hill. The drive was arranged by Winkelmann's Alan Rees, the man who had first spotted Rindt, and the car was the one crashed by Max Mosley that May on the Nürburgring. Ronnie qualified eighth in the Friday qualifying session, and was sensationally third fastest when it rained on the Saturday. After being dominated by Jackie Stewart, until his Matra lost its engine, the race was won by Hill, with Rindt third and Ronnie fifth, the interlopers being Matras raced by Johnny Servoz-Gavin and Henri Pescarolo. Among the envious onlookers were his regular Formula 3 rivals, including Tim Schenken and Reine Wisell, who finished first and second in the support race. In a meeting with Rees during the evening, Ronnie verbally agreed a three-year deal with the new March Engineering company.

ABOVE Ronnie hounds James Hunt during their race-long dice on the début of March Engineering at Cadwell Park. A slow puncture hampered Ronnie but he managed to pip Hunt for third place behind Tim Schenken's works Brabham and Howden Ganley's Chevron. The following week, March sent him to Montlhéry for the Coupe du Salon event coinciding with the Paris Motor Show. Ronnie put the March on pole position, ahead of Emerson Fittipaldi's Lotus, the Tecnos of François Mazet and Jean-Pierre Jaussaud, Reine Wisell's Chevron and Schenken. But he made a poor start and, in trying to recover, clipped a straw bale on the exit of a chicane that slowed the cars as they came off the banking. The impact flipped the March over and a broken suspension wishbone punctured the fuel cell, causing a big fire. Marshals were instantly at work with extinguishers and March chief mechanic Ray Wardell sprinted from the pits to help them pull Ronnie out of the upturned car. Ronnie was fortunate to survive this accident, but was hospitalised for two days with burns on his arms and wrists – a bad end to such an outstanding Formula 3 career. However one of the visitors to his ward was Alan Rees, with a three-year March contract in his hand instead of a bunch of grapes. Ronnie signed it...

RIGHT Alan Rees had had a hidden agenda in inviting Ronnie to do a Formula 2 race with Winkelmann Racing: he wanted to secure the services of this prodigious talent for March Engineering. Ronnie gained the distinction of becoming the very first driver to race a March when the ambitious new company made its début in September 1969 in a British Formula 3 race at Cadwell Park. Rees convened with the other March founders, Max Mosley, Graham Coaker and Robin Herd, to see Ronnie in the prototype of their 703 model. Ronnie put it on the front row of the grid alongside Tim Schenken's new works Brabham BT28 (nearest camera) and Jean-Pierre Jaussaud's Tecno.

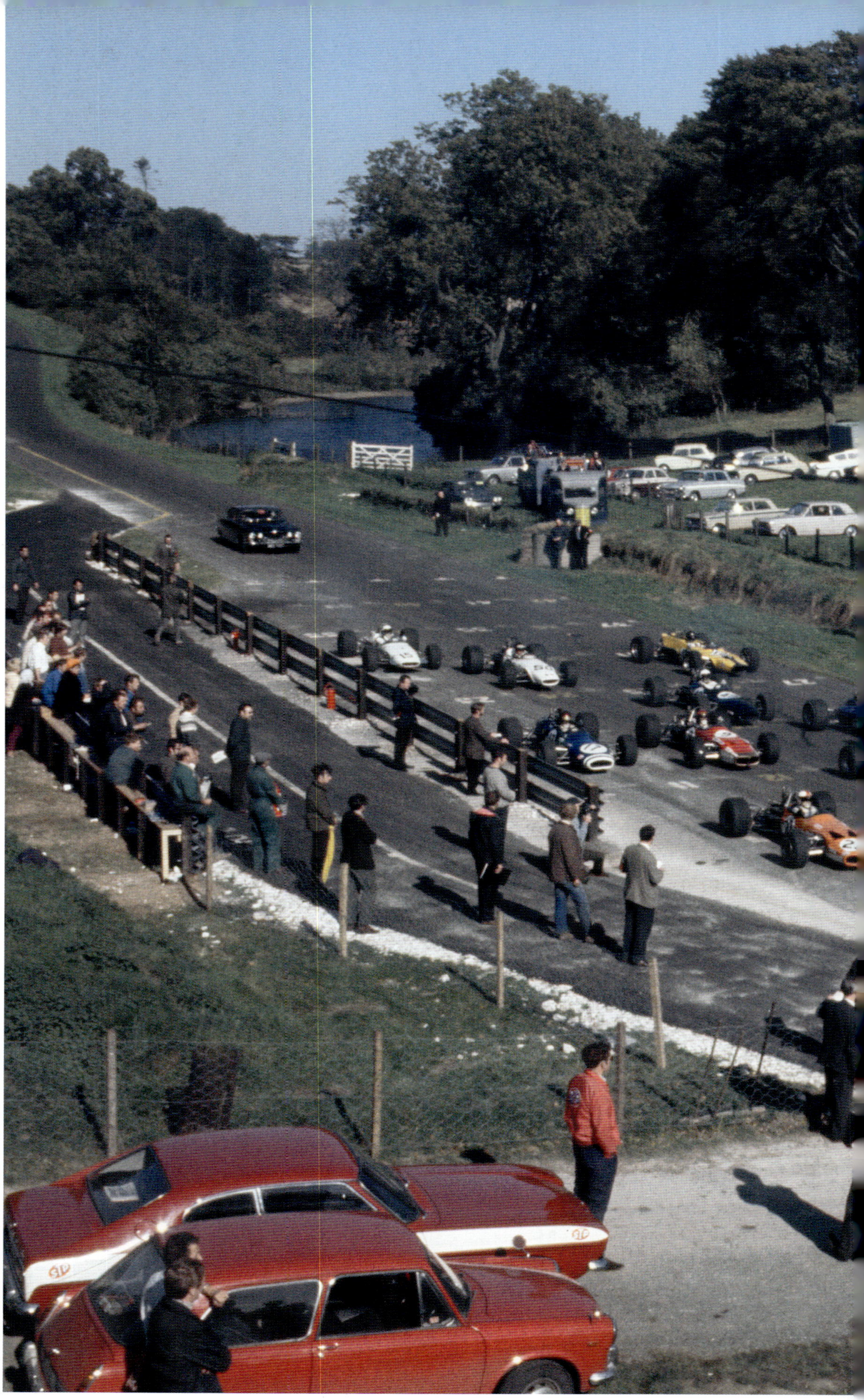

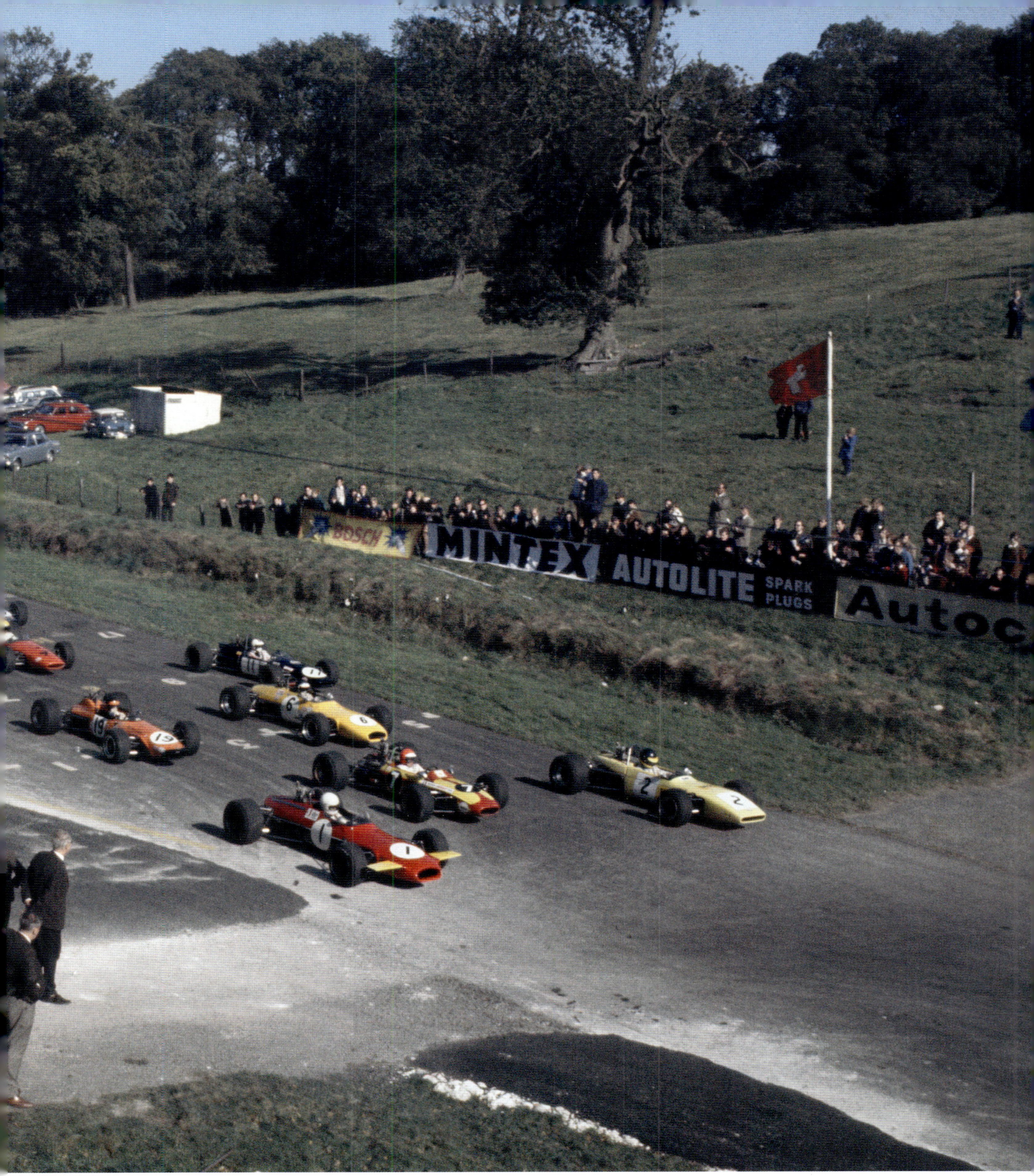
BOSCH
MINTEX
AUTOLITE
SPARK PLUGS
Autoc

1970

MARCHED SIDEWAYS TO GRAND PRIX RACING

Once they knew that Ronnie was going to be OK after his horrific Formula 3 accident at Montlhéry, the directors of March Engineering might have optimised their hot new property for the 1970 season. But commercial pressures led to front-line drivers Chris Amon and Jo Siffert being assigned the works Formula 1 cars. Eventually a way to run Ronnie was found with British entrant Colin Crabbe. His was one of seven March 701s this season, the others including Ken Tyrrell's cars for Jackie Stewart and François Cevert, and Andy Granatelli's for Mario Andretti. It seemed Ronnie had the chance to prove himself against exalted company. But Crabbe's team was not a March priority, and there were no points from nine Grands Prix. Adding to Ronnie's dismay, the Formula 2 March turned out to be a dog...

RIGHT Ronnie negotiates the Casino Square in Monaco during his maiden Formula 1 race. The new Antique Automobiles March 701 was taken to the principality after the briefest shakedown at Silverstone, but Ronnie qualified it despite inadequate brakes. He was in line to score on début when he lost sixth place eight laps out from the finish to the delayed BRM P153 of Pedro Rodriguez.

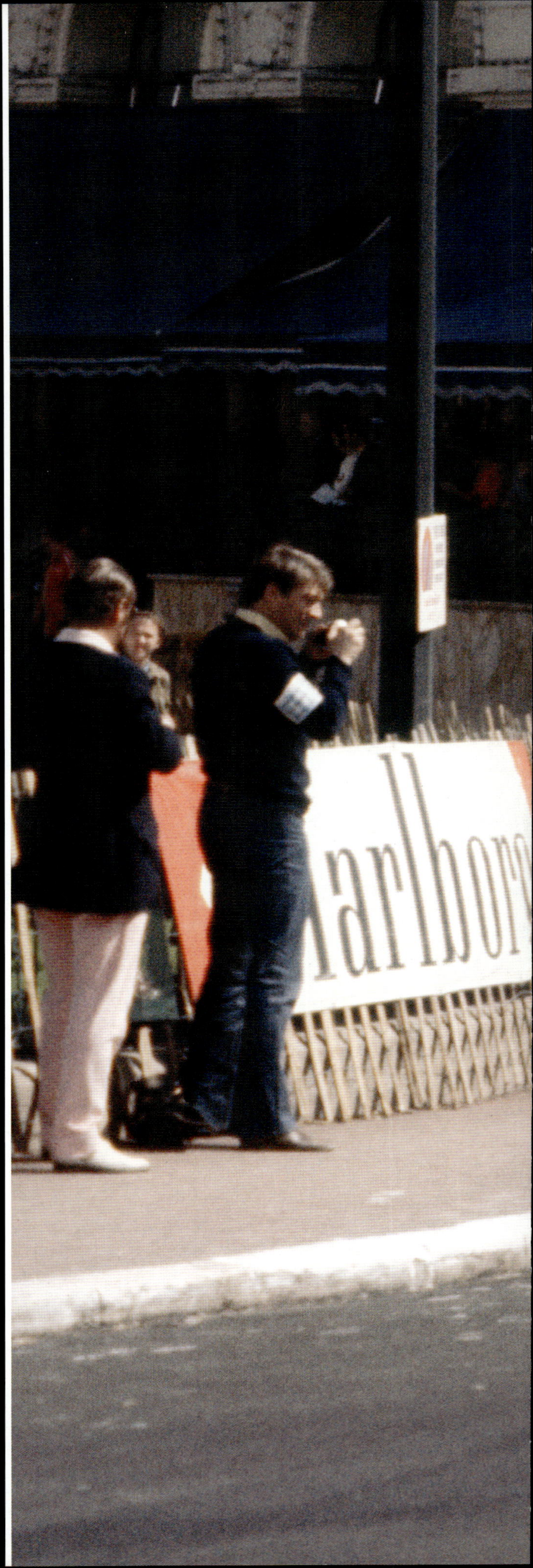

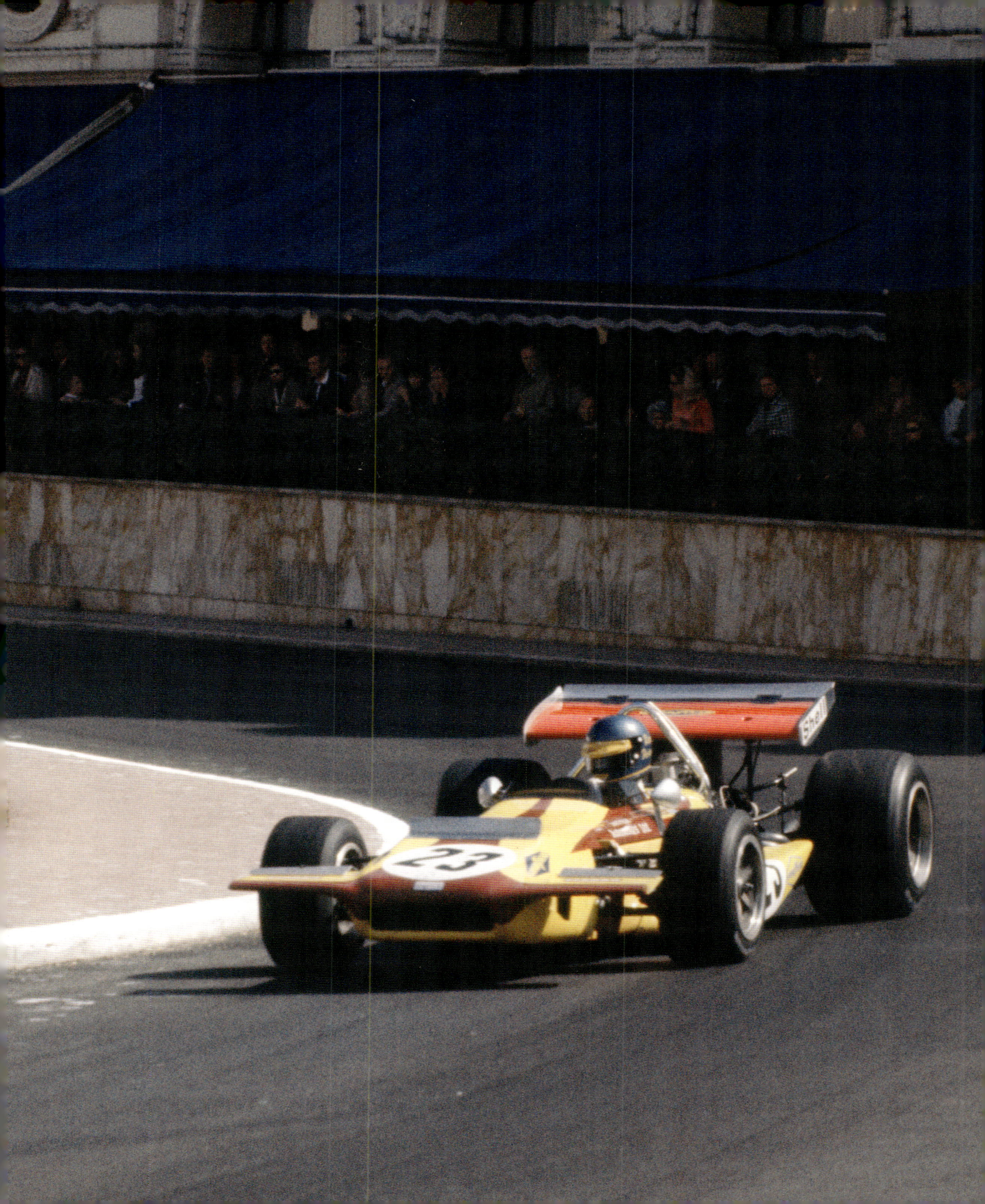

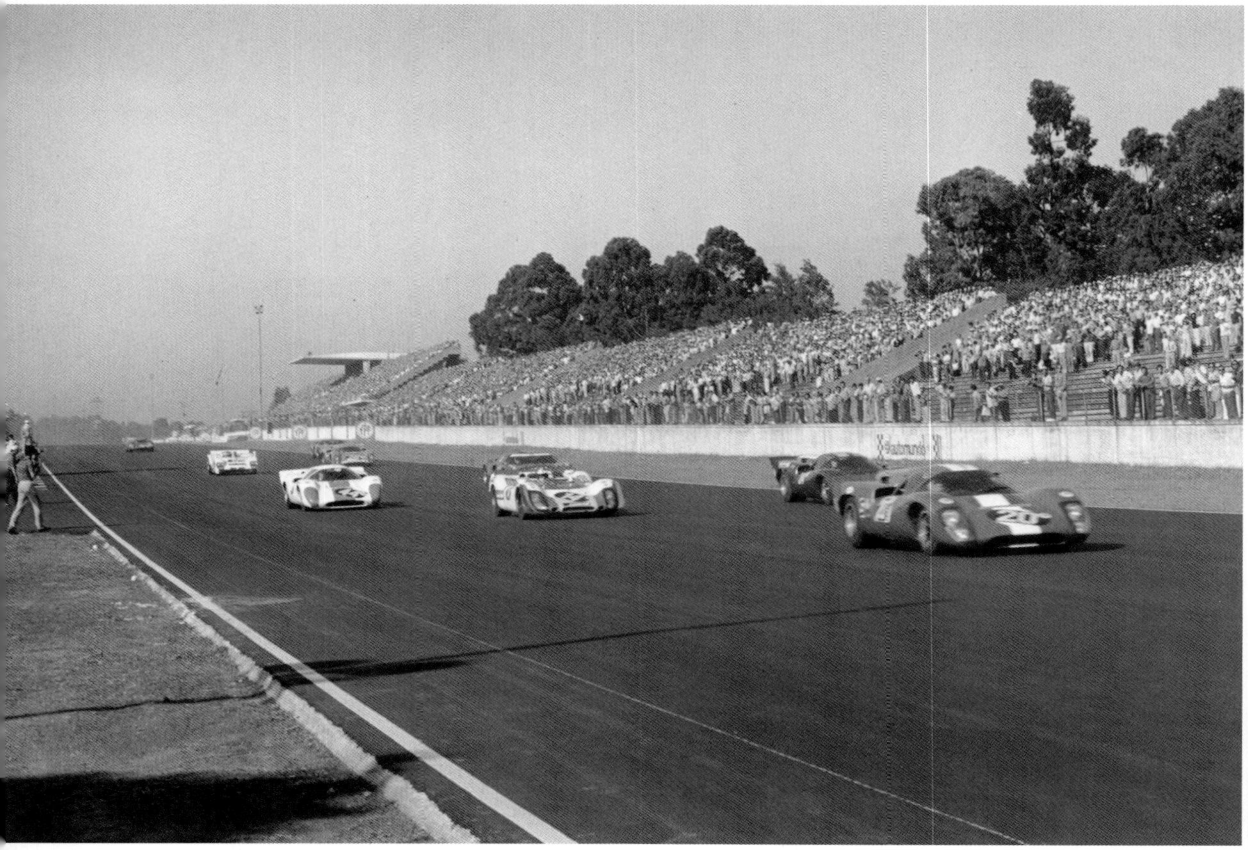

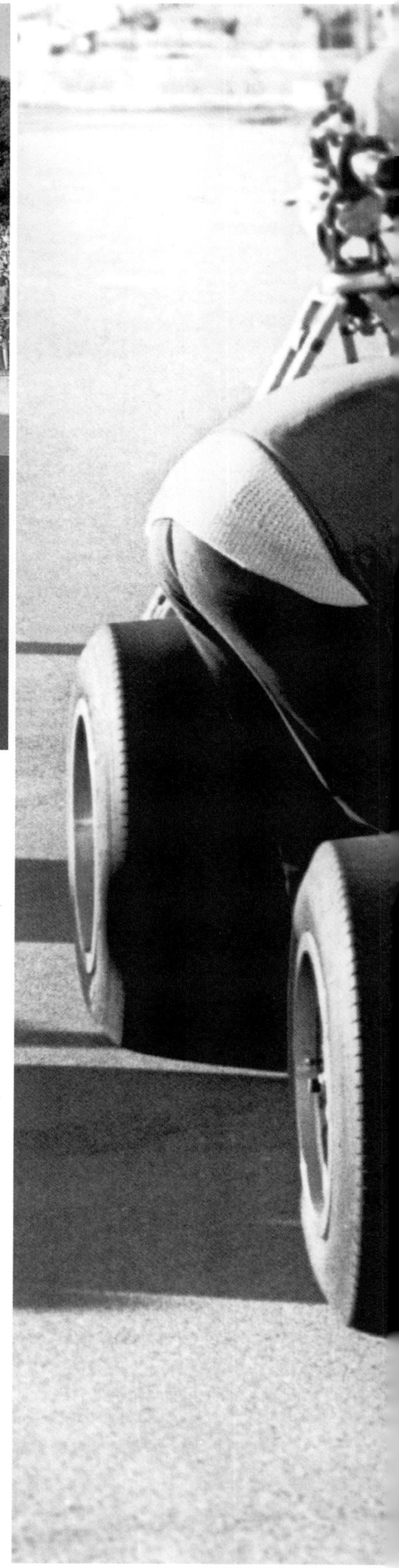

ABOVE The most important season of Ronnie's career to date began with a South American commitment to Jo Bonnier, who had entered two Lola T70 sportscars for the big 1000-kilometre race at Buenos Aires in January. Bonnier himself co-drove one with Reine Wisell, while Ronnie shared the other with Argentine road racer Jorge Cupeiro. The all-Swedish pairing was halted by an engine failure but Ronnie's car finished sixth overall. Here pursued by Jose Juncadella's Porsche 908, flanked by the Lolas of Jacques Rey (left) and Richard Attwood, their car finished second in class behind the Team VDS Lola of Teddy Pilette and Nestor Garcia. This race was marred during practice when a marshal was killed by Richard Brostrom's Porsche 908/2. It was won by Henri Pescarolo and Jean-Pierre Beltoise with a works Matra MS650 from two more Porsche 908s. Ronnie raced the Ecurie Bonnier Lola again at Keimola in Finland later in the season, finishing third overall.

RIGHT Ronnie had to borrow a helmet to drive a few laps in Chris Amon's works STP March 701 during the media launch of the new team in February, although someone had found a Smog decal for the benefit of the Swedish TV coverage. This was the first time Ronnie had ever driven a Formula 1 car. The assembled media were told that he would make his début in the Race of Champions at Brands Hatch the following month Actually March had yet found no entrant for him – nor even built his car.

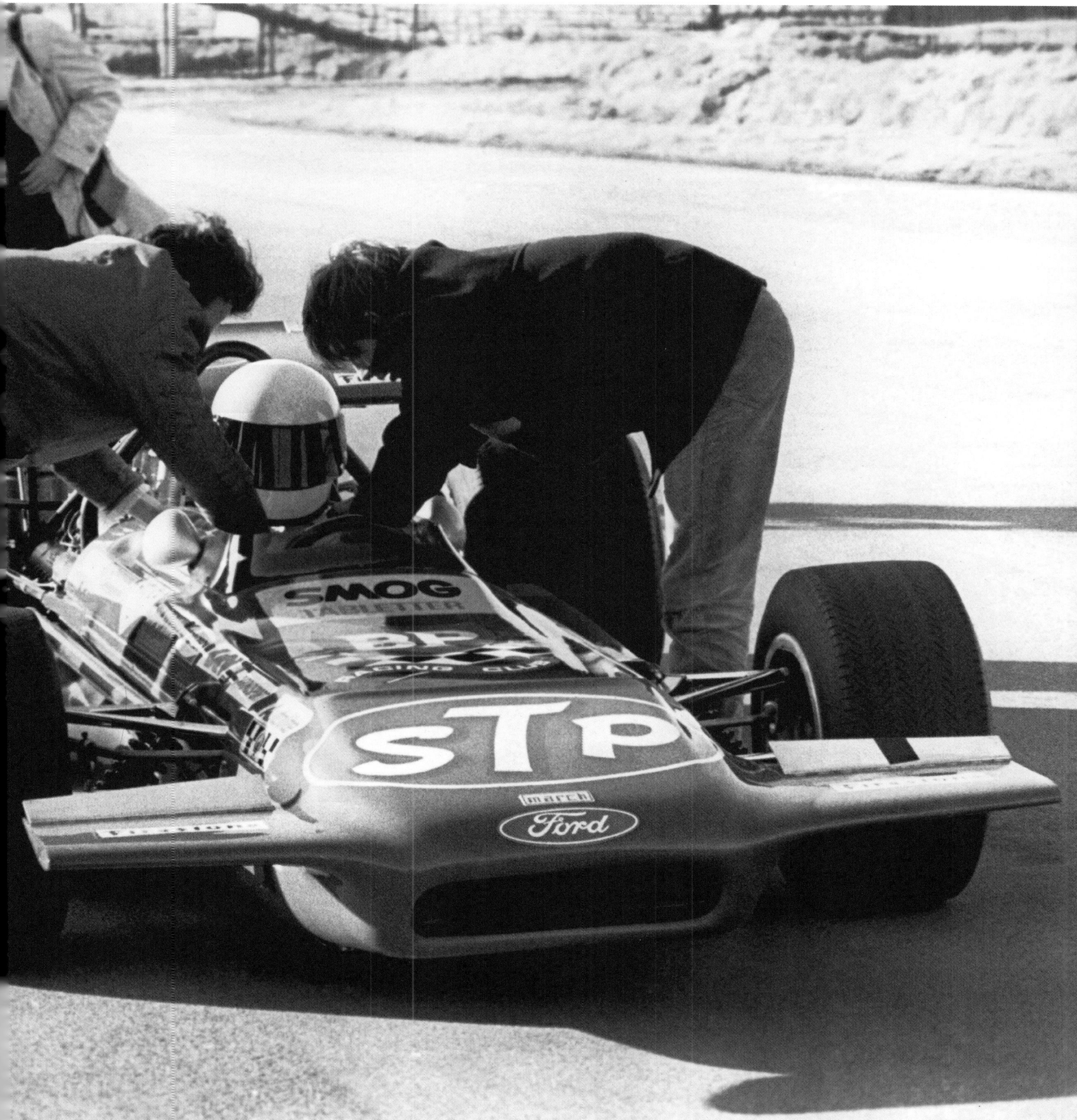
SMOG
BP
STP
march
Ford

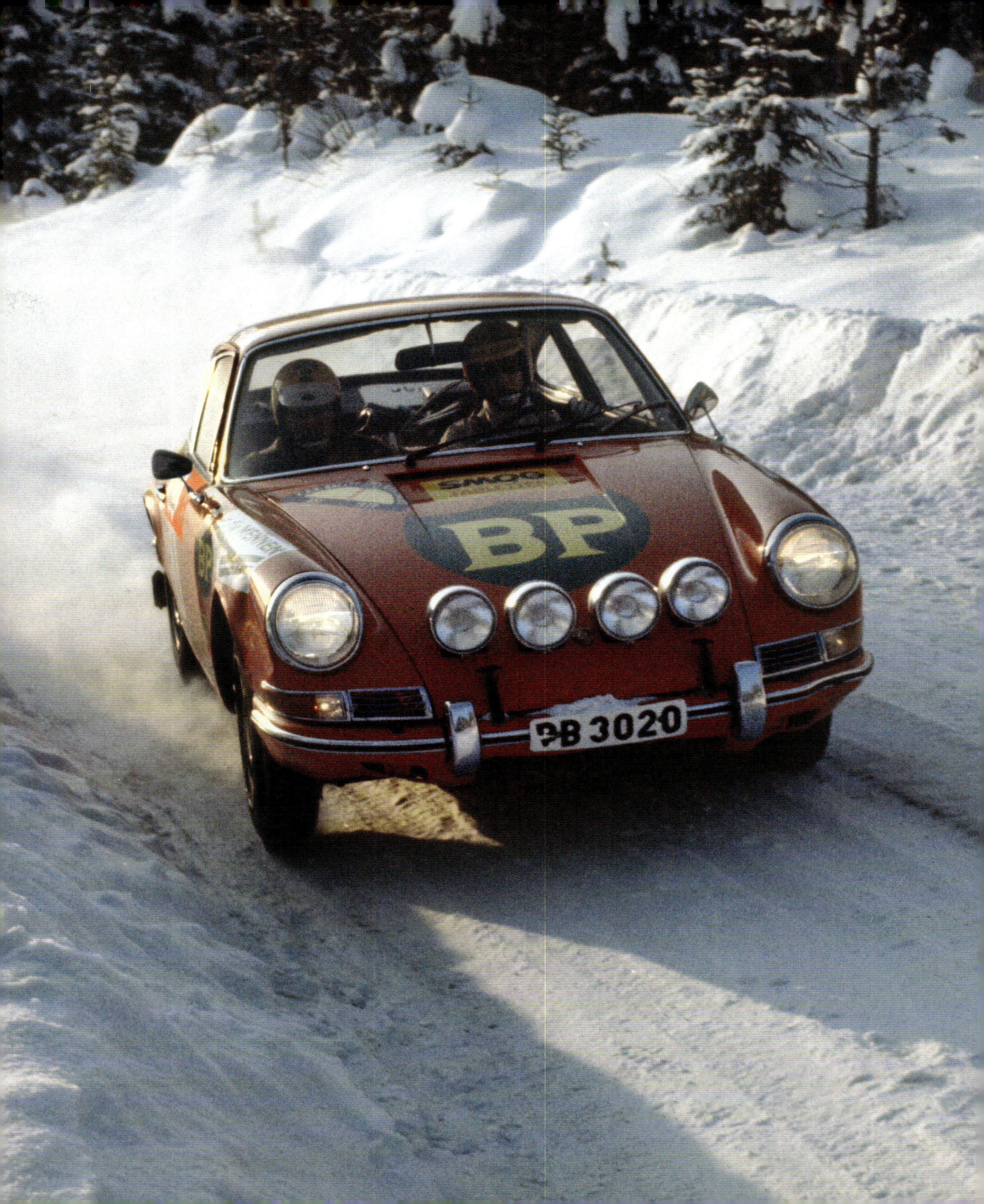
BP

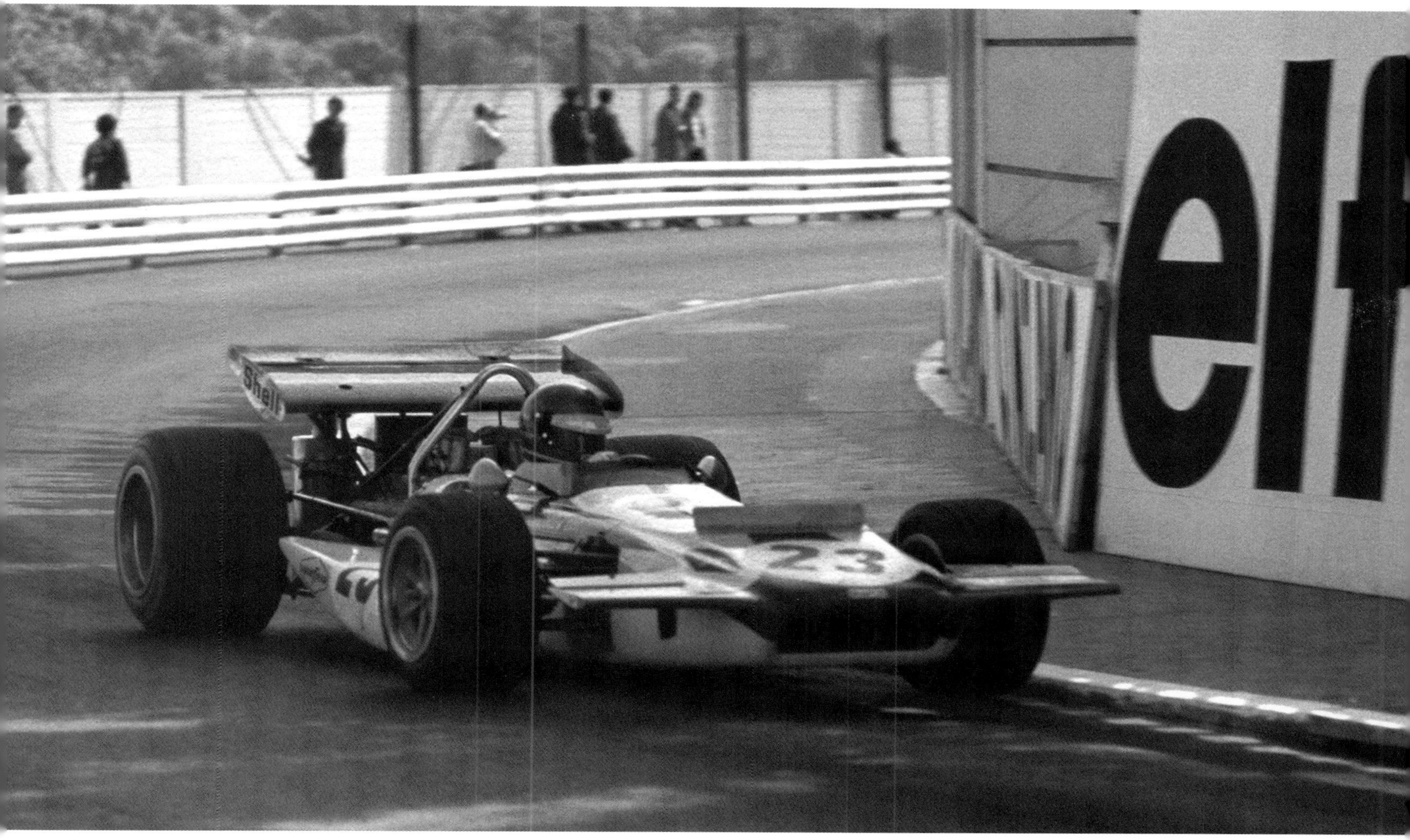

LEFT Porsche Sweden hired Ronnie to drive an almost standard 911L in the KAK Swedish Rally, the opening round of the 1970 FIA European Championship in February. He was to have been co-driven by Torsten Palm, his friend and rival from Swedish Formula 3. However Palm was rushed into hospital for a gallstone operation just before the start, and replaced by Sven-Olaf Svedberg. Rallying was not really Ronnie's thing. This event was dominated by Bjorn Waldegard with another Porsche, but Ronnie was languishing in 20th position when his car's transmission broke.

ABOVE Ronnie was not really fit enough to make his Formula 1 début at Monaco. Less than three weeks before, testing a March-Alfa Formula 1 prototype at Silverstone, he had had a big accident caused by jammed throttle slides, and spent a night in hospital with cracked ribs. In agony, but telling no one, he had gone straight to Barcelona for a Formula 2 race, and then on to another at the Nürburging, where he had a high-speed crash in qualifying. Come Monaco, the pain had subsided – until his safety harness was tightened. A Formula 3 star here in 1968 and 1969, he caused a minor sensation when he went fourth fastest in the second (wet) practice session with a car hampered by poor stopping performance – the only March still fitted with the original outboard brakes. He ultimately qualified 12th of the 21 runners, far from the front-row pace on the 16-car grid of Jackie Stewart and Chris Amon in similar cars. Ronnie kept out of trouble on Sunday afternoon and brought the 701 safely home in seventh position – the only March driver to finish the race, which is famous for Jochen Rindt's astonishing victory over Jack Brabham. It turned out to be the best result of Ronnie's season.

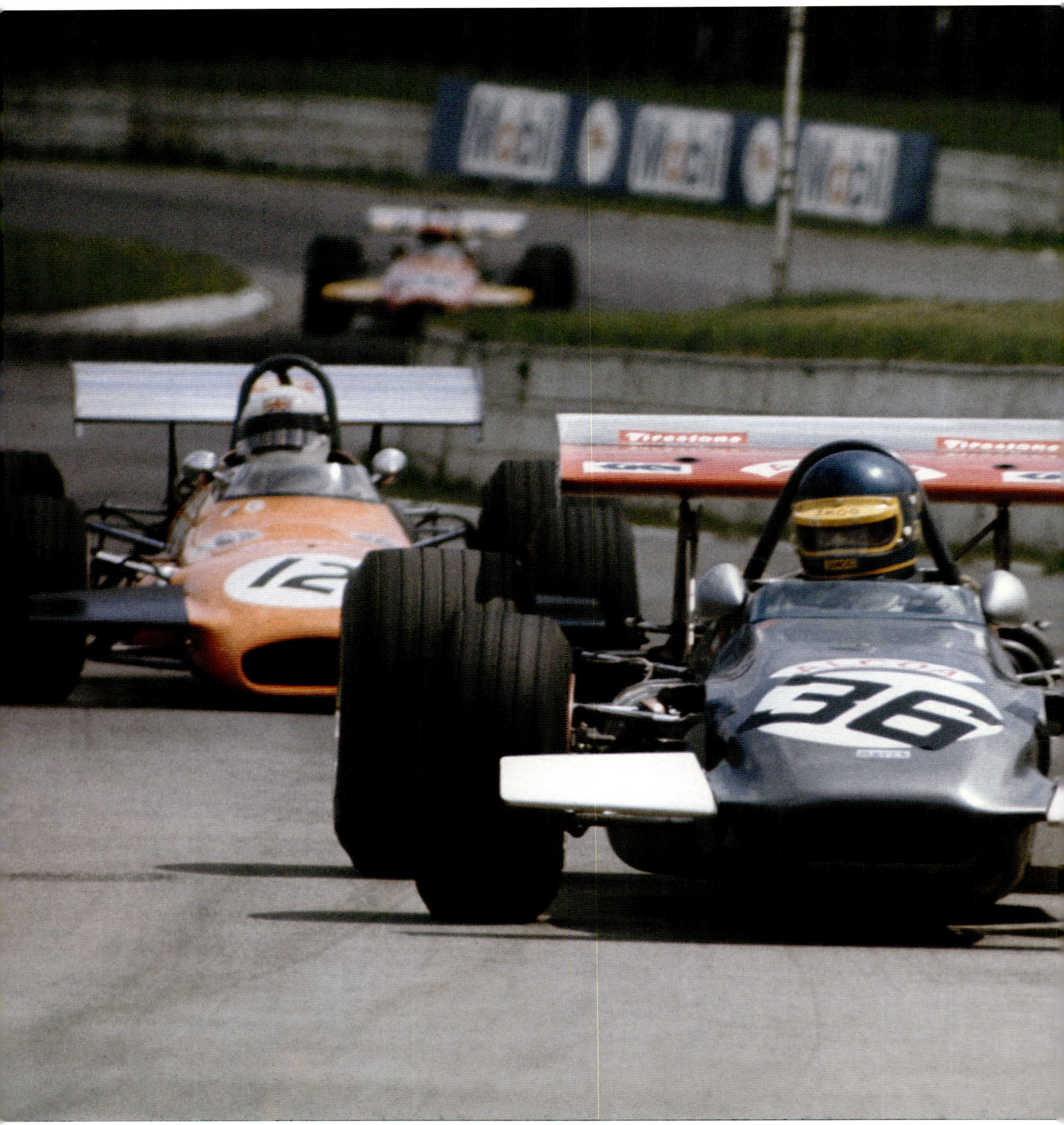
Mobil
Mobil
Mobil
Firestone
Firestone
12
36

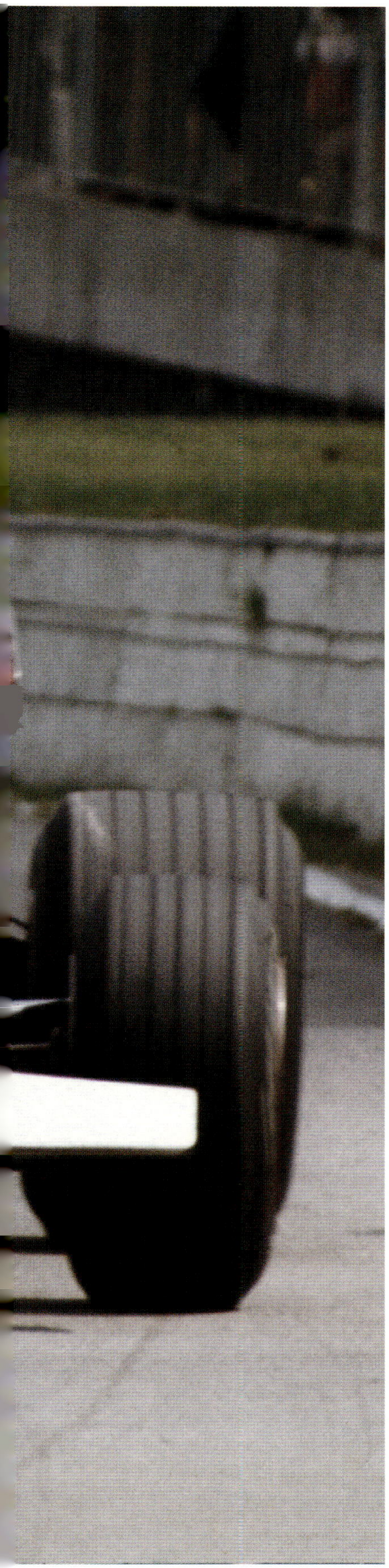

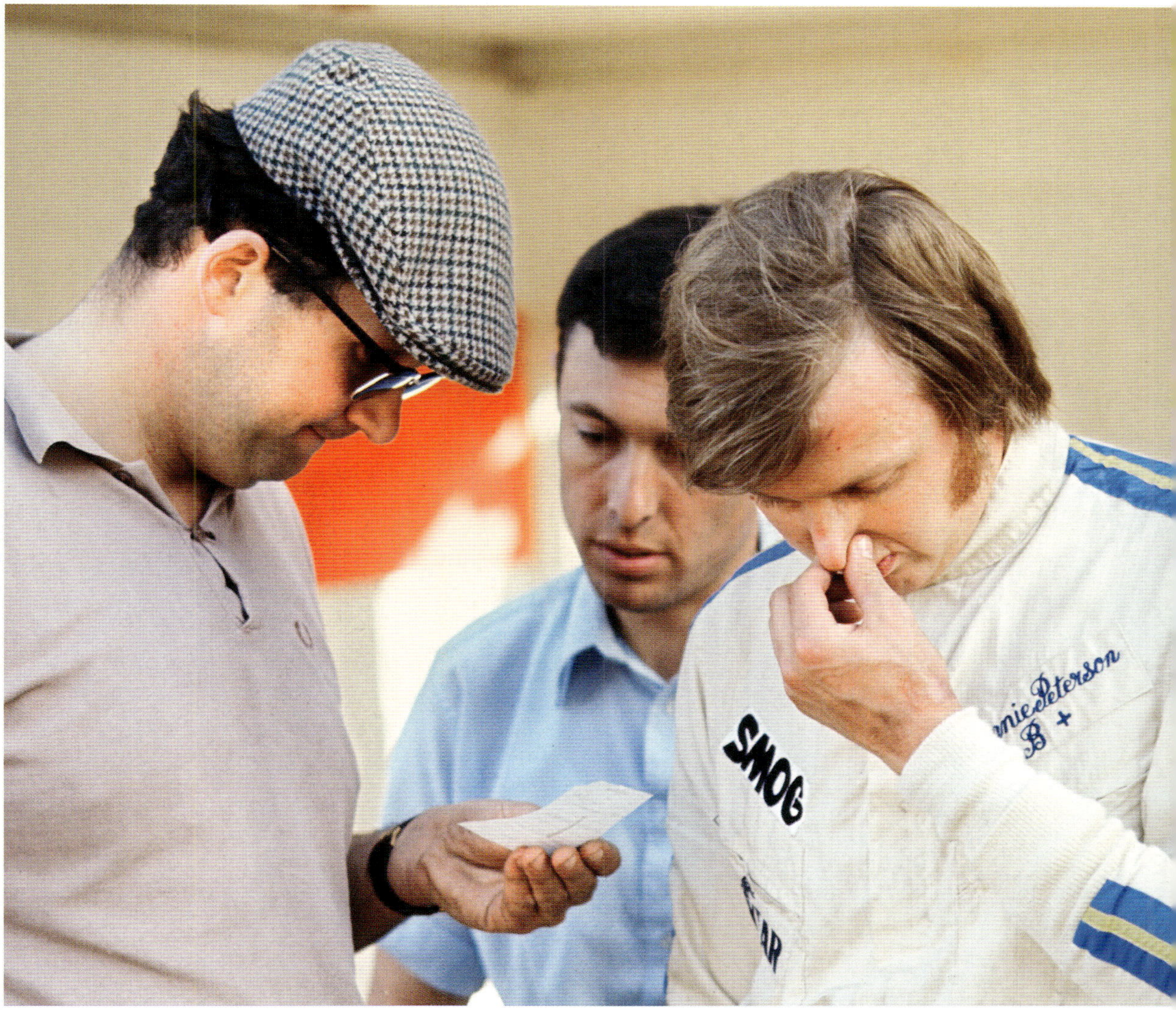

LEFT Ronnie had a dreadful start to his Formula 2 career with the March 702: he fell victim to a crash at Hockenheim, a clutch malfunction in Barcelona, another crash during practice on the Nürburgring, engine overheating at Zolder. Here is he trying again in the London Trophy, a non-championship race at Crystal Palace. The 702 was unworthy of the engineering talent that March had assembled, although this was a much-modified new chassis and Ronnie qualified it sixth for his heat. Here he leads Derek Bell in Tom Wheatcroft's Brabham BT30 into South Tower corner. Bell passed him but, when John Watson tried with another Brabham, he smeared the March against the wall...

ABOVE With his first Formula 1 entrant, Colin Crabbe, during the Belgian Grand Prix meeting. Ronnie had expected to be racing a works STP March, but had lost out when Porsche offered to pay for Jo Siffert's drive to prevent him defecting to Ferrari, its big rival in sportscar racing. Crabbe was the owner of Antique Automobiles, a vintage car restoration business based in a converted Methodist chapel in Baston, Peterborough. He had entered a Cooper and a McLaren for Vic Elford in a few races in 1969, and had accepted when March offered to loan him a car for a full 1970 programme, taking in nine races in which he would split the start money with his driver. Crabbe almost had no driver at Spa-Francorchamps. Ronnie got caught up in a traffic jam on race morning, and jumped the queue. A policeman tried to stop him, and Ronnie inadvertently ran over his foot. He was taken into custody and released, at the request of the race organisers, only at the last minute.

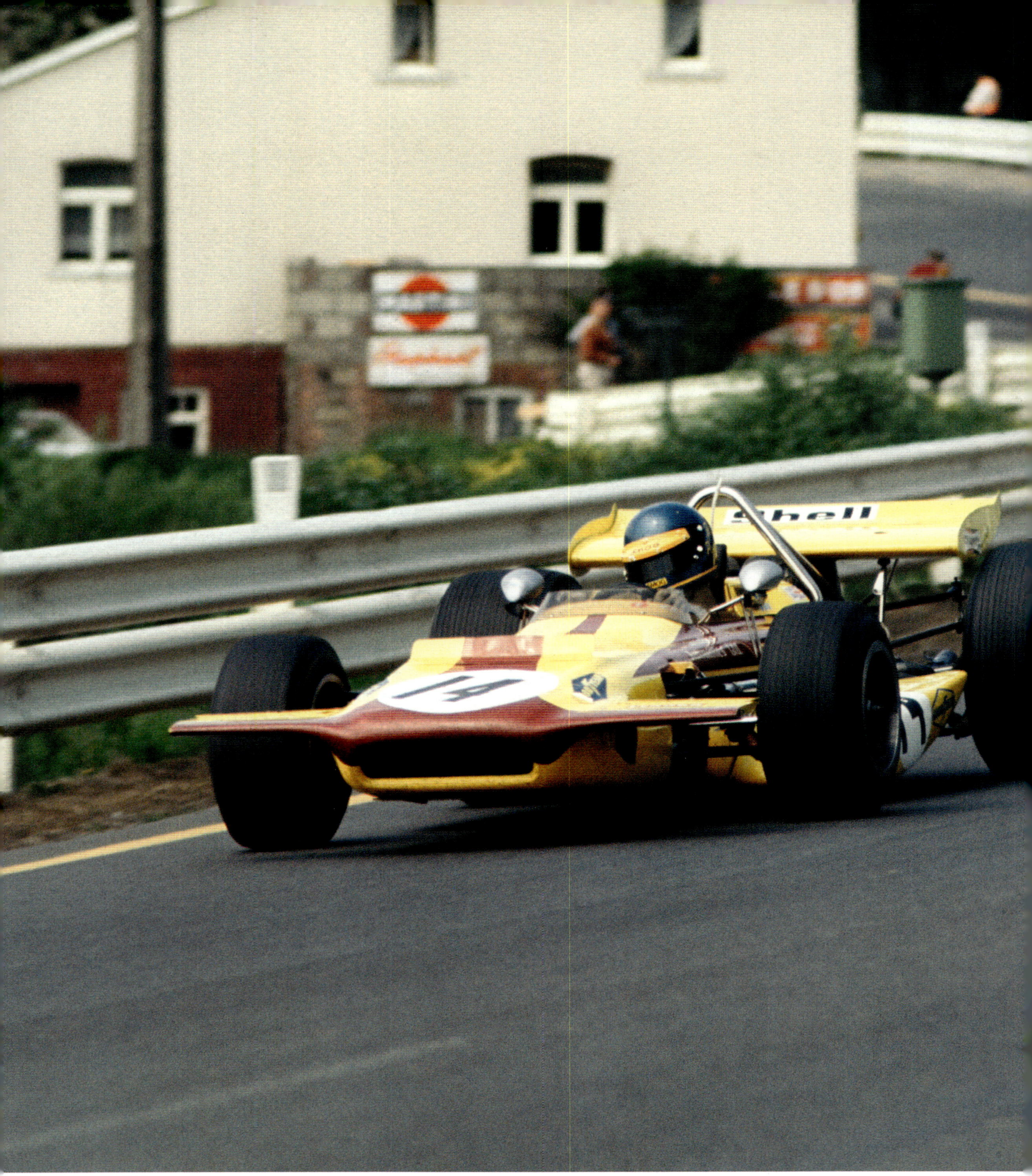
Shell
14

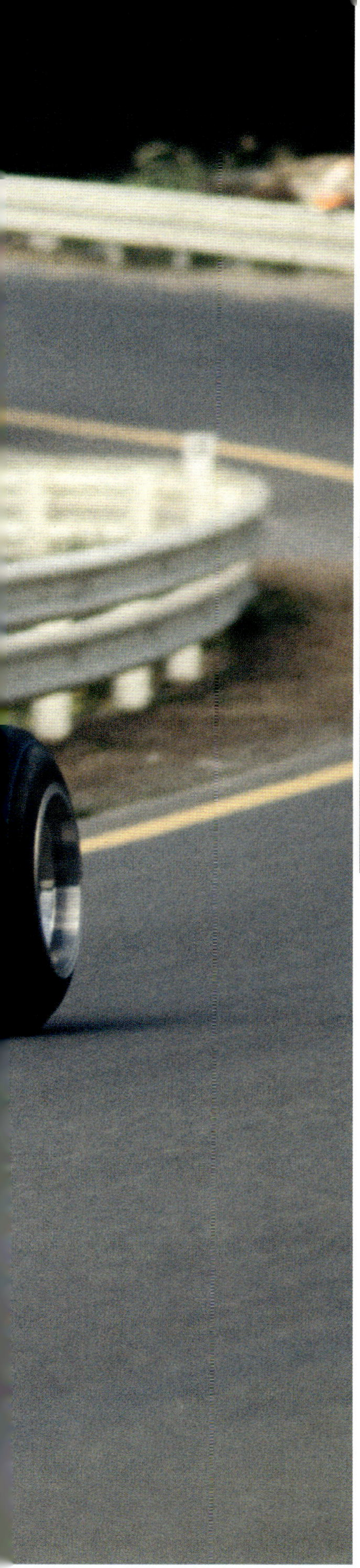

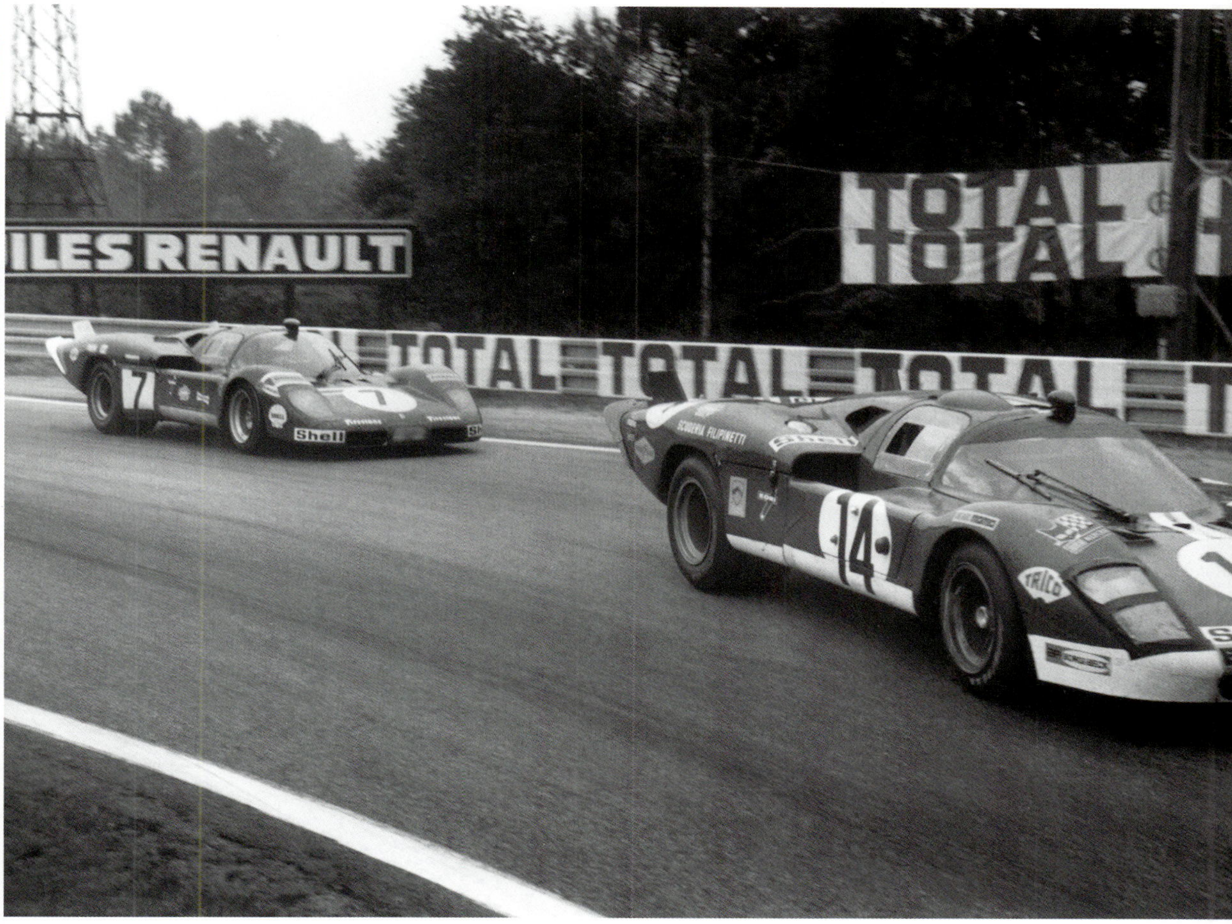

LEFT Ronnie hurtles through the very fast Burnenville right-hander on the full road course at Spa-Francorchamps. The Antique Automobiles entry was the eighth March to be built and here, for its second race, it had been brought up to the latest specification, with inboard rear brakes and parallel-link suspension. Ronnie qualified ninth and was racing in that position, hampered by a broken exhaust pipe, when he pitted for a replacement. The delay cost eight laps and he was not classified as a finisher. Afterwards he was arrested by the police and spent two days in jail for his traffic offence.

ABOVE Ronnie raced only once in the Le Mans 24 Hours, when he was hired to drive a works Ferrari 512S in the 1970 race with fellow débutant Derek Bell. None of the four factory cars from Maranello survived even until halfway, and theirs was halted by an engine failure during the fifth hour. Here Ronnie follows his friend Reine Wisell in Ecurie Filipinetti's 512. At the end of the season, Ronnie was invited to Goodwood with Bell and Peter Gethin to be tested by JW Automotive's works Gulf Porsche sportscar team. It was Bell who landed the career-changing opportunity to race alongside Jo Siffert, Pedro Rodriguez and Jackie Oliver in 1971.

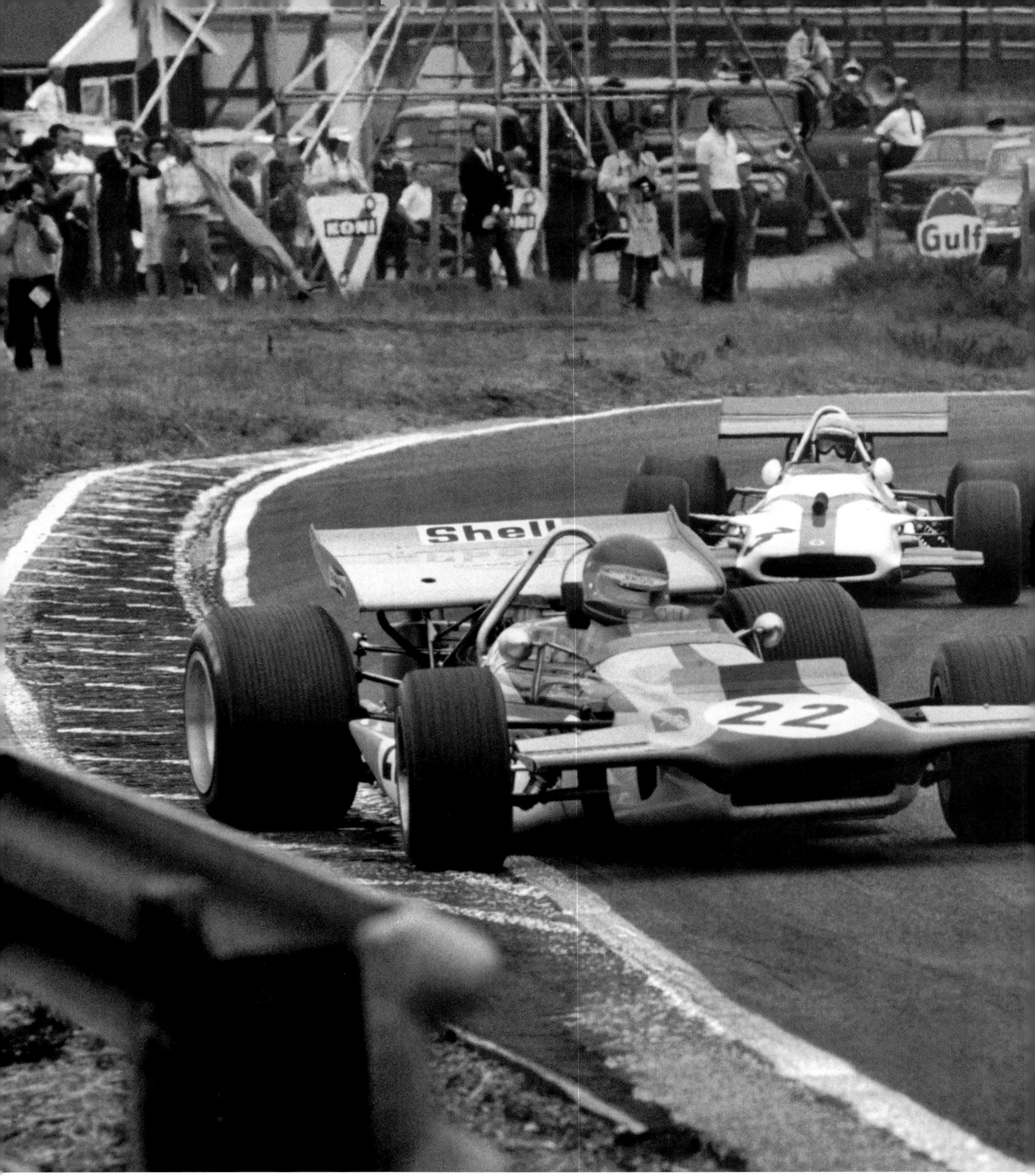
KONI
Gulf
Shell
22

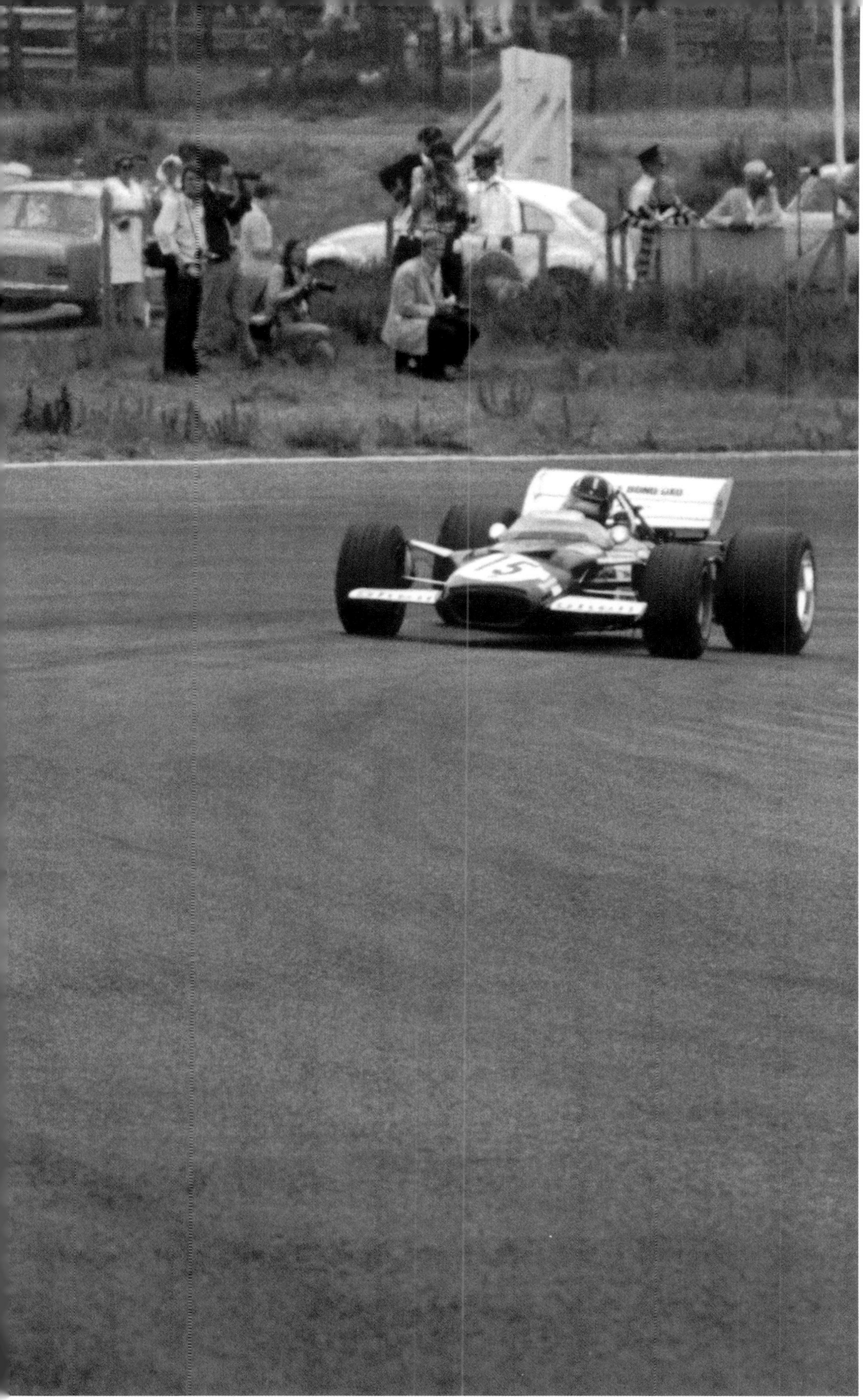

LEFT Ronnie gets a wheel on the dirt in the Hunzerug corner early in the Dutch Grand Prix, striving to keep the Antique Automobiles March ahead of George Eaton in a fourth works BRM and Graham Hill, who had replaced Jo Siffert in Rob Walker's Lotus 49. Ronnie, ninth, was March's only finisher in this race, which was dreadfully marred by the fatal accident that befell Piers Courage in Frank Williams's De Tomaso.

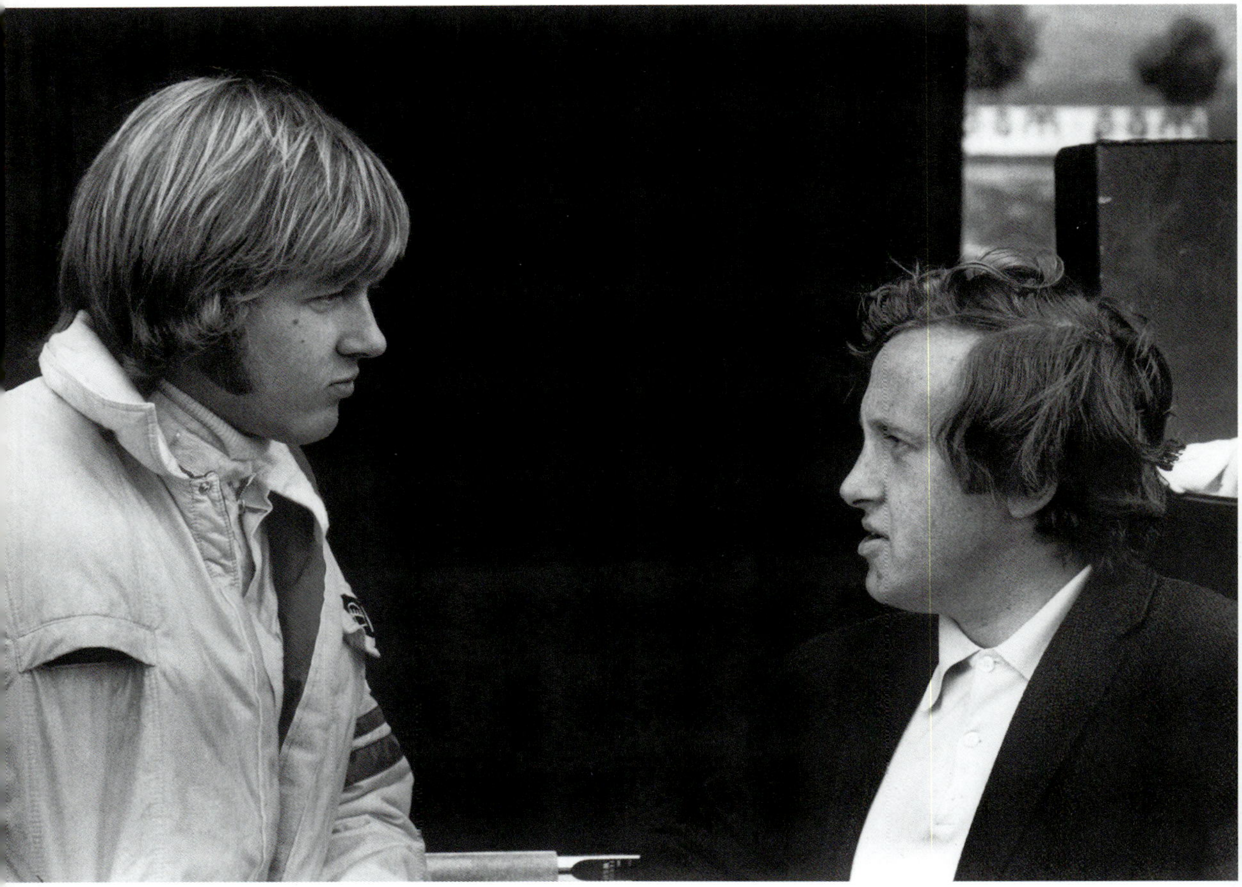

ABOVE With Alan Rees, formerly the driver turned manager of Roy Winkelmann's Formula 2 team, now a director of March Engineering. It was Rees who resolved to sign Ronnie for the new company after witnessing his victory in the epic Formula 3 race at Monaco the previous May.

RIGHT Ronnie gets his March 702 sideways on the cobbles as he negotiates the hairpin at the bottom of the hill at Rouen in June. March had been embarrassed by the 702 and had engineered a brand new car for this race. The change in fortunes was spectacular, and in an exceptionally strong field, Ronnie finished a close second in his heat (pictured) after a race-long battle with Jo Siffert's BMW and Jack Brabham's Brabham, which ran without a rear wing. For the final, Ronnie also had his wing removed, but it proved his undoing. He made a bad start and got away ninth but, with a decent car at last, his skills on this difficult road circuit shone through. After 19 laps, he was in the lead, battling once again with Siffert. Here at Nouveau Monde on the last lap, having failed to adjust the front:rear brake ratio to take the absent wing into account, he spun the lead away. But at least he finally finished a Formula 2 race, sixth behind Siffert, Clay Regazzoni (Tecno), Emerson Fittipaldi (Lotus), Jacky Ickx in the other BMW and Tim Schenken (Brabham).

PAGE 58–59 Ronnie stayed in France after Rouen for the Formula 1 Grand Prix at Clermont-Ferrand. He qualified ninth (seven places ahead of Jo Siffert with the works 701) and was racing in seventh position when the transmission broke shortly before half-distance.

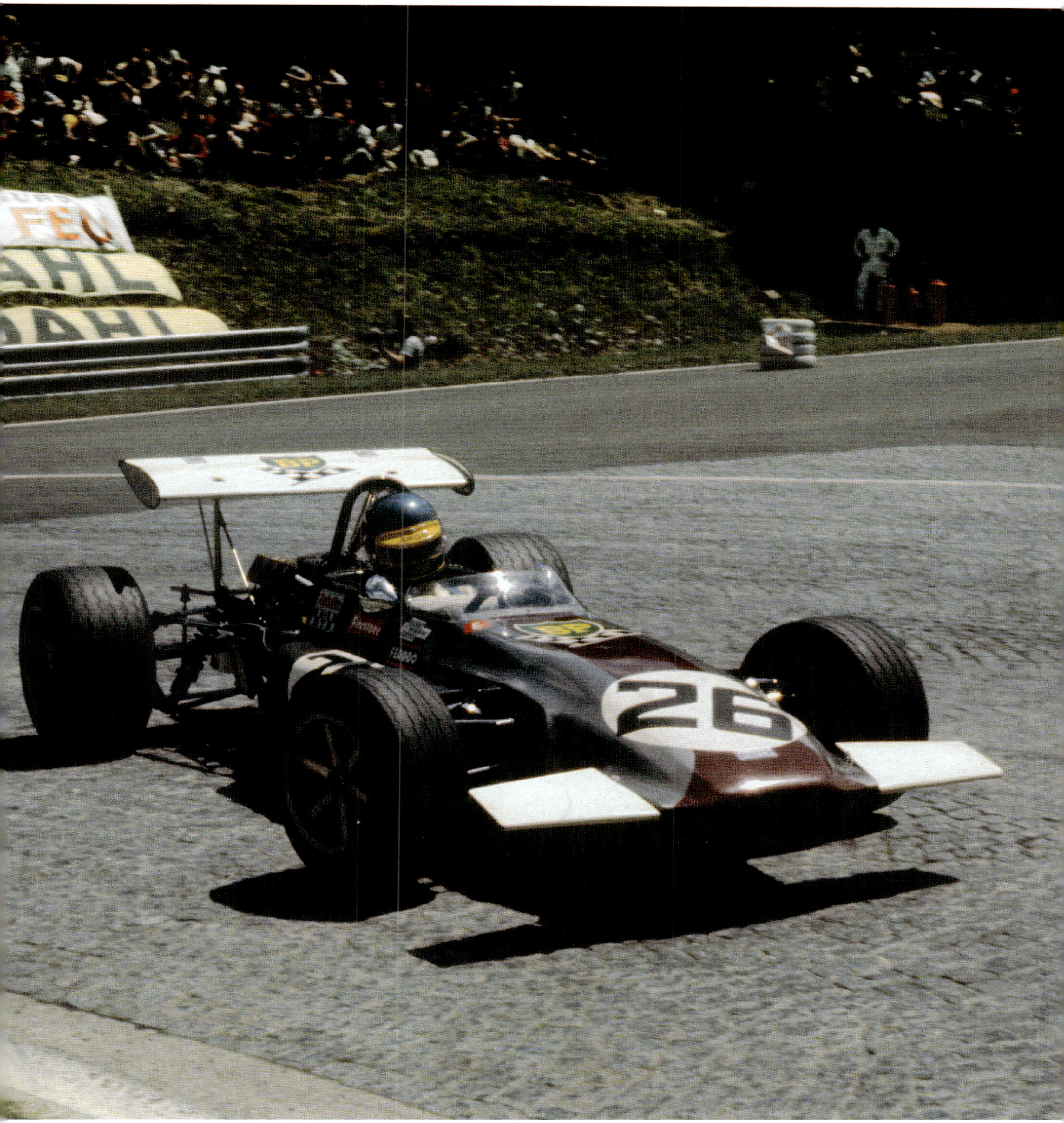
26
Firestone
FERODO

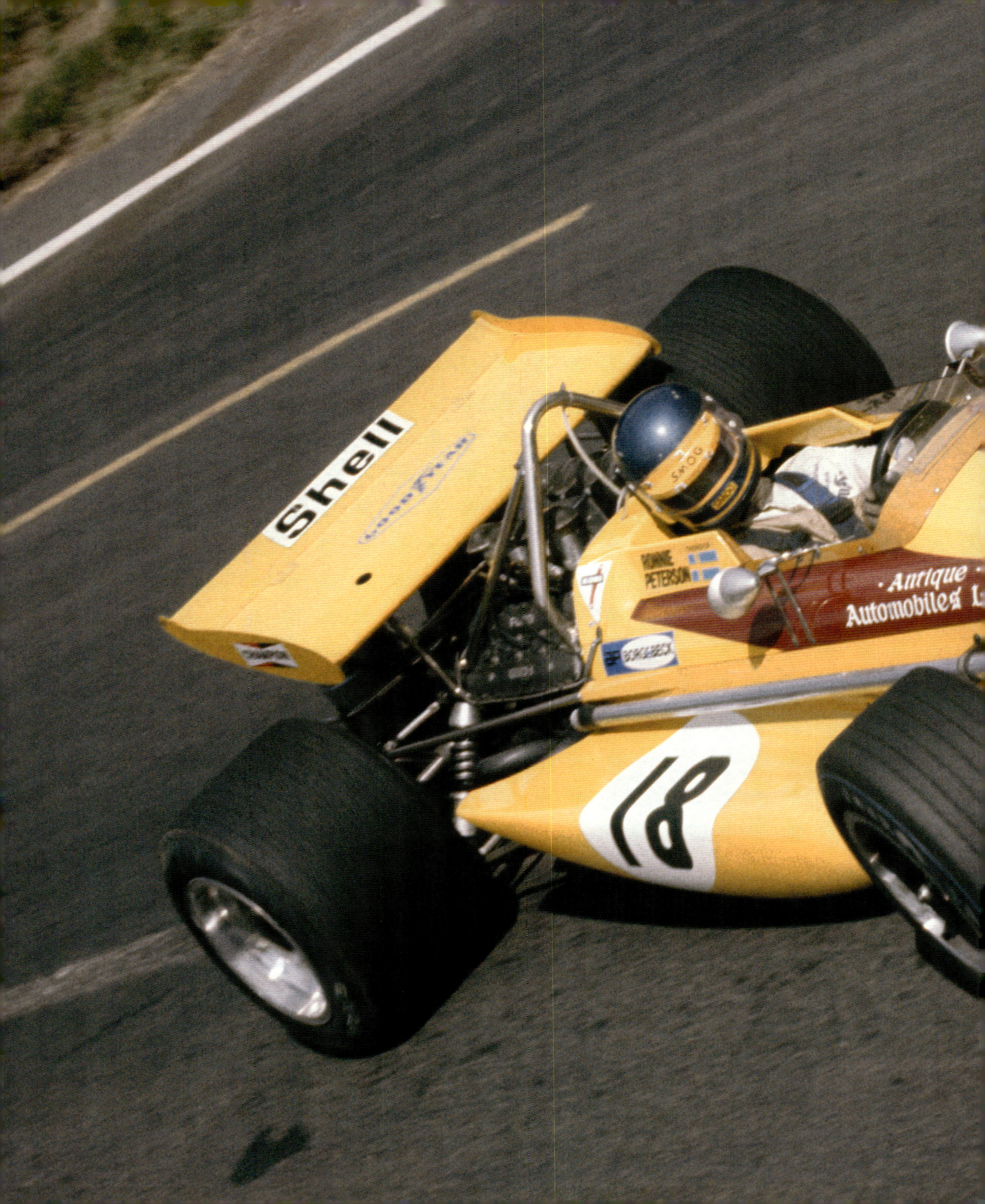
Shell
GOOD YEAR
RONNIE
PETERSON
· Antique ·
Automobiles L
BORGEBECK
CHAMPION
18

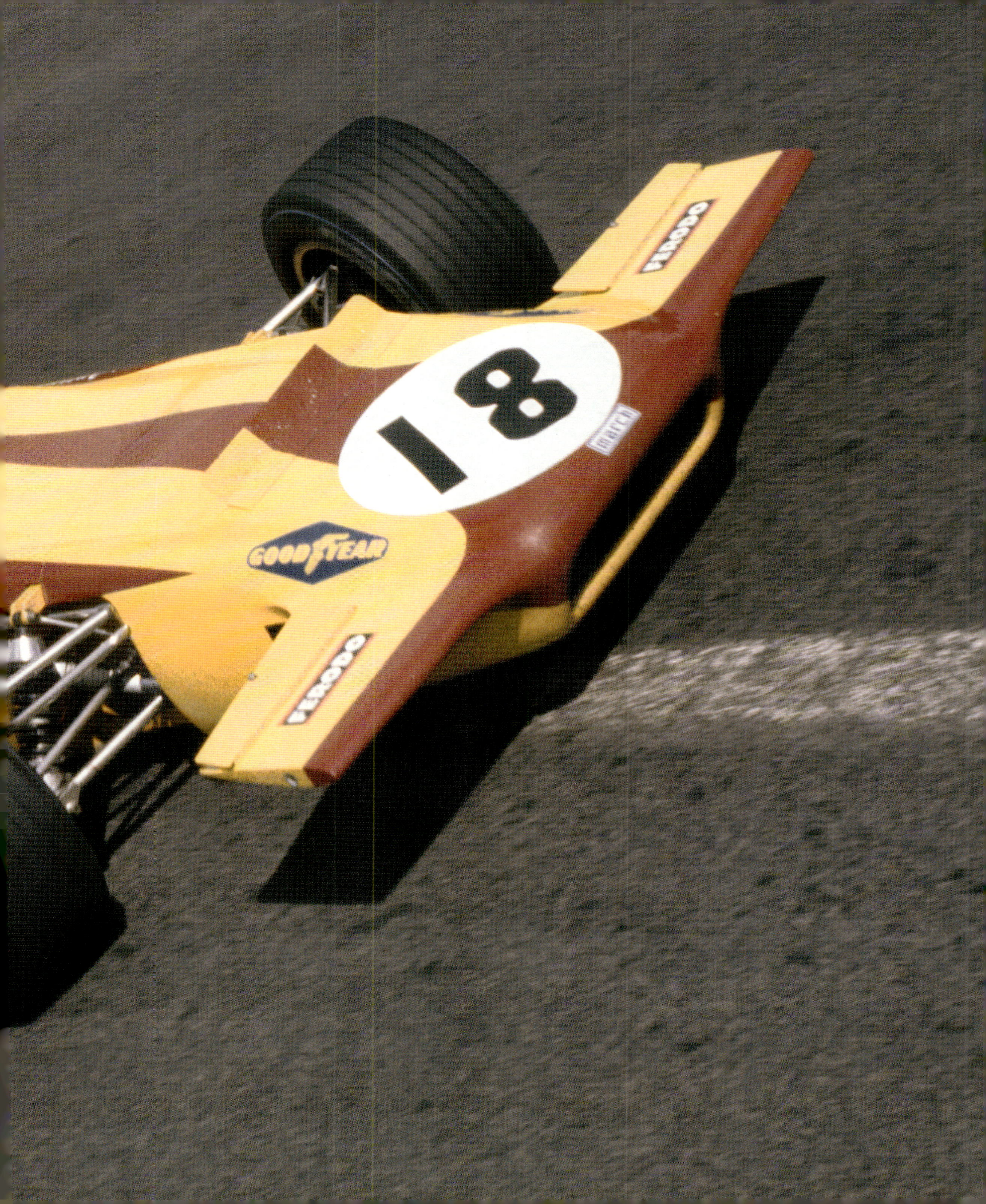
FERODO
18
march
GOODYEAR
FERODO

RIGHT Leading Jo Siffert's STP March 701 down the hill from the Druids hairpin during the British Grand Prix. Ronnie consistently outqualified the Swiss who had taken his promised works drive, and such was again the case here at Brands Hatch. In the race, despite a slipping clutch, he even led Chris Amon in the other works car in a group that included Dan Gurney (McLaren), Graham Hill in Rob Walker's Lotus and François Cevert in Ken Tyrrell's March. However a puncture sent him into pit-lane just before halfway – and the clutch had to be repaired before he could rejoin, seven laps behind them.

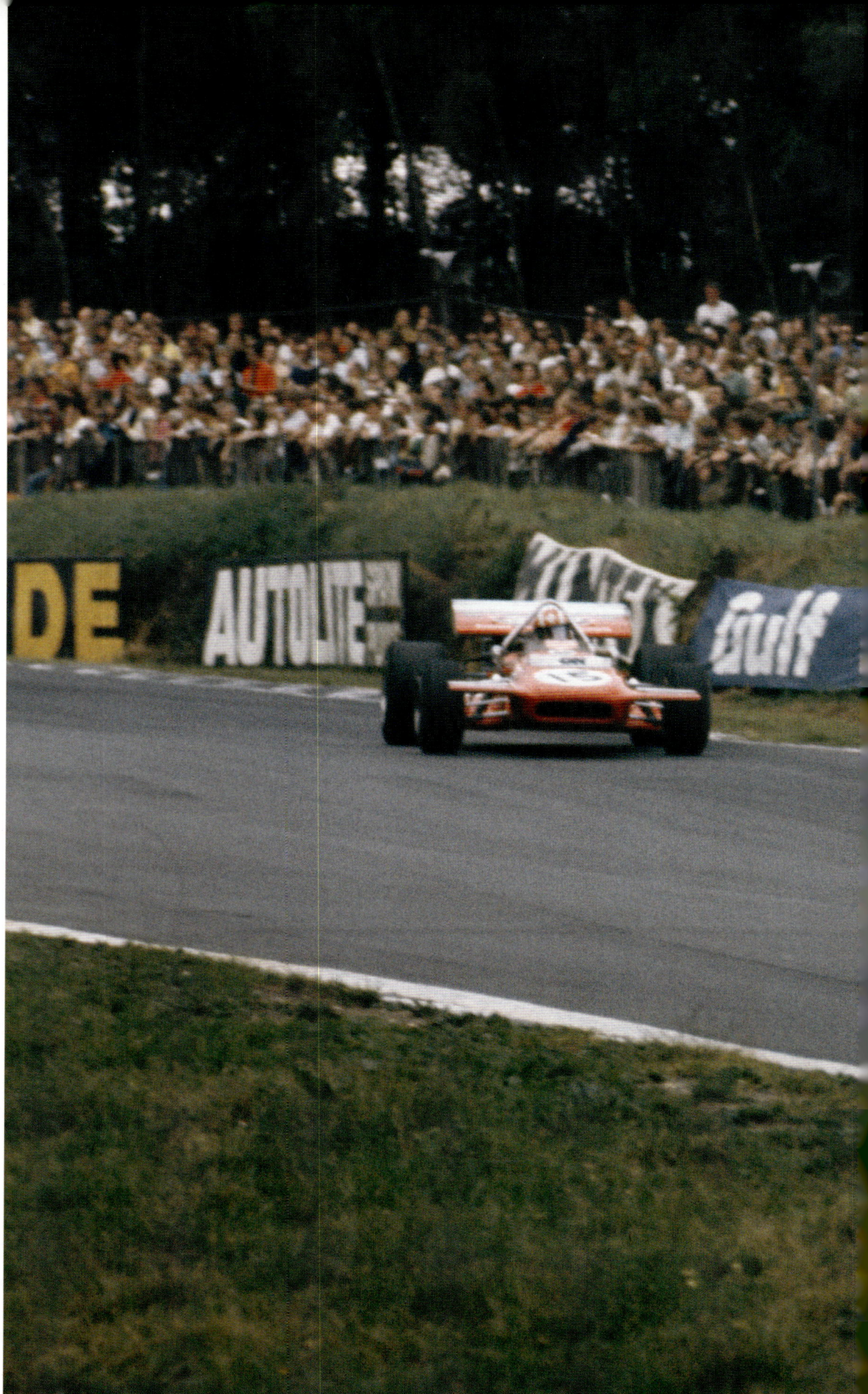

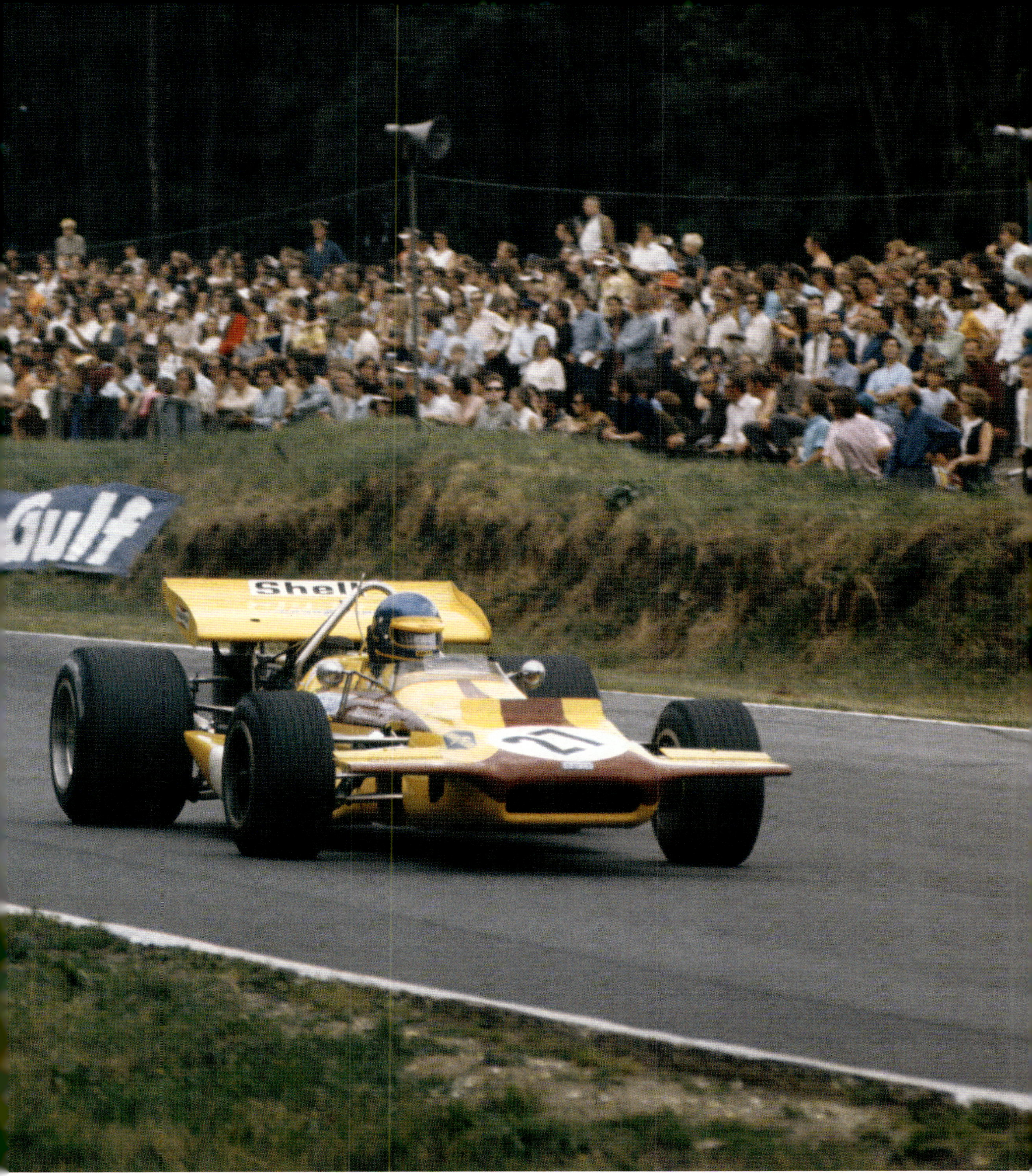
Gulf
Shell

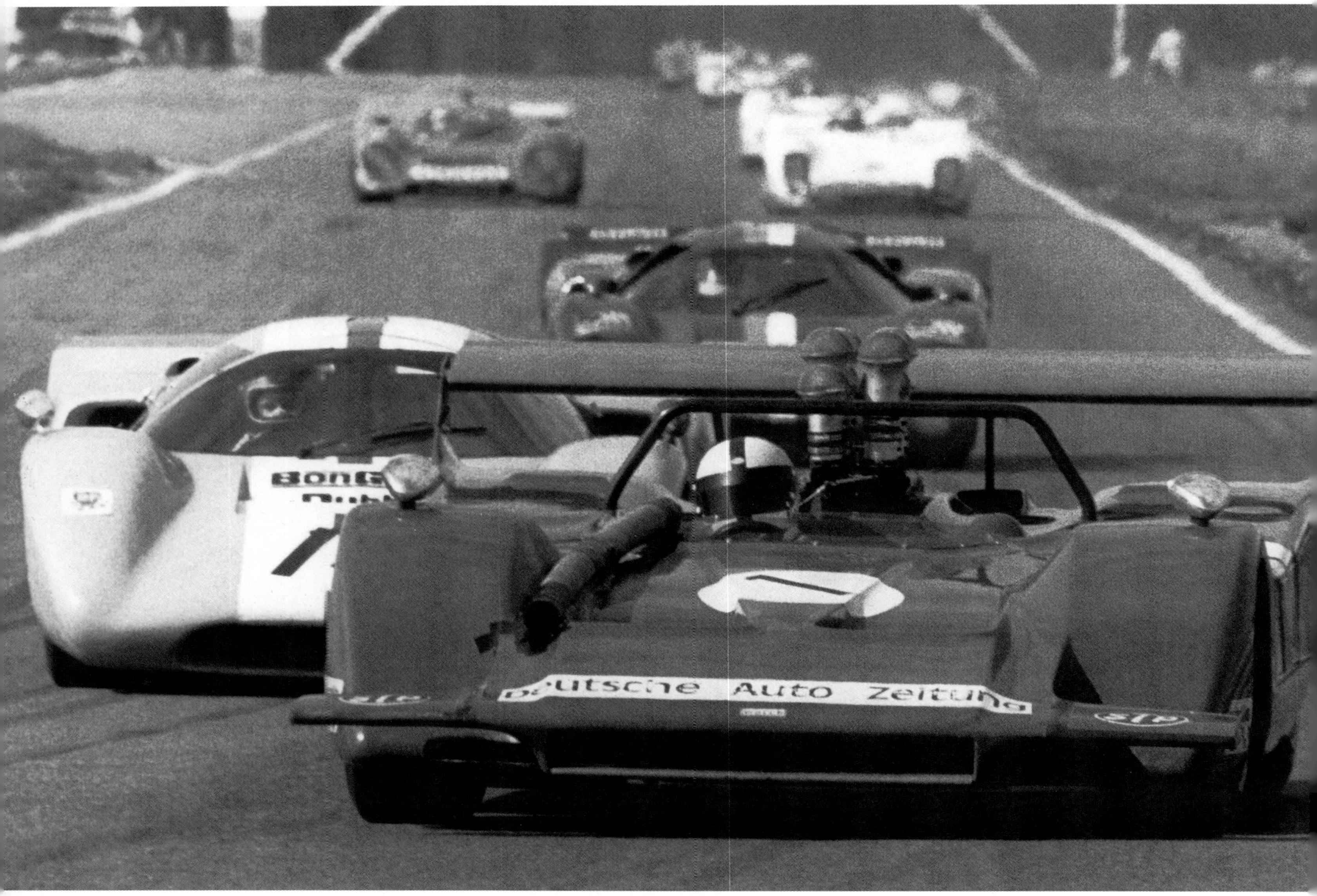

ABOVE Entrant/driver Richard Brostrom invited Ronnie to race his Porsche 908/2 in the Swedish Grand Prix, then a sportscar race on the Karlskoga circuit, and he startled the sportscar racing community by qualifying third. The front-runners were Chris Craft's DFV-powered Ecurie Evergreen McLaren M8C and Helmut Marko's Porsche 908 Spyder, a lightweight special built by the works-backed Martini Racing team. After leading at first, Ronnie was racing strongly with these two when a driveshaft broke. Two weeks later, when the Interserie visited Keimola in Finland, Ronnie was back in Jo Bonnier's Lola. He is pictured vainly trying to find a way past Helmut Kelleners's colossal March 707 CanAm sports-racer.

RIGHT With Reine Wisell and the ever-immaculate Jo Bonnier in the pit garages at Watkins Glen. The United States Grand Prix meeting that closed the 1970 Formula 1 season was the first contested by three Swedish drivers. Bonnier – still the only Swede ever to win a Grand Prix – was aware that his standing back home was being diminished by the success of these two young chargers, but nonetheless he helped them whenever he could. This event brought Emerson Fittipaldi his maiden victory (in his fourth race) and Reine, his Gold Leaf Team Lotus team-mate, finished a strong third behind Pedro Rodriguez (BRM). Another puncture delayed Ronnie, and 40-year-old Bonnier failed to finish in his privately entered McLaren. Wisell lost a lot of heart for racing two years later after Bonnier's fatal accident at Le Mans.

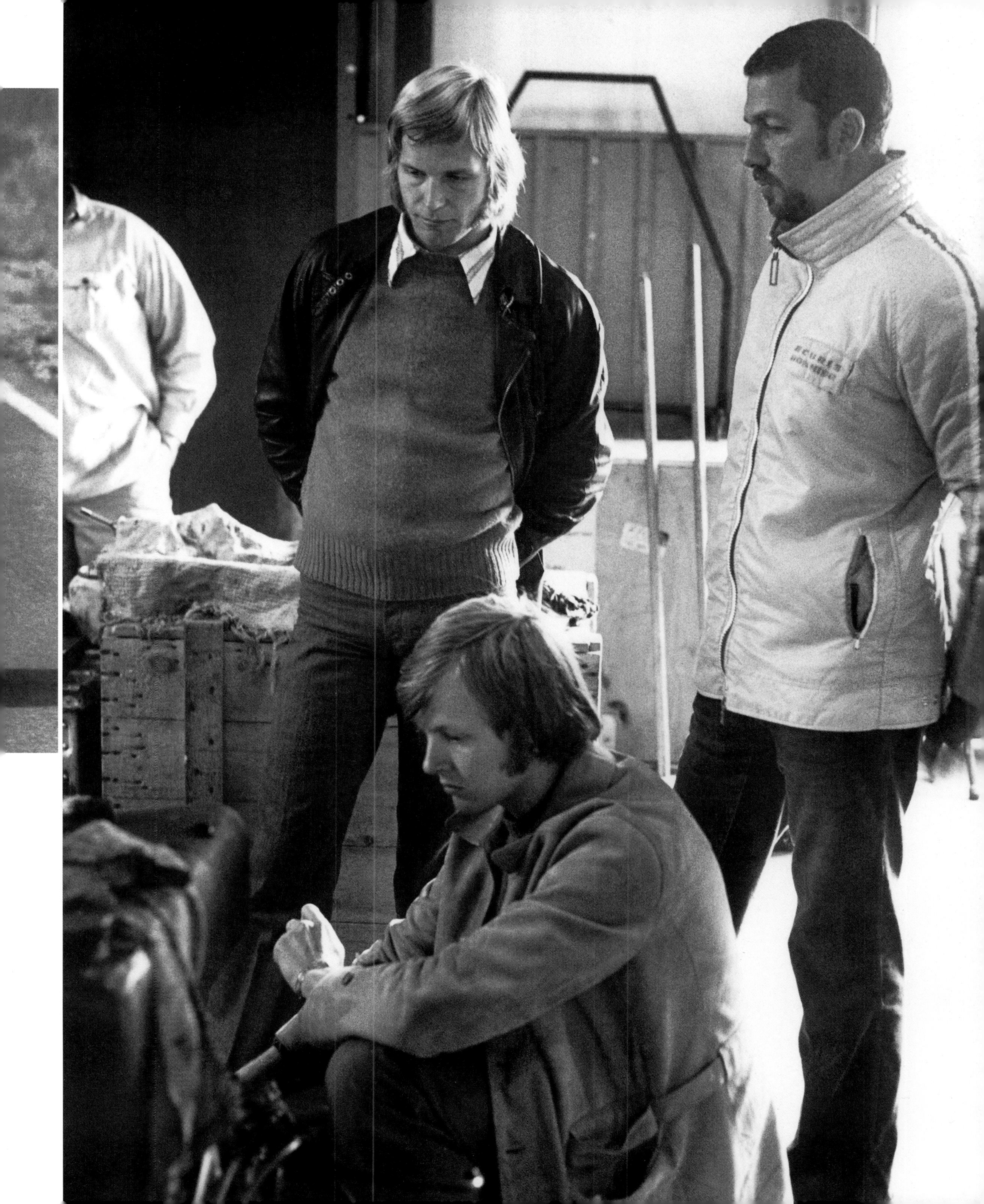

1971

RUNNER-UP BUT NOT YET A RACE WINNER

Ronnie was promoted to the works STP March team for his first full Formula 1 season, with number one status facilitated by the departures of both Chris Amon and Jo Siffert. The highly distinctive March 711 was on the pace as soon as Ronnie got his hands on the latest, Series 11 Cosworth DFV. Some great drives, particularly at Monaco and Monza, showed that he was already one of the fastest men in Formula 1, and four second places made him the runner-up in the World Championship. And he dominated the second half of the European Formula 2 series, beating Carlos Reutemann to the title with a race to spare. Before the season was done, he had been approached by almost all the front-running Grand Prix teams, but typically chose to honour his March contract and stay for a third term in 1972.

RIGHT Running his March 711 without its front wing, Ronnie throws the car through the Parabolica curve at Monza, striving to break the tow to Chris Amon's V12 Matra. The 1971 Italian Grand Prix stood for 32 years as the fastest in history and came down to a breathless dash to the line, where the five-car leading group was covered by 0.6sec. Ronnie lost by a nose to Peter Gethin's BRM.

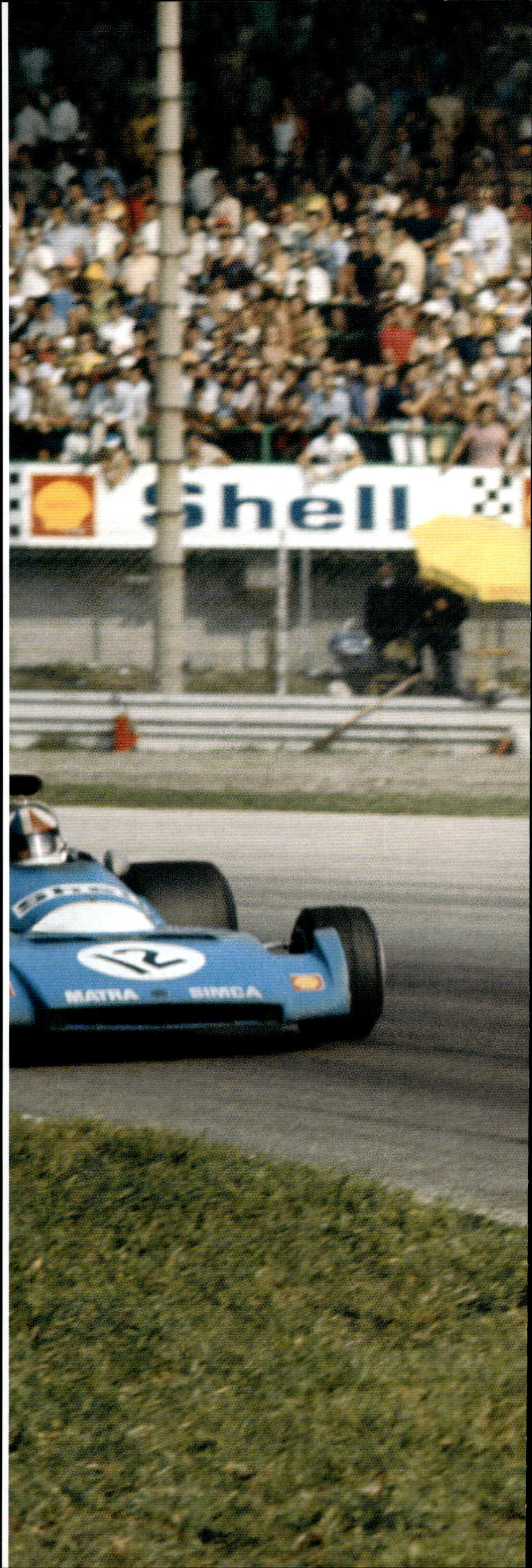

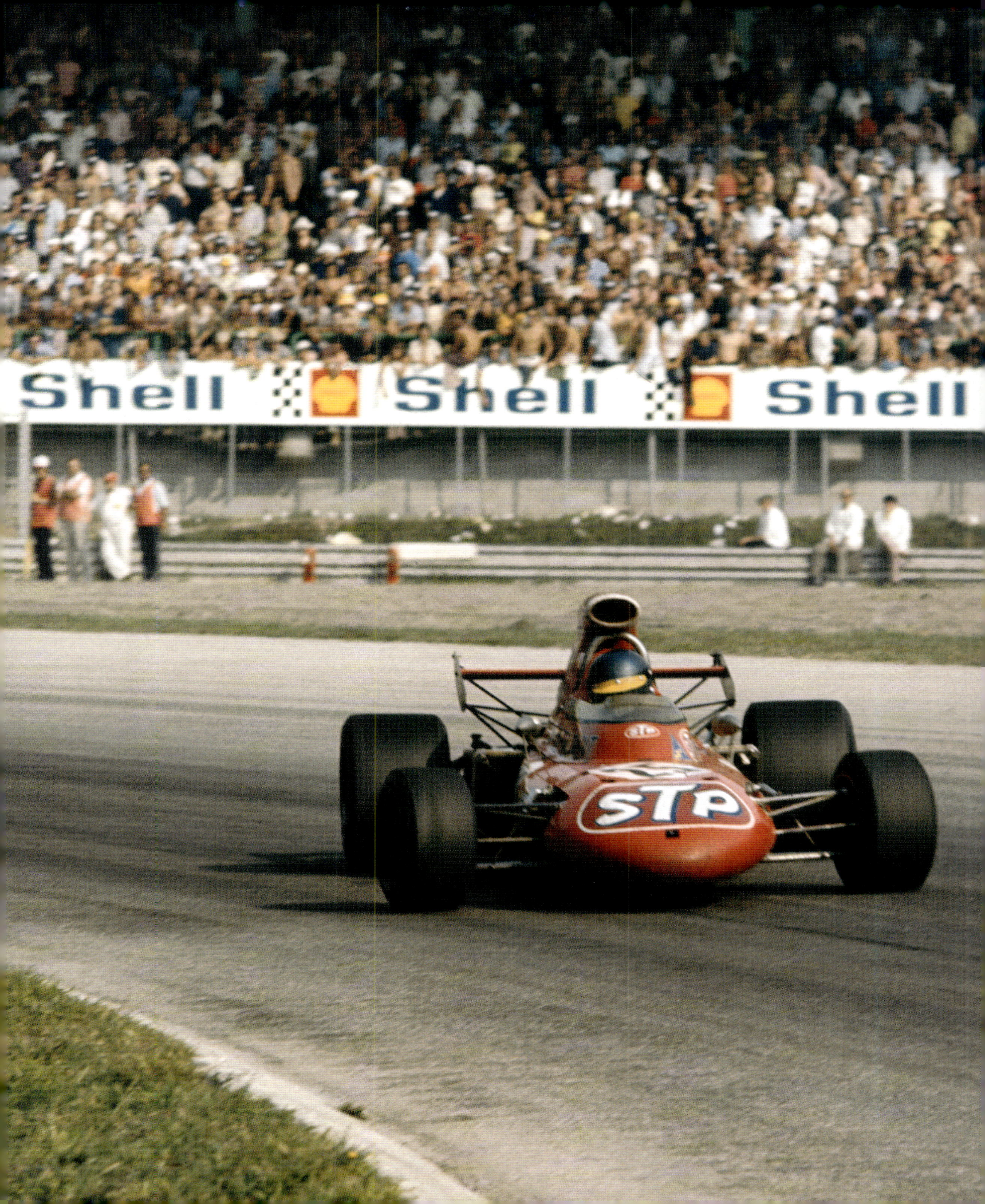
Shell
Shell
Shell
STP

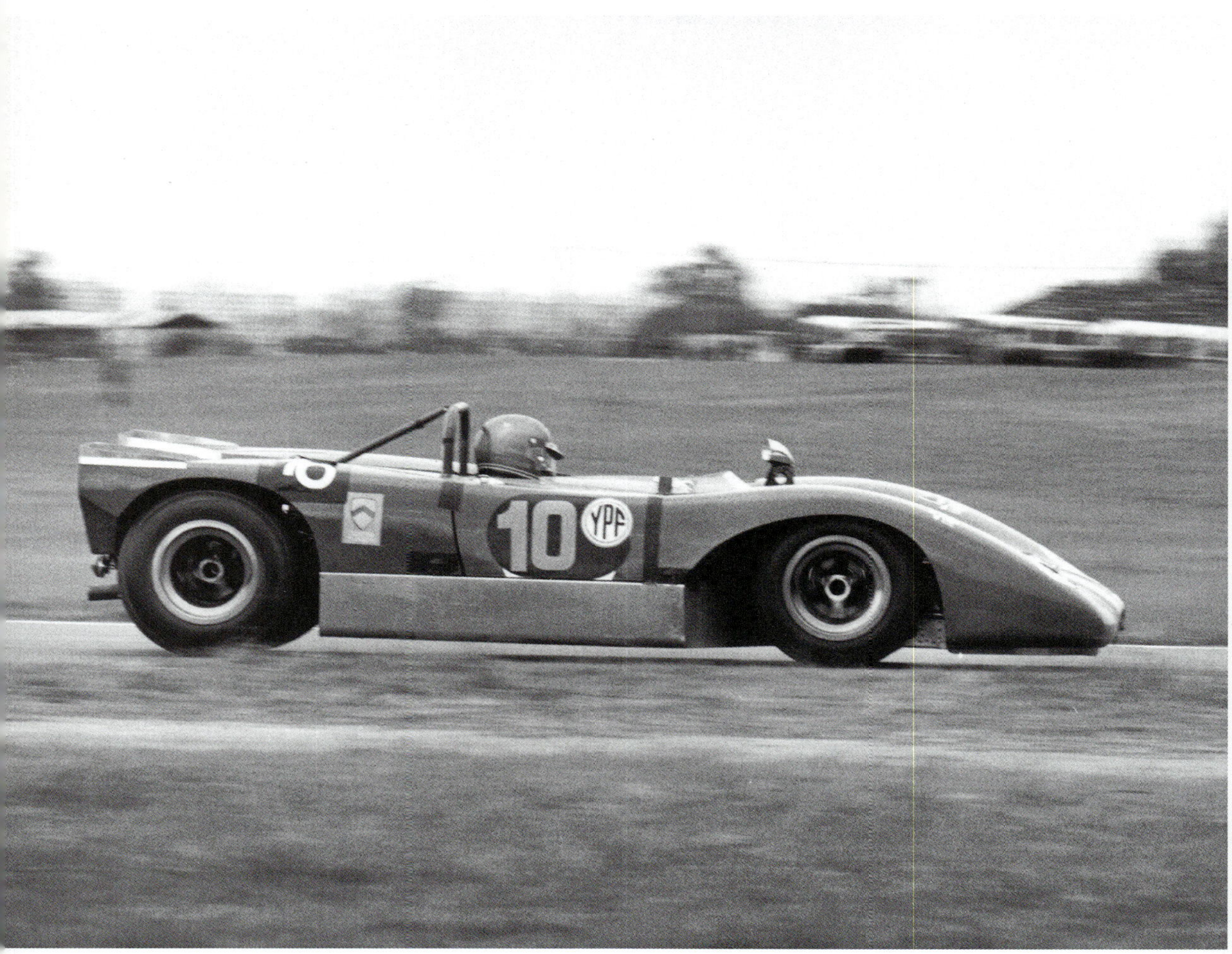

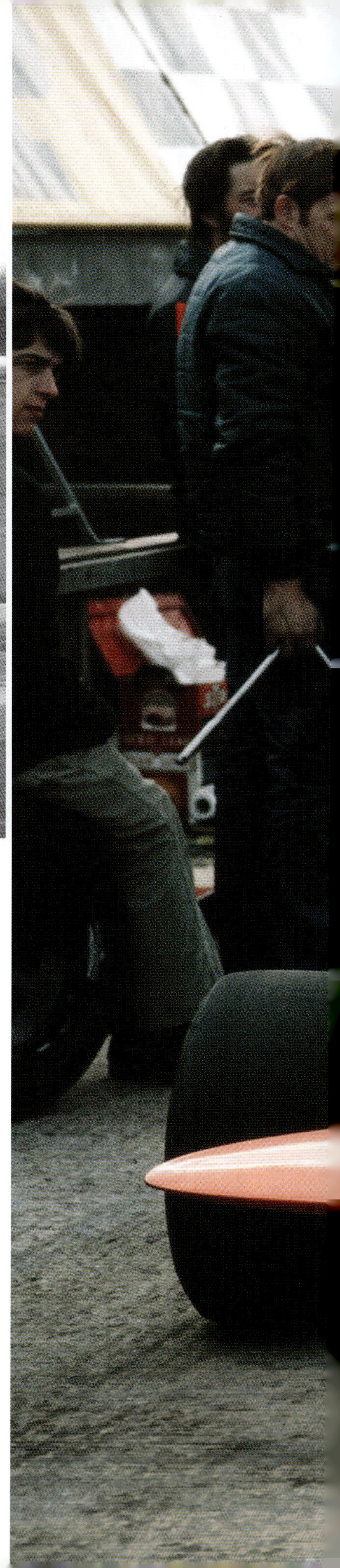

ABOVE Ronnie's 1971 season began with two accidents in one race meeting when Jo Bonnier arranged a drive for him with Georges Filipinetti's Swiss-based team in the opening round of the World Championship of Makes, in Buenos Aires. First, during practice, Ronnie crashed the team's Ferrari 512S, so he was switched to a brand new, Cosworth FVC powered Lola T212. Co-driven by Jorge Cupeiro, Ronnie was one of the stars of the 1000km race, leading the 2-litre class by miles. In fact, he was holding down fifth place overall when a sudden tyre deflation sent him into another high-speed crash. The car was classified in 12th position at the finish, second in the class. This race delivered a 1–2 for the works Gulf Porsche team, Jo Siffert/Derek Bell ahead of Pedro Rodriguez/Jackie Oliver, but is best remembered for the tragic début of the new Ferrari 312P. Ignazio Giunti received fatal head injuries when he struck a works Matra that had run out of fuel and was being pushed across the track by its driver, Jean-Pierre Beltoise.

RIGHT Hands in pockets, March designer Robin Herd looks nonchalant during a pre-season test with Ronnie in the distinctive 711 Formula 1 car at Silverstone. The rounded fuselage and 'tea-tray' front wing, with its single mounting post, was the concept of aerodynamic consultant Frank Costin, and was designed to generate high front-end downforce with minimal drag. The high cockpit enclosure was also a Costin feature. Although it signalled a period of over-confident experimentation on the part of the team that would have disastrous consequences in 1972, this concept worked pretty well. March principal Max Mosley had done a deal to access Alfa Romeo V8s, as well as Cosworths, which allowed the team to field three cars in every race. This is one of the Italian engined cars.

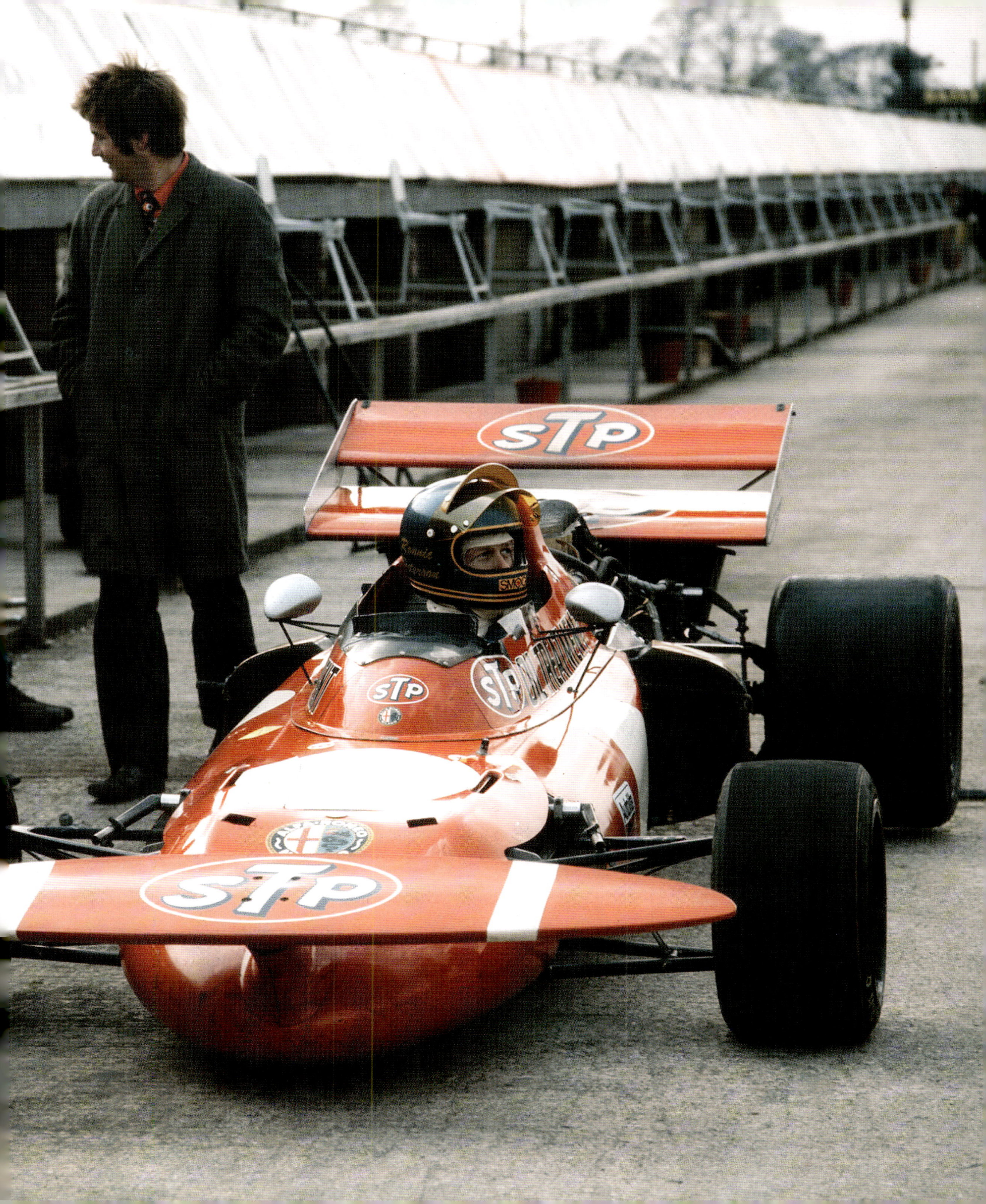
STP
STP
STP

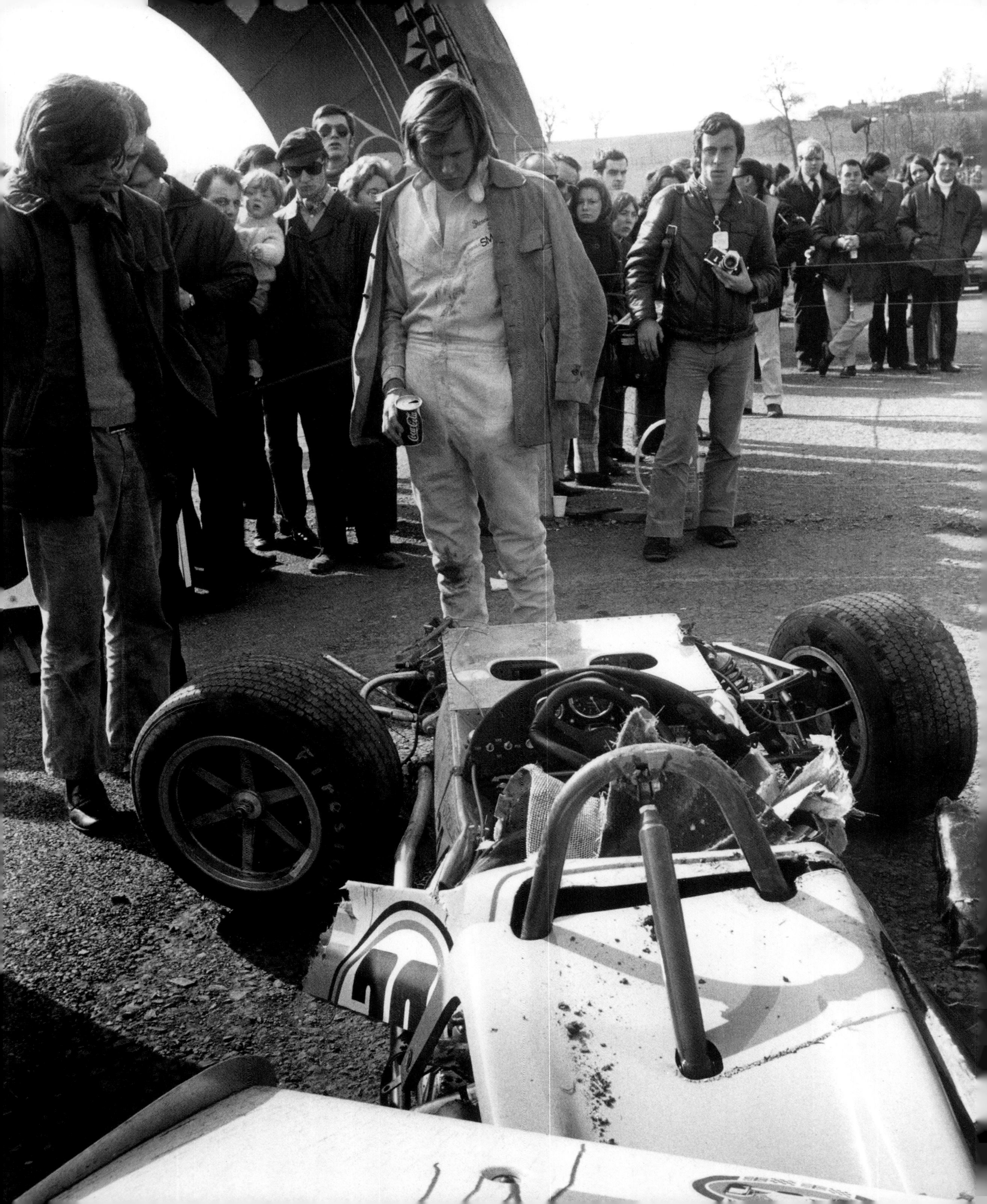

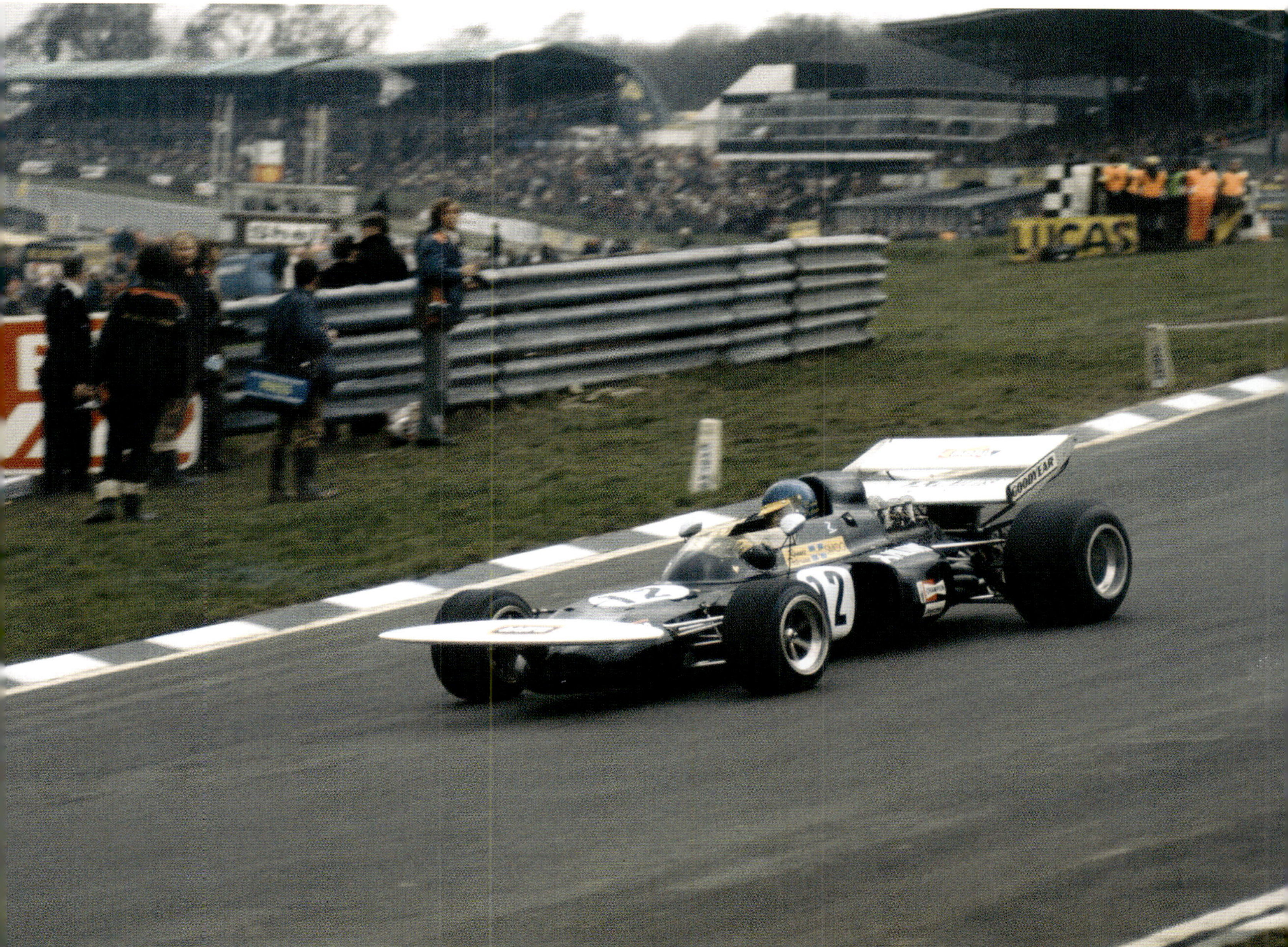

LEFT Ronnie ruefully surveys the results of a big crash at Mallory Park during a non-championship Formula 2 race in mid-March, on début with the March 712M. A ball-joint in the car's steering seized, making him a helpless passenger. He escaped with painful bruising but was mortified when told that a small boy in the crowd had been cut by a piece of flying debris. He autographed one of the front aerofoils from the wreck and sent it to the youth.

ABOVE A week after his accident at Mallory, Ronnie was asked to race Frank Williams's new, Motul sponsored March-Cosworth in the Race of Champions at Brands Hatch, in the absence of regular driver Henri Pescarolo. The car arrived in Kent in boxes and was built up during the qualifying sessions, but he was permitted to start from the back of the sparse, 15-car grid with a 10sec penalty. Racing the completely unsorted car with 'slick' tyres on a damp track, Ronnie had caught and passed four of the cars ahead when, on the 14th lap, one of the inboard front brake shafts broke.

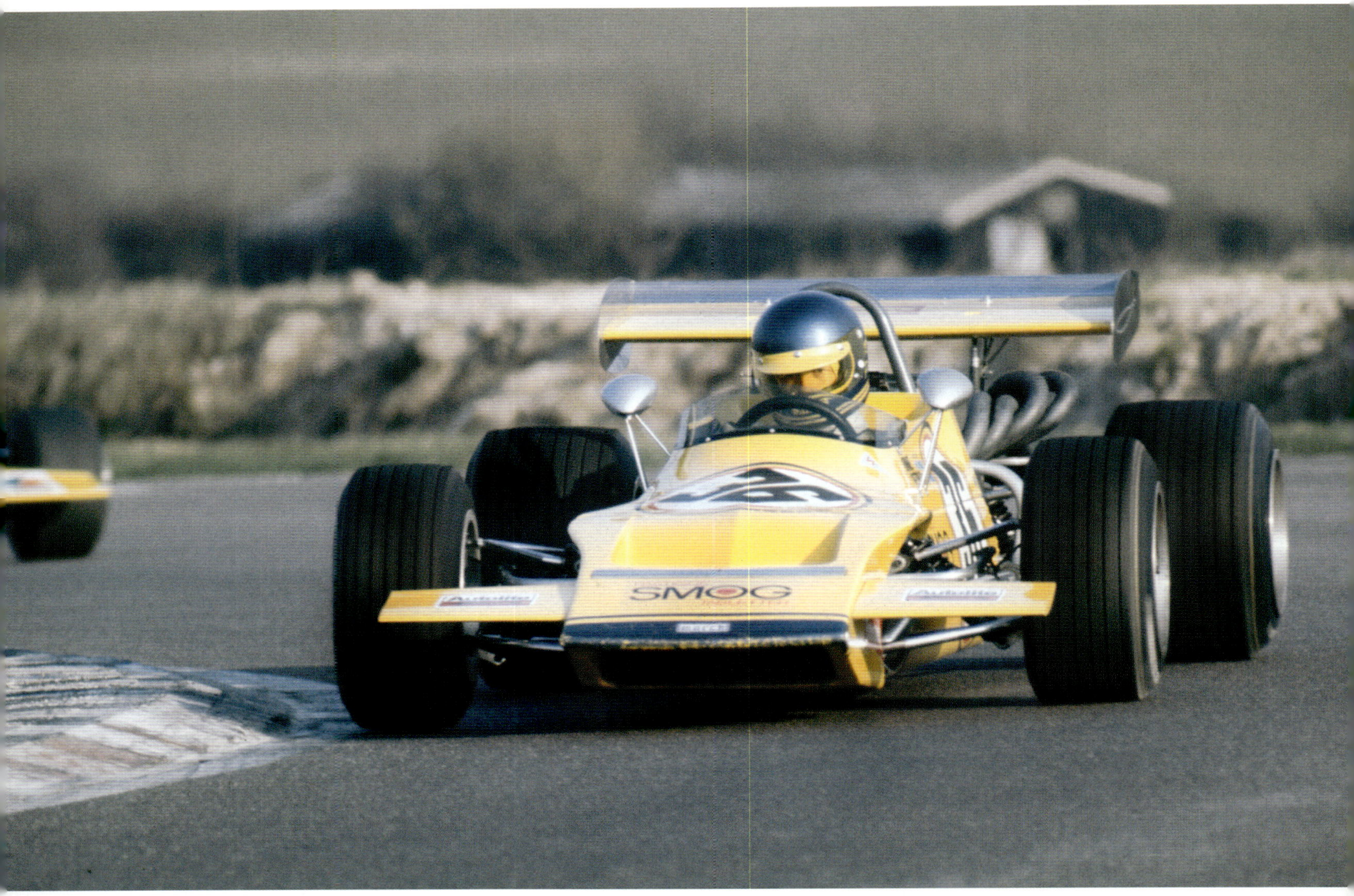

ABOVE The European Formula 2 Championship visited Thruxton a week after a rare Cosworth FVA engine failure had ended Ronnie's run in the opening round at Hockenheim. A broken gearlever cost him the lead in his heat at the UK venue, and he finished second behind Henri Pescarolo in Frank Williams's privateer March 712M. In the final, Ronnie hunted down the other heat winner, Graham Hill in Ron Dennis's Brabham, and got on his tail after 33 of the 50 laps. He left his move until lap 49, outbraking Hill at the chicane. Midway round the final lap, a backmarker put Ronnie on the grass verge. Hill was through in an instant and held on to win by 0.6sec. And Ronnie had to wait some more for his maiden Formula 2 victory.

RIGHT Having finished a delayed 10th in the 1971 series-opening Formula 1 race in South Africa, due to a puncture, Ronnie hoped for better things when the teams assembled six weeks later for the second round in Barcelona. He drove his March 711 in typical, opposite-lock style on the Montjuic street course, but could qualify and race only in the midfield. He was about to be lapped by Spanish Grand Prix winner Jackie Stewart's Tyrrell when his ignition system packed up. This was not looking good – and in his next Formula 1 race, it got worse. Ronnie tried one of the Alfa Romeo V8 cars for the International Trophy at Silverstone but crashed heavily when the throttle jammed wide open, and was knocked briefly unconscious by a detached front wheel.

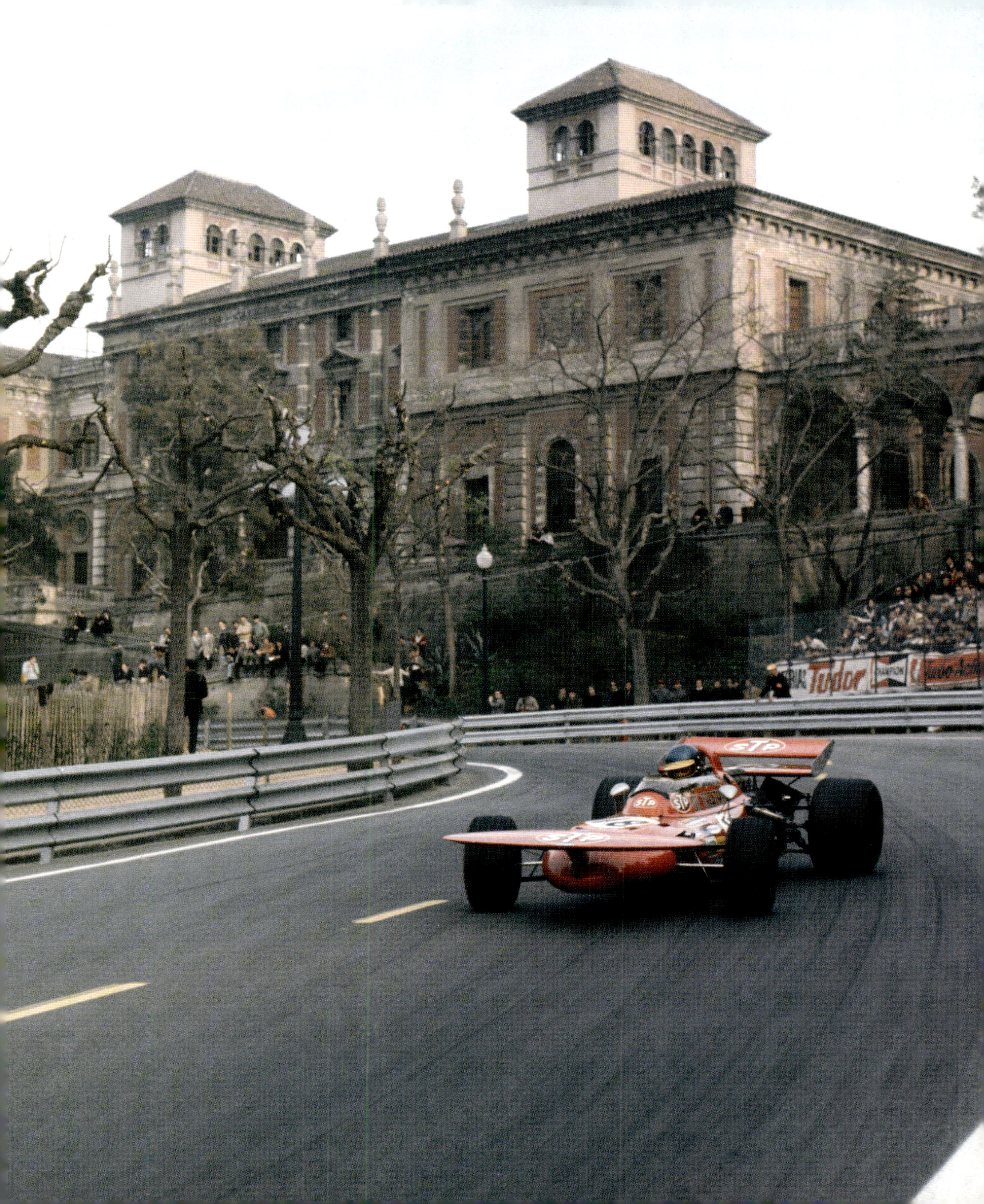

STP
Tudor

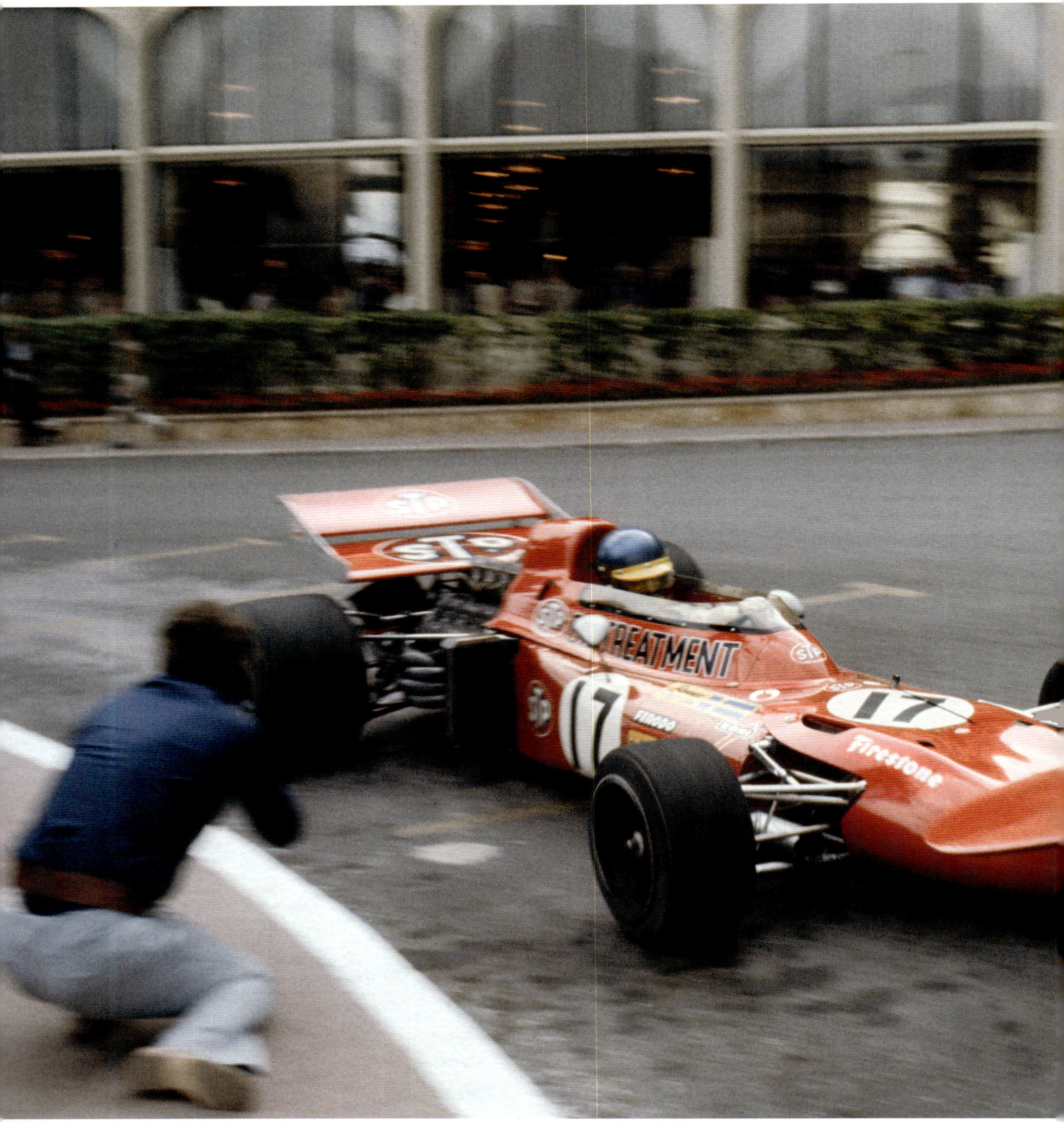
TREATMENT
17
Firestone

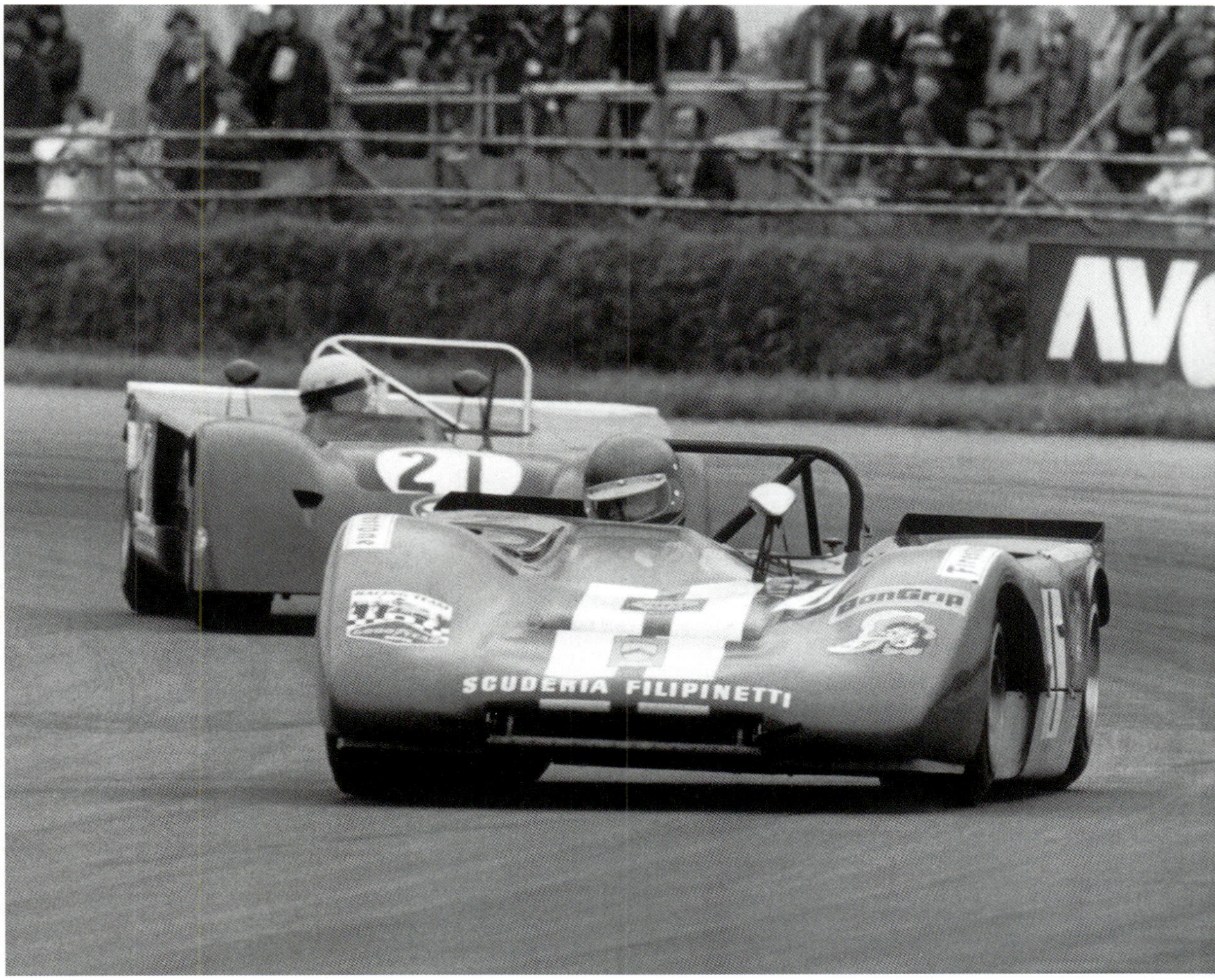

LEFT The STP March Formula 1 programme took a sudden and unexpected upswing when, out of nowhere, Ronnie produced a sensational drive at Monaco. He qualified eighth, but went straight into fifth place. Although passed by Denny Hulme's McLaren M19A, he took the place back and, after Pedro Rodriguez had pitted his BRM P160, picked off Jacky Ickx's Ferrari 312B2 and Jo Siffert's BRM. There was no catching Jackie Stewart's Tyrrell, but this second place was greeted with a standing ovation from the crowd, the uncomfortably close attention of the photographic media, and ecstacy from his team. This was some way to score the first World Championship points of his career. Sadly, the team's joy was tempered by the death the very same day of one of its founders, Graham Coaker, from complications that set in after he had broken a leg in a Formula 2 crash at Silverstone.

ABOVE The popular 2-litre sports-racing cars of the early 1970s were nimble and chuckable, and could have been made to suit Ronnie's press-on style. He was blindingly quick in Ecurie Filipinetti's Lola T212, and never more so than in the 1971 Martini Trophy event at Silverstone. He was a last-minute replacement for an unwell Jo Bonnier, and missed qualifying. One of Ronnie's former karting adversaries, Toine Hezemans won the first heat from Helmut Marko (Lola) and British champion John Lepp (Chevron), with Ronnie a fantastic fourth after starting 33rd and last. Here he has just taken the lead of the second heat from Hezemans, and went on to win easily. But Hezemans could afford to cruise into third place behind DART Chevron team-mate John Miles and still win on aggregate, with Ronnie second.

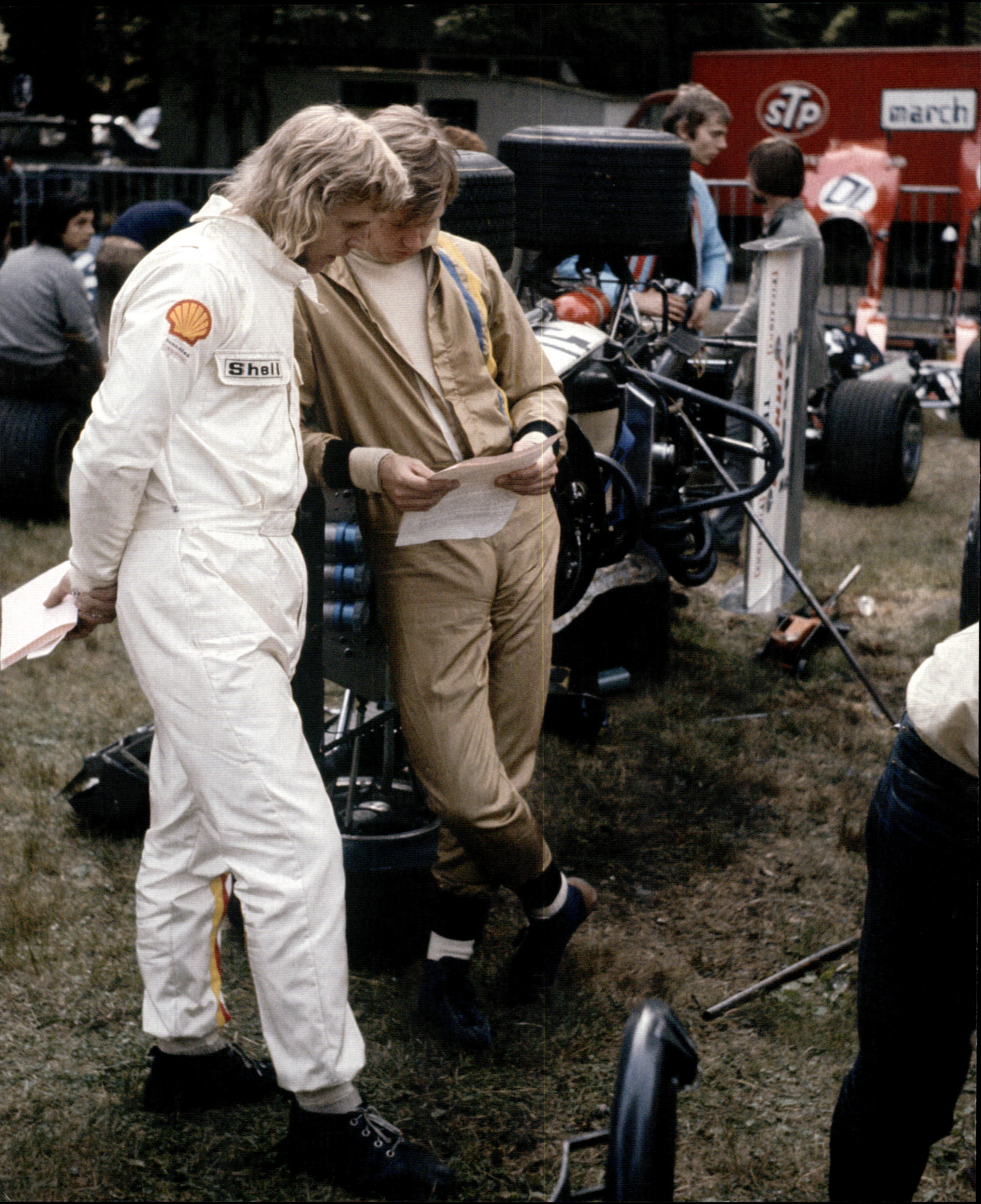
STP
march
Shell

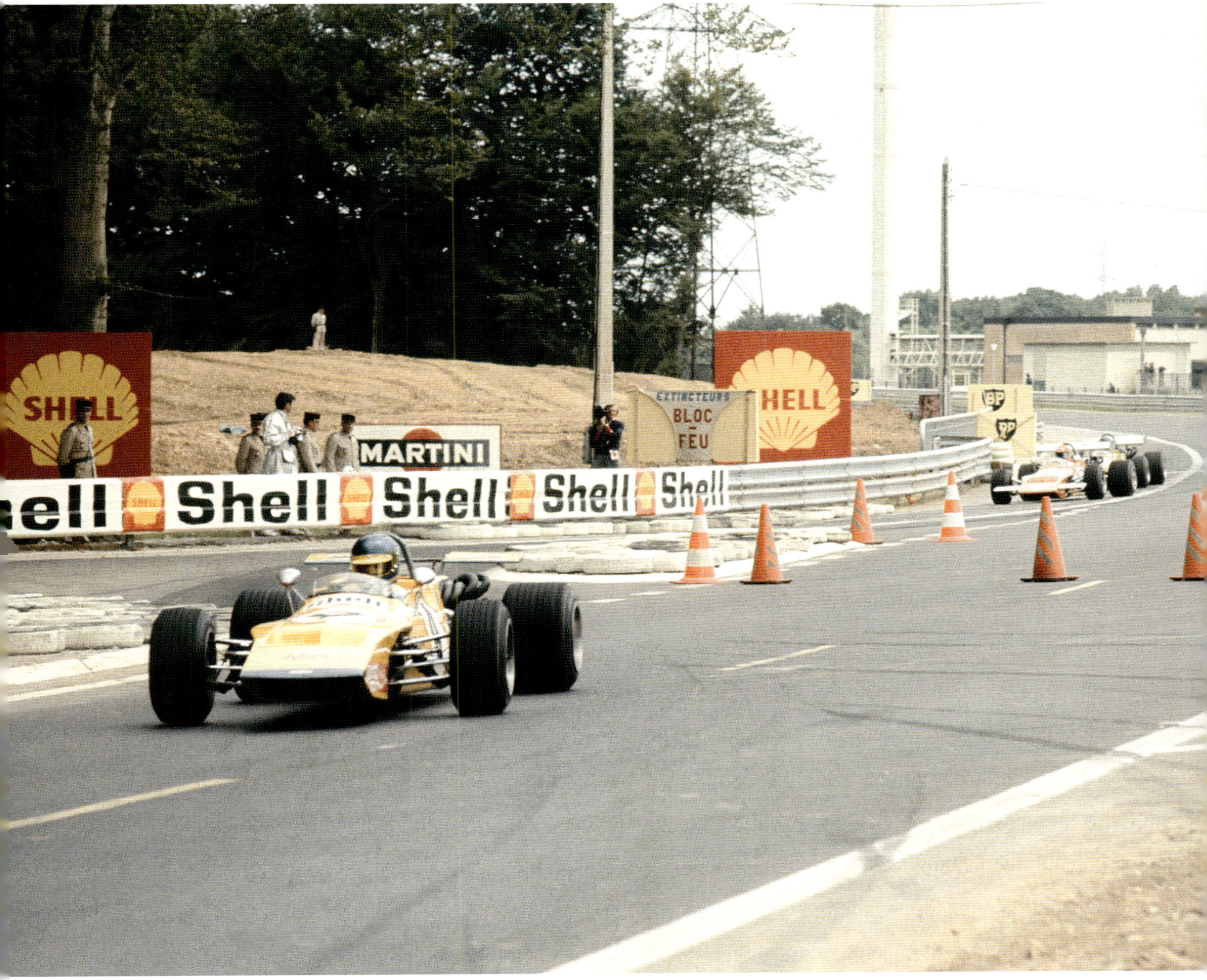

LEFT Ronnie and Reine study the qualifying lap-times in the paddock at Rouen-les-Essarts. The Grand Prix de Rouen was to be Ronnie's 21st Formula 2 event, and he had yet to win one. He was fastest in both the qualifying sessions with the Hart-engined works March 712M, while Reine would line up ninth with the UK-owned Team LIRA Lotus 69.

ABOVE Ronnie exits a makeshift chicane at Rouen, well ahead of Niki Lauda and Mike Beuttler with two more March 712Ms. He led this heat for the entire distance and, at the front of the final, engaged championship leader François Cevert in a torrid battle that ended with the Tecno in the barrier. Finally Ronnie broke his Formula 2 jinx. This was the first of four consecutive victories in the European Championship that delivered the title in the penultimate round.

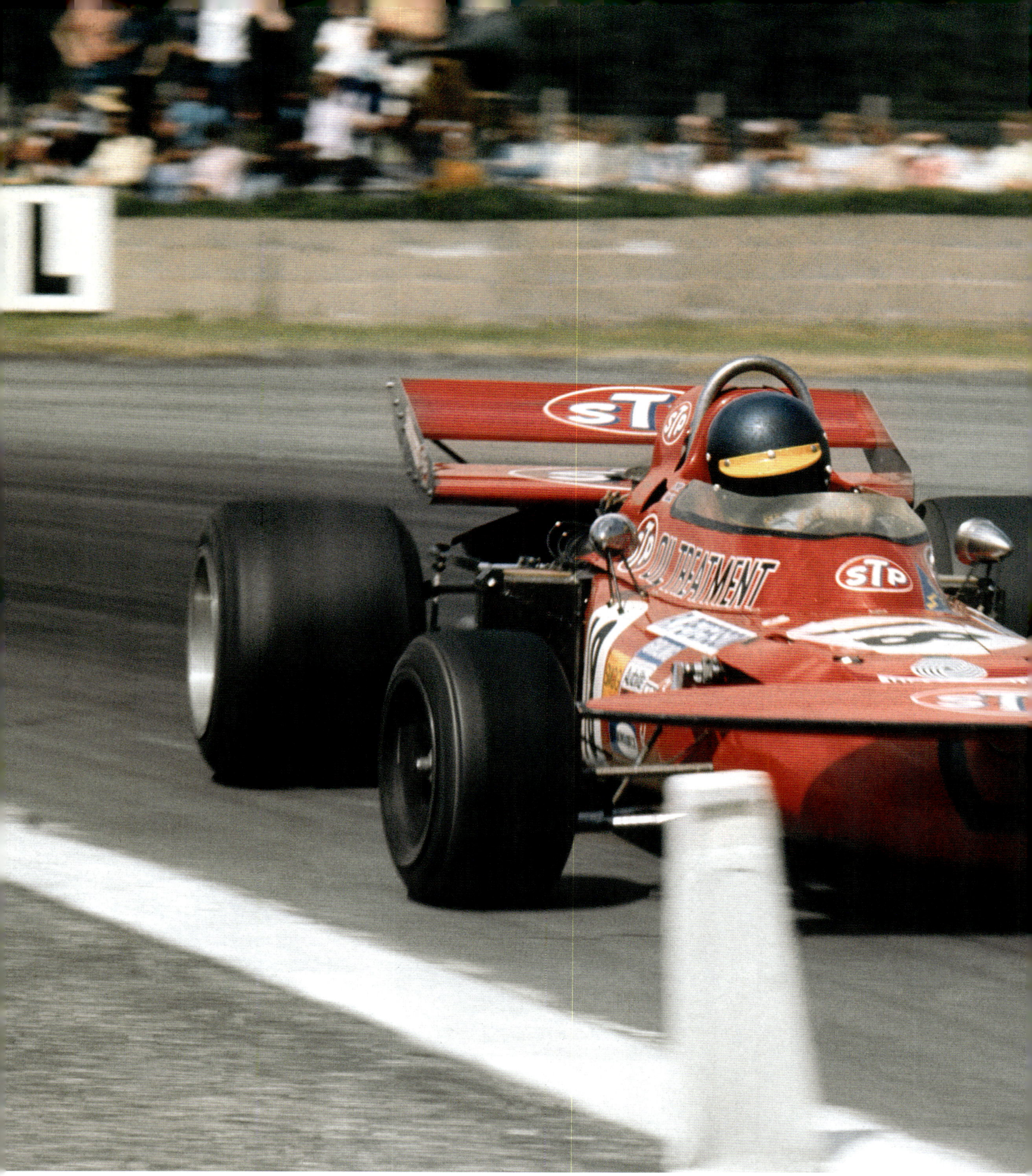
STP
OIL TREATMENT

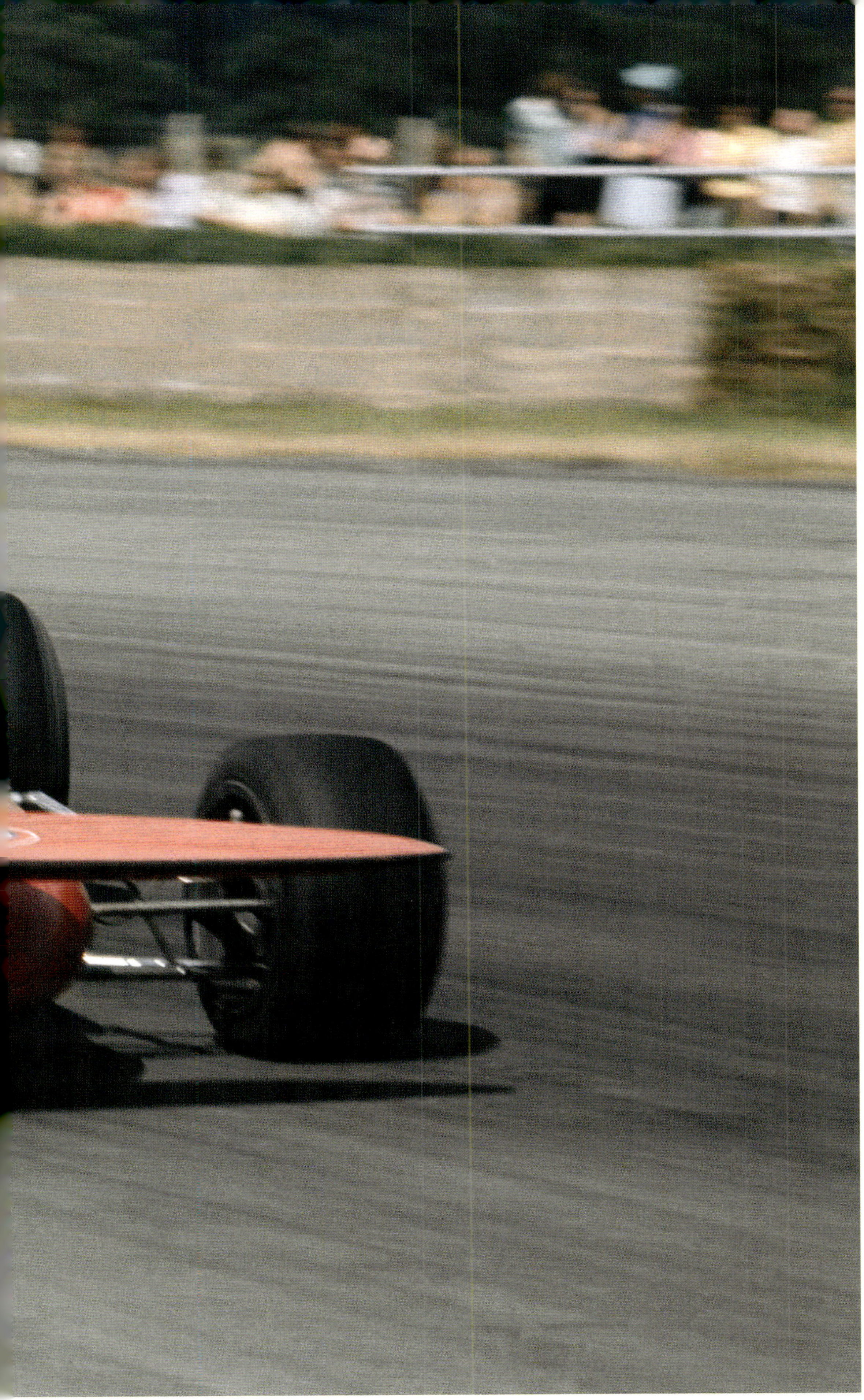

LEFT Ronnie qualified fifth for the British Grand Prix at Silverstone and produced another top-class performance on race day. After a closely fought battle with Emerson Fittipaldi's Lotus 72D, he moved ahead in mid-race, passed Tim Schenken's Brabham and, when Clay Regazzoni's Ferrari lost its engine, emerged in second place. Jackie Stewart's winning Tyrrell was again far out of his reach, but suddenly Ronnie was third in the championship.

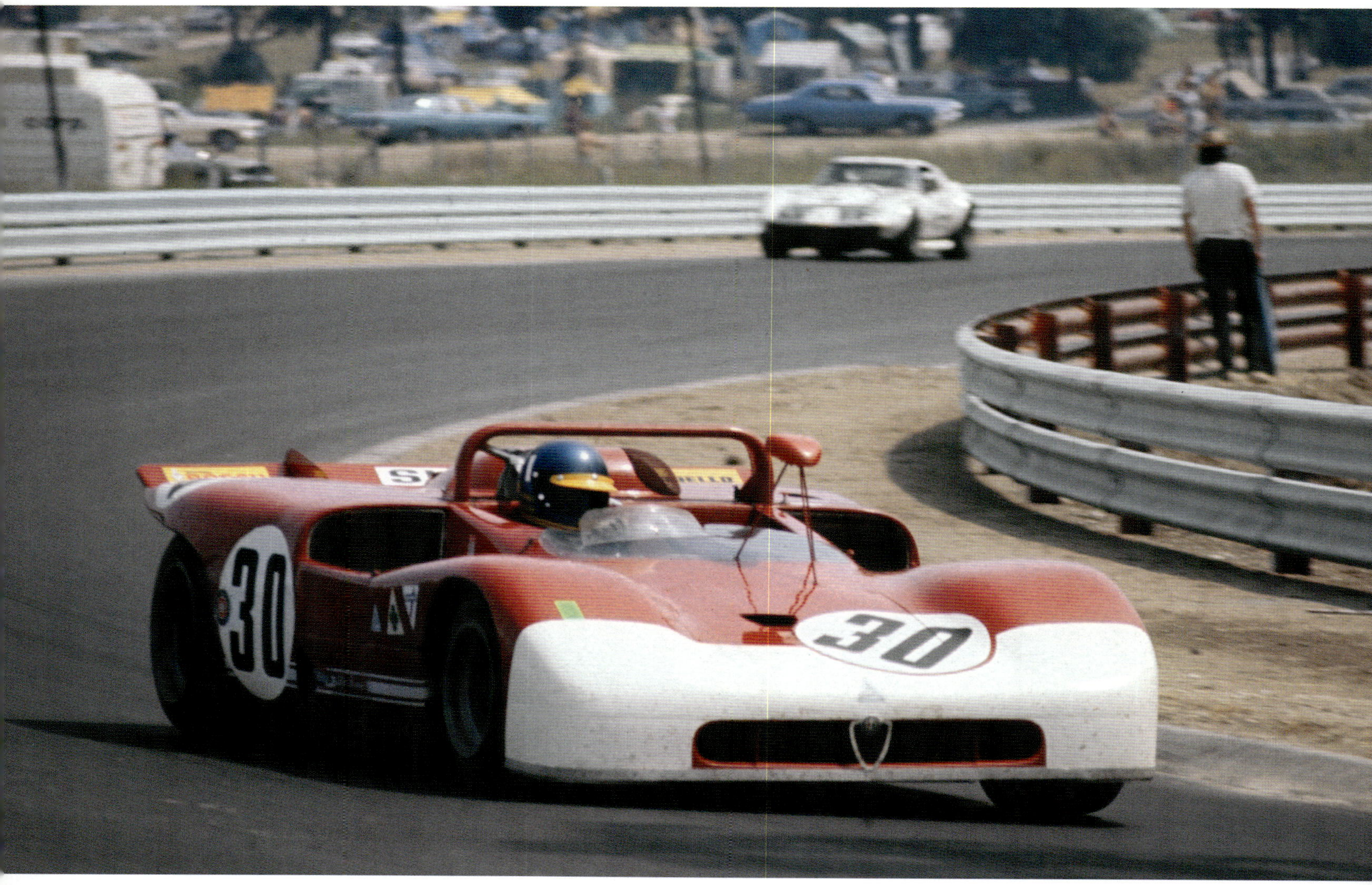

ABOVE Ronnie raced this 3-litre Alfa Romeo T33/3 sports-prototype in the Watkins Glen 6 Hours as part of the commercial arrangement between March Engineering and Alfa Romeo. He co-drove Andrea de Adamich, who did seven Grands Prix this season in Alfa V8 powered March single-seaters. No one expected a victory in the American round of the World Championship of Makes, but that is what happened. This was a race of high attrition in which the faster Porsche 917s and Ferrari 512s, and a solo Ferrari 312P, were eliminated or delayed by all manner of mechanical failures. Treacherous track conditions under heavy rain accounted for other front-runners, including the other two Alfa Romeos. The all-conquering 5-litre JW/Gulf Porsches, delayed by five punctures between them, finished 2–3 in their last competitive outing prior to the introduction of a new formula in 1972.

RIGHT Sweden's finest contest the midfield on the Osterreichring, far behind flag-to-flag leader Jo Siffert's BRM. Reine Wisell's Gold Leaf Lotus 72 leads Graham Hill's Brabham, Ronnie's March, Denny Hulme's McLaren and Henri Pescarolo's Frank Williams entered March in a battle over eighth position. Attrition ahead put Reine in fourth place at the finish, ahead of Hill and Pescarolo, while Ronnie ended up eighth behind Rolf Stommelen's Surtees. It was Ronnie, however, whose career was on the up. Reine would be dropped by Lotus at the end of this season and, after an unhappy sojourn with BRM, would drift away from the sport.

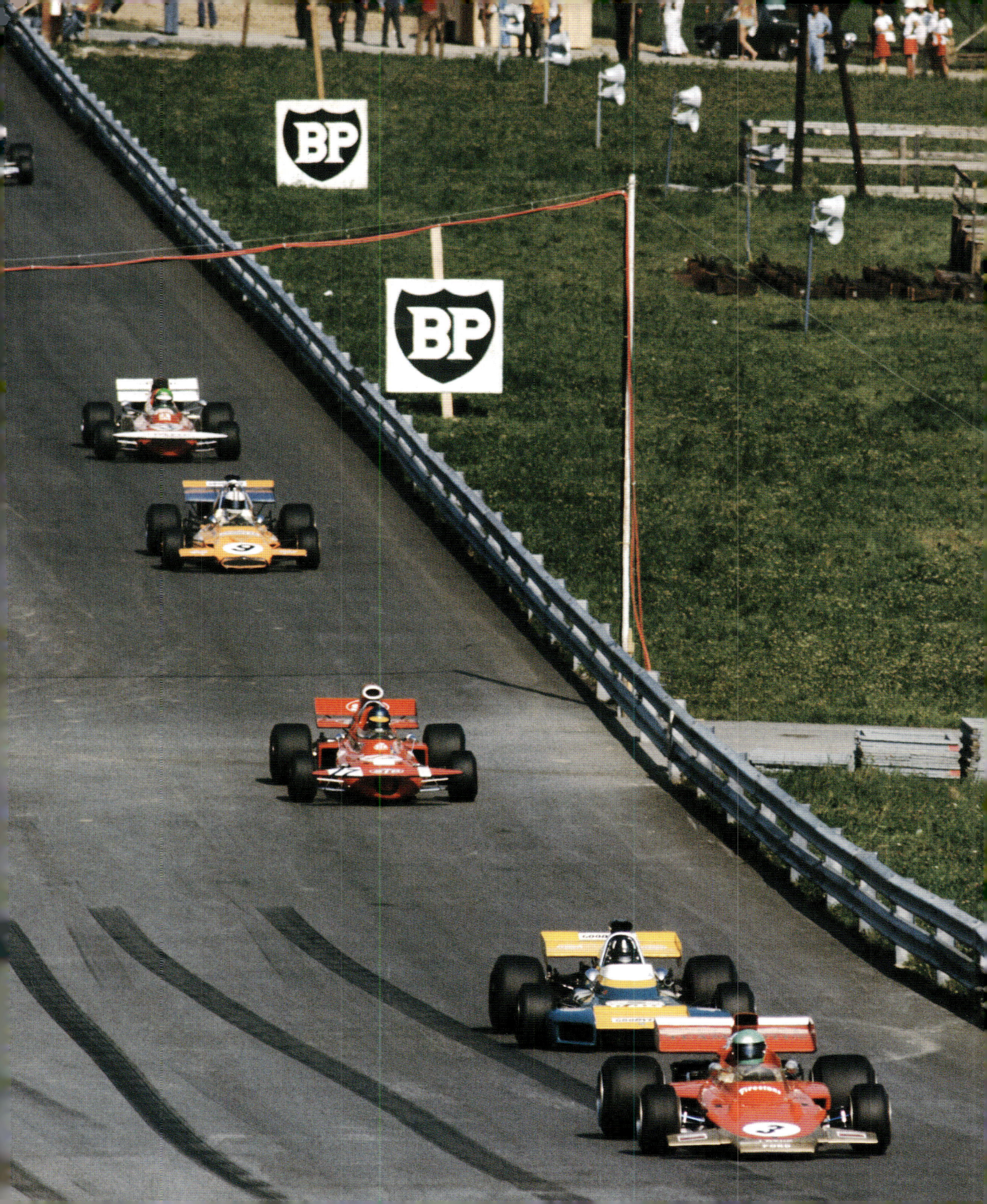
BP
BP

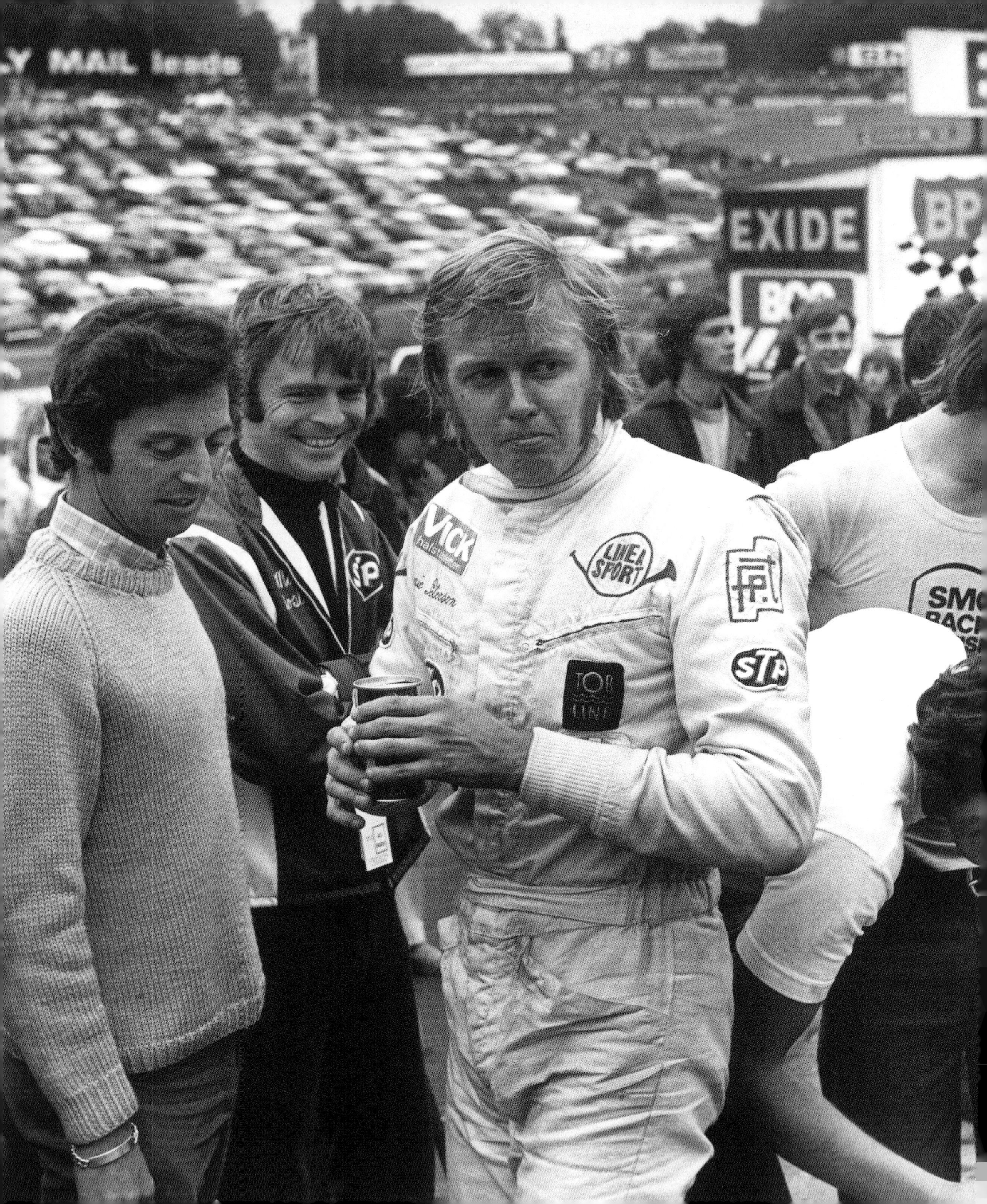
MAIL
EXIDE
BP
VICK
LINEA SPORT
STP
TOR LINE

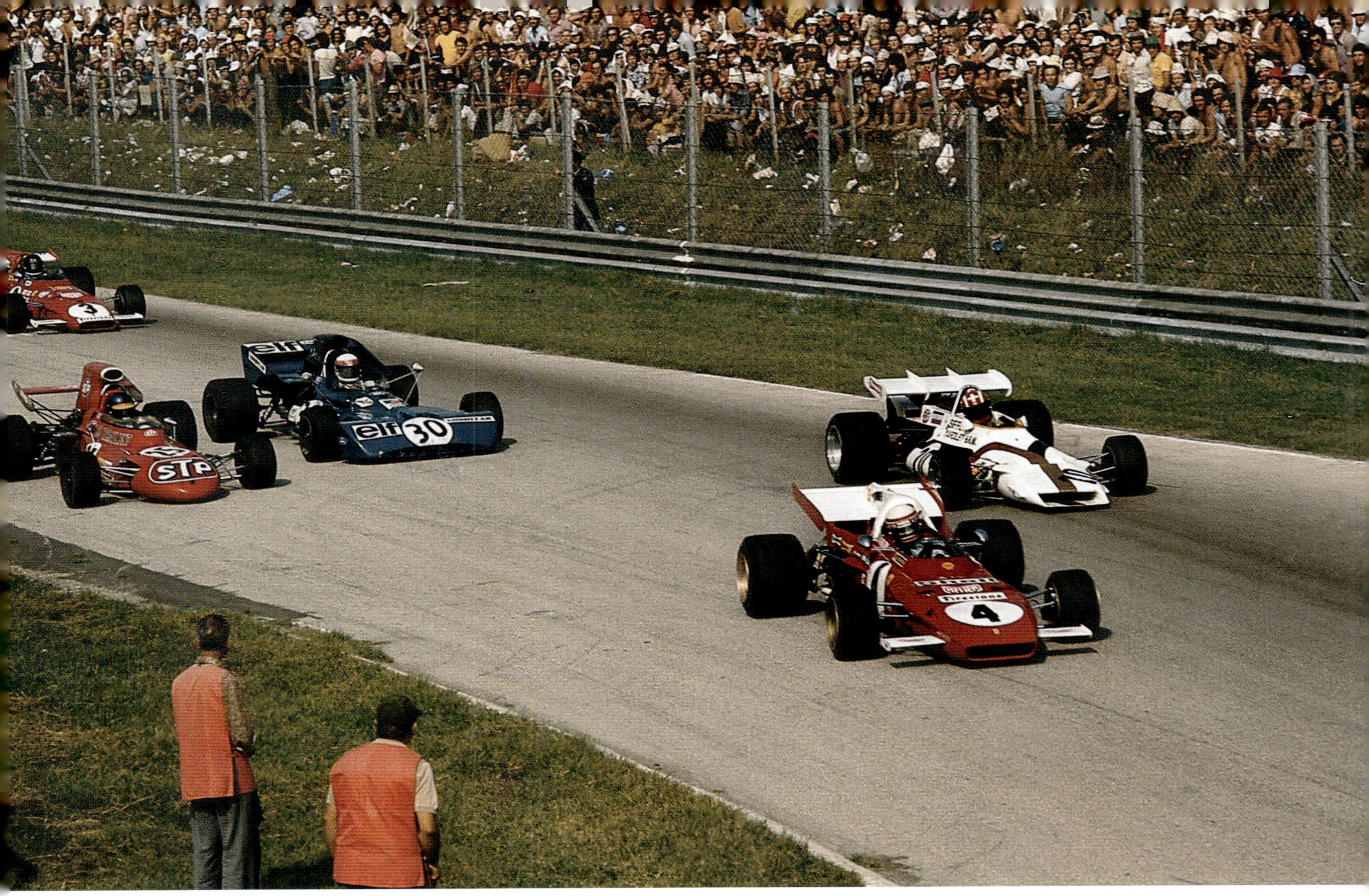

LEFT With a beaming Max Mosley and photojournalist Max Le Granc at the August Bank Holiday Brands Hatch meeting. Ronnie has just won the Formula 2 race from a pole position driven 0.2sec under the outright lap record, and 1.4sec faster than Graham Hill in Ron Dennis's Brabham and Emerson Fittipaldi in the Team Bardahl Lotus. His margin of victory over Hill was almost 15sec. Ronnie had recently renewed his acquaintance with the beautiful Barbro Edvardsson, whom he had first met two years before, and would shortly relocate from rented accommodation near the March factory in Bicester to share a new house with her in Cookham Dean, near Maidenhead, Berkshire.

ABOVE The 1971 Italian Grand Prix was one of the races of the decade, an unrelenting, high-speed slipstreaming battle that transfixed onlookers as the leaders swapped places constantly. Equipped for the first time with the latest, Series 11 Cosworth DFV, Ronnie qualified sixth but got himself in the lead of a 15-car 'train' on the fourth lap. Ronnie was always in contention and led on eight separate occasions, but the frantic pace of this race took its toll on others. It was too much for the engines in Jackie Stewart's Tyrrell and the Ferraris of Clay Regazzoni (leading here) and Jacky Ickx, while Jo Siffert's BRM fell back with a malfunctioning gearbox. Later Chris Amon, leading in the Matra, went to tear off a single visor strip and instead removed all of them, leaving his eyes unprotected. Meanwhile Peter Gethin famously decided to ignore the rev-limit of his BRM V12 and sailed up to join the leading group. At the last corner, two wheels on the grass, Gethin got himself between Ronnie and Tyrrell's François Cevert, sent them off-line and led them over the finish-line with Mike Hailwood's Surtees and Howden Ganley's BRM still in the tow. The fifth-placed BRM was 0.61sec behind the winner, whose race average of 150.75mph was an all-time Formula 1 record. After the race, March discovered that one of Ronnie's exhaust-headers had broken, costing him a few precious horsepower...

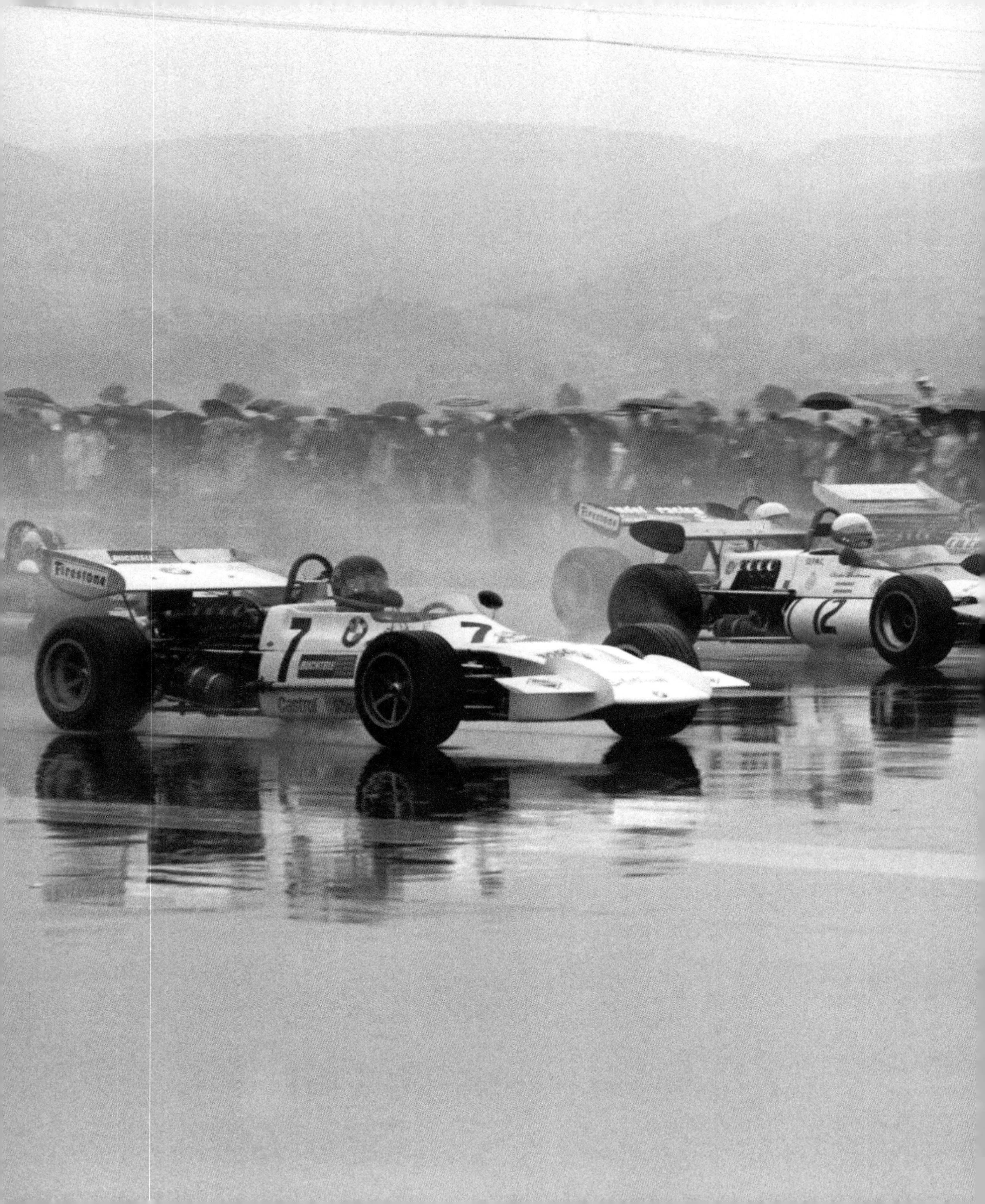
Firestone
Castrol

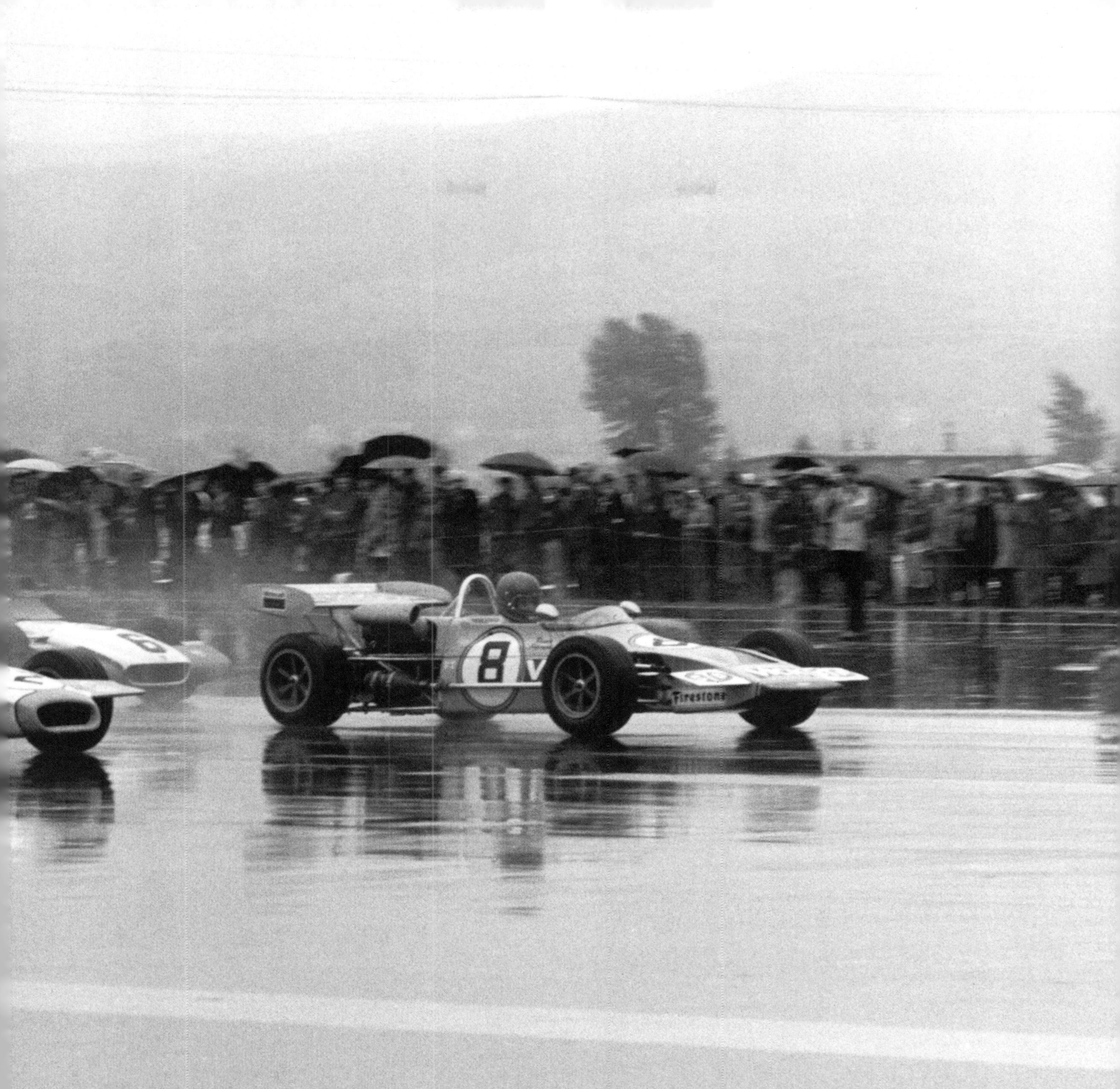

From pole position, Ronnie's March-Cosworth (at right) gets the drop on Carlos Reutemann's Brabham and Dieter Quester's March-BMW (7) on a saturated Tulln-Langenlebarn airfield circuit. This is the start of the first part of Austria's round of the European Formula 2 Championship, and Ronnie won it easily. In the second race, he was sure of victory on aggregate as he closely followed leader Tim Schenken into the last lap. Then Schenken spun his Rondel Racing Brabham, so the works March driver was victorious in both races. A month later, Ronnie clinched the title by winning again at Vallelunga.

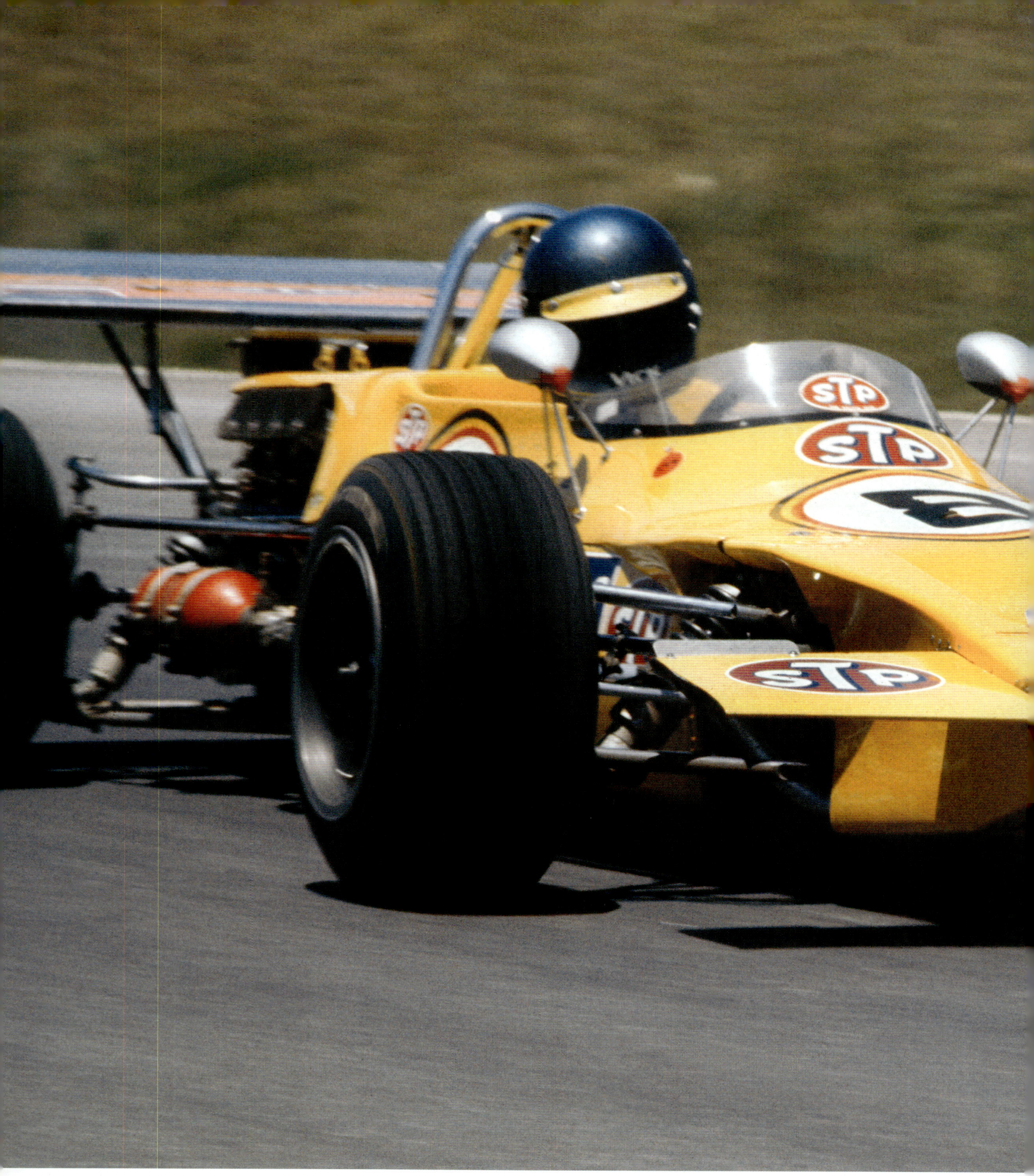
STP
STP
STP

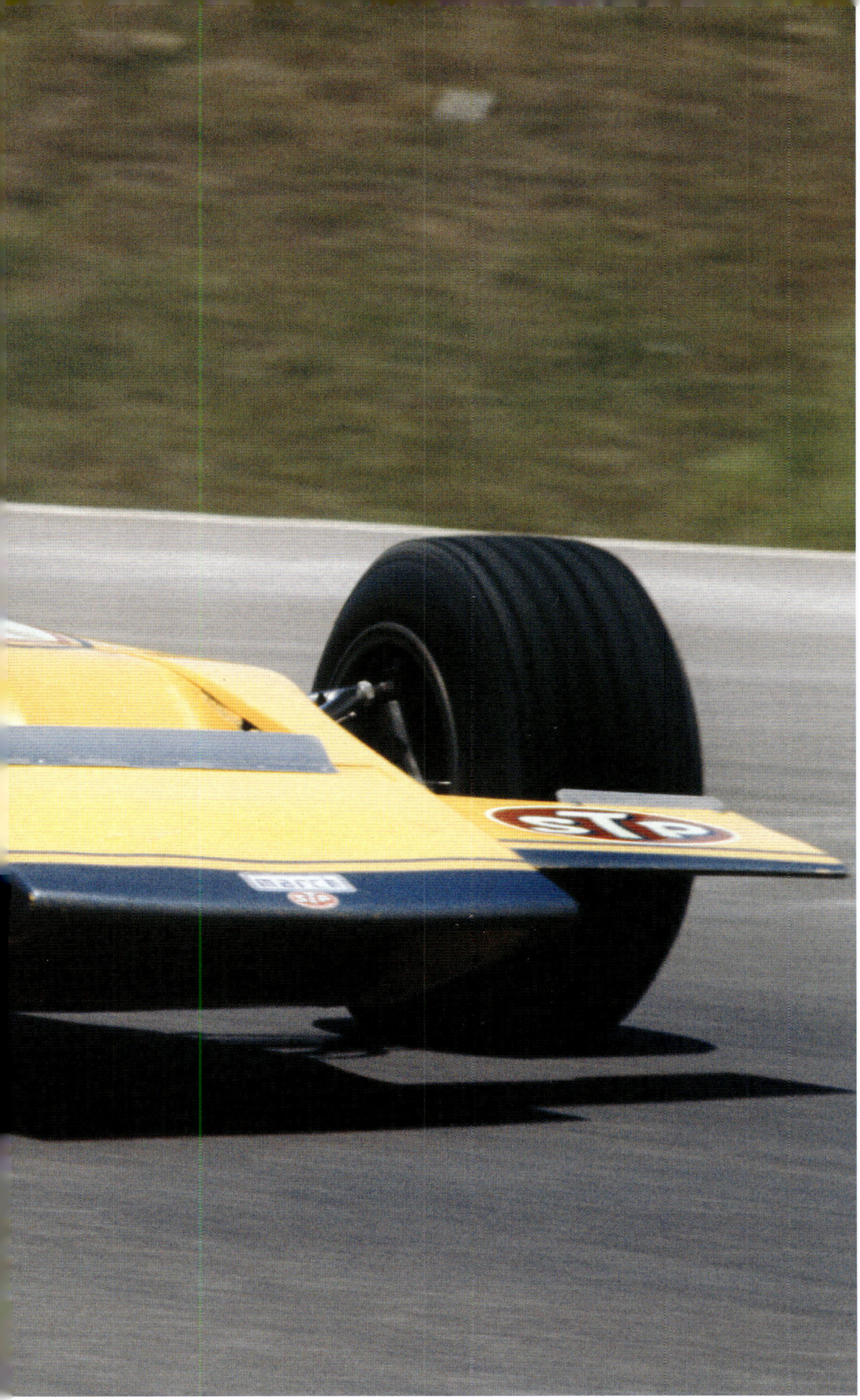

LEFT Ronnie ended an excellent season with a month in South America, contesting four two-heat Formula 2 events in the Brazilian-based 'Torneio'. The campaign began well at Interlagos, where Ronnie engaged his March 712M in exciting battles throughout with local hero Emerson Fittipaldi's Bardahl Lotus 69, finishing second on aggregate after being held up by a backmarker. But it went sharply downhill from there. Back in Sao Paulo the following week, he was again leading Fittipaldi in the first heat when his ignition cut out, costing him seven laps, and was narrowly beaten in the second heat after leading. At Porto Allegre, where Giovanni Salvati was killed in his Ala d'Oro team March, Ronnie struck a tyre marker and retired. Finally, leading again at Cordoba in Argentina, a broken engine took him out early in the action.

1972

FERRARI RESCUES A DISMAL SUMMER

Ronnie was optimistic that March would produce technical improvements for his second Formula 1 season in the works team, now partnered full-time by pay-driver Niki Lauda. But experimentation by the design engineers let him down. March started out with the 721, a conventional evolution of the 1971 car, but replaced it after three races with the 721X, an all-new concept based on the latest theories about weight distribution. It was an unmitigated disaster, and was itself replaced after three races with a hastily upgraded Formula 2 chassis. The 721G put Ronnie more or less back on the pace but, by that time, he had lost patience with March, and soon signed to race for Team Lotus in 1973. Meanwhile his confidence was sustained by a successful, nine-race sportscar campaign with Scuderia Ferrari.

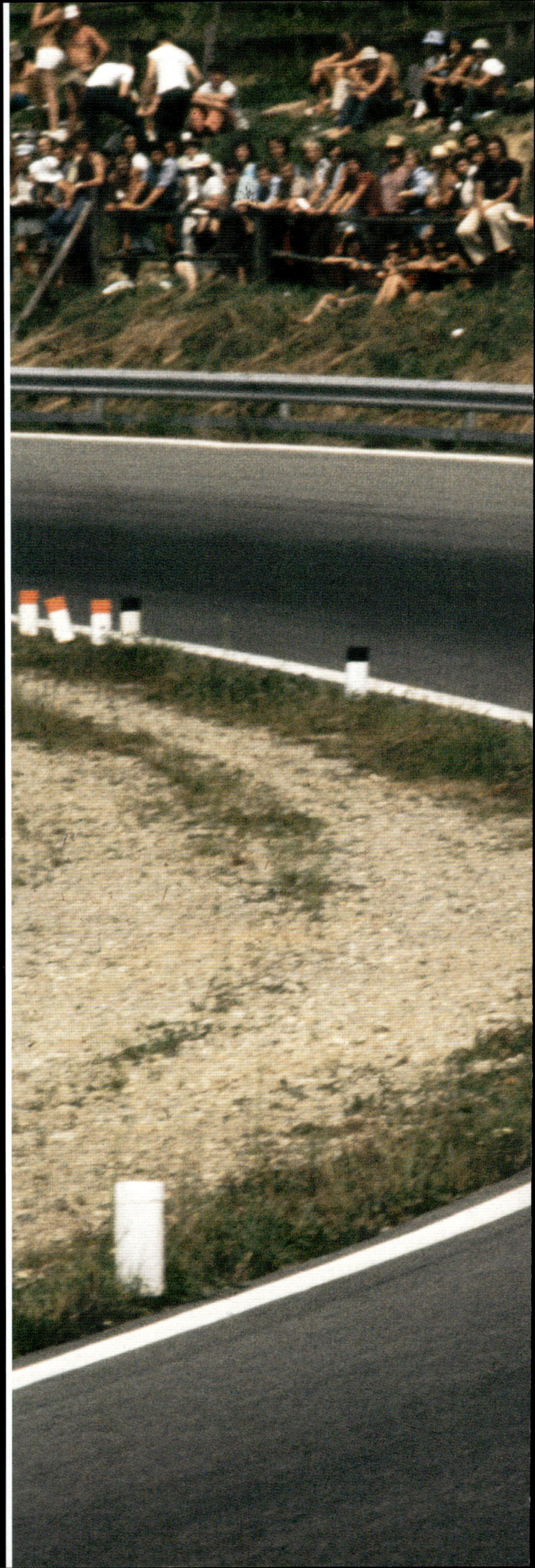

RIGHT The 721G, a modified Formula 2 chassis, dramatically improved the fortunes of the STP March team in the second half of the 1972 season. Here Ronnie has just taken third place from defending World Champion Jackie Stewart's ill-handling Tyrrell 005 midway through the Austrian Grand Prix, in front of 160,000 spectators on the majestic Osterreichring. Fuel starvation spoiled a great run.

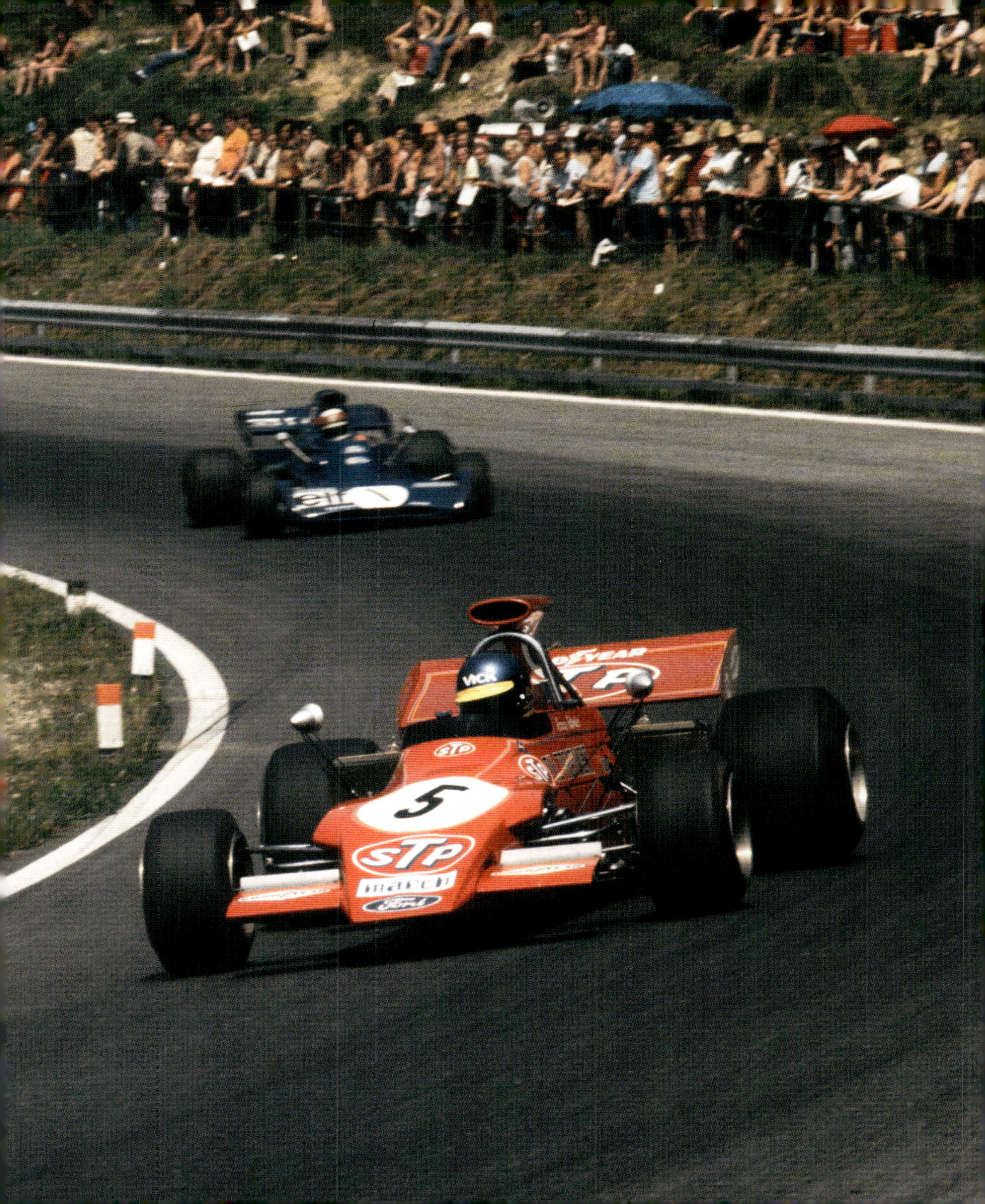

5
STP
march
Ford
VICK

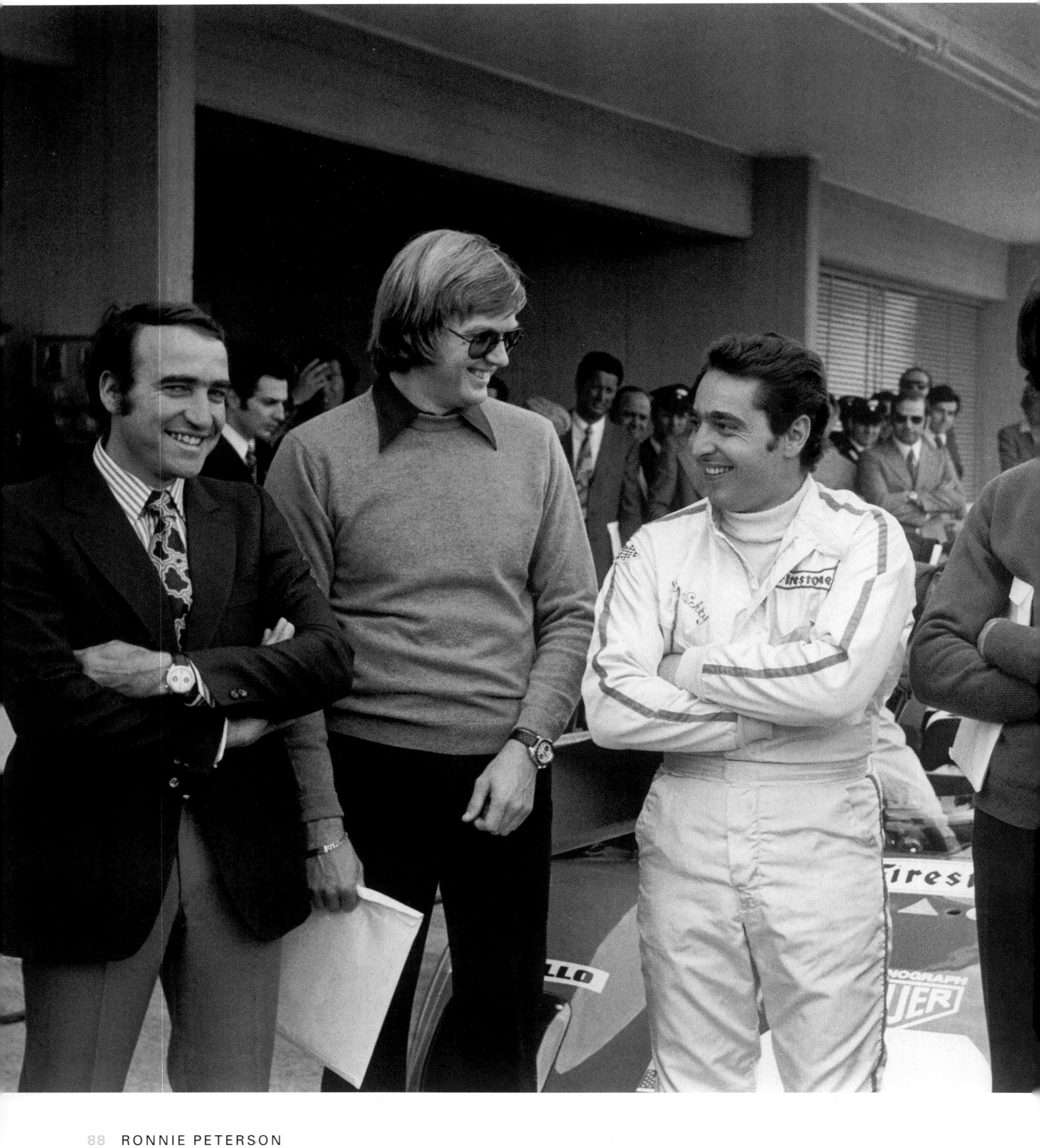
Firestone
UER

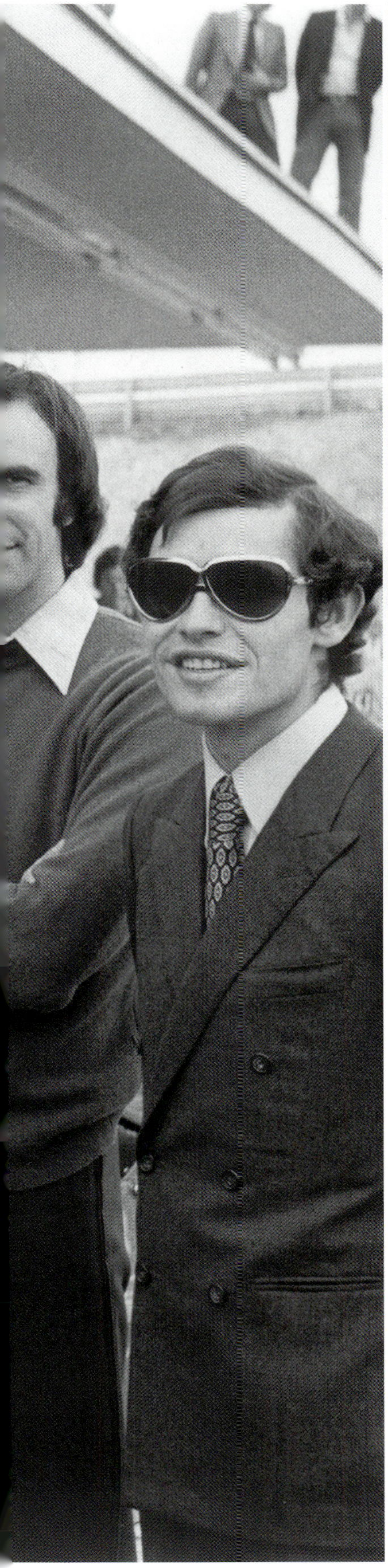

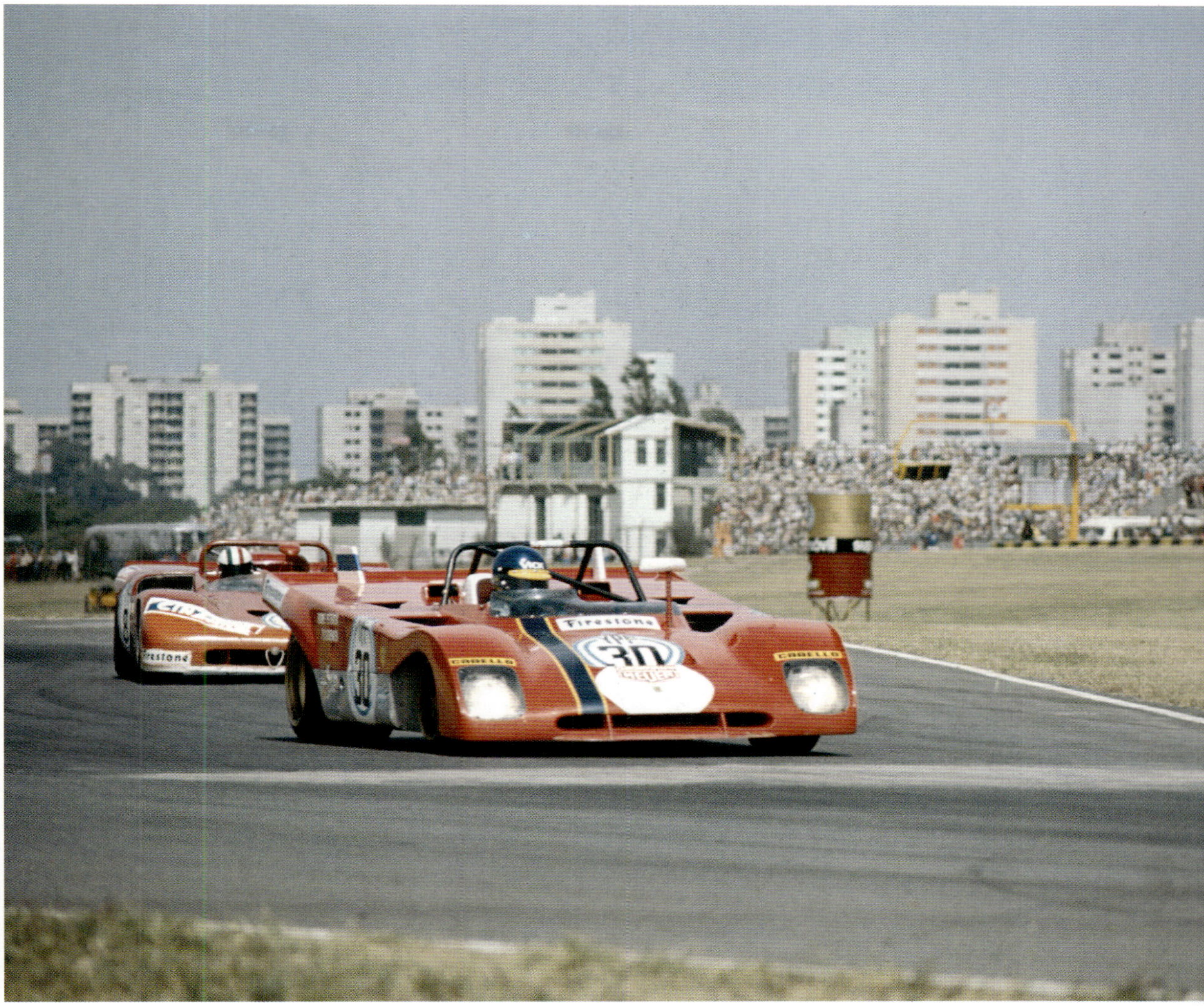

LEFT Ronnie's March contract allowed him to accept an offer from Scuderia Ferrari to join its team for a full programme in the 1972 World Championship of Makes. There were no date clashes with Formula 1, but the opportunity meant that he could not defend his Formula 2 title. The deal excluded the Targa Florio, for which Ferrari entered only one car at the last minute, and employed specialist drivers. Here is Ronnie at Fiorano, Ferrari's private test circuit, with (left to right) Clay Regazzoni, team manager *cum* test driver Peter Schetty, Tim Schenken and Jacky Ickx. His other team-mates in the red cars were to be Mario Andretti, Brian Redman and the Targa winners, Arturo Merzario and Sandro Munari.

ABOVE It was Ronnie's Ferrari sports car drive that made his 1972 season worthwhile. Teamed for every race with Tim Schenken in the new, 3-litre flat-12 Ferrari 312PB sports-prototypes, Ronnie beat Jacky Ickx to pole position first-time-out here in Buenos Aires and, in the race, defeated team-mates Clay Regazzoni/Brian Redman by almost a lap. The car behind is Nino Vaccarella's Autodelta team Alfa Romeo T33/3. A month later, Schenken was leading the six-hour race at Daytona with 15 minutes remaining when he picked up a puncture, dropping their car to second place behind Ickx and Mario Andretti. The same 1–2 formation would be repeated in the Sebring 12 Hours and the BOAC 1000 at Brands Hatch. In total this season, the Peterson/Schenken partnership secured two victories, four second places and two thirds. The pair had only one DNF all year, thanks to outstanding mechanical preparation under a team led by the accomplished Ermanno Cuoghi.

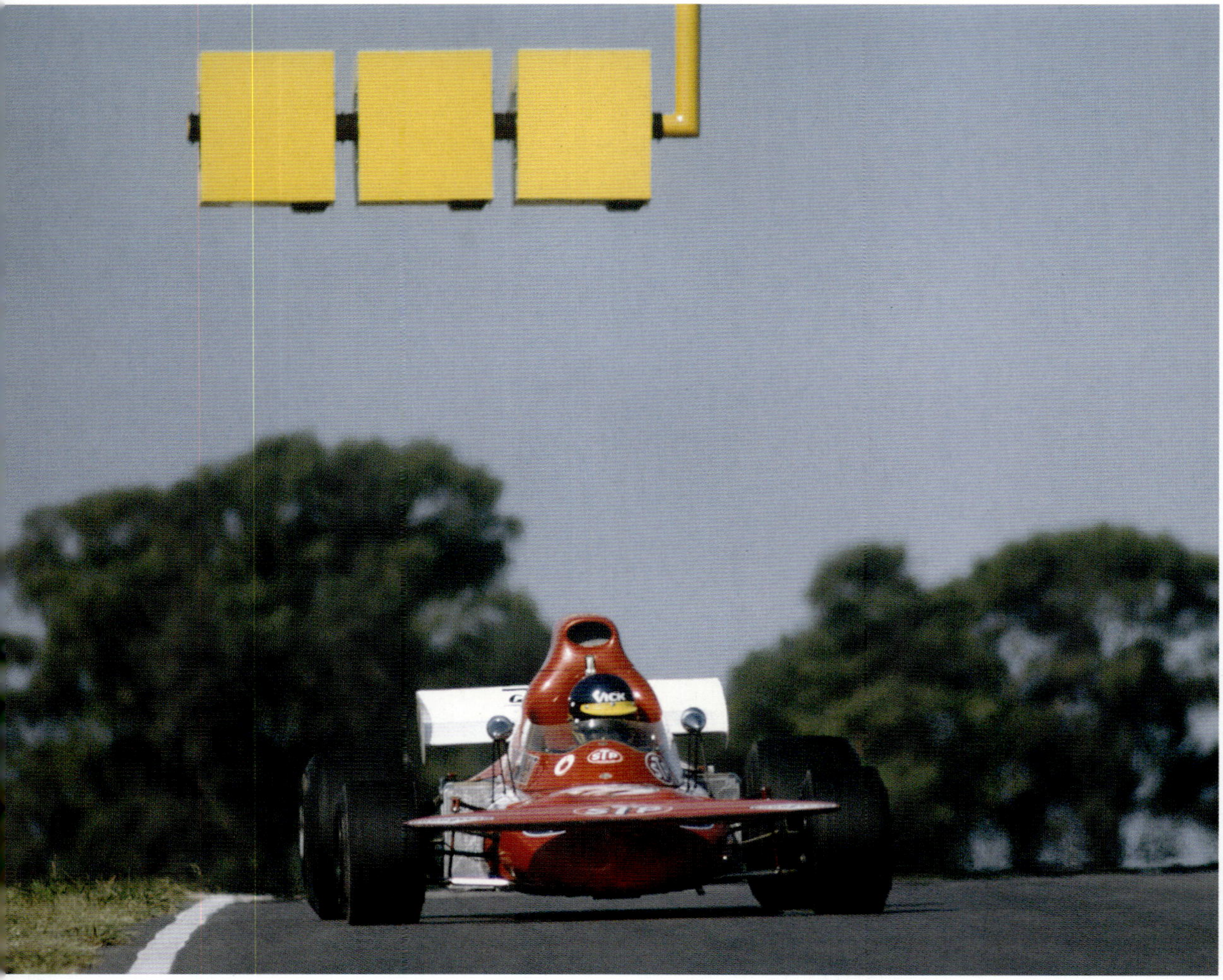

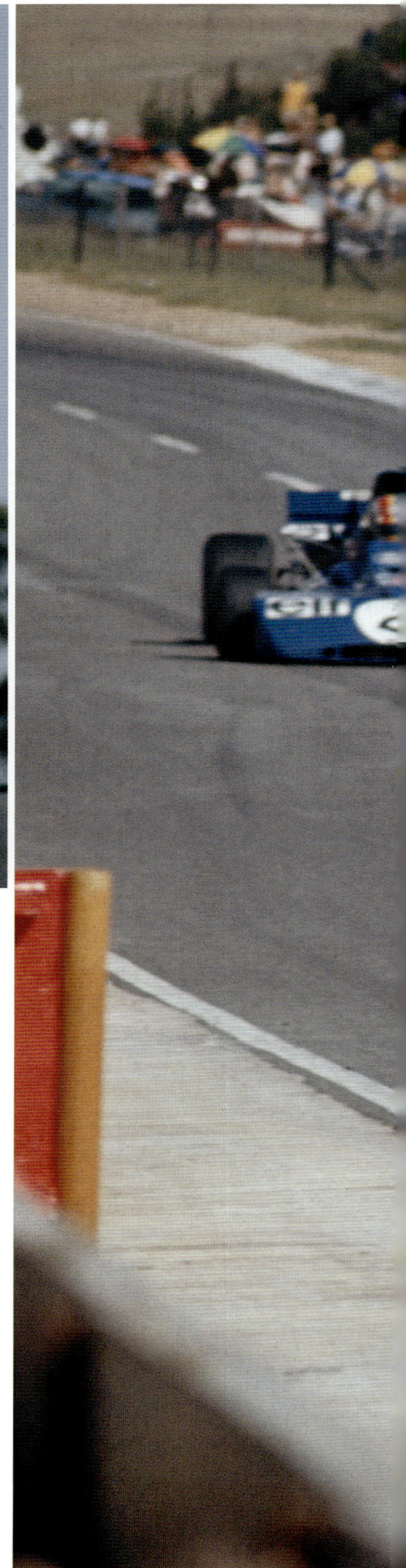

ABOVE A couple of weeks after winning Argentina's round of the World Championship of Makes, Ronnie returned to the nation's capital for the opening round of the Formula 1 World Championship, armed with the new March 721. The car had a new monocoque and bodywork but retained the distinctive front-end layout of the 711. Ronnie was smitten by a stomach ailment, and advised by doctors not to take part, but he put the new car 10th on the grid and was soon embroiled on race day in a long battle for sixth place with his friend Tim Schenken's Surtees, just behind the Ferraris of Clay Regazzoni and Jacky Ickx. Tripped into a spin when lapping Helmut Marko's BRM, Ronnie was passed by Schenken but recovered to finish sixth.

RIGHT Come Kyalami, the March 721 appeared with a square nose that had been tried on a 711 the previous season. Ronnie qualified ninth for the South African Grand Prix, but the early-race form he had found in Argentina was repeated. He gained fifth place inside the first 10 laps, at the expense of François Cevert's Tyrrell 002 and Jean-Pierre Beltoise's BRM P160B (pictured). He was promoted to third on the retirements of Mike Hailwood (after his best race for Team Surtees) and Jackie Stewart with the race-leading Tyrrell. Then a rear aerofoil stay broke. Ronnie brought the car home in fifth place, 50sec behind Denny Hulme's winning McLaren M19A.

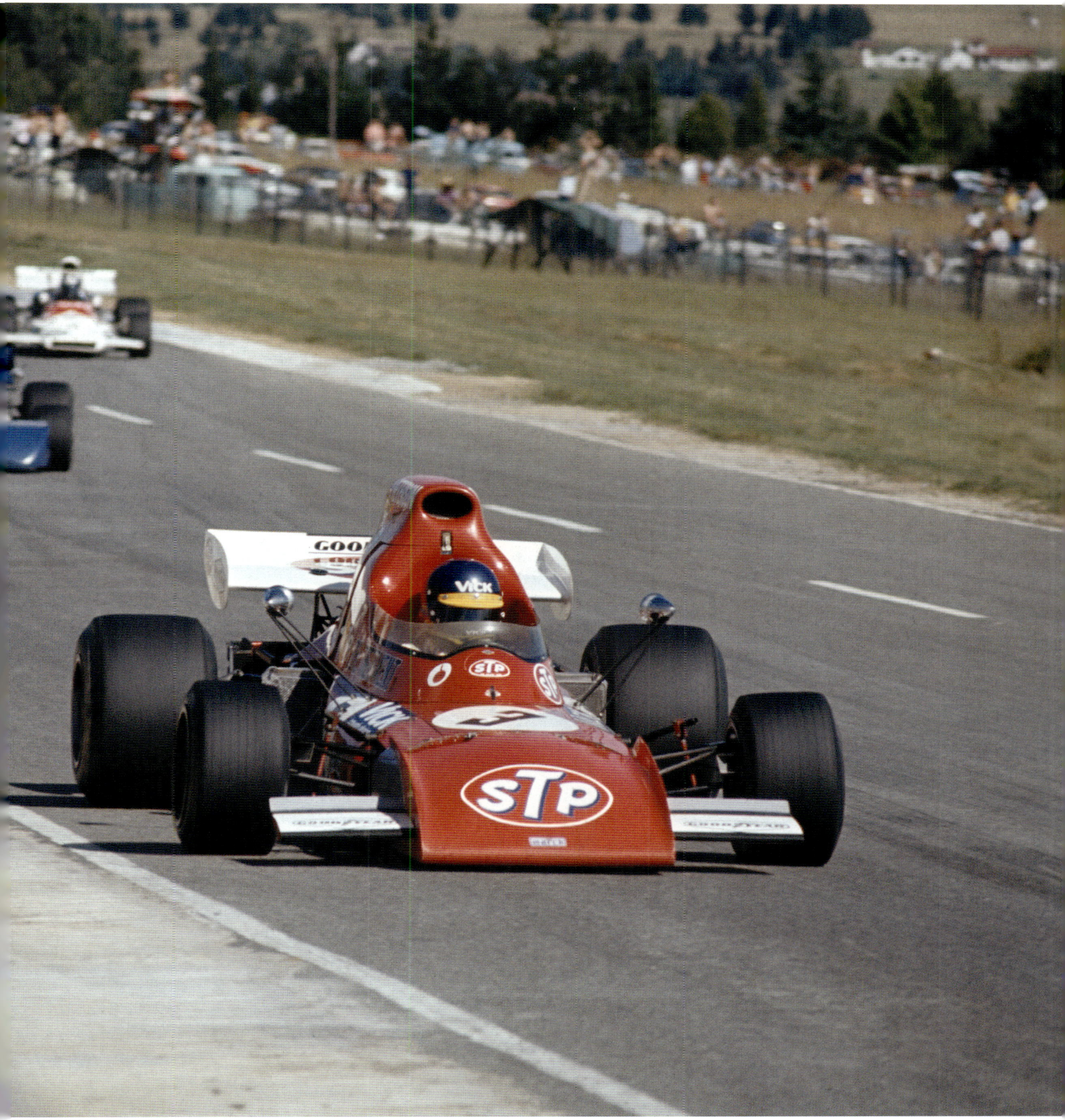
STP
VICK

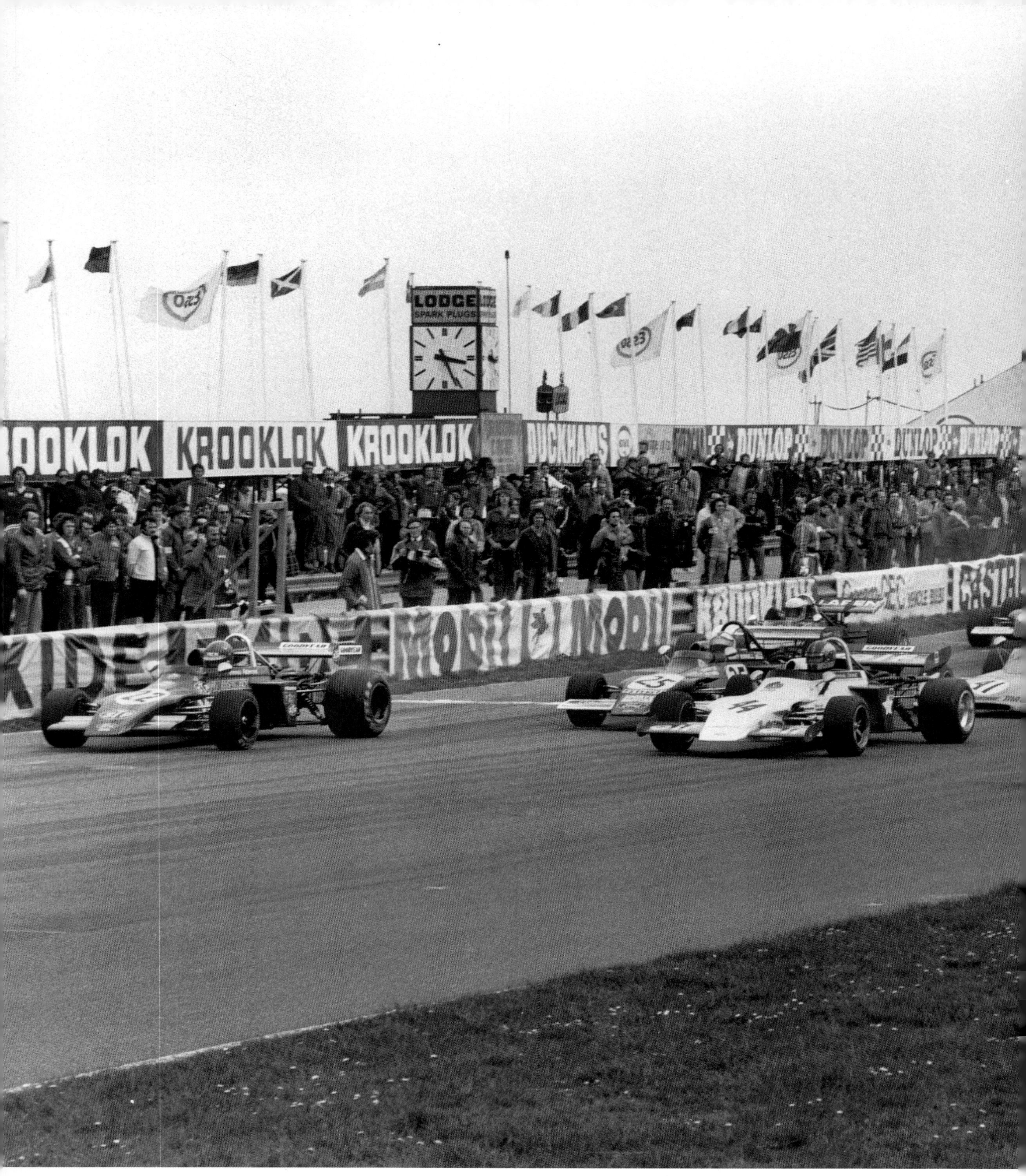
LODGE
SPARK PLUGS
KROOKLOK
KROOKLOK
KROOKLOK
DUCKHAMS
DUNLOP
DUNLOP
DUNLOP
DUNLOP
GOODYEAR

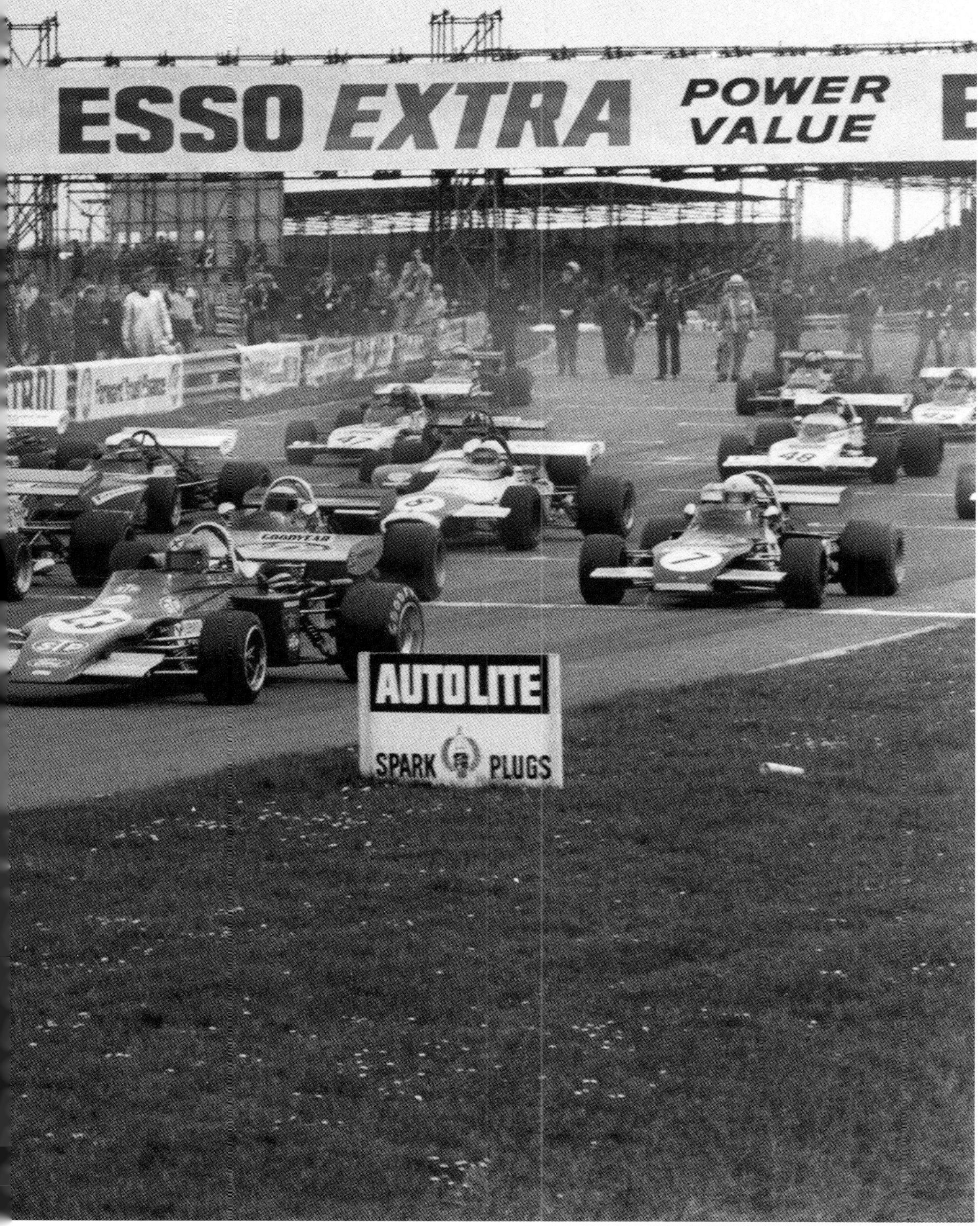

LEFT Clashing sportscar dates severely limited Ronnie's Formula 2 drives in 1972, but he was free to do the opening round of the European and British championships at Mallory Park, the scene of his big crash the year before. His pole position underlined his status as the reigning champion but otherwise meant nothing, because a loose fuel line sent him to the pits after only three laps of the first heat and, after rejoining, he was stopped by a faulty metering unit. In the second heat, he went way off-line in an outrageous attempt to pass three cars at once around the outside of the Gerards corner, slipped up on some mud, and had another major accident... However he was available again over Easter to do the Jochen Rindt Memorial Trophy race here at Thruxton. The regular drivers were understandably dismayed when Ronnie easily won his heat from pole position. In the final, his STP March 722 (at left) got the jump on François Cevert in John Coombs's March and Niki Lauda in the second works entry, and was never seen again. His margin of victory over Cevert was more than 24sec and he came away with a new outright lap record.

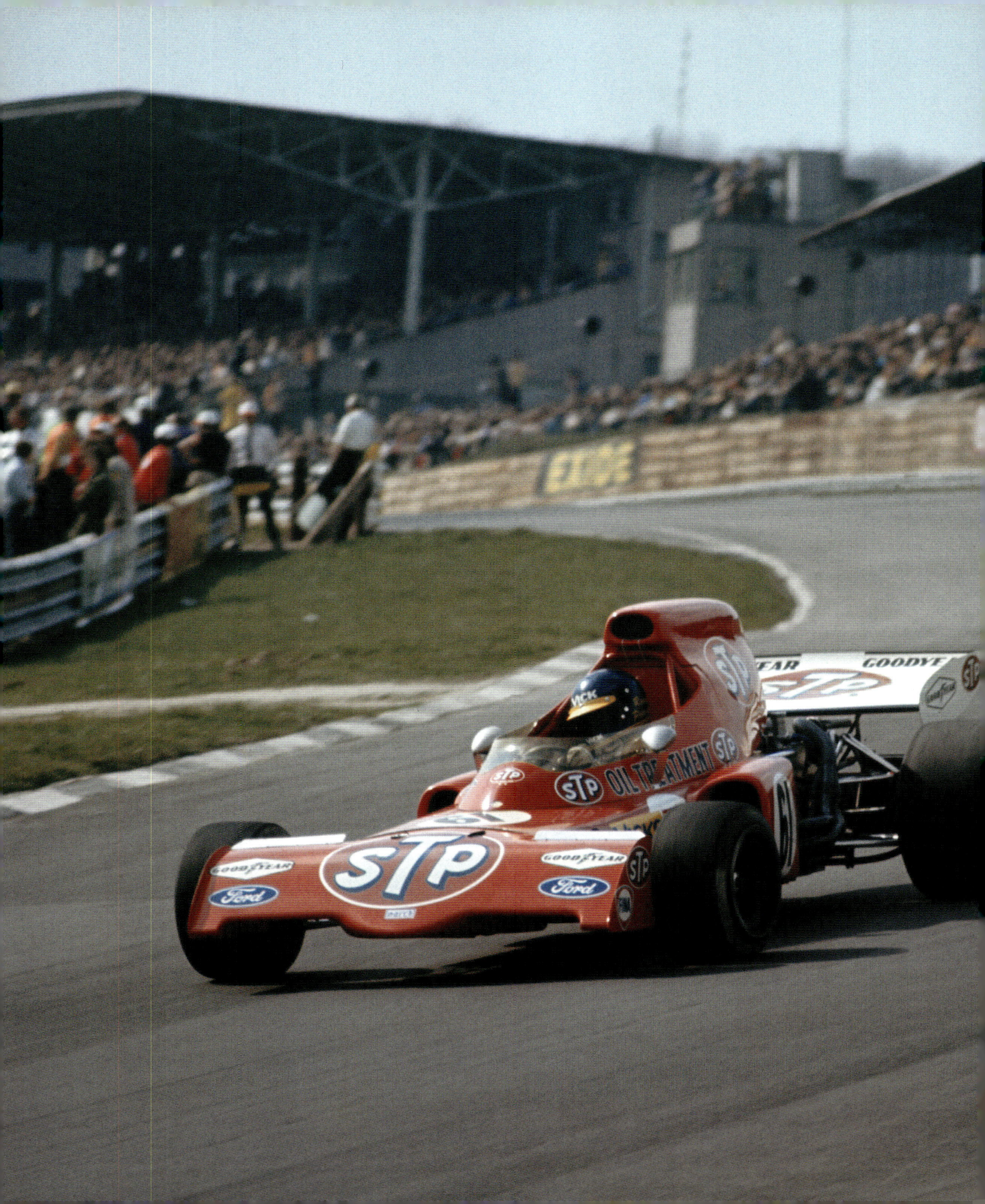
EXIDE
STP
STP OIL TREATMENT
GOODYEAR
Ford
61

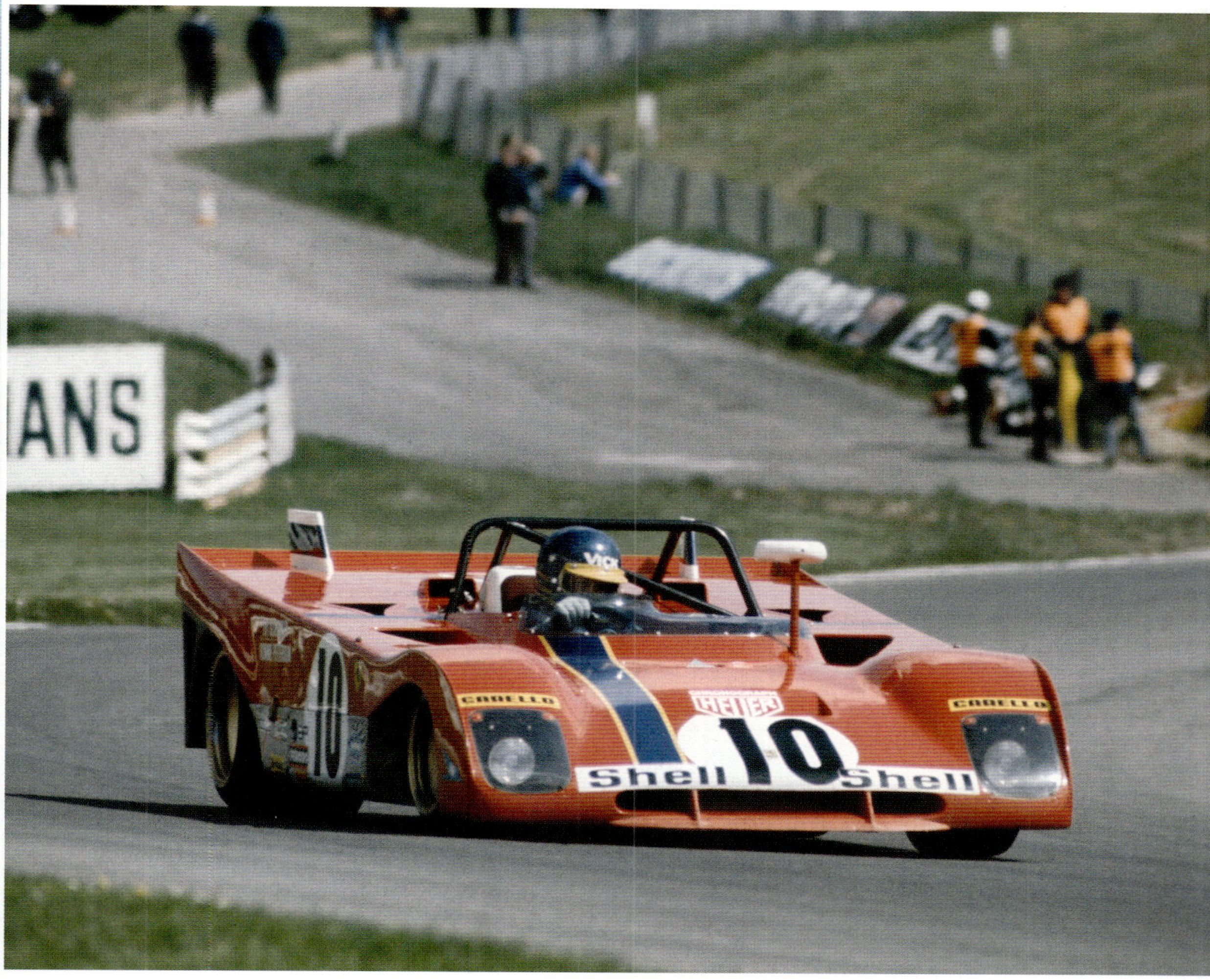

LEFT The début of the radical March 721X came two weeks after Kyalami, in the non-championship Race of Champions at Brands Hatch, where the team's worst fears were confirmed. With its entire powertrain mounted ahead of the rear axle line to reduce its polar moment of inertia, the hideous 721X was supposed to revolutionise handling. Instead the layout served merely to overload the car's front tyres, resulting in gross understeer – the opposite of the characteristic needed by a driver with Ronnie's uncanny skills of car control. The experience frustrated Ronnie and it often showed in his driving in this car. He finished its maiden race in 12th place after an unnecessary pitstop, caused when an observer mistakenly reported that a road wheel was loose.

ABOVE Ronnie corners a brand new Ferrari 312PB during the BOAC 1000 at Brands Hatch, where he and Tim Schenken, grappling understeer, finished a distant second behind team-mates Jacky Ickx and Mario Andretti. This was a fourth 1–2 humiliation of what had seemed to be a powerful challenge from Alfa Romeo which, with Porsche gone to the CanAm, had intended to dominate the World Championship of Makes. Instead, Ferrari won all 10 FIA Group 5 races it entered. The ultimate blow for Alfa Romeo came with defeat by Matra-Simca in the Le Mans 24 Hours, the only event Ferrari missed – and the only one contested by the French team.

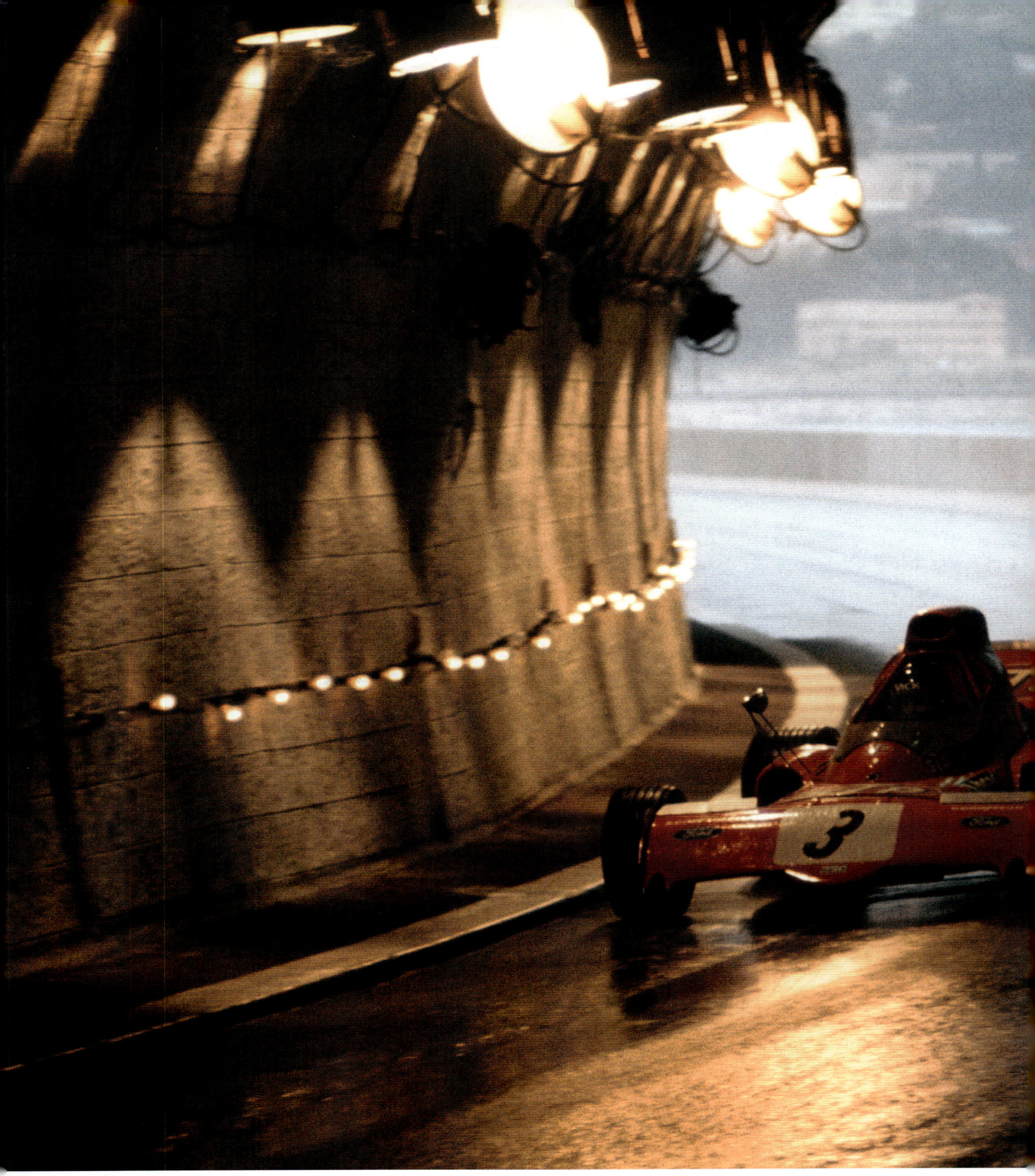

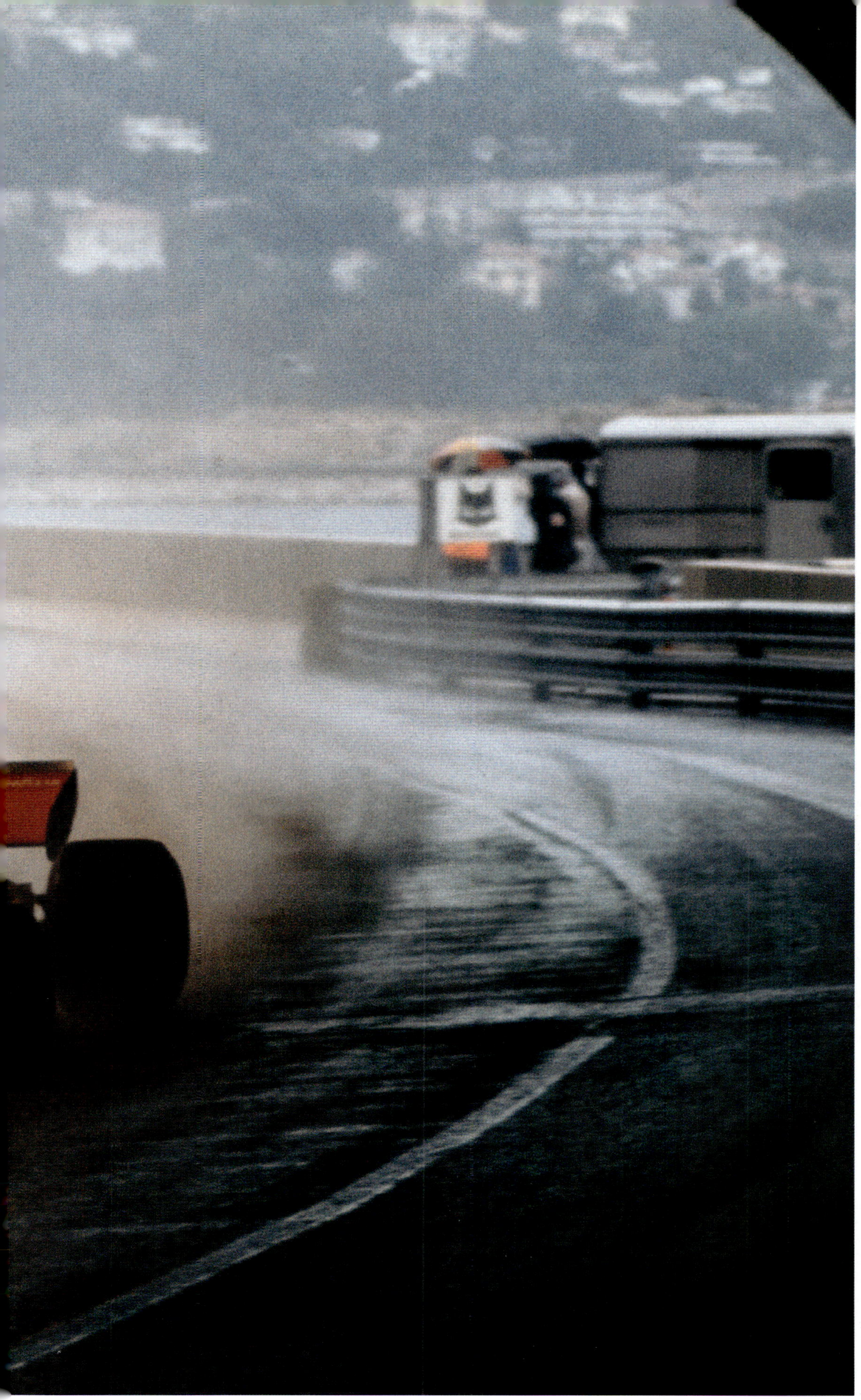

LEFT The only driver unfazed by the constant rain in Monaco seemed to be Jean-Pierre Beltoise, who famously won the Grand Prix with his BRM more or less as he liked, with only Jacky Ickx's Ferrari on the same lap. Ronnie worked wonders to qualify 15th with the recalcitrant March 721X, which arrived here with different transmission and suspension set-ups, but handled as badly as ever. He raced as best he could and finished 11th after a pitstop to secure a loose steering wheel.

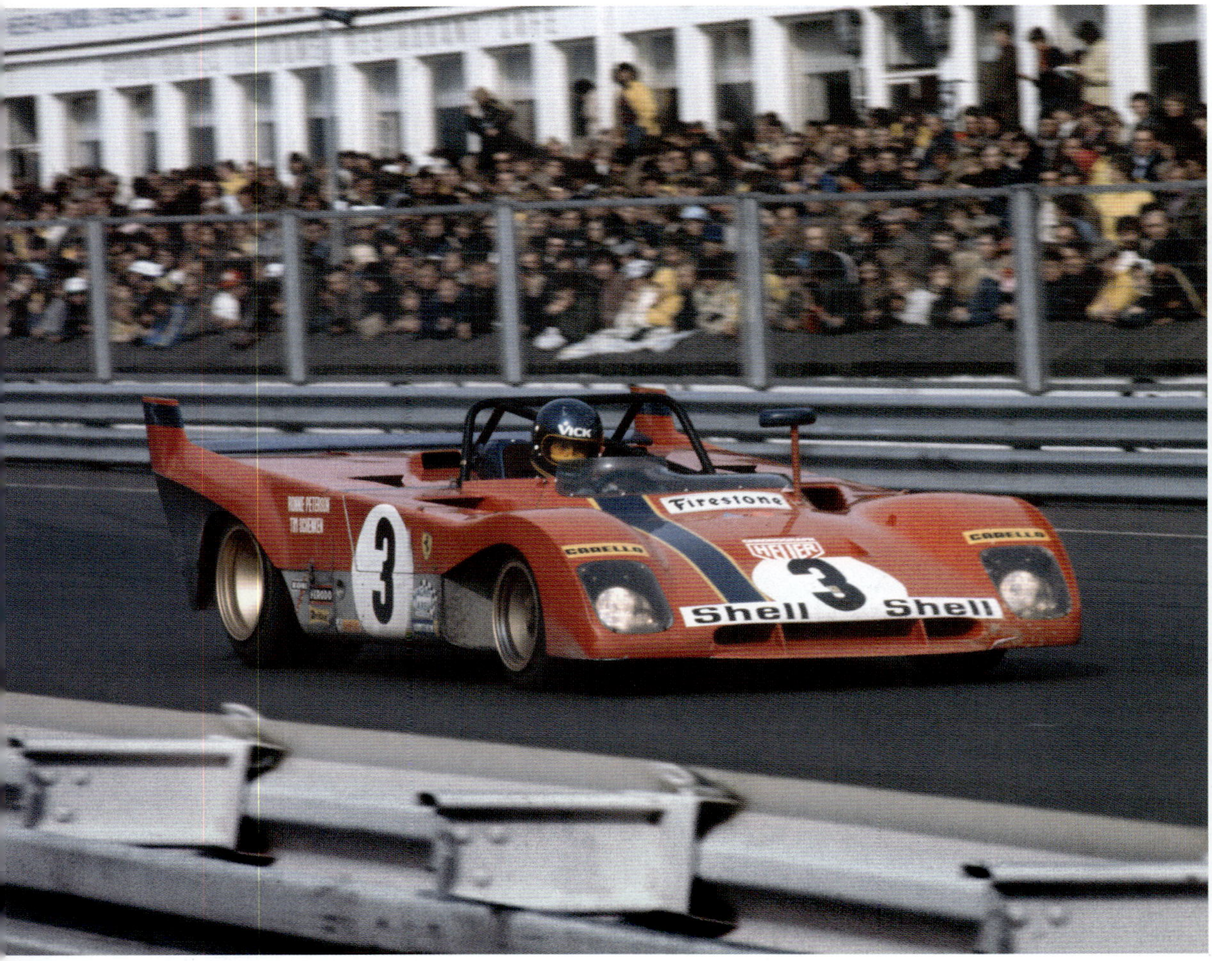

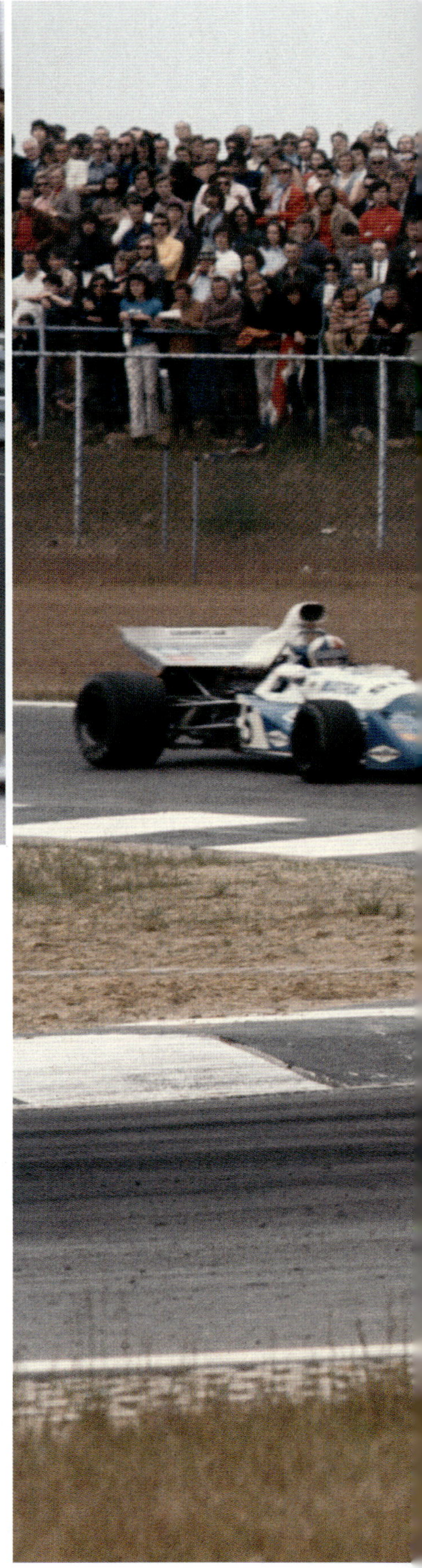

ABOVE Ronnie speeds past the pits on the Nürburgring on his way to another emphatic victory with Tim Schenken, although on this occasion Gulf Mirage drivers Derek Bell and Gijs van Lennep almost prevented a Ferrari 1–2. The DFV powered car was second until blowing its engine with only two laps remaining, so Brian Redman/Arturo Merzario took the place, with the best Alfa Romeo third as usual. This result clinched the 1972 Makes title for Ferrari and, the following week, the team withdrew its entries for the Le Mans 24 Hours, having found that its cars were no faster than the Matras during the test day in mid-March.

RIGHT The March 721X failed to respond when it was subjected to many more modifications. No Formula 1 driver was inherently faster than Ronnie in 1972 – and none had a worse racecar. Here at Nivelles he leads Rolf Stommelen's modified Eifelland-March as the third-place duel, featuring Clay Regazzoni's Ferrari 312B2 and Chris Amon's Matra MS120C, come up to lap them both long before halfway in the Belgian Grand Prix. Ronnie finished a thoroughly disgusted ninth and the March 721X was thrown away after this race.

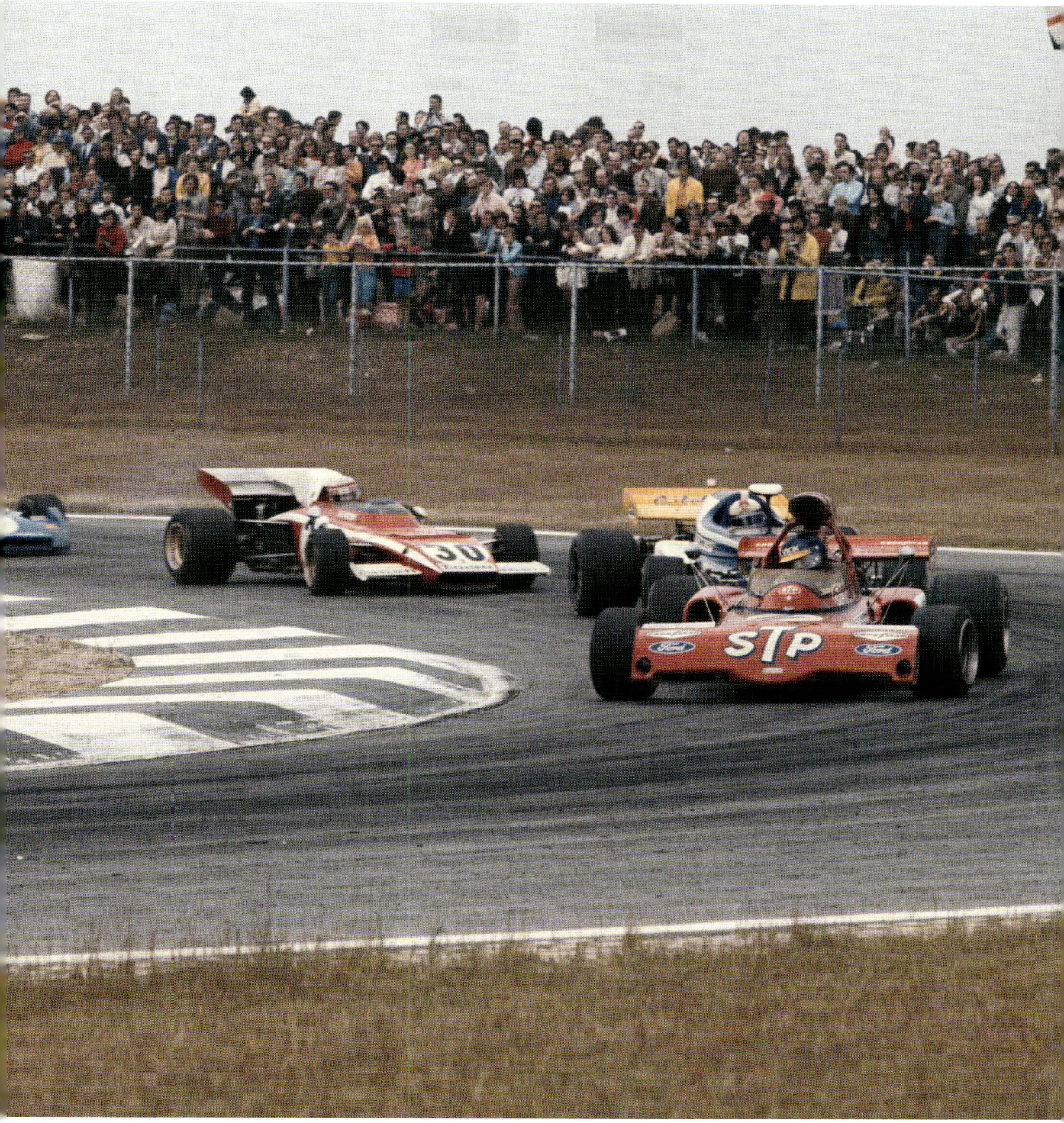
30
STP
Ford
Ford

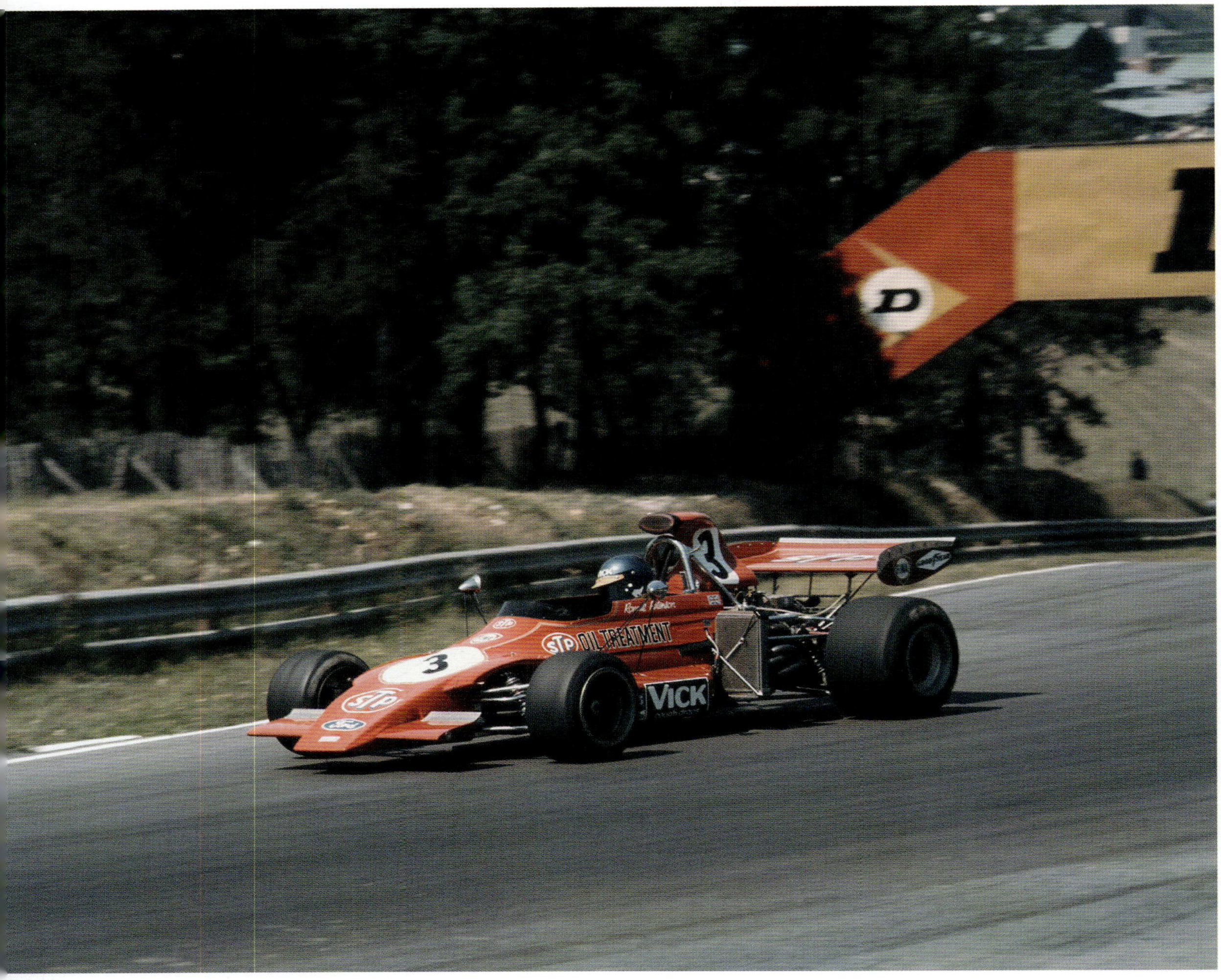

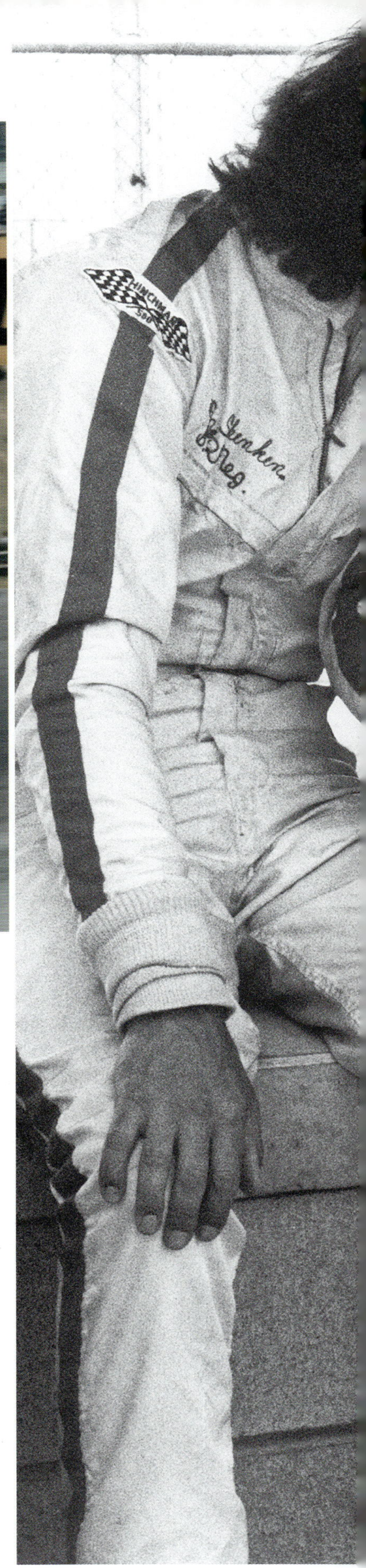

ABOVE March had paved a way for a 721X replacement by building up a much-modified, DFV powered Formula 2 chassis for a privateer Formula 1 team, Clarke-Morduant-Guthrie, for Mike Beuttler to drive. Ronnie had pleaded to borrow this car on more than one occasion but had to wait until July for the works team's own version, which had more than 30 revisions to the 'customer' specification. He and Niki Lauda got their hands on this much more manageable hardware at the French Grand Prix at Clermont, where Ronnie was robbed of third place by a broken roll-bar mounting. Next time out, here at Brands Hatch for the British Grand Prix, Ronnie climbed from eighth on the grid into fourth position, only to run low on fuel in the closing stages. With three cars close behind him, he chose to gamble by staying out of the pits. On the final lap, the engine abruptly died at the apex of Paddock Hill Bend, and sent him off the track and into two cars that had been adandoned there earlier.

RIGHT Catching up on the latest news with (left to right) Tim Schenken, Brian Redman and Arturo Merzario at Watkins Glen for the final round of the World Championship of Makes. The Scuderia Ferrari sportscar racing programme brought happy times for Ronnie. While the racing itself was not very competitive in terms of the opposition, he enjoyed some good-natured intra-team rivalry, and above all the opportunity to win races. On this occasion in upstate New York, team manager Peter Schetty threw away the team orders and let his drivers race for the hell of it. It was Schenken's turn to win pole position, and their car led until the final shifts. Then Ronnie found himself with locking brakes and could not resist when Jacky Ickx came along to grab the victory with six laps remaining.

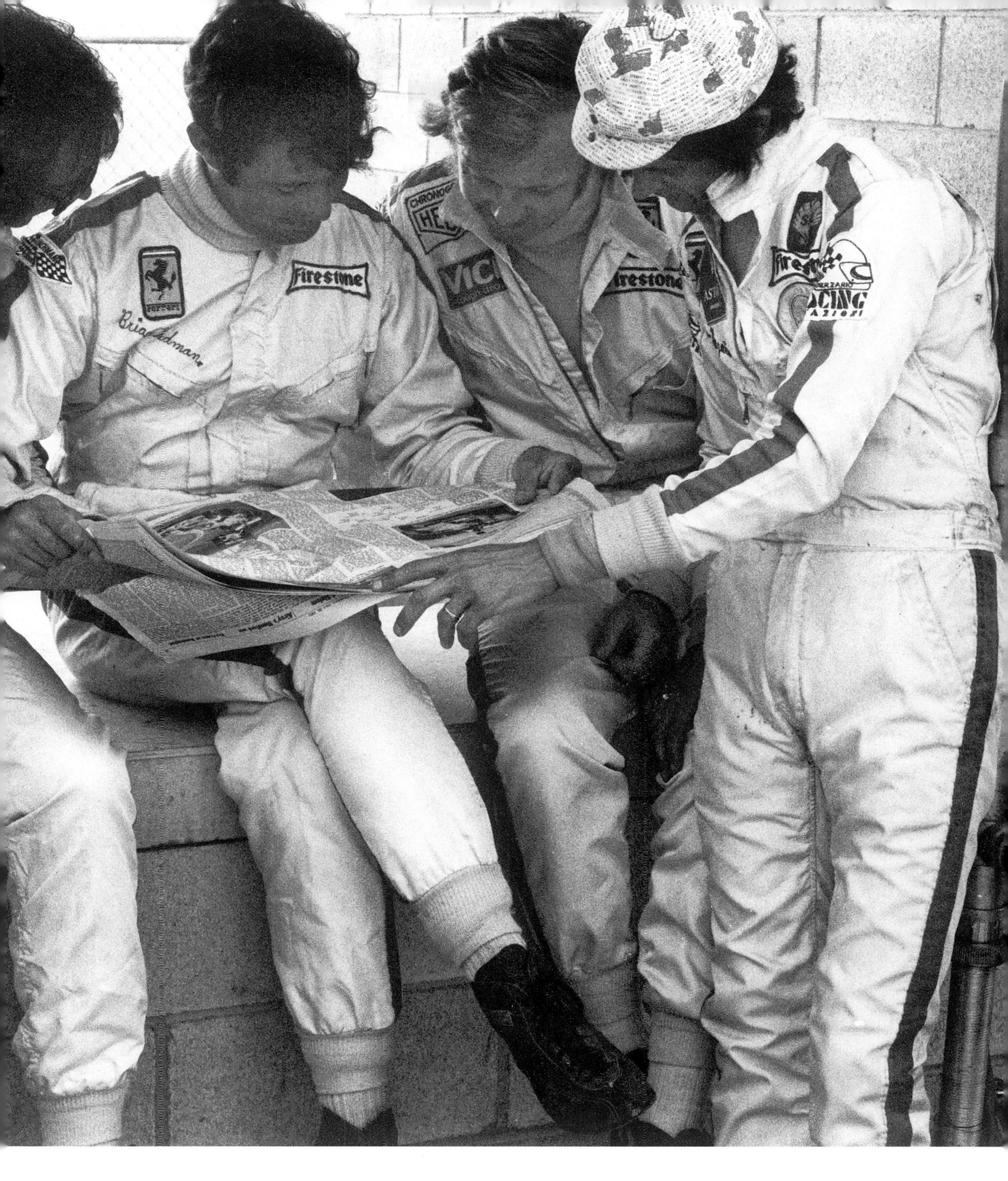
Firestone
Firestone
RACING

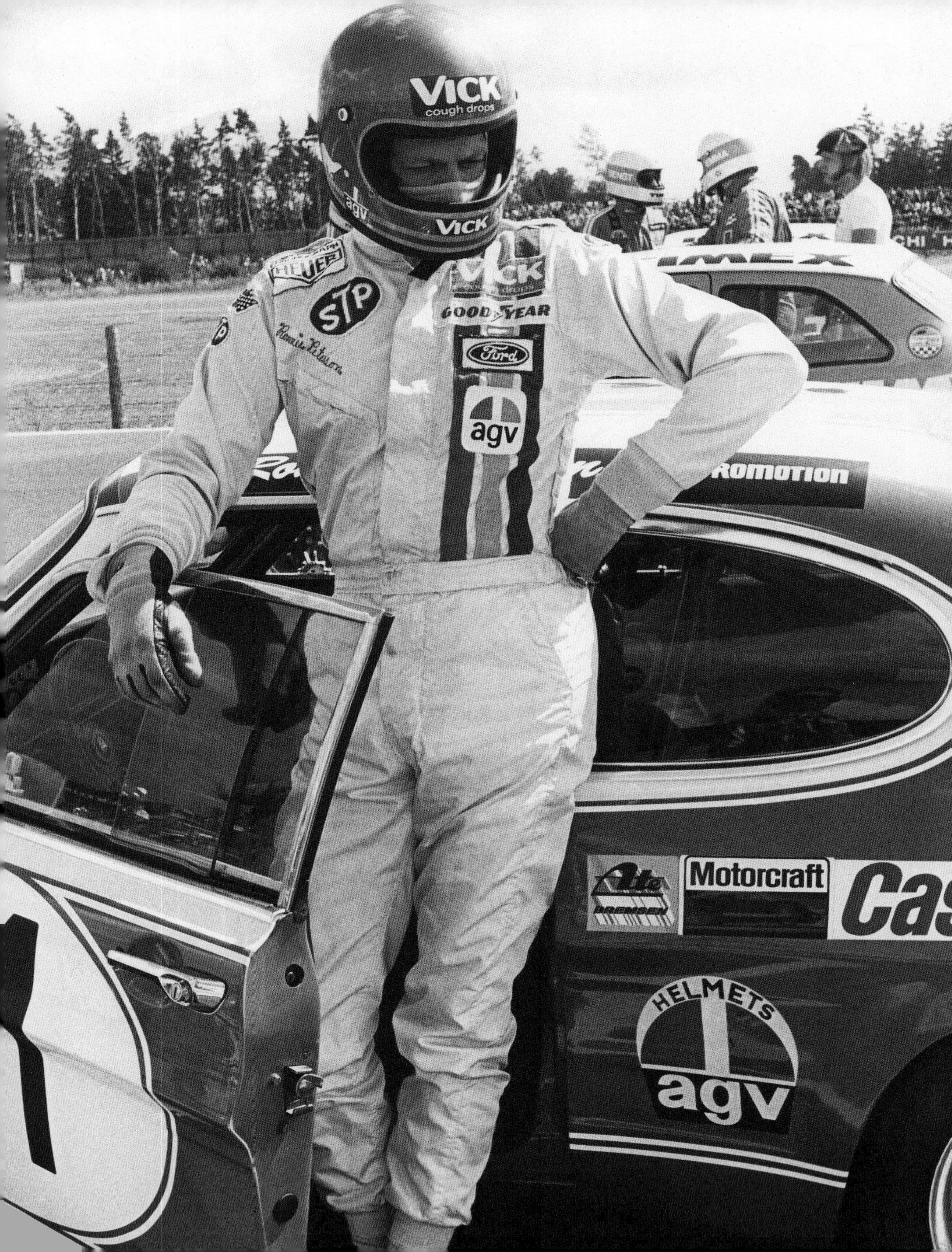
VICK
cough drops
agv
VICK
HEUER
STP
GOODYEAR
Ford
agv
ROMOTION
Motorcraft
BREMSEN
HELMETS
agv

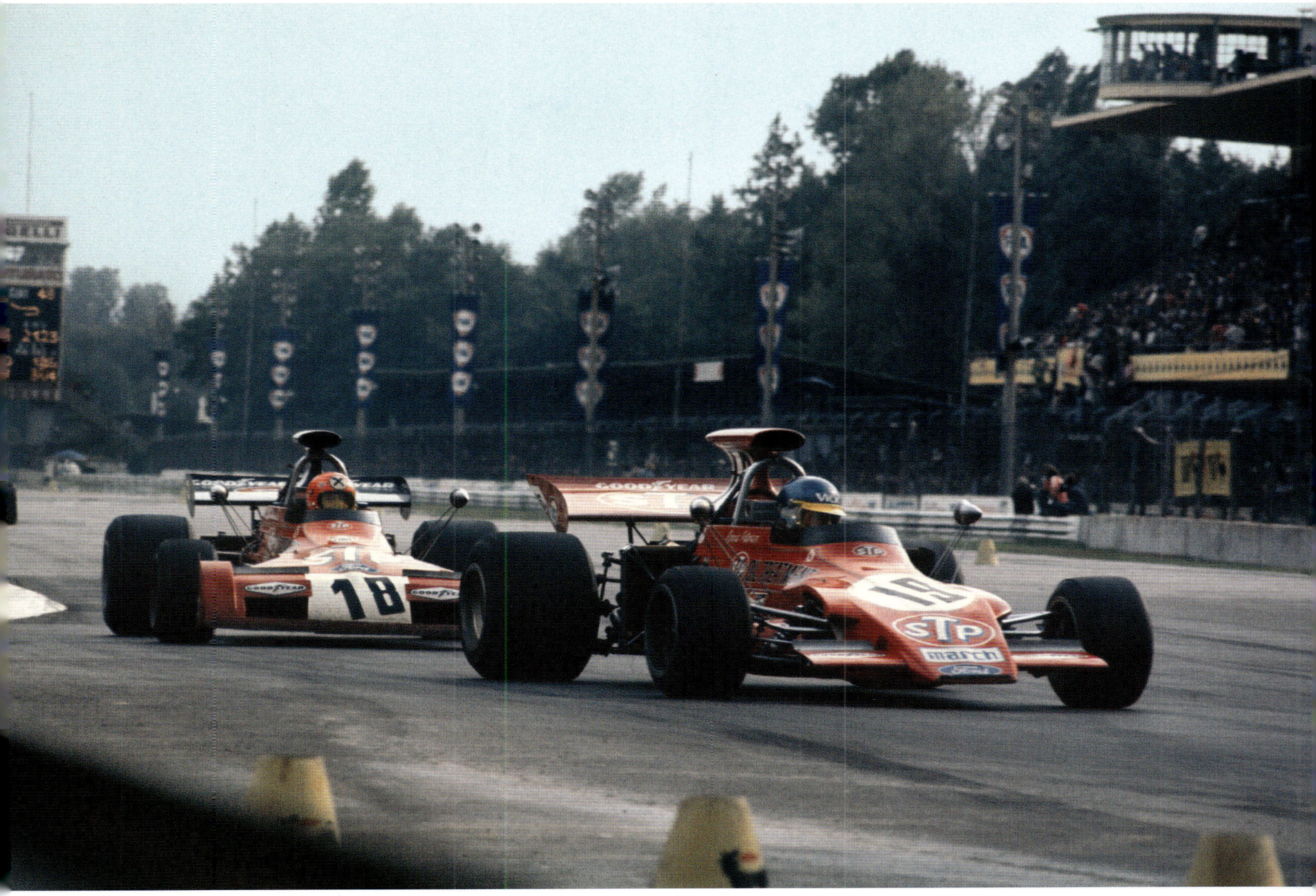

LEFT Engine problems brought a DNF for Ronnie in his home Formula 2 race at Mantorp Park, but he alleviated his disappointment with a victory in the supporting race for touring cars. He was asked to take the wheel of a works Ford Capri RS2600 entered by Ford Köln, and personally overseen by competitions director Mike Kranefuss. Ronnie smashed the front of the ex-Le Mans Capri during practice when he went off on oil from the blown engine of a Chevrolet Camaro, but he won the race easily from much-admired Ford Escort driver Bon Emanuelsson.

ABOVE Three March 721Gs at Monza in the Italian Grand Prix. Ronnie leads works team-mate Niki Lauda, whose car is fitted with a full-width nose section housing the radiators, and Mike Beuttler in the Clarke-Morduant-Guthrie entry. This was Ronnie's first Grand Prix since signing his new Team Lotus contract, and he had no cause to regret the move. He was hampered by engine problems on the Friday and crashed in the Vialone chicane on the Saturday, so he started from the back of the grid. He made up seven places in the first two laps, but damaged a road wheel on the eighth in another chicane, and had to stop for a replacement. He continued to finish ninth. Beuttler was 10th at the chequer and Lauda 13th, delayed by sticking throttle slides. Emerson Fittipaldi's fifth victory of the season clinched the title for John Player Team Lotus.

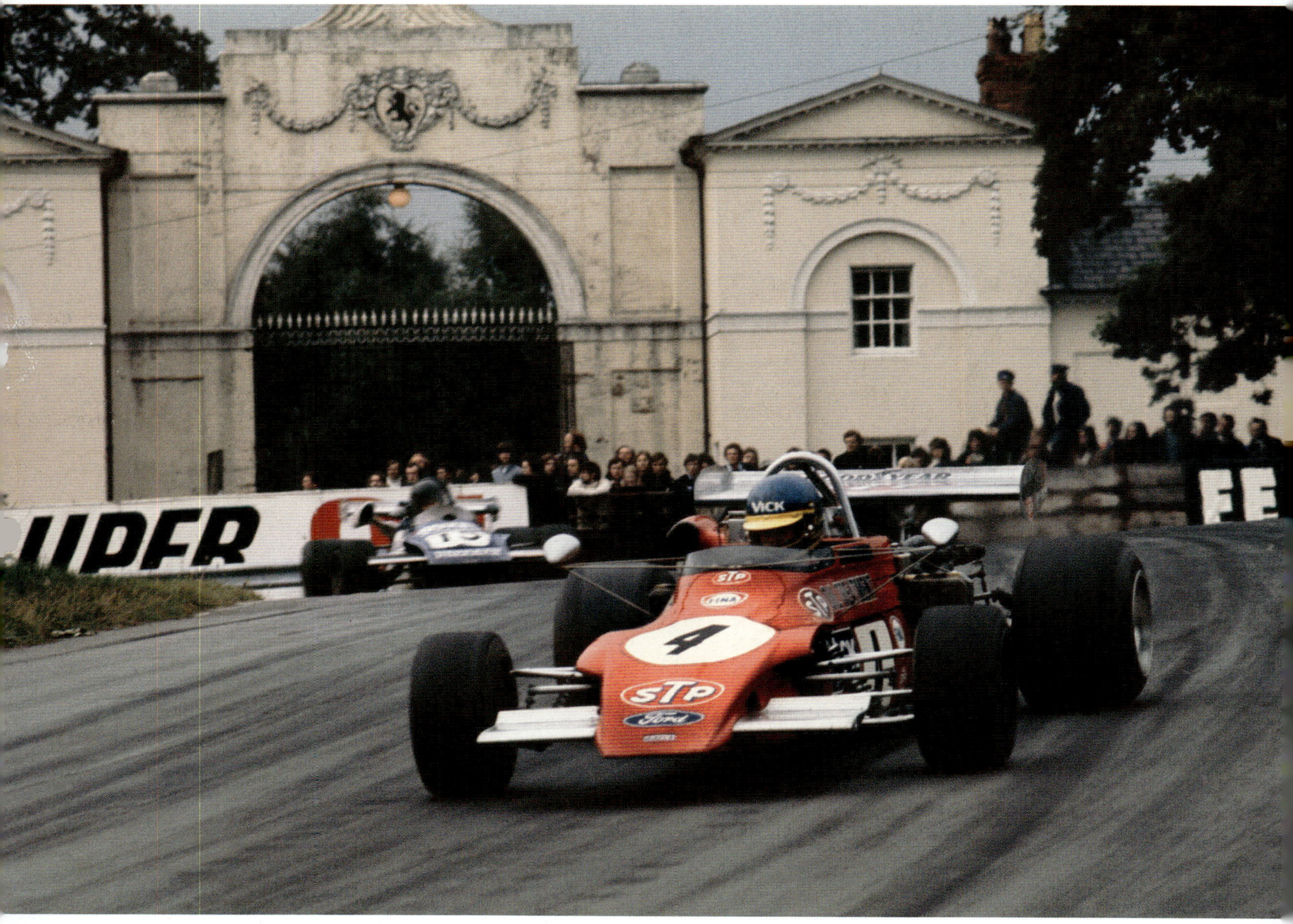

ABOVE One of the most satisfying races of Ronnie's entire season came at Oulton Park, in the final round of the John Player British Formula 2 Championship. The works March team encountered strong challenges here from new boys Jody Scheckter in the one-off McLaren, Vern Schuppan in his modified Formula Atlantic March, and James Hunt in Alexander Hesketh's year-old March 712M. Schuppan and Scheckter both led but retired, leaving Hunt to harry the STP March drivers. Pictured hunting Ronnie through the Old Hall corner, Hunt passed him to take the lead six laps out from the finish, but Ronnie forced him into a spin next time round. He then held off a charge by team-mate Niki Lauda to win by 0.2sec, with Hunt third. The race result was reversed in the championship, in which Lauda pipped Ronnie by two points.

RIGHT Peter Warr, the team manager of John Player Team Lotus, chats with his new driver on the pit-wall in a quiet moment during the 1972 series-closing US Grand Prix meeting at Watkins Glen. Warr and Lotus founder Colin Chapman had been trying to sign Ronnie for more than a year. At the end of August, during a four-week gap between the Austrian and Italian Grands Prix, they finally had his signature on a two-year contract.

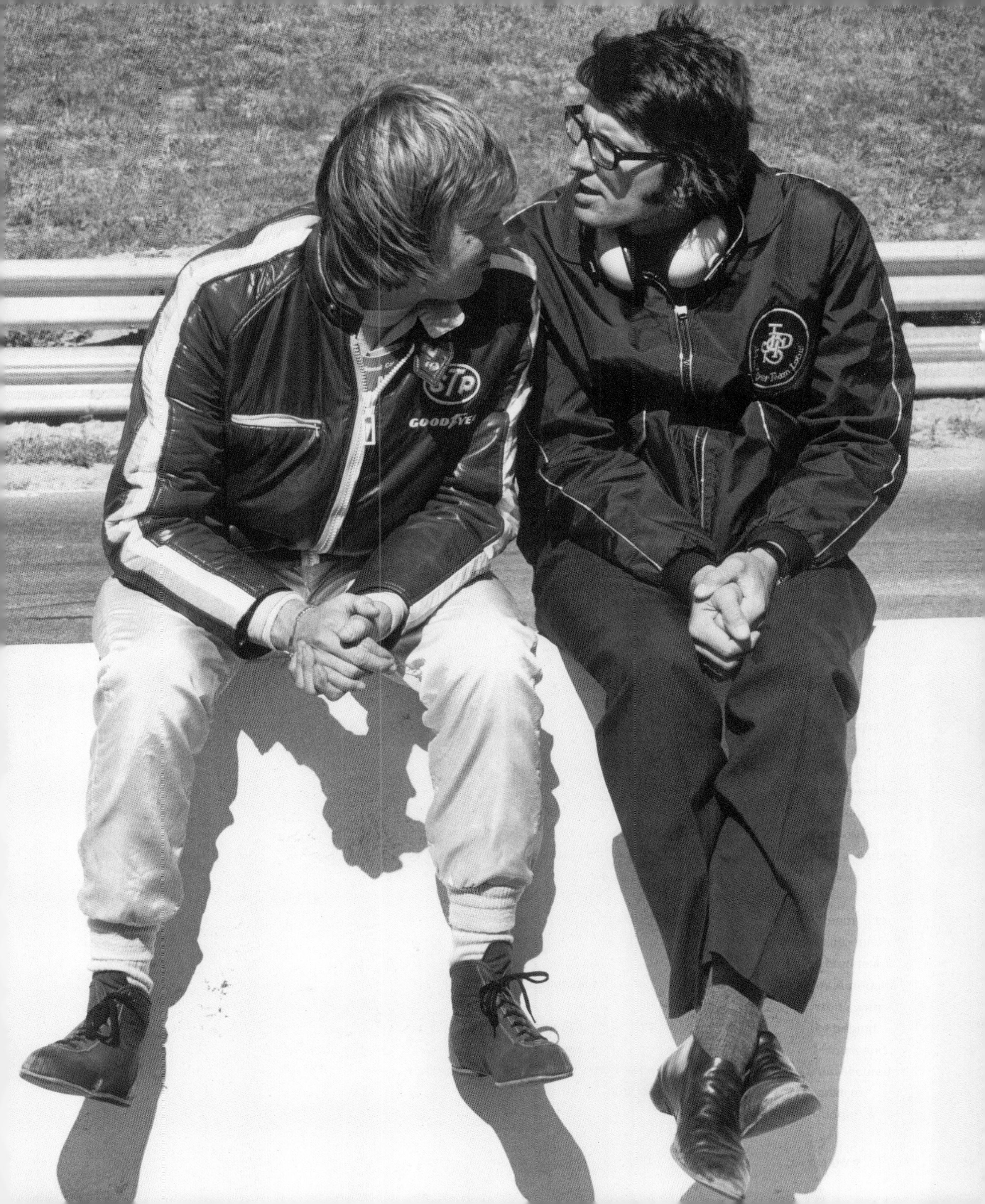
STP

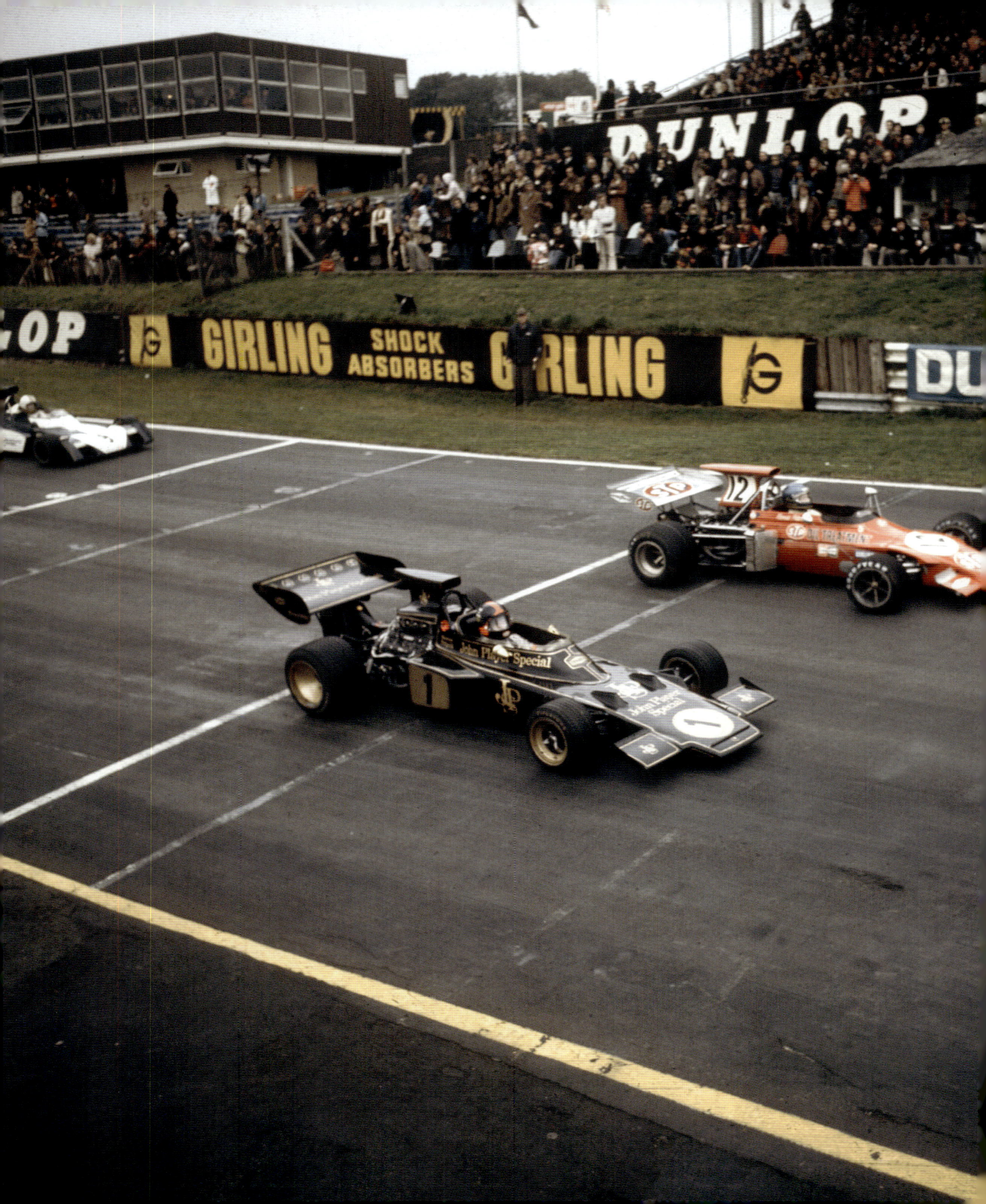
DUNLOP
GIRLING
SHOCK ABSORBERS
John Player Special

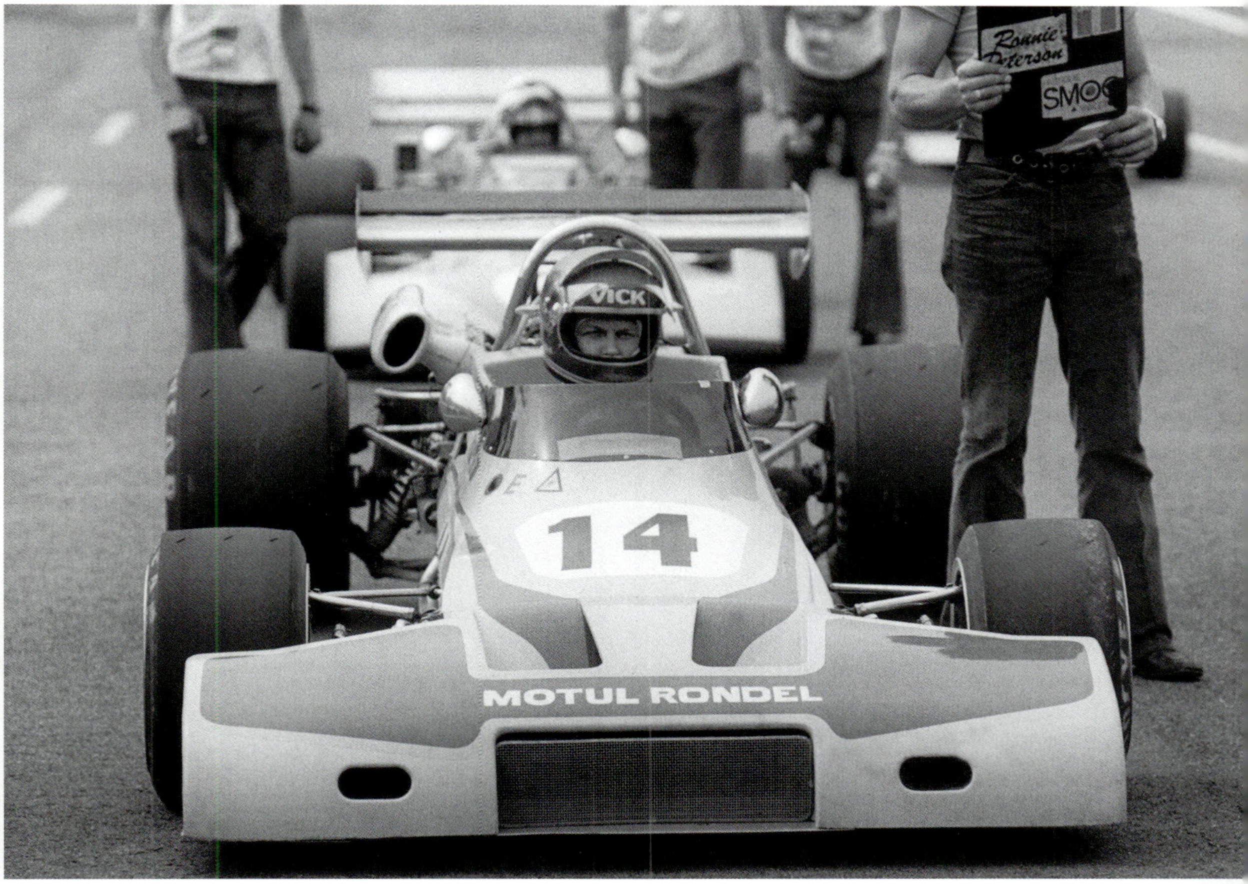

LEFT John Webb, the brilliantly opportunistic promoter at Brands Hatch, saw a chance to stage a third Formula 1 race on his circuit in 1972, and approached John Player & Sons to sponsor an October event to celebrate the World Championship double by John Player Team Lotus. The March 721G was working well here and Ronnie qualified second behind the Lotus 72 of Emerson Fittipaldi, the new World Champion who would be his team-mate the next time they raced Grand Prix cars. The other car in the picture is Mike Hailwood's Surtees TS9B. The race began under a fine drizzle and these three chose wet-weather tyres, which turned out to be the wrong decision. Ronnie led at first, with Hailwood and Fittipaldi in his wake, but the track began to dry out and along came Monaco winner Jean-Pierre Beltoise, with his Marlboro BRM P180 on intermediates. When the three leaders had to stop for slicks, it was all over. Beltoise won from the other Surtees drivers, Carlos Pace and Andrea de Adamich, with Ronnie eighth, Hailwood ninth and Emerson parked with a broken engine.

ABOVE Ronnie's 1972 season ended with three two-race events at Interlagos making up Brazil's 'Torneio' series, which was strongly supported by most of the European Formula 2 teams, but not by March. Instead Ronnie found himself teamed once more with Tim Schenken, this time along with Bob Wollek in Brabham BT38s entered by Ron Dennis's Rondel Racing. This South American campaign turned out to be as disappointing for Ronnie as the one the year before. A spin late in the first meeting cost him third place, a blown engine eliminated him early in the action the following week, and the foray ended with more engine problems the week after that. The three two-part events were won by Emerson Fittipaldi (Lotus 69) and Surtees TS15 drivers Carlos Pace and Mike Hailwood. Fittipaldi clinched the championship with Hailwood second, Schenken third, Pace fourth and Ronnie nowhere.

1973

A FORMULA 1 WINNER AT LAST WITH LOTUS

Ronnie's move to John Player Team Lotus at last gave him Formula 1 equipment commensurate with his ability. The Lotus 72 was one of the best packages in the field and he often outshone his team-mate, Emerson Fittipaldi, the defending champion. He secured his first Formula 1 pole in the second race, in Brazil, and his first victory in the eighth, in France. He took nine pole positions in 15 attempts, never qualifying lower than fourth, and won again in Austria, Italy and the USA. However, his season began with a dismal series of five DNFs, which condemned him to an effort to help Fittipaldi to the title. It was won by the more reliable Tyrrell of Jackie Stewart, with Emerson and Ronnie second and third. Their seven wins landed Lotus some consolation in the form of the Constructors' title.

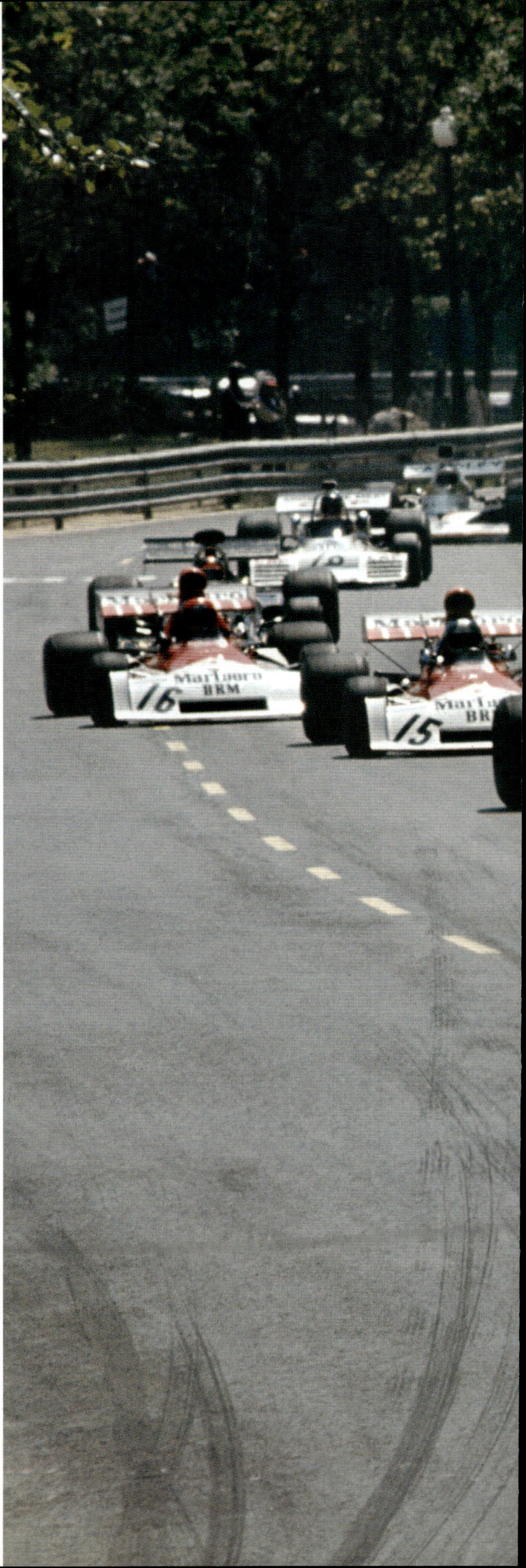

RIGHT From the pole, Ronnie leads the Spanish Grand Prix on the awesome road course in Montjuic Park, overlooking the city of Barcelona. His JPS Lotus 72E is chased by Denny Hulme's McLaren M23, the Tyrrells of François Cevert and Jackie Stewart, and the BRM P160Es of Jean-Pierre Beltoise and Niki Lauda. Ronnie's new team-mate, Emerson Fittipaldi, is seventh – but will go on to win.

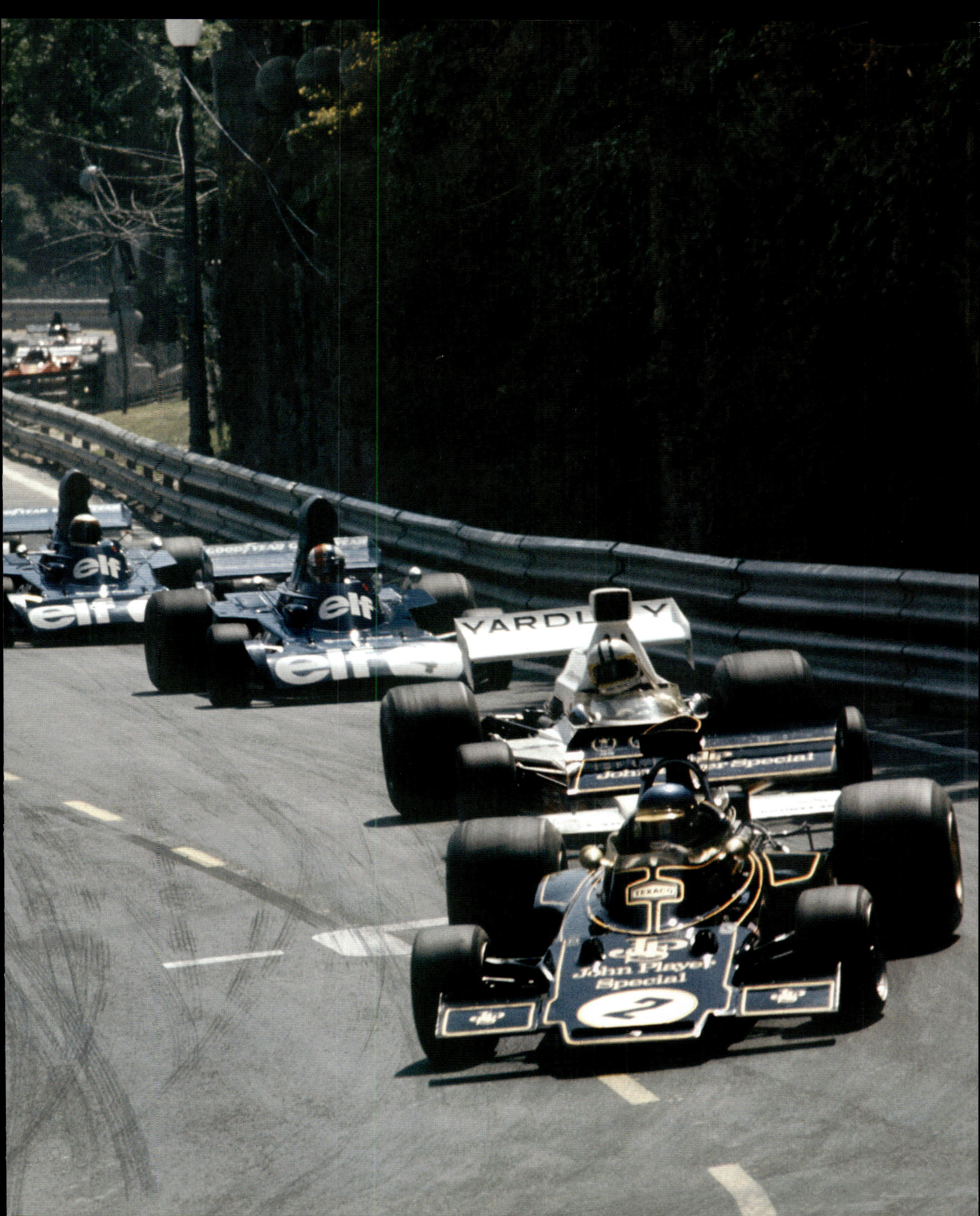
elf
elf
elf
elf
John Player Special
2

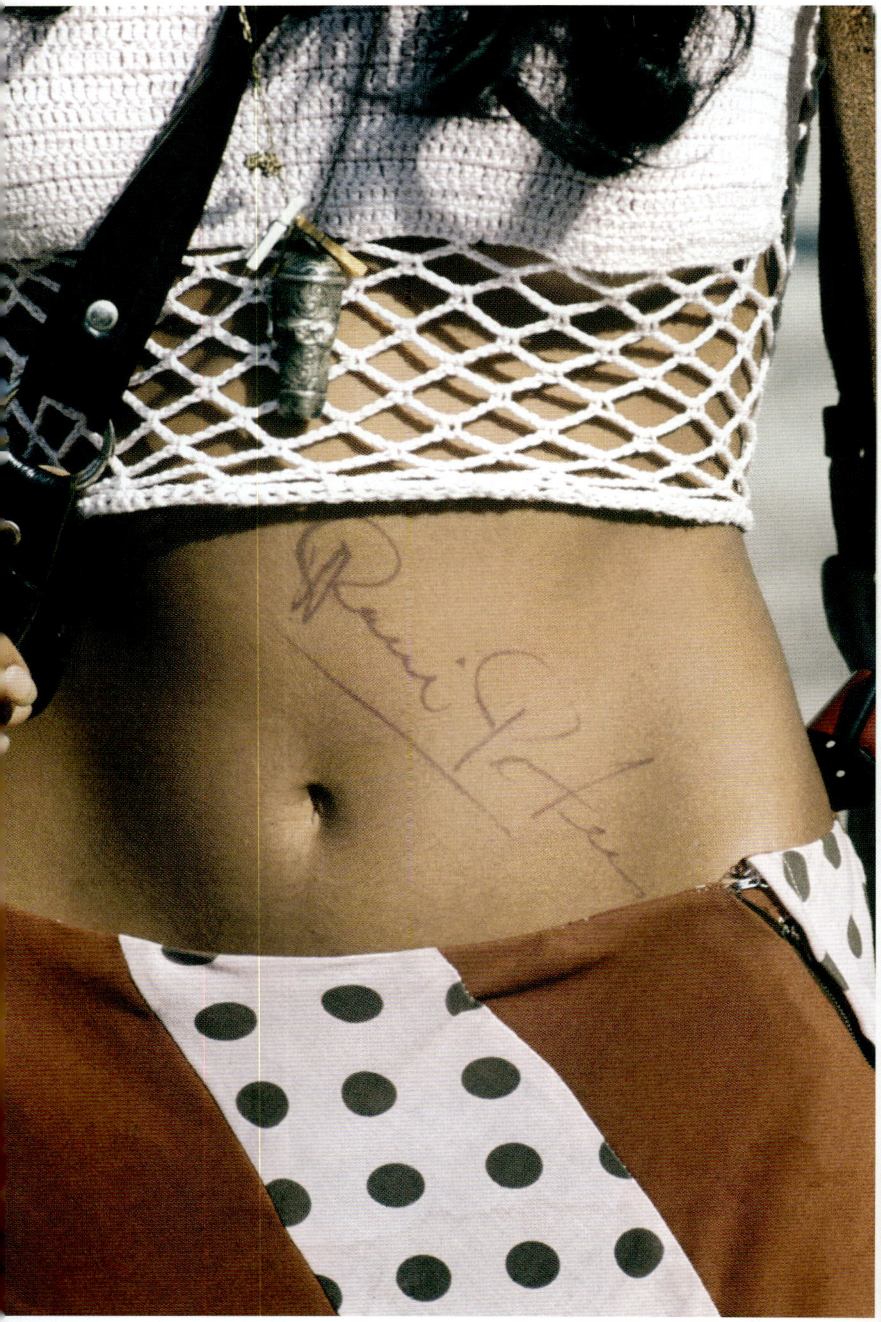

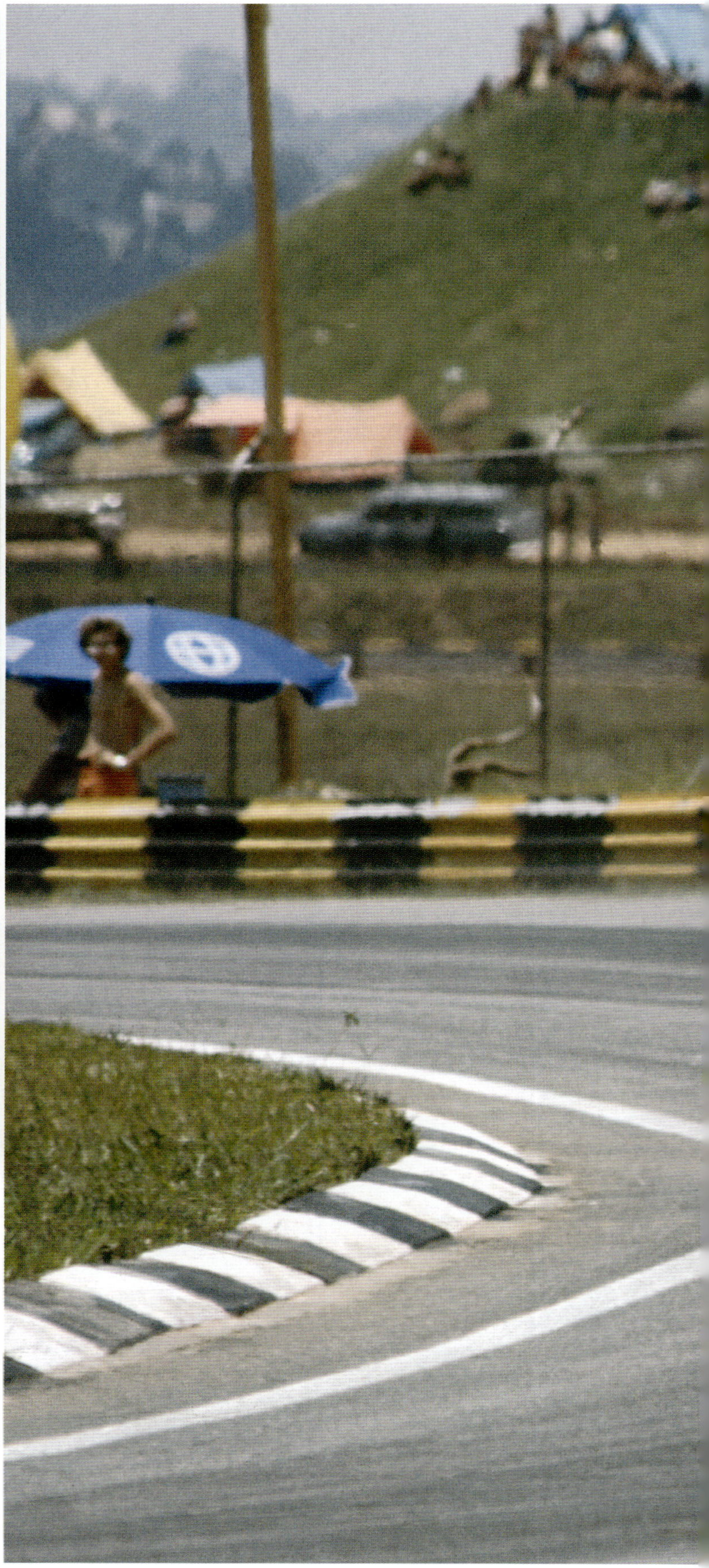

ABOVE AND RIGHT Pictured passing local driver Luis Bueno's rented Surtees, Ronnie secured his first Formula 1 pole position in the 1973 Brazilian Grand Prix, rendering his autograph more desirable – and, in some cases, much more fun to write. Over the course of this season, Ronnie justified description as the fastest driver in Formula 1 by outqualifying Emerson Fittipaldi, his team-mate and the defending World Champion, at 11 of the 15 venues.

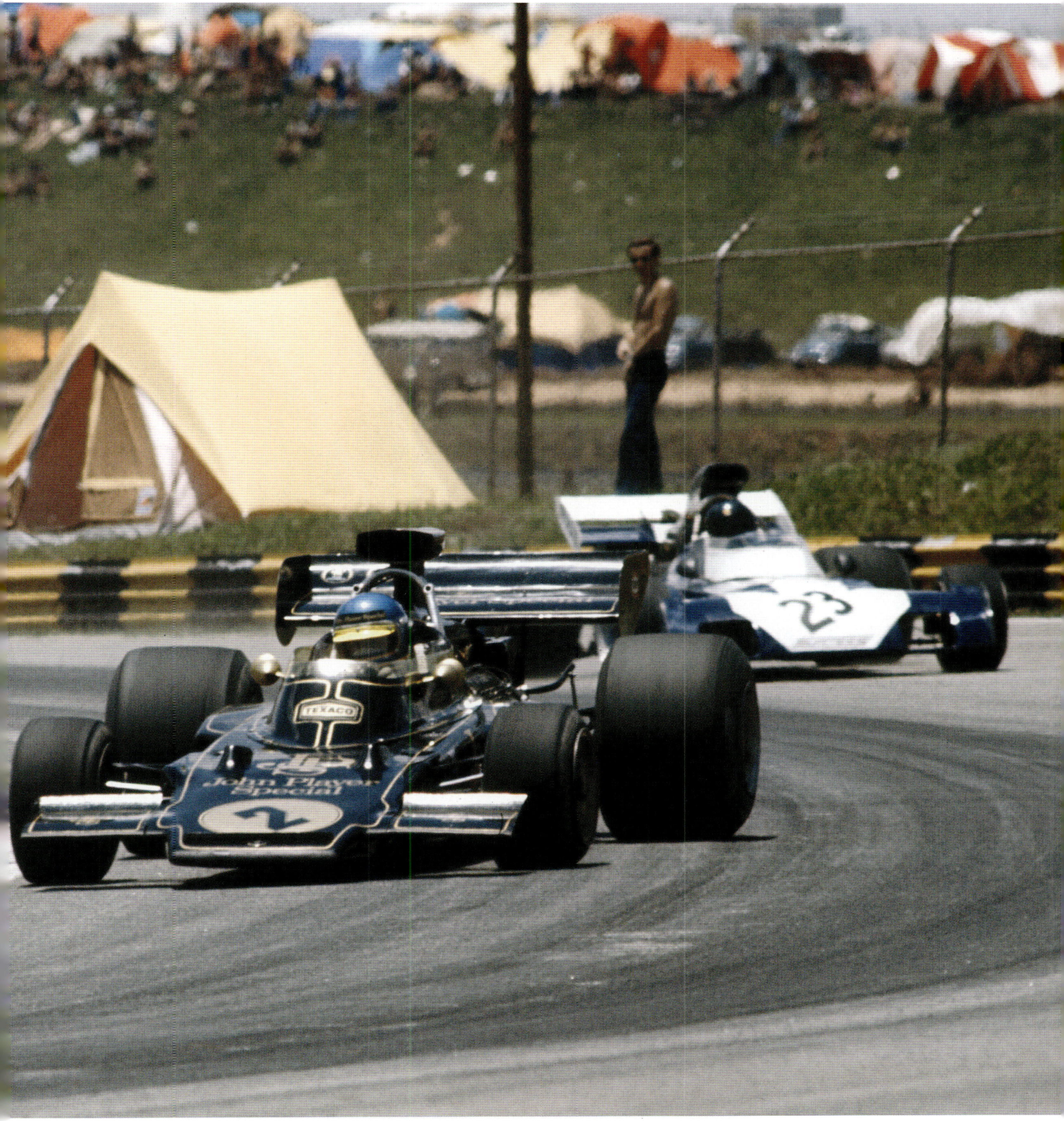
TEXACO
John Player Special
2
23

RIGHT Ronnie and the débutant E-version of the JPS Lotus 72 were clearly the fastest combination in Montjuic Park, and annexed pole position with 0.7sec to spare. So Colin Chapman ordered him to build up a 4sec lead and hold it there, to conserve his tyres. Ronnie did just that, driving well within himself. When, after 46 of the 75 laps, Jackie Stewart parked his Tyrrell with a detached brake disc, the second-placed man was Emerson Fittipaldi, up from seventh on the grid with the other Lotus. This, surely, was to be Ronnie's maiden victory. Ten laps later, Ronnie's gearbox broke. Emerson successfully nursed a deflating rear tyre, and won the Spanish Grand Prix. Incredibly, it would be his last victory of the season...

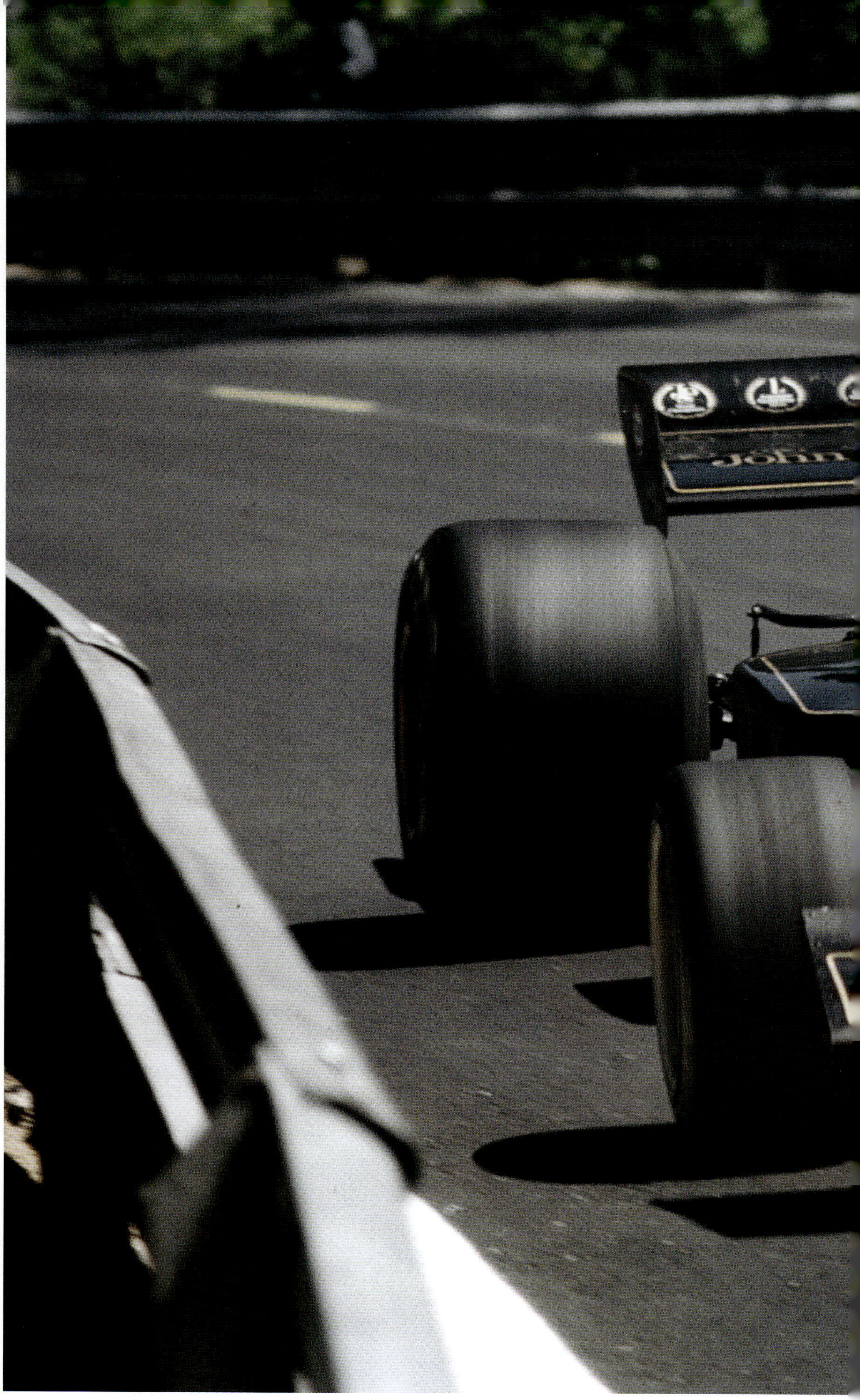

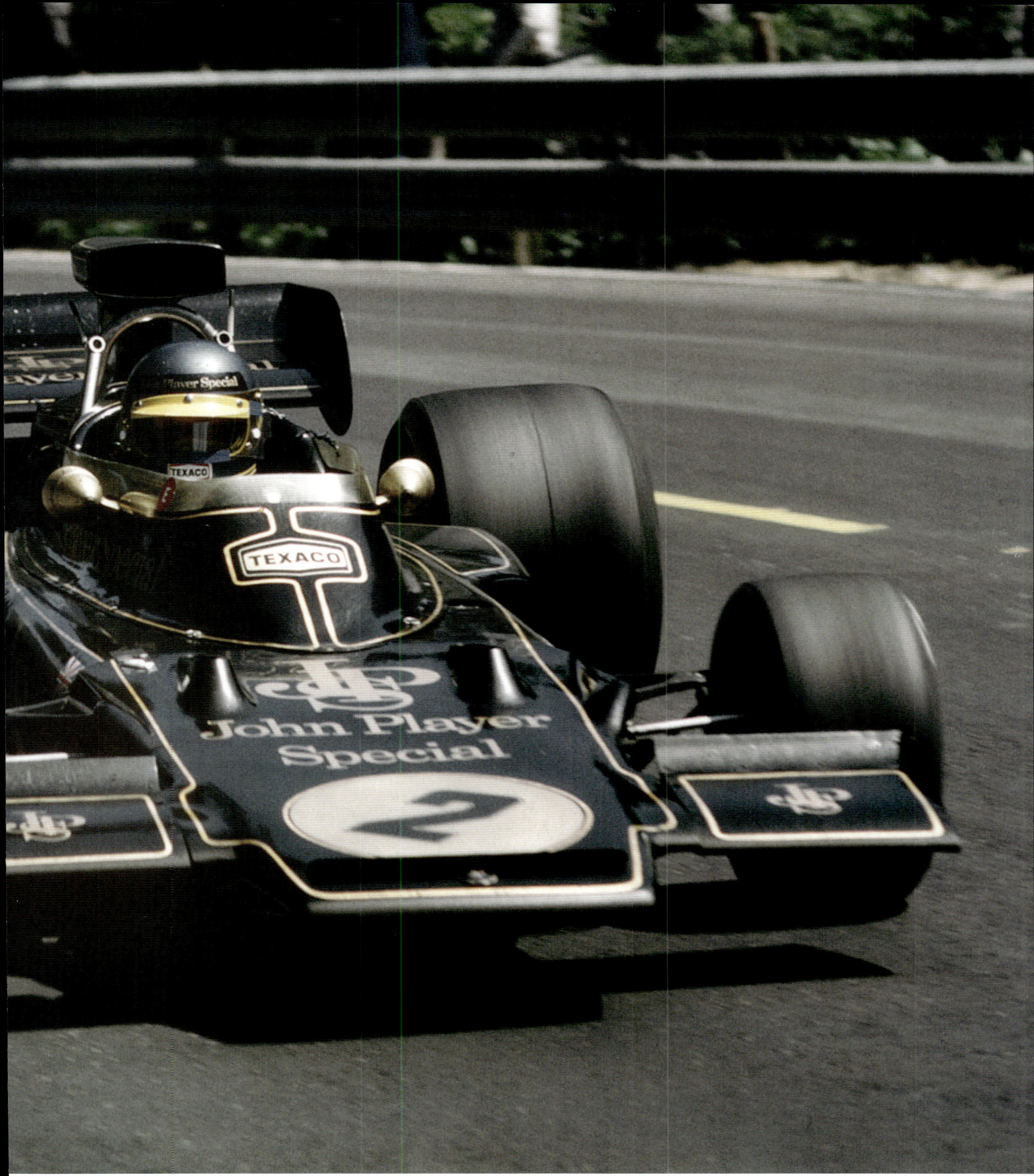
Player Special
TEXACO
TEXACO
John Player
Special
2

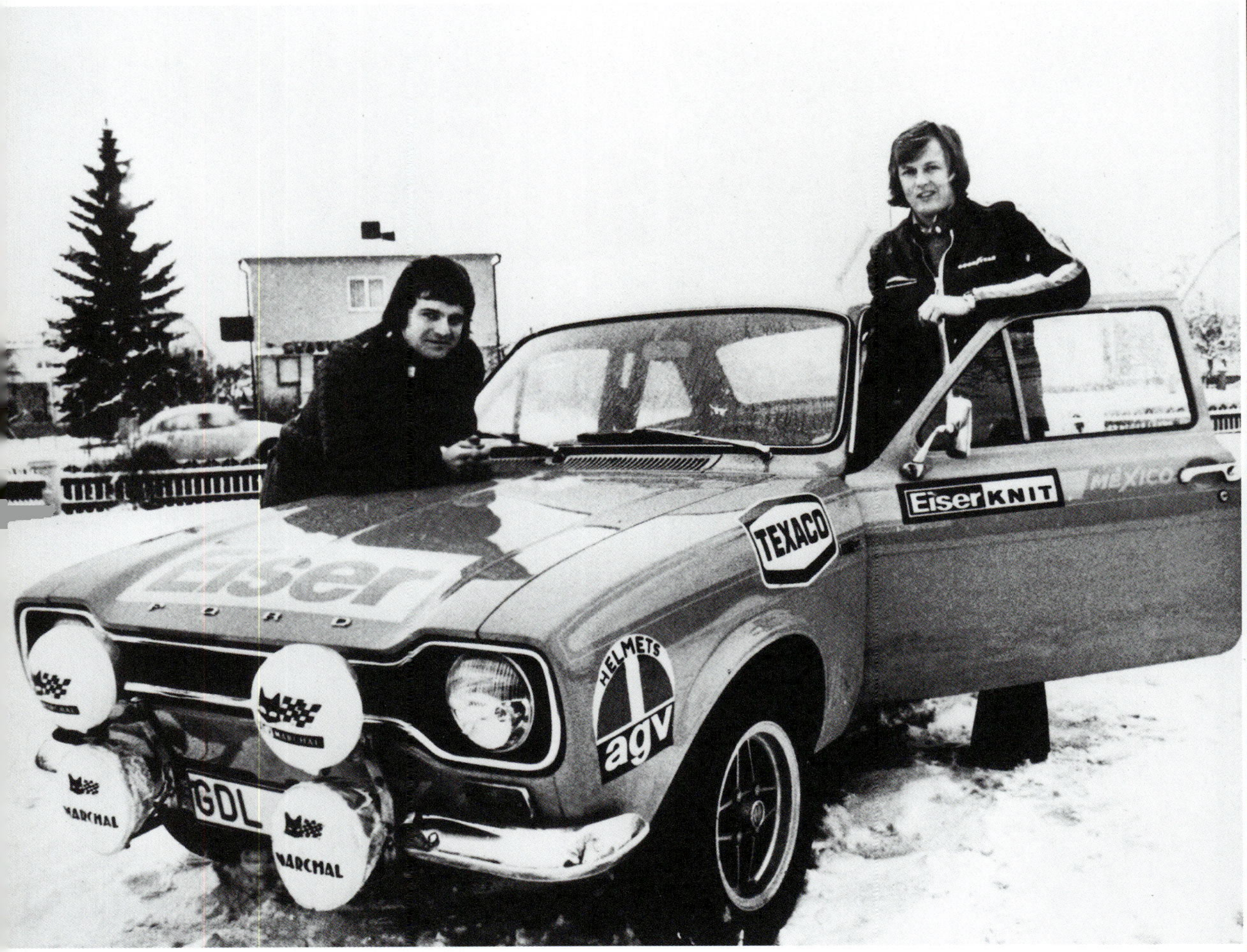

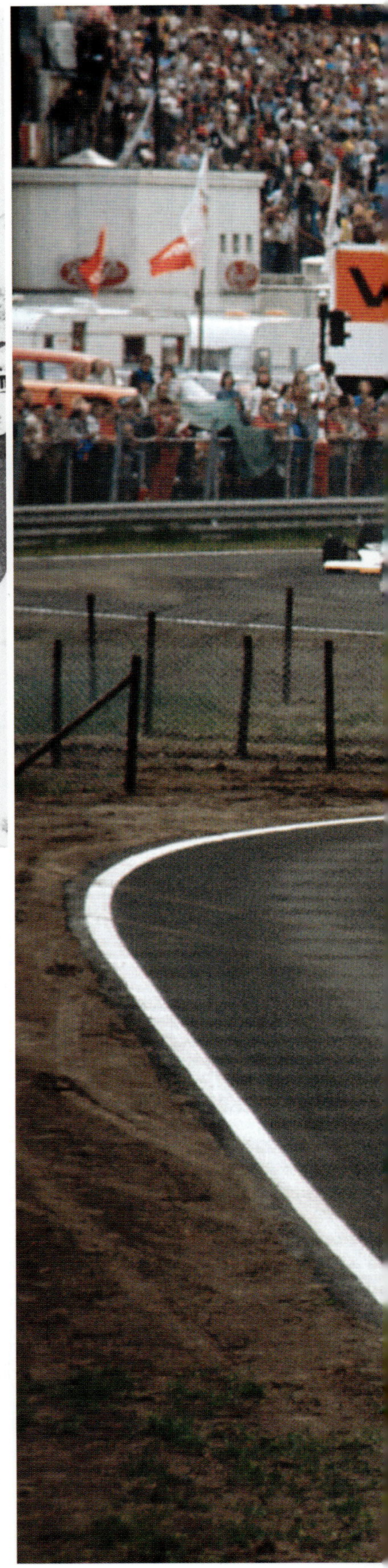

ABOVE Ronnie with co-driver Torsten Palm before another brief encounter with the sport of rallying. The Ford Escort Mexico had established itself as one of the most popular competition cars in Europe this year and a special event for them was arranged by the KAK, the organiser of the Swedish Rally. The Mexico crews were to contest the second half of the rally and Ford Stockholm prepared two cars for Ronnie and Reine Wisell, the latter co-driven by Gunnar Trygg. Reine beat Ronnie into second place when the action began on a trotting track in Karlstad, and then Ronnie flew off the road on the first special stage proper. Reine got to the finish, sixth in the class.

RIGHT Ronnie was suffering from a heavy cold during the European Grand Prix meeting on the Zolder circuit in Belgium, which was almost cancelled when a new track surface broke up badly. And he crashed three times in one day... He put his JPS Lotus 72E on pole position but, on race morning, he embarked on the warm-up session with a 100deg fever, and went off. He returned to the pits for the spare car – and crashed that too. The Team Lotus mechanics took the undamaged rear end of one car and the undamaged front of the other, and cobbled together something for him to race. Here he is pursued on the opening lap by François Cevert's Tyrrell, Jacky Ickx's Ferrari 312B3, Denny Hulme's McLaren M23, Carlos Reutemann's Brabham BT42 and Jean-Pierre Beltoise's BRM P160E. The hastily reassembled Lotus oversteered viciously and Ronnie crashed out of fifth place after 42 laps. The race was won by Jackie Stewart (eighth in the picture) in the first of three Tyrrell 1–2s with Cevert, with Emerson Fittipaldi's Lotus third.

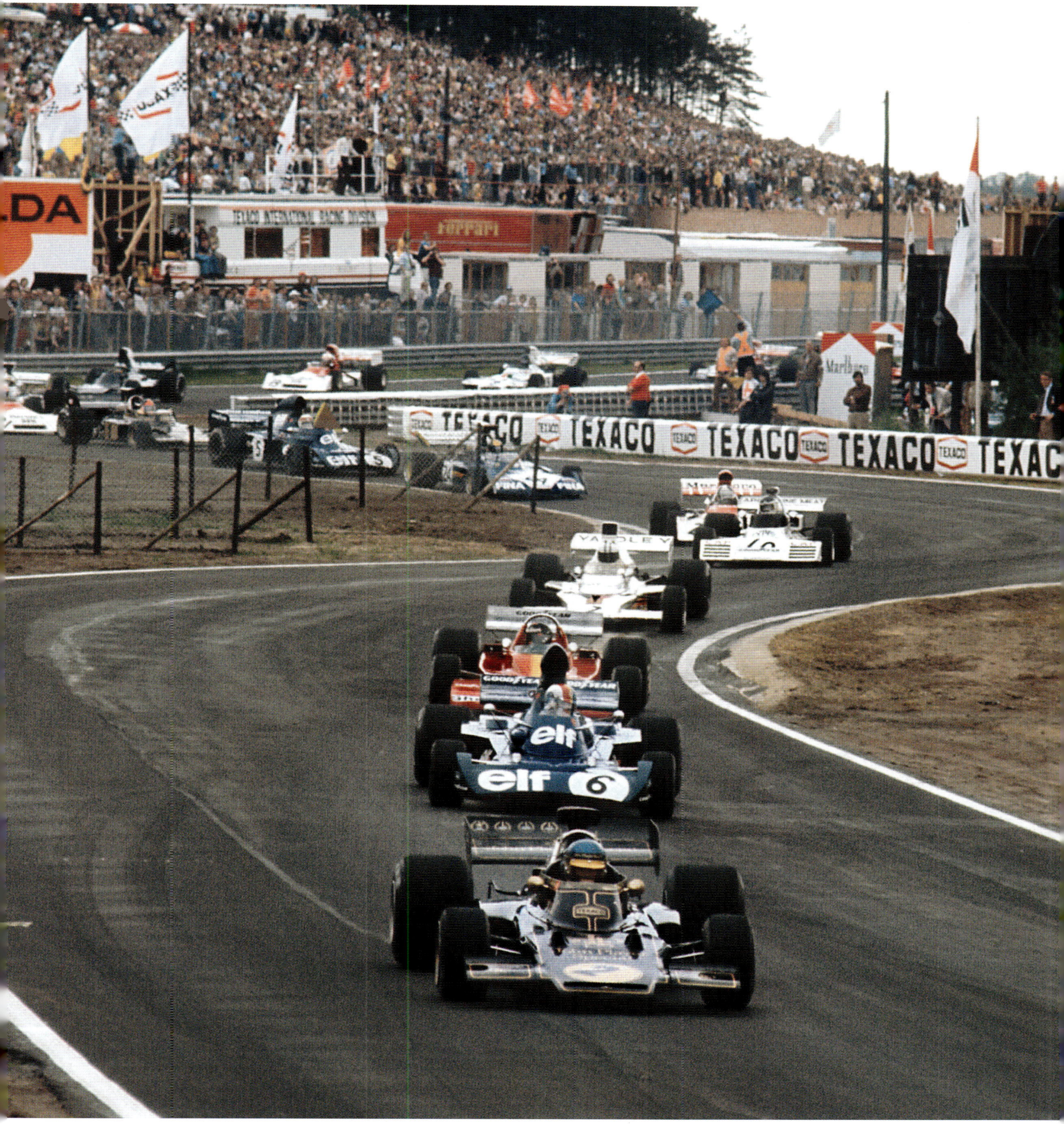
TEXACO
TEXACO
TEXACO
TEXAC
elf
elf 6

RIGHT At Monaco with Emerson Fittipaldi and Team Lotus founder Colin Chapman. Emerson was already worried about the pace of his team-mate, who had outqualified him 3–2 so far. And Ronnie made it 4–2 here, lining up on the front row alongside Jackie Stewart's Tyrrell, with Emerson fifth. Ronnie passed Stewart on the second lap and led the race until the eighth, when his Cosworth DFV engine lost fuel pressure. Emerson harried JYS but finished second, with Ronnie a lapped third. The four points represented Ronnie's first score of the season, but Emerson left the principality leading Stewart 41–37. It was clear which of Chapman's drivers would now have to be favoured in the championship.

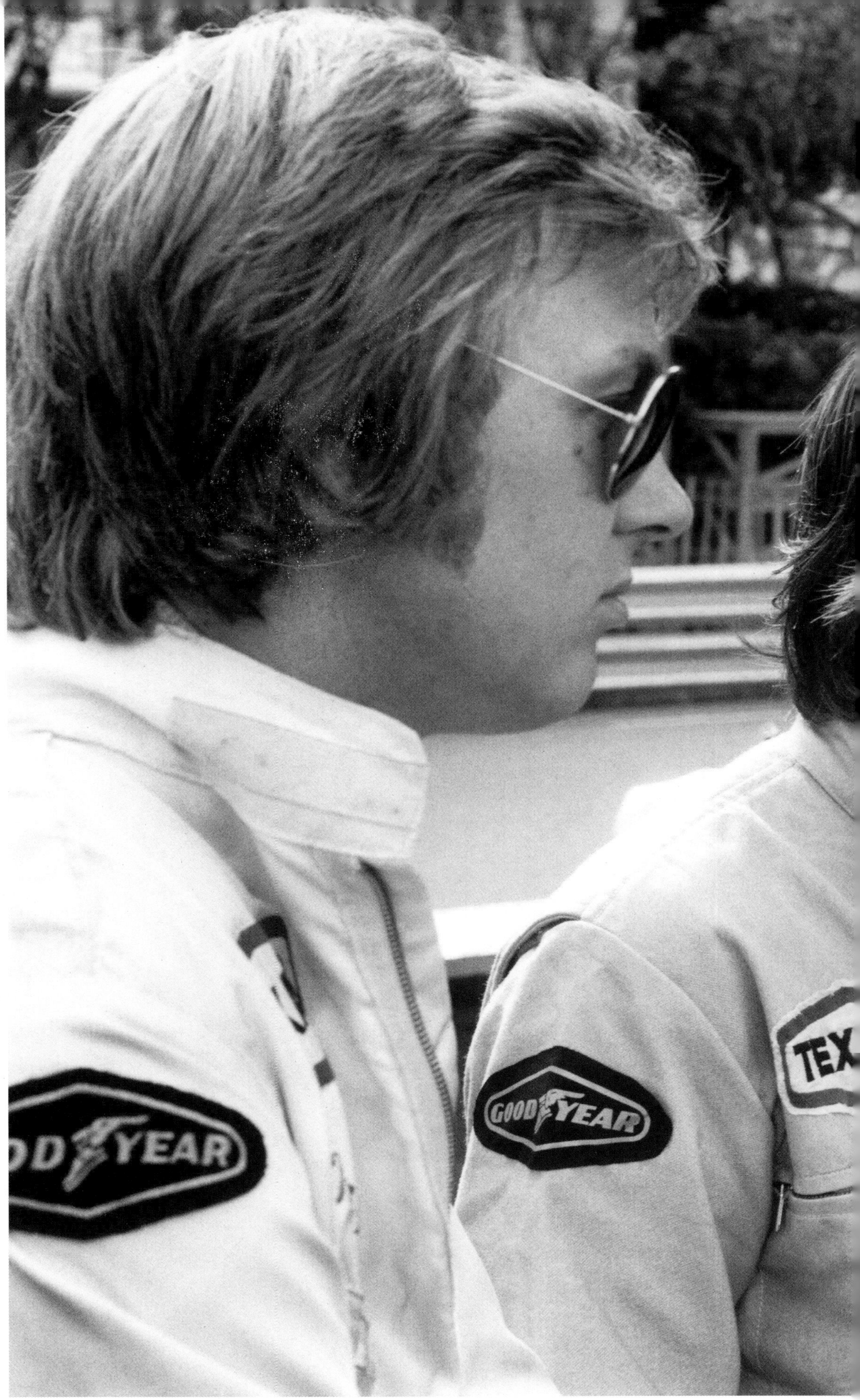

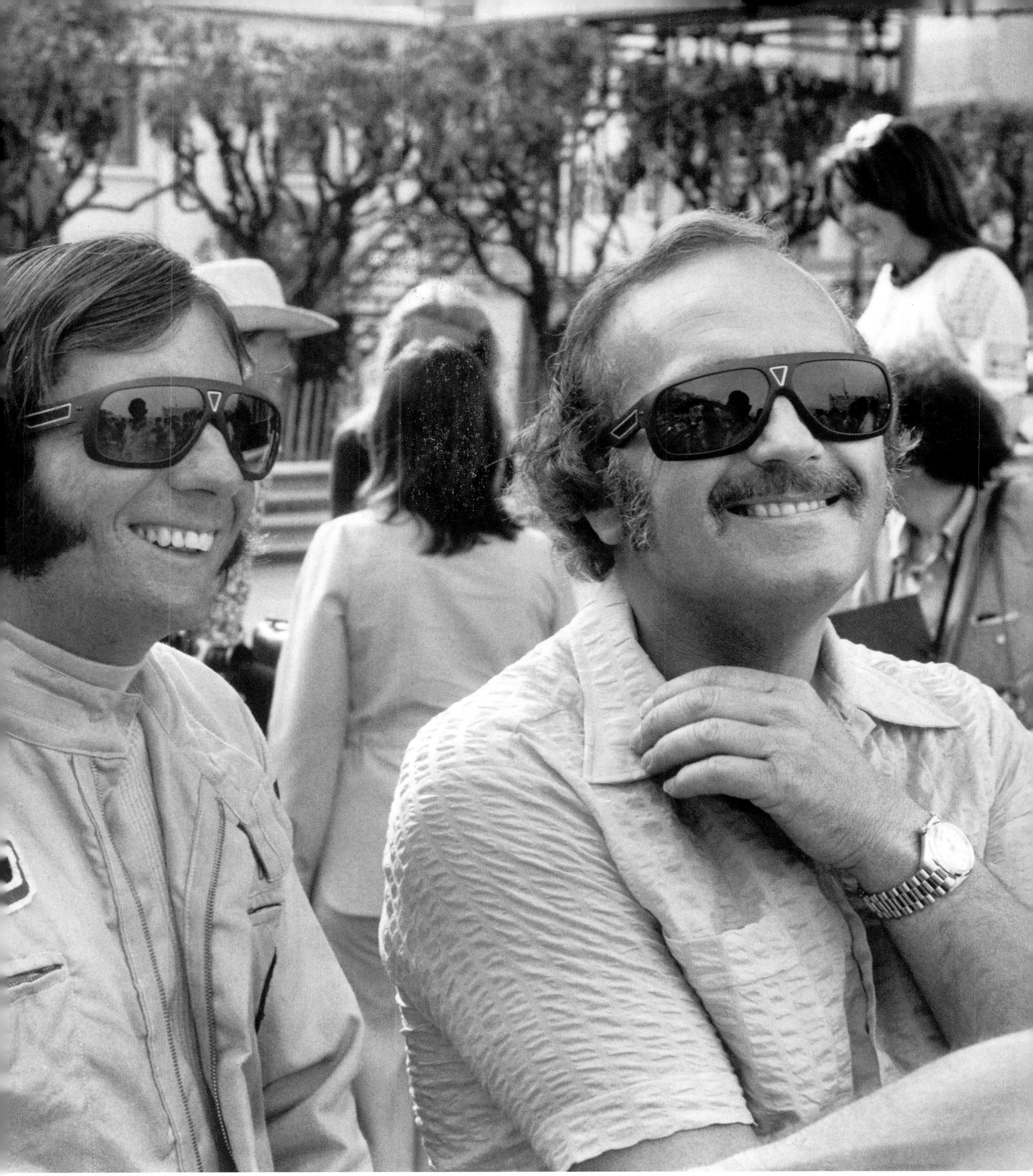

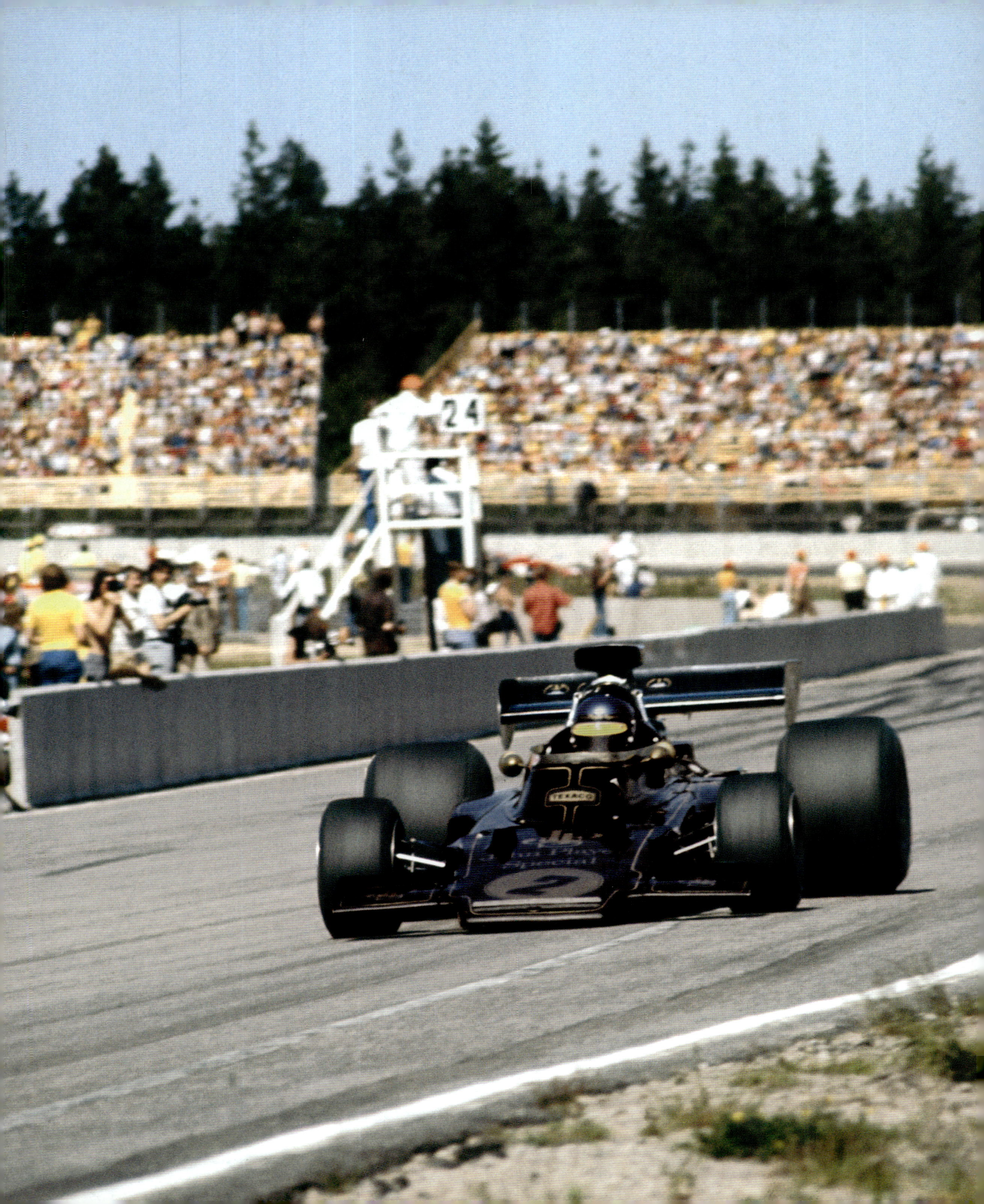
24
TEXACO

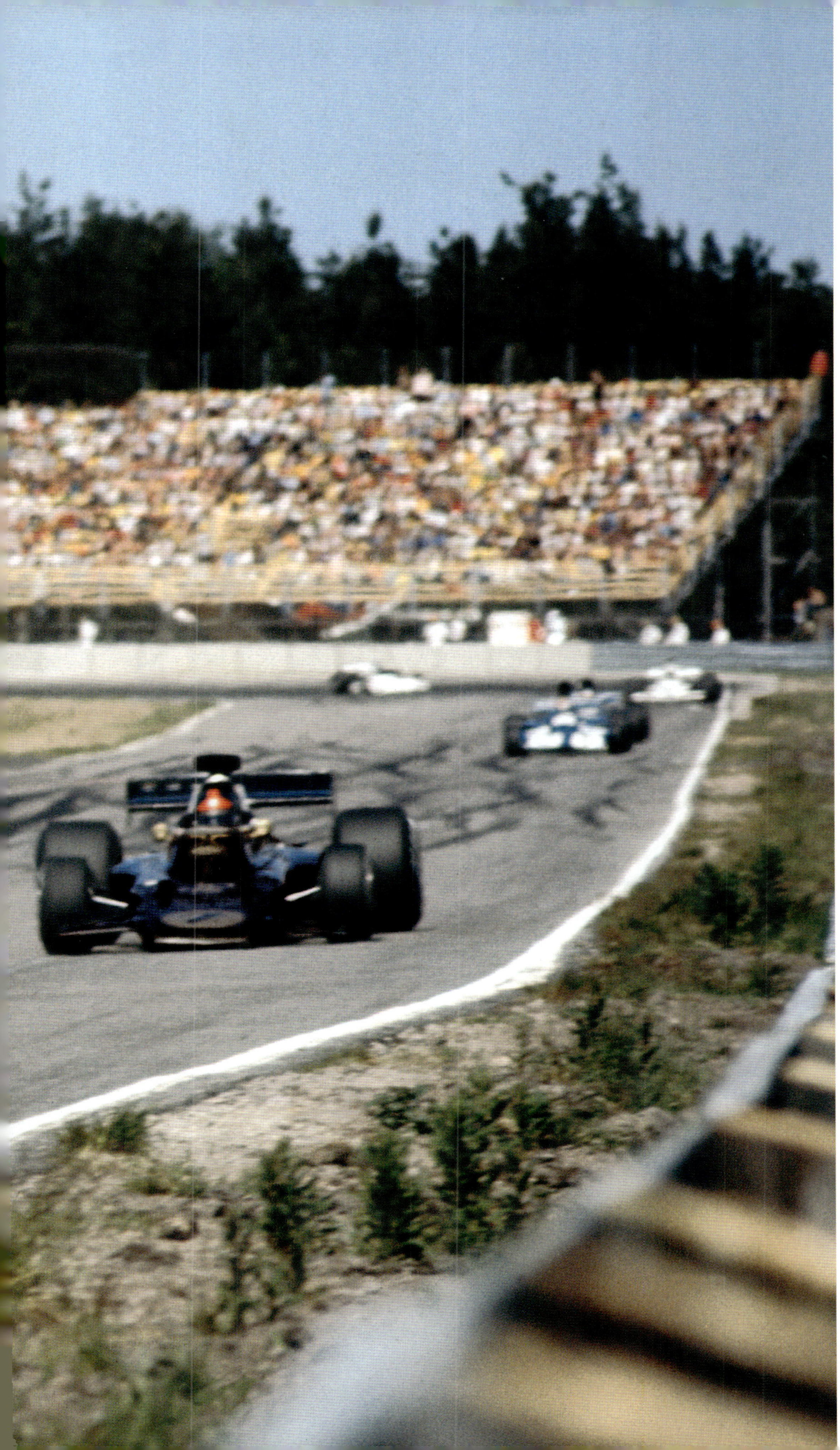

LEFT Ronnie brought massive crowds to the Scandinavian Raceway at Anderstorp for the Swedish Grand Prix, and he delighted his fans with pole position ahead of the Tyrrell drivers and team-mate Emerson Fittipaldi. Before the season, the joint Lotus number ones had agreed that each would help the other to win his home Grand Prix. Ronnie had been in no position to honour his side of the bargain at Interlagos, but Emerson had won anyway. Here he is protecting Ronnie's tail from any assault from Tyrrell drivers François Cevert and Jackie Stewart early in the race. If this was to be the scene of Ronnie's maiden victory, he could not have chosen better. With just over a lap to run, he was stymied by a puncture. With Emerson out with a broken transmission, and the Tyrrells hampered by fading brakes and severe tyre vibrations, the surprised winner was Denny Hulme with his Yardley McLaren M23. Ronnie followed across the line 4sec later, with Cevert still a distant third.

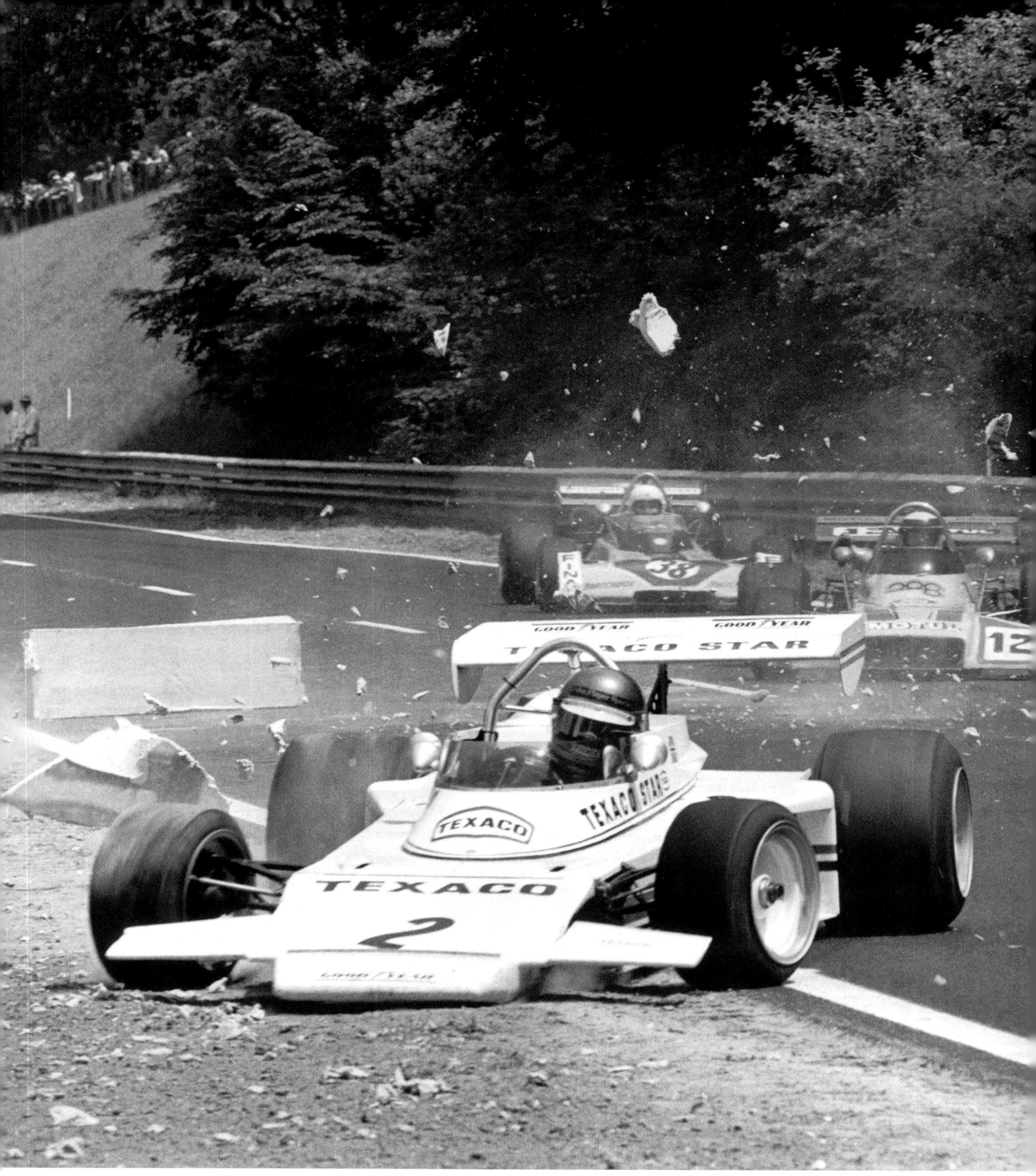
GOOD YEAR
GOOD YEAR
TEXACO STAR
TEXACO STAR
TEXACO
TEXACO
2
38
12

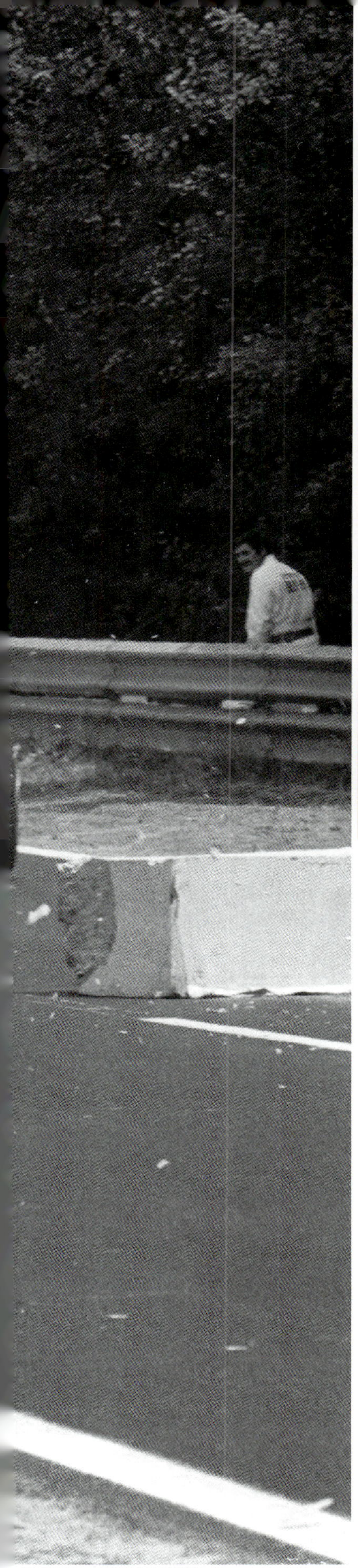

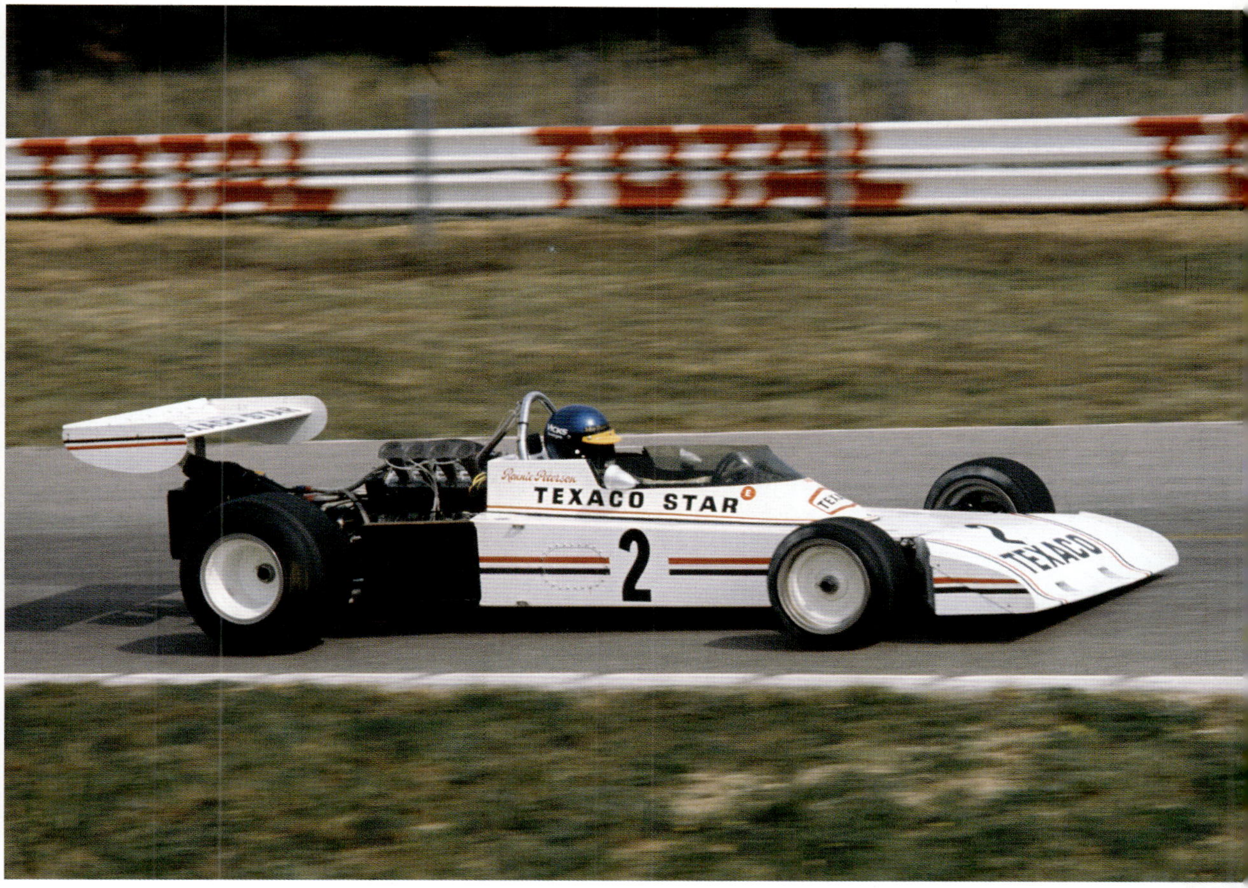

ABOVE Both Ronnie and Emerson were under contract with Team Lotus to race in Formula 2 in a 1973 programme sponsored by Texaco. The Lotus 74 was the work of newly recruited design engineer Ralph Bellamy, who had been hired to help with the Lotus 76 that was projected for Formula 1. Pictured at Albi, its second race, the 'Texaco Star' turned out to be a disastrously bad car, underpowered by its Novamotor-prepared Lotus BDA engine, and barely competitive with the latest chassis from Alpine, Chevron, March, Motul and Surtees. Ronnie hated the car and, in the end, did only seven races with it, finishing only two. Jean-Pierre Jarier dominated the European Championship with the works STP March team, for which Ronnie had raced the previous season.

LEFT Ronnie got his line through a chicane a tad wrong in the Formula 2 race on the road circuit at Rouen... The organisers hastily built this barrier from polystyrene blocks to slow the cars before the famous downhill section, on which poor Gerry Birrell had been killed the day before while qualifying his works Chevron. Ronnie was racing in the midfield in the final when he clipped one of the blocks. The impact dislodged the steering rack and this turned into a major accident, in which Ronnie was lucky not to go over the Armco. The drivers with the best view are Jean-Pierre Jaussaud in Ron Dennis's Motul M1 and Jose Dolhem (Surtees TS15).

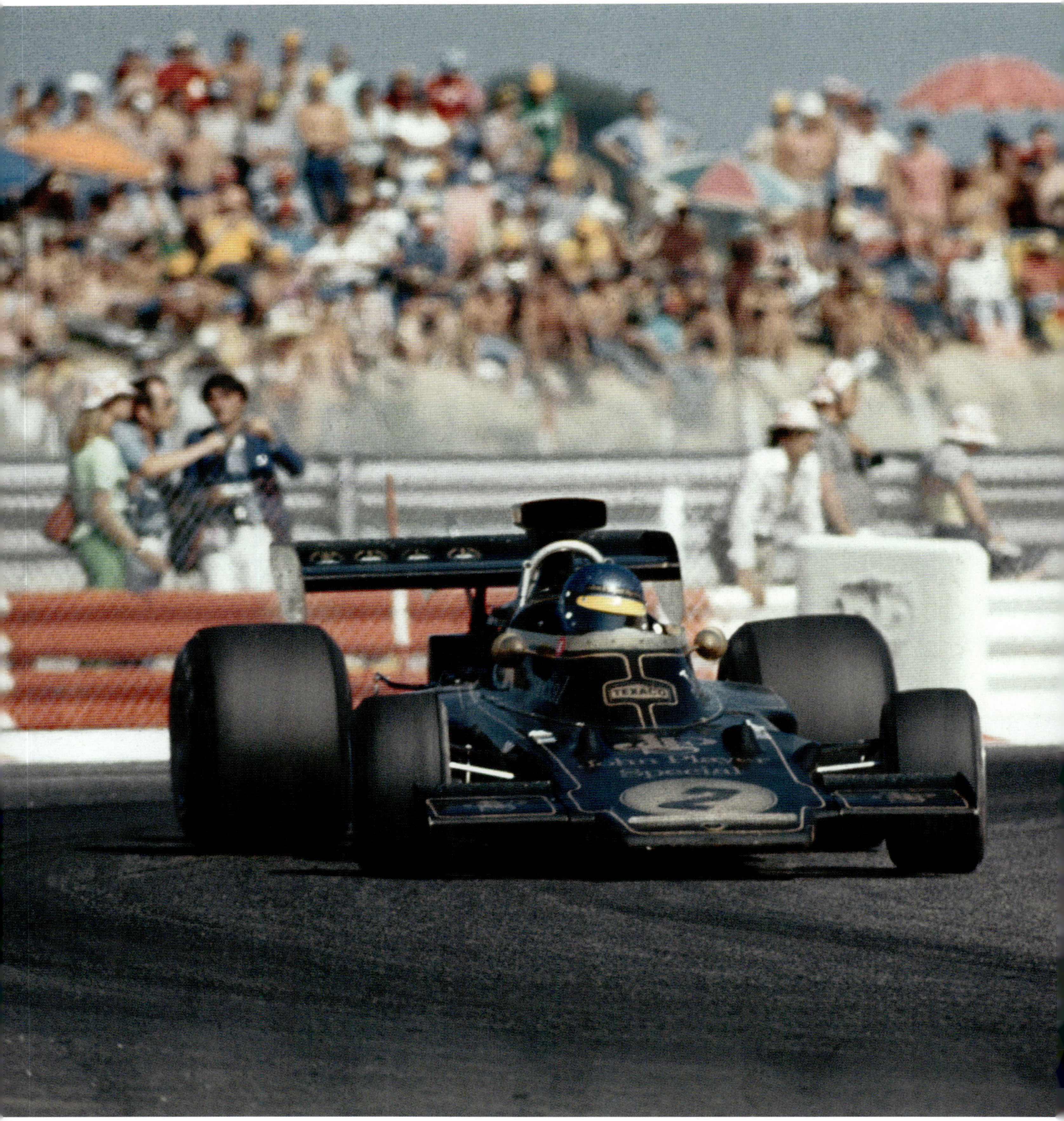

LEFT A fortnight after the huge disappointment of Anderstorp, and a week after his nasty crash at Rouen, Ronnie went from Normandy to the Mediterranean coast for the French Grand Prix. There was an interloper at Paul Ricard: Jody Scheckter, McLaren's new hotshoe, deputising for Peter Revson who had an American commitment. And Scheckter led the motor race, resisting all Ronnie's efforts to get around him, quick on the long straights, canny in the turns. After 21 frustrating laps, Ronnie waved Emerson past so that he could have a go. It worked a treat, because 21 laps turned out to be enough for Emerson, too. As the two leaders braked behind a backmarker for the tight right-hand corner leading onto the main straight, completing their 42nd lap, Emerson lunged at Scheckter, they collided, and both were out of the race. Ronnie inherited an enormous lead over François Cevert's Tyrrell, and this time the Lotus stayed in one piece through the remaining 12 laps to the chequer. It was Ronnie's 40th Grand Prix start, but the wait was finally over...

BELOW Wedges at Silverstone. Having beaten the McLarens of Denny Hulme and Peter Revson to pole position for the British Grand Prix, Ronnie leads them off the line at a restart caused by a multiple accident. A third M23 was entered here for Jody Scheckter, the sensation of Paul Ricard a fortnight before, but he lost control at the end of the opening lap, causing mayhem. A red flag was thrown for the track to be cleared of nine wrecked cars. Fortunately only one driver was hurt: Andrea de Adamich, with whom Ronnie had won a sportscar race for Alfa Romeo two years before, suffered a broken leg, ending his career. Ronnie led this race with a viciously oversteering car until, on the 39th of 67 laps, a slight drizzle demanded caution even from him. Revson passed into a lead he never lost, so Formula 1 had two new winners in as many races. Ronnie, his Lotus increasingly skittish, had to fight as hard as he knew to keep second place, but just held it to the finish-line under frantic pressure from Hulme and James Hunt in Hesketh Racing's very effective March 731.

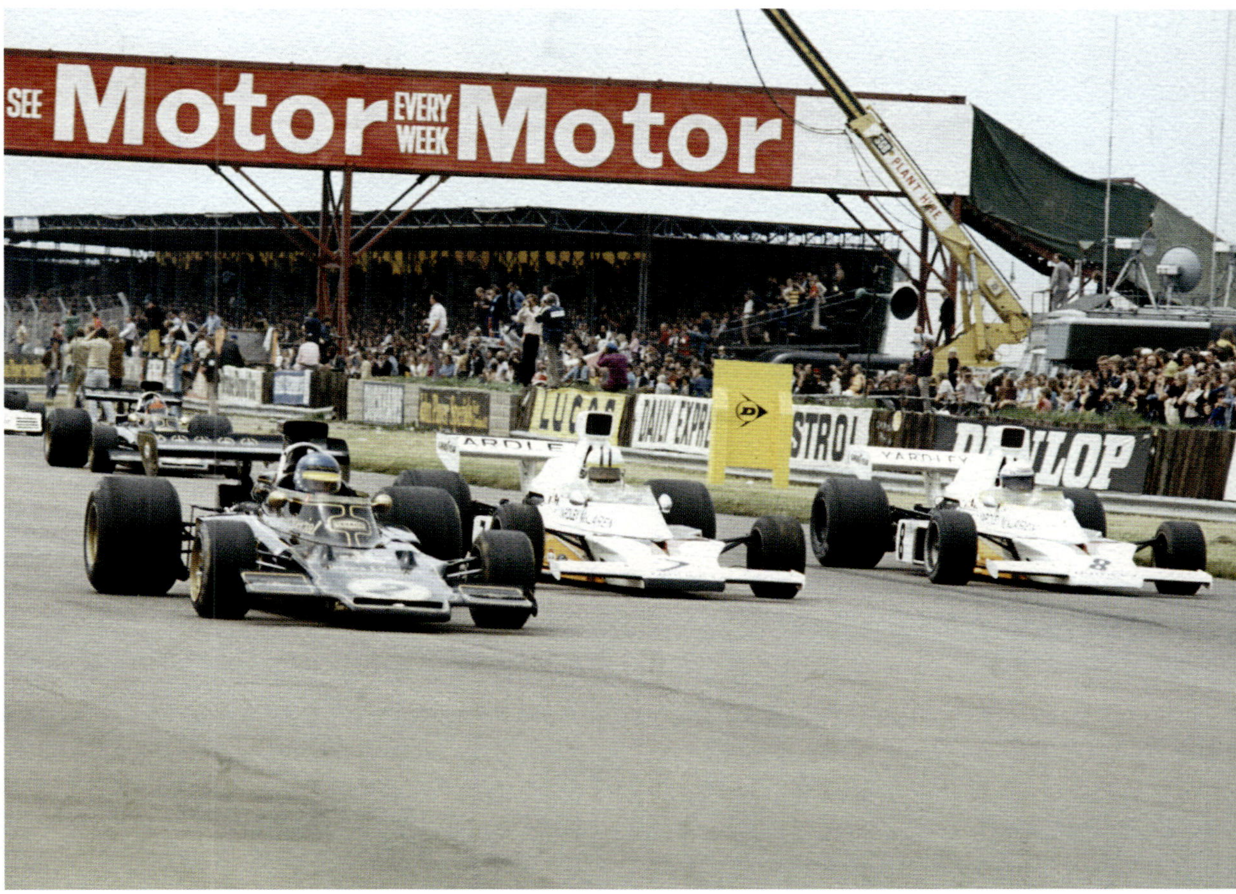

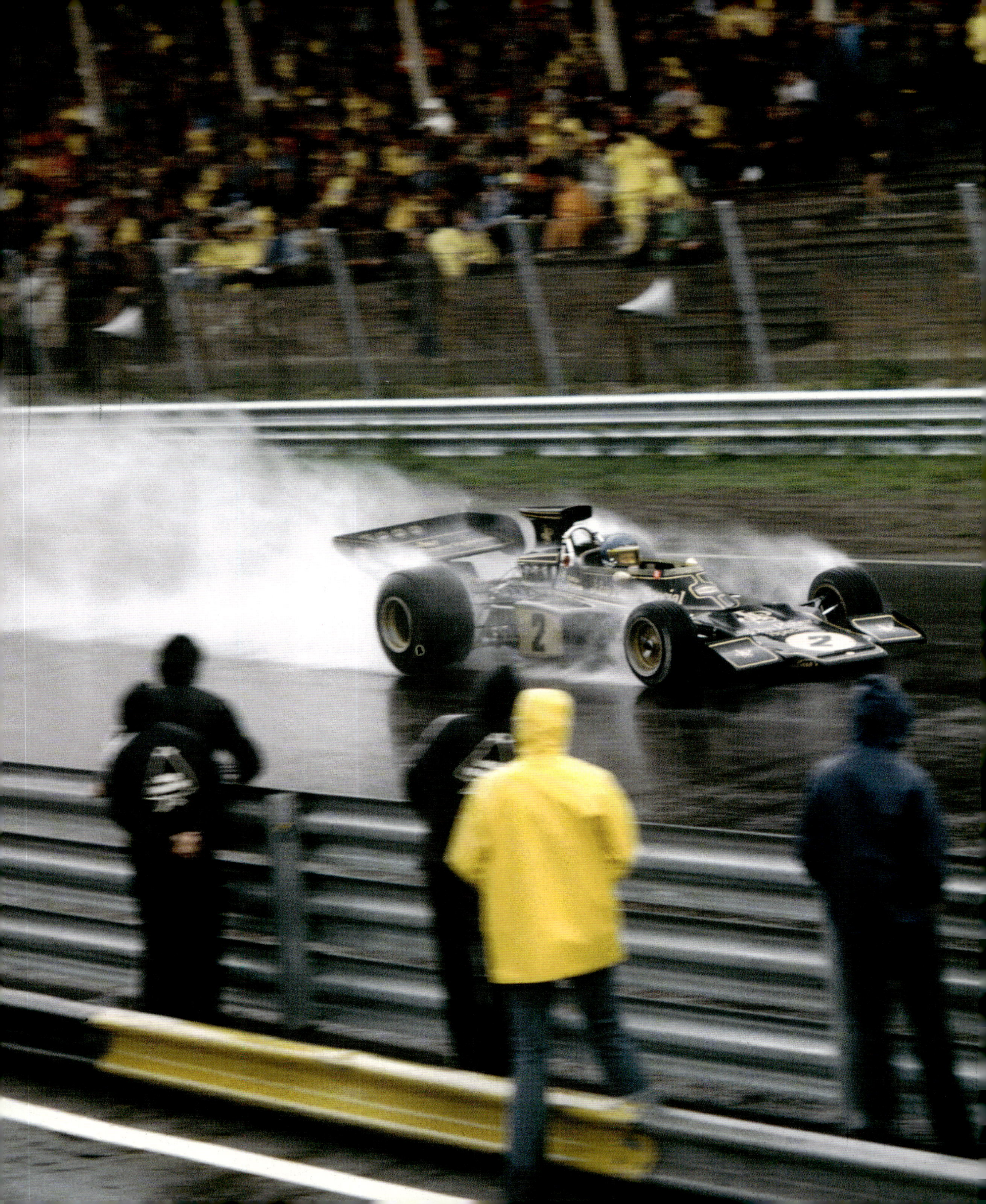
2
2

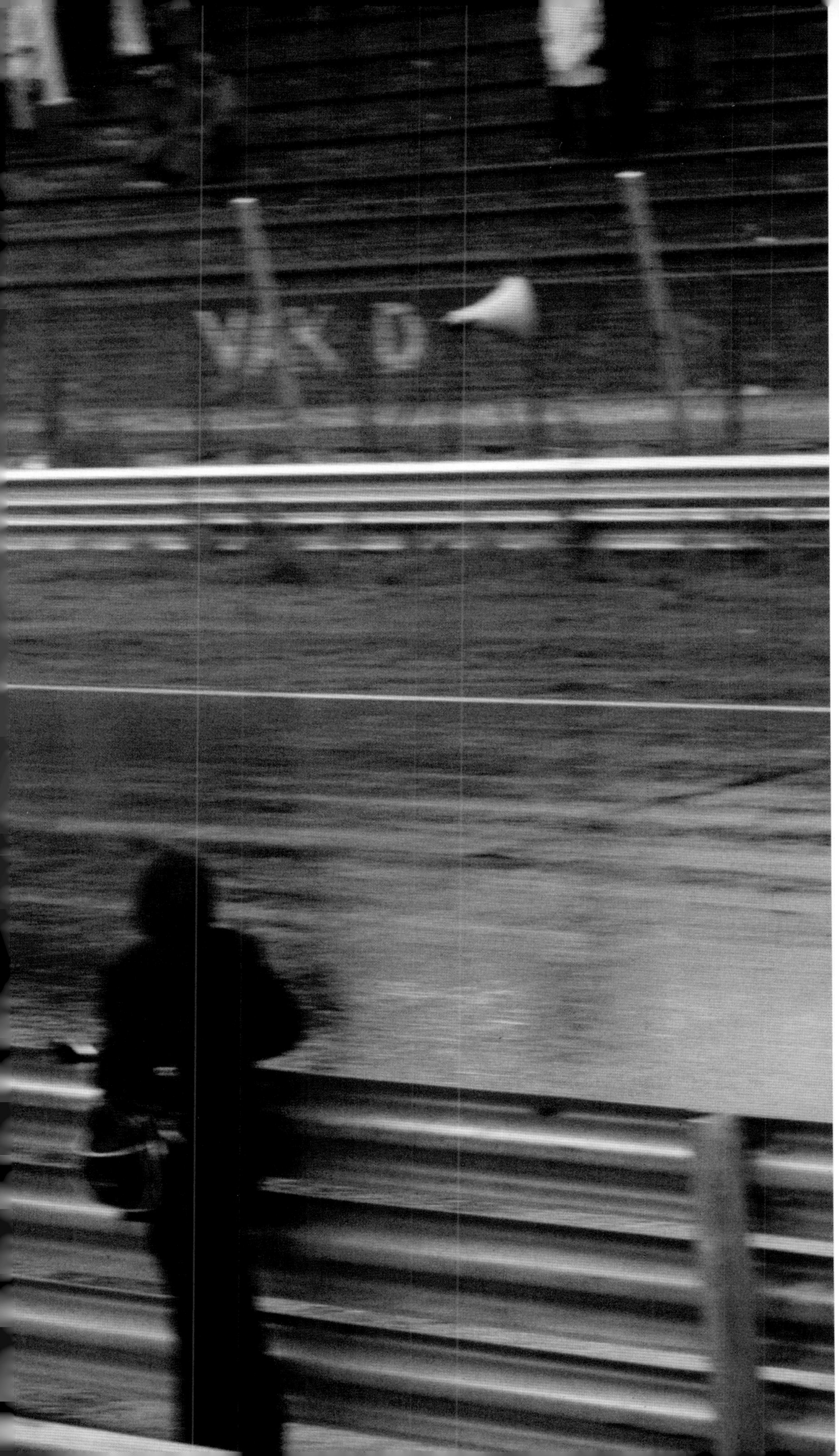

LEFT A Grand Prix driver earning his money. Ronnie copes with atrocious track conditions on the opening day at Zandvoort. The following day, he secured another pole position, while team-mate Emerson Fittipaldi had a big accident when a front wheel parted company with his Lotus, and tore ligaments in his left leg. Ronnie built up a 14sec lead on race day over the Tyrrell twins, but both Jackie Stewart and François Cevert came back at him when he lost the use of second and fourth gears. With nine of the 72 laps remaining, Ronnie retired with an engine problem. Emerson started the race but could not continue, and this was his fourth consecutive DNF. Suddenly Stewart had a 10-point lead in the championship. The Dutch Grand Prix should have been stopped after only eight laps when Roger Williamson hit a guardrail with such force that it flipped his STP March, which caught fire with its driver trapped inside. Despite the heroic efforts of David Purley, who stopped his own March at the scene, poor Williamson lost his life.

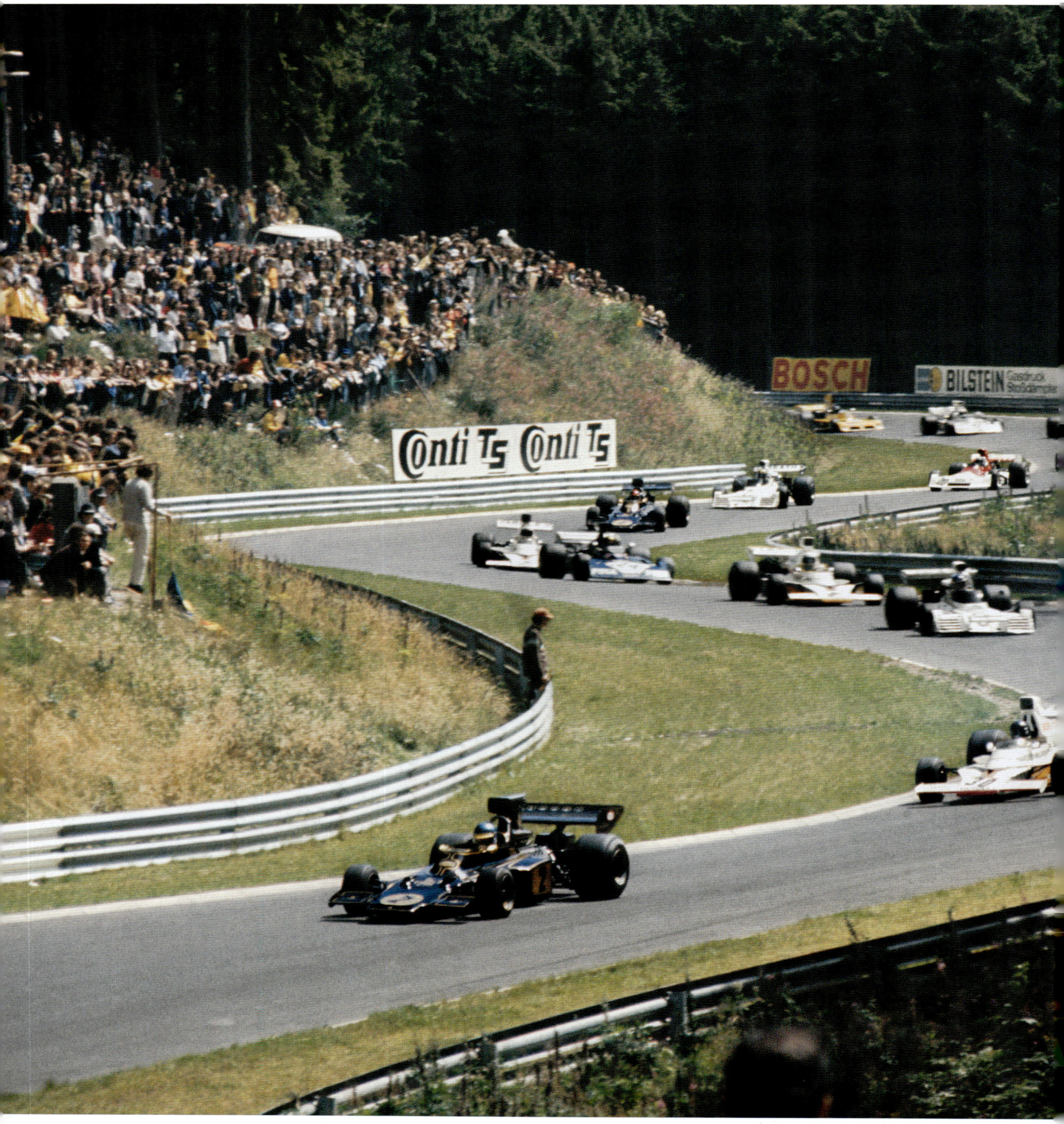
BOSCH
BILSTEIN
Conti TS Conti TS

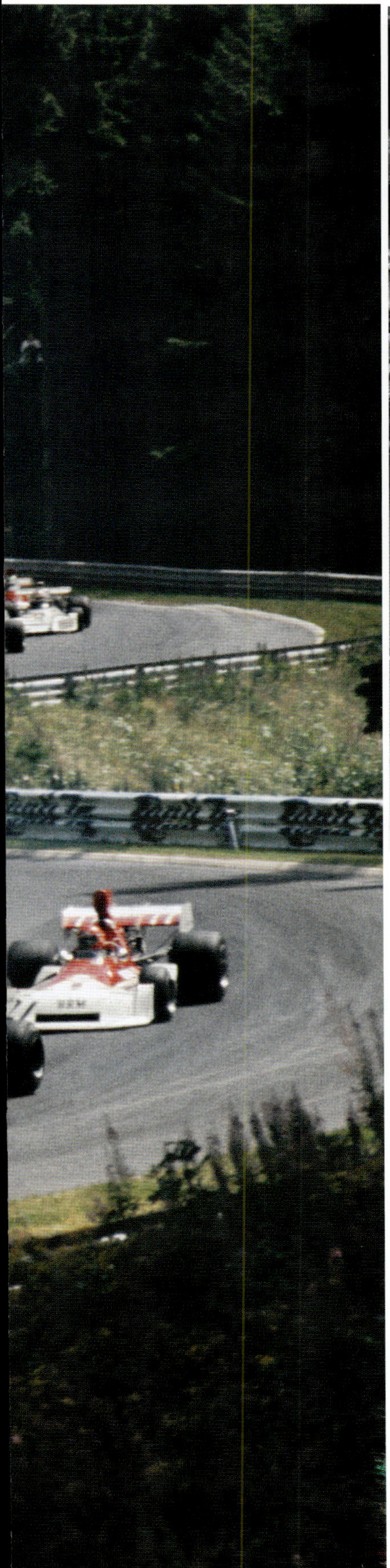

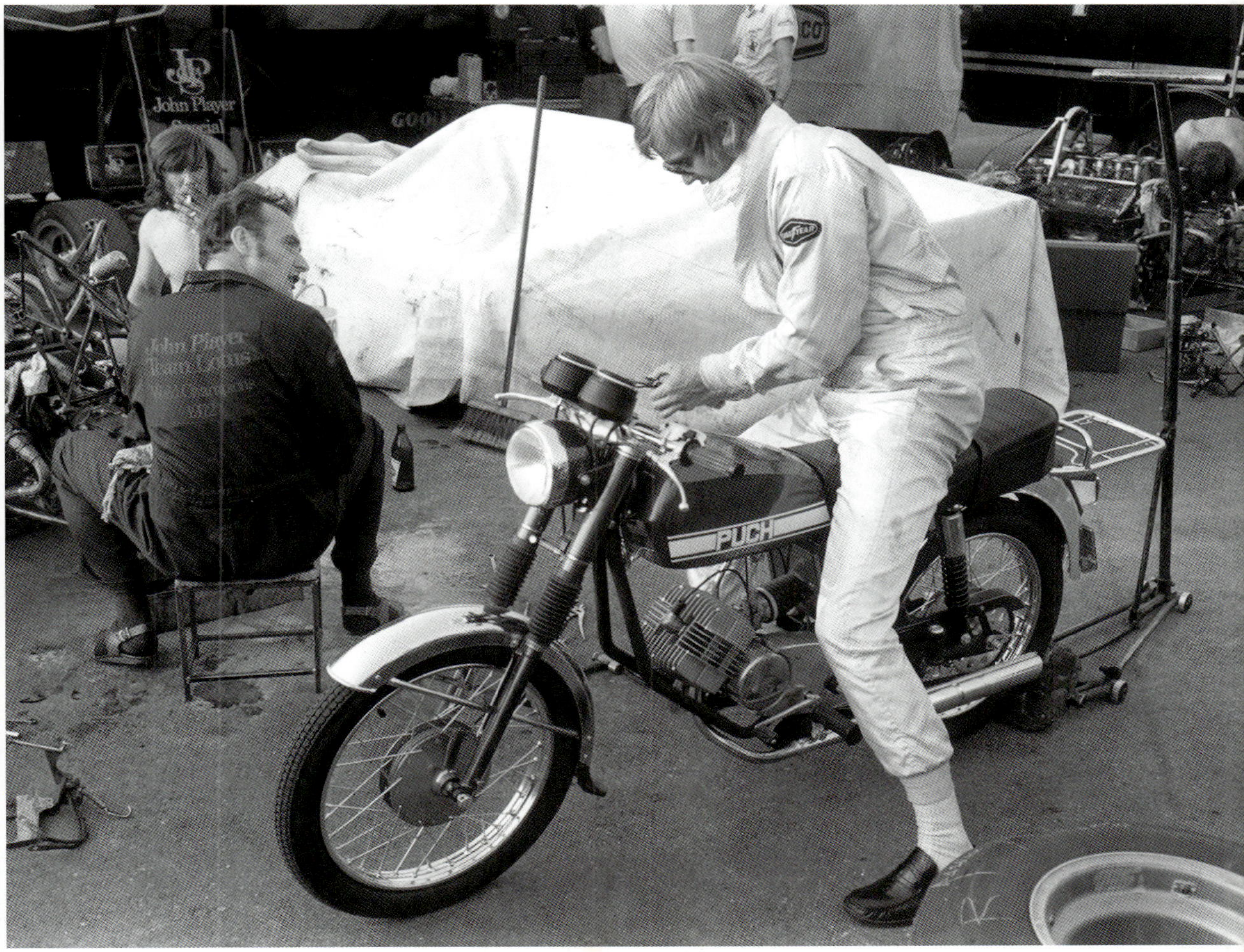

LEFT The Nürburgring, and Ronnie holds third place behind the already departed Tyrrells as the field snakes through the swerves at Wehrseifen on the opening lap of the German Grand Prix. Ronnie had survived a terrifying incident during practice on the Nordschleife when his car's front suspension broke as it was in mid-air on a 'yump' near Pflantzgarten. Following are Jacky Ickx, entered in a third McLaren M23, Niki Lauda (BRM P160E), Carlos Reutemann (Brabham BT42), Peter Revson (McLaren), Carlos Pace (Surtees TS14A), Denny Hulme (McLaren) and Emerson Fittipaldi in the other Lotus 72E. This didn't last. Ronnie is about to pull off the circuit with a broken distributor. Jackie Stewart and François Cevert completed a Tyrrell 1–2 but Emerson, in great pain from his injured leg, finished a heroic sixth.

ABOVE Ronnie reacquaints himself with a Puch motorcycle in the paddock at the Osterreichring. His first ever race on anything with an engine had been a motorcycle scramble with a 50cc Puch moped, aged 15 back in 1959. He had loved that bike and had been upset when it was stolen in the centre of Orebro. Bengt Peterson had refused to replace it but had consoled Ronnie with an offer to build him a racing kart...

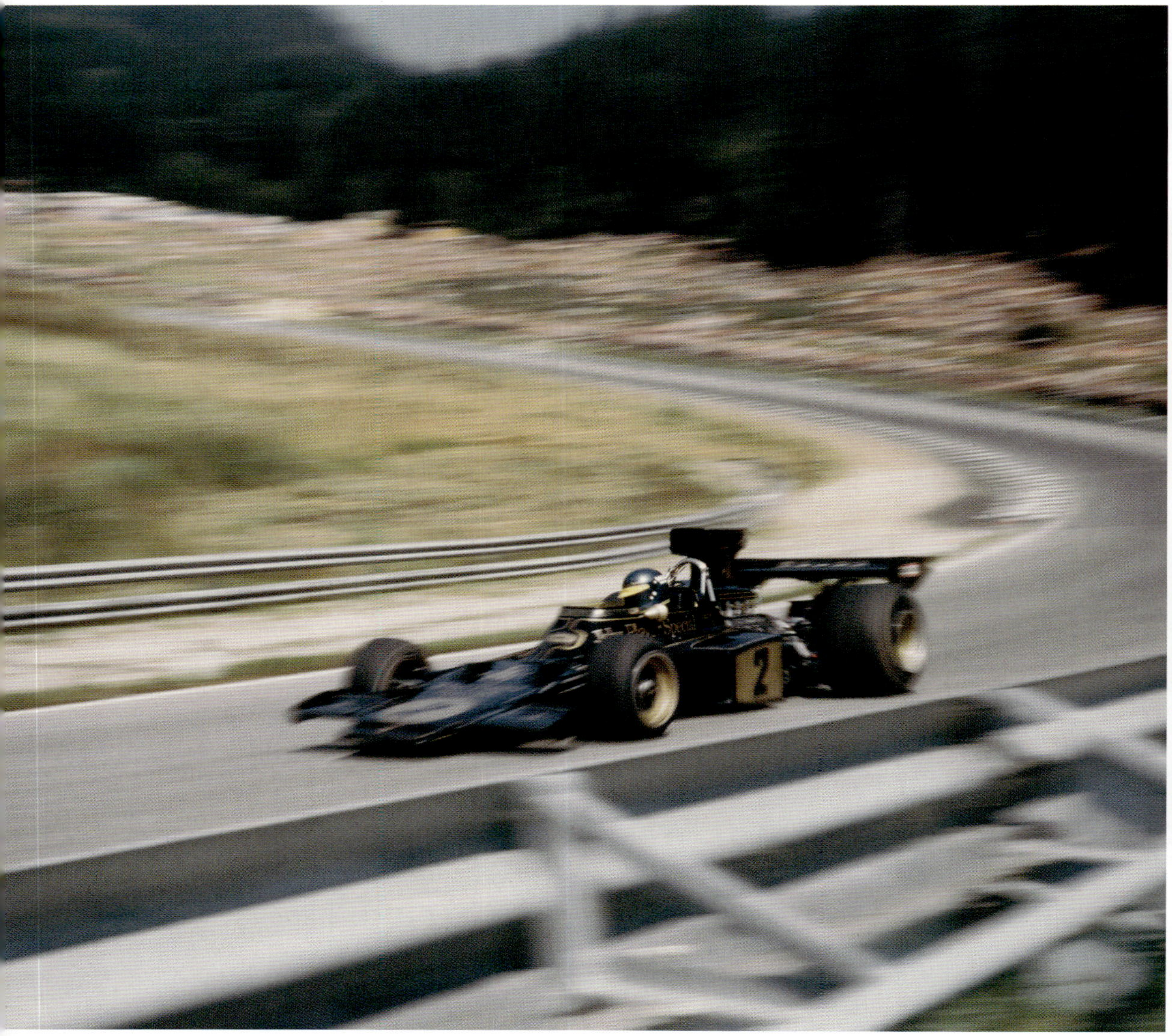

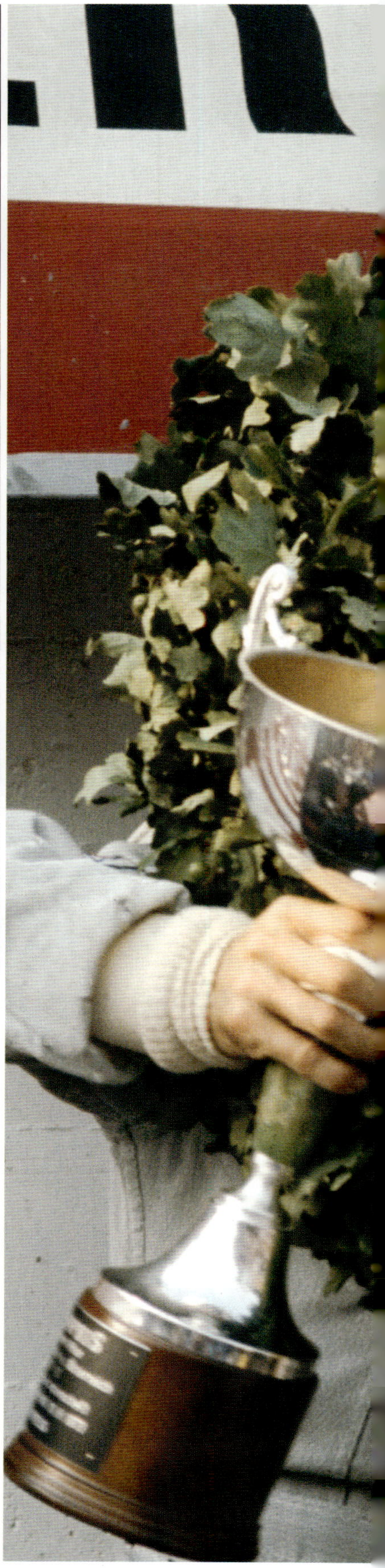

ABOVE An outstanding study of Ronnie and the JPS Lotus 72E on their way to victory on the magnificent Osterreichring. Emerson Fittipaldi pulled off his first pole position of the season in Austria, 0.39sec quicker than Ronnie, with the McLarens on the second row at a venue where the slow-turn handling virtues of the series-leading Tyrrells delivered no advantage. Emerson was the only Lotus driver with enough points to challenge for the title. After leading for 16 laps, and with their only real challenger, Denny Hulme's McLaren, in pit-lane to replace a detached sparkplug lead, Ronnie loyally moved over for him to take the lead. The black cars maintained 1–2 station until six laps out from the chequer, when Emerson was abruptly halted by a detached fuel-line. Ronnie raced on and crossed the line 9sec ahead of Jackie Stewart.

RIGHT Ronnie seems unimpressed as his huge Austrian Grand Prix laurel wreath is invaded by Jackie Stewart and the third-placed Team Surtees driver, Carlos Pace. Stewart knows that his third World Championship is in the bag. With only three Grands Prix remaining, his lead over Emerson Fittipaldi now stands at 24 points.

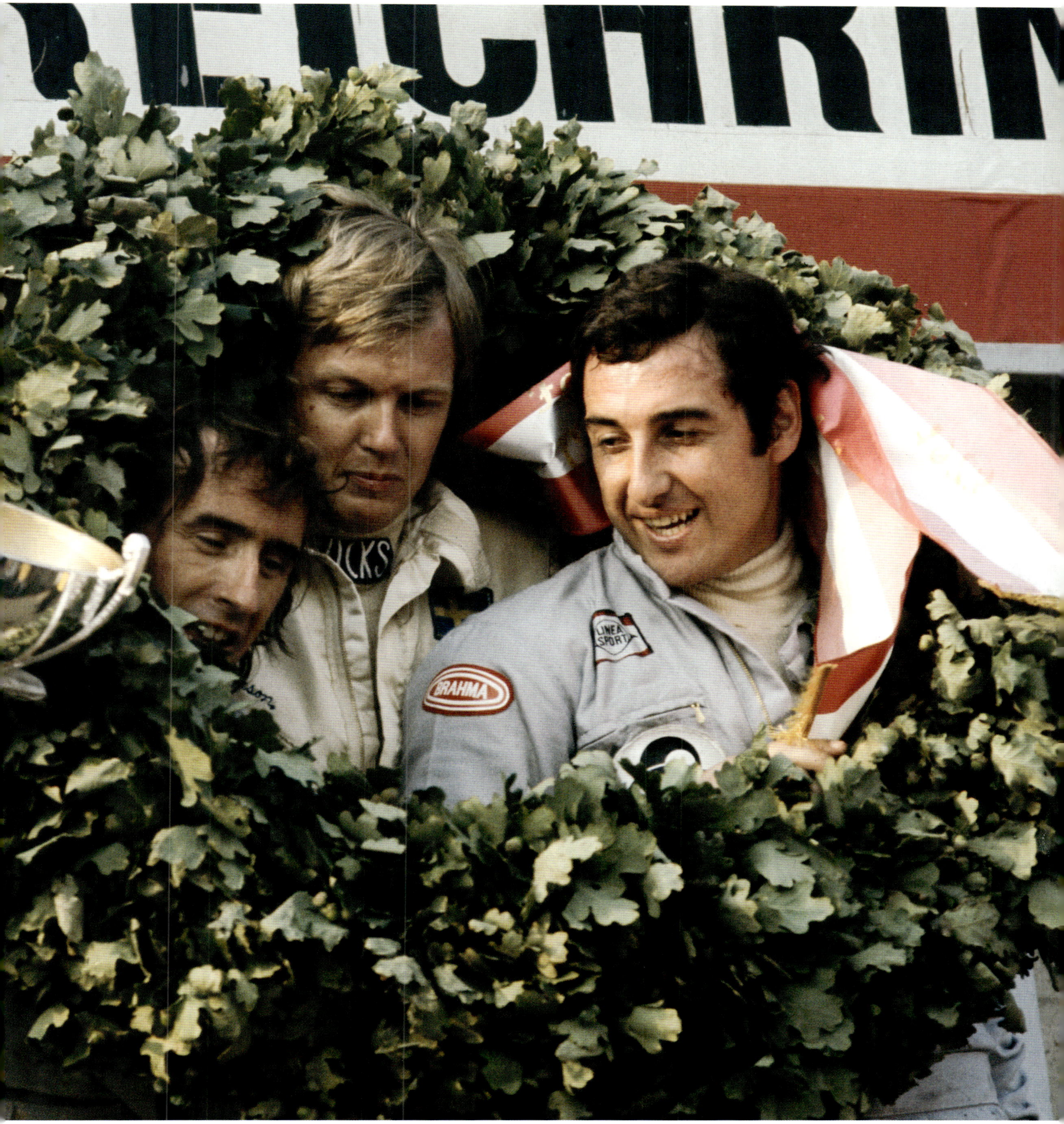
LINEA SPORT
BRAHMA

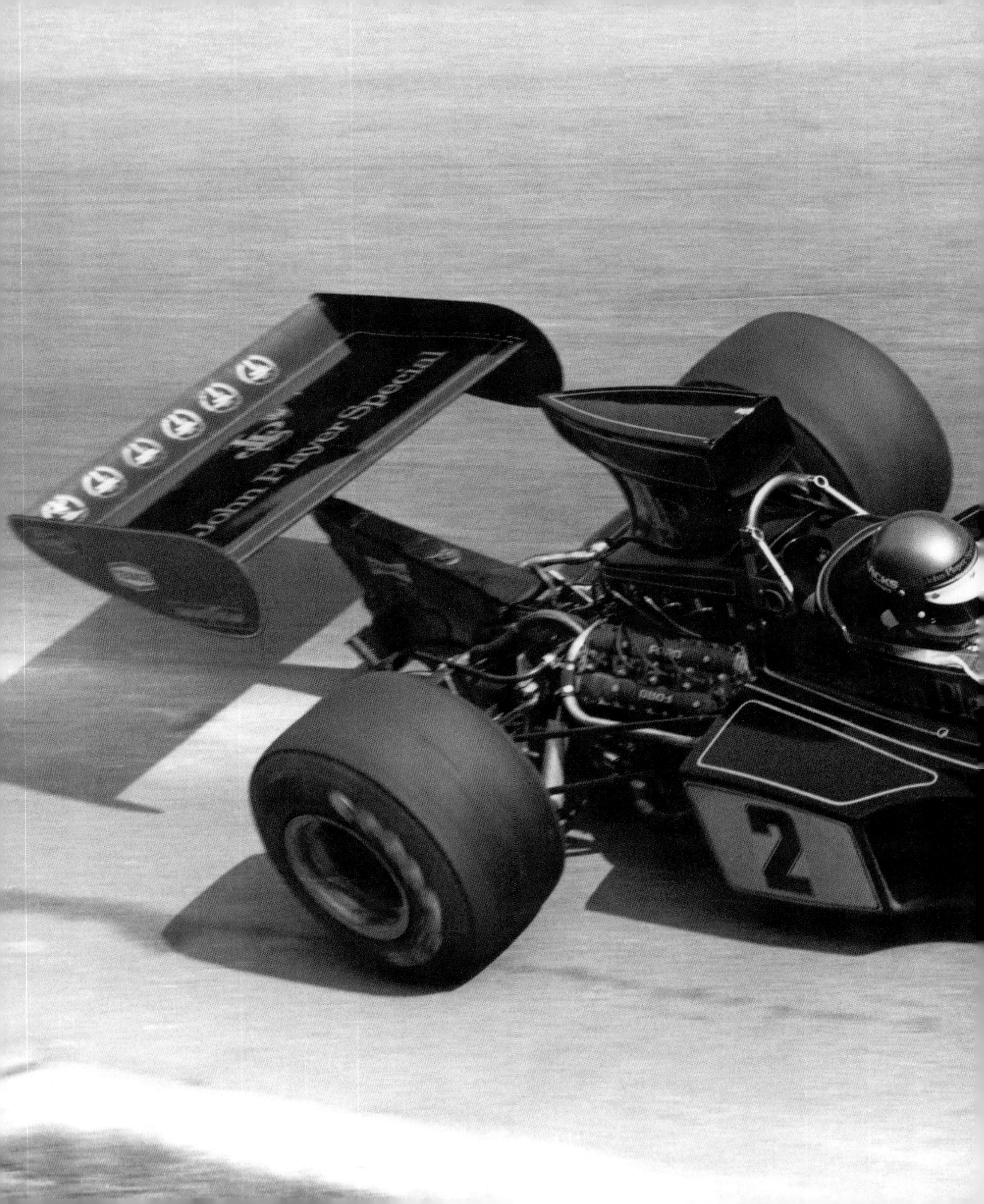
John Player Special
2

The John Player Special drivers, like fighter pilots, liked to boast about their 'kills'. Those JPS stickers on Ronnie's rear wing signify Grand Prix victories. Jackie Stewart needed to finish in the top four in the Italian Grand Prix to clinch the title, so Colin Chapman's instruction was that Ronnie would let Emerson past if the Tyrrell driver was placed fifth or lower. Ronnie was on pole with Emerson fourth, but they had their 1-2 before the end of the opening lap. JYS was delayed by a puncture but fought back with one of the greatest drives of his career, arriving in fourth place with six laps to run. JPS Team Lotus staged a defiant formation finish, line astern, Ronnie still ahead.

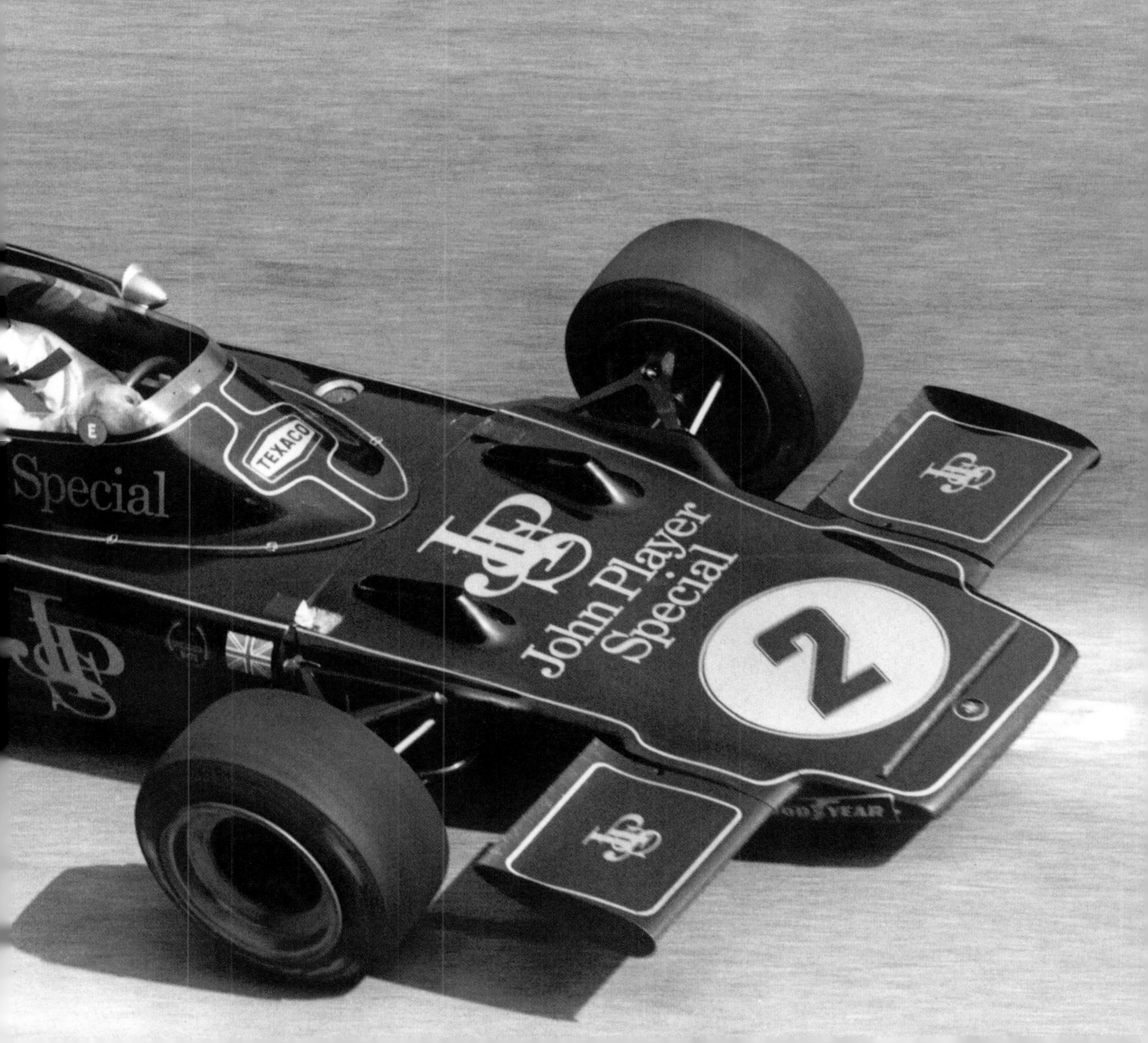

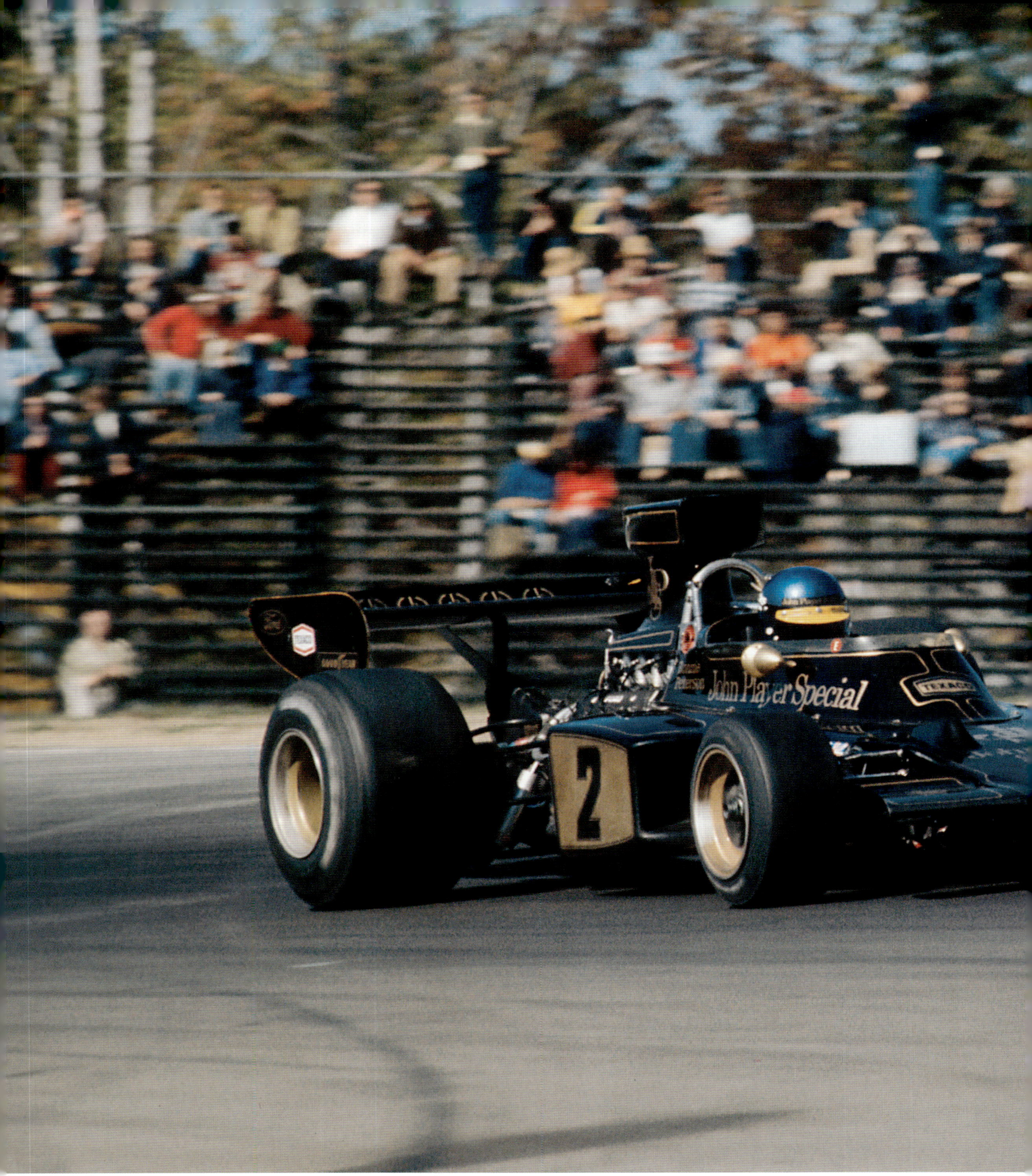
John Player Special
2
TEXACO

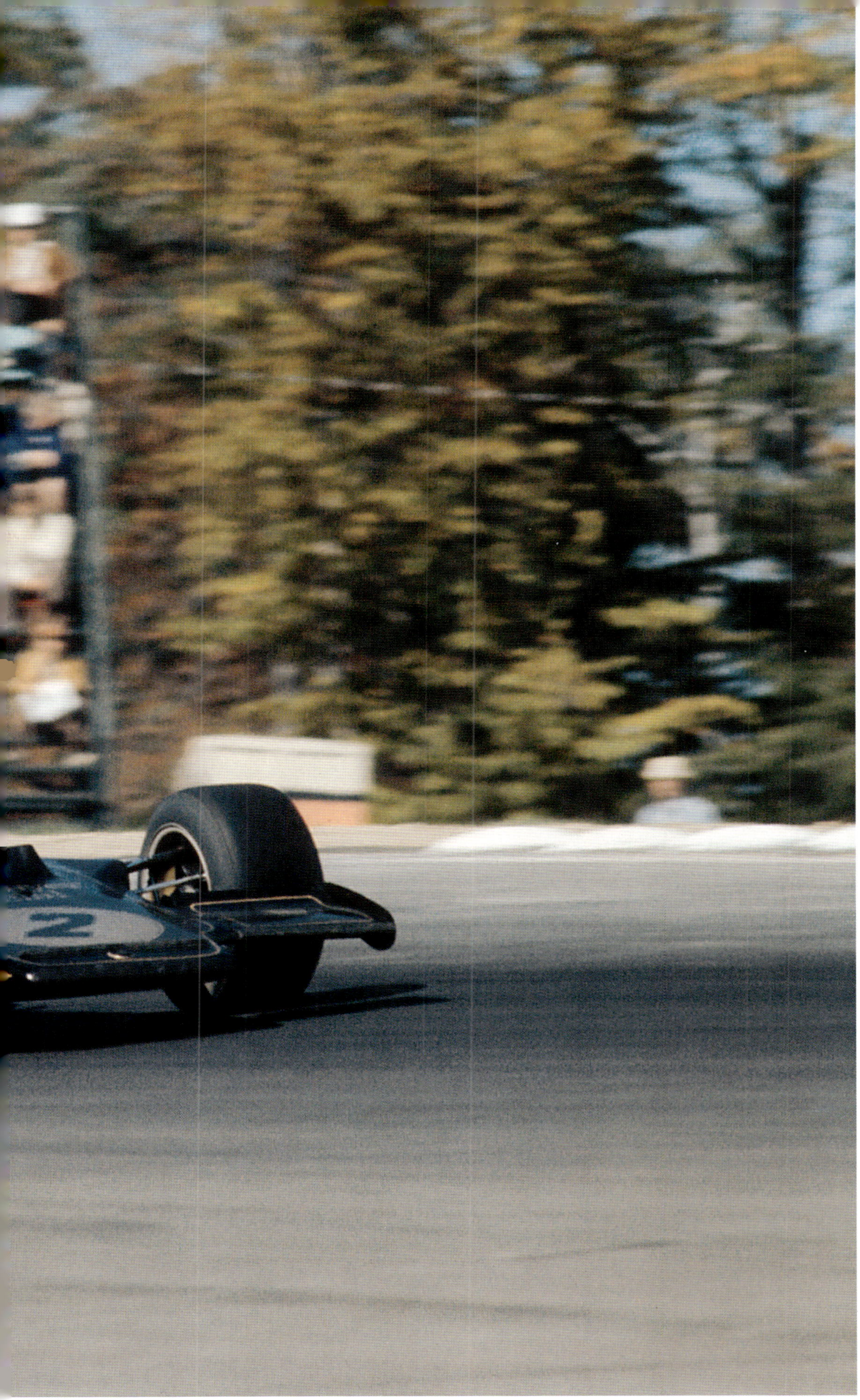

LEFT With the Drivers' championship settled, the North American races that closed the season were for the Constructors' title, with only Lotus and Tyrrell involved. Ronnie had pole position in Mosport Park but was running second behind Niki Lauda's BRM when a burst tyre hurled him into a guardrail. Emerson finished second behind Peter Revson's McLaren, and Jackie Stewart fifth in the best-placed of three Tyrrells, so they left Canada with Lotus ahead 83–82. As it transpired, this was enough, because Elf Team Tyrrell sadly withdrew from the finale here at Watkins Glen when François Cevert lost his life in an accident during practice. Ronnie scored a narrow victory over an inspired James Hunt in Hesketh Racing's March 731, with Emerson sixth after a tyre stop.

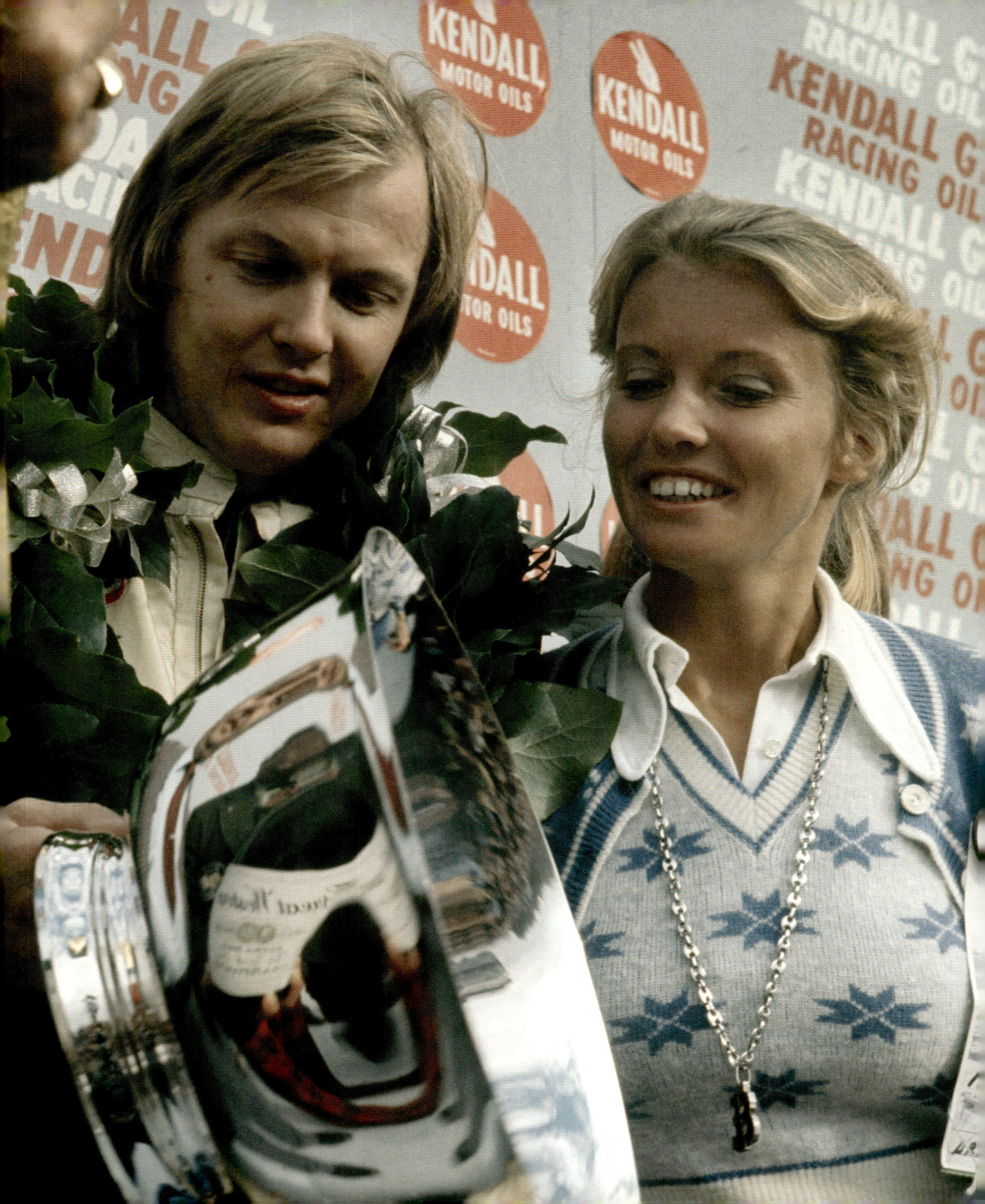
KENDALL
MOTOR OILS
KENDALL
MOTOR OILS
KENDALL
MOTOR OILS
RACING OILS

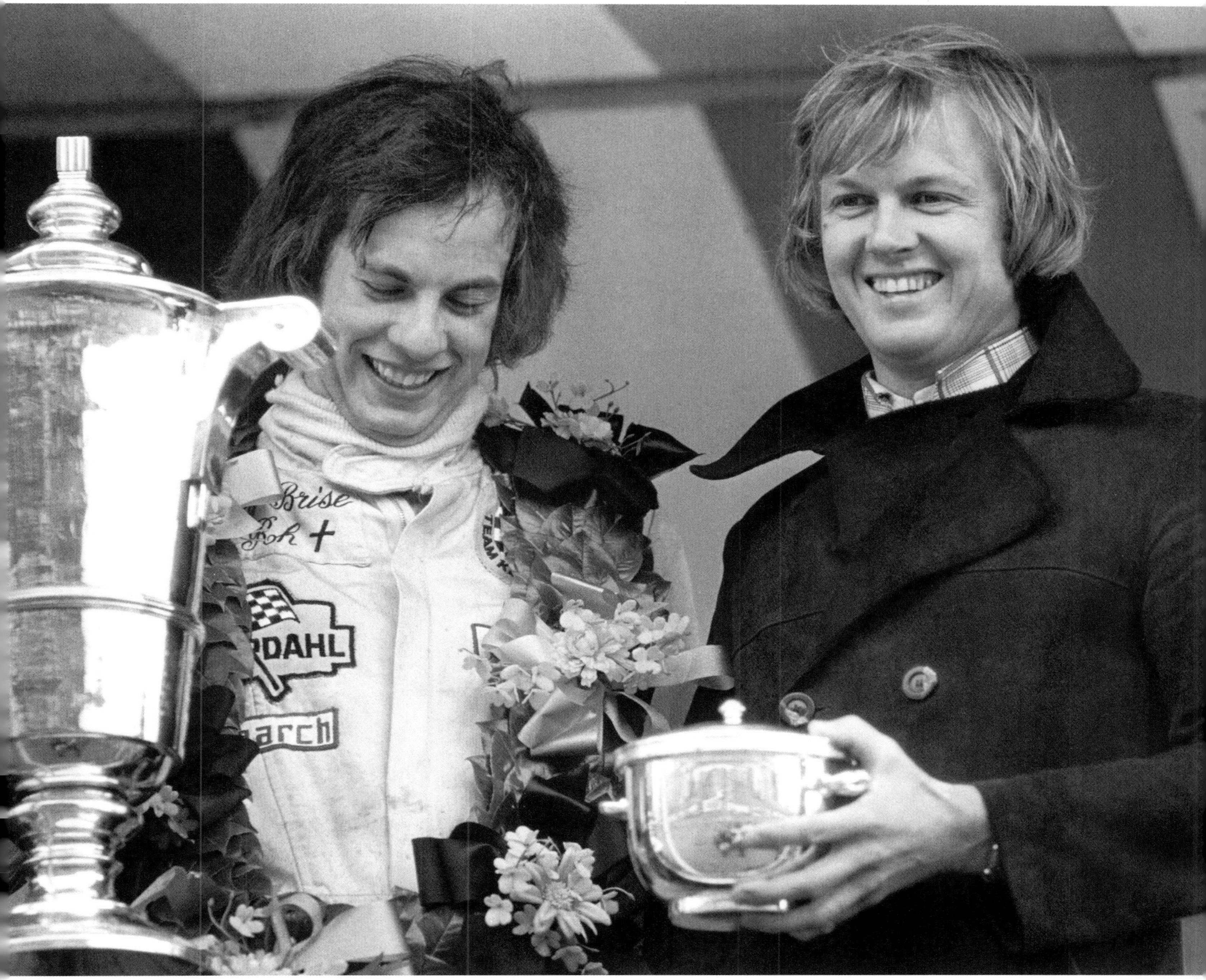

LEFT Ronnie and Barbro on the podium together after his hard-won success in the United States Grand Prix that closed the season. It was his fourth victory (to Emerson Fittipaldi's three) but it left him three points shy of the runner-up position in the World Championship.

ABOVE Ronnie was the guest of honour at Brands Hatch for the Motor Show 200 meeting in October, when he presented the John Player British Formula 3 Championship trophy to Tony Brise. Ronnie had been an F3 champion only four seasons before. Now he was a superstar. The gifted Brise was going exactly the same way but, two years later, would lose his life in an airplane accident returning from a test session at Paul Ricard with Graham Hill and three other members of his Formula 1 team.

1974

THREE VICTORIES BUT IT IS NOT ENOUGH

Ronnie had intruded on Emerson Fittipaldi's territory at Team Lotus throughout 1973, and was installed for a second season. And Fittipaldi had had enough of the fragility of Colin Chapman's Formula 1 cars. He departed Team Lotus after four years, and was replaced by the declining Jacky Ickx. The team did not start testing its new car, the Lotus 76, until after its return from the South American races, and its complexity generated a formidable job-list that would have been beyond the capabilities of any team once the season was under way. After only three Grands Prix, the new car was discarded, and Ronnie never raced it again. In a season that produced seven different winners, only he and Fittipaldi won three times. And Emerson became the World Champion once again with the reliable McLaren M23...

RIGHT After struggling manfully with the overly complex new Lotus 76, Ronnie and Jacky Ickx persuaded Team Lotus principal Colin Chapman to revert to the faithful 72E for the Monaco Grand Prix. Pictured just as the car goes light on the downhill exit of Casino Square, Ronnie qualified third behind the Ferraris, and went on to land one of the most memorable victories of his career.

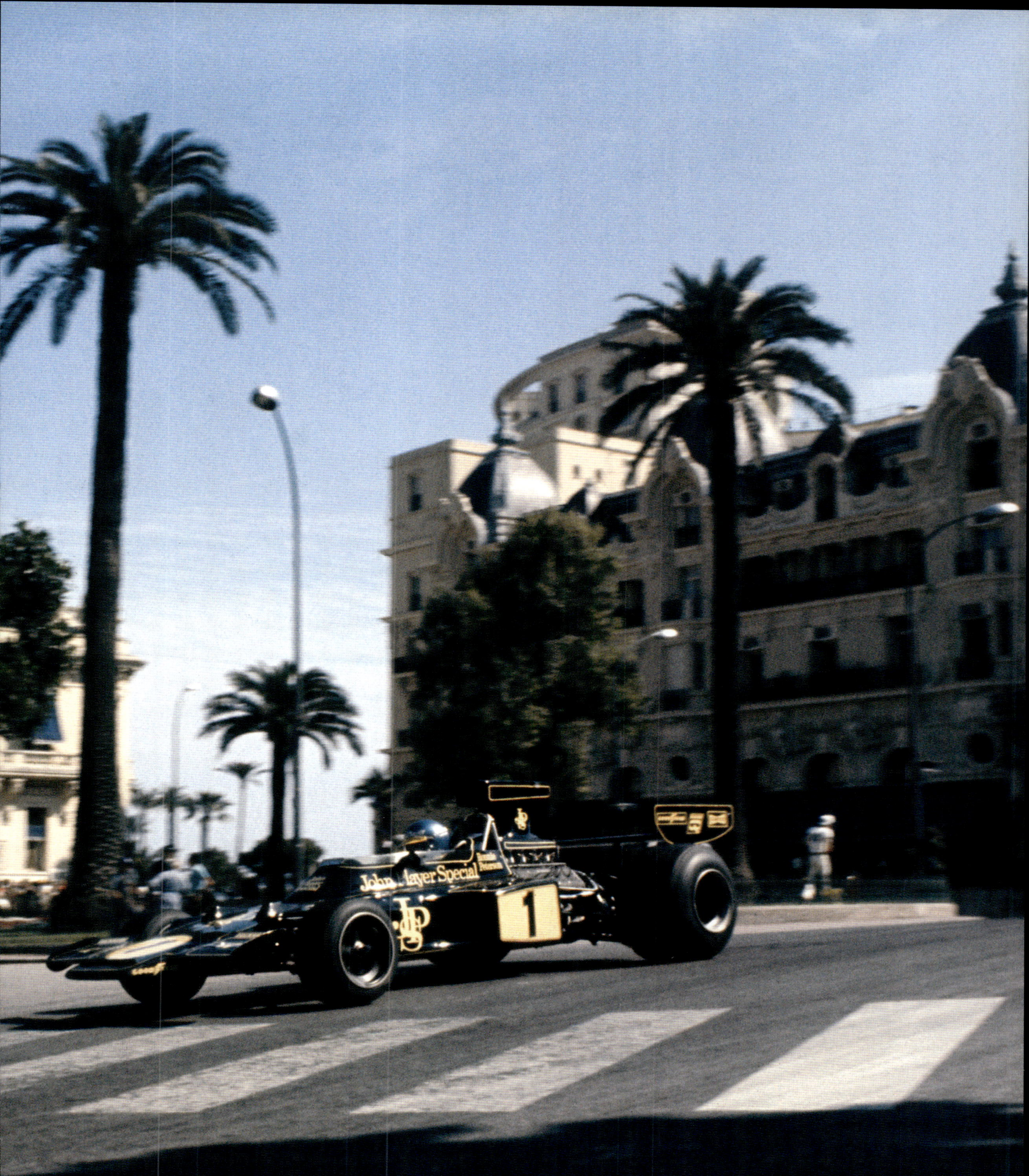

John Player Special
1

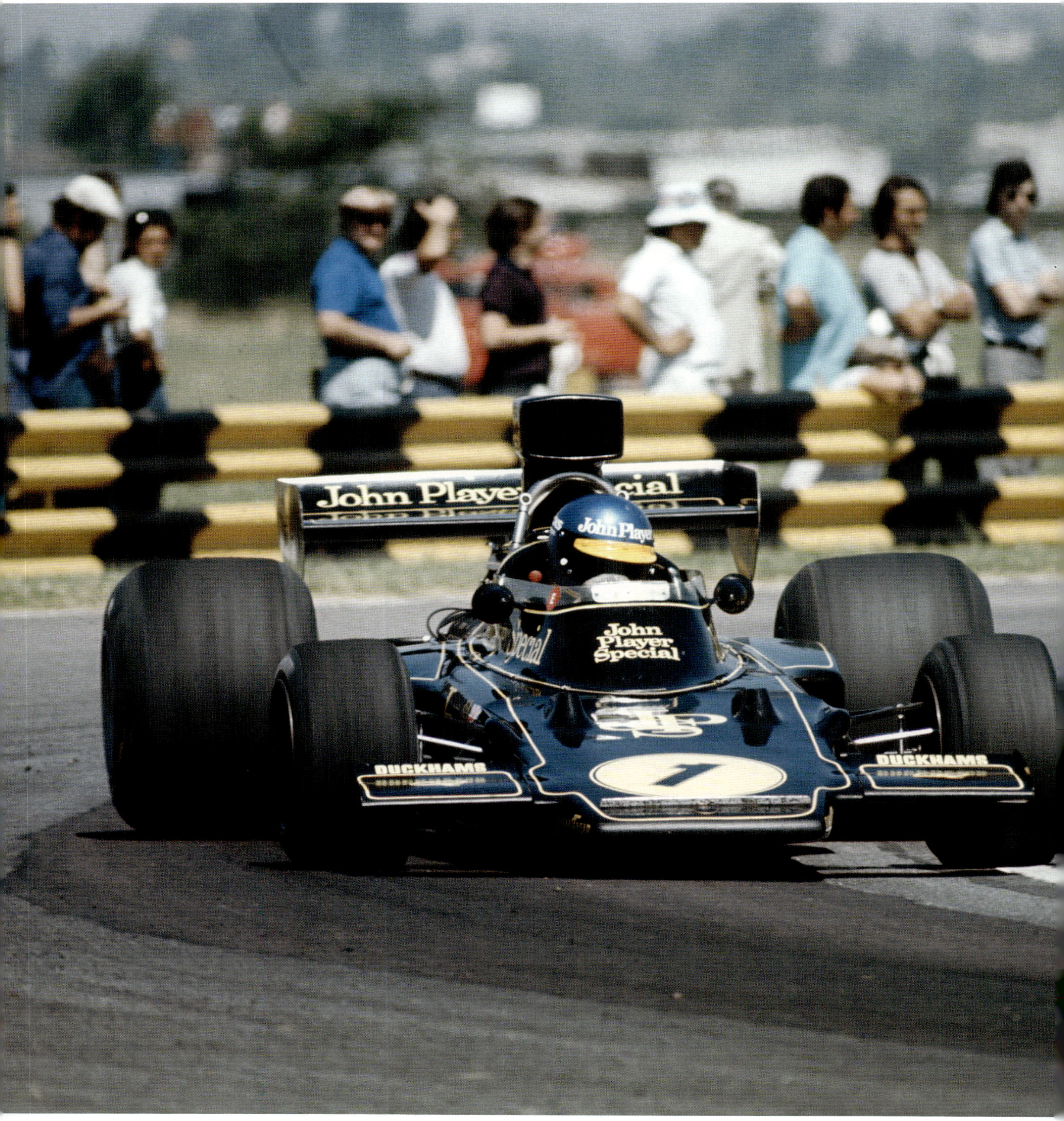
John Player Special
John Player
John Player Special
DUCKHAMS
DUCKHAMS
1

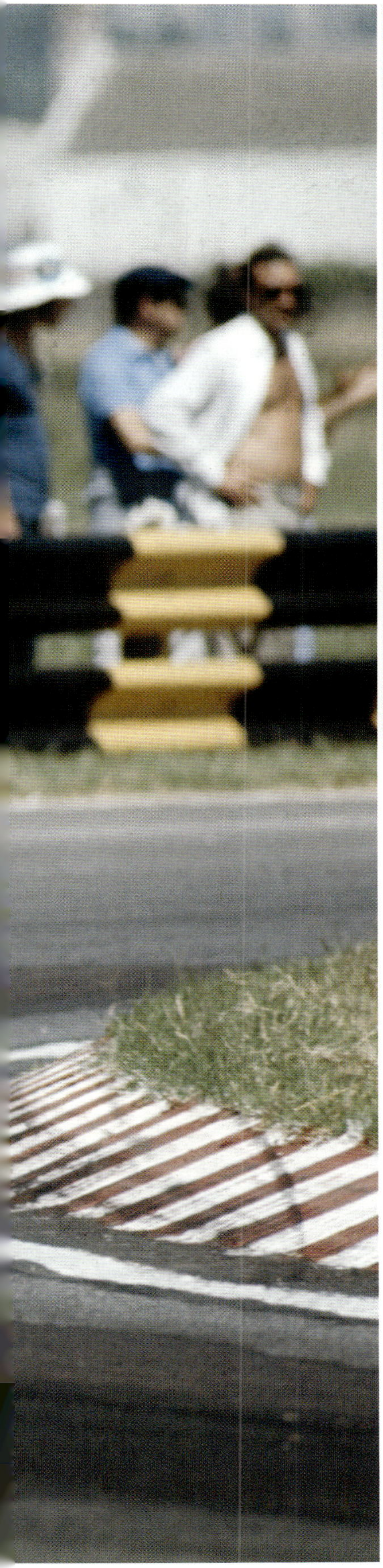

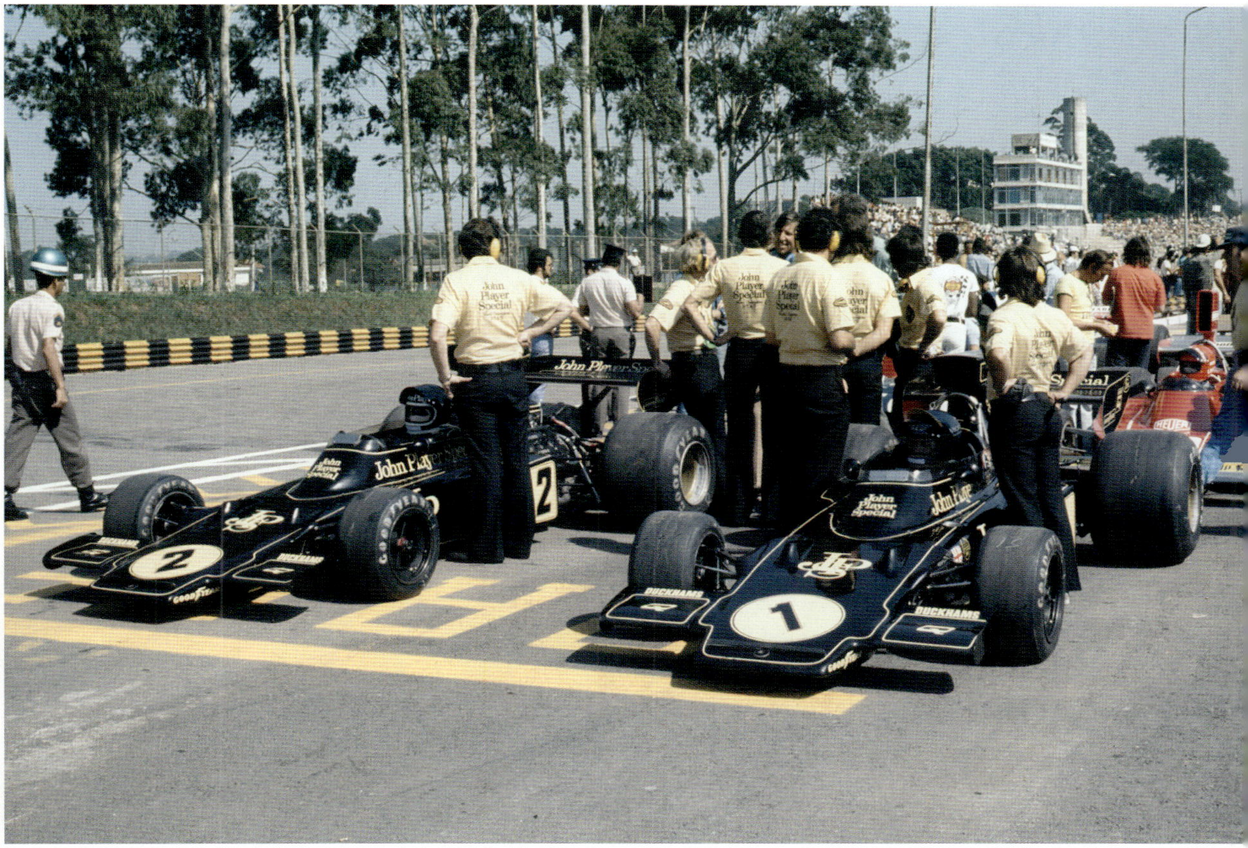

LEFT The season began with another Peterson pole position, but Ronnie did not meet President Peron on the podium. He led from the standing start in Buenos Aires under challenge from James Hunt in the Hesketh March who – as at Oulton Park two years before – was suckered into a spin as soon as he challenged Ronnie for the lead. But a loose battery pack and fading brakes sent the Lotus steadily down the field, and later a pitstop for new tyres left Ronnie 13th and last. Jacky Ickx's Lotus début was halted by a transmission failure and clearly the team was ready for a new, more reliable car. This race was dominated by local hero Carlos Reutemann's new Brabham BT44 until a loose pluglead caused a misfire and ran him out of fuel on the very last lap. Denny Hulme won for McLaren, and the emerging Ferrari team was next with Niki Lauda and Clay Regazzoni.

ABOVE John Player Team Lotus in the assembly area at Interlagos before the Brazilian Grand Prix. The Lotus 72Es qualified fourth and fifth, Ronnie ahead. In the race, Ronnie had a narrow lead over Emerson Fittipaldi's McLaren until the local hero suddenly took over on the 16th lap – Ronnie was headed to pit-lane with a deflating rear tyre. He rejoined 10th and could only recover sixth place before the end.

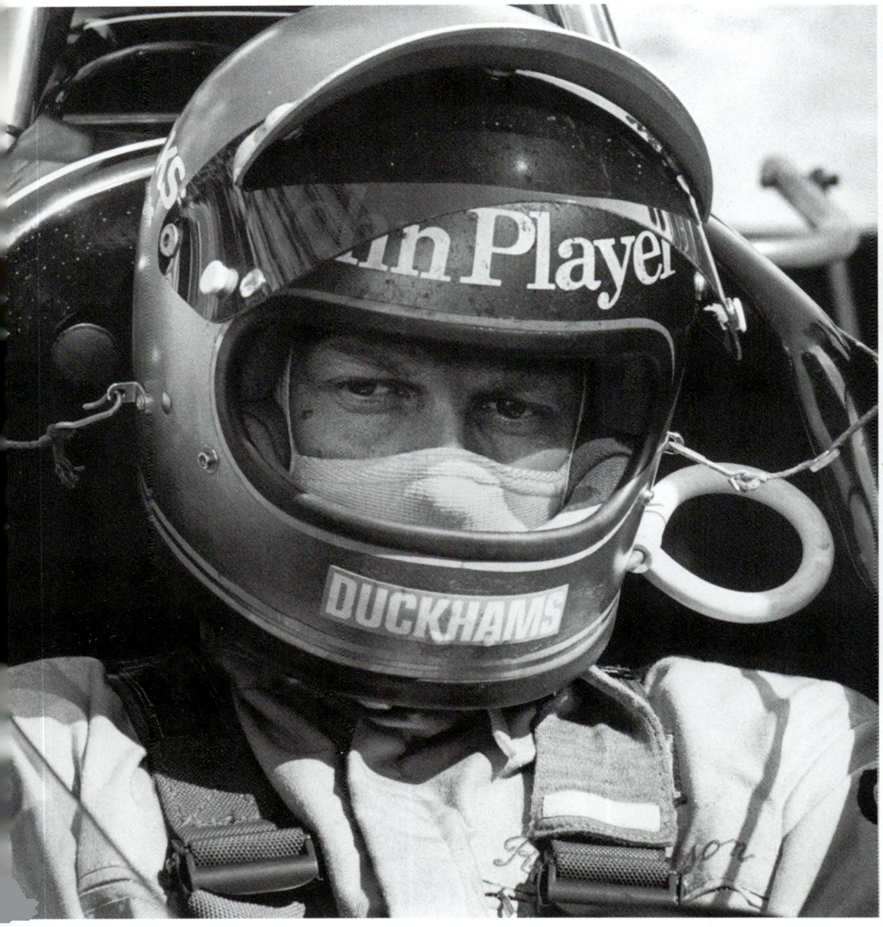

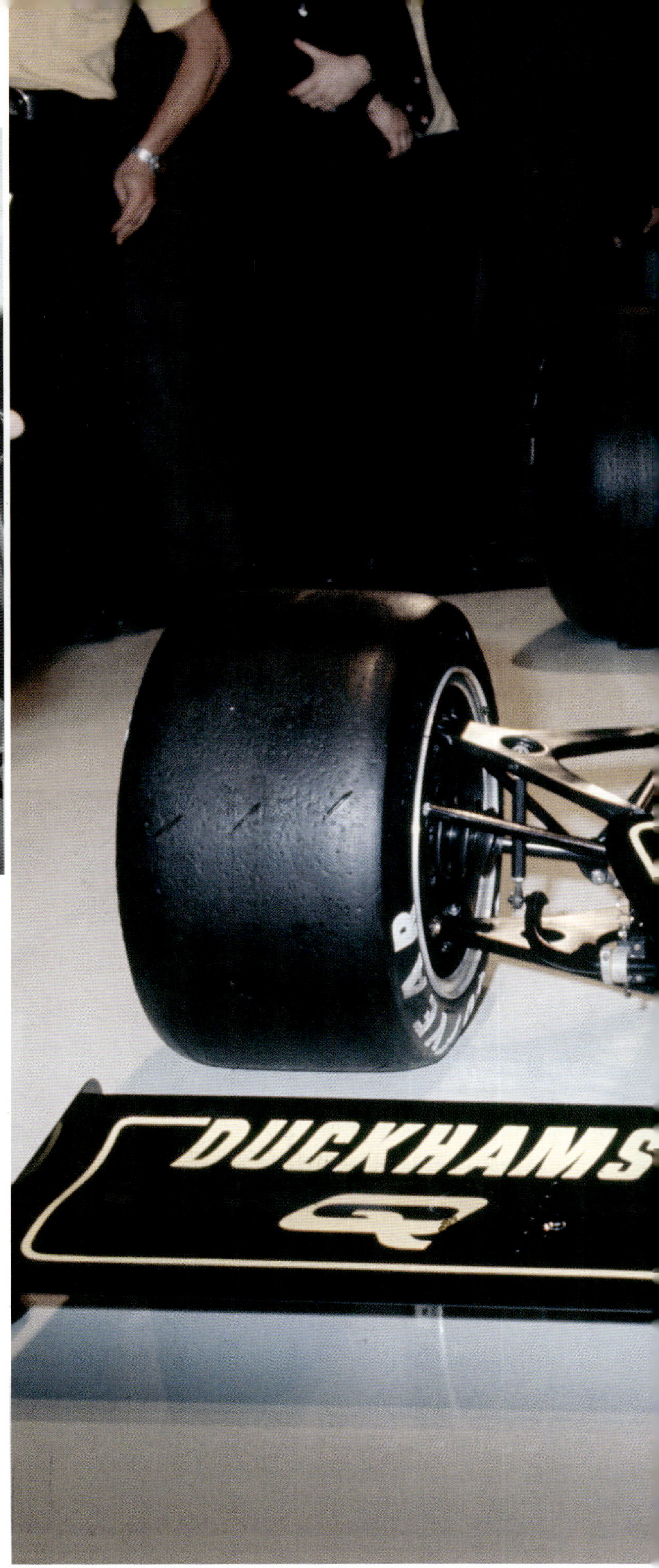

ABOVE In the cockpit of the Lotus 72E, preparing for the Brazilian Grand Prix. Note the lanyards attaching his helmet to the cockpit sides: lateral G-forces were already a problem for the drivers this early in the development of high-downforce, slick-tyred cars.

RIGHT Two weeks after the Brazilian Grand Prix, Colin Chapman summoned his drivers to London for the launch of the new JPS/9 (Lotus 76), which was preceded by a shakedown at Silverstone. The build of the new car was seriously hampered by the imposition of a three-day working week in Britain, caused by the energy crisis. The 76 was supposed to be 200kg lighter than the five-year-old 72. Chapman had asked Ralph Bellamy to retain the basic layout of the 72 but had given him a free hand on design details. Bellamy came up with a chisel-nose, sharply angled sidepods housing radiators either side of the engine, twin rear aerofoils, variable-rate suspension and a trick electro-hydraulic clutch control mechanism. Activated with a button on top of the gearlever, this was intended to free up the driver's left foot, and there were two brake pedals as well as a backup clutch pedal, the throttle and a footrest. In circumstances demanding that Lotus urgently acquired the virtue of durability, it all seemed rather elaborate.

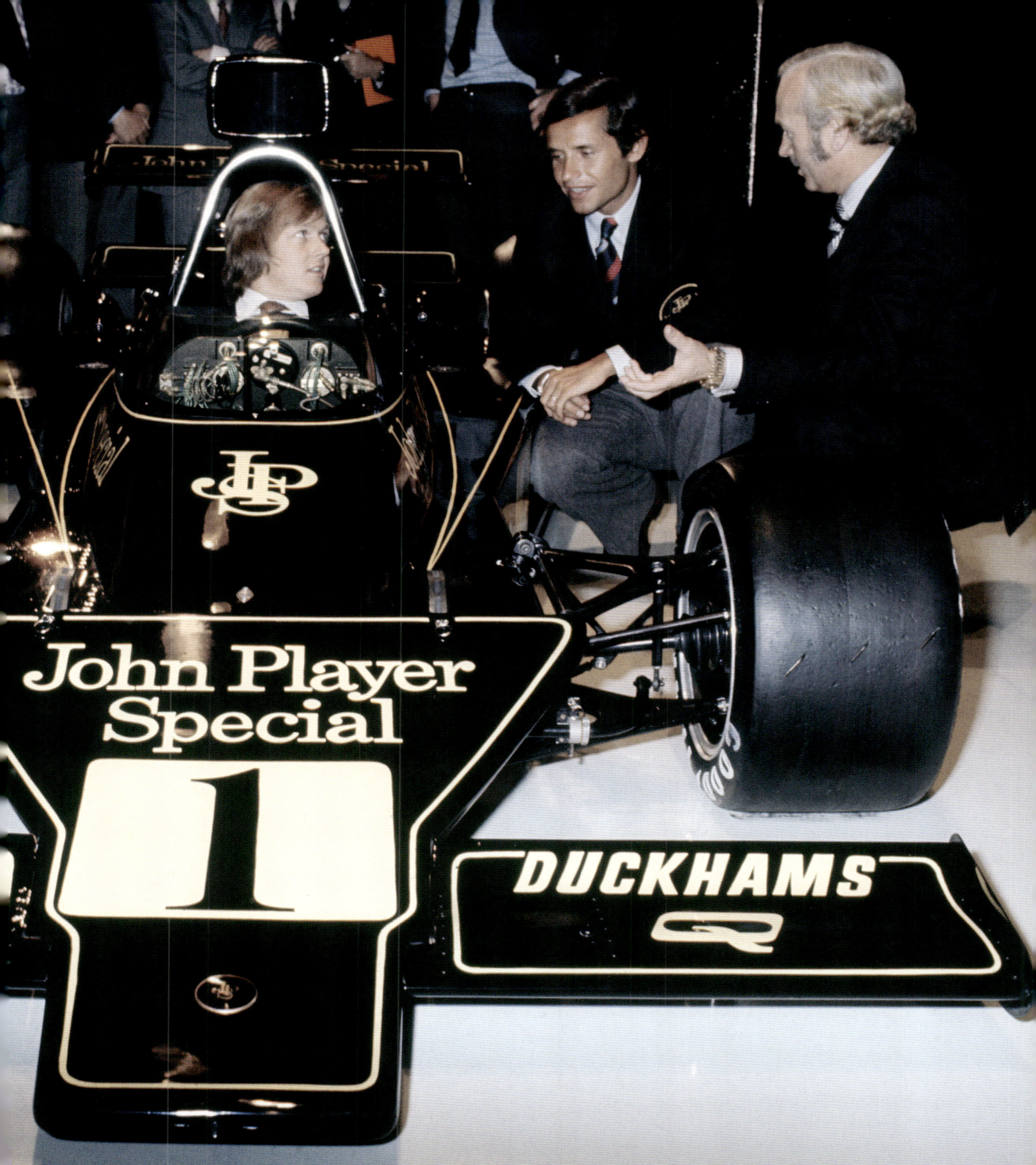
John Player
Special
1
DUCKHAMS
Q

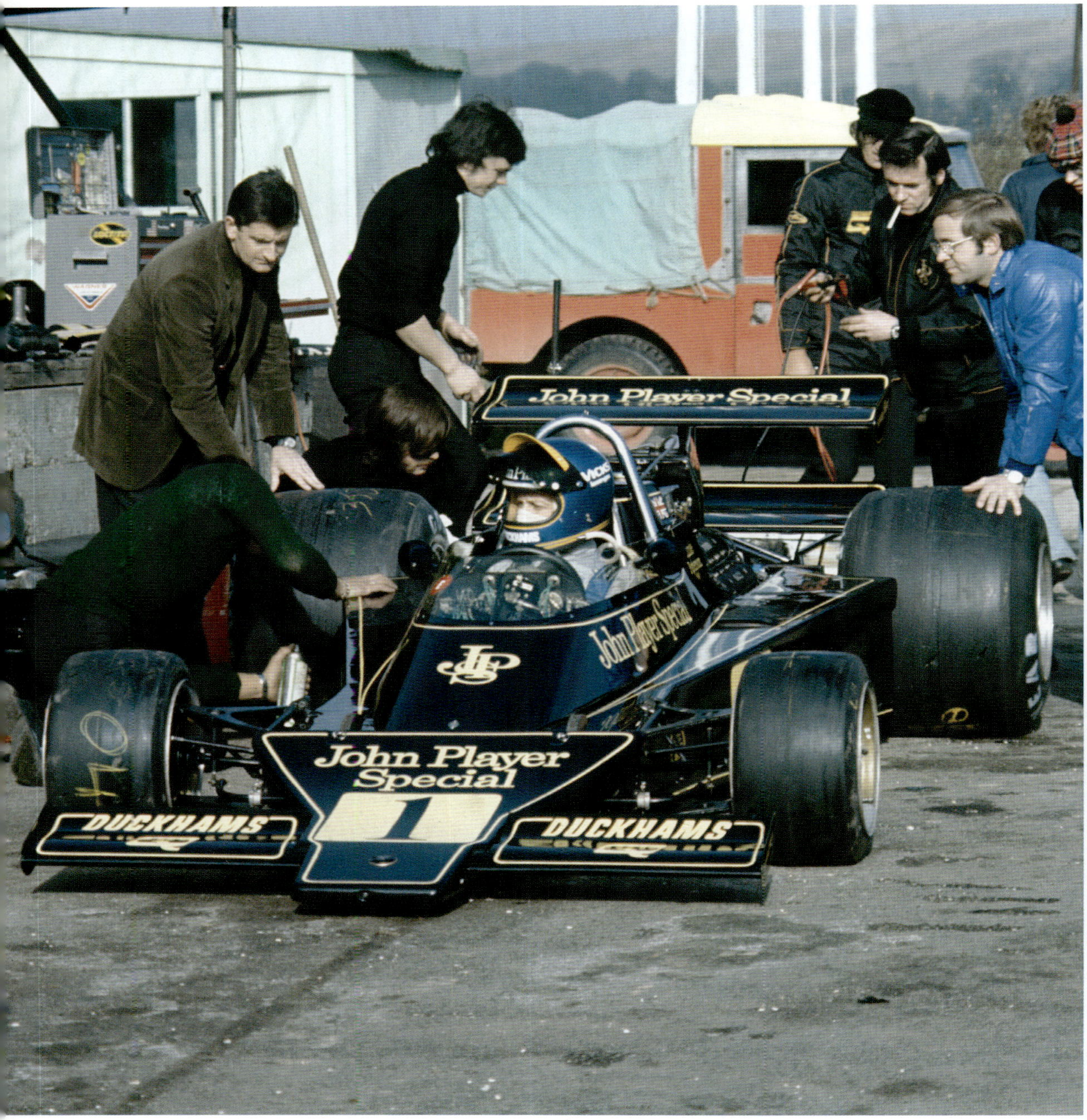

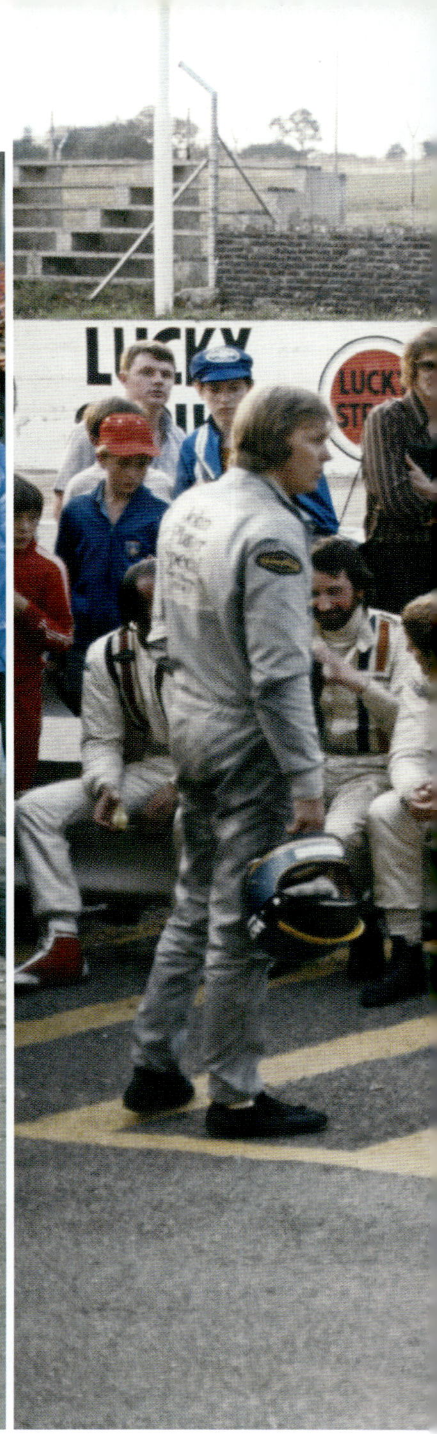

ABOVE The Lotus 76 was taken straight from the launch for track-testing at Goodwood, where Ronnie got himself used to the intricacies of the design and came to like the facility for left-foot braking. Car development was never his forte. In fact, his ability to drive round or through set-up problems often perplexed the Lotus engineering team. But he began the job of sorting the new John Player Special as best he could, and came away from Goodwood believing that the handling deficiencies would be rectified by detail work with the settings.

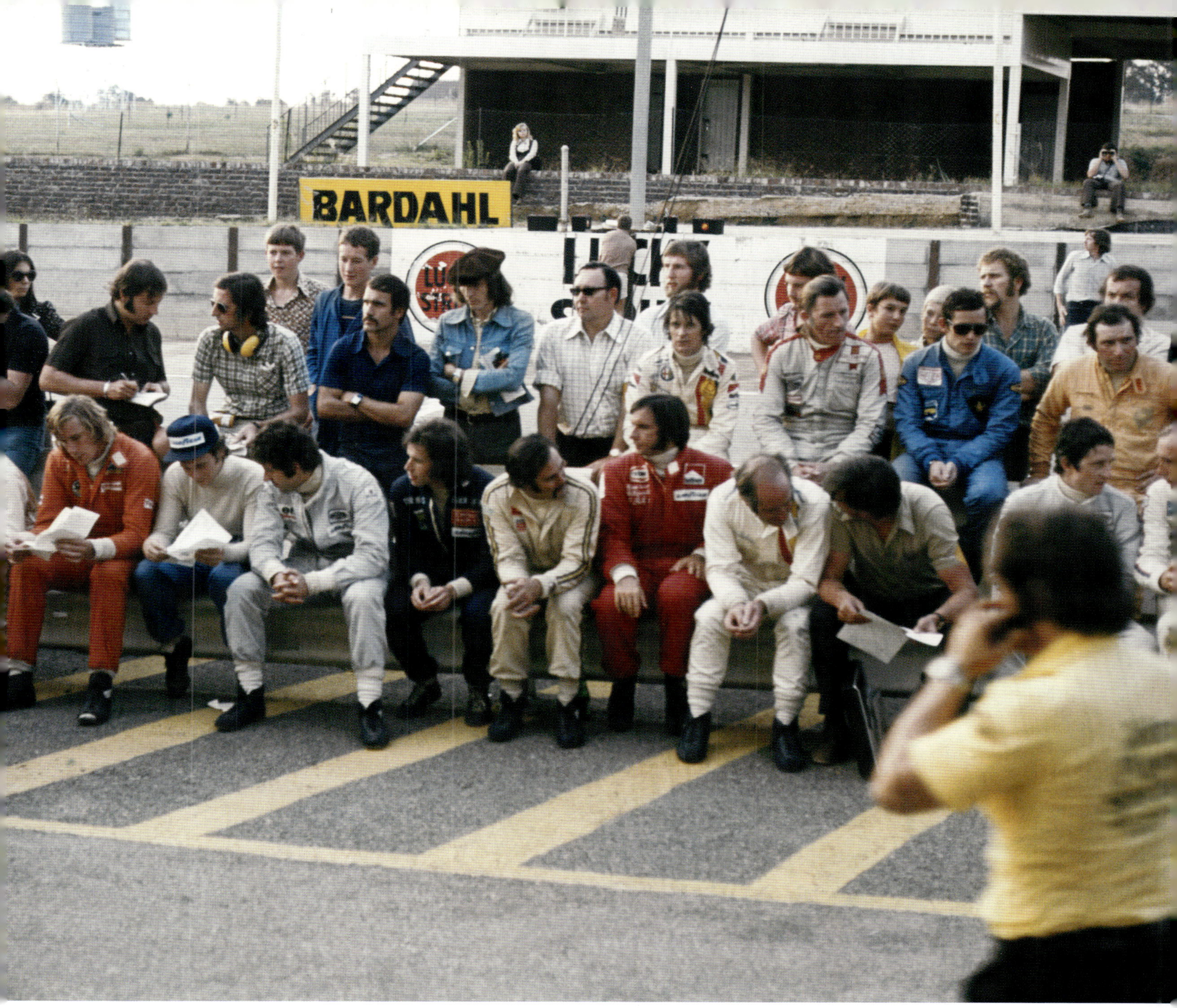

ABOVE Musical chairs at Kyalami – and Ronnie is the last man standing. With the additions of locals, the South African Grand Prix was contested by 27 drivers, and the photograph shows 16 of them. They are (front row, left to right) Mike Hailwood, John Watson, Ian Scheckter, James Hunt, Niki Lauda, Jody Scheckter, Eddie Keizan, Paddy Driver, Emerson Fittipaldi, Denny Hulme, Patrick Depailler and Hans-Joachim Stuck; and (second row, right to left) Vittorio Brambilla, Jacky Ickx, Graham Hill and Arturo Merzario. Missing is poor Peter Revson, the victim of a fatal accident at the track in pre-race testing at the end of the previous week.

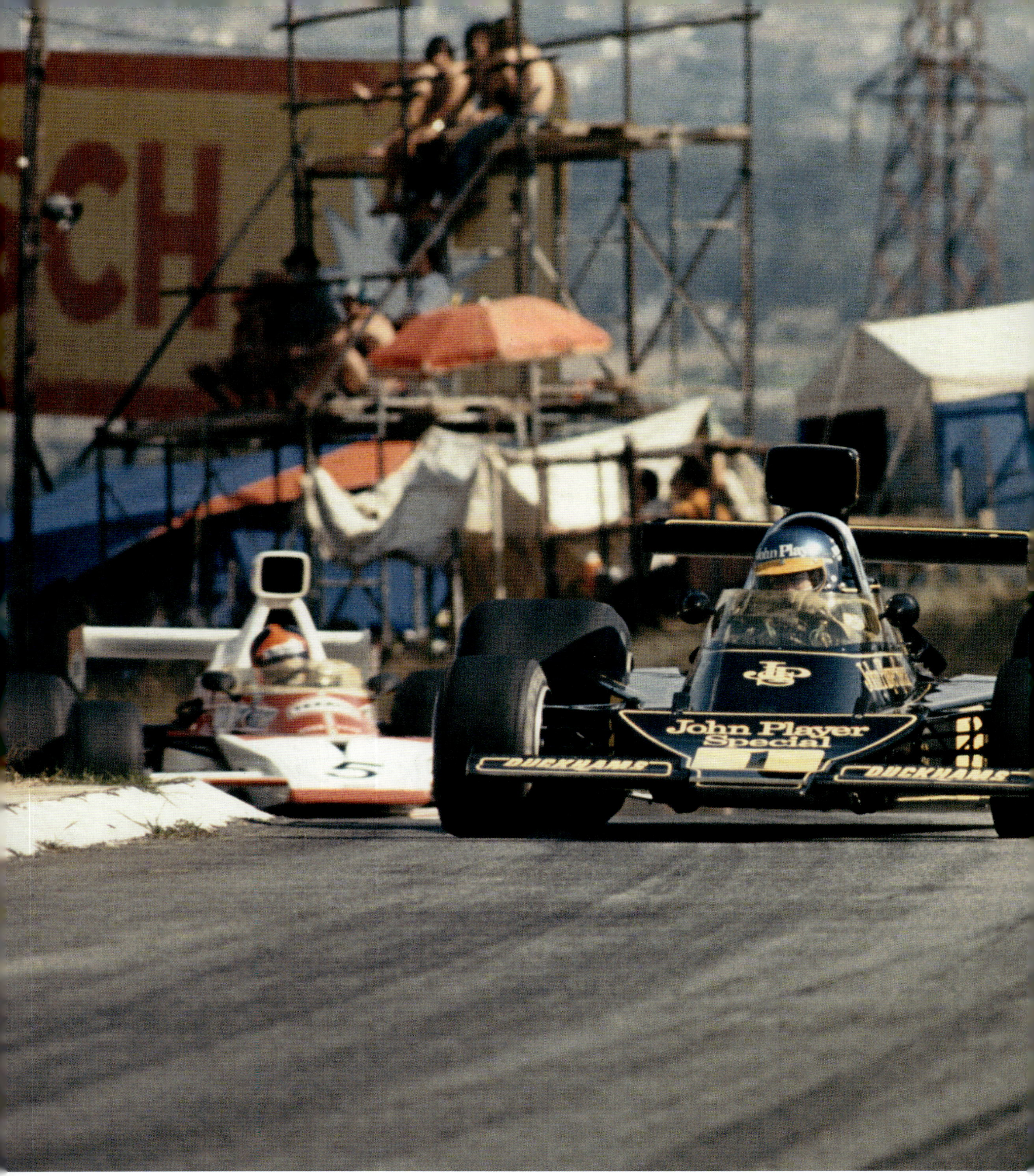
John Player
Special
DUCKHAMS
DUCKHAMS

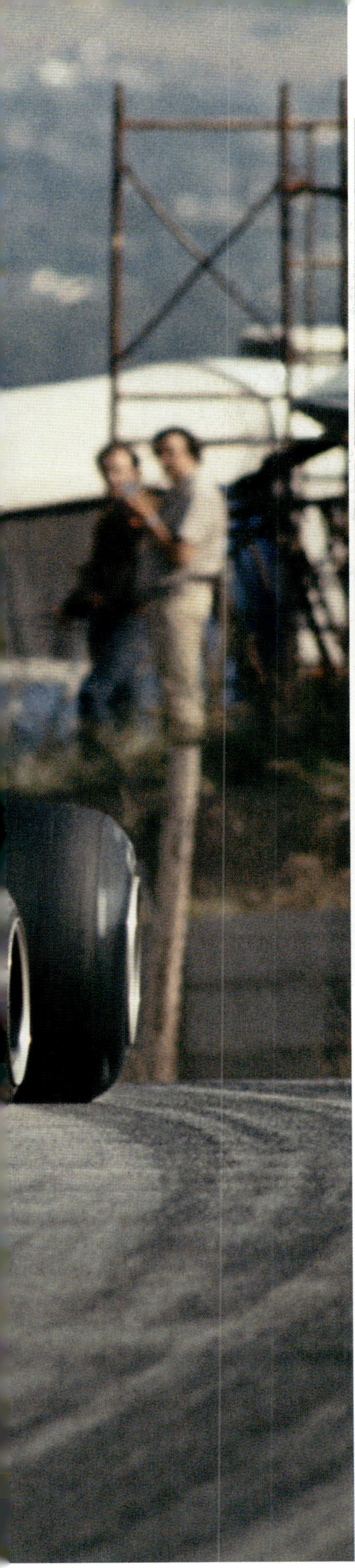

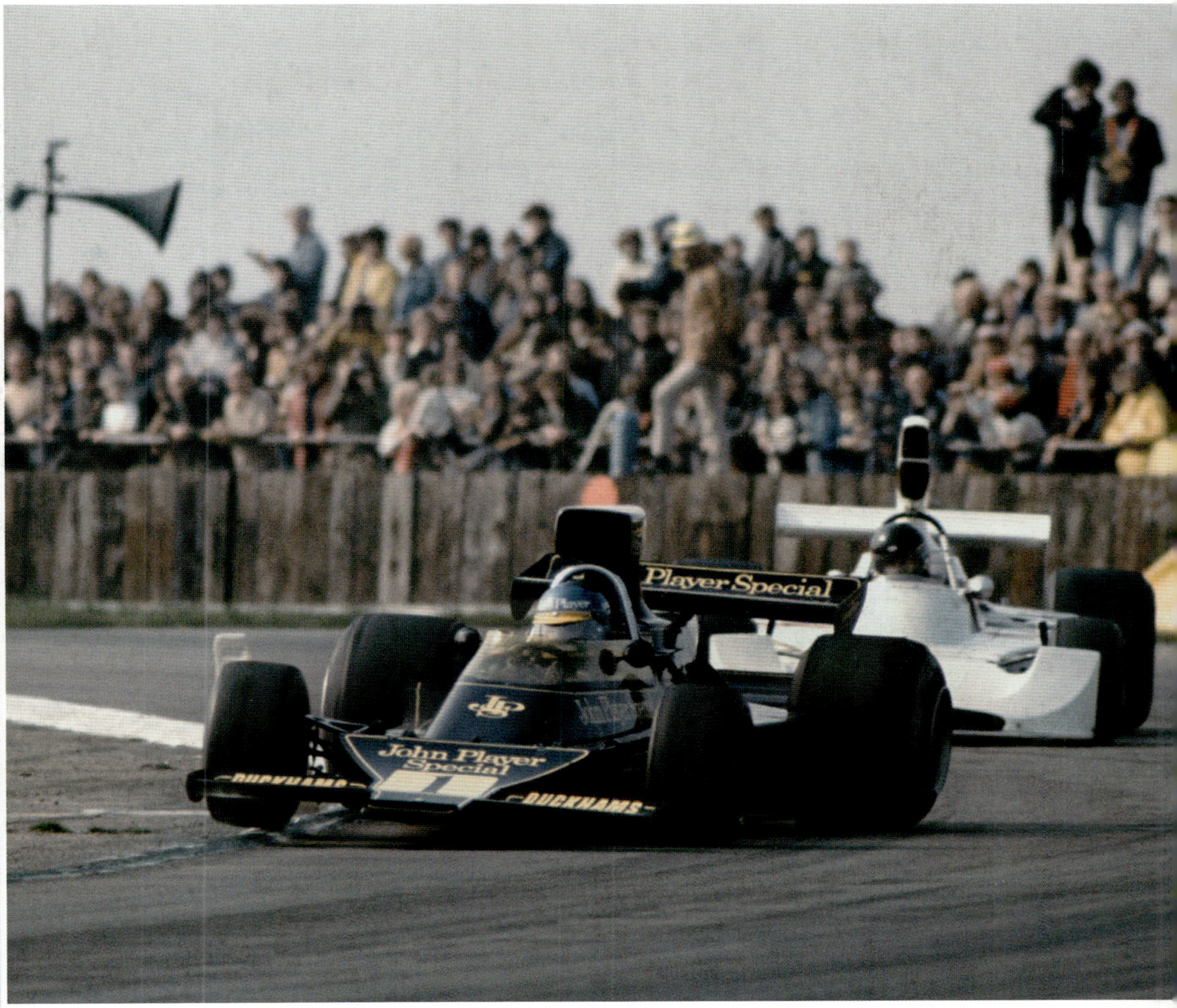

LEFT The début of the Lotus 76 came at Kyalami, a couple of weeks after Jacky Ickx had taken a 72 to victory in the horribly wet Race of Champions at Brands Hatch, making a famous pass at Paddock Hill Bend in wresting the lead from Niki Lauda's Ferrari. In contrast, Johannesburg was dry but John Player Team Lotus had a miserable weekend. The new car's electro-hydraulic clutch activator proved troublesome: in one of the sessions, the clutch button killed the engine. The system was completely removed before race day, but the car's front:rear brake balance defied a satisfactory set-up. Ronnie, pictured ahead of Emerson Fittipaldi's McLaren, could qualify only 16th. The next day, his race endured as far as the first corner. He arrived at Crowthorne with his throttles jammed wide open, all four tyres smoking, and smote the other new Lotus a hefty blow. Jacky Ickx continued but was in and out of the pits before joining him in the paddock 30 laps later.

ABOVE The week after Kyalami, Ronnie was entered in a solo 76 for the International Trophy – and put it on the front row! The car was running with a conventional, three-pedal set-up but, as depicted in the photograph, its handling was dire. This is lap 28 and the left rear tyre is already chunking. Ronnie is about to lose the lead to James Hunt, who had started on pole position with the new Hesketh 308, but had made a poor start. Hunt drove on to a famous victory but Ronnie soon parked the Lotus when he felt the engine seizing up. The team stayed on at Silverstone for some intense track testing and did not leave until Ronnie finally felt they had got it to handle.

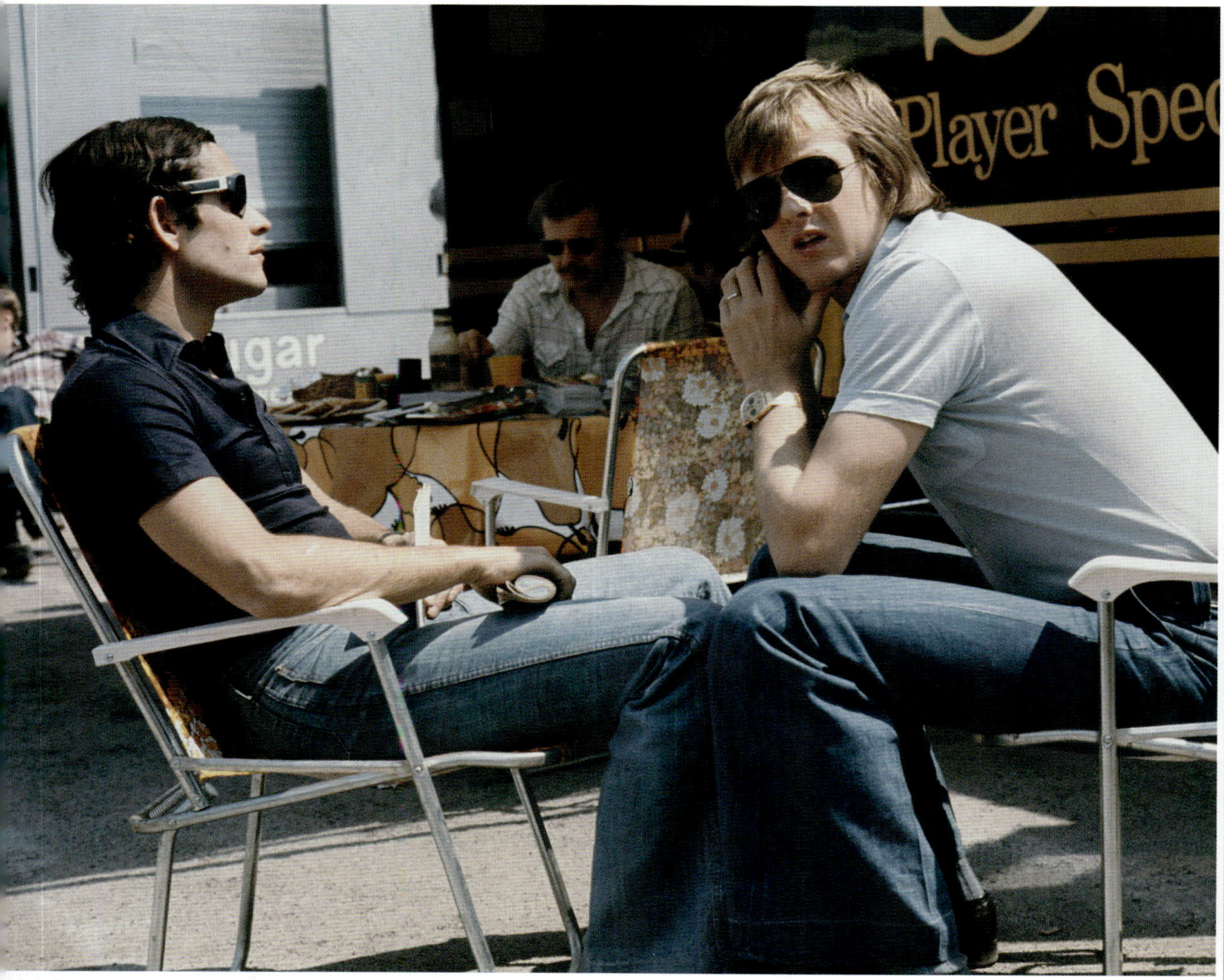

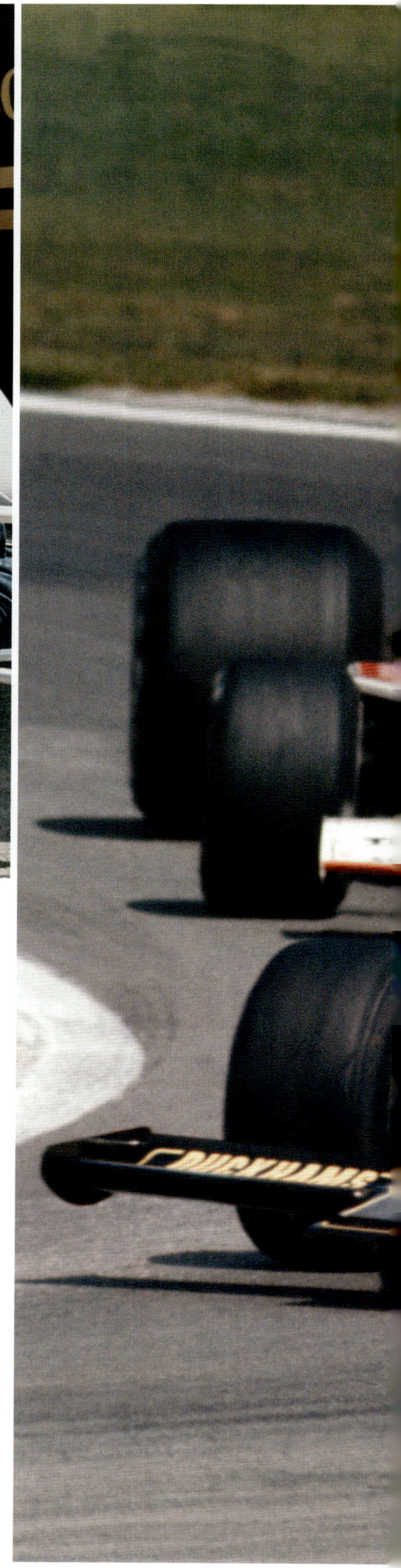

ABOVE With Jacky Ickx in the paddock at Jarama, which was alternating with Barcelona as the venue of the Spanish Grand Prix. Now running the new cars with monoplane rear wings, Ronnie qualified second here behind Niki Lauda's Ferrari, with Ickx fifth. Rain on race day might have brought the race to Ronnie, but it was not to be. He led the first 20 laps, keeping Lauda firmly behind him, with Ickx fourth behind Clay Regazzoni in the other red car. But the rain ceased, and the track surface dried. All stopped for slick tyres but, within a few laps, both the Lotus drivers were out, Ronnie with an overheated DFV and Jacky with a brake fluid leak. The Ferraris finished 1–2.

RIGHT The Lotus 76 wants to spin, but Ronnie is on the case. Emerson Fittipaldi, no doubt relieved to be in the cockpit of a Texaco Marlboro McLaren M23, gets a close-up view of the deficiencies of the new John Player Special during practice on the Nivelles circuit. Fittipaldi won the Belgian Grand Prix after a closely fought race with the Ferraris. Ronnie failed to finish again, the victim this time of a leaking fuel cell after racing in fifth position for 37 laps. Jacky Ickx was off the pace with the other new Lotus and was stopped by a brake system failure.

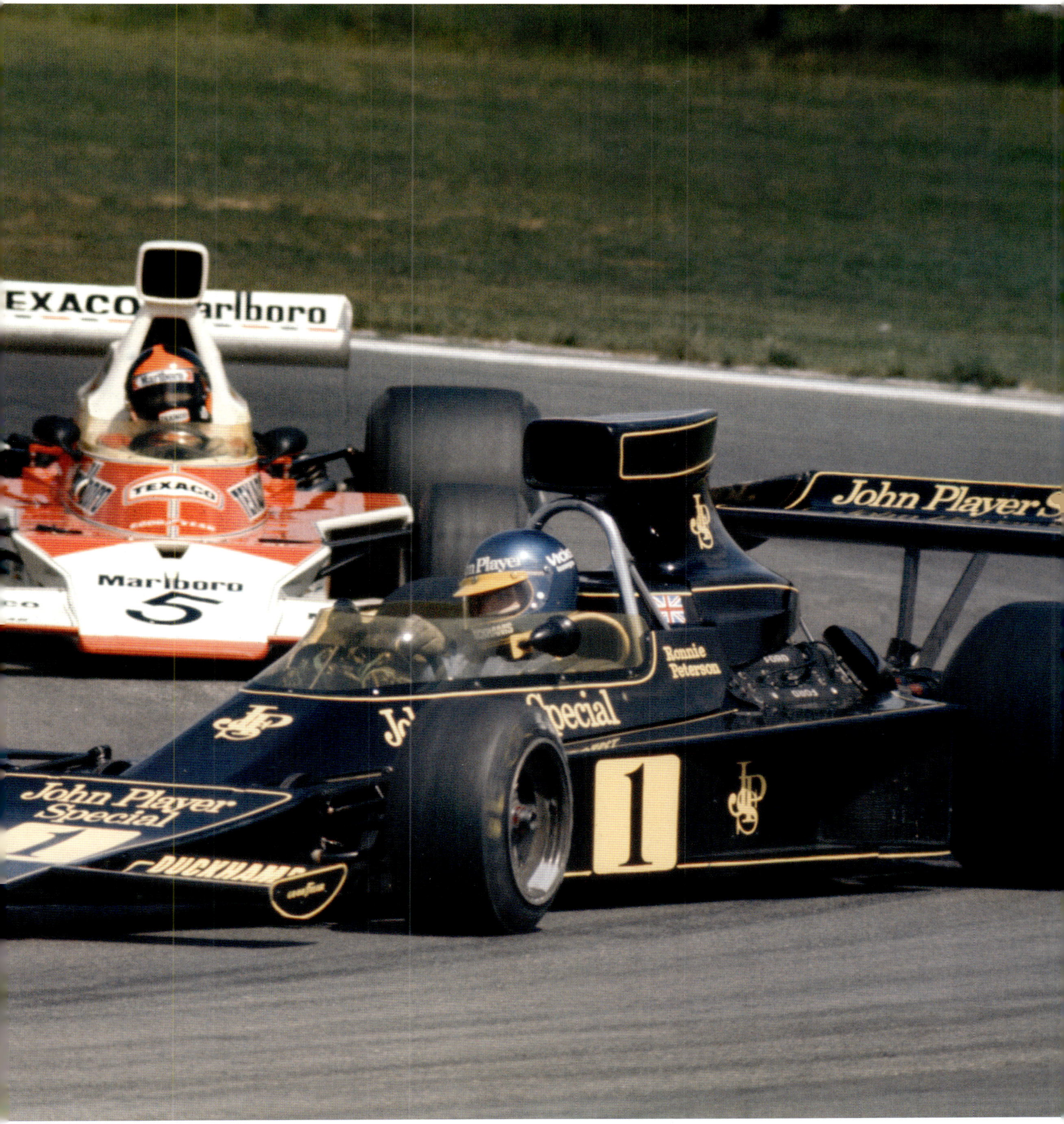
EXACO
arlboro
TEXACO
Marlboro
5
John Player S
Ronnie
Peterson
Special
1
John Player
Special
DUCKHAMS

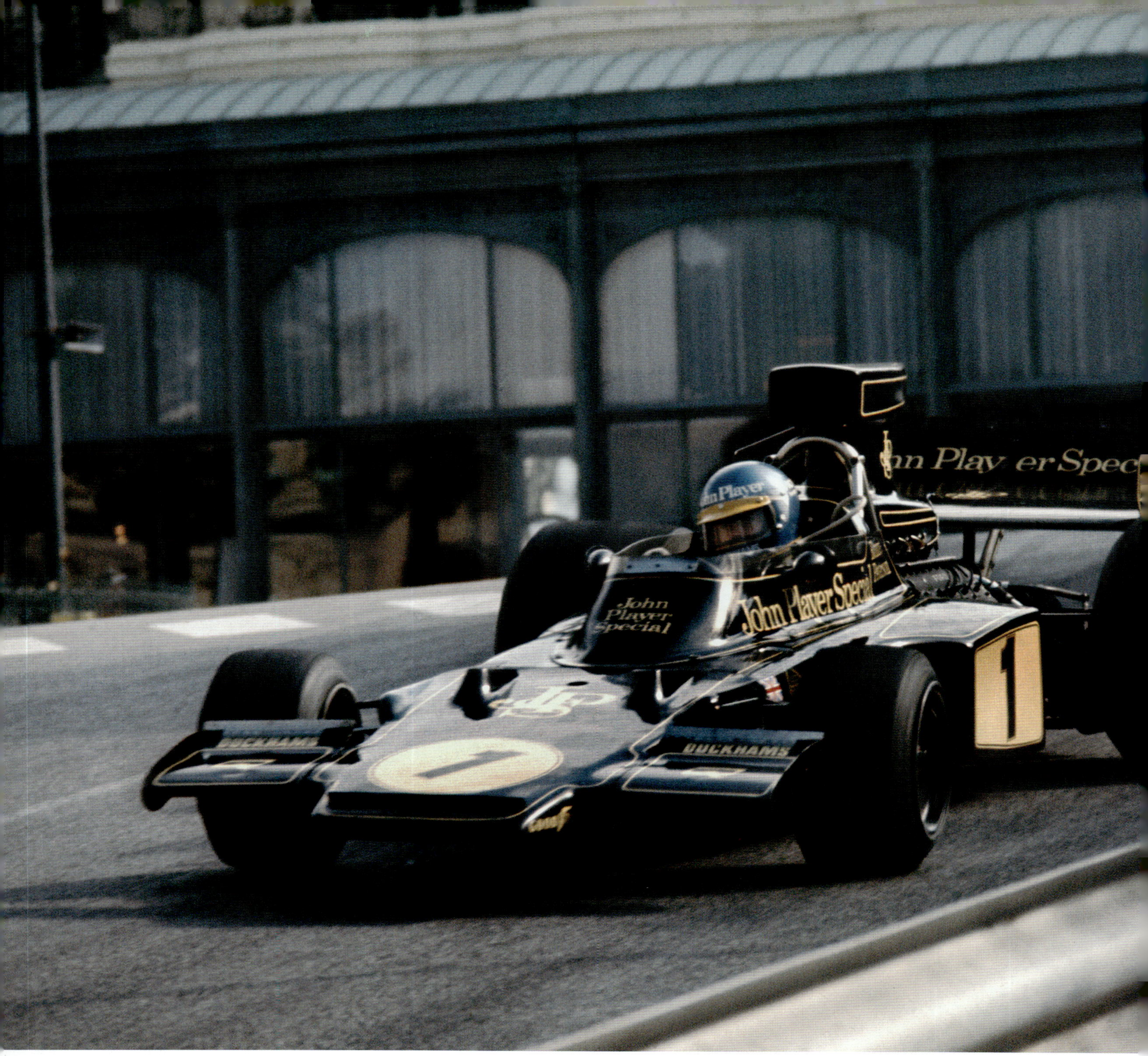

ABOVE When neither of the Lotus 76 cars finished the Belgian Grand Prix, Colin Chapman had had enough. He had established that the 76 weighed more or less the same as the old 72, partly as a consequence of beefing up various suspect components, and was aghast at the number of things that needed sorting out. His instincts told him, as he described it, that the 76 had become a 72 with 50 new problems. Clearly a car with a lot of potential had simply arrived too late for proper development, and the mid-season was almost upon the team. It was not difficult for Ronnie to convince Chapman that the 72E would be a more trustworthy proposition on the unforgiving streets of Monaco. And the decision to revert to the old car was immediately vindicated when Ronnie produced a much-needed victory.

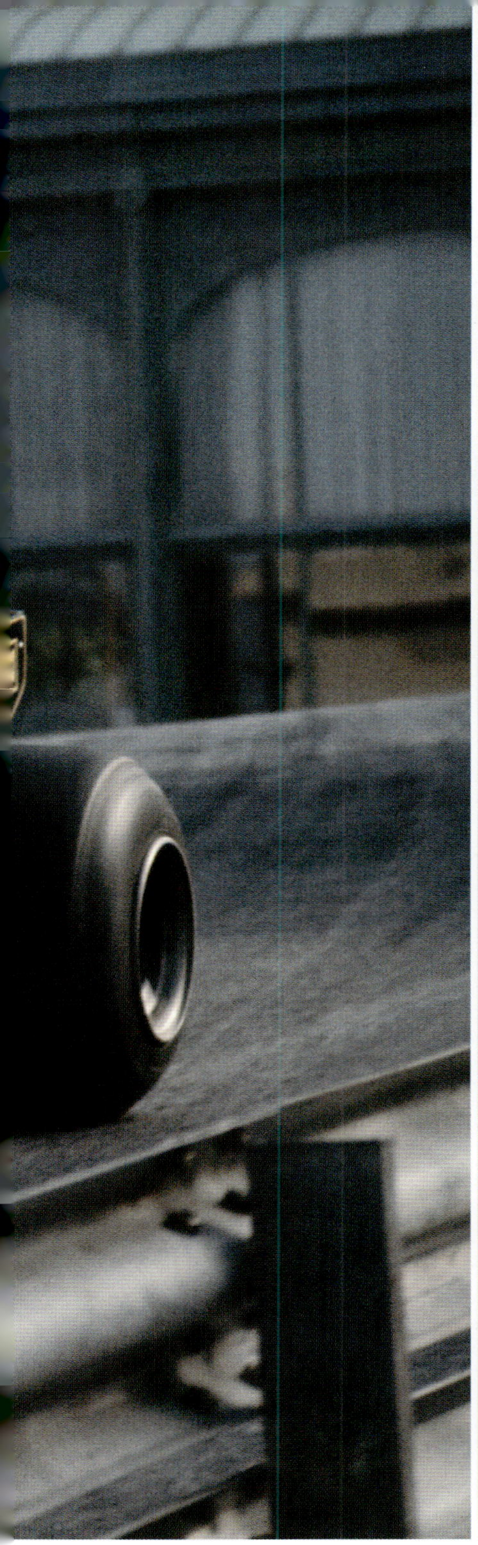

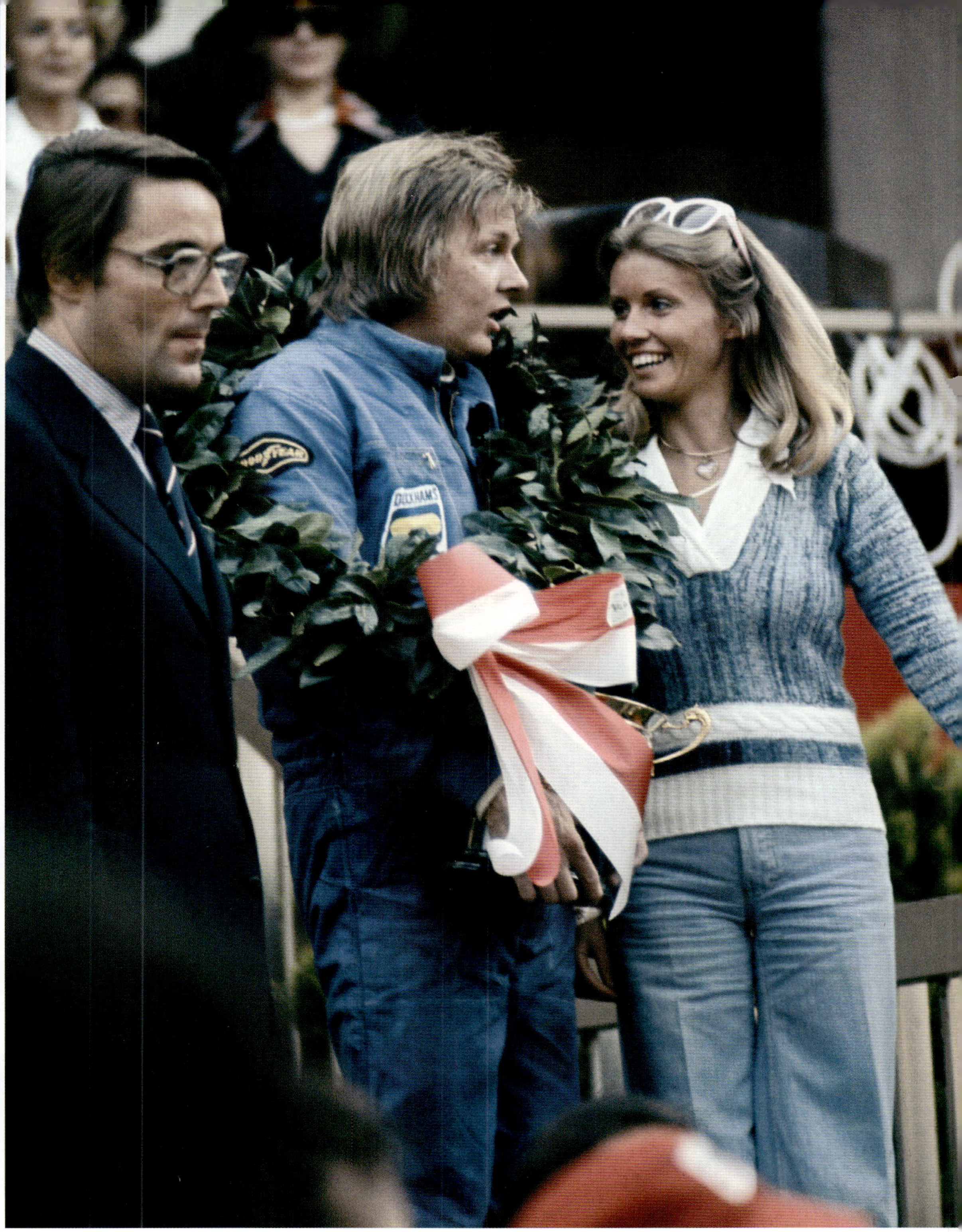

ABOVE Fancy meeting you here! Barbro tries to convince Ronnie that he has, indeed, won the Monaco Grand Prix. Outqualified only by the Ferraris, he was hot in pursuit early in the race when he lurched very wide at Rascasse. In rejoining the track, he inadvertently took out Carlos Reutemann's Brabham, but resumed in sixth place. That became fifth when Mike Hailwood crashed his McLaren, and Ronnie subsequently overcame Jody Scheckter (Tyrrell 007) and Jean-Pierre Jarier (Shadow DN3). One Ferrari failed, then the other, and he swept into the lead on the 33rd of the 78 laps. It was reminiscent of Monaco 1970, when the Lotus 72 had been the recalcitrant new car, and Jochen Rindt had switched to the old 49 and won the motor race. Ickx's 72E was retired from eighth place with a gearbox failure.

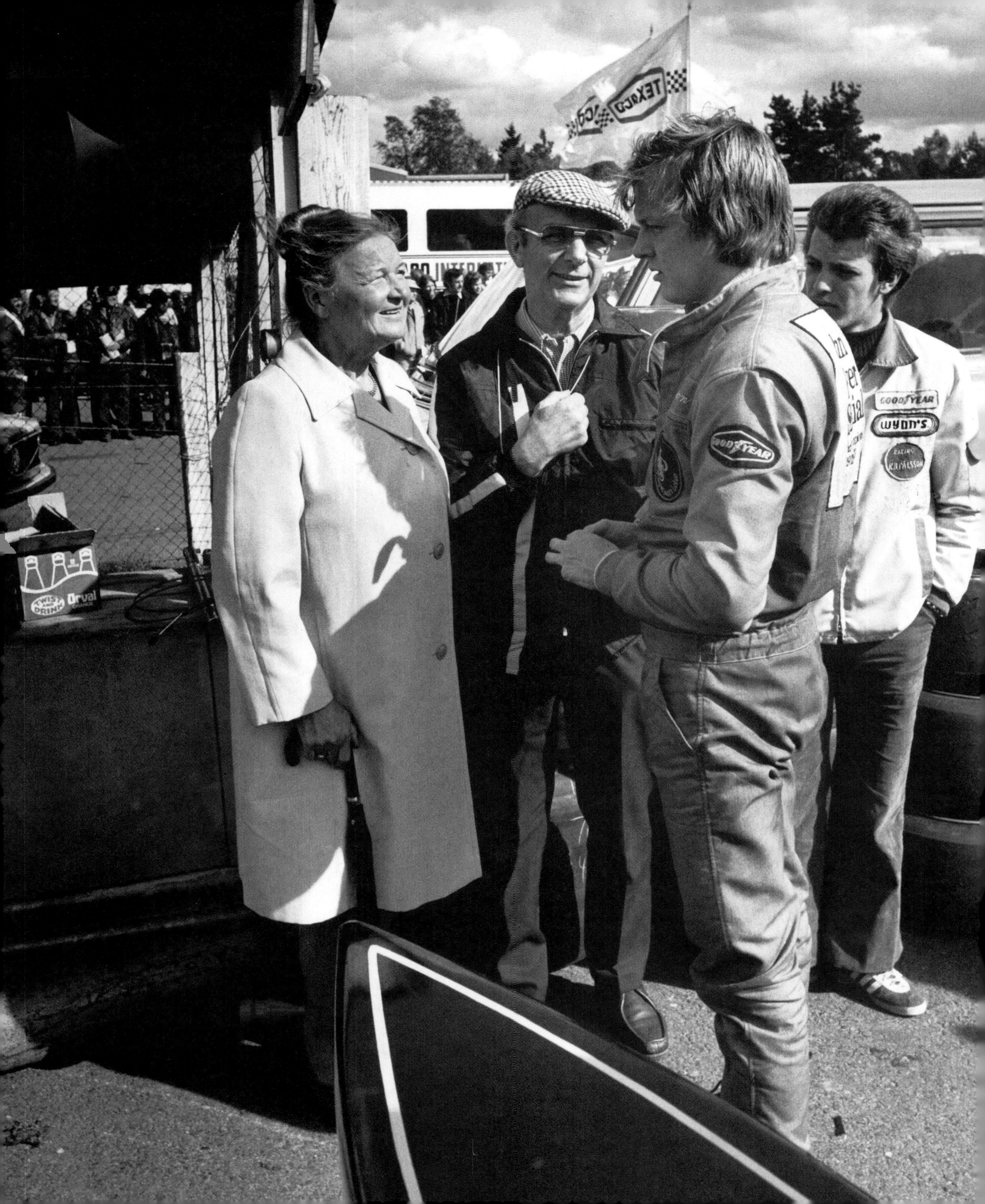
TEXACO
GOODYEAR
GOODYEAR
WYNN'S
Orval

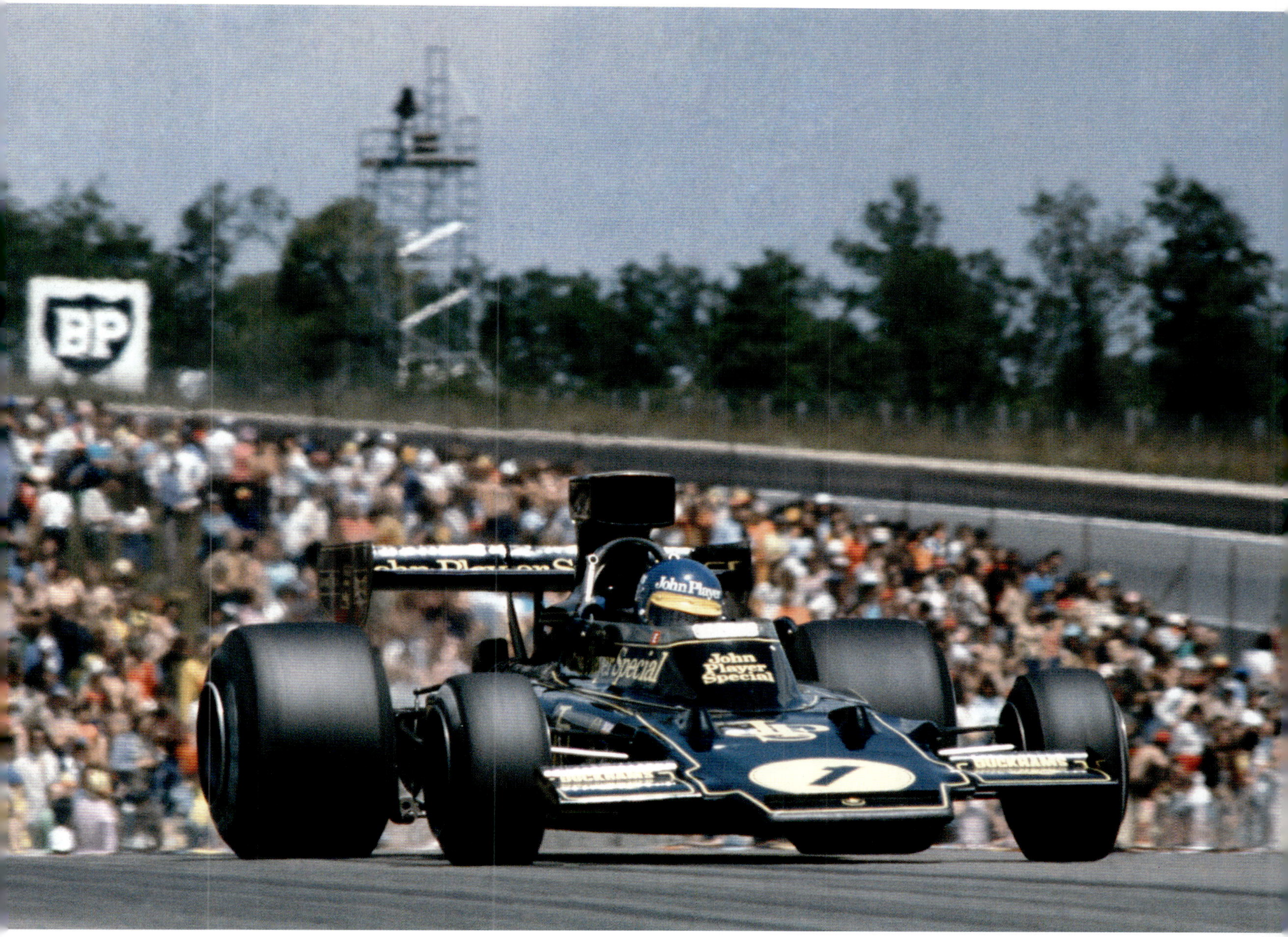

LEFT Ronnie with his parents, May-Britt and Bengt, and brother Tommy at Anderstorp, a fortnight after his Monaco success. The team stayed with the Lotus 72Es for the Swedish Grand Prix and Ronnie qualified fifth, again behind the Ferraris which were themselves outpaced here by Tyrrell drivers Jody Scheckter and Patrick Depailler. He vaulted the Ferraris with a stupendous start that placed him between the Tyrrells, but this family- and crowd-pleasing performance was over after only eight laps when a driveshaft failed. Ken Tyrrell's new boys delivered a 1–2.

ABOVE The JPS Lotus 72s were never in the hunt at Zandvoort but Ronnie came back with gusto, driving his heart out when the Dijon-Prénois circuit took its turn to stage the French Grand Prix. With his 72E equipped here with a four-inch wider front track, he shared the front row with Niki Lauda, harried the Ferrari over the opening 16 laps, and then coolly outbraked it to take the lead. There was simply no catching him and he extended his advantage to more than 20sec when the 80th lap signalled the end of the race. Jacky Ickx, completely overshadowed, finished another 18sec behind in fifth place.

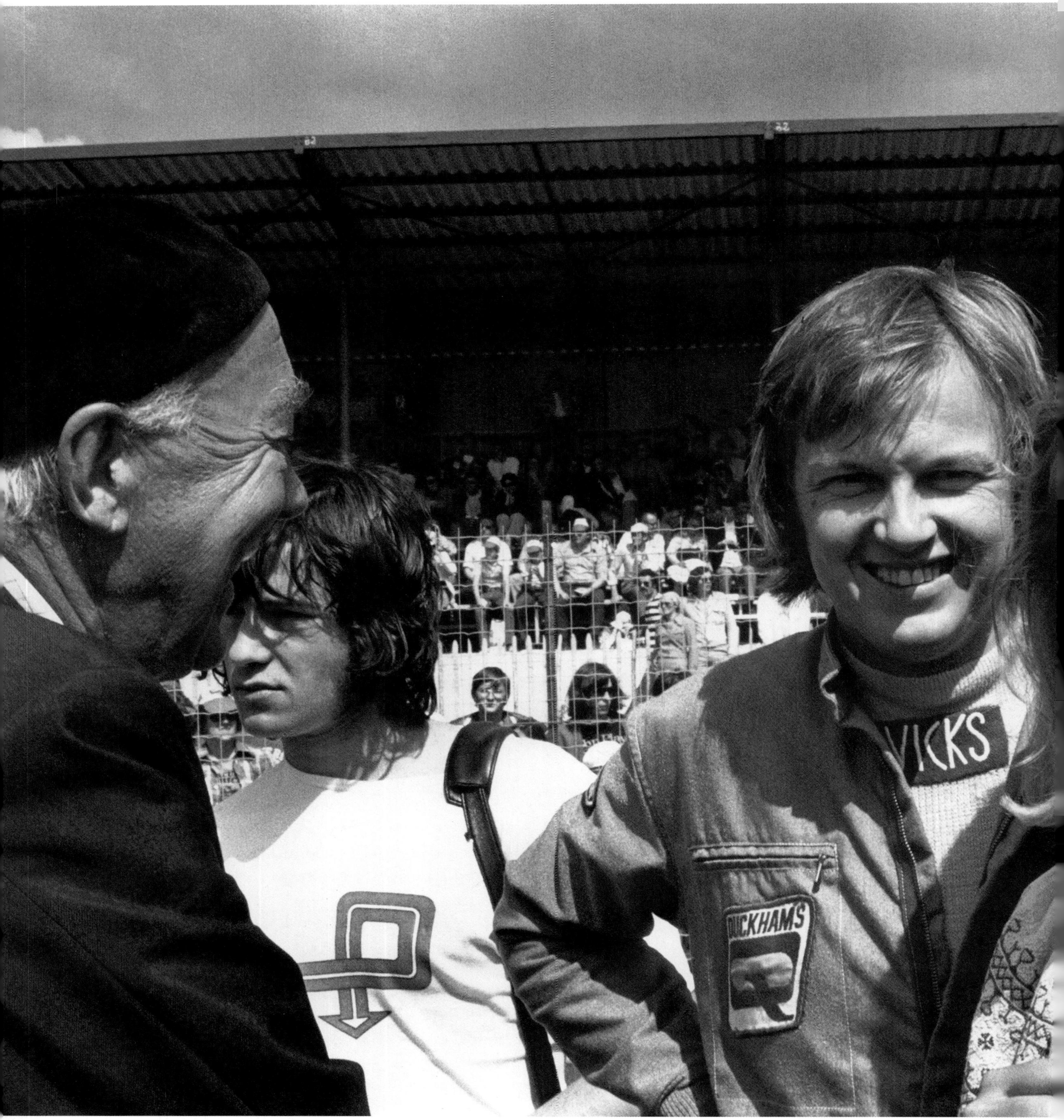
VICKS
UCKHAMS

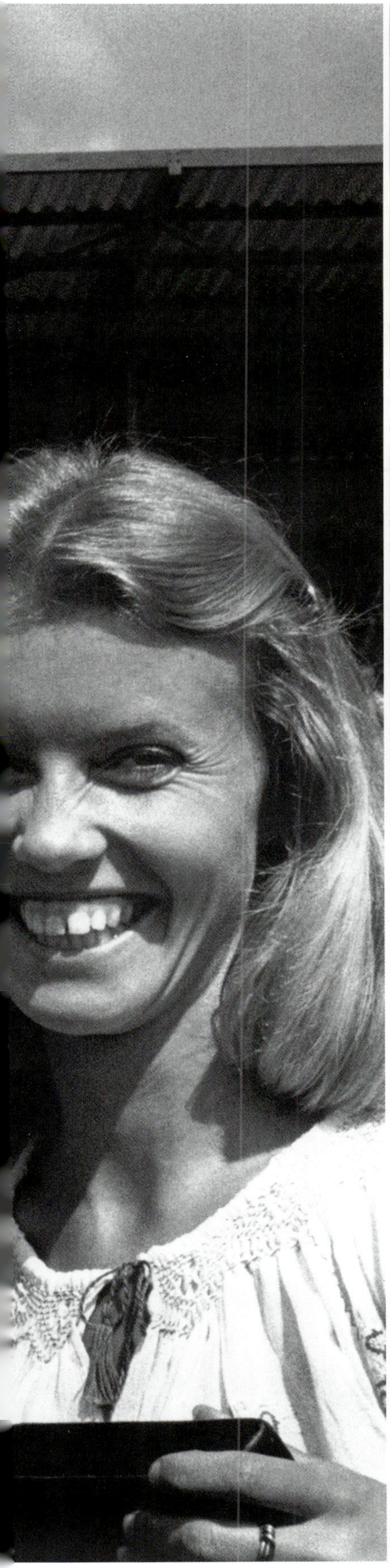

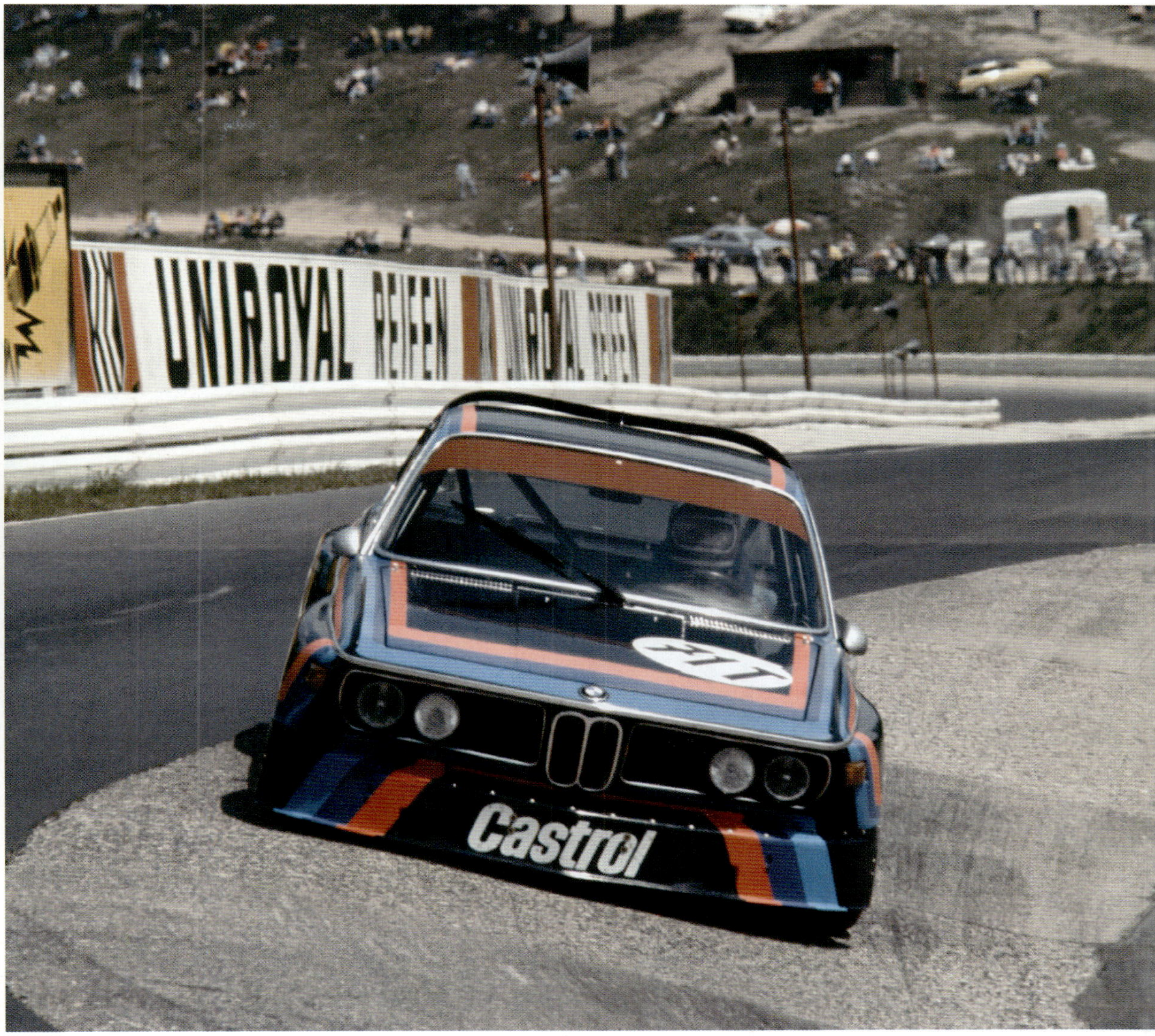

LEFT Ronnie was one step above Scuderia Ferrari's Clay Regazzoni and Niki Lauda more or less all the way in the French Grand Prix. After nine races, thoughts might even have been entertained about the World Championship. No one driver had emerged as a clear favourite so far in this curious season, although several had individually dominated some of the events. After Dijon, Lauda had won two races but only led his winless team-mate 36–32. With two wins, Emerson Fittipaldi lay third on 31 points with the super-reliable McLaren M23. Ronnie also now had two wins, and 19 points. Six Grands Prix remained. Was it possible?

ABOVE For Ronnie, motor racing was everything, and he enjoyed relief from the pressures of Formula 1 by driving quick sportscars and touring cars whenever he could. He did three races with BMW during 1974, the first here on the Nürburgring. His co-driver in the 6 Hours round of the European Touring Car Championship was Hans-Joachim Stuck. It was a formidable partnership, and Stuck put their car on the pole ahead of Jochen Mass in a works Ford Capri, Toine Hezemans in another Capri shared with Niki Lauda, and Jacky Ickx in another 3-litre BMW CSL. Hans-Joachim, pictured leading the race, had to pit for suspension repairs after 10 laps of the Nordschleife, and later the car broke its gearbox. Klaus Ludwig and Hans Heyer won with a Zakspeed Ford Escort.

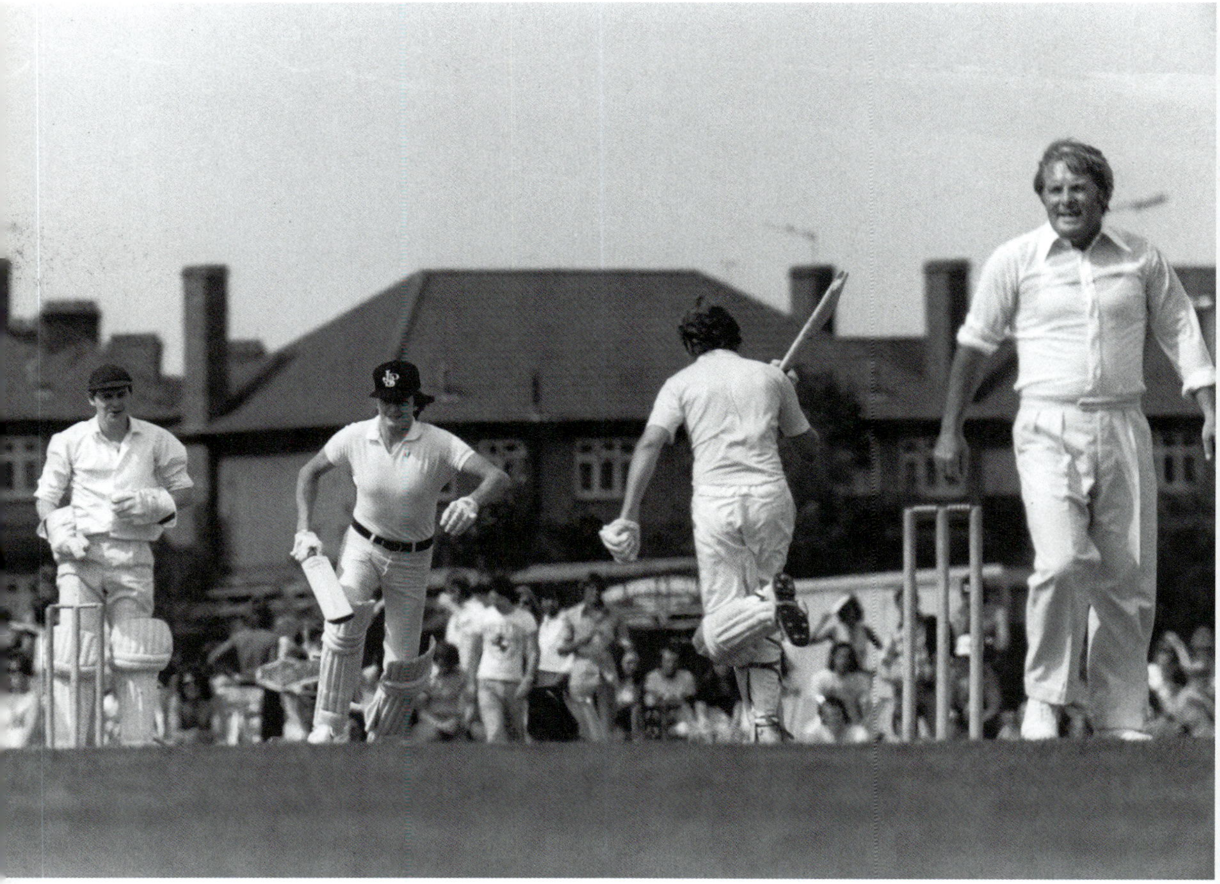

ABOVE Niki Lauda, having struck a ball from bowler Ernie Wise through the covers, calls Ronnie back for a second run during the traditional annual charity cricket match in British Grand Prix week. These two then went to Brands Hatch and annexed the front row of the grid, each with an identical lap-time, the Ferrari on pole position having done it first. But both were delayed by punctures and Jody Scheckter won the race for Tyrrell.

RIGHT Happy campers look on as Ronnie leads Tyrrell's Patrick Depailler and team-mate Jacky Ickx on the Nürburging, early in the German Grand Prix. Colin Chapman's men were never in contention on this dank day in the Eifel hills. Clay Regazzoni led all the way in the only Ferrari to complete the first lap. Niki Lauda crashed when trying to outbrake Jody Scheckter's Tyrrell, which then raced in second place throughout, with Carlos Reutemann third for Brabham. Ronnie and Jacky had a brief battle with Mike Hailwood that ended when the McLaren landed awkwardly from the 'yump' at the Pflanzgarten and slammed into the barriers. Hailwood broke a leg in three places and never raced again. Ronnie finished fourth, only a second behind Reutemann, and Jacky fifth.

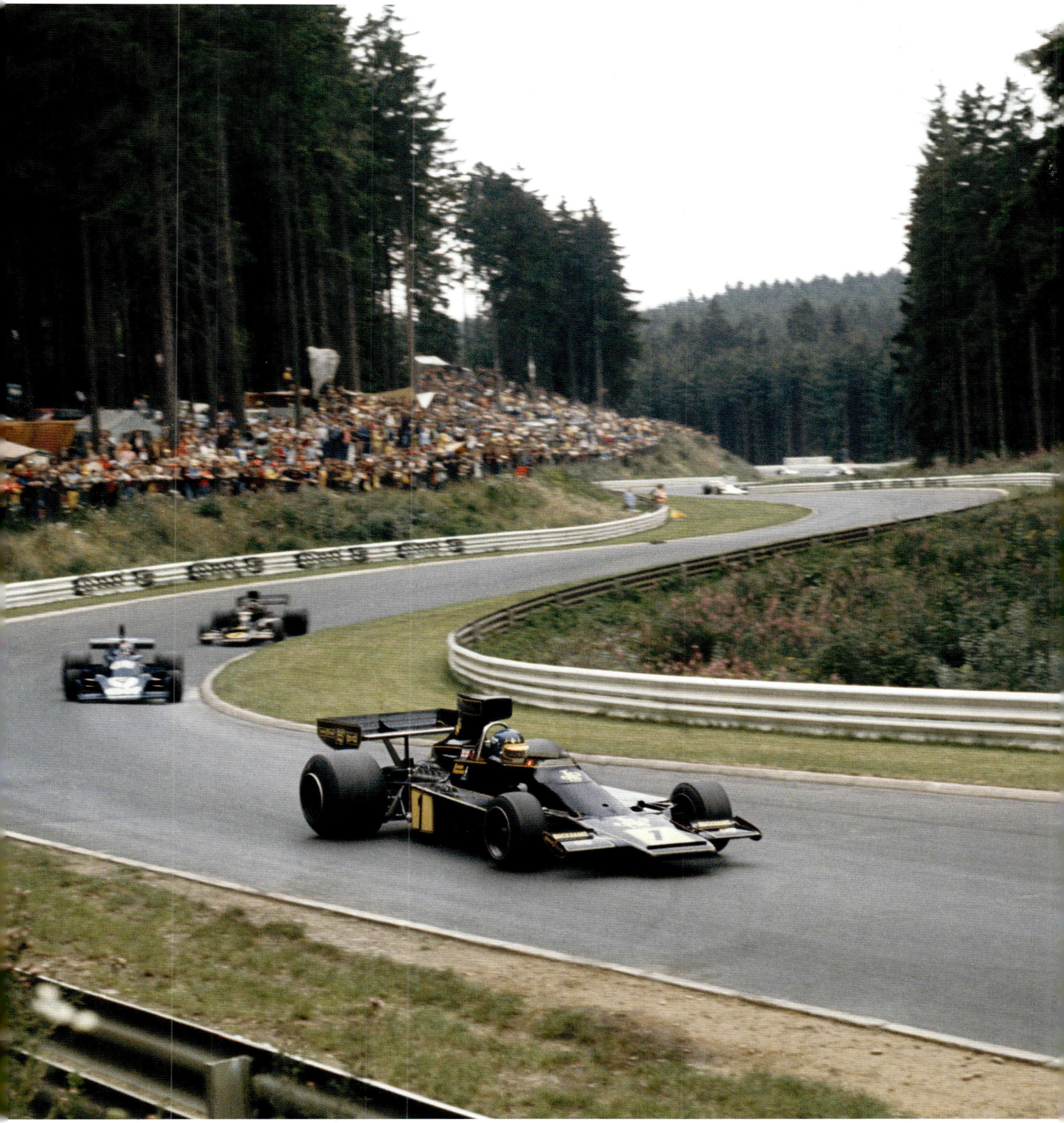

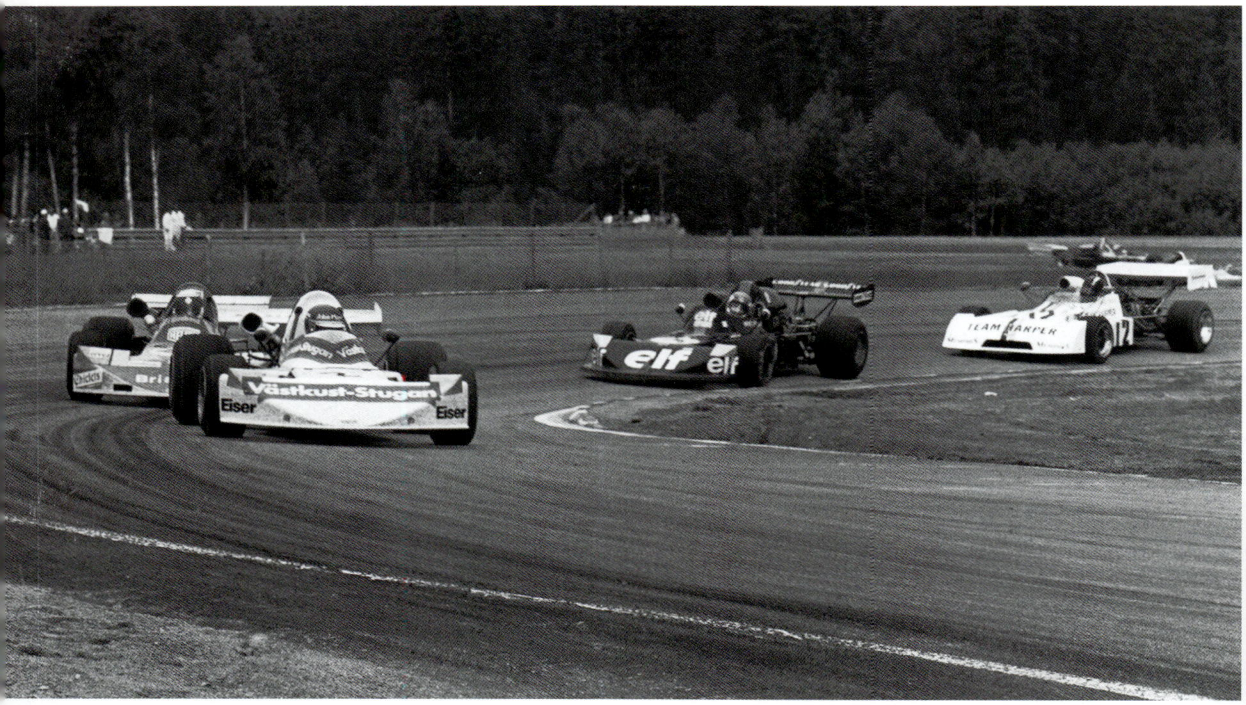

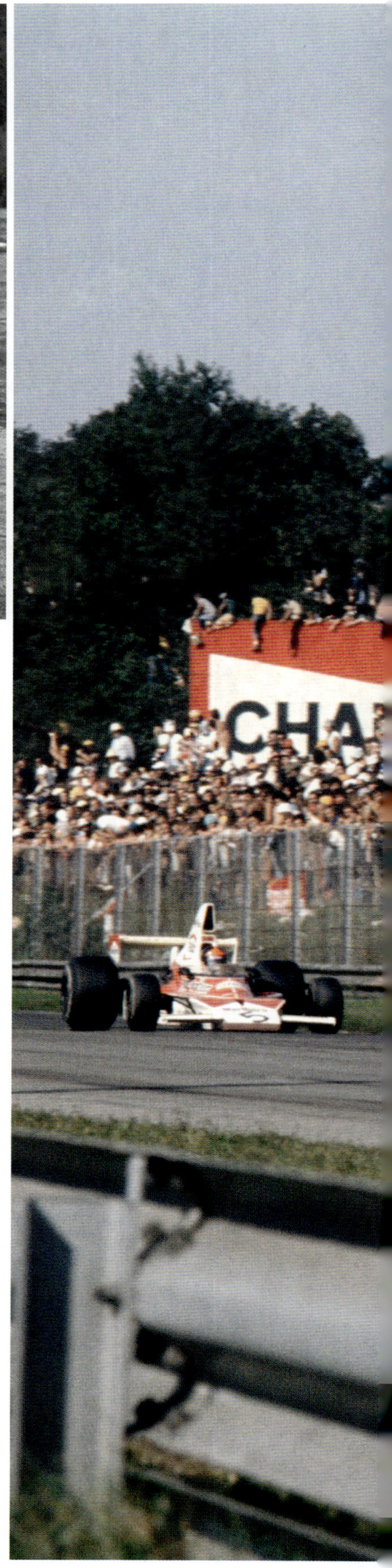

ABOVE Ronnie took up an invitation from March Engineering to race in the 1974 Formula 2 Kanonloppet at Karlskoga, Sweden's round of the FIA European Championship. The British works team was again the one to beat this season, with factory BMW engines for drivers Patrick Depailler and Hans-Joachim Stuck, and entered a third car for Ronnie here. He had a problematical qualifying and lined up eighth on the grid, but it took him only five laps to appear on the gearbox of Depailler's Elf-liveried car, which was leading from pole position. As a graded driver, Ronnie was ineligible for championship points, so Depailler waved him by and raced to the finish in his wheeltracks. Here the works March 742 BMWs lap two backmarkers, Carlos Jarque in a Trivellato team March (at left) and David Purley in the white Team Harper Chevron. This was Ronnie's first Formula 2 victory since Oulton Park two years before, and his last. The result left Depailler in the lead of the championship and he went on to win it.

RIGHT The discarded Lotus 76 had not raced since the Belgian Grand Prix in mid-May, but had been tested when time allowed, and one had been taken to all the race meetings. Definite progress was made, so two were deployed at Monza in early September, along with a single 72E as the spare car. Ronnie tried both in qualifying and the old car was about a second quicker than the new, so he decided to race it. After qualifying, the front spacers were removed to restore the original front track dimension, and the next day Ronnie lined it up seventh on the grid. The Ferraris dominated the early action, along with three Brabhams, but in turn Carlos Pace, John Watson and Carlos Reutemann were hampered by mechanical problems. By lap 12, they were gone, and Ronnie was in third place behind NIki Lauda and Clay Regazzoni. Later the engines of both Ferraris broke and suddenly this race-long duel between Ronnie and Emerson Fittipaldi was for the lead, with 11 laps to go. Most of the disgruntled Italian fans stayed to watch it, and were rewarded well. Ronnie's DFV sounded awful due to a cracked exhaust pipe, but there was no significant loss of power and his main problem was 'soft' front brakes. Emerson got on his tail and outbraked him in the chicane, but Ronnie repassed and the two staged a frantic battle throughout the final three laps. Ronnie held on by 0.8sec, thus becoming the first driver to win more than twice all season, with Jody Scheckter's Tyrrell a distant third.

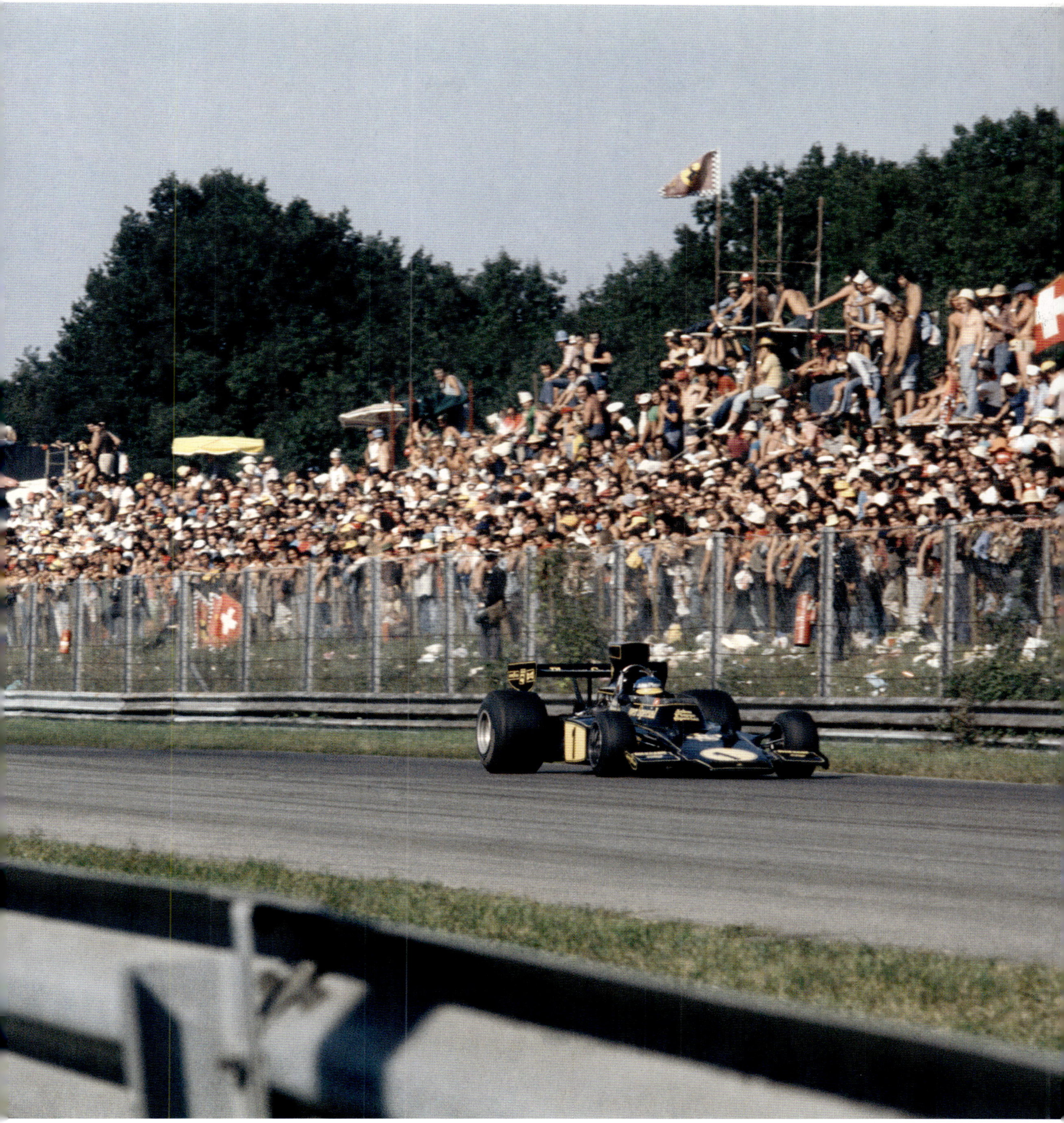

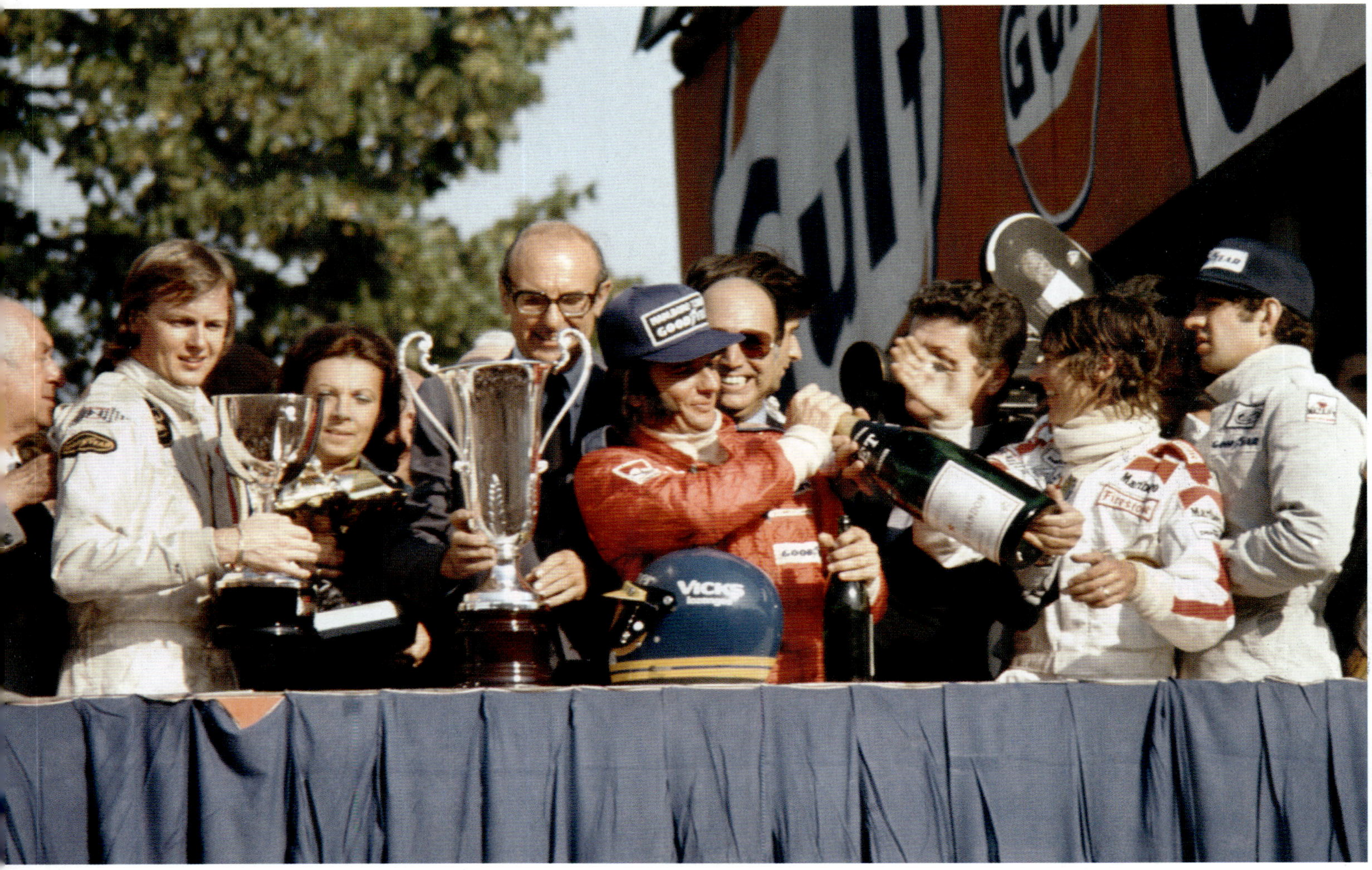

ABOVE The Italian Grand Prix result was difficult for Ronnie's former team-mate to take but, on the other hand, it propelled Emerson Fittipaldi into third place in the championship, just three points behind Clay Regazzoni and two behind Jody Scheckter, with only Canada and the USA to come. On the chaotic Monza podium, a clearly outraged Scheckter is being shoved into the background by a shameless interloper. Arturo Merzario had qualified 15th with Frank Williams's 'Iso-Marlboro' (a mite quicker than Jacky Ickx in the JPS Lotus 76) but a clutch problem meant that he got away dead last of the 26 starters. A terrific recovery drive placed him fourth of the 11 finishers, on the winner's lap. Without the Ferraris to cheer, the crowd absolutely loved it. No way was anyone going to keep little Art off the podium...

RIGHT After Ronnie had driven probably his best race of the season at Mosport Park, finishing a close third behind Emerson Fittipaldi's McLaren and Clay Regazzoni's Ferrrari with a damaged front wing, the 1974 World Championship ended on a dark note when Team Surtees driver Helmuth Koinigg was killed early in the US Grand Prix. For Team Lotus, the event at Watkins Glen was an especially gloomy occasion. Neither of its cars finished, and Ronnie's was never higher than ninth. Here Ronnie and Colin Chapman reflect on a season ruined by the late arrival of the Lotus 76, and by all too familiar reliability issues after Chapman had decided to revert to the 72E. Ronnie had started the year as one of the favourites for the title, but had ended it in fifth place behind Emerson Fittipaldi, Clay Regazzoni, Jody Scheckter and Niki Lauda. His three victories were among only six finishes in the points. But perhaps the apparent potential of the Lotus 76 could be realised after a winter's testing, and Chapman was talking about another new car, anyway. Ronnie signed up for another season at John Player Team Lotus.

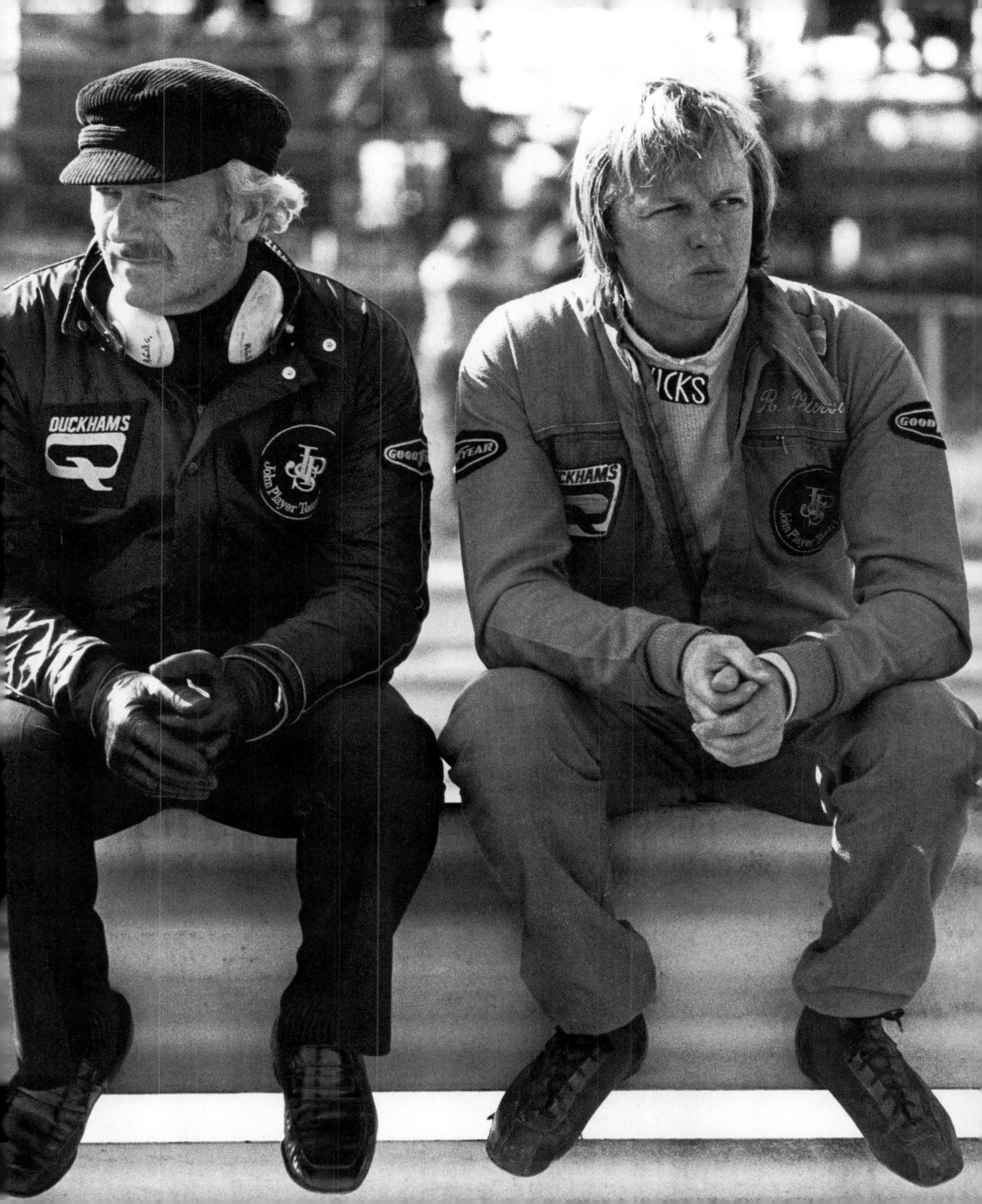
DUCKHAMS

1975

TEAM LOTUS WASTES ITS GREATEST ASSET

Before the 1975 World Championship began, and even while the teams were in South America, Ronnie had second thoughts about staying with Team Lotus. He made a serious attempt to switch to UOP Shadow, but this came to nothing. Ronnie was pacified by a salary increase from JPS, the team's title sponsor, but even then he might have quit had he known that he would spend all season with the increasingly uncompetitive Lotus 72. Now in its sixth summer, the car was completely unsuited to the latest tyres, which were being developed by Goodyear with the Brabham, Ferrari, McLaren and Tyrrell teams for their new cars. The Lotus often delivered lap-times slower than in 1974, and this was a rotten year. The promised new car never materialised and Ronnie's best Grand Prix result was fourth in Monaco.

RIGHT To the utter amazement of the Formula 1 community, the outstanding team of the 1960s found itself in a position where it had to race its 1970 design six seasons later. Not even Ronnie's prodigious ability could overcome the deficiencies of the JPS Lotus 72E, although he usually showed a clean pair of heels to Jacky Ickx, here at Zolder for his team-mate's home Grand Prix.

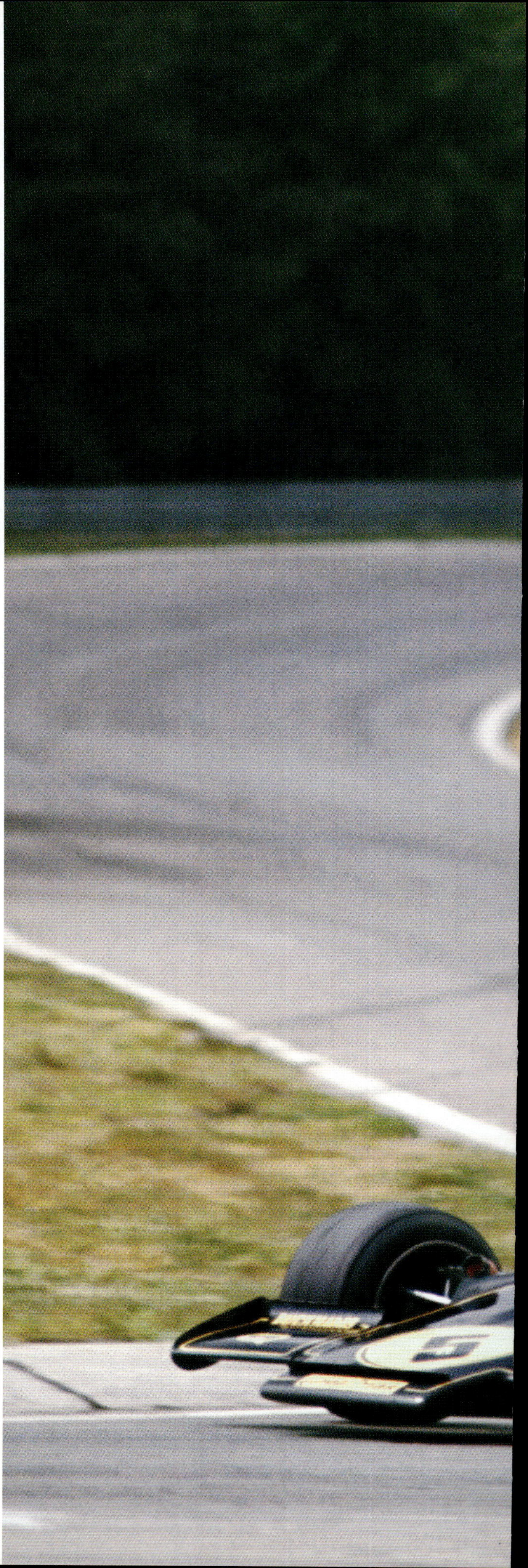

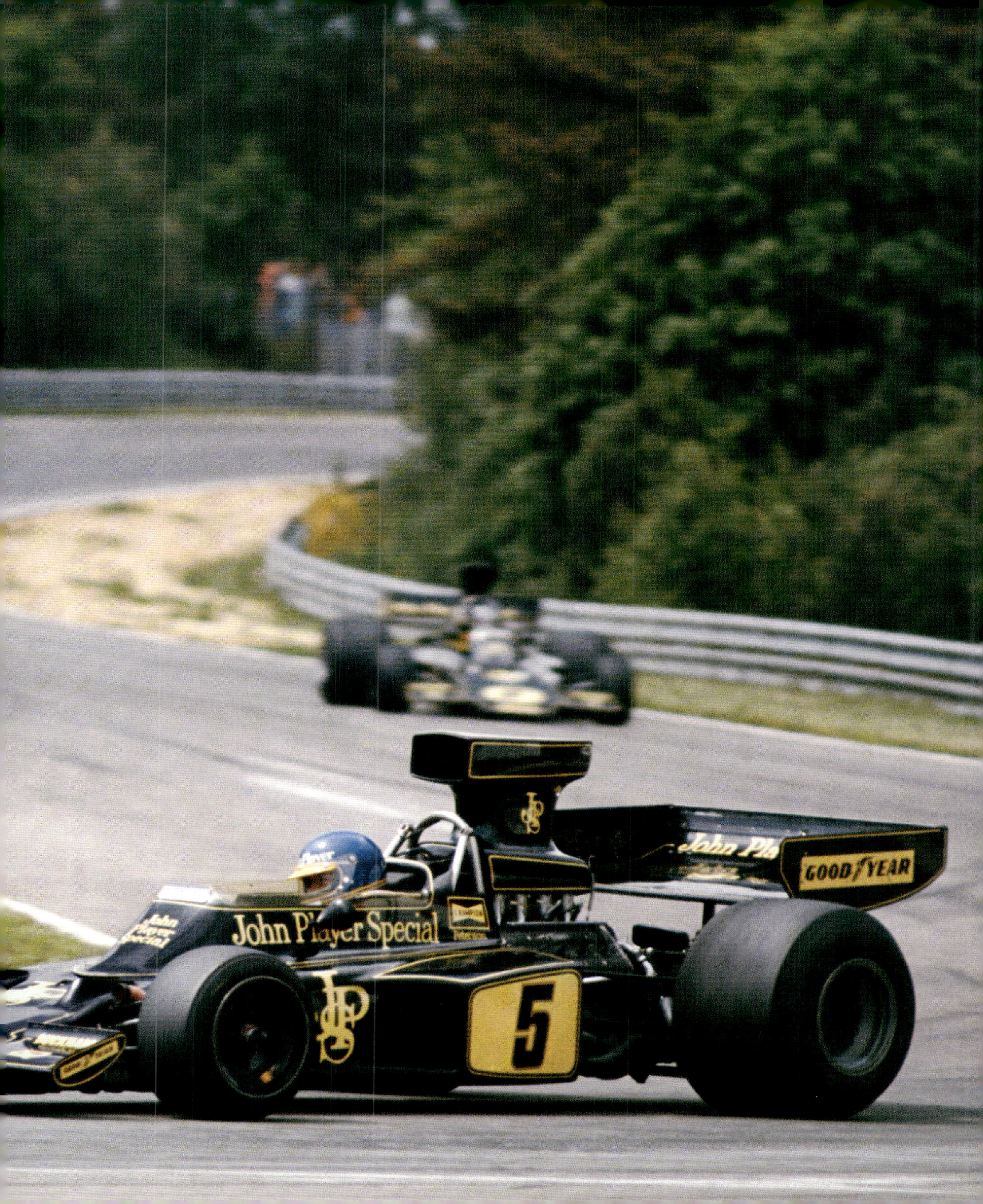
John Player Special
GOOD YEAR
5

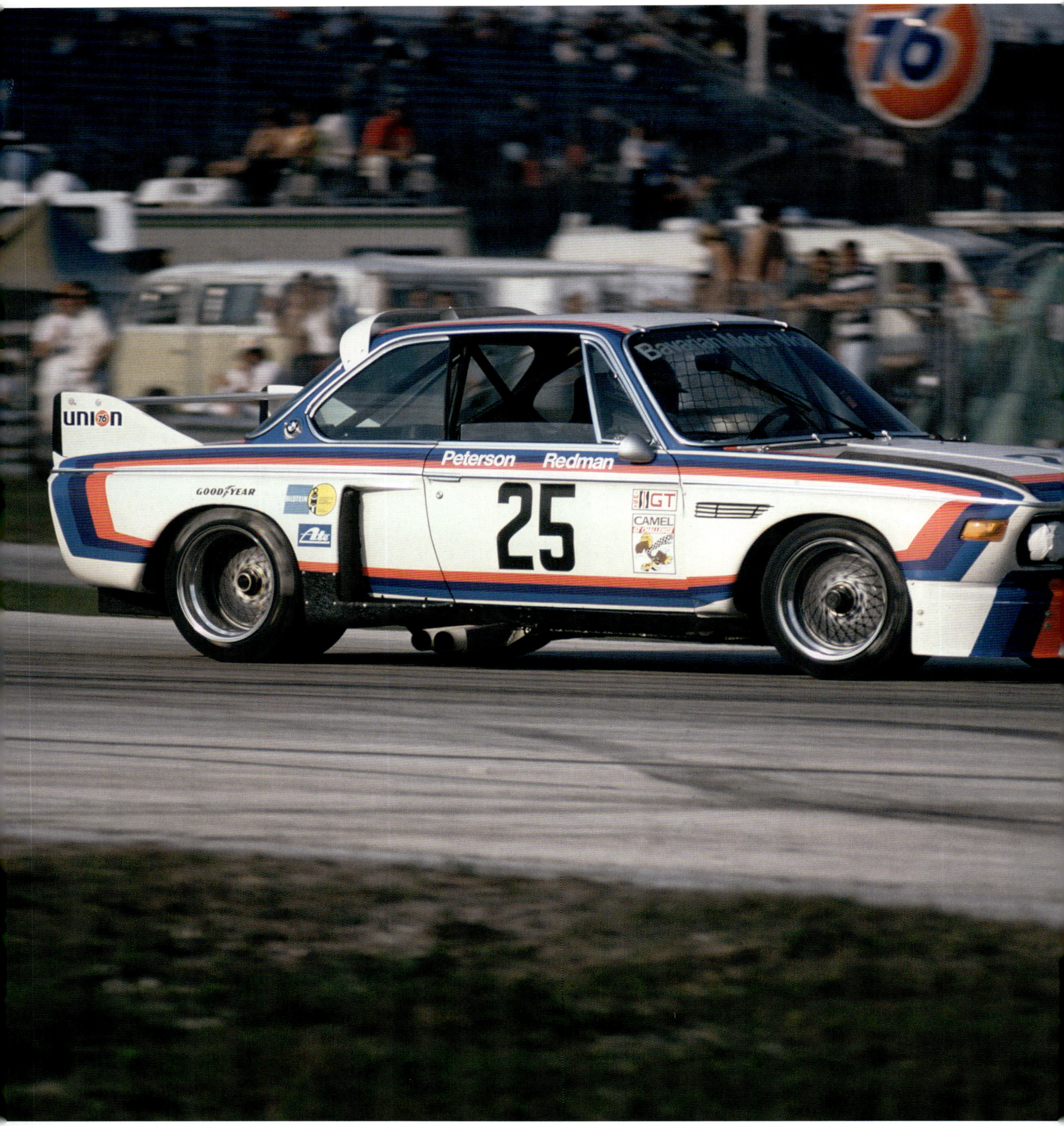
76
union
GOODYEAR
Peterson
Redman
25
GT
CAMEL

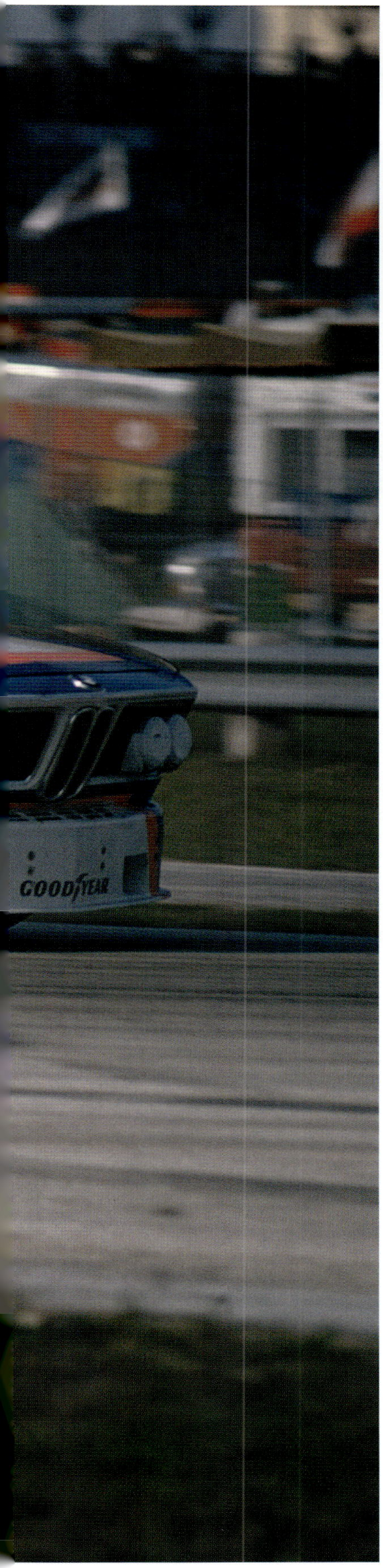

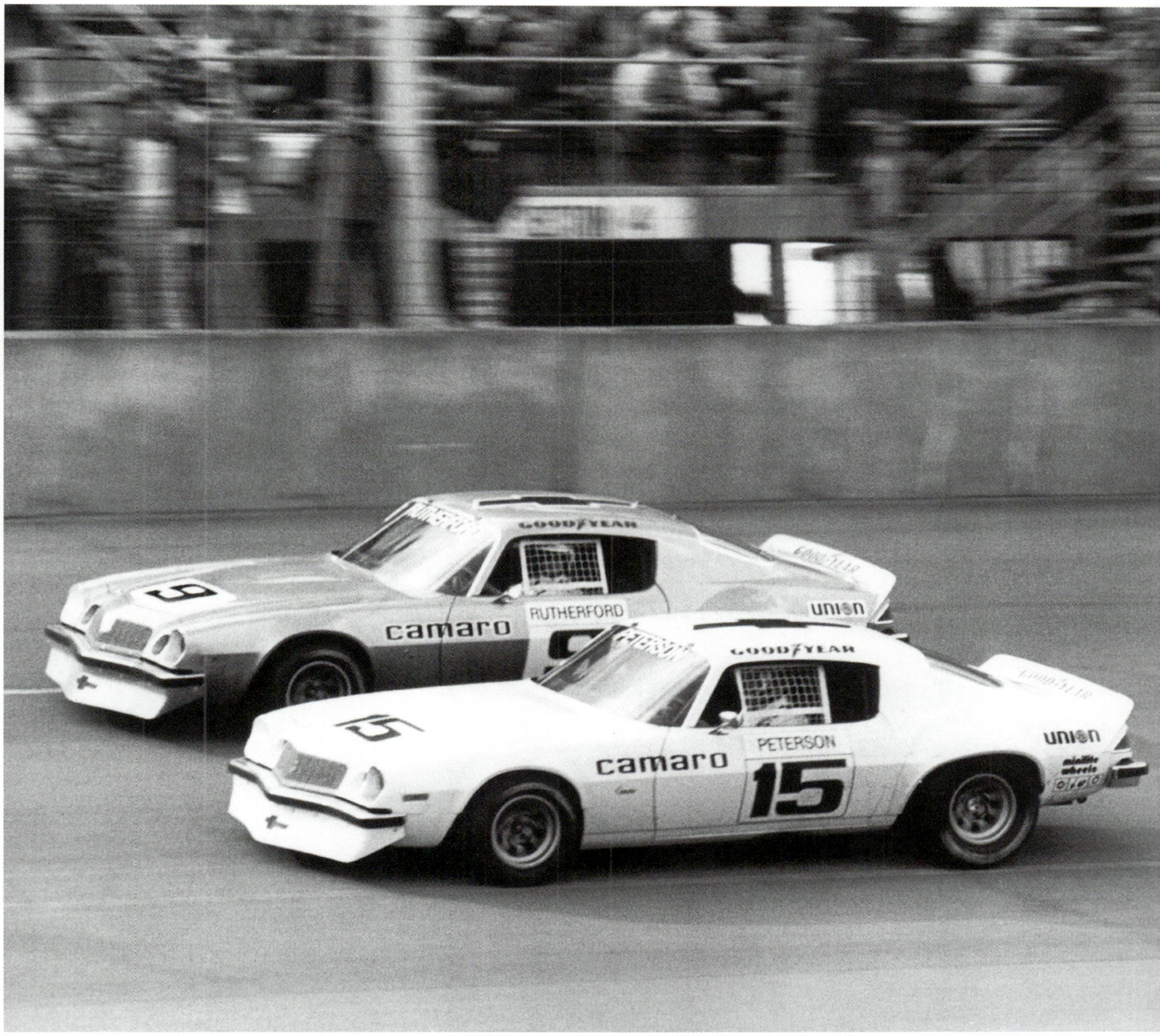

LEFT After failing to feature in the season-opening Argentine and Brazilian Grands Prix, from midfield qualifying positions, Ronnie flew to Florida to race one of two works BMW 3.0 CSLs in the Daytona 24 Hours. Sharing his 3.5-litre car with Brian Redman, he put it on the front row with a lap-time beaten only by John Greenwood's fearsome 7-litre Chevrolet Corvette, with Hans-Joachim Stuck third fastest in the other BMW, co-driven by Sam Posey. The long race was hardly under way when Ronnie was black-flagged with inoperable brake lights, and shortly afterwards his engine broke its camshaft drive. The sister car led until halted by a broken conrod, the Corvette was destroyed in a crash, and Porsche Carreras filled the first six places.

ABOVE Ronnie stayed on in Florida for the International Race of Champions final at Daytona the weekend after the 24 Hours, and was joined by Emerson Fittipaldi, the only other non-American in the invitational field. Both were going well when Johnny Rutherford (alongside Ronnie in the picture) collided with George Follmer, and the cars of both Formula 1 drivers were hit by flying debris, breaking their windscreens. The race was red-flagged and, after the restart, Ronnie eliminated himself by spinning at 160mph and smiting the wall 500 yards down the road. Emerson finished fifth with a puncture, far behind IROC winner Bobby Unser.

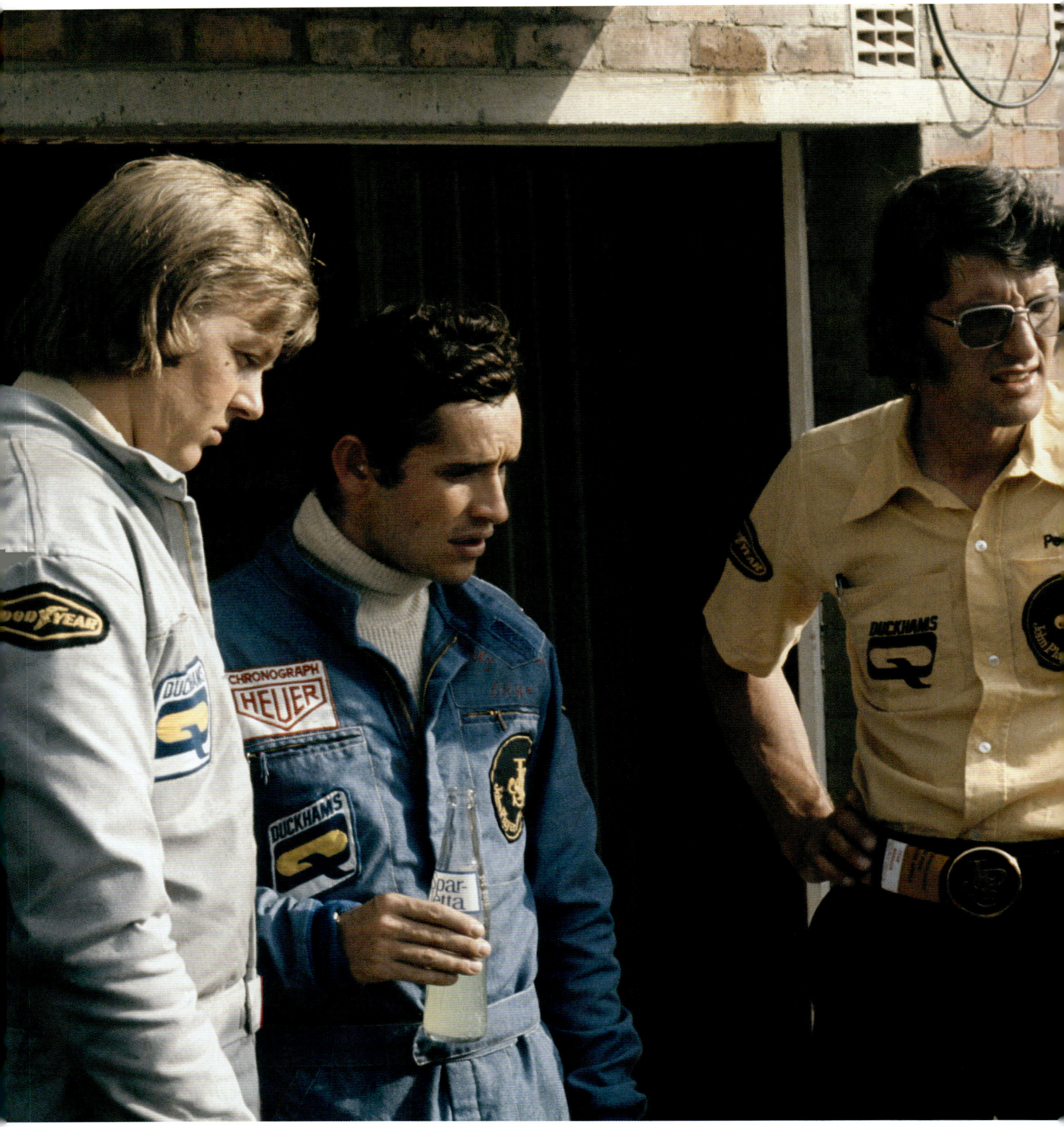
CHRONOGRAPH
HEUER
DUCKHAMS
DUCKHAMS

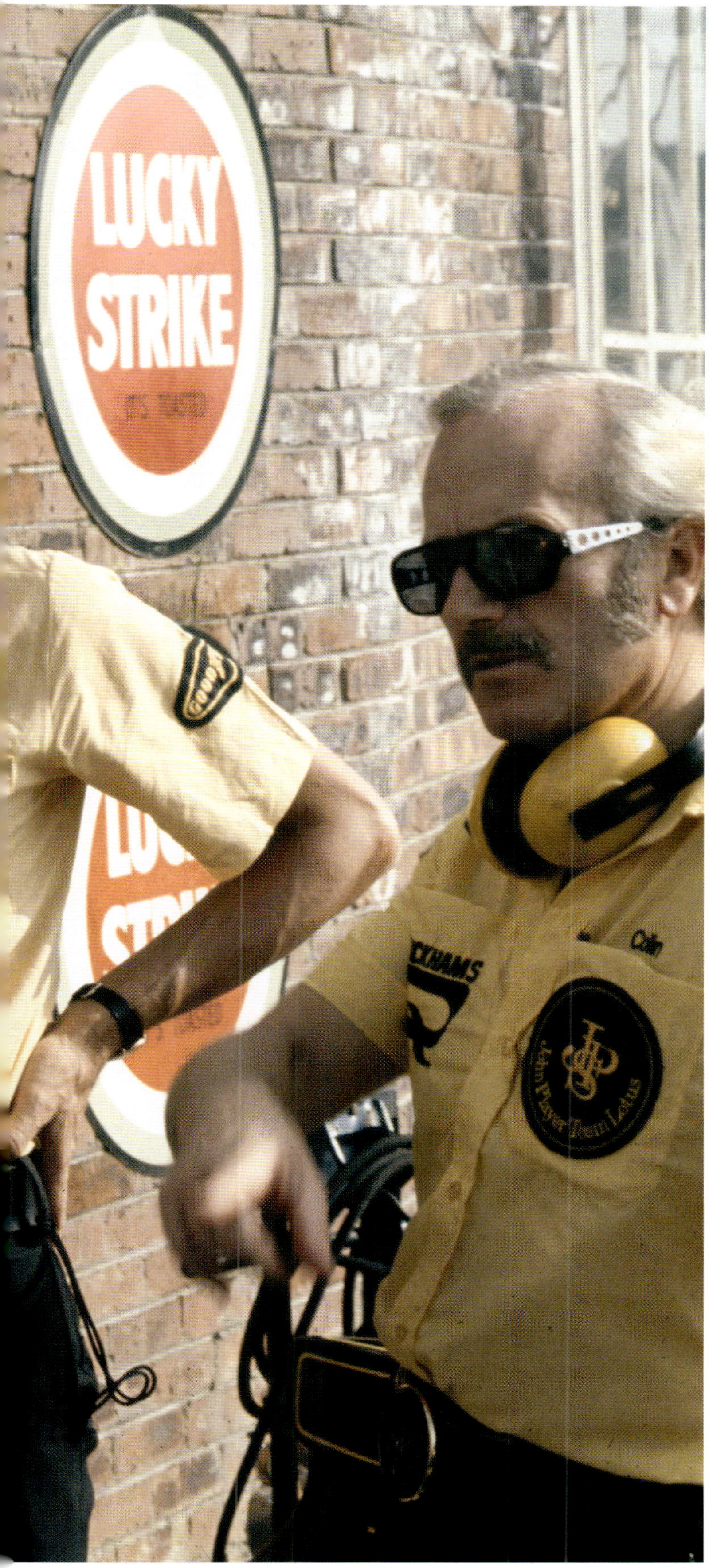

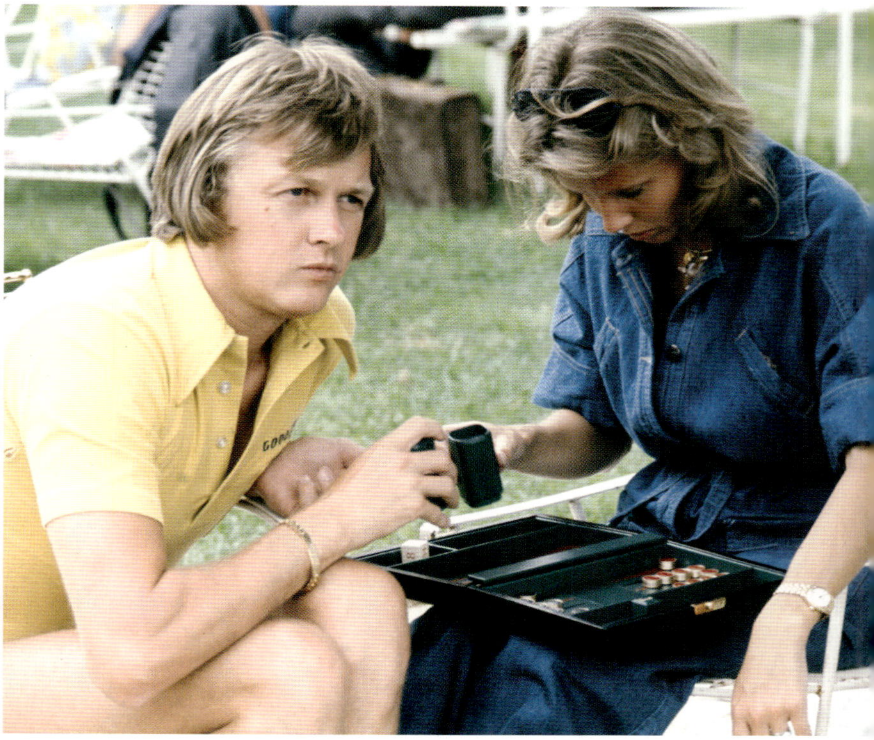

LEFT With Jacky Ickx, team manager Peter Warr and Colin Chapman at Kyalami for the South African Grand Prix. At this stage of his business life, Chapman was distracted by an expansion of his empire into boat building and other fields, and his drivers had already begun to doubt that the new Lotus 77 project would be in metal for a while yet. Ickx will quit Team Lotus in disgust after the French Grand Prix, and thereafter Ronnie's team-mates will be variously Jim Crawford, John Watson and Brian Henton.

ABOVE Ronnie is pensive in the garden of the Kyalami Ranch, and he is not thinking about the backgammon game with Barbro – not even a couple of weeks before their marriage. He is wondering why the dice had fallen so badly for him in his Formula 1 career. Until shortly before this photograph was taken, former March director Alan Rees was engaged in negotiations to switch him to the Shadow team, in a swap deal involving Tom Pryce. Ronnie even had a seat fitting, but ultimately it all came to nothing – after he had seen the new Shadow DN5 outpacing allcomers in both Argentina and Brazil, in the hands of Jean-Pierre Jarier.

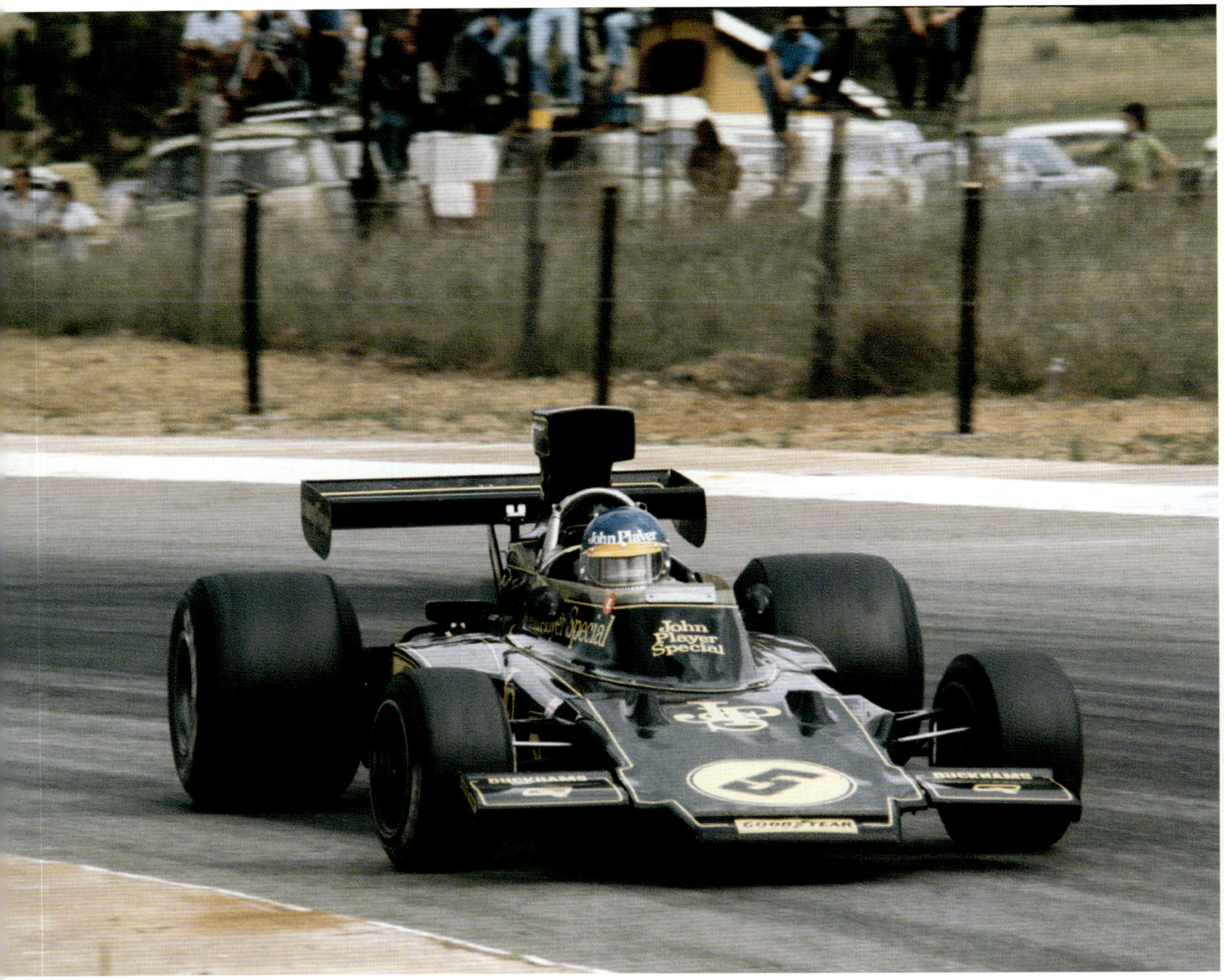

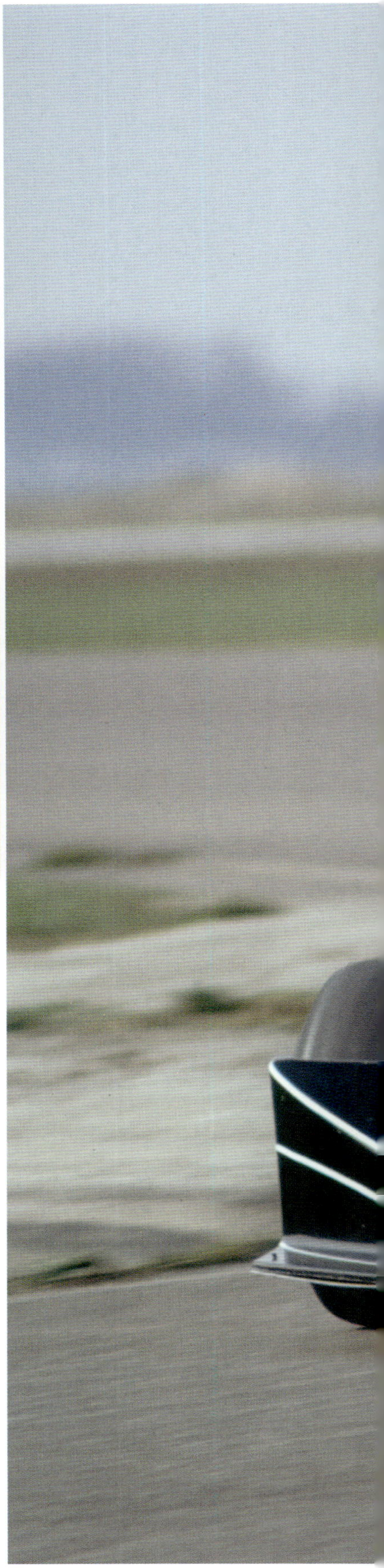

ABOVE John Player Team Lotus built a new 72E for Ronnie's use, and he had it in time for the South African Grand Prix. Both the team's cars were equipped with a new rear suspension set-up and Ronnie qualified eighth – an encouraging performance after his experiences in South America. He made a tremendous start, rocketing into third place on the run down to Crowthorne, but he couldn't hold it. Steadily he lost track position, hampered by gross understeer, having to pitch it sideways just to get round the turns. A pitstop for new front tyres and front wing adjustments did not cure the problem. He finished 10th, a lap down on Jody Scheckter's winning Tyrrell 007.

RIGHT After a deceptively strong result in the Formula 1 Race of Champions, finishing third on the gearbox of John Watson's Surtees, Ronnie did the only Formula 2 event of his 1975 season over the Easter weekend at Thruxton. The race promoters paid to get him behind the wheel of this black March 752 BMW, which was run on behalf of the factory by Ron Dennis's newly formed Project 3 team. The car was brand new and handled like a dog throughout practice. Ronnie spun often and, at one stage, broke the nose splitter (pictured). He could qualify only seventh and, in the first of the two heats, was running sixth when he spun again. He rejoined in 17th place and then showed the crowd why he was there, manfully climbing back to ninth. But his race ended in a violent accident when his was one of two cars that struck a Formula Atlantic Chevron that had spun and stalled in the chicane. The shunt ultimately involved five other cars but Ronnie escaped unscathed. The event was won by Jacques Laffite's Martini-BMW and the supporting Formula 3 race by a new, up-and-coming Swedish driver, Gunnar Nilsson.

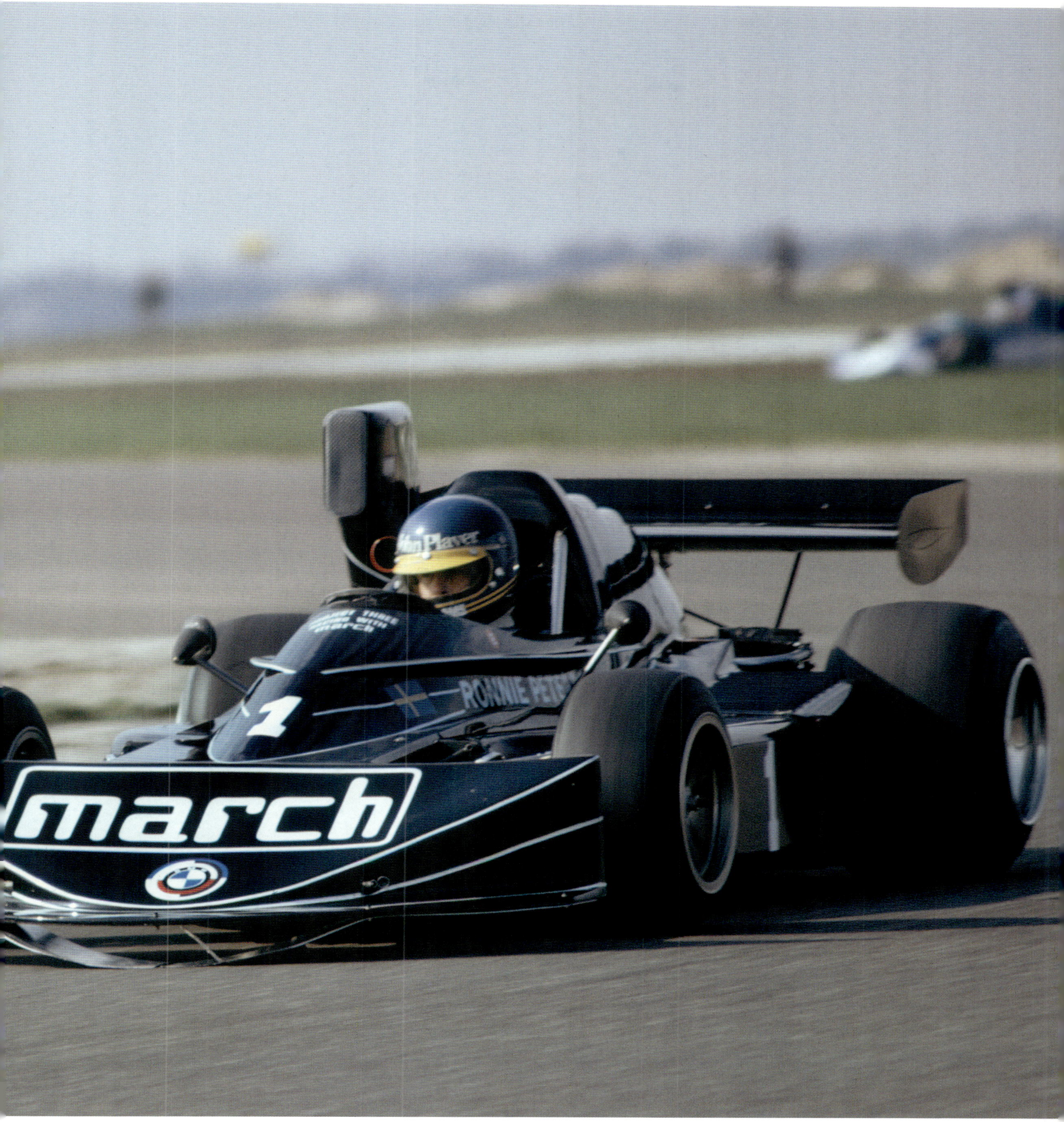
march
1

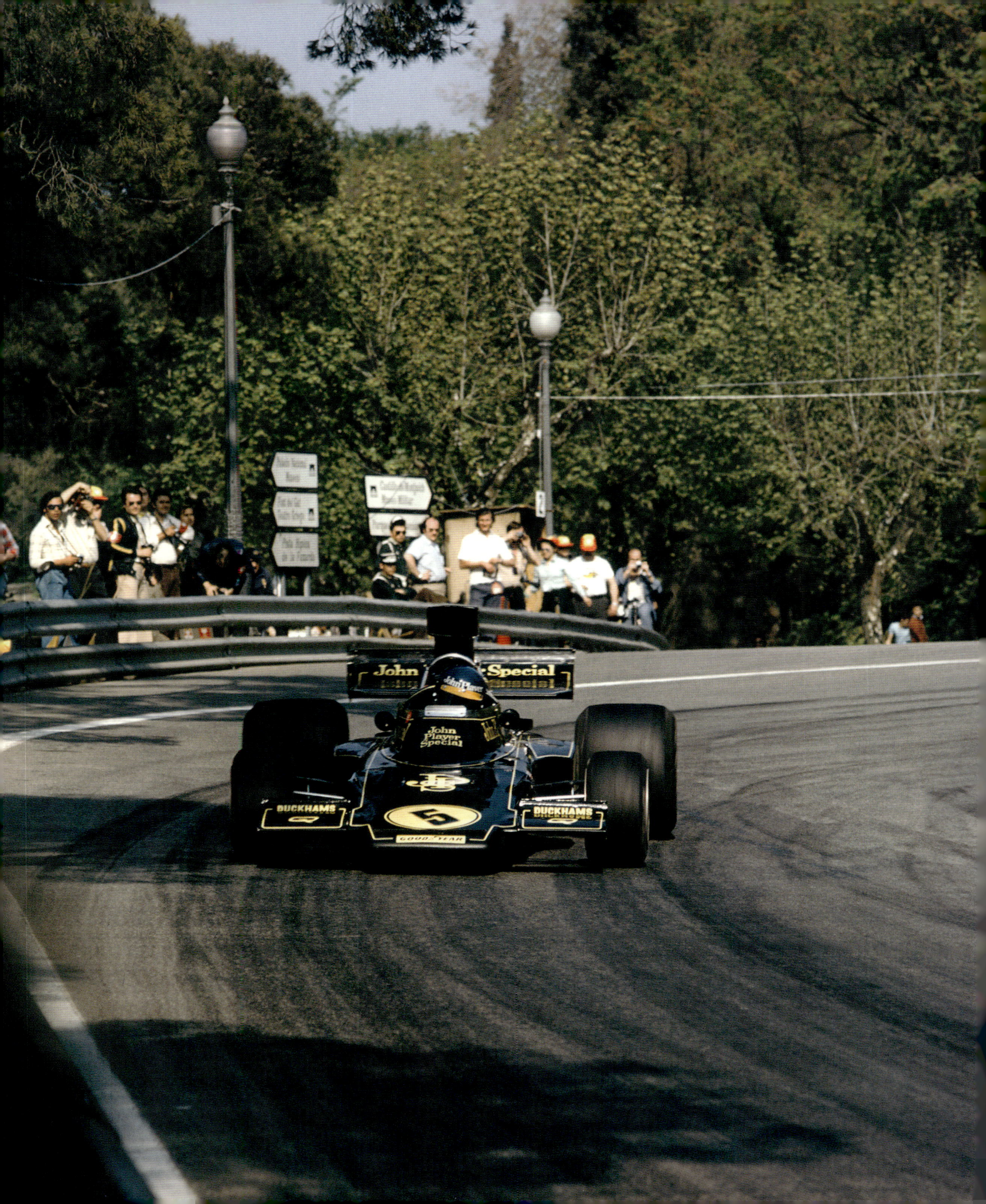
John Player Special
John Player Special
BUCKHAMS
5
BUCKHAMS

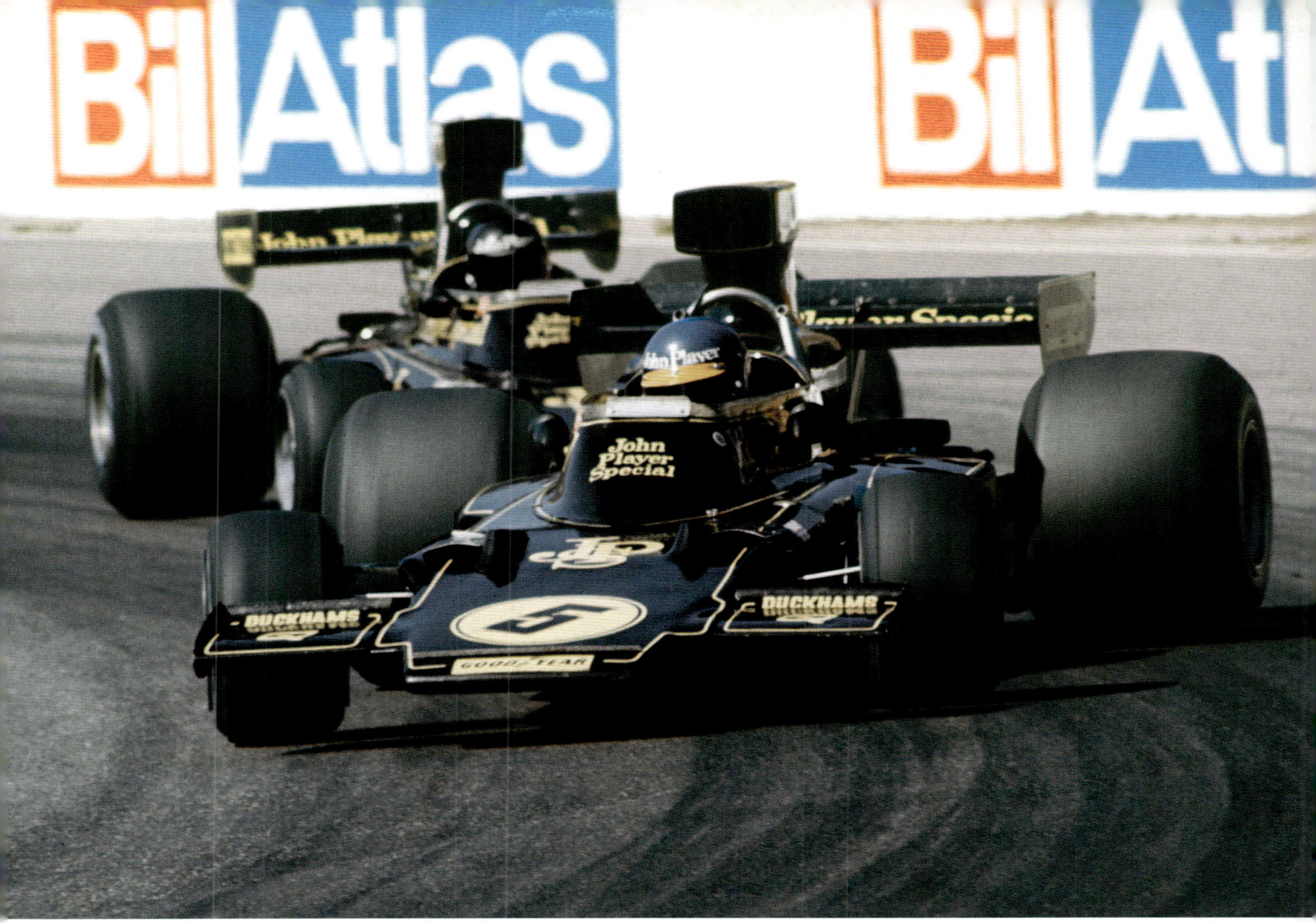

LEFT Having picked up his first points of the season with a solid fourth place in Monaco, and then crashed at Zolder (again!) due to a brake failure, Ronnie returned to Montjuic Park for the Spanish Grand Prix in Barcelona. He could do no better than 12th in the single qualifying session. This was a famously farcical race meeting, initially because the very fast street circuit was in a dangerous condition, the barriers inadequately secured. Most of the drivers refused to practise on the first day, but the organisers threatened to impound all the teams' equipment if they failed to honour their contracts. So the teams organised work parties to secure the barriers, and eventually the drivers relented. On race day, the farce continued with many crashes and collisions, all of which helped Ronnie's progress. He was up in third place on the 24th lap when he collided with François Migault's lapped Embassy Lola GH1. Three laps later, the farce turned to tragedy. Rolf Stommelen, an unlikely leader with Graham Hill's other GH1, lost his rear wing on the start-finish straight and careened over one of the barriers, killing five bystanders and breaking a leg. After a disgraceful delay, the race was stopped with Jochen Mass's McLaren leading.

ABOVE Ronnie hams it up for his home crowd at Anderstorp, fending off team-mate Jacky Ickx in the midfield of the Swedish Grand Prix. Unable to find a good balance, he had qualified his Lotus 72E in eighth place and, as shown, continued to wrestle with the car on race day. He brought it home in eighth position, a lap behind winner Niki Lauda, whose third straight victory for Ferrari cemented his grip on the championship. Ronnie's arrival at JPS Team Lotus had been the catalyst that created this event two years before, and it was last run in 1978. Ronnie never did win here on the Scandinavian Raceway.

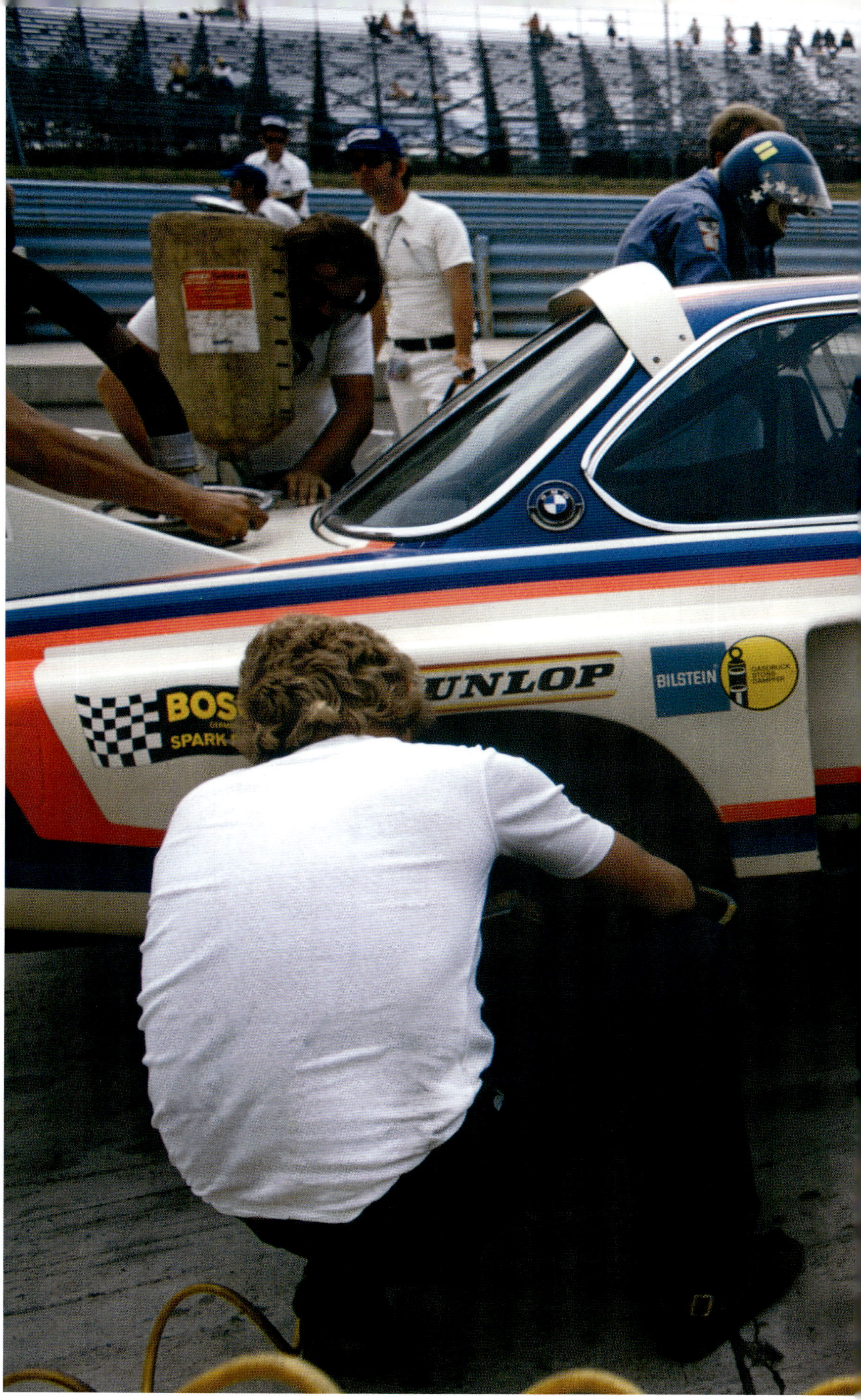

RIGHT The week after more disappointment in the French Grand Prix, Ronnie rejoined the works BMW Motorsport team for the six-hour World Championship of Makes race at Watkins Glen, in rural New York state. This was the third of only four outings this season with the 3.5-litre BMW 3.0 CSL and his co-driver here was Hans-Joachim Stuck, a regular team driver with Brian Redman and Sam Posey in BMW's IMSA campaign in America. Stuck took on the qualifying duties, and the two BMWs, built to comply with the FIA Group 2 regulations, lined up on the fourth row behind the faster Renault-Alpine, Alfa Romeo and Porsche Group 6 sports-prototypes. The BMWs dominated the Porsche Carreras and Chevrolet Corvettes in their class and here Ronnie takes over from Stuck in the first routine pitstop. Midway through Stuck's second shift, under a sudden torrential rainstorm, he collided with a Corvette and damaged the rear of the BMW. The flooded race was red-flagged and Jochen Neerpsach's crew was able to make repairs before the restart, but did not notice that the fuel tank had been ruptured. And this was also the third of four DNFs this year for Ronnie and BMW...

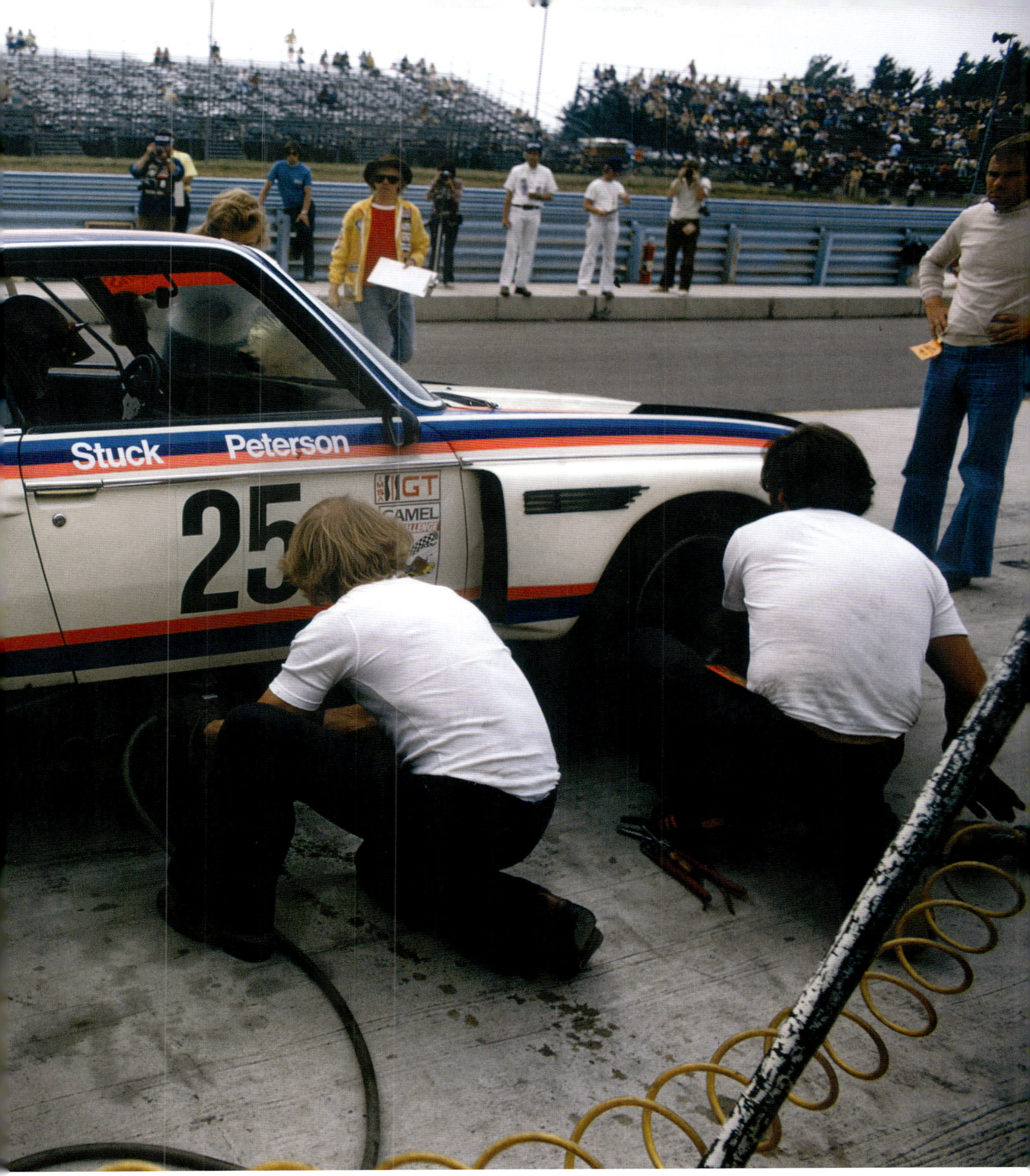
Stuck
Peterson
25
IMSA GT
CAMEL

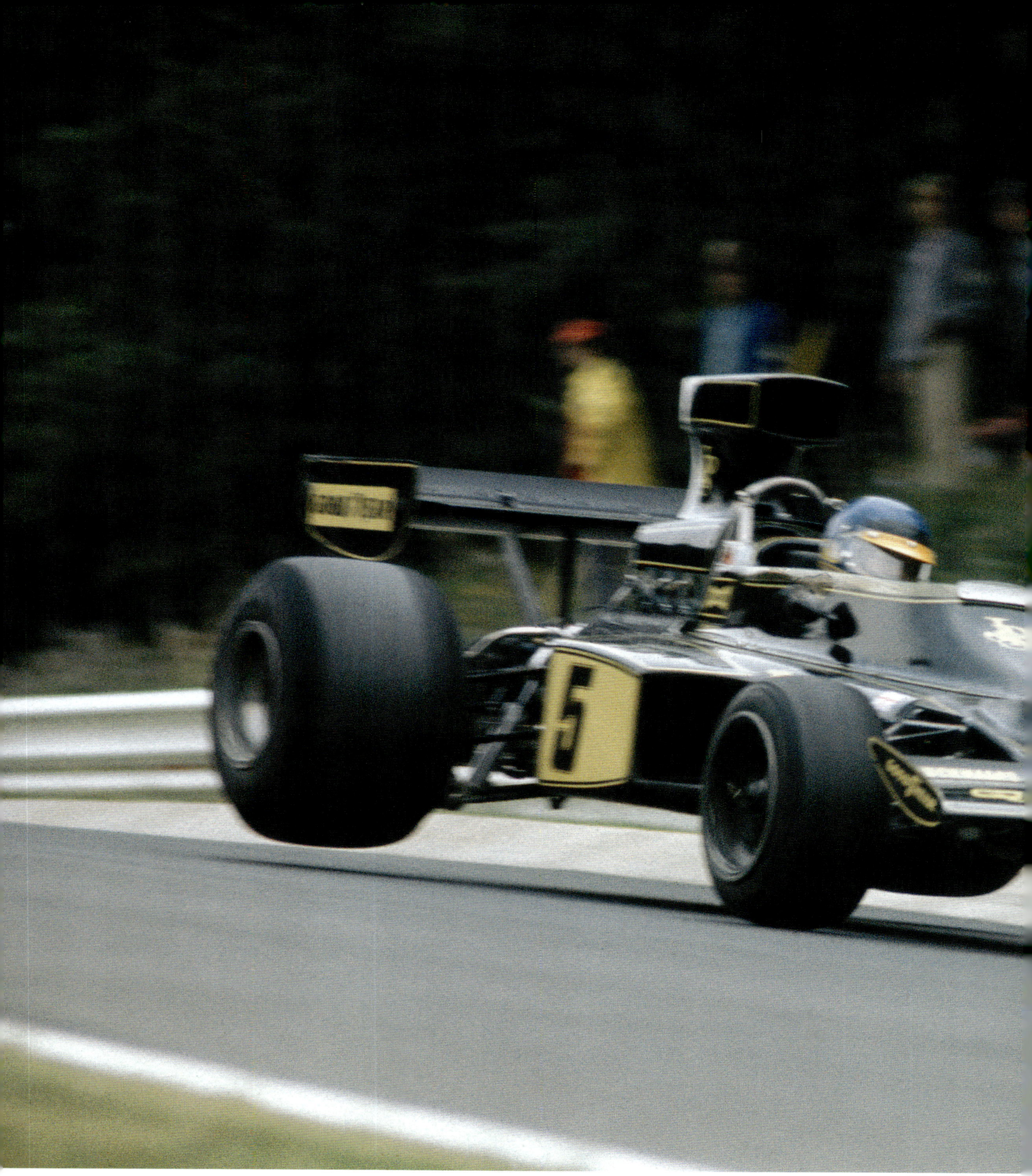

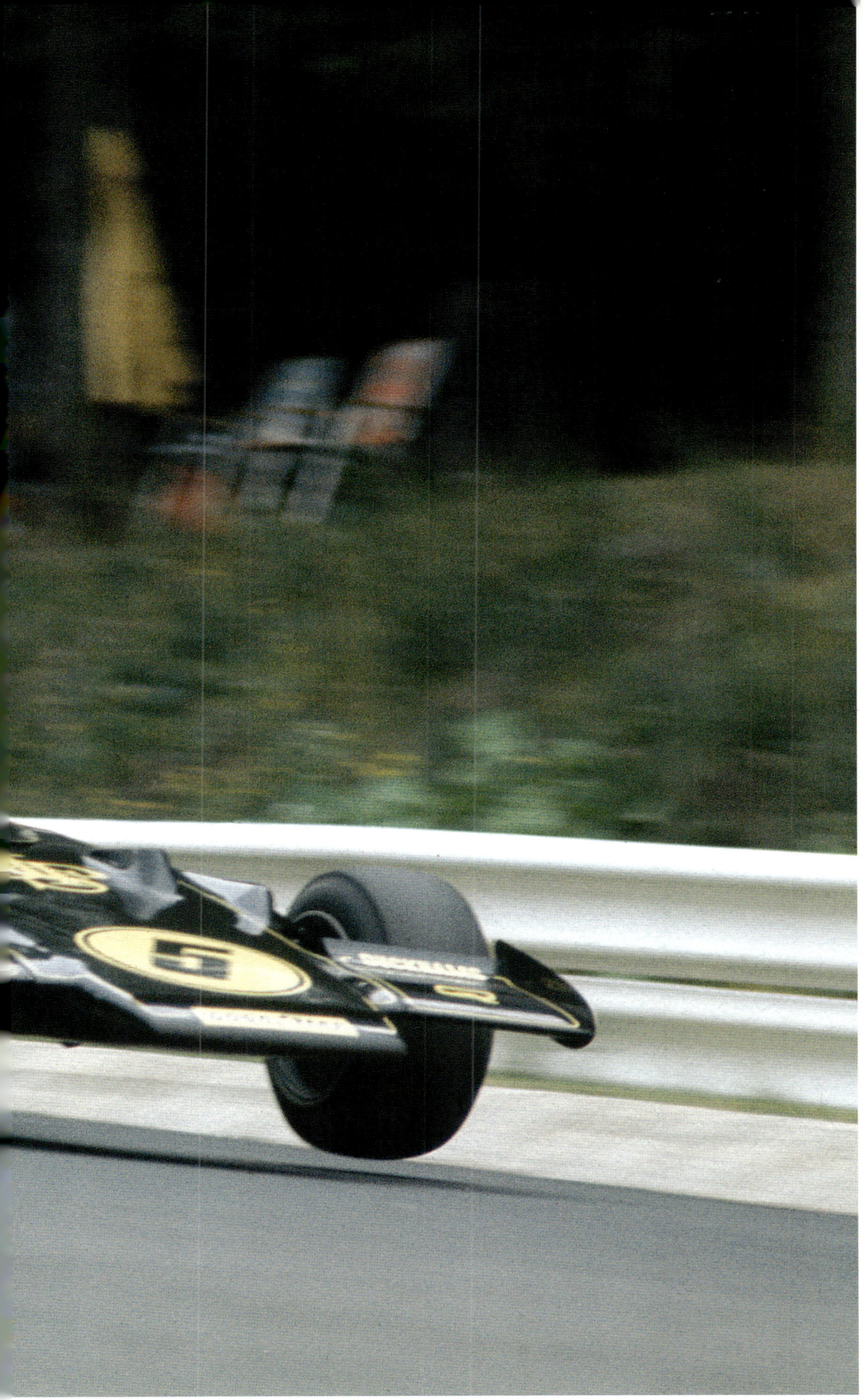

LEFT A one-point landing shows how hard Ronnie is trying with his uncompetitive old Lotus on the Nürburgring. After yet another mechanical failure at Paul Ricard, Jacky Ickx shrugged his shoulders and walked away from Team Lotus. In his place, Colin Chapman had run Jim Crawford at Silverstone and was using John Watson here. But the German Grand Prix turned out to be the nadir of this woeful season for Chapman's team. Both men qualified towards the back of the grid, Ronnie was out with a clutch failure after only a lap, and Watson with broken suspension after only two...

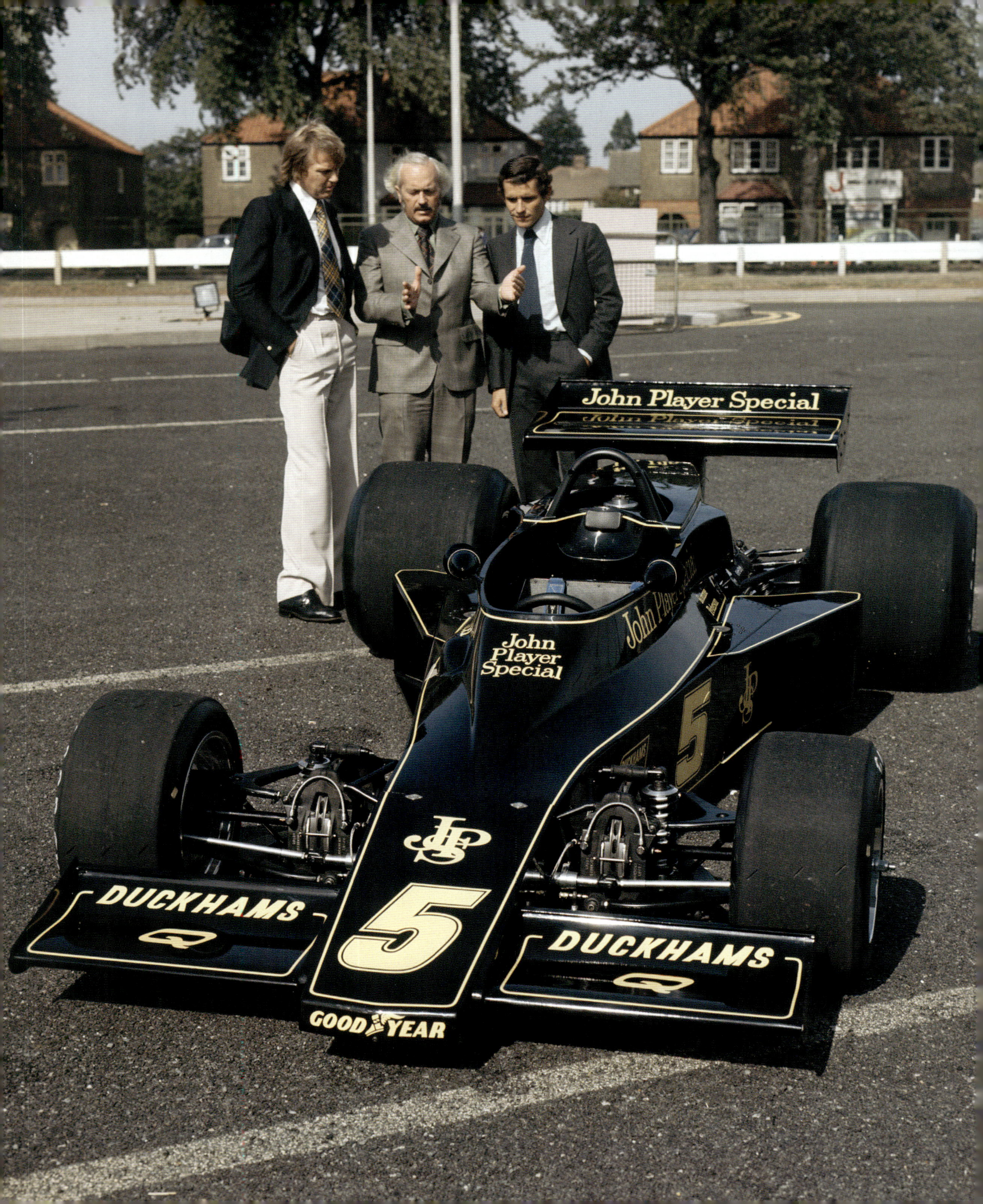
John Player Special
John Player Special
John Player Special
5
DUCKHAMS
DUCKHAMS
GOODYEAR
5

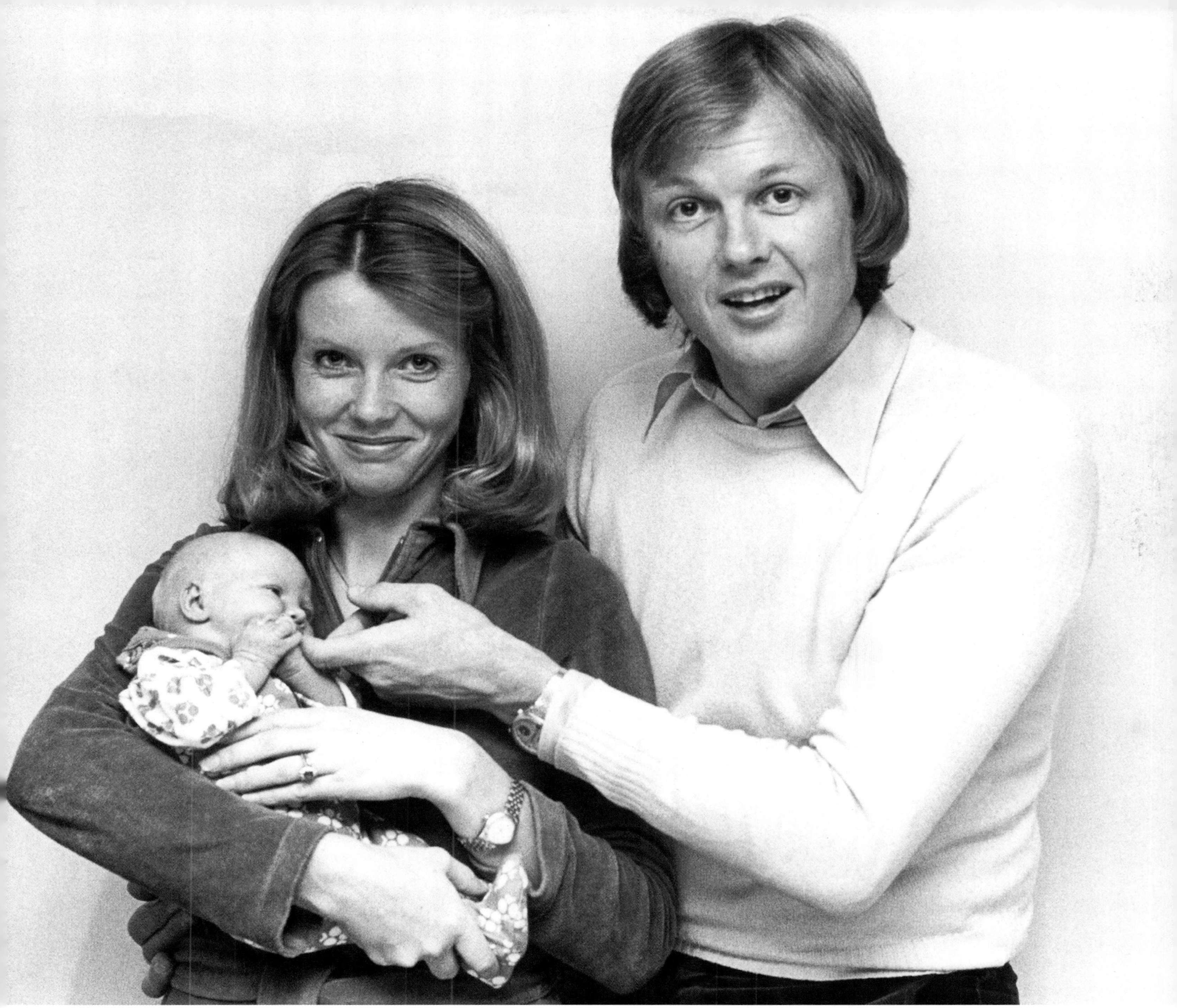

LEFT The first all-new JPS Lotus 77 was not on its wheels until mid-September, when it was unveiled to the media at a London Heathrow hotel. Colin Chapman persuaded Jacky Ickx to come to the launch. Here Chapman explains to his intended 1976 drivers that the keynote of the 77 was wide-ranging adjustability not only of the suspension and wing settings, but also the track, the wheelbase and the weight distribution. Both drivers look unconvinced. Ronnie signed a new contract for the following season, but Ickx declined, and ultimately raced for Frank Williams. Note the massive inboard brake assemblies in the airflow, a solution that would make a modern Formula 1 aerodynamicist weep. When Ronnie tested the car at Silverstone, they slowed the car in a straight line and clearly there was an enormous amount of work to be done over the coming winter.

ABOVE Ronnie and Barbro, the love of his life, were married in March 1975 after a four-year relationship and, in November, she gave birth to their daughter, Nina. With a season that had delivered only eight finishes from 23 racing starts fresh in his memory, Ronnie is clearly cheered by this event. Things are now looking better for him, with a reinvented family life, a new second home in Monaco, another Team Lotus contract in his pocket, and the firm prospect of a new Grand Prix car at last.

1976

BACK TO MARCH – AND THE WINNER'S CIRCLE

One race meeting with Team Lotus was more than enough for Ronnie in 1976. The radical new Lotus 77 was disappointing in testing in England, and again in practice at Interlagos – where a component failure caused him to crash it after only three laps. The incident led to a public row with Colin Chapman and Ronnie immediately accepted an offer to return to March. He raced for his former team, alongside Vittorio Brambilla and Hans-Joachim Stuck, for the duration of the season. Ronnie started out with a chassis that was found to be cracked but, once with a new tub, he was increasingly competitive and managed to lead five races before securing a memorable victory at Monza – his first for exactly two years. By then, however, he was committed to a one-year contract in 1977 with Elf Team Tyrrell.

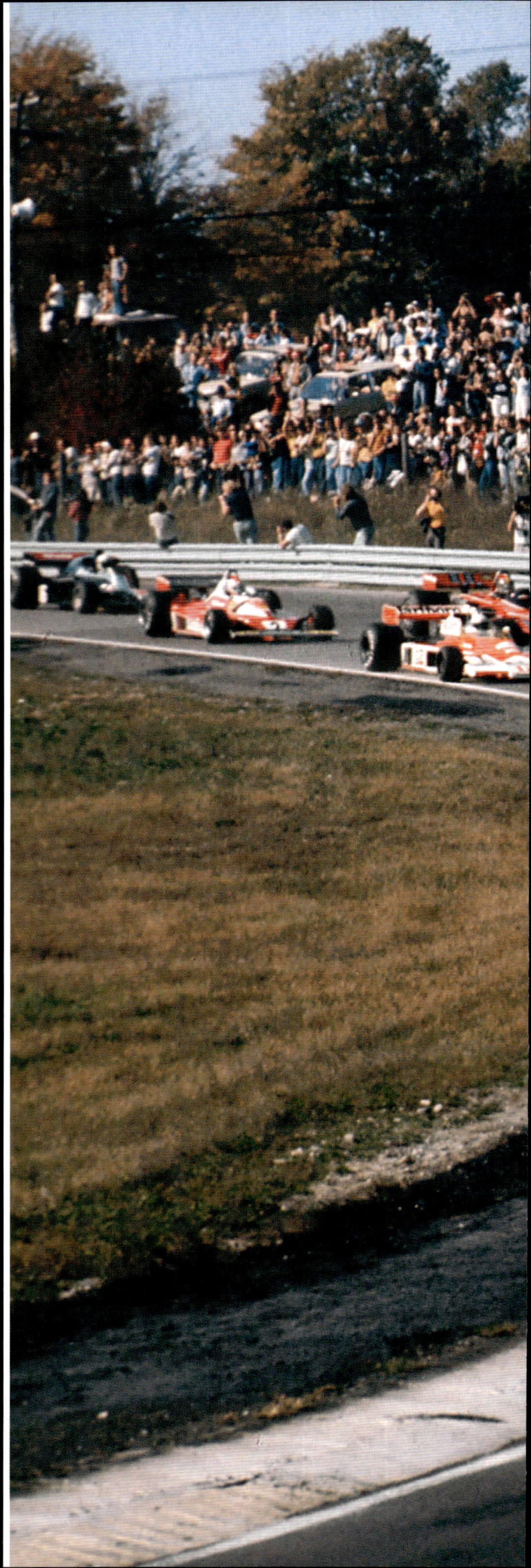

RIGHT Encouraged by a great victory at Monza, Ronnie qualified his March 761 second on the grid for the Canadian Grand Prix on the scenic Mosport Park road circuit, but grabbed the lead at the start of the race from James Hunt's pole position McLaren M23, Vittorio Brambilla's March, Patrick Depailler's Tyrrell P34, Mario Andretti's Lotus 77, Niki Lauda's Ferrari 312T2 and the rest.

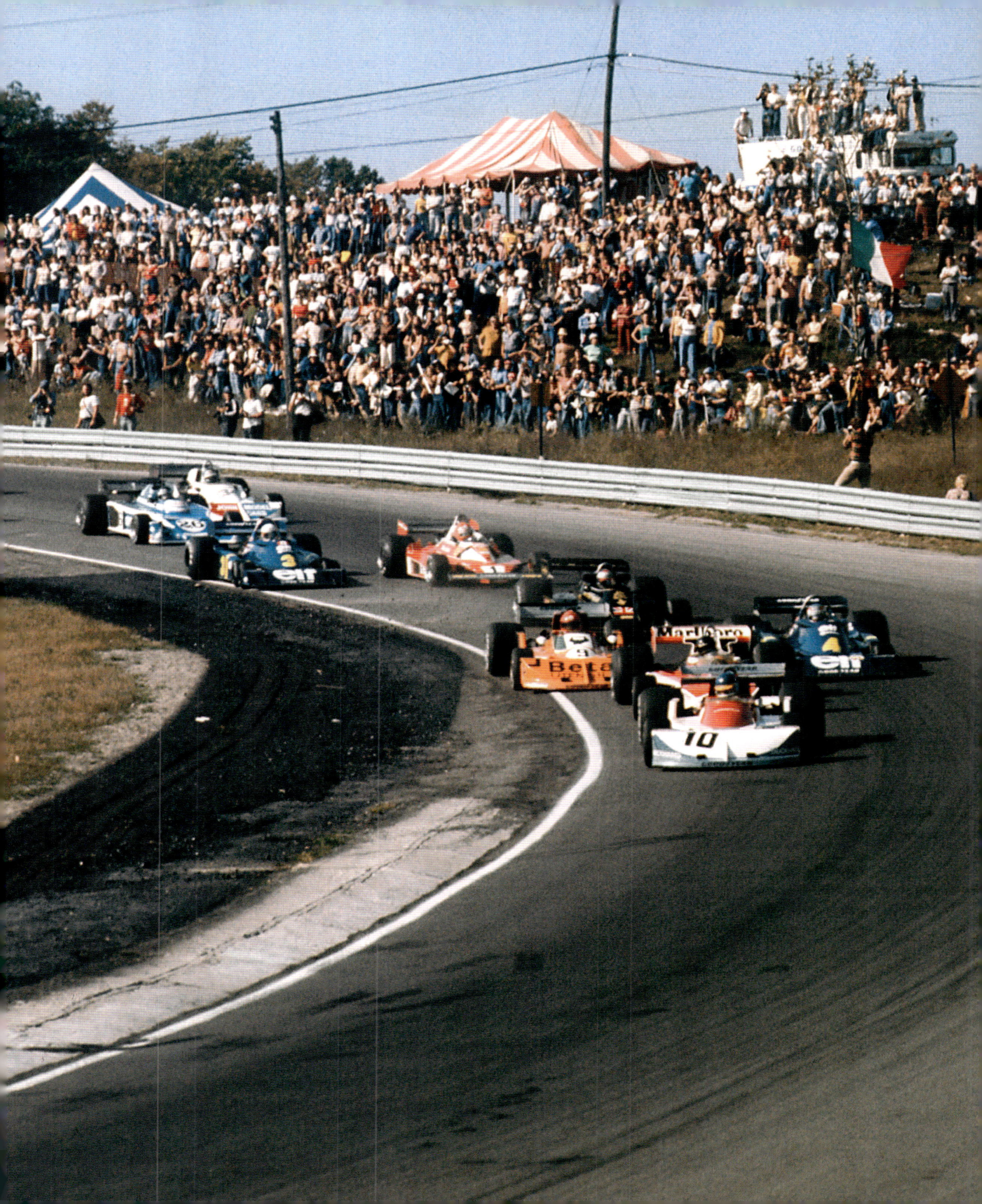
elf
3
Beta
Marlboro
elf
4
10

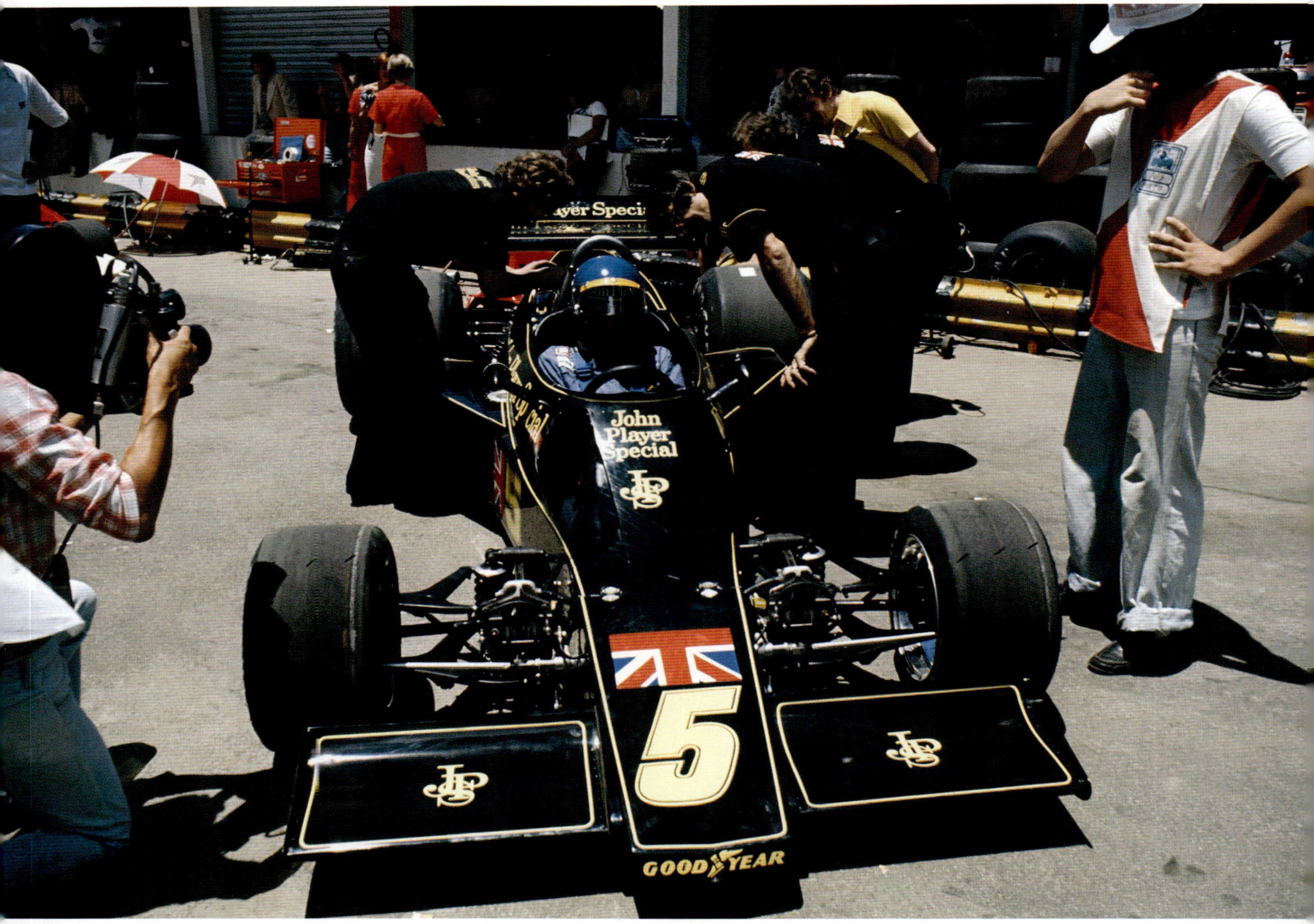

ABOVE Ronnie prepares to practise his JPS Lotus 77 at Interlagos for the season-opening Brazilian Grand Prix. He and Jim Crawford had done the bulk of the pre-season testing of the team's new equipment, and had found it inadequate in terms of straight-line speed and chassis rigidity.

OPPOSITE TOP Ronnie damaged his new Lotus only three laps into the first practice session at Interlagos when a water line detached itself and sprayed the liquid over a rear tyre, causing a head-on crash into the catchfencing. He was not impressed...

OPPOSITE BOTTOM John Player Team Lotus in consultation in pit-lane after qualifying at Interlagos. Mario Andretti, here for a one-off drive pending the completion of Parnelli Jones's new US-built Formula 1 car, had qualified 16th and his disappointment with the performance of the Lotus 77 shows clearly. Ronnie was to start two places even further back. Nursing a painful finger after his accident, he is not paying attention to Colin Chapman, distracted by his decision to quit his job. That evening, he and his boss had a blazing row during a reception in Sao Paulo. The next day, Mario misjudged a pass on Carlos Pace's Brabham on the seventh lap, and took himself and Ronnie out of the Brazilian Grand Prix.

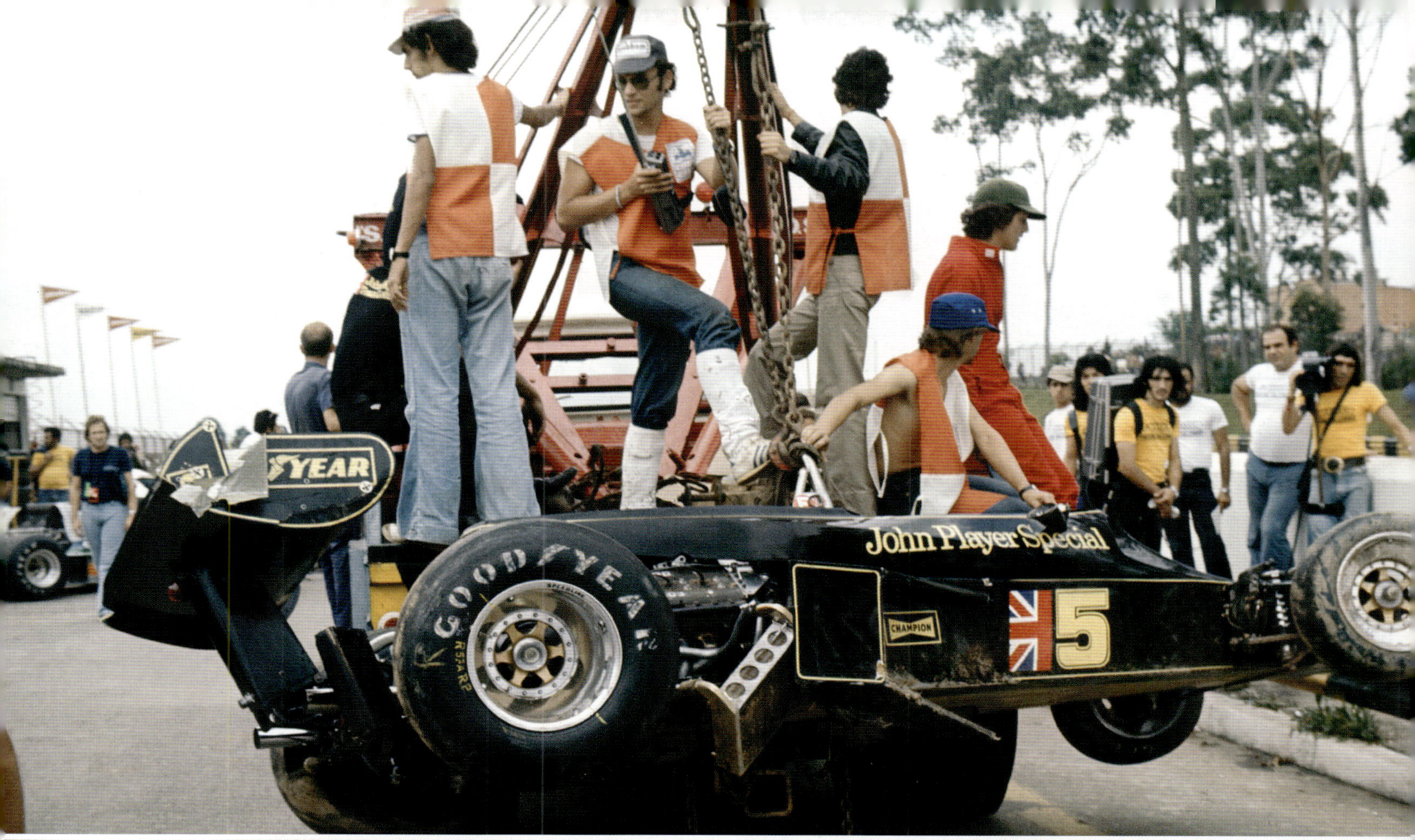
GOODYEAR
John Player Special
CHAMPION
5

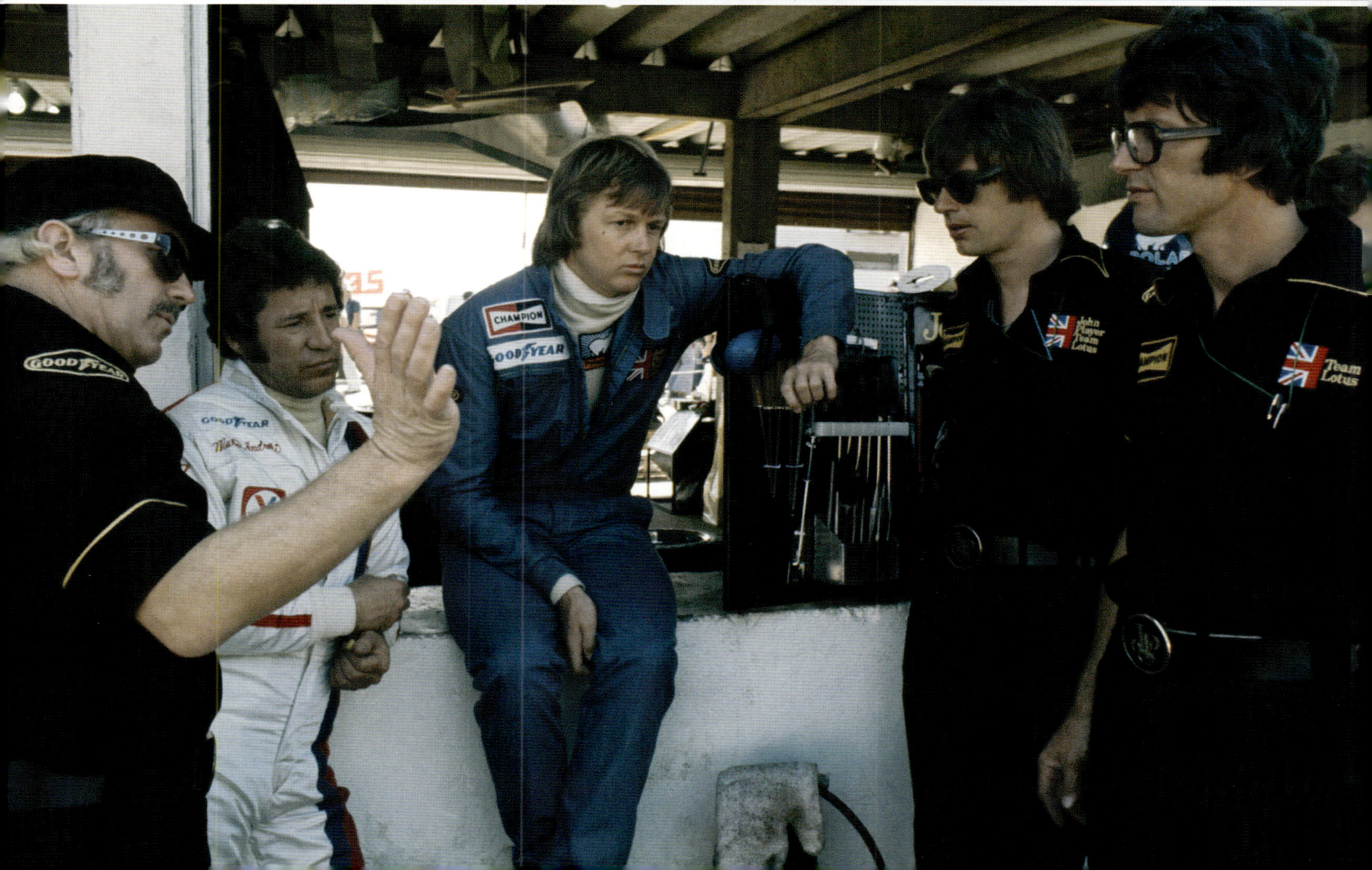
CHAMPION
GOODYEAR
John Player Team Lotus
Team Lotus

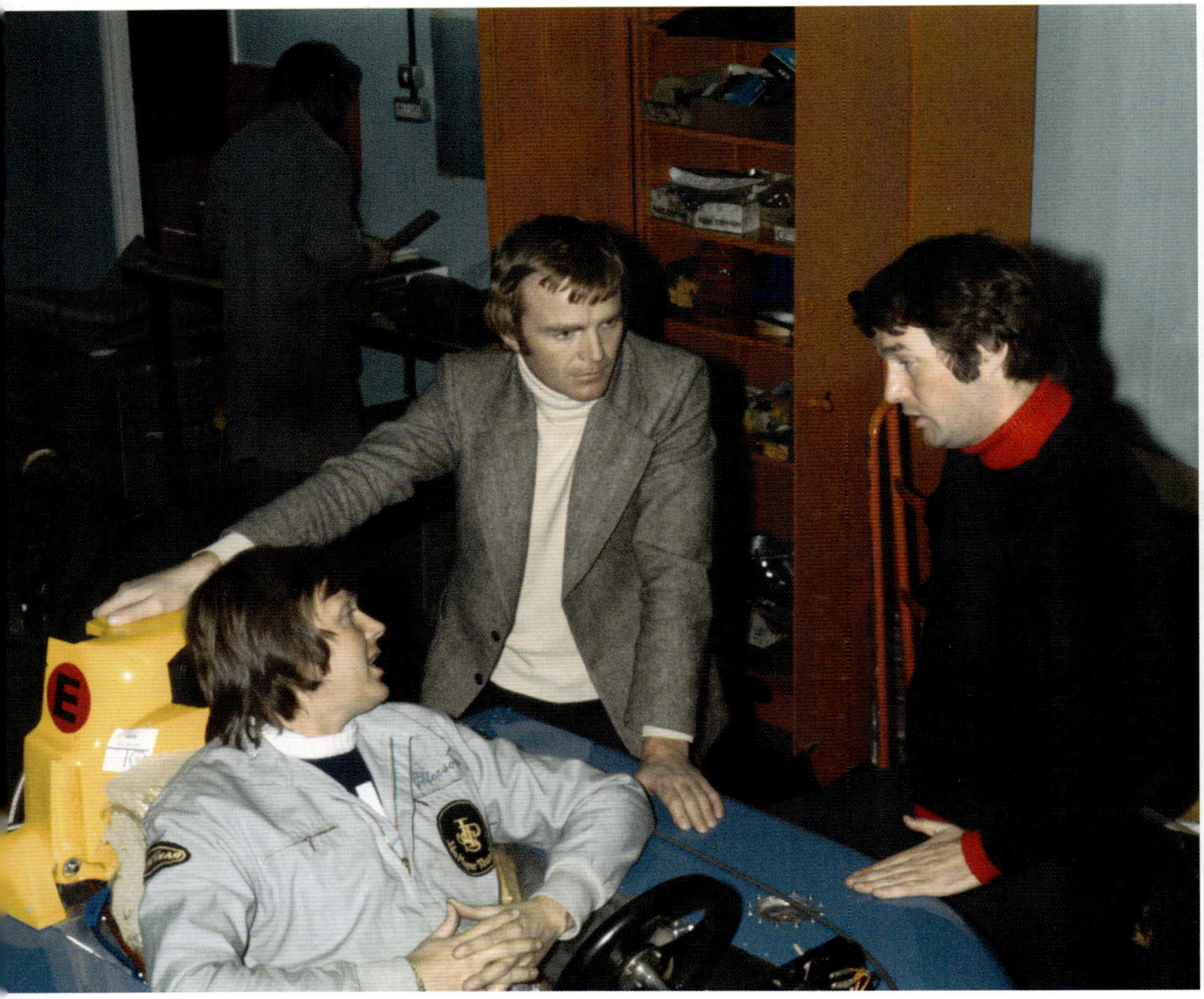

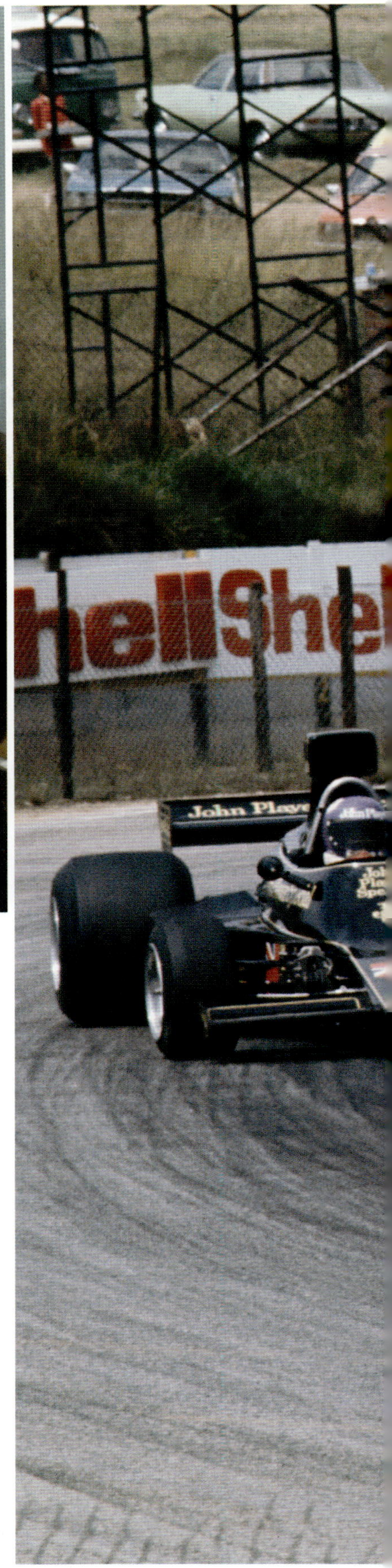

ABOVE Max Mosley and Robin Herd look on as Ronnie has a seat fitting in the 761 in March Engineering's factory in Bicester, less than two weeks after returning from Brazil. This was all done in secrecy but a journalist learned that Lella Lombardi's car had already been liveried in the colours of Sweden. Challenged with this information, Mosley said it might be because blue and yellow were the municipal colours of Turin, Lombardi's home town (where all the residents thought they were red and silver). The switch was financed by Polar Caravans and, ironically, by Count 'Googhie' Zanon, who had paid for Lombardi's drive but was also an avid Peterson fan. The deal, brokered by Ronnie's faithful manager, Stefan Svenby, involved the release of Gunnar Nilsson, who was under contract to join the March Formula 2 team, so that he could race for Team Lotus in Ronnie's place.

RIGHT During practice at Kyalami, Ronnie leads Gunnar Nilsson, his young compatriot who had replaced him in the Lotus 77, and Jody Scheckter in his Tyrrell 007. Ronnie qualified seventh for the South African Grand Prix, surprised to be behind Vittorio Brambilla in the other works March 761. In the race, however, he swiftly ascended to fifth position and was shaping up to pass Brambilla on the 17th lap when he was taken out of the race by Patrick Depailler, who spun the other Tyrrell and broke the March's suspension in the process. Nilsson, on his Grand Prix début, qualified last and retired early on with a clutch failure. Nothing had changed at Team Lotus. Yet...

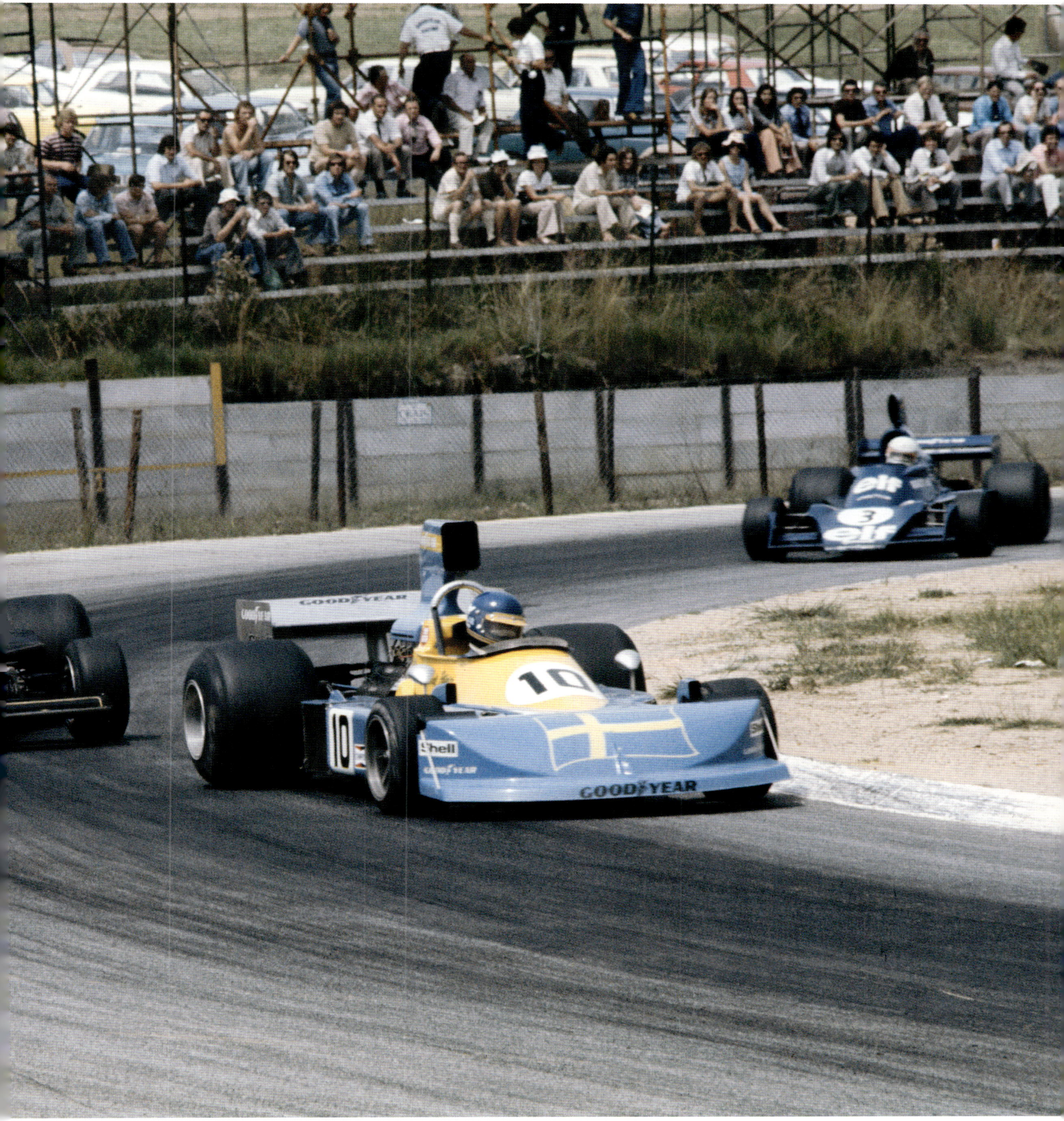
GOODYEAR
Shell
10
elf
3

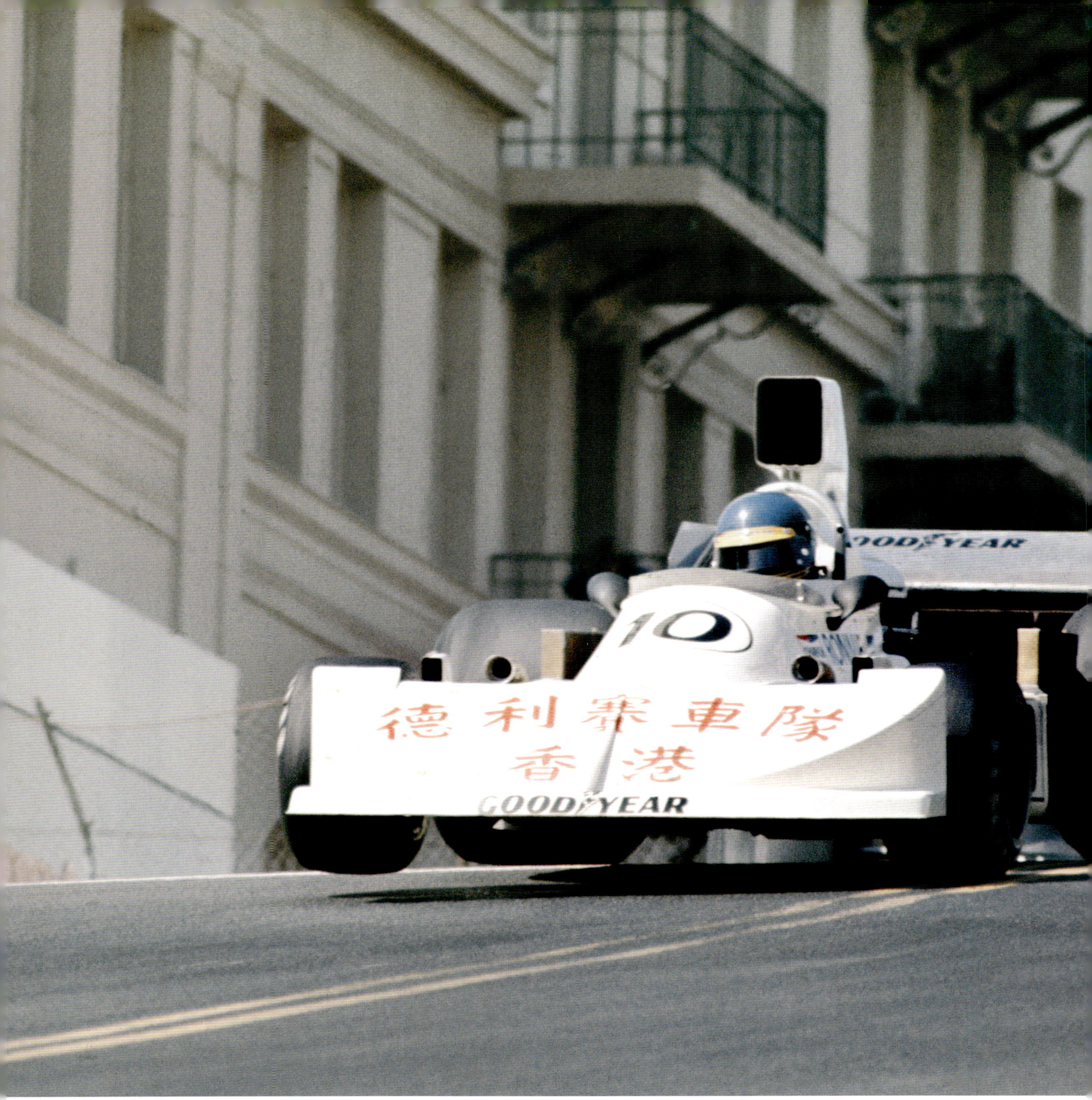

ABOVE Wealthy Hong Kong entrepreneur Teddy Yip, who was preparing to establish his Theodore Racing Formula 1 team, sponsored two of four works Marches in Long Beach. Ronnie's was the fastest in qualifying, in sixth place. On race day, he climbed into fourth, dicing with the Shadows of Tom Pryce and Jean-Pierre Jarier, but had to pit when his brake fluid boiled. He resumed to finish last, three laps down on the Ferrari 1–2 at the front of the 10 survivors.

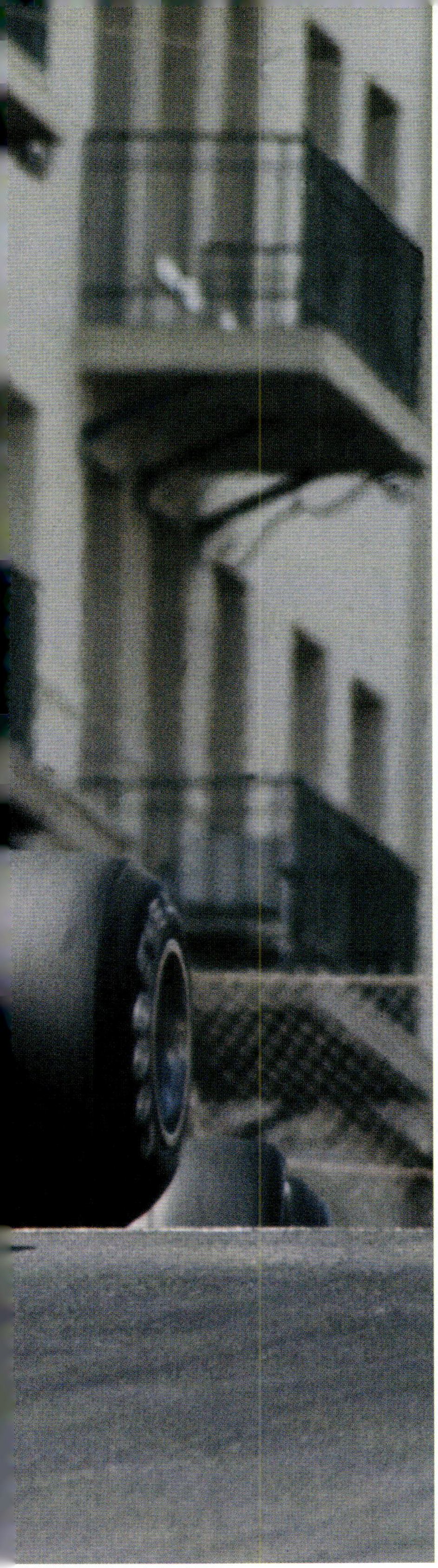

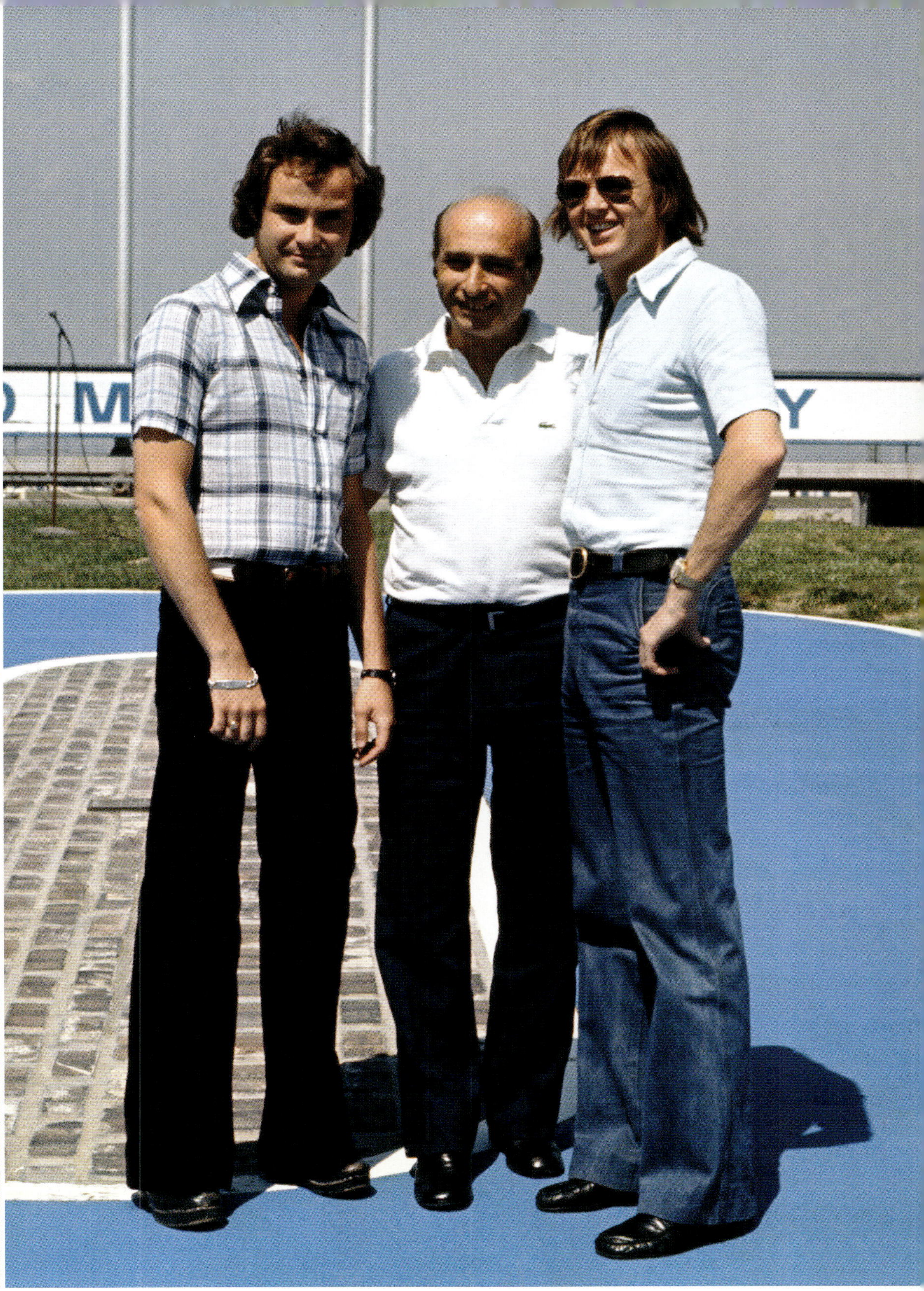

ABOVE Ronnie and Gunnar Nilsson got to meet the incomparable Juan Manuel Fangio at Ontario Motor Speedway while they were in California for the inaugural USA Grand Prix West on the new Long Beach street course. The five-time World Champion later drove a 1955 Mercedes-Benz W196 in the celebrity event.

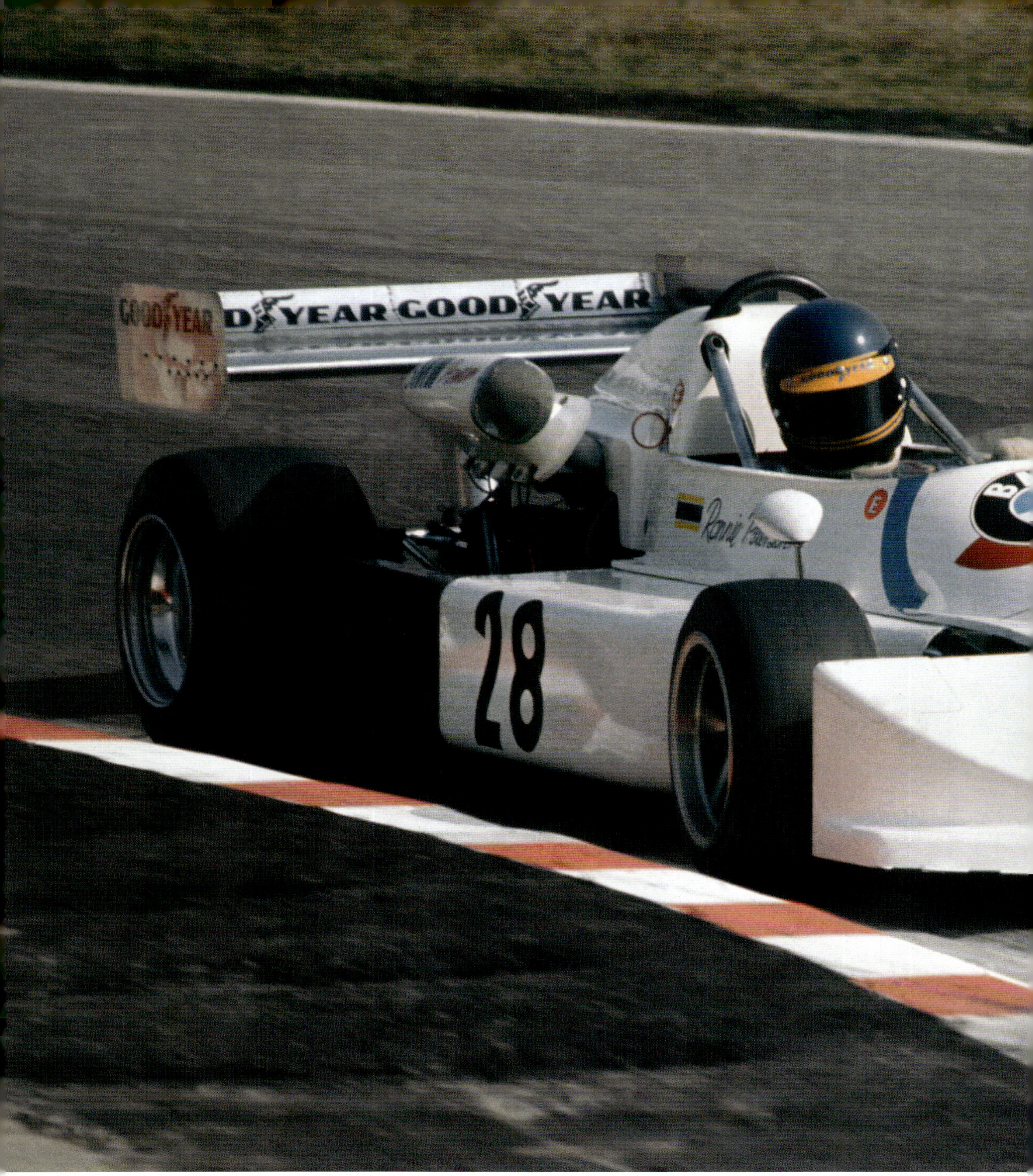
GOODYEAR
28

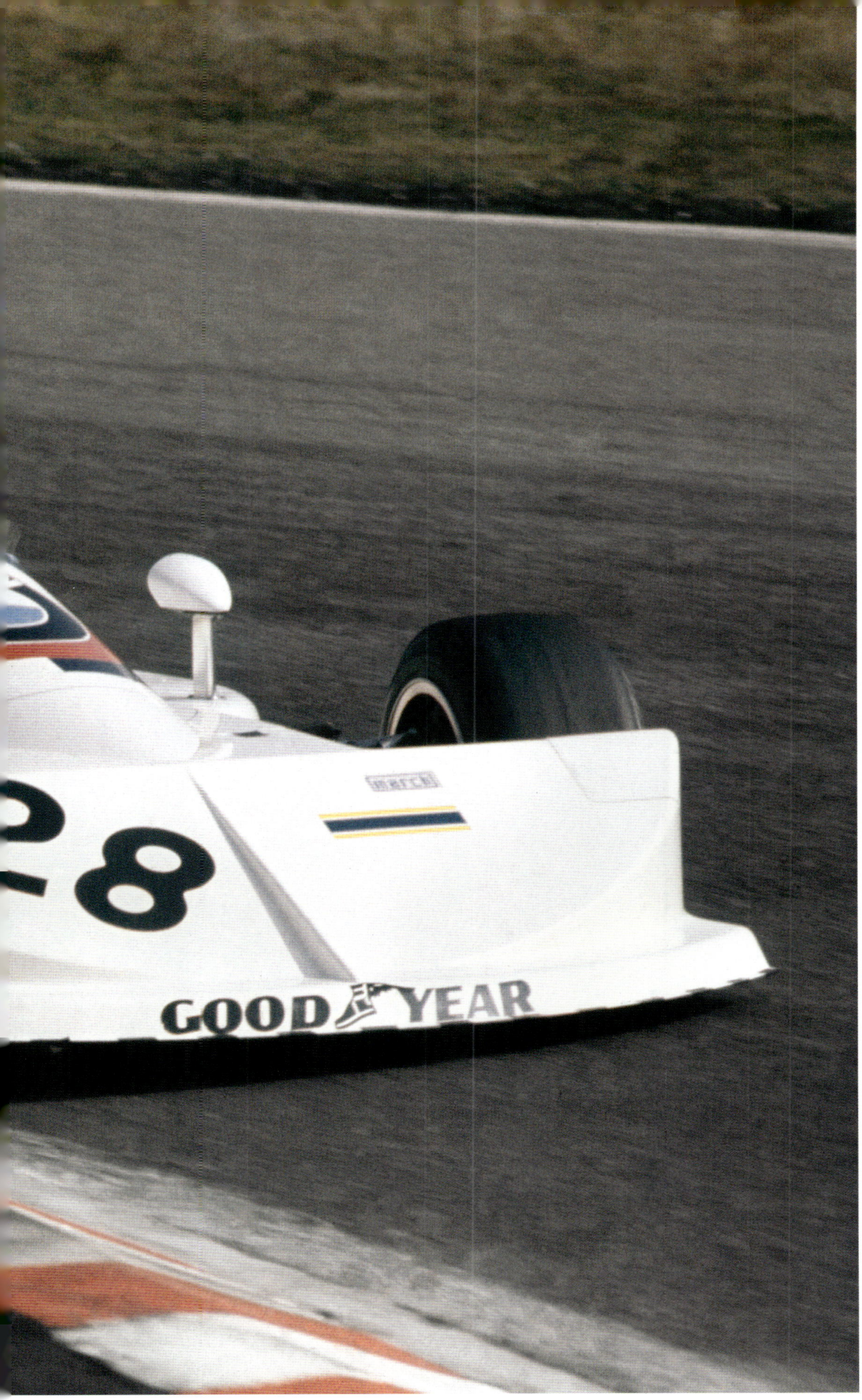

LEFT For Ronnie, part of the attraction of March was that he wanted to do some Formula 2 races. However, ultimately he did only one, the Jim Clark Trophy event at Hockenheim midway through the five-week gap between the USA West and Spanish Grands Prix. The 50th and last Formula 2 event of Ronnie's career was a miserable experience. March provided him with a brand new 762-BMW and he qualified it third on the grid behind team-mate Hans-Joachim Stuck and Jean-Pierre Jabouille with the quickest Elf-Renault V6. It all went downhill from there. In the first heat, Ronnie's clutch exploded on the third lap. In the second heat, his fuel pressure zeroed – on the third lap. Stuck won both the heats as he liked.

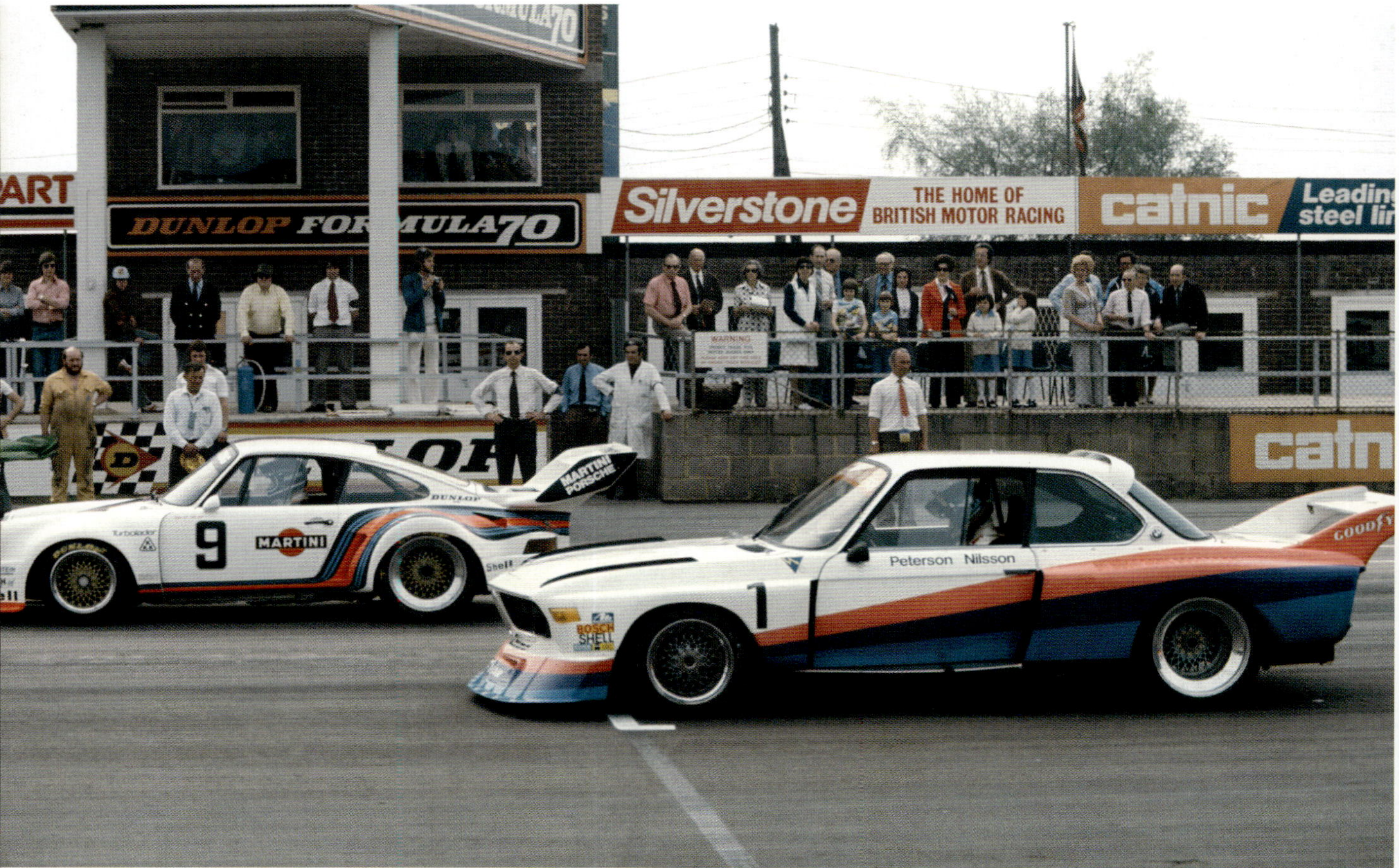

ABOVE BMW Motorsport entered Ronnie for the Silverstone 6 Hours round of the World Championship of Makes, wishing to show the potential of a twin-turbocharged, 3.2-litre CSL with which it intended to challenge Porsche. Sharing the new car with Gunnar Nilsson, Ronnie produced a series of spectacular qualifying laps to put it on the front row alongside Jacky Ickx in the rival factory team's new Martini Porsche 935. Ickx's clutch burned out at the start and Ronnie built up a big lead over the Kremer Porsche of Bob Wollek – only to pit for new tyres before the race was half an hour old. He rejoined sixth and treated the crowd to a wonderful drive. He had recovered second place when the gearbox broke shortly before his first scheduled pitstop.

RIGHT Ronnie prepares for the start of the Monaco Grand Prix. He always revelled in the many challenges of the world's most famous street circuit, and this time he made the March punch far above its weight. He put it third on the grid, behind the Ferraris of Niki Lauda and Clay Regazzoni, and just ahead of the six-wheel Tyrrells of Patrick Depailler and Jody Scheckter. Polar Caravans, a long-established Swedish company that had sponsored Torsten Palm's Hesketh in a couple of Formula 1 races the previous season, had financed Ronnie's sudden move from Lotus to March, along with Count 'Googhie' Zanon.

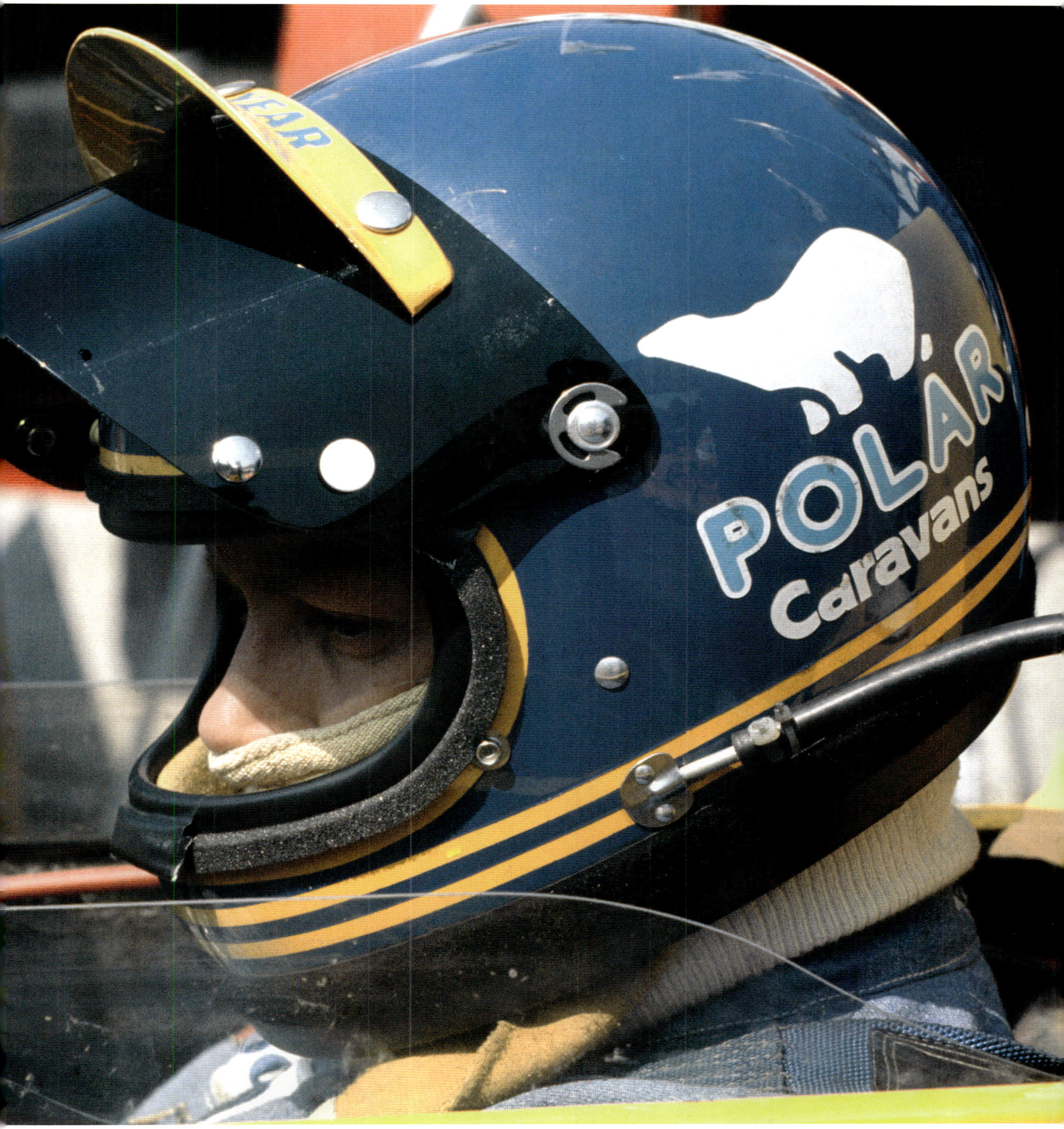
POLAR
Caravans

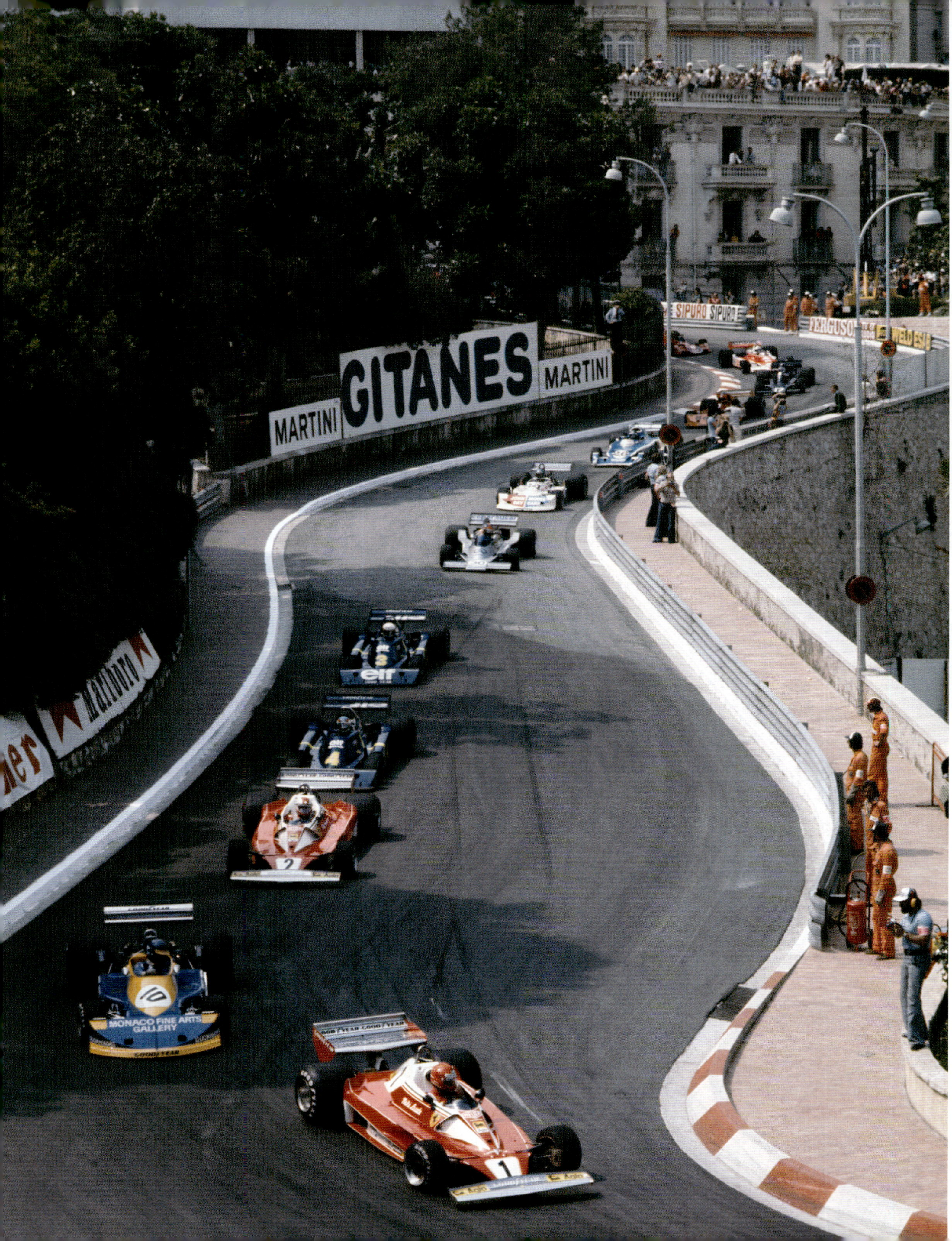
GITANES
MARTINI
MARTINI
SIPURO SIPURO
FERGUSON
Marlboro
elf
MONACO FINE ARTS GALLERY
GOOD YEAR

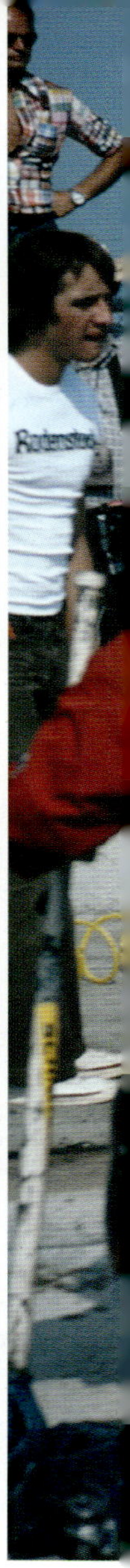

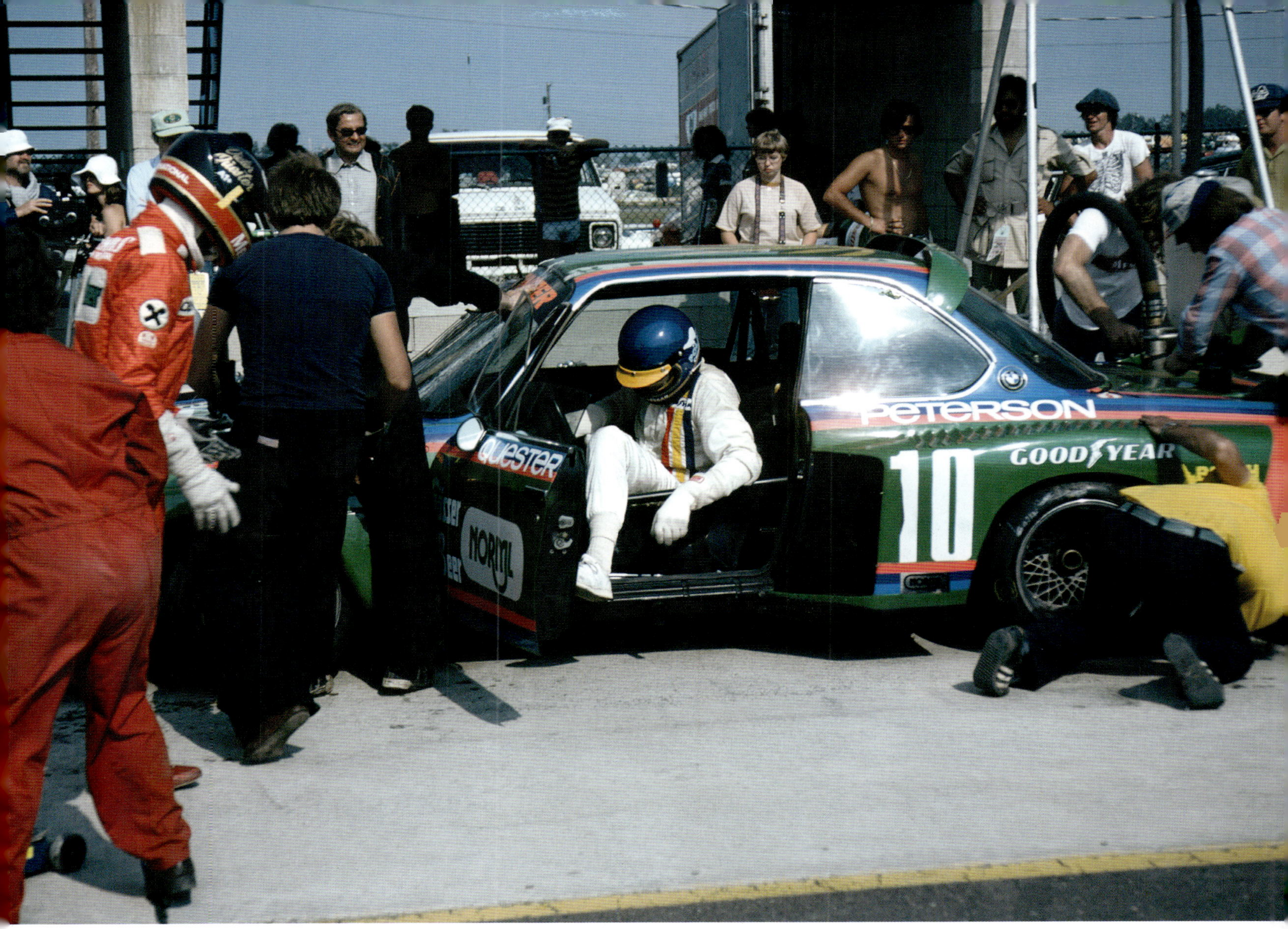

LEFT Ronnie beat Clay Regazzoni in the short drag race to Ste Devote and inserted his March firmly between the Ferraris. As Niki Lauda leads the field into the Station hairpin for the first time, Patrick Depailler has fourth place ahead of Tyrrell team-mate Jody Scheckter, Emerson Fittipaldi (Copersucar), Hans Stuck in the second works March and Jacques Laffite in his Ligier JS5. Ronnie was still splitting the Ferraris when, on the 29th lap, he came across some oil in the harbourfront chicane from the broken engine of James Hunt's McLaren. Ronnie held a big slide but, unaware that his tyres had been liberally greased by the oil, spun into the wall when he tried to turn into Tabac. Lauda won this with the Tyrrells second and third.

ABOVE The third of Ronnie's four 1976 races with BMW Motorsport was the Watkins Glen 6 Hours, which he had won with an Alfa Romeo sports-prototype five years previously. And this was the only one he finished, sharing a Schnitzer-operated 3.0 CSL with Dieter Quester and later Brian Redman, after his car had been retired. Although BMW's Group 5 teams arrived in America with three wins in the bag, to Porsche's two, this race was dominated by the Porsche 935s of the works and Evertz teams. Ronnie qualified seventh but had his car racing along in fourth place early in the action. Here he pits the car for the first handover to Quester. Later, their BMW was delayed in the pits with a gear selection fault. Ronnie rejoined in seventh position and but could recover only two of the lost places during the final hour, finishing fifth.

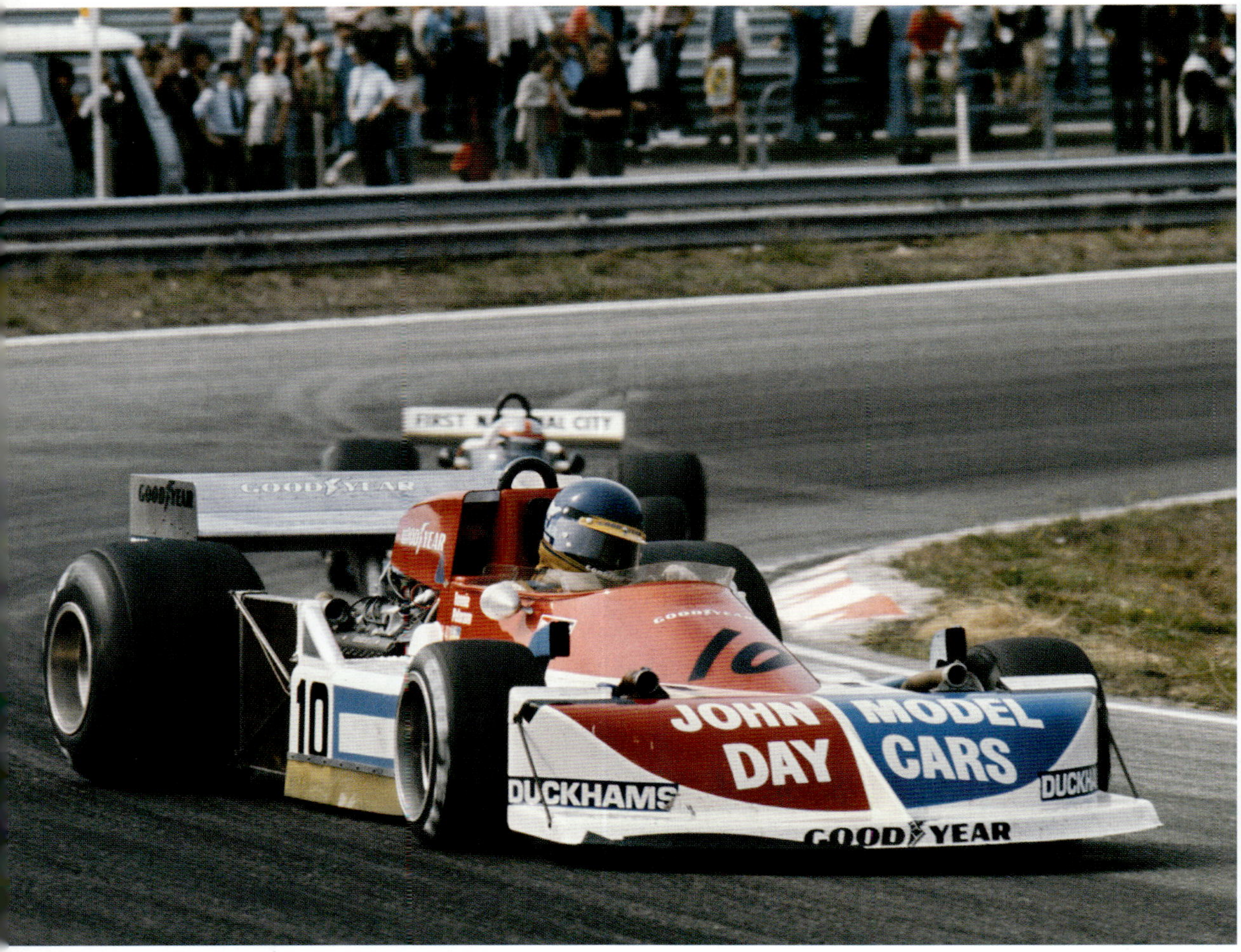

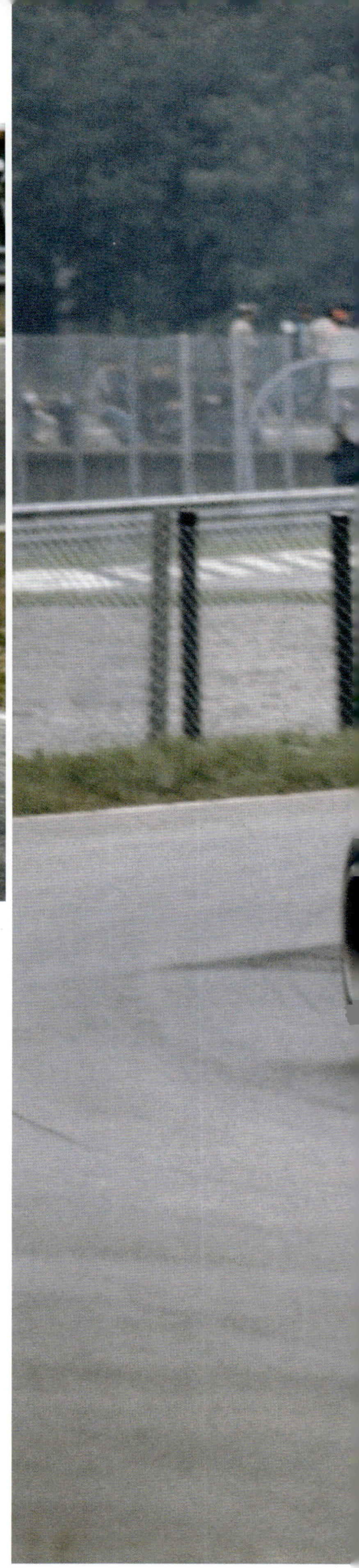

ABOVE The only pole position of Ronnie's season came at Zandvoort, where he narrowly outqualified one of the regular pacesetters of 1976, James Hunt, in the absence of the other, Niki Lauda, who had been badly injured on the Nürburgring four weeks before. Ronnie led the Dutch Grand Prix from the start but was soon having to do everything he could with an understeering car to fend off John Watson's Penske PC4 (pictured) and then Hunt's McLaren M23. It wasn't enough and, not without a struggle, they outbraked him on laps 12 and 13. Five laps later, Ronnie was also overtaken by Clay Regazzoni's Ferrari. But he held down fourth place until lap 48, when the Penske's gearbox broke and he was promoted to third. Only four laps later, Ronnie's engine failed. Hunt won from Regazzoni, and Ronnie's place on the podium was taken by Mario Andretti with the JPS Lotus 77 he had discarded at the start of the season.

RIGHT Ronnie qualified the March eighth on the grid at Monza but made a familiar charge away from the line, straight into fourth place behind Jody Scheckter (Tyrrell P34), poleman Jacques Laffite (Ligier-Matra) and Patrick Depailler in the other six-wheel device. After 10 laps, he was past all of them and narrowly leading the race. The lead battle was soon joined by Clay Regazzoni for Ferrari. It raged on into the second half of the Grand Prix, through a brief shower of rain that came just at the right moment to cool Ronnie's overworked tyres. Both the Tyrrells fell back with misfiring engines, but Ronnie had to work hard to keep Regazzoni and Laffite in his mirrors. He handled the pressure perfectly and won by just over 2sec after beating Laffite's pole position time on the 50th of the 52 laps. The Tyrrells were demoted to fifth and sixth by the heroic Niki Lauda, returning to the cockpit of his Ferrari only six weeks after an horrific accident on the Nürburgring.

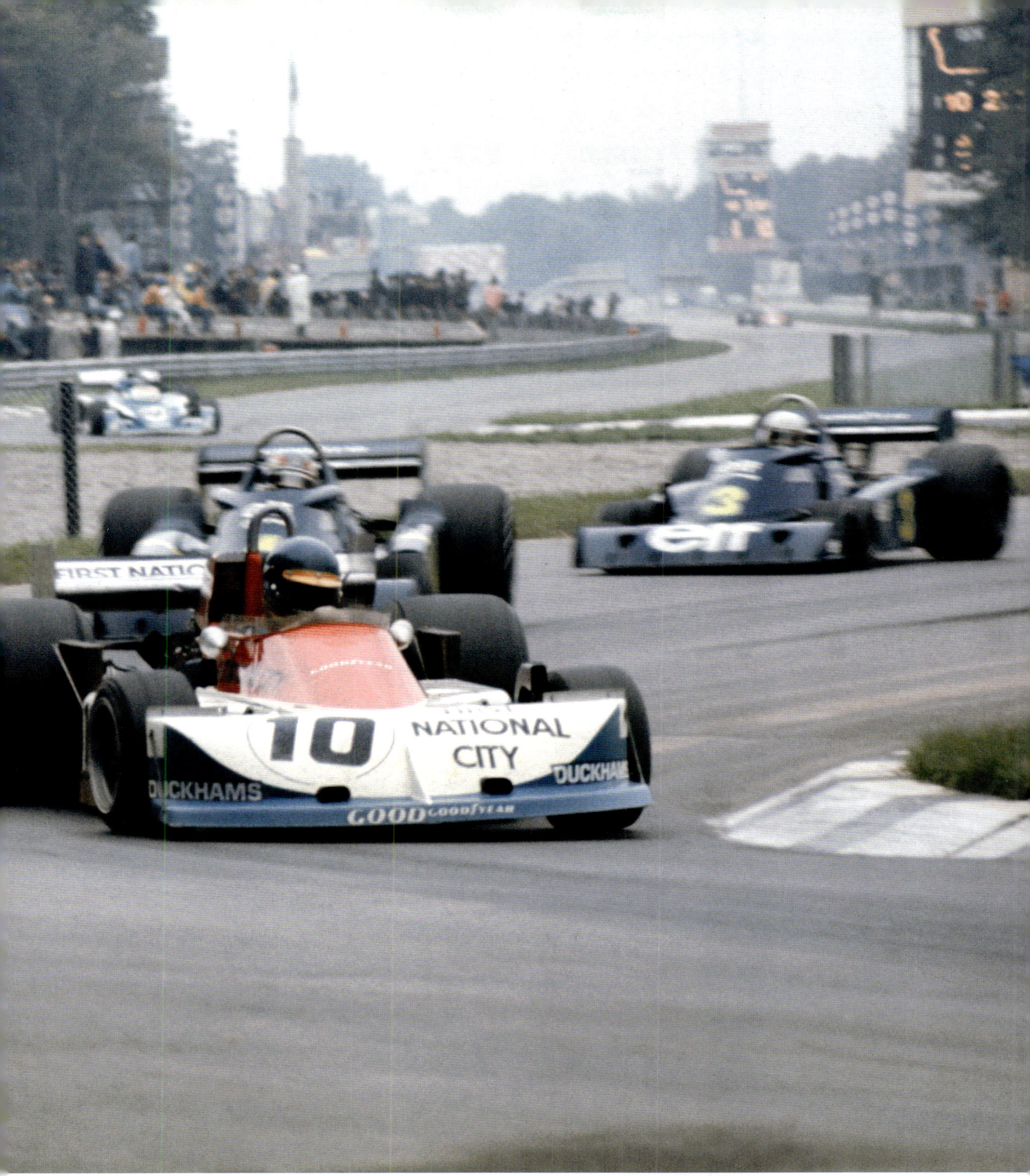
FIRST NATIO
10
NATIONAL
CITY
DUCKHAMS
DUCKHAMS
GOODYEAR
elf
3

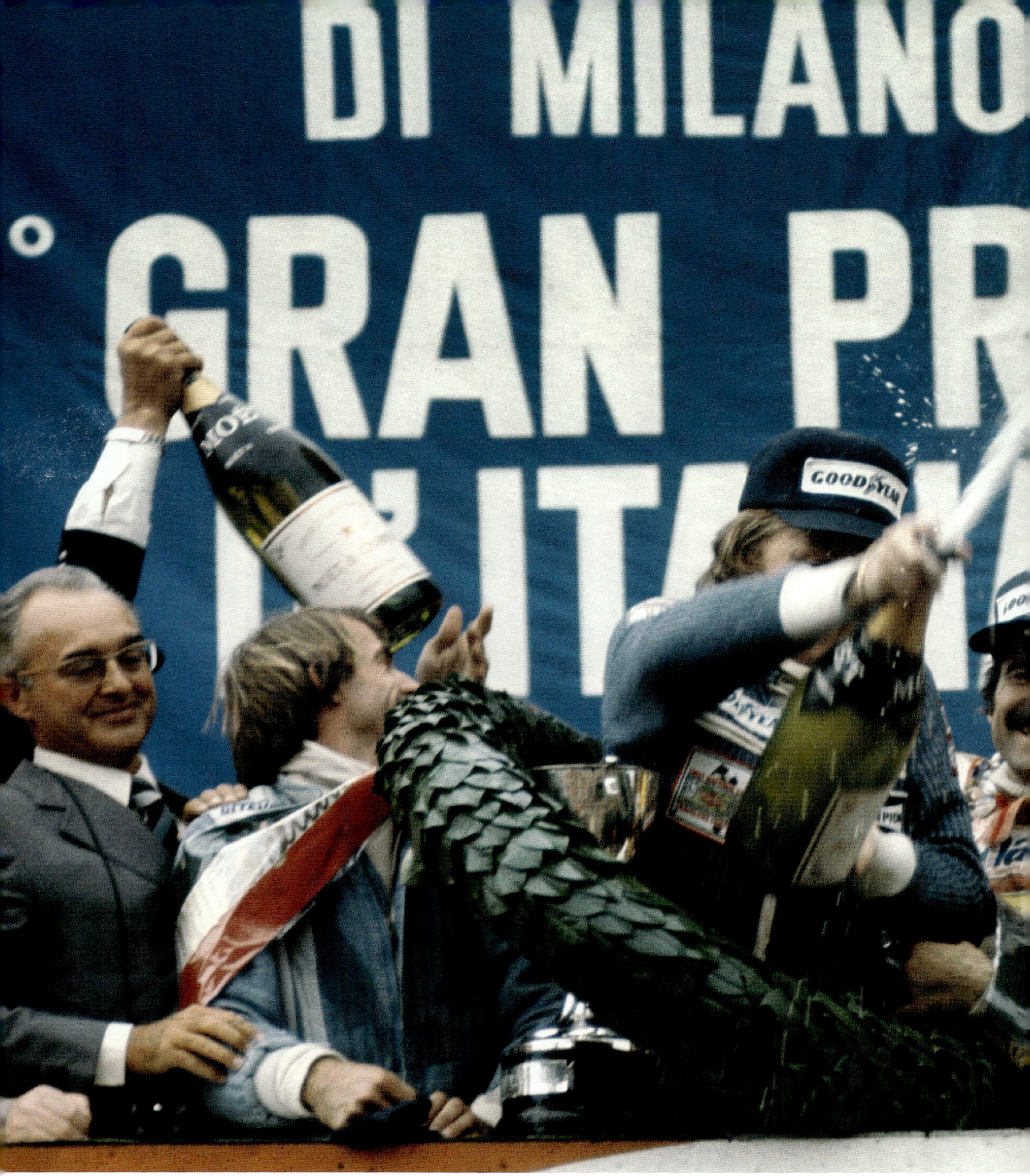
DI MILANO
GRAN PR
GOODYEAR

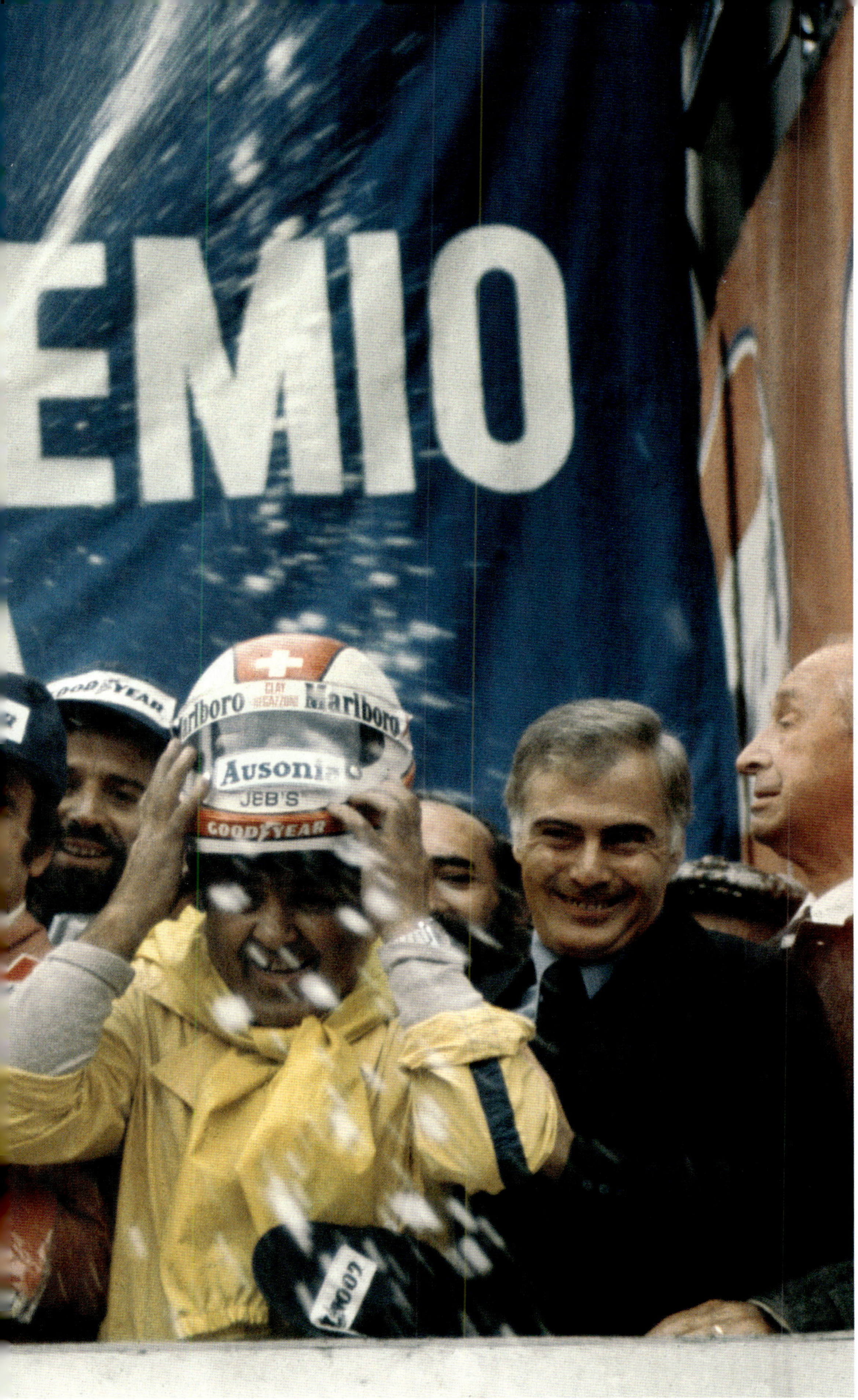

LEFT Ronnie celebrates with Clay Regazzoni, Jacques Laffite and the great and good of the Automobile Club di Milano after winning a thoroughly exciting Italian Grand Prix. This was only the third Grand Prix victory for March Engineering, and the last.

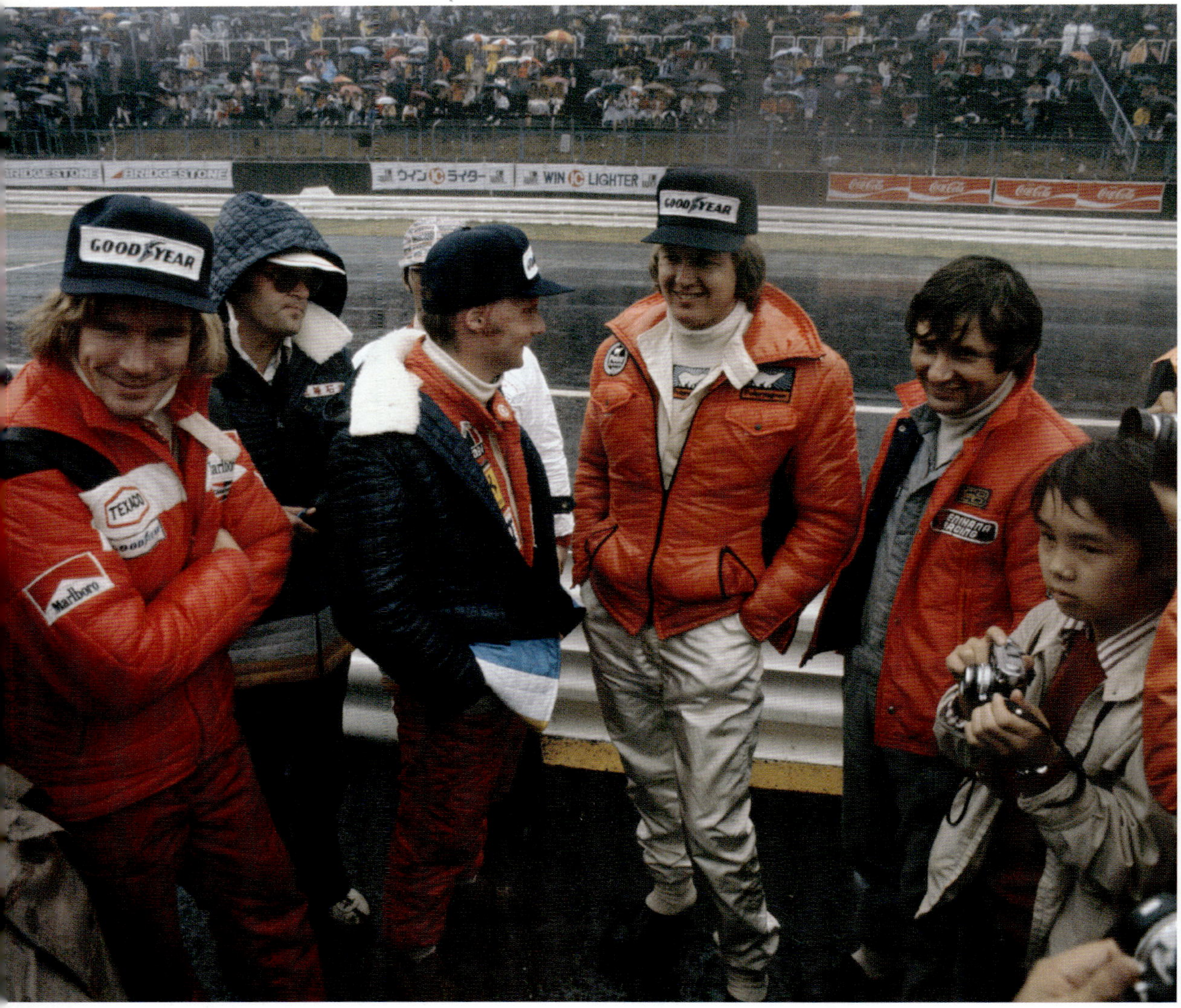

ABOVE The 1976 World Championship ended in dramatic circumstances at Fuji International Raceway. Rainy and misty weather on race day almost caused the inaugural Japanese Grand Prix to be postponed, and the drivers were alarmed by the standing water on the circuit even between the showers. Here James Hunt, Niki Lauda, Ronnie and Jean-Pierre Jarier discuss the situation. Eventually the race was started, but Lauda famously parked his Ferrari after only two laps, declaring the conditions unacceptably hazardous. This meant that Hunt would win the title if he finished in the top three, and he drove his McLaren M23 into third place behind Mario Andretti's Lotus 77 and Patrick Depailler's six-wheel Tyrrell P34.

RIGHT Ronnie was out of the rain-drenched Japanese Grand Prix even before Niki Lauda, the victim of soaked electrics. His season had produced the Monza victory and a sixth place in Austria, but no other finishes in the points with yet another unreliable car. Meanwhile Team Lotus had developed the 77 to the point where Mario Andretti could qualify on pole position here, and win by a whole lap... A return to Lotus was out of the question, but Ronnie had been impressed by the durability of the Tyrrell P34.

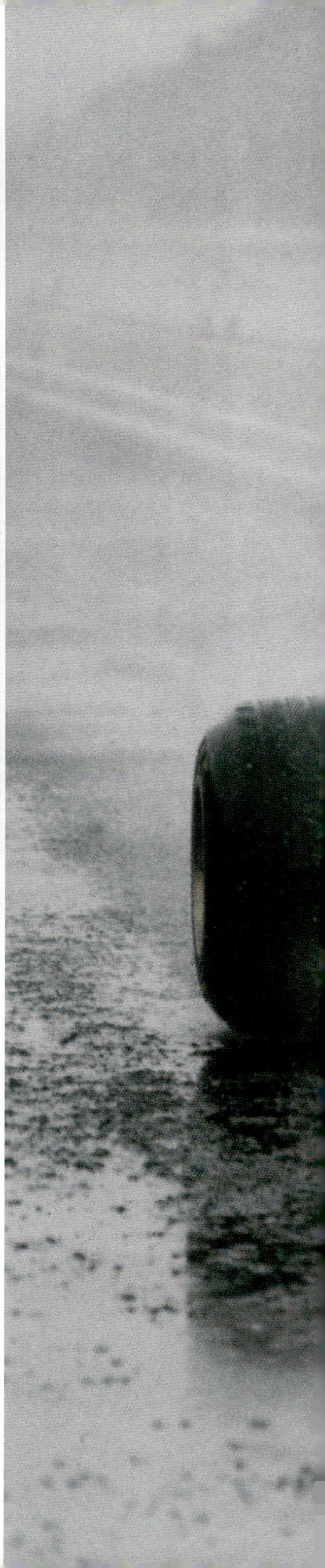

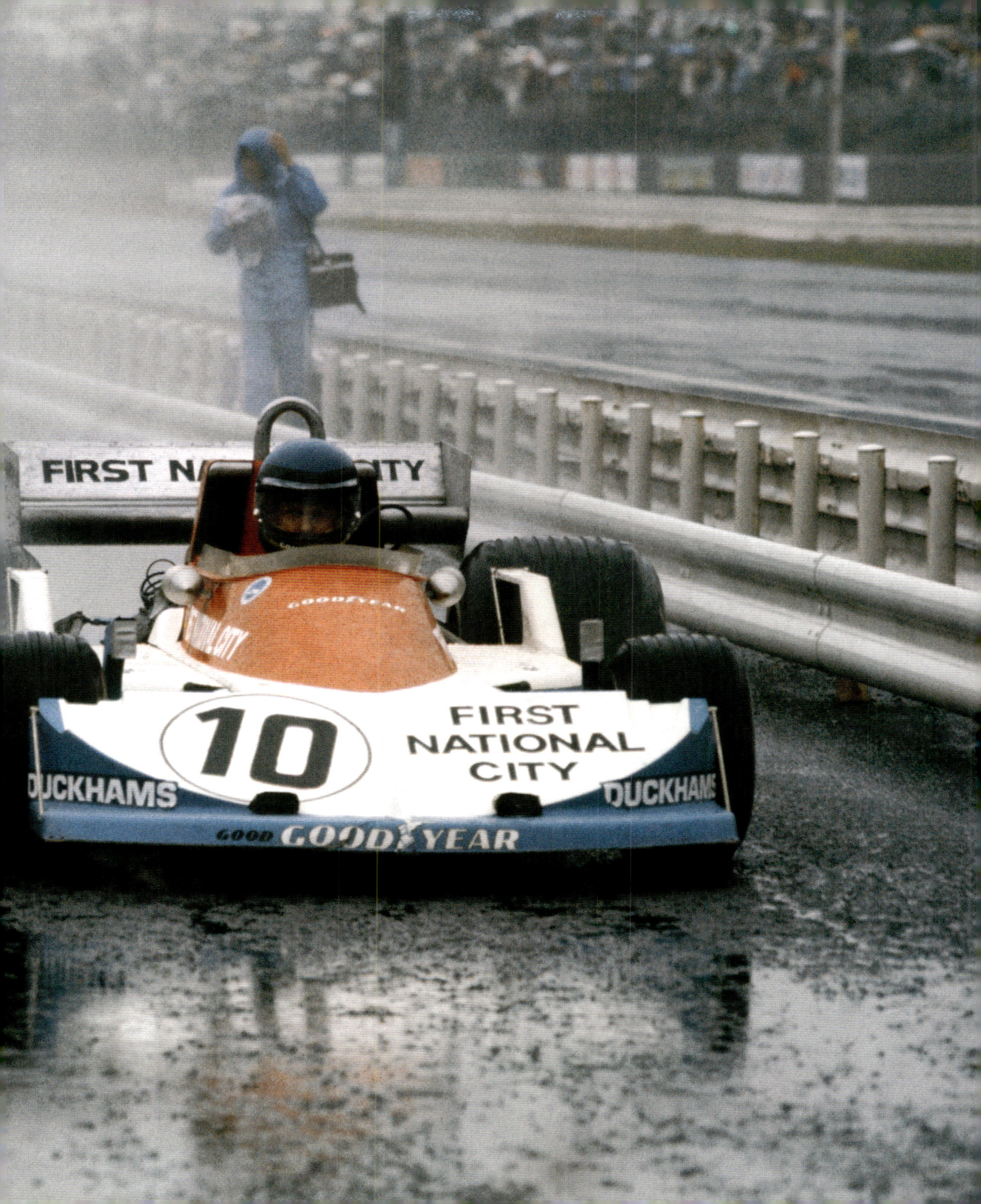
10
FIRST NATIONAL CITY
DUCKHAMS
DUCKHAMS
GOODYEAR

1977

A DESPERATE SEASON WITH SIX WHEELS

Jody Scheckter's departure to Walter Wolf's new Formula 1 team left a 1977 vacancy at Elf Team Tyrrell, alongside Patrick Depailler. Ken Tyrrell had long admired Ronnie and knew that he was frustrated after three seasons with unreliable equipment. During 1976, the unique, six-wheel Tyrrell P34s had finished in the points on 20 occasions from 32 starts, so it did not take long for 'SuperSwede' to be convinced. But Ronnie brought his bad luck along with him. In 1977, he and Depailler could only achieve eight points-scoring finishes between them, from 34 starts, and Ronnie was on the podium only once. Thoroughly disillusioned, he startled the Formula 1 community when, before the season finale in Japan, he agreed to return to Team Lotus for 1978, effectively as the number two to Mario Andretti.

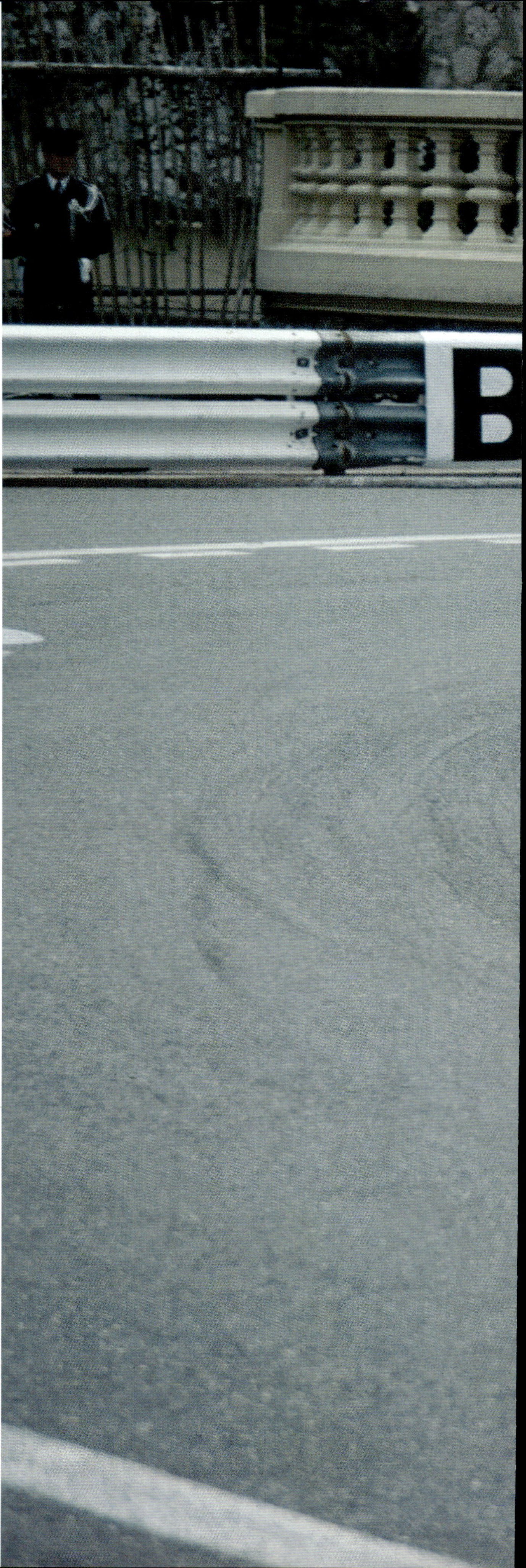

RIGHT Yet again, Ronnie's class shone through in Monaco, compensating for some of the inadequacies of his equipment. After qualifying ahead of eventual champion Niki Lauda, he kept his overweight Tyrrell P34 firmly in front of the Ferrari 312T2 (here at the Station hairpin) – until the 10-lap mark, when his brakes had already had enough punishment, and he became the first retirement.

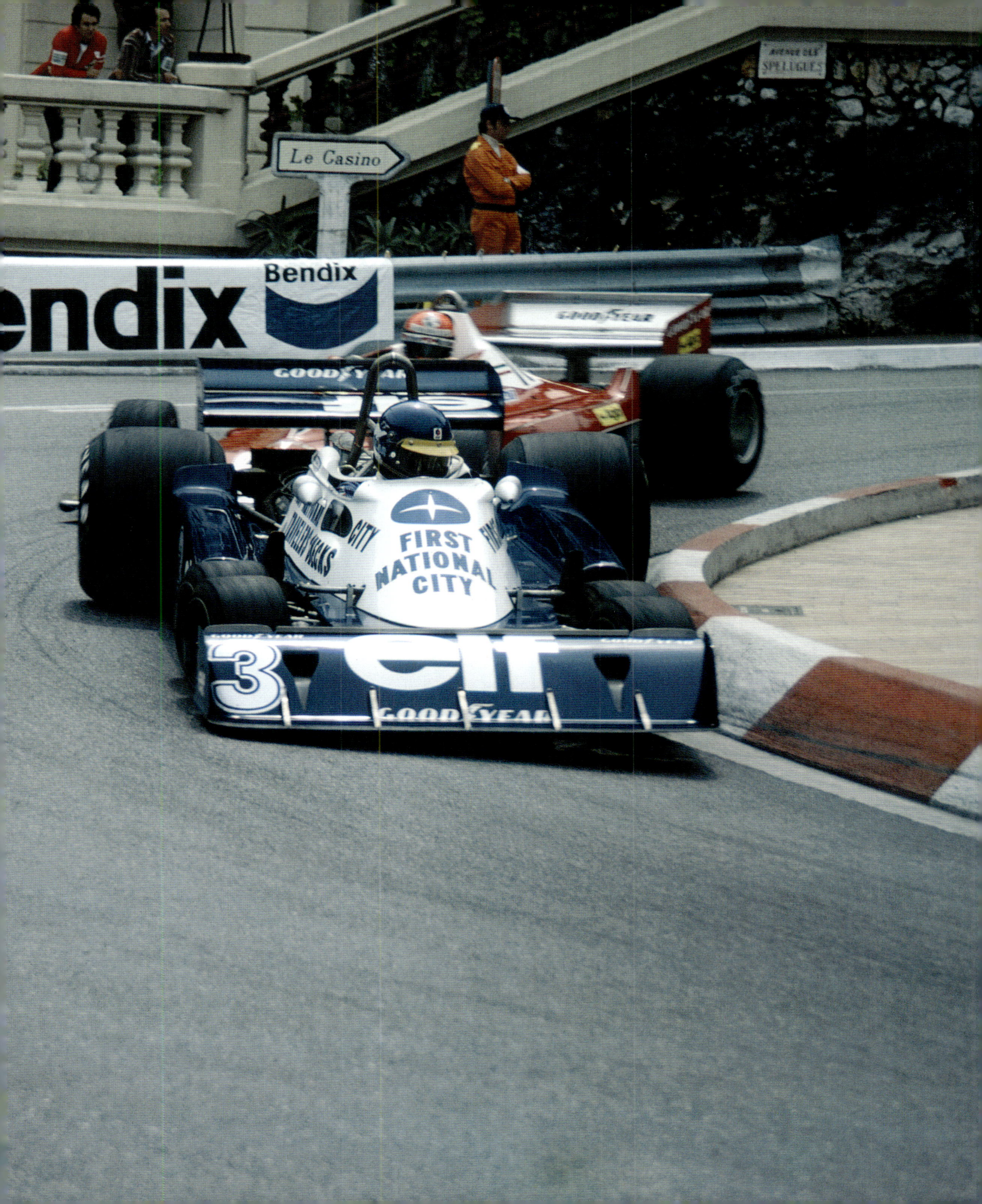
Le Casino
Bendix
endix
GOODYEAR
FIRST
NATIONAL
CITY
3
elf
GOODYEAR

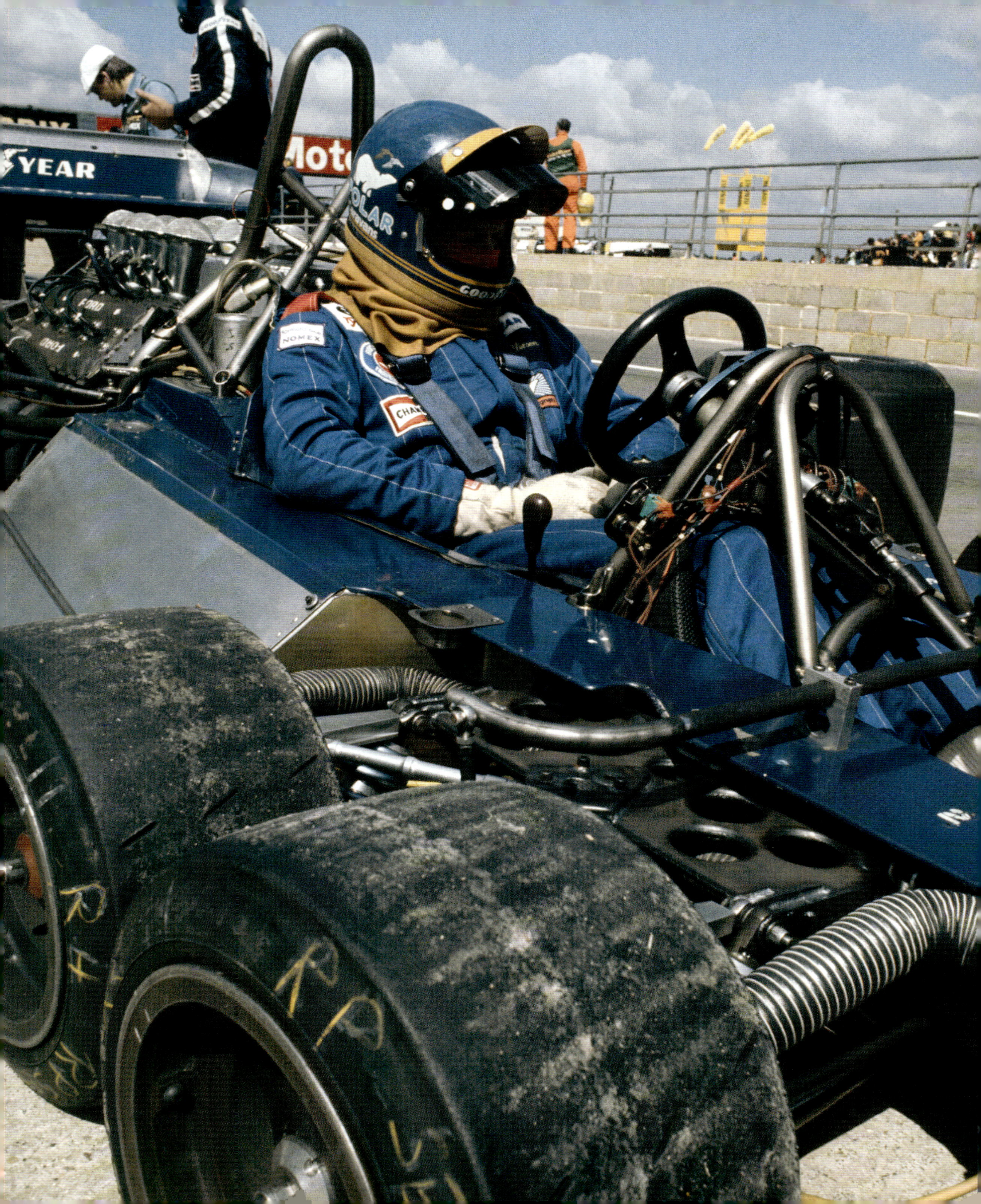
YEAR
NOMEX

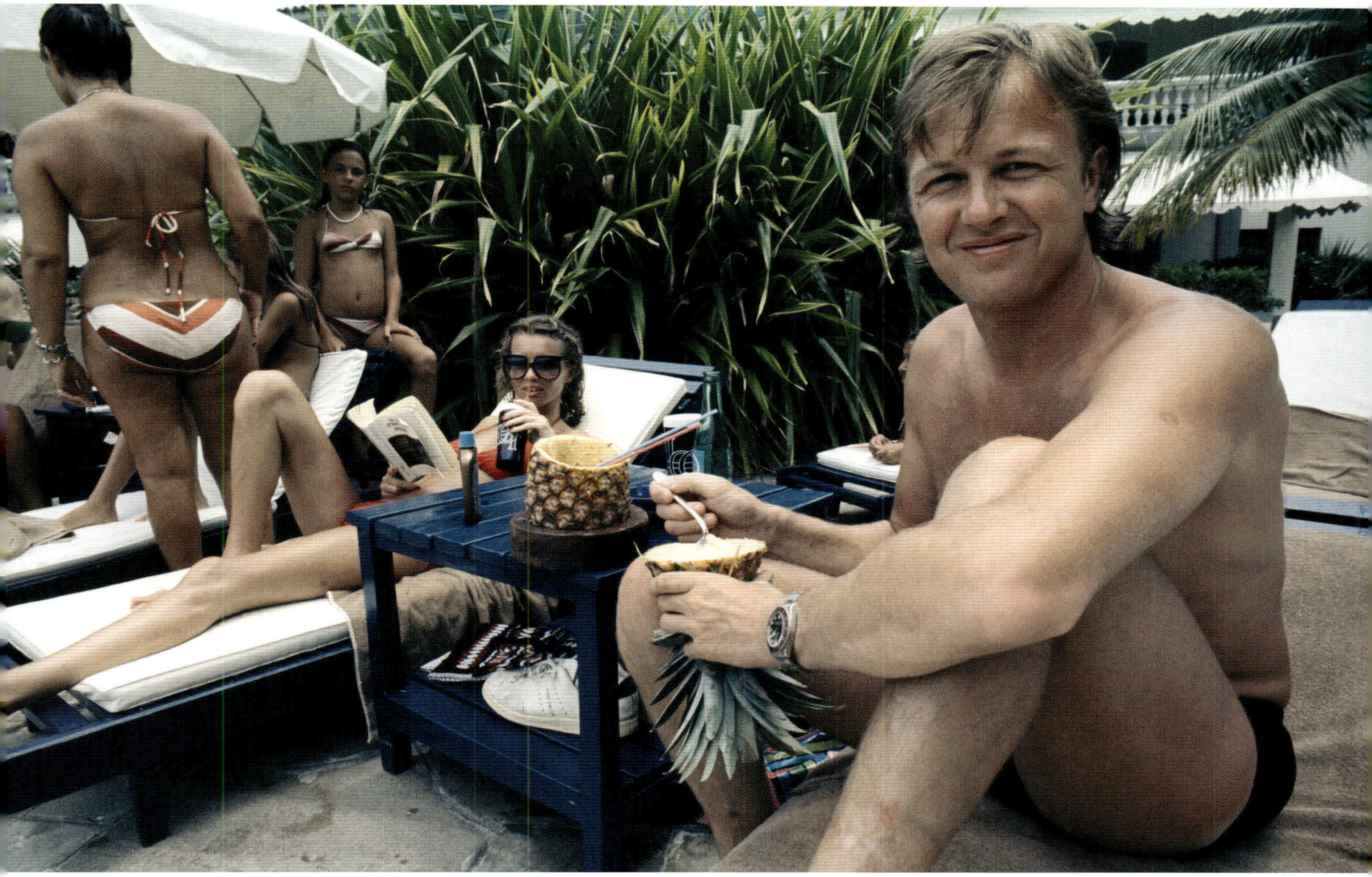

LEFT The Cosworth DFV powered P34 was the concept of Tyrrell designer Derek Gardner, who noticed that nowhere in the Formula 1 Technical Regulations did it say that a car had to have four wheels. The idea was to reduce frontal area while maintaining more or less the same area of contact patch. Once Goodyear had agreed to supply special tyres for the 10-inch diameter front wheels, the team set about getting the concept into metal. The car had been very competitive through 1976, winning with a 1–2 at Anderstorp, and Ronnie had been impressed with both its pace and its durability all that season. However the 1977 version had redesigned aerodynamics and other revisions that added more than 100kg to its weight, making it the heaviest car on the grid. Meanwhile Goodyear, under new challenge from Michelin, concentrated its development resources on conventional front tyres. As the other teams advanced, the P34 was no longer a competitive proposition, and it was not long before Ronnie realised he had made another costly mistake.

ABOVE Ronnie's season began in Buenos Aires with qualification in the midfield, followed by a spin into retirement on race day when he lost concentration in a severely overheated cockpit. Nevertheless, he seems happy enough with life as he relaxes with Barbro in their hotel prior to the second Grand Prix here in Sao Paulo. He put his six-wheeler eighth on the grid at Interlagos (a six-place improvement) but his Brazilian Grand Prix ended in the wall when, struggling with a braking imbalance, he could not avoid accident debris from Jochen Mass's McLaren and Clay Regazzoni's Ensign.

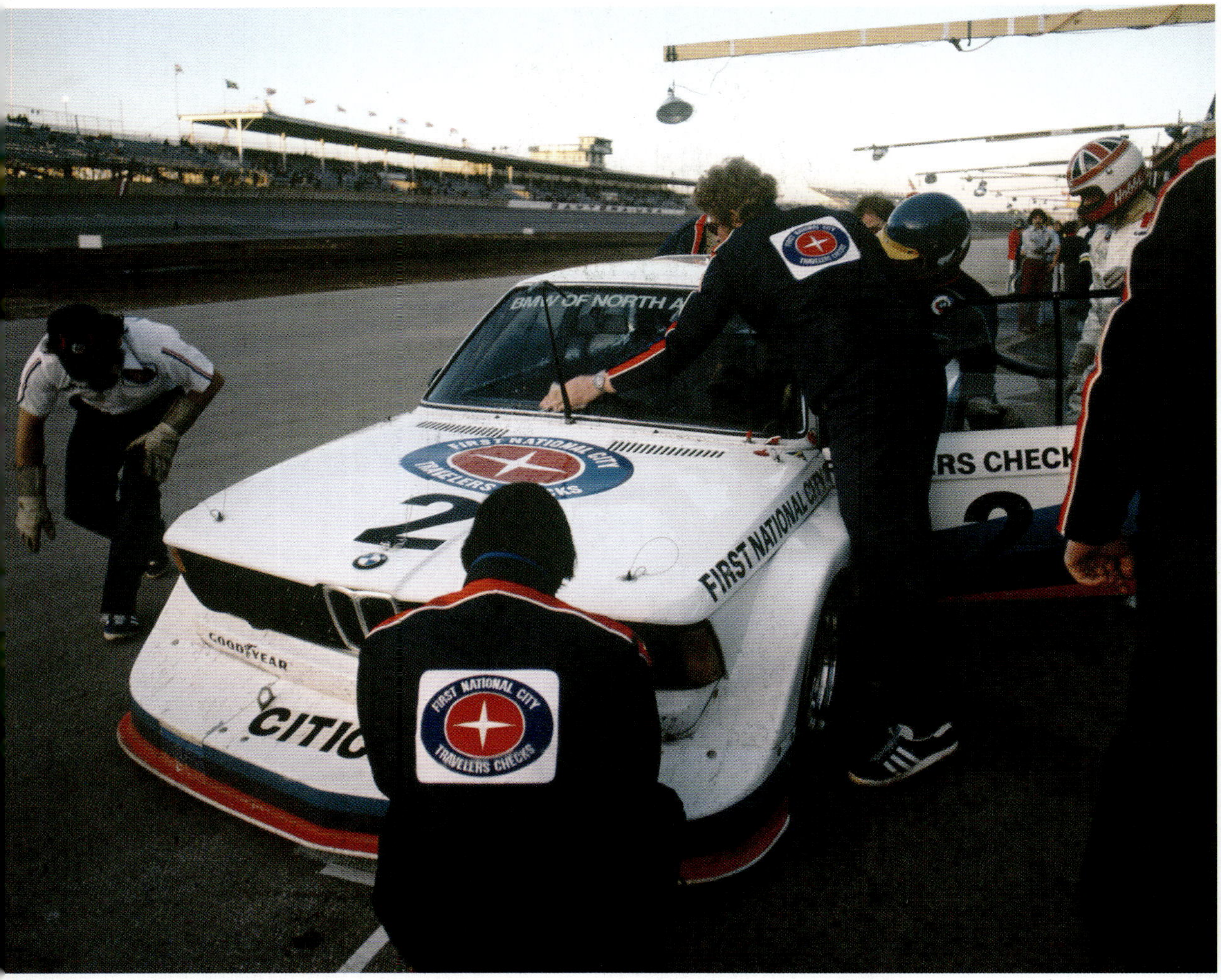

ABOVE Alongside his Elf Team Tyrrell deal, Ronnie signed for a full season of seven 1977 endurance races with BMW Motorsport, starting with the Daytona 24 Hours on the way home from South America. His co-drivers here were Sam Posey and David Hobbs, and their car was a new, lightweight, FIA Group 5 BMW 320i to be operated in the IMSA series by Team McLaren. The car was super-quick on the infield road course but the team's turbocharged engine was not ready, and the 'atmo' Formula 2 engine was not up to the job on the speedway sections. Here, with the car solidly placed in the top 10, Ronnie hands over to the patriotically helmeted Hobbs. Soon after Posey had taken the wheel, the engine tightened and the car was parked, leaving a squadron of Porsches almost unopposed.

RIGHT After a month's break, Ronnie was in Johannesburg for the South African Grand Prix at Kyalami, where he was again outqualified by team-mate Patrick Depailler. The six-wheeler evidently took some getting used to. Ronnie was out inside six laps with no fuel pressure. This race is remembered for the appalling fatality of Tom Pryce, killed in the cockpit of his Shadow when it struck a marshal who was foolishly running across the track, carrying a heavy fire extinguisher. After the South American successes for Jody Scheckter's Wolf in Argentina and Carlos Reutemann's Ferrari in Brazil, Niki Lauda became the third winner from the opening three races, but Ronnie returned to Europe without a point to his name.

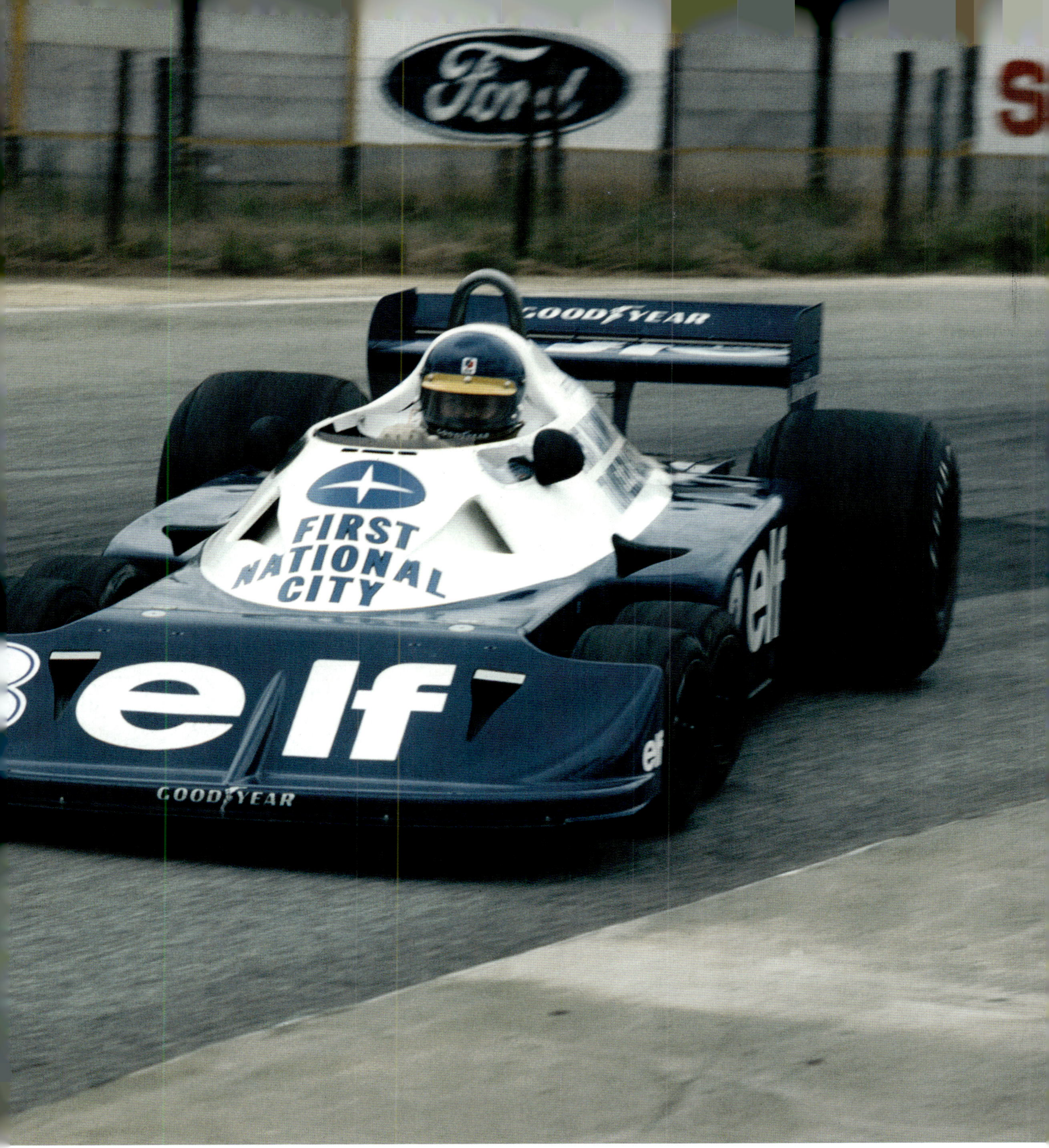
Ford
GOODYEAR
FIRST NATIONAL CITY
elf
GOODYEAR

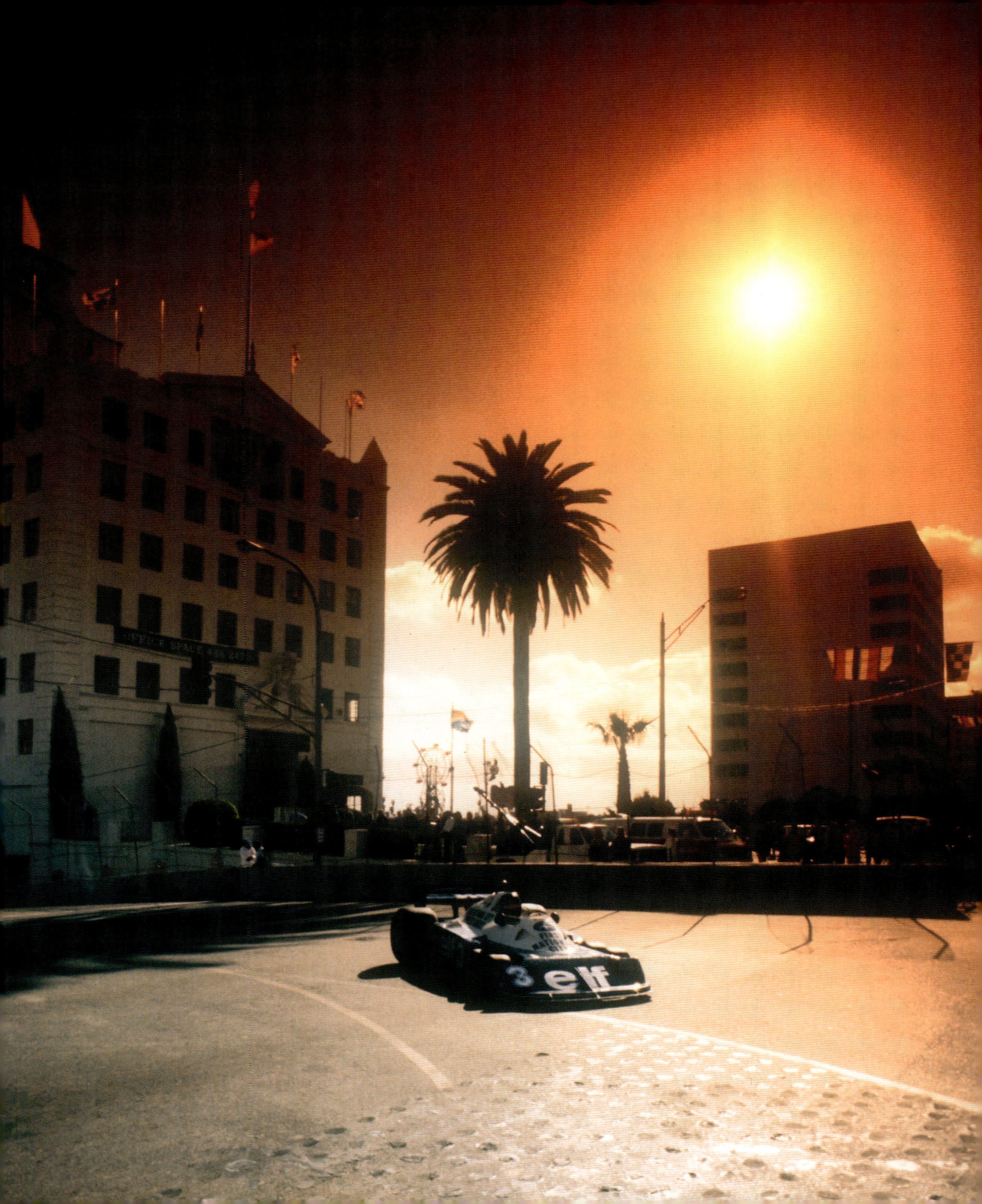
3 elf

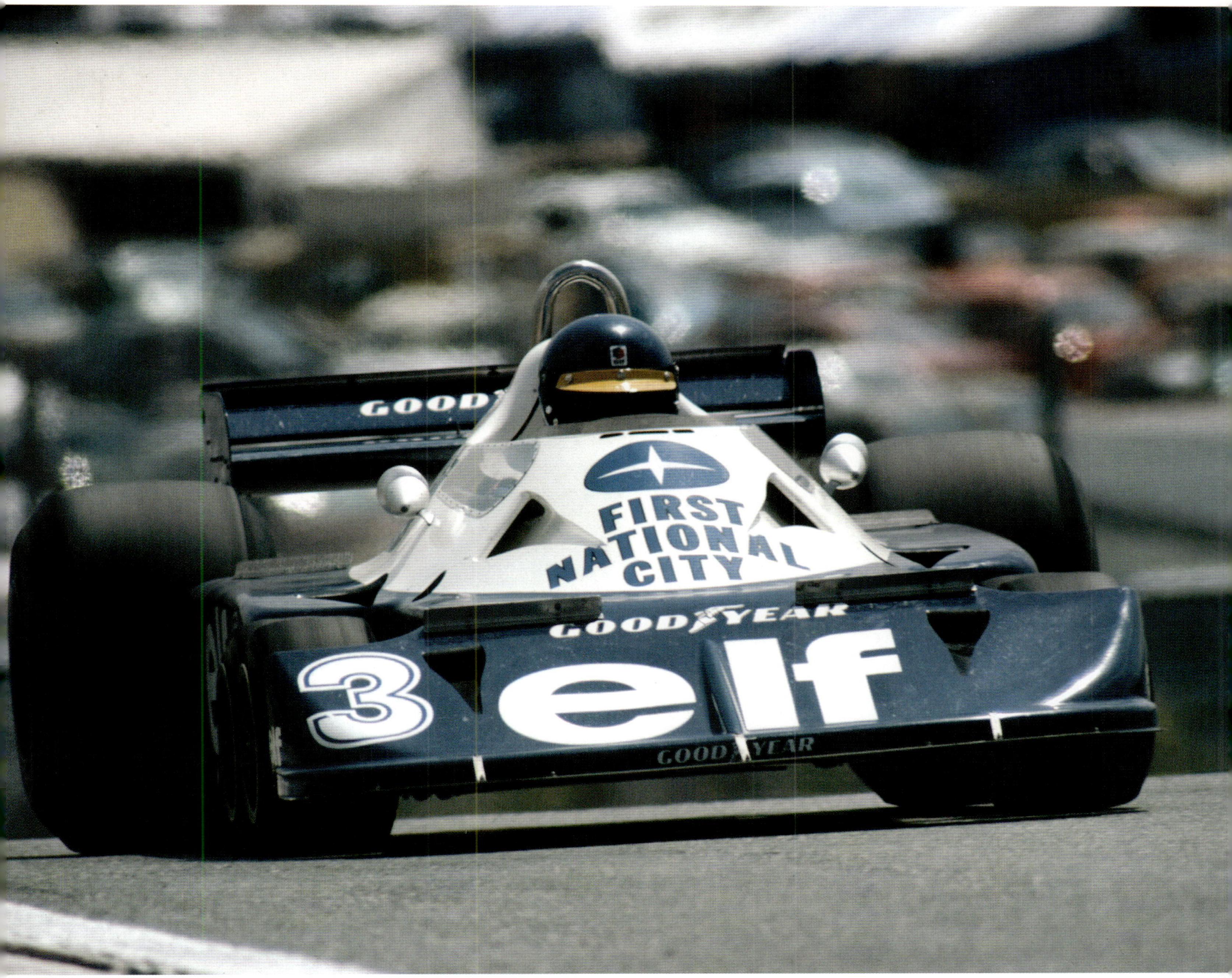

LEFT The fourth round of the Formula 1 World Championship was the US Grand Prix West at Long Beach, and it produced a fourth winner – but it was not a Tyrrell P34. It was the new Lotus 78, driven by Mario Andretti... Ronnie outqualified Patrick Depailler for the first time but had to pit halfway through the race when a braking problem caused a badly flat-spotted tyre. His team-mate progressed into fourth place behind Niki Lauda (Ferrari) and Jody Scheckter (Wolf) but, after rejoining the race, Ronnie rolled to a halt with a ruptured fuel-line.

ABOVE The Spanish Grand Prix at Jarama produced a dominant performance by Mario Andretti, who led from flag to flag from pole position with a brand-new Lotus 78. Ronnie only saw Mario once, when the Tyrrell was being lapped 20 laps out from the end. He was classified in eighth place – but at least he had finally finished a race with a P34.

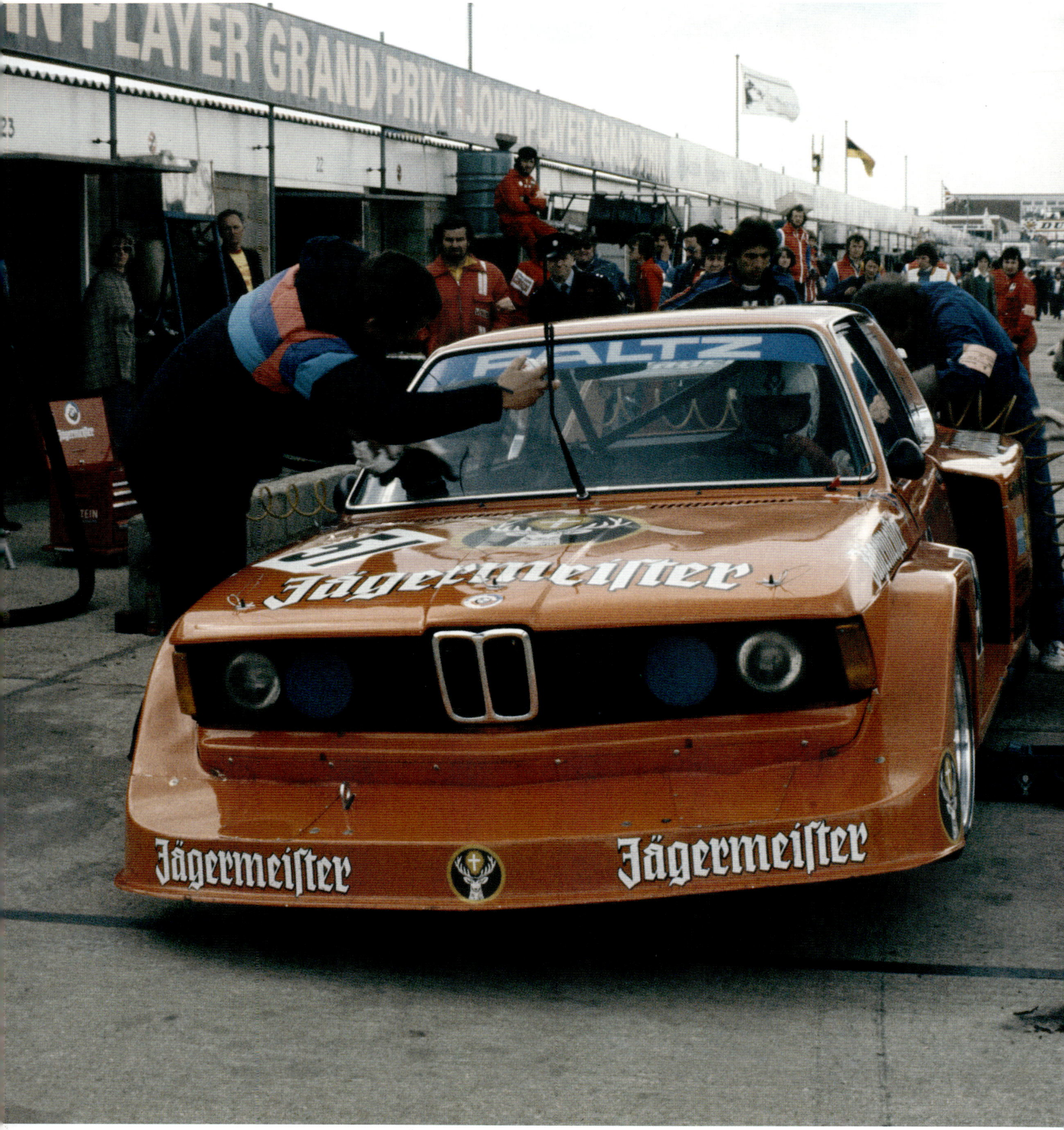
PLAYER GRAND PRIX
JOHN PLAYER GRAND PRIX
Jägermeister
Jägermeister
Jägermeister

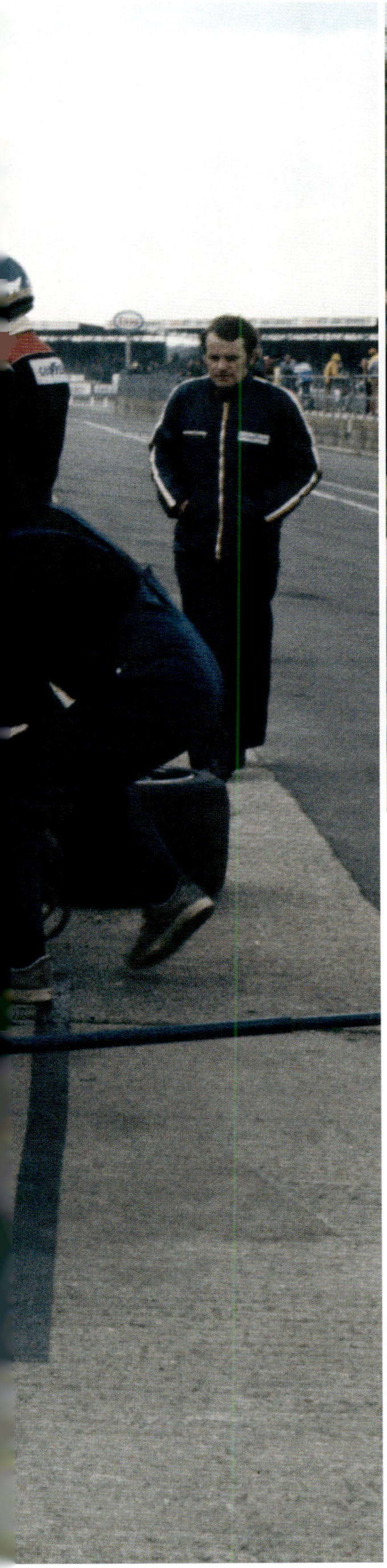

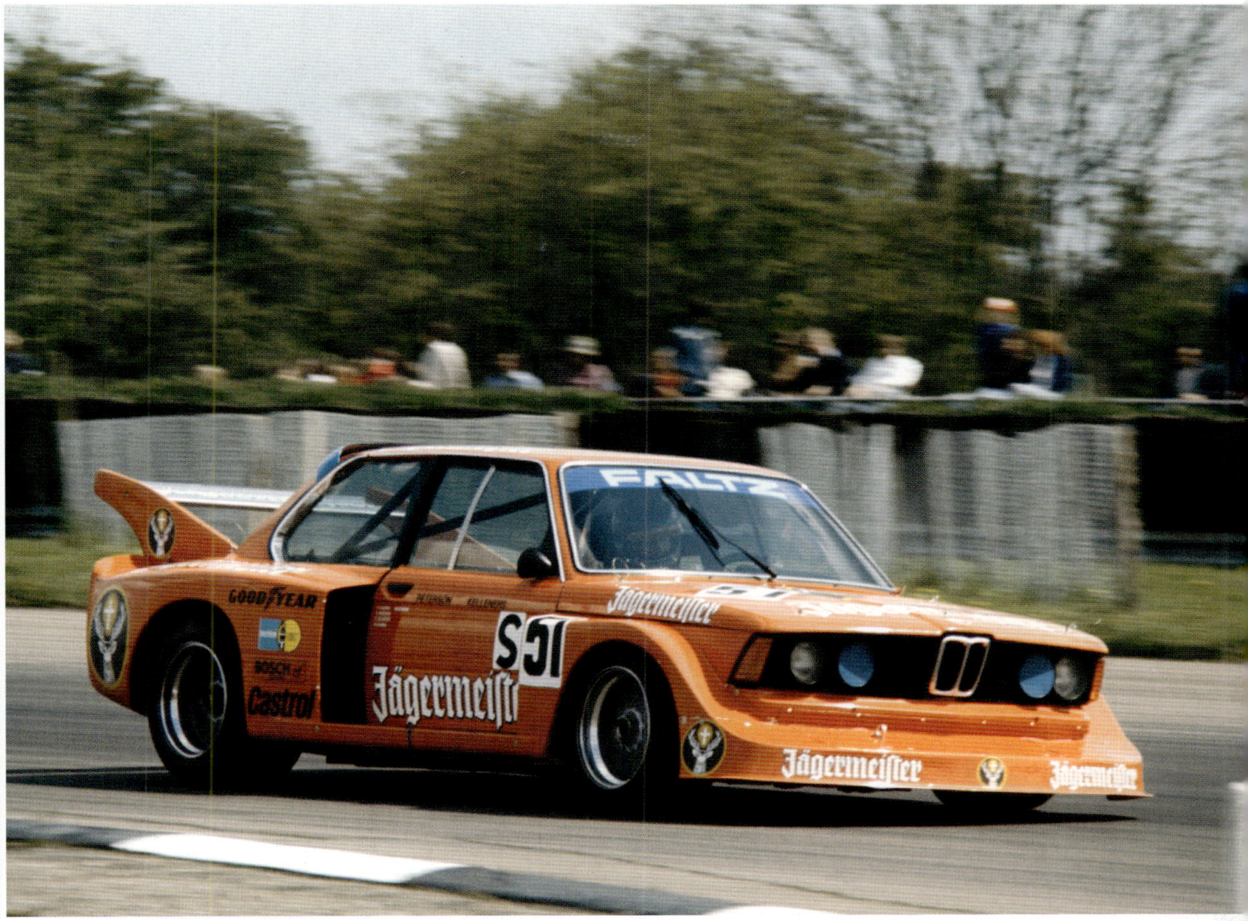

LEFT The week after Jarama, Ronnie was at Silverstone for the annual six-hour World Championship of Makes event, having been asked to share Rüdiger Faltz's factory-supported BMW 320i with regular driver Helmut Kelleners. This is a handover during qualifying, in which the 2-litre Formula 2 engine, as expected, proved to be hopelessly underpowered relative to half a dozen of the new, turbocharged Porsche 935s. Among these, the latest factory car of Jochen Mass and Jacky Ickx annexed pole position, and would go on to win the race.

ABOVE Ronnie heads the Faltz BMW towards fourth place in the Silverstone 6 Hours, the only non-Porsche among the top 14 finishers – and the class winner by no less than 88 laps! Early on he had transfixed the crowd in brutal battle with Vittorio Brambilla, eventually passing the Surtees Formula 1 driver's Porsche 934, pulling away and consistently breaking the 2-litre lap record by as much as 4sec. But it was the final hour that made him the hero of the day. When it rained, Ronnie stayed on slicks, just for the hell of it, and the BMW was rarely pointing dead ahead. The people loved it, and gave him a standing ovation.

PAGES 206–7 Ronnie always gave his all, but it was never more evident than at Monaco. Smoke pouring from a front brake is testament to his vain effort to resist Jochen Mass's McLaren M23 and Jody Scheckter's Wolf WR1 at the Mirabeau hairpin during qualifying. But it was also a warning... Ultimately Ronnie qualified a terrific fourth, beaten only by John Watson (Brabham-Alfa), Scheckter and Carlos Reutemann (Ferrari), and four-tenths faster here than team-mate Patrick Depailler. On race day, he was running fifth when the P34's brakes gave up the ghost after only 10 laps. Scheckter's victory here was the 100th for the Cosworth DFV engine.

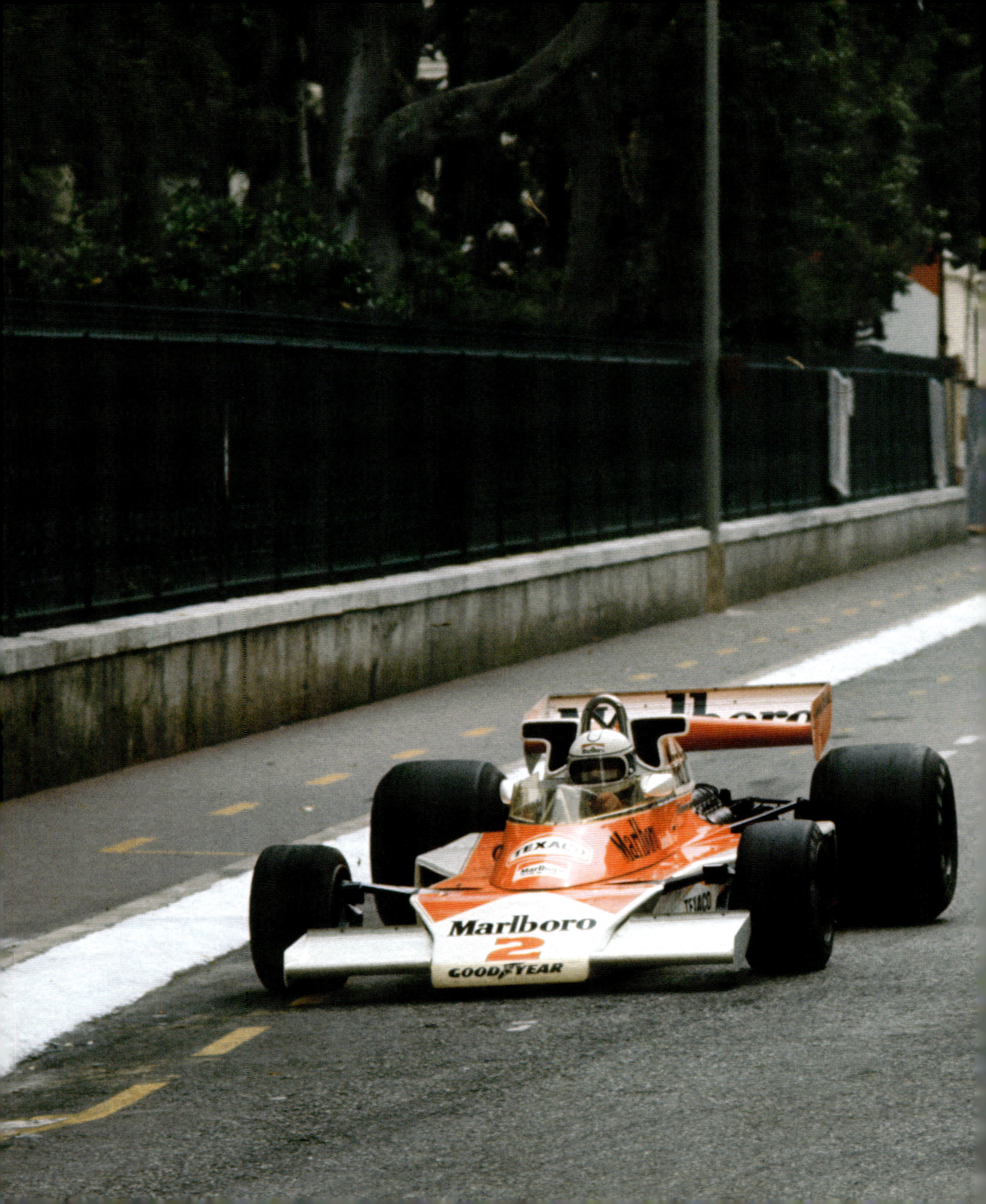

Marlboro
2
GOODYEAR
TEXACO

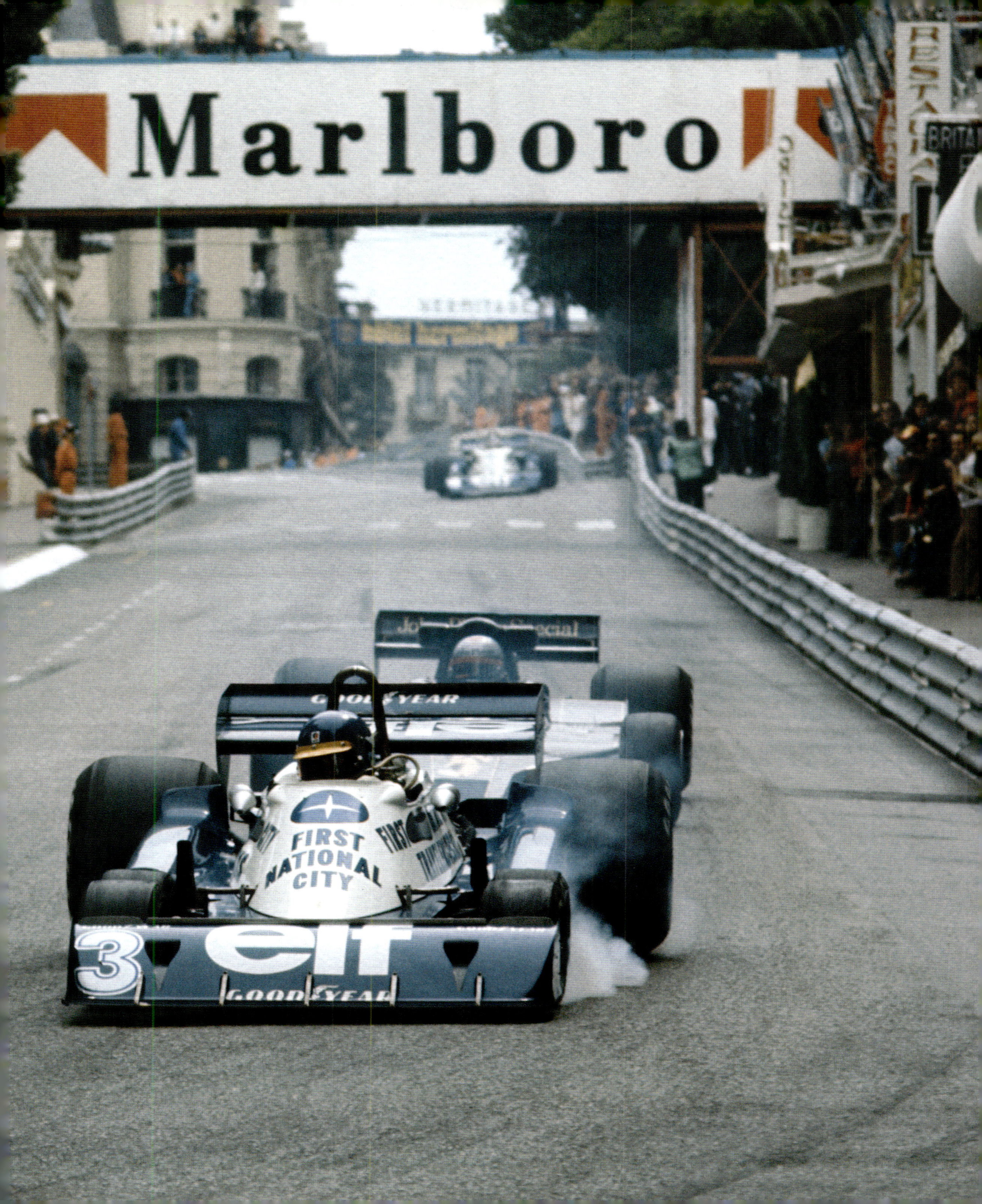
Marlboro
GOODYEAR
FIRST NATIONAL CITY
3
elf
GOODYEAR

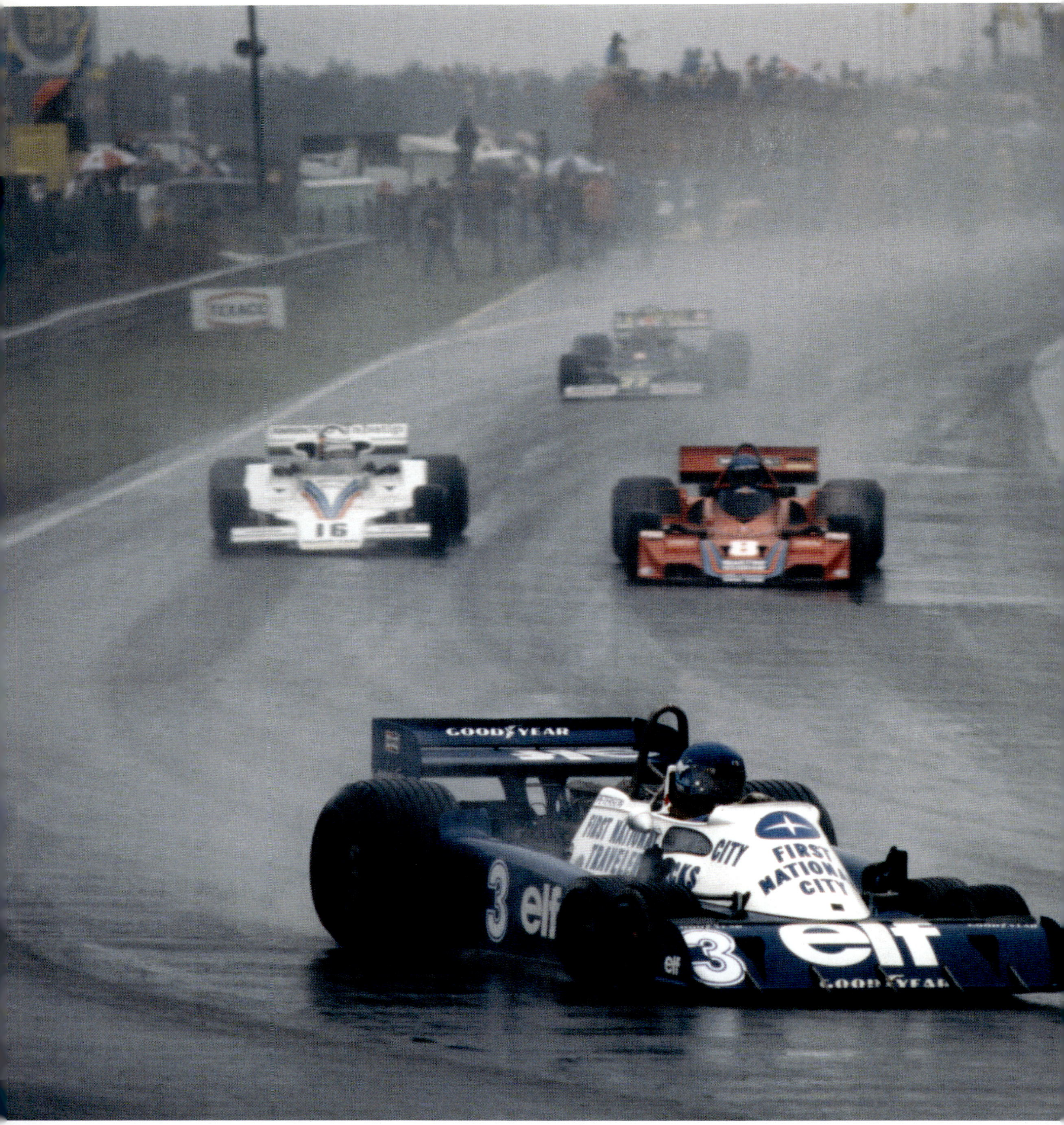
GOODYEAR
3
elf
FIRST NATIONAL CITY
3
elf
GOODYEAR

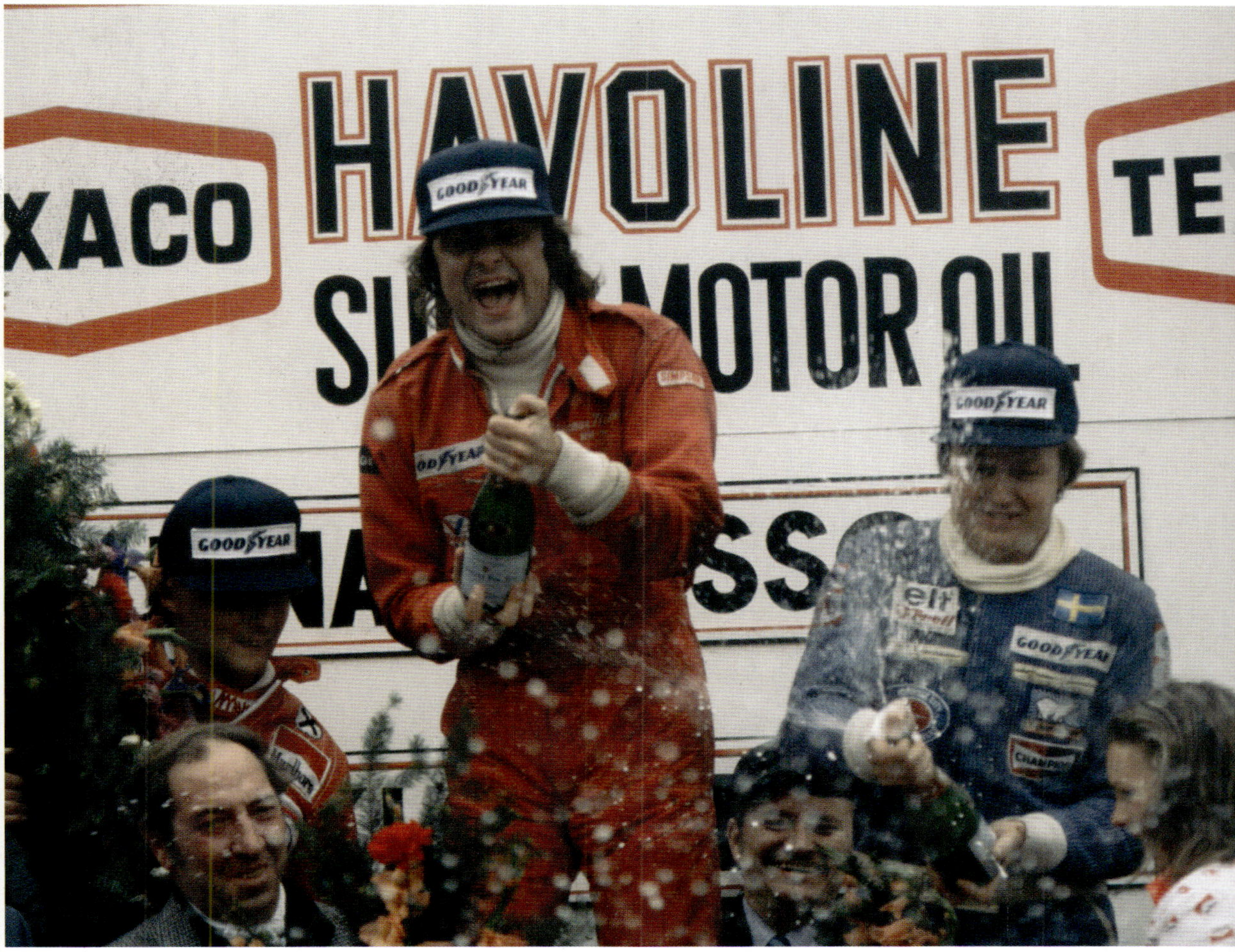

LEFT The highlight of another desperately frustrating season was a very fine third place in the rain at Zolder. Ronnie qualified eighth for the Belgian Grand Prix but, in the wet–dry conditions, kept pace with the leaders for much of race day. He is pictured ahead of Hans Stuck's Brabham-Alfa, rookie Riccardo Patrese's Shadow and Clay Regazzoni's Ensign. Passed early on by Vittorio Brambilla's bravely driven Surtees, he got his own back towards the end and emerged from a frantic, attritional race with the first points of his season. He knew very well, though, that a victory was out of the question. This would be the first year in which Ken Tyrrell's team failed to win a race since he had become a constructor at the start of the decade.

ABOVE Mixed feelings for Ronnie on the podium at Zolder. He was happy to have finished third in the Belgian Grand Prix, about 6sec behind Niki Lauda's Ferrari. And he was happy for his young compatriot, Gunnar Nilsson, who had been victorious. But his joy was tempered by the knowledge that he might so easily have been the winning Swede in the very effective new Lotus 'wing-car'.

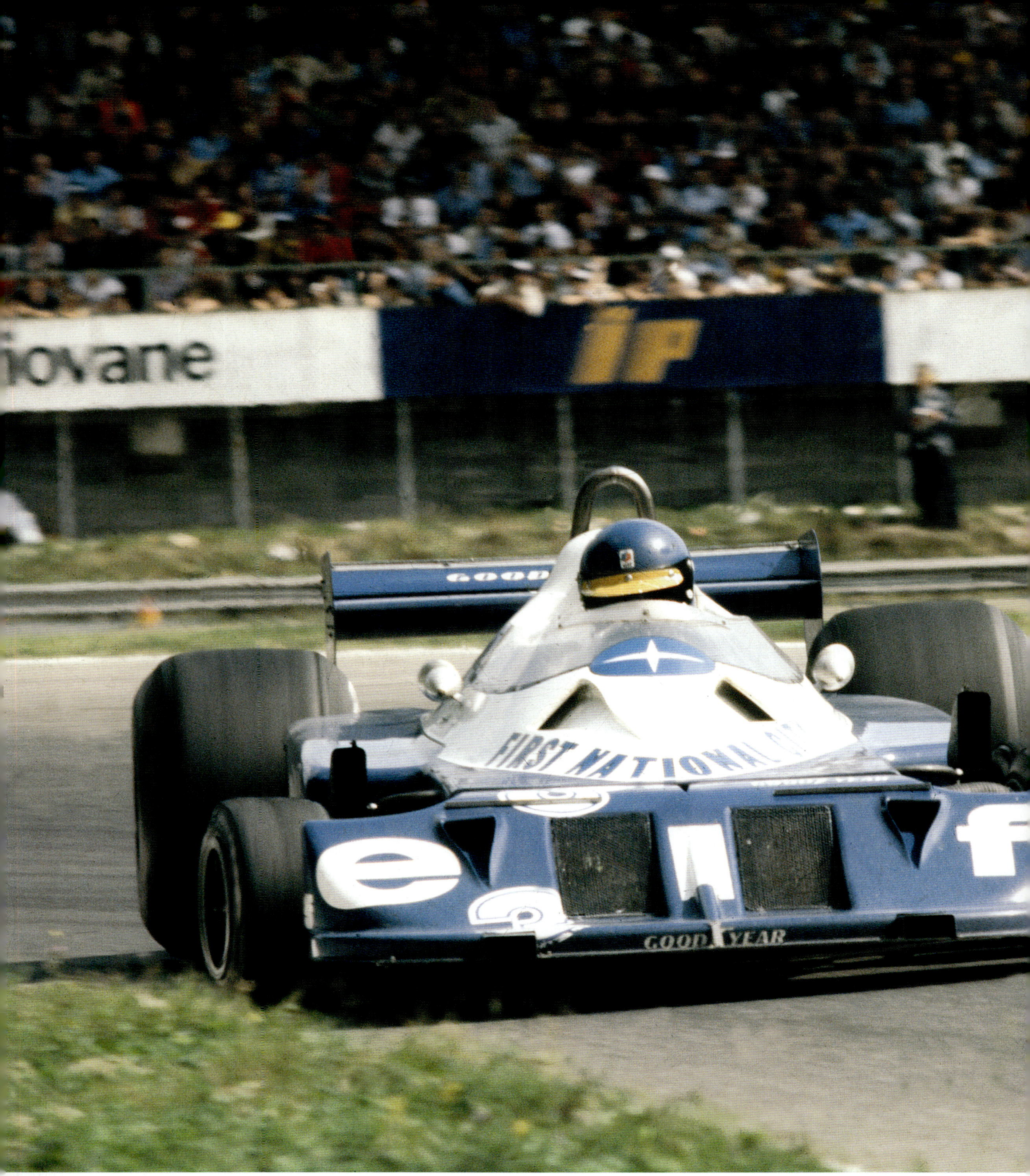
FIRST NATIONAL
GOOD YEAR

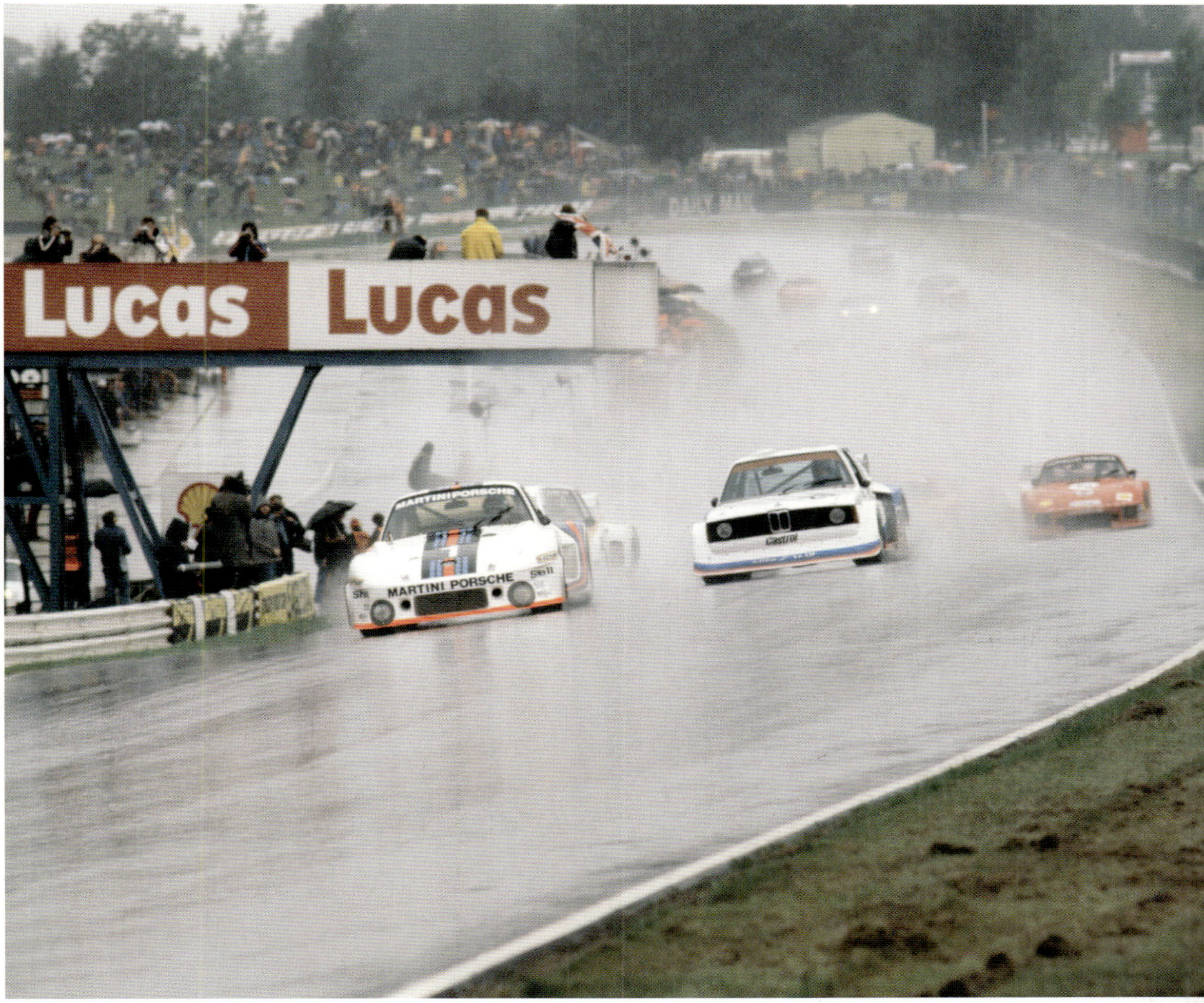

LEFT As the P34's competitiveness waned, Ronnie's driving became increasingly desperate, as shown here as he attacks the Parabolica on Italy's Autodromo Nazionale. The extra weight of the 1977 P34 posed an additional problem because of the car's inherently minimal front suspension travel. As soon as the car was turned in to a corner, the assembly now locked solid and pitched the rear into oversteer. The six Grands Prix intervening between Zolder and Monza had been eminently forgettable for Ronnie, although there had been a fortuitous fifth-place finish on the Osterreichring. He qualified 12th here but came in sixth for his third (and final) points-scoring finish of the year, Elf Team Tyrrell's sixth. For JPS Team Lotus, the Italian Grand Prix delivered a 12th scoring finish – and a fifth victory. Ronnie's season with Ken Tyrrell would end with his unwitting involvement in Gilles Villeneuve's accident in the Japanese Grand Prix, in which two spectators lost their lives.

ABOVE Having done a couple of American races with Team McLaren's BMW 320i turbo, co-driving David Hobbs, Ronnie came to Brands Hatch in September to race the blown version of the 2-litre car for the first time in Europe. The World Championship of Makes had been dominated by the works Martini Porsche 935-77, but Ronnie made Jacky Ickx work very hard in qualifying. The BMW's best lap was hampered by traffic but it was only a tenth away from pole position. Hans Stuck was entrusted with the car for the first shift in this six-hour race, took the lead from Ickx midway round the fourth lap – and promptly crashed.

1978

A CAREER RETRIEVED – AND A FUTURE LOST

Ronnie was clear about his reasons for returning to Team Lotus on a one-year contract in 1978. He was now 33, and had never raced a Formula 1 car with both the pace and durability to deliver the title. Colin Chapman convinced him that, in the revolutionary, ground-effect Lotus 79, he and Mario Andretti would have by far the best car. The American would have the number one status but, after three seasons that had produced a total of 23 championship points, this was still an opportunity for Ronnie to rebuild his reputation. It meant riding shotgun for Mario, but it worked. Early in September, with two more Grand Prix victories to his name, Ronnie agreed a number one deal with McLaren for 1979. A week later, he was dead, after sustaining injuries at Monza that had not appeared life-threatening.

RIGHT Curiously, the 1978 Austrian Grand Prix delivered the only 'perfect' performance of Ronnie's entire Formula 1 career – pole position, a flag-to-flag victory, fastest lap. At the first start, he leads Carlos Reutemann (Ferrari) and Mario Andretti in the other Lotus 79 (destined to collide midway round the lap), with Jacques Laffite (Ligier) and Jody Scheckter (Wolf) on the inside.

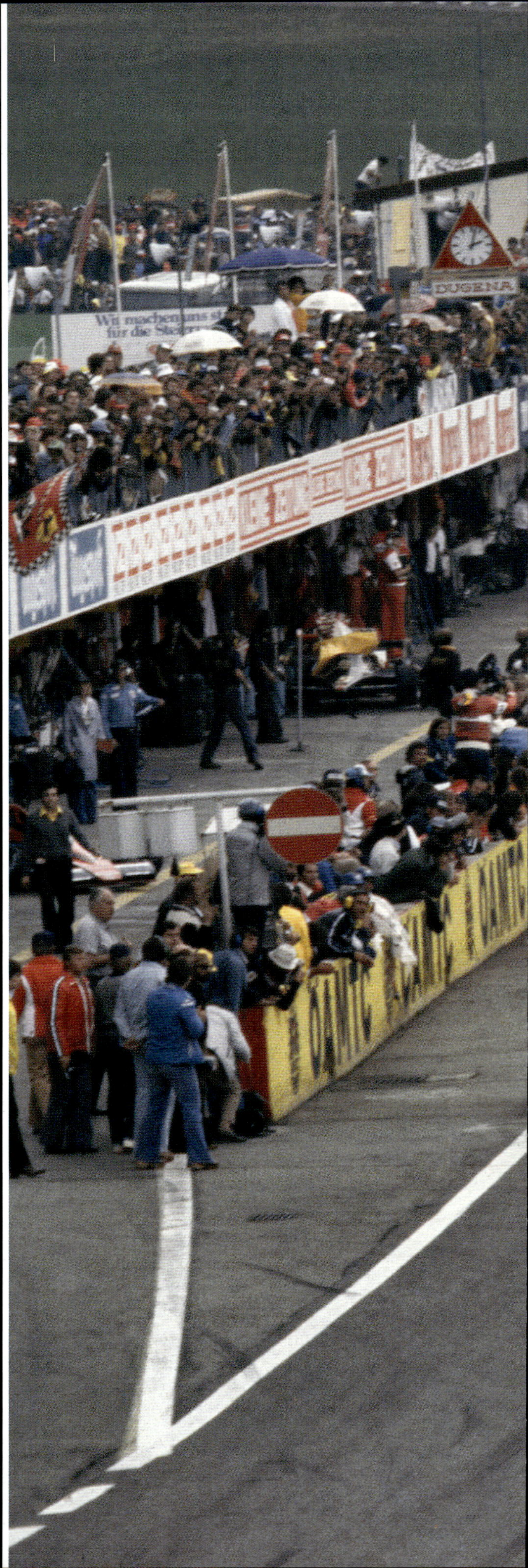

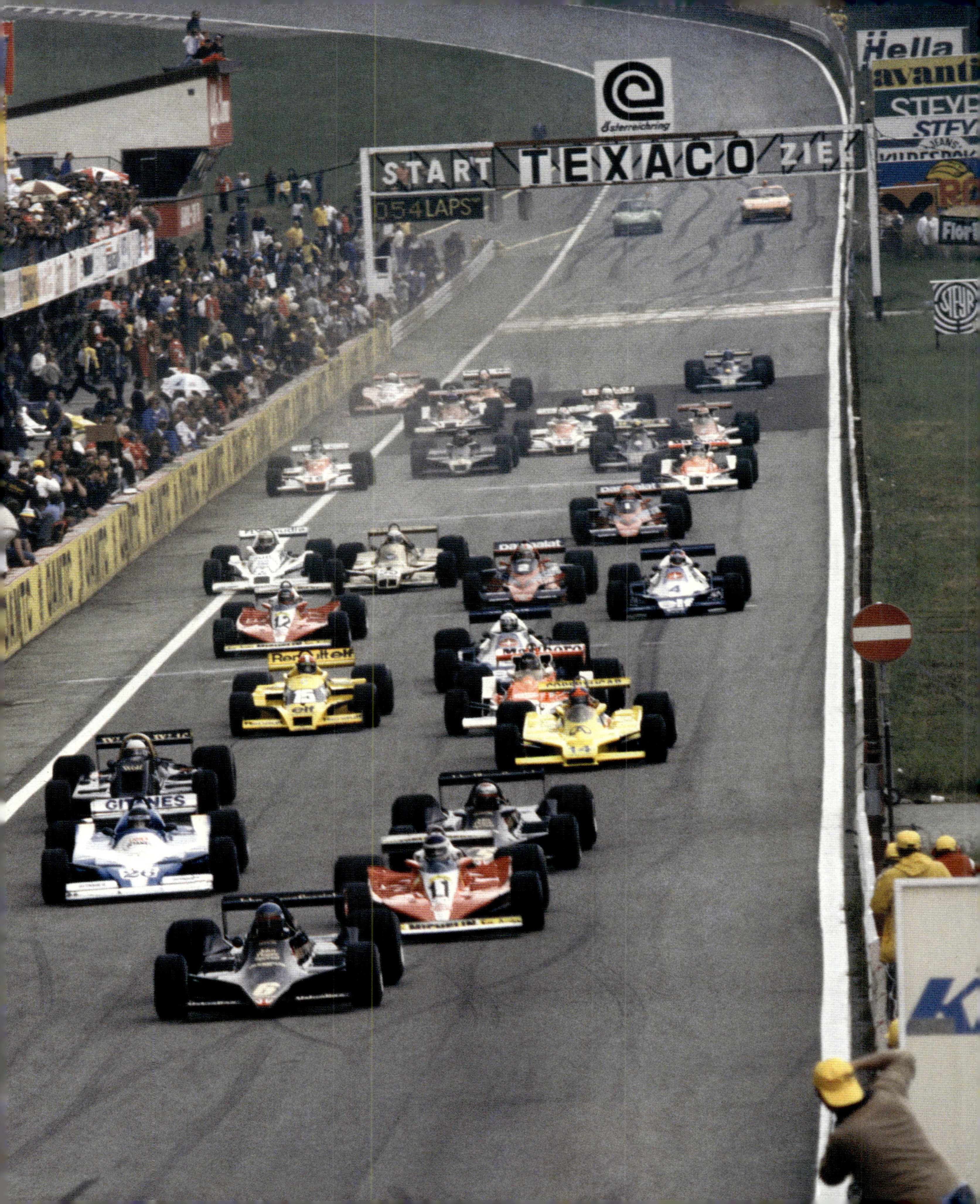
START
TEXACO
Hella
avanti
STEYR
GITANES

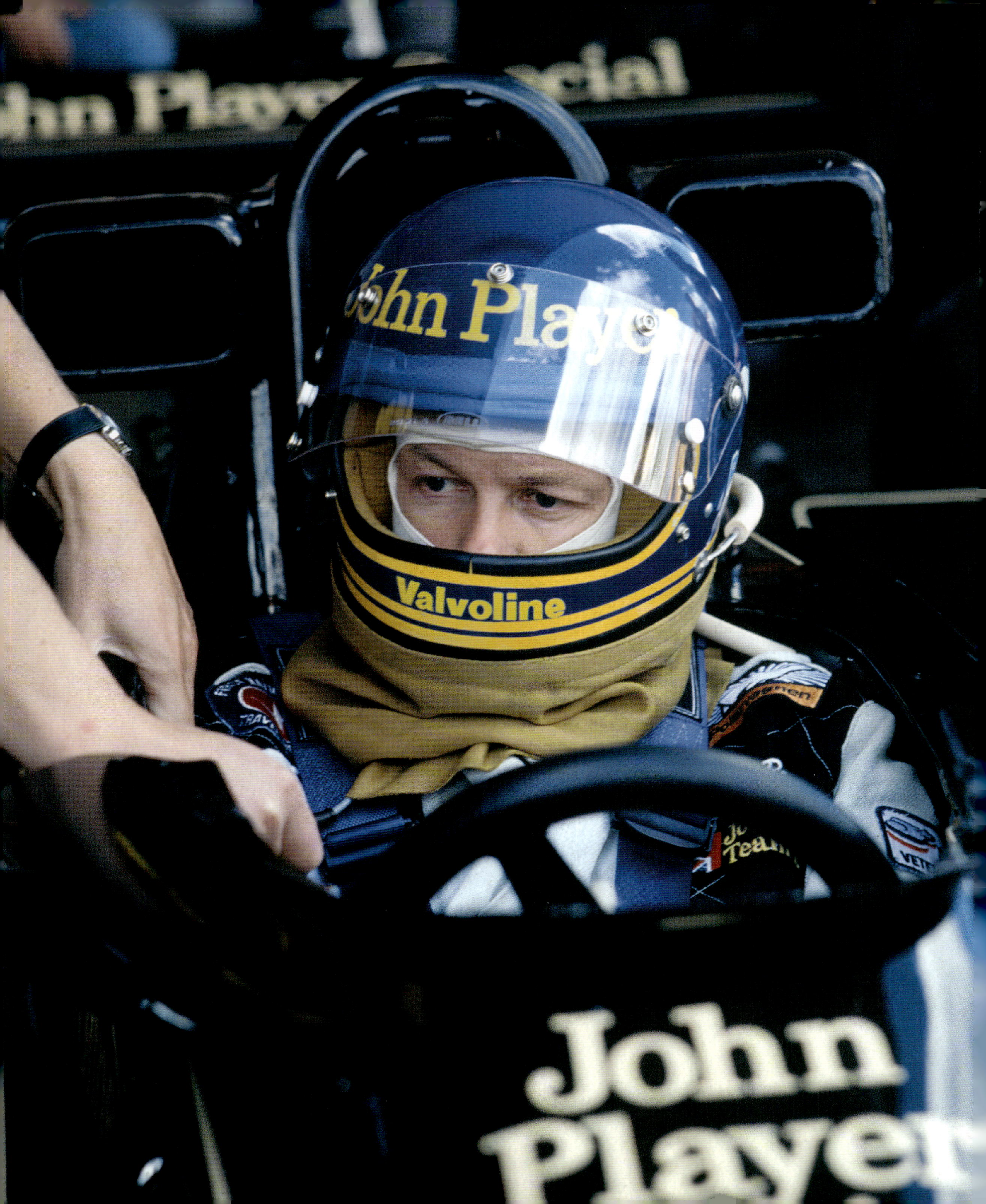
Valvoline
John Player

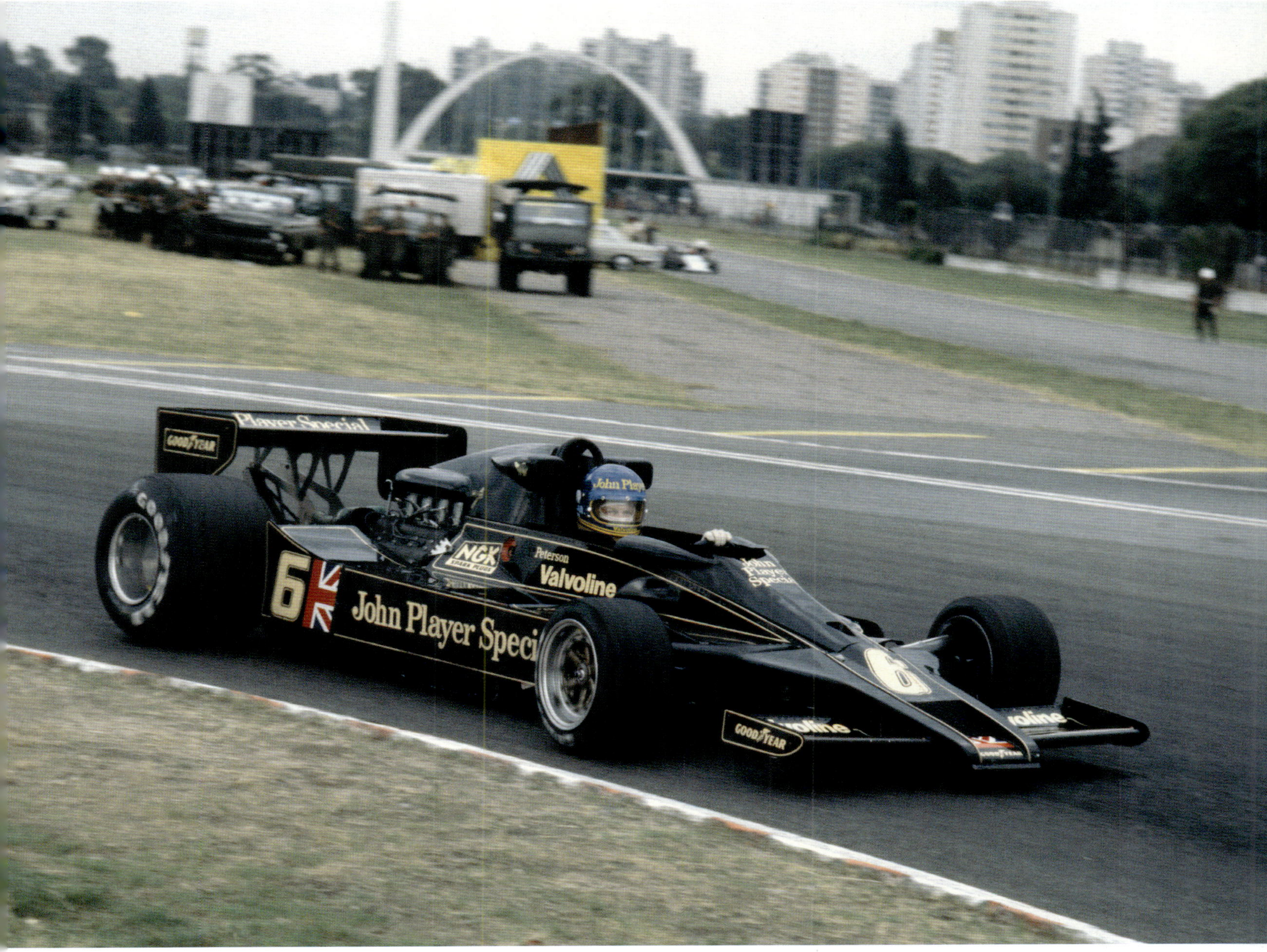

LEFT Ronnie's fourth full season with Team Lotus began in Argentina, where both he and Mario Andretti were equipped with updated versions of the Lotus 78. The team's first 'wing-car', the 78 had won five times the year before while Ronnie had struggled with the six-wheel Tyrrell, and remained highly competitive into the new season.

ABOVE Ronnie in action on the autodromo in Buenos Aires, where national hero Juan Manuel Fangio accepted the honour of flagging the Argentine Grand Prix. With a new and more effective rear end on the sister car, Mario Andretti led all the way from pole position, but from third on the grid Ronnie grappled all afternoon with understeer and blistering tyres. He could not match Niki Lauda's Brabham-Alfa, Patrick Depailler's Tyrrell or James Hunt's McLaren. He finished fifth, but only just. Fangio mistook his car for Mario's and showed him the chequered flag first. Ronnie thought the race was over, eased off, and was almost caught by Patrick Tambay in the other McLaren M26.

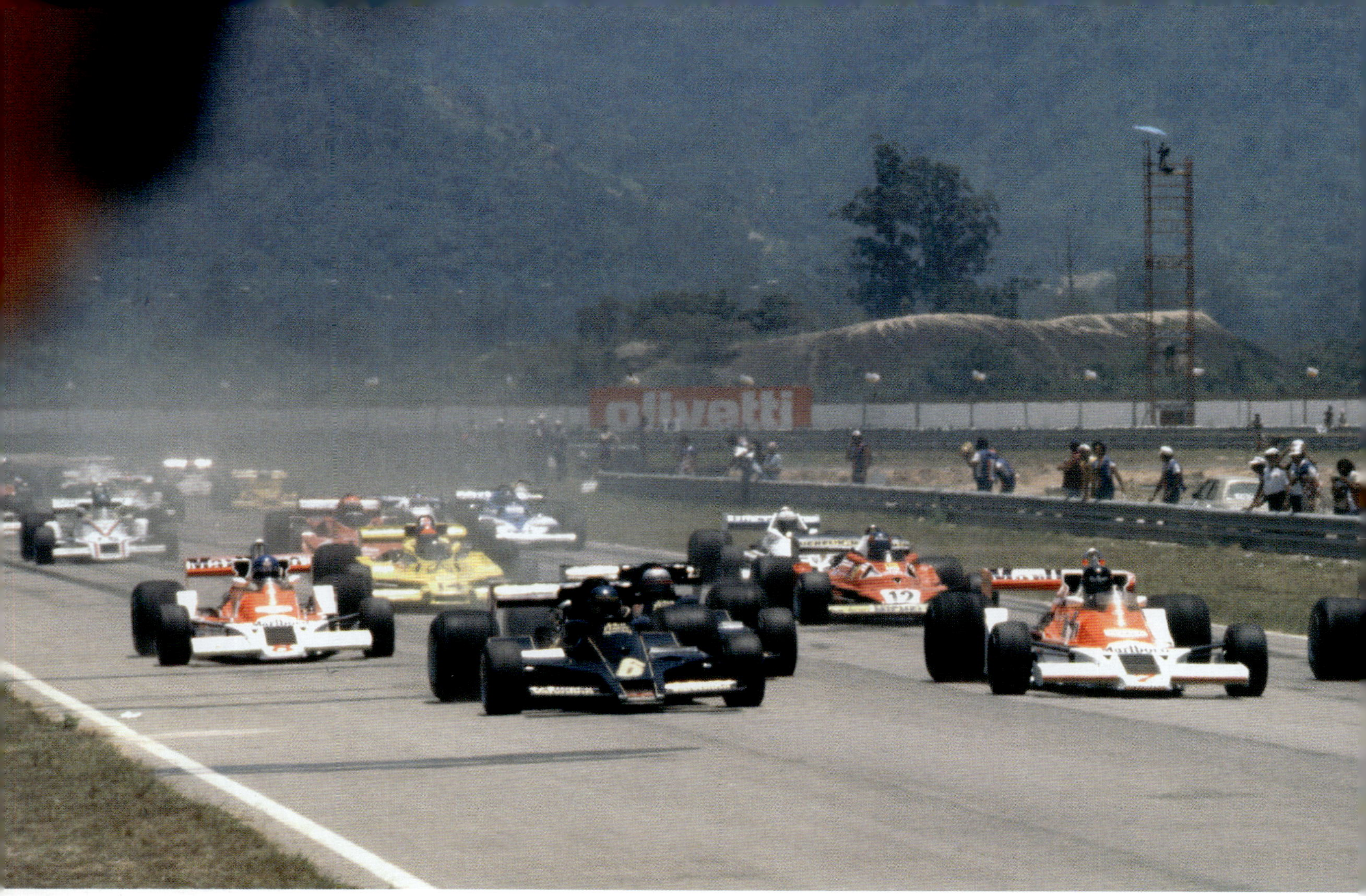

ABOVE A fortnight after Argentina, Ronnie took his turn to claim pole position in searing heat on the Jacarepagua circuit near Rio de Janeiro. He lost out at the start when his rear wheels were spun by a pool of water left by his own engine on the dummy grid, and Carlos Reutemann took his Ferrari round James Hunt's McLaren and into the lead. 'Lole' went on to win the Brazilian Grand Prix comfortably. Ronnie again found his progress seriously hampered by understeer and was running fourth when, after 15 laps, he was struck by Ferrari's hard-charging Gilles Villeneuve, damaging his left rear suspension. He continued after a pitstop, but then the suspension collapsed.

OPPOSITE TOP Ronnie was stymied by a gearbox failure during qualifying at Kyalami. As Mario Andretti lined up the sister car second on the grid behind Niki Lauda's Brabham-Alfa, he found himself back in 12th position. But the South African Grand Prix was an attritional and ultimately Ronnie won a very exciting race. It was led by Andretti, until a tyre problem slowed him. Jody Scheckter's Wolf took over, but had to give way to an inspired performance by Formula 1 rookie Riccardo Patrese in the new Arrows FA1. Fifteen laps from the end, Patrese lost his engine, and Patrick Depailler, from 11th on the grid, took the lead. But Ronnie – pictured leading Alan Jones (Williams FW06) and Gilles Villeneuve (Ferrari 312B2) into Crowthorne corner at the end of the long straightaway – had also been making up places. When his team-mate had to make a last-gasp pitstop for fuel, Ronnie swept past into second place, now hard after the leading Tyrrell, which was hampered by an intermittent fuel pickup fault. On the final lap, after twice banging wheels with his 1977 team-mate, he forced his way past and held on to win by half a second.

OPPOSITE BOTTOM Elf Team Tyrrell had abandoned its six-wheel project and reverted to a conventional car, the 008, with which Patrick Depailler, in his fifth season with the team, so nearly won the South African Grand Prix. Ronnie looks mightily relieved: what would he have thought about his decision to return to Lotus if Depailler had beaten him?

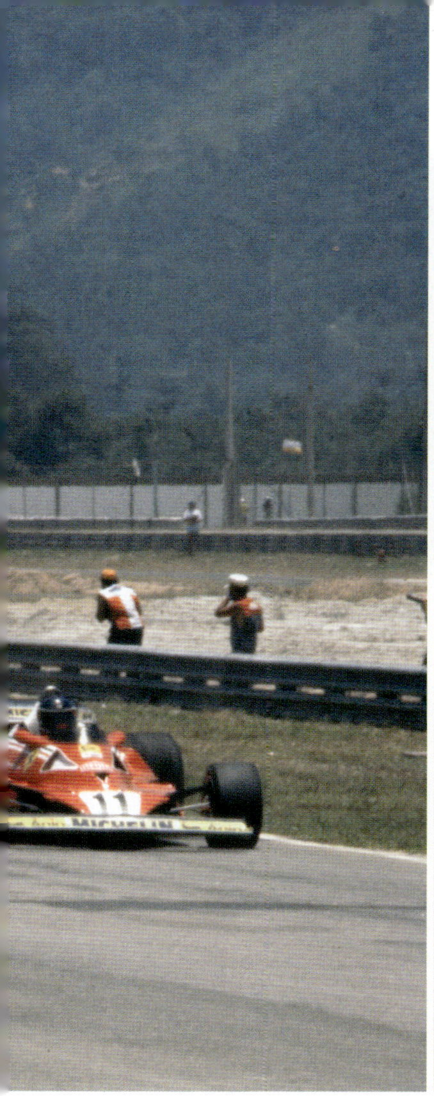

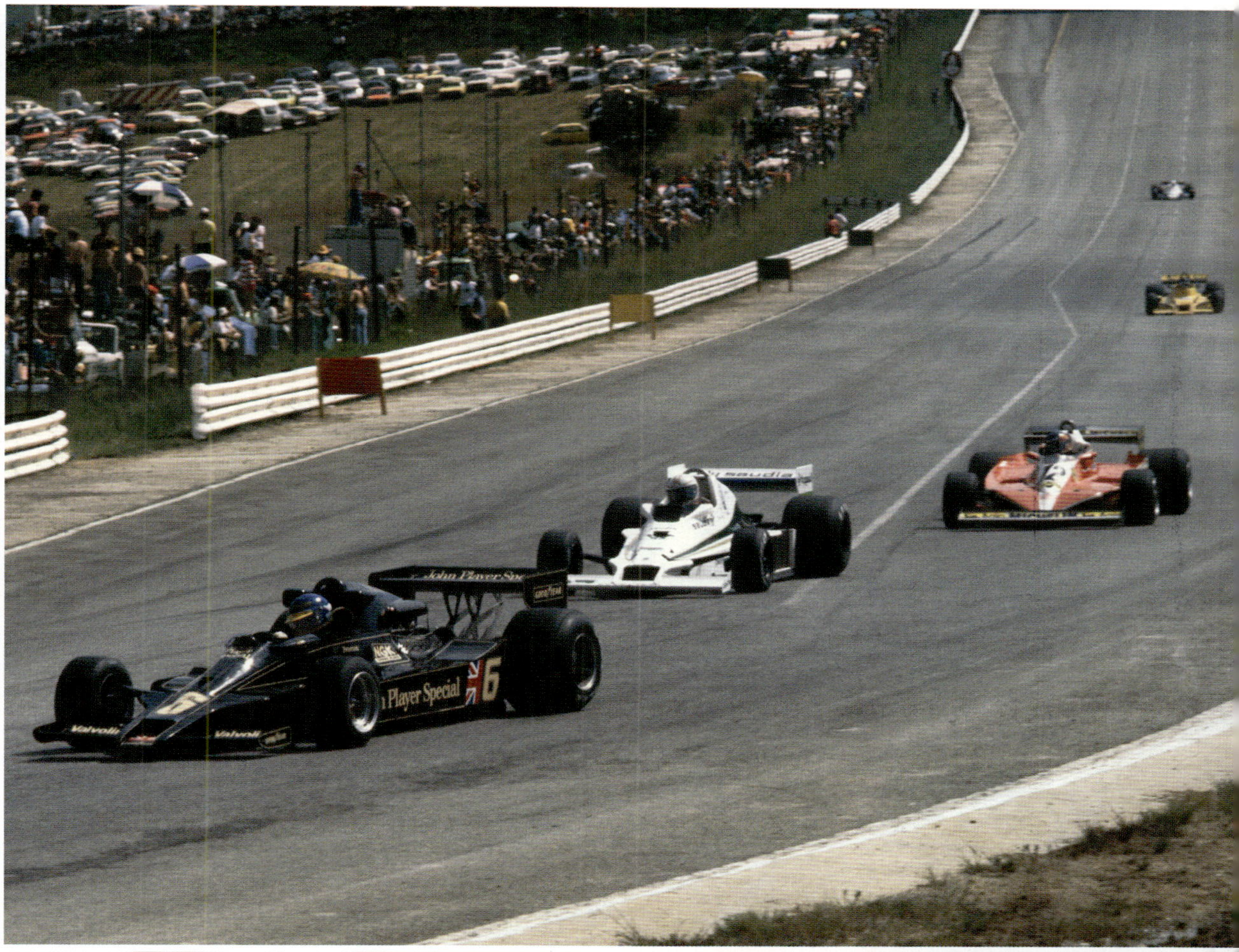
Player Special

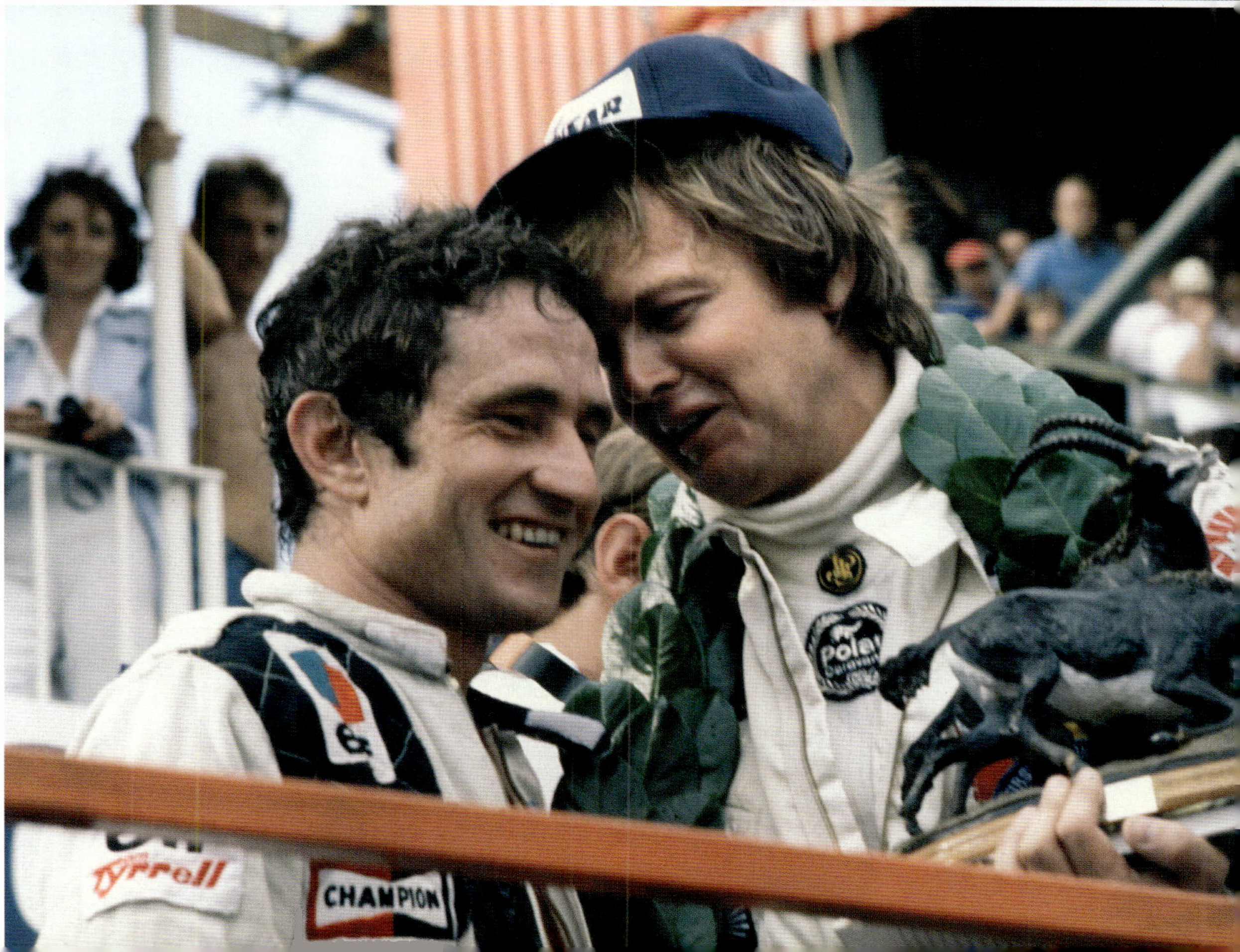
Tyrrell
CHAMPION

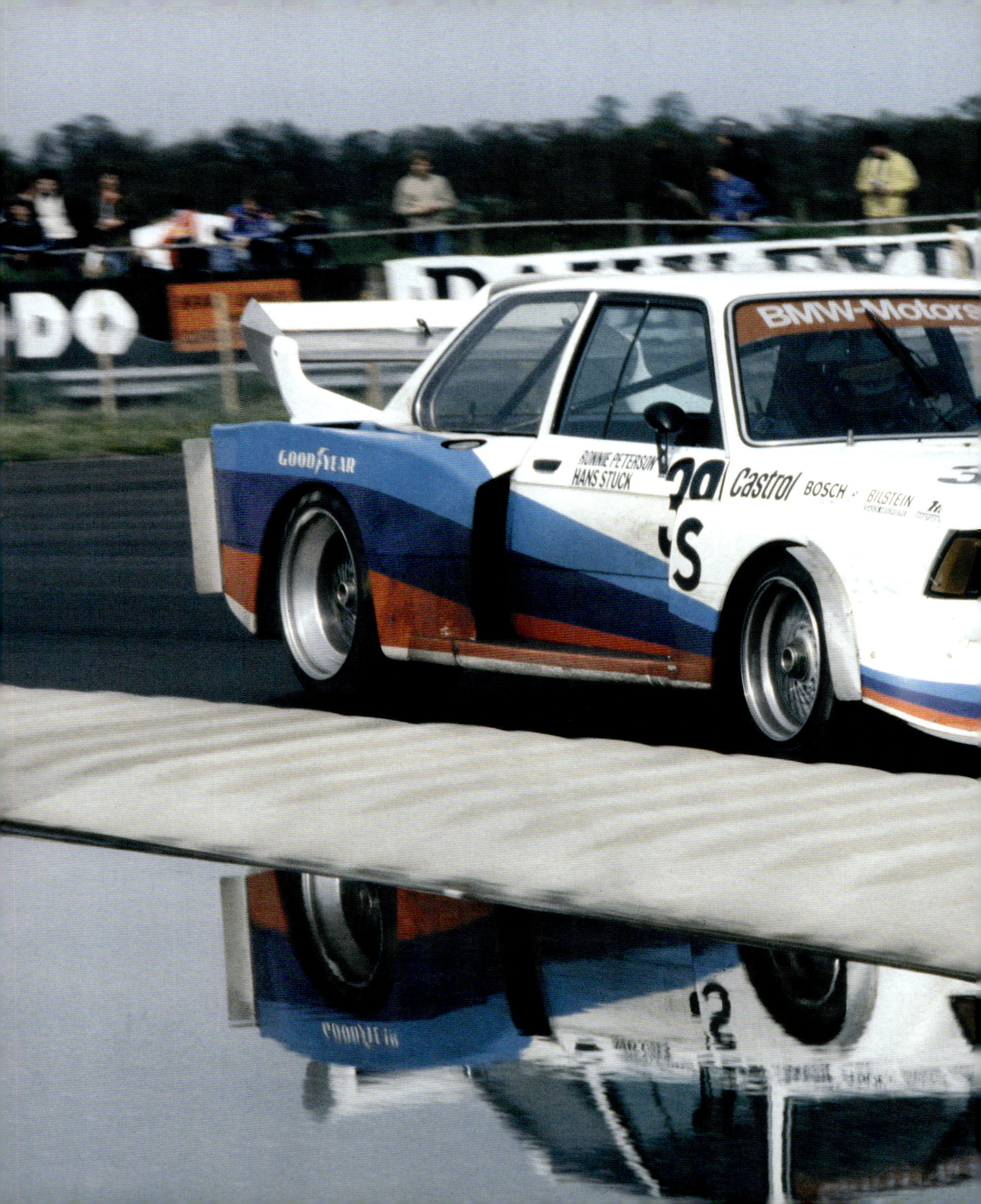
BMW-Motors
GOODYEAR
RONNIE PETERSON
HANS STUCK
Castrol
BOSCH
BILSTEIN

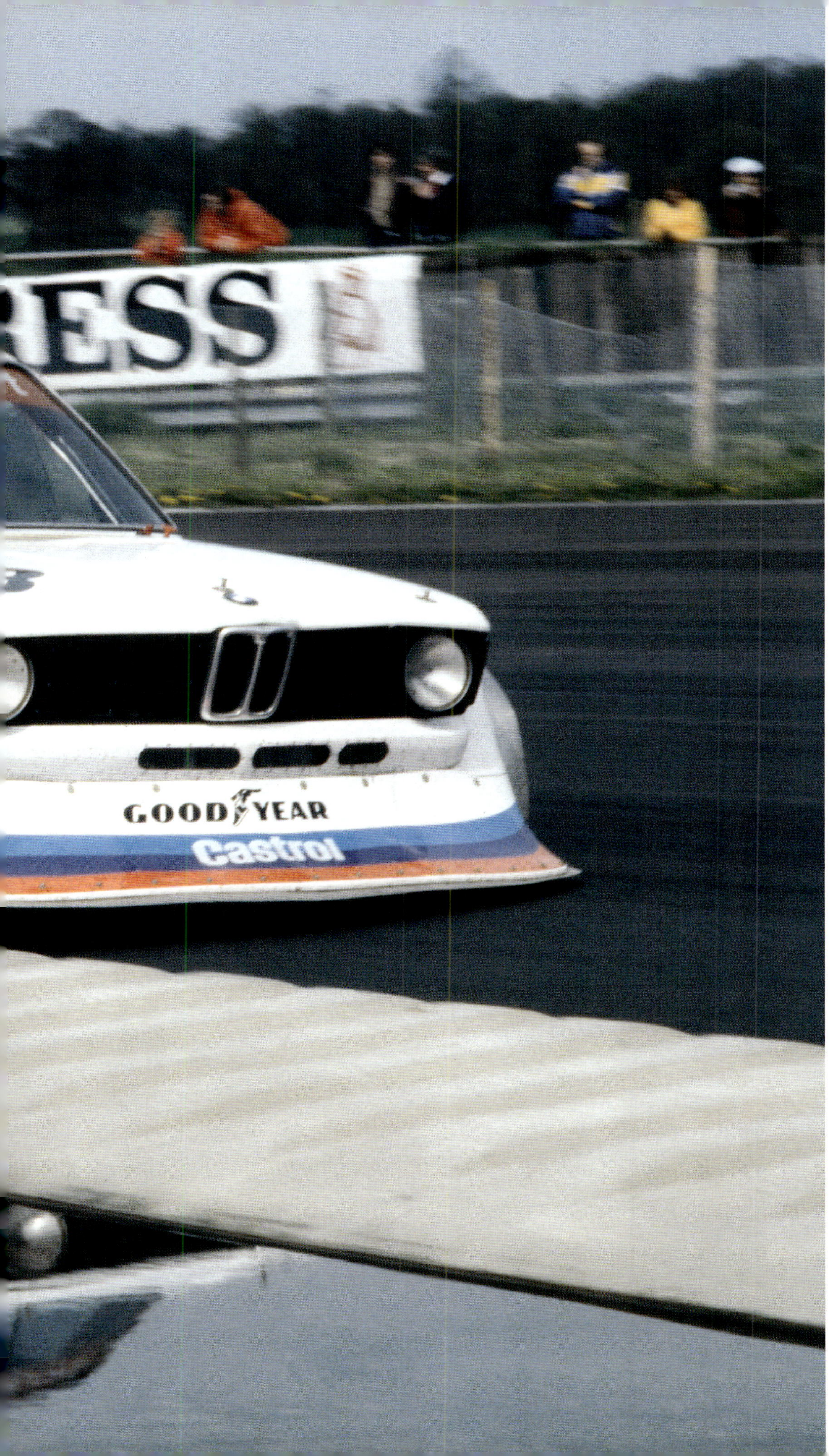

LEFT For a fourth season, Ronnie was retained by BMW Motorsport to race in the World Championship of Makes when available. After doing the Daytona 24 Hours in February with McLaren North America, and a German championship event on the Nürburgring (where he had written off his car), his next date was at Silverstone for the annual six-hour race in May, again co-driving Hans Stuck. Perhaps in the light of their experience at Brands Hatch eight months before, this time Stuck was asked to qualify the 600bhp BMW 320i turbo (sixth), and Ronnie to drive the first shift. The race was dominated by the brand-new, 800bhp 'Moby Dick' Porsche 935-78 of factory drivers Jochen Mass and Jacky Ickx, but Ronnie had the BMW solidly in contention with the various privateer Porsches when he handed it over to Stuck after 40 laps. Hans-Joachim, and then Ronnie again, both drove superbly and established the car in an unlikely second place. Early in Stuck's next shift, after 150 laps, a broken oil pump drive seized the rear axle.

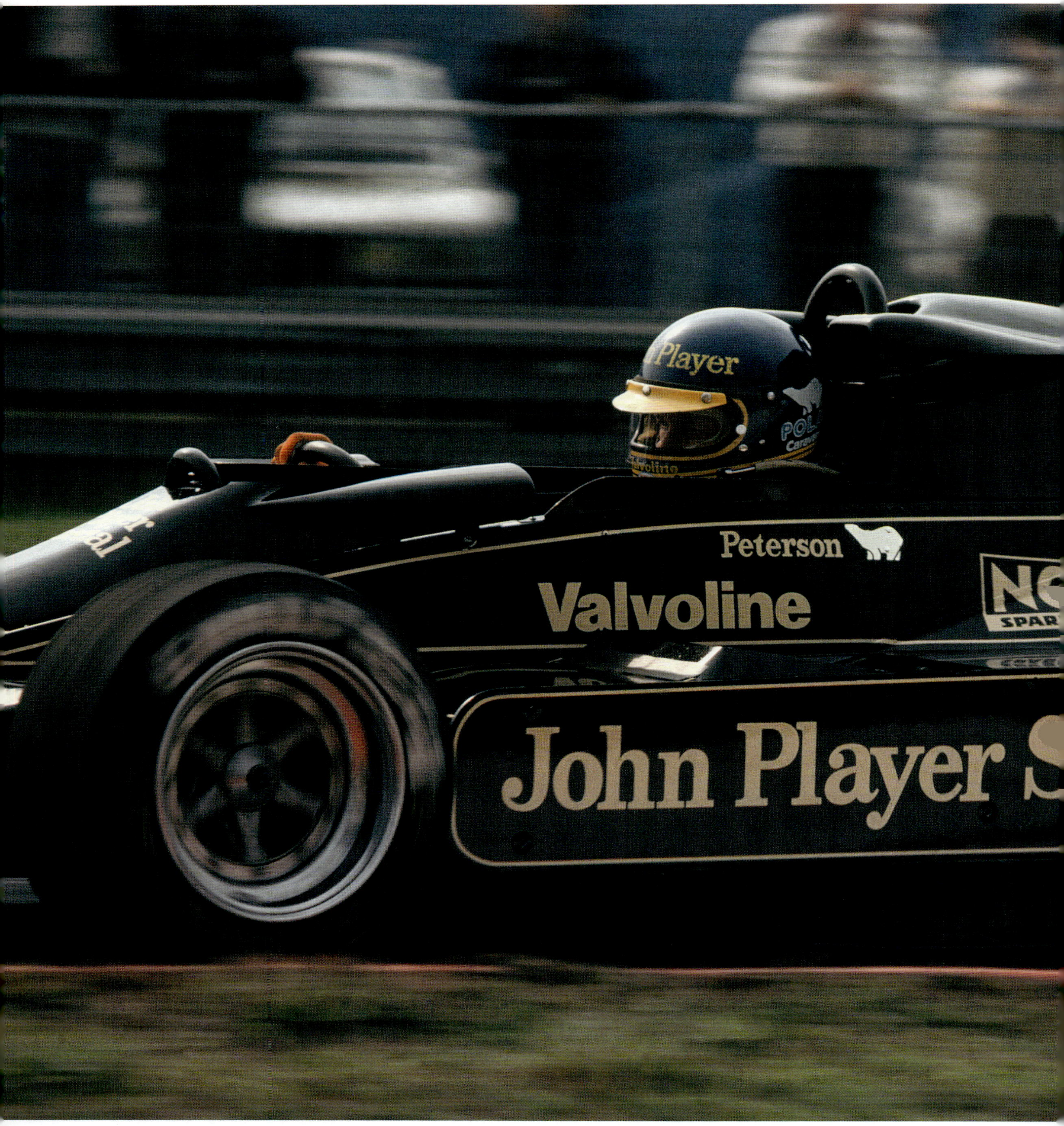
Player
Peterson
Valvoline
John Player

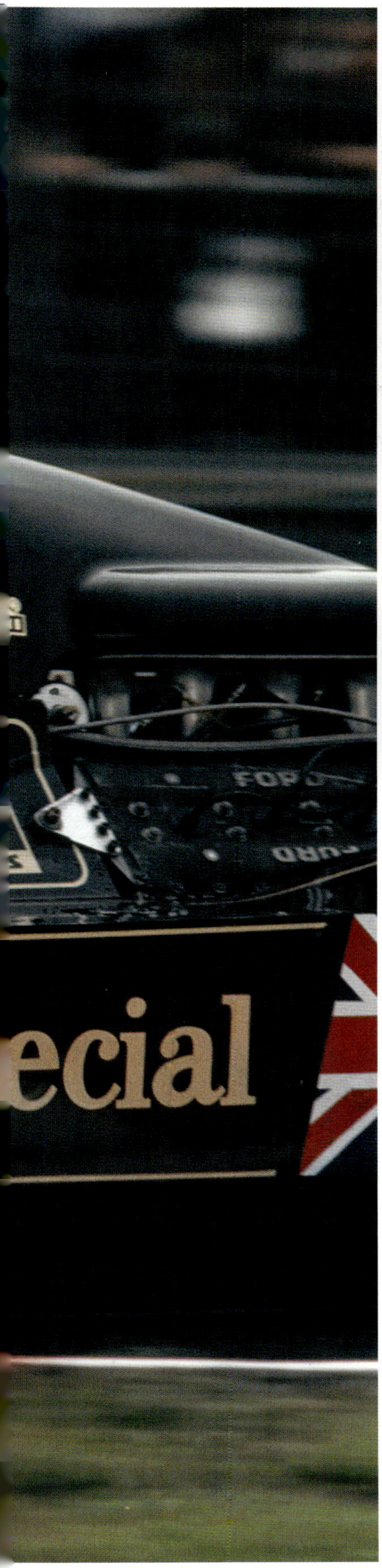

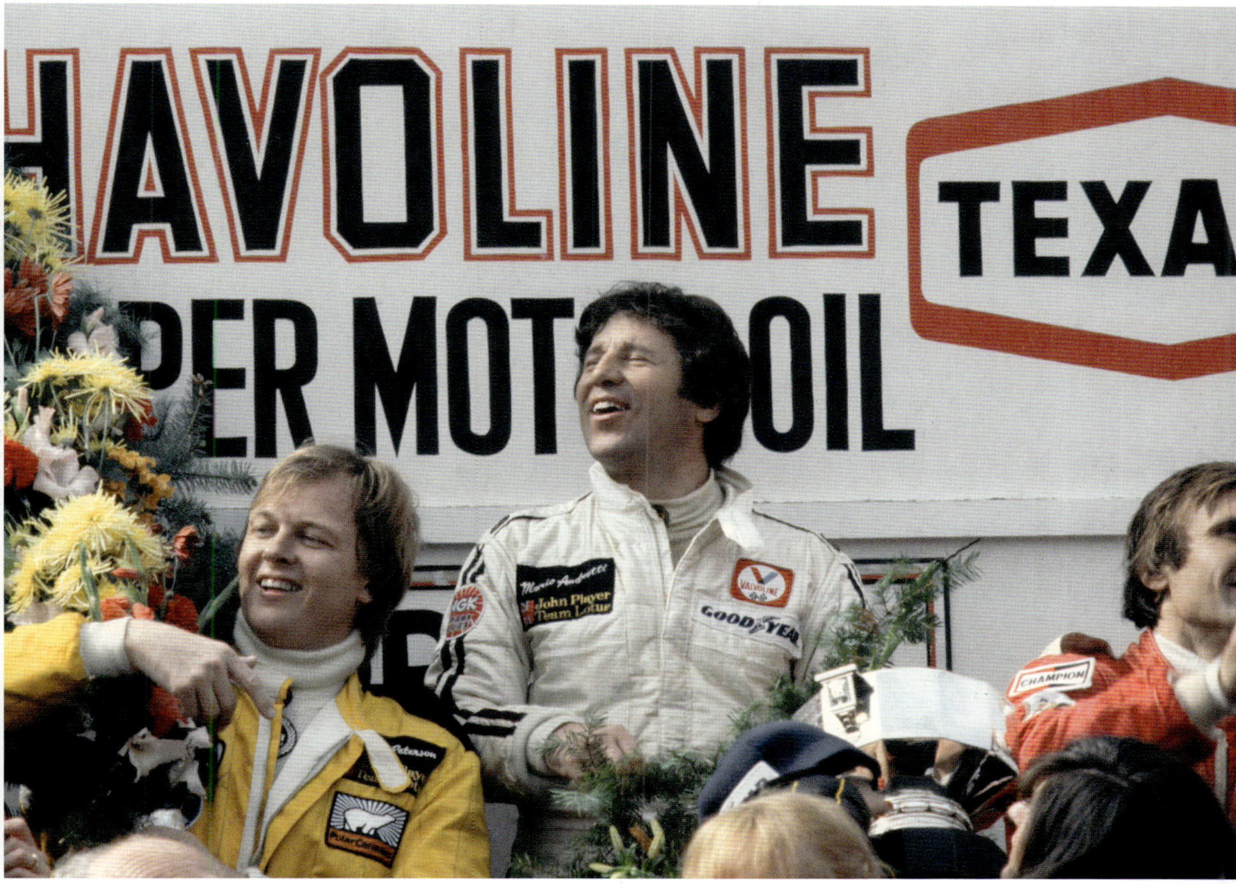

LEFT Ronnie was running second in the Belgian Grand Prix when he had to stop for a new tyre with 15 laps remaining. The delay dropped him to fourth and made him angry. On rejoining, his driving was simply fabulous. Ronnie repassed Jacques Laffite's Ligier-Matra within five laps, putting him third, 7sec behind Carlos Reutemann's Ferrari. Repeatedly demolishing the Zolder track record, by well over 2sec, he was back in second place only three laps later. The winner, from pole position, was his team mate, Mario Andretti, racing the sensational new Lotus 79 for the first time.

ABOVE The Belgian Grand Prix delivered the first John Player Team Lotus 1–2 of the season, the new car winning from the old. The ground-effect Lotus 79 was so good in every department that, after only six races, Mario Andretti already knew that the championship was his for the taking. Third man Carlos Reutemann knew that, for Ferrari, the game was up. And Ronnie knew that, in a fortnight's time, he would be racing a 79 too.

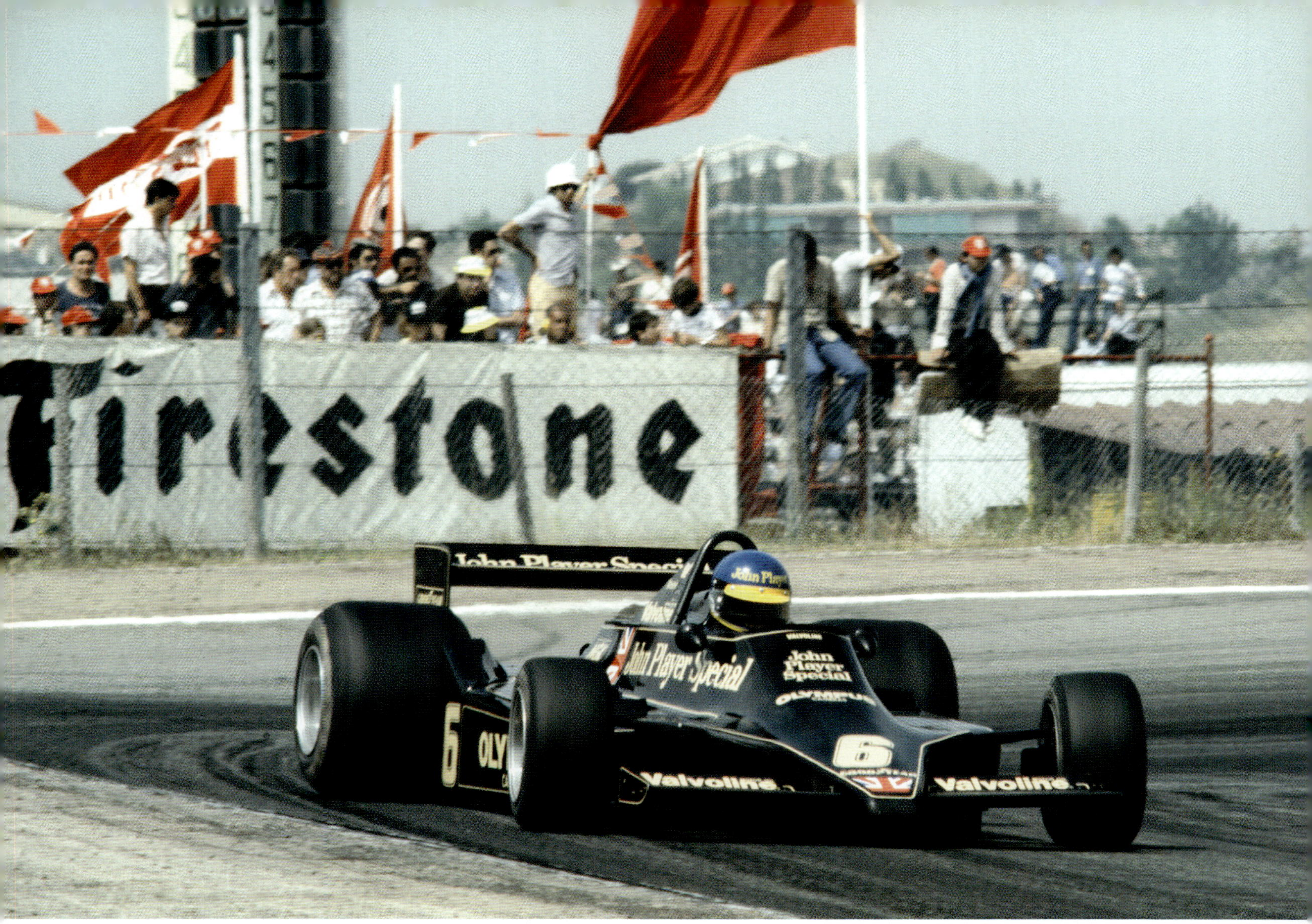

ABOVE Ronnie first raced the superb Lotus 79 at Jarama on the first Sunday in June. He qualified second, a tad slower than Mario Andretti in the sister car. On race day, he was watching policemen clearing the last people from the grid when the start signal was given... Ronnie was taken completely by surprise, and was not even in gear. Others were also not ready, but James Hunt was, and took full advantage, taking the lead of the Spanish Grand Prix from the second row. Mario took only four laps to hunt down the McLaren M26 and take the lead, but Ronnie's poor start had put him down in ninth place. It took him 53 of the 75 laps to regain second place.

RIGHT Ronnie's popularity in his native Sweden reached new dimensions during a fantastic drive at Anderstorp that had a capacity crowd shouting with excitement. This was the race won by Niki Lauda in the 'fan-car' – Brabham's outrageous answer to the ground-effect Lotus. The fully skirted BT46B was sucked onto the track surface by a huge fan. It was blatantly a movable aerodynamic device, and therefore illegal, but the justification was that, since the Alfa Romeo flat-12 would overheat without it, engine cooling was its 'primary purpose'. Mario Andretti lost the lead to Lauda several laps before parking up with a broken engine. Ronnie had been racing in third position behind these two when, after 11 laps, he was in pit-lane with a punctured tyre. The stop dropped him to 17th but, in the third Grand Prix running, he produced a sensational comeback drive. By the time Mario's retirement promoted Riccardo Patrese to second place, on lap 47, Ronnie was third. Try as he did over the remaining 23 laps, however, he could not dislodge the weaving Arrows. The two finished side-by-side, Patrese still just ahead. They were half a minute behind the Brabham, which was never raced again. It was banned shortly afterwards, although Lauda's win was allowed to stand.

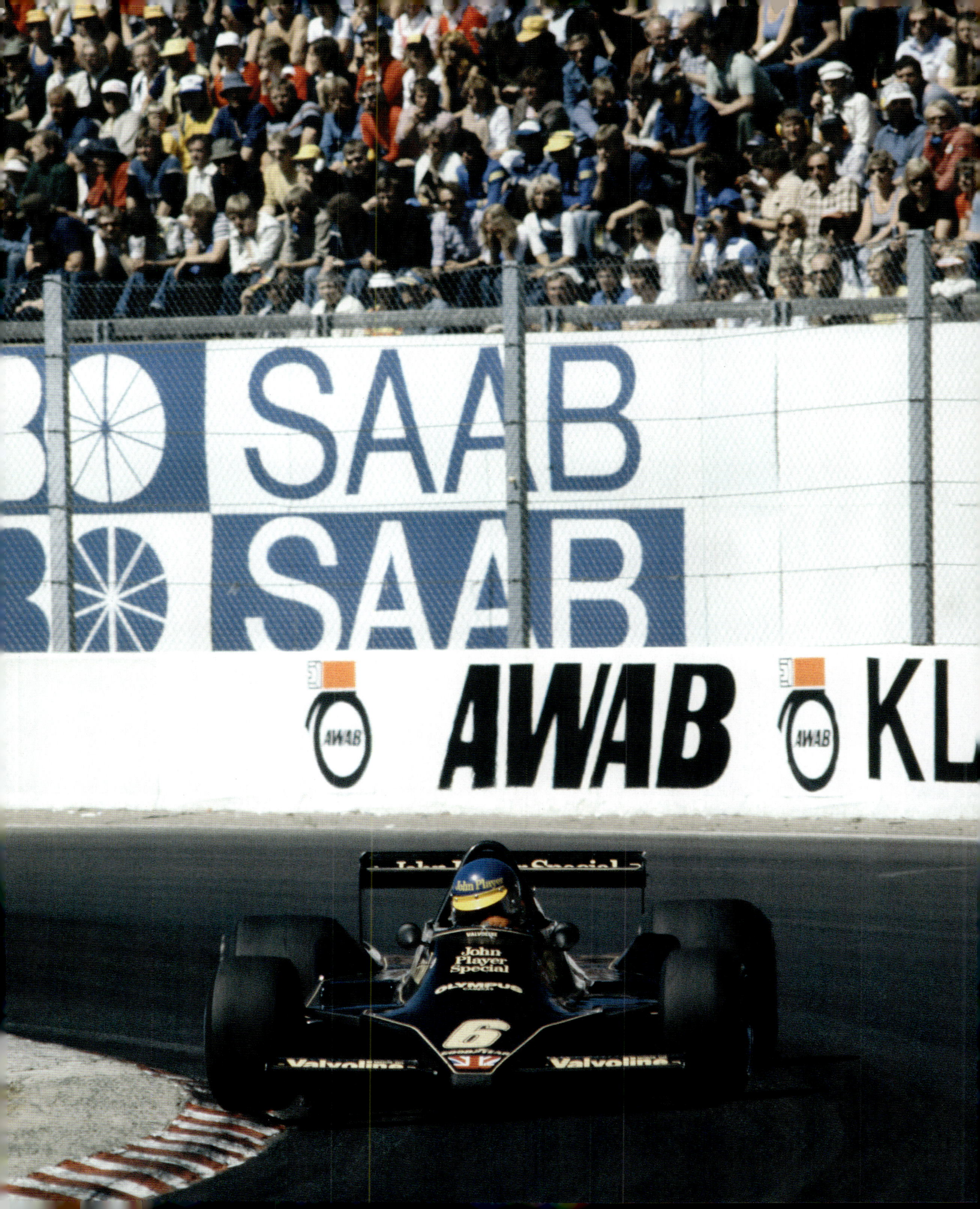
SAAB
SAAB
AWAB
AWAB
AWAB
KL
John Player
John Player Special
Valvoline
Valvoline
6

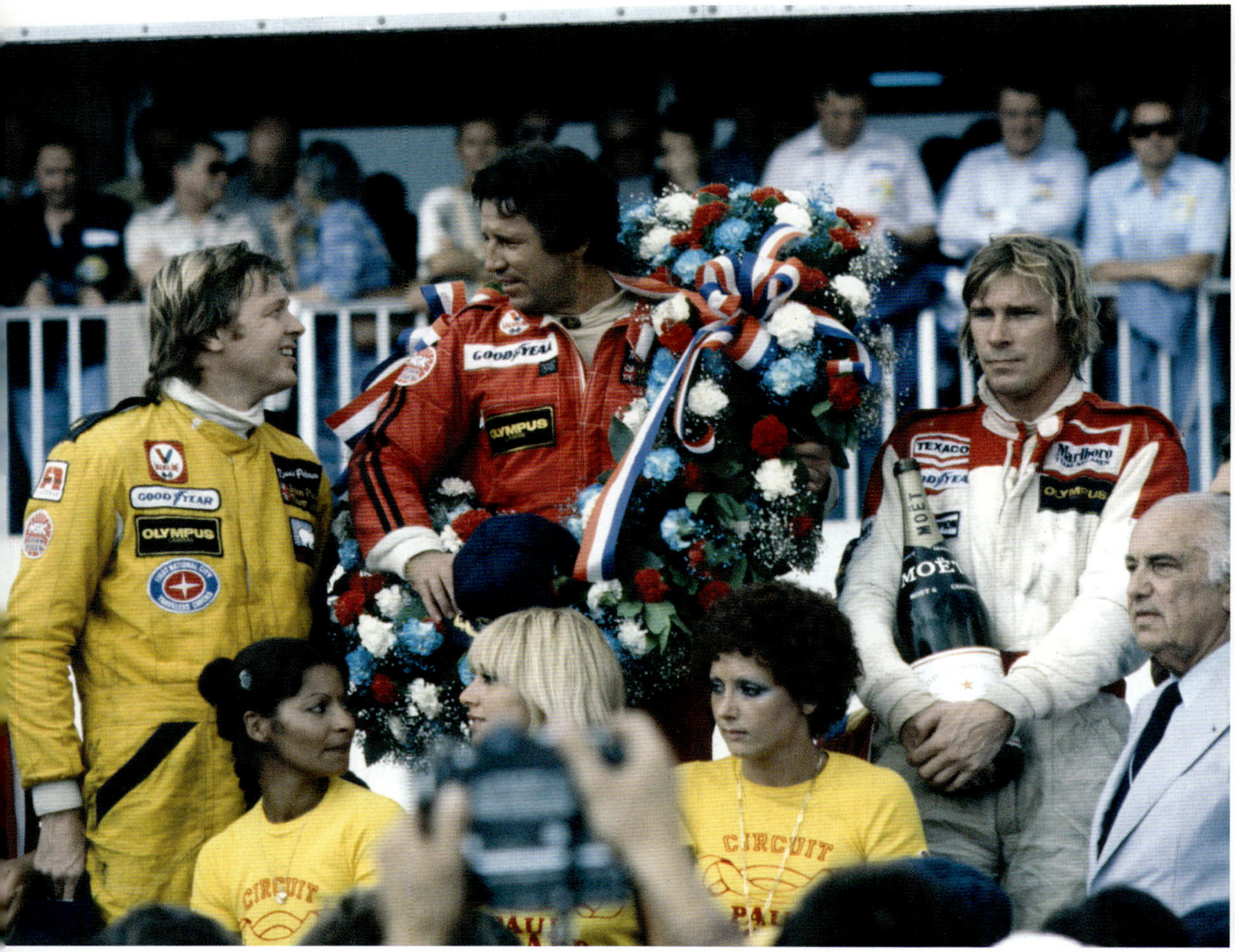

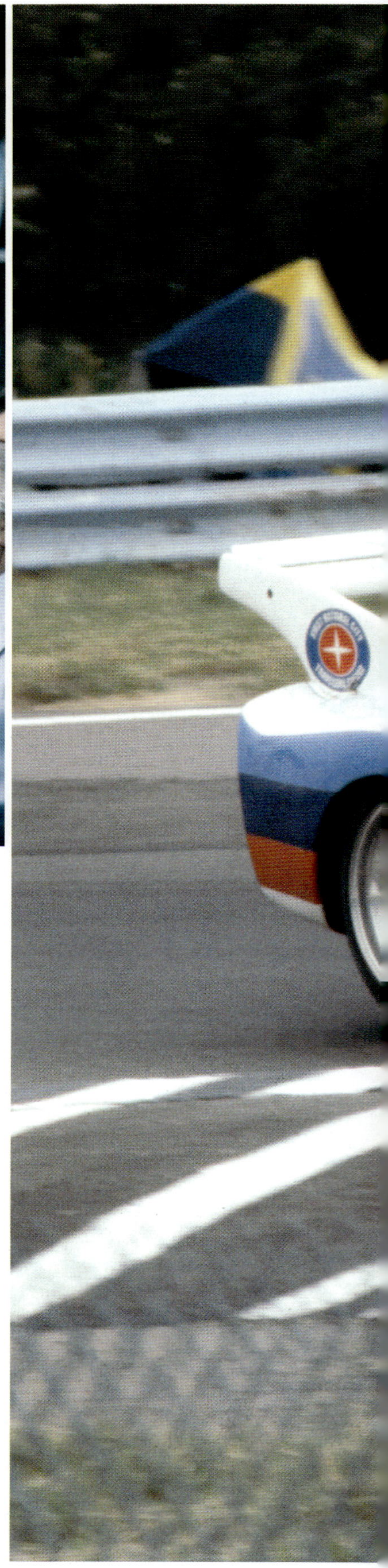

ABOVE Ronnie and Mario pulled off a third 1–2 in four races for Colin Chapman in the French Grand Prix at Paul Ricard, although Ronnie found himself grappling with excessive oversteer and spent much of the race under severe pressure from James Hunt's McLaren. Here on the podium, Hunt appears uncharacteristically disgruntled. In fact, he had vomited in the cockpit on the final lap, dropping off Ronnie's gearbox and leaving him in the clear.

RIGHT Ronnie had another run in McLaren North America's BMW 320i turbo in the Watkins Glen 6 Hours. The team had two cars at this event, one a much-modified and lighter new version. When the new model developed a turbocharger problem during practice, it was decided to start both, David Hobbs from fifth on the grid in the new car, Ronnie from the back in the older one. Sure enough, the turbo immediately played up again on the new car, and Hobbs parked it. Meanwhile Ronnie made astonishing progress through the 44-car field (pictured), emerging in sixth place after only four laps! He was challenging one of the Porsche 935s for fifth position when the engine broke. In all, Ronnie did 29 races with BMW's touring cars, and failed to finish 24 of them...

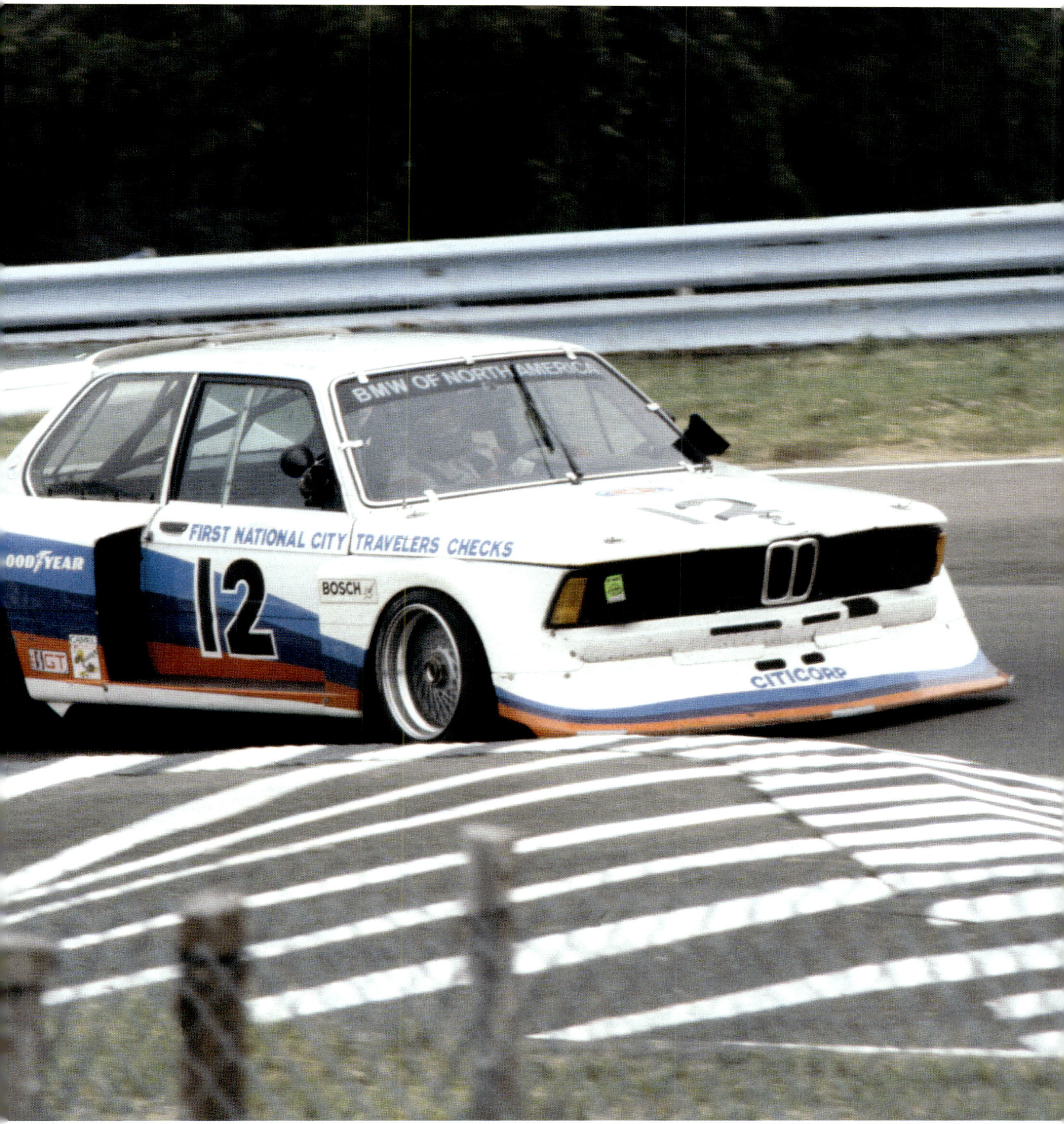
BMW OF NORTH AMERICA
FIRST NATIONAL CITY
TRAVELERS CHECKS
GOODYEAR
12
BOSCH
CITICORP

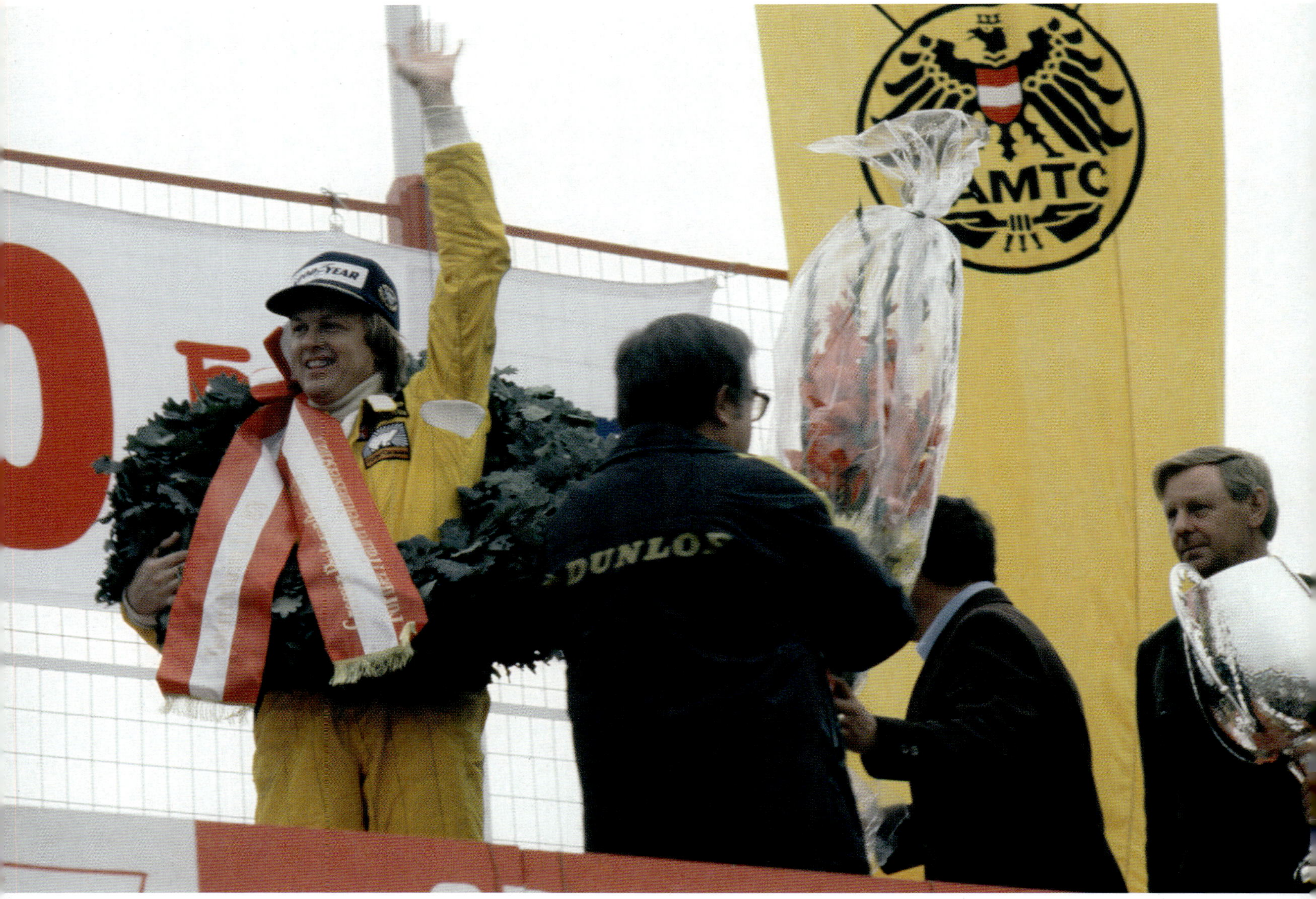

ABOVE Ronnie, understandably elated, completes his perfect weekend on the Osterreichring by acknowledging the plaudits from the crowd. As so often, the Austrian Grand Prix delivered an unusual race, being red-flagged after only seven laps due to a sudden cloudburst. Ronnie had led all the way so far, and did that again after the restart. The question of seniority never arose, because Mario Andretti had crashed the other Lotus 79 in trying to pass Carlos Reutemann's Ferrari on the opening lap. This weekend produced the 14th and last pole position of Ronnie's 122-race Formula 1 career, the ninth fastest lap, and the 10th and final victory.

RIGHT There was no unforeseen problem for either of the Team Lotus men at Zandvoort, and they swiftly adopted a 1–2 formation, doggedly pursued by Niki Lauda's Brabham BT46. Occasionally when these formations were established, Ronnie would place his car alongside Mario's, just to wind him up, and he did this often on the long straightaway here. Later in the Dutch Grand Prix, Ronnie's integrity was tested when, with Lauda closing on them both, Mario's engine began to lose revs due to a broken exhaust. But a severe vibration hampered Lauda, and Colin Chapman's men completed the race line astern. Now the Constructors' title was clinched, and only Mario and Ronnie could win the Drivers' championship.

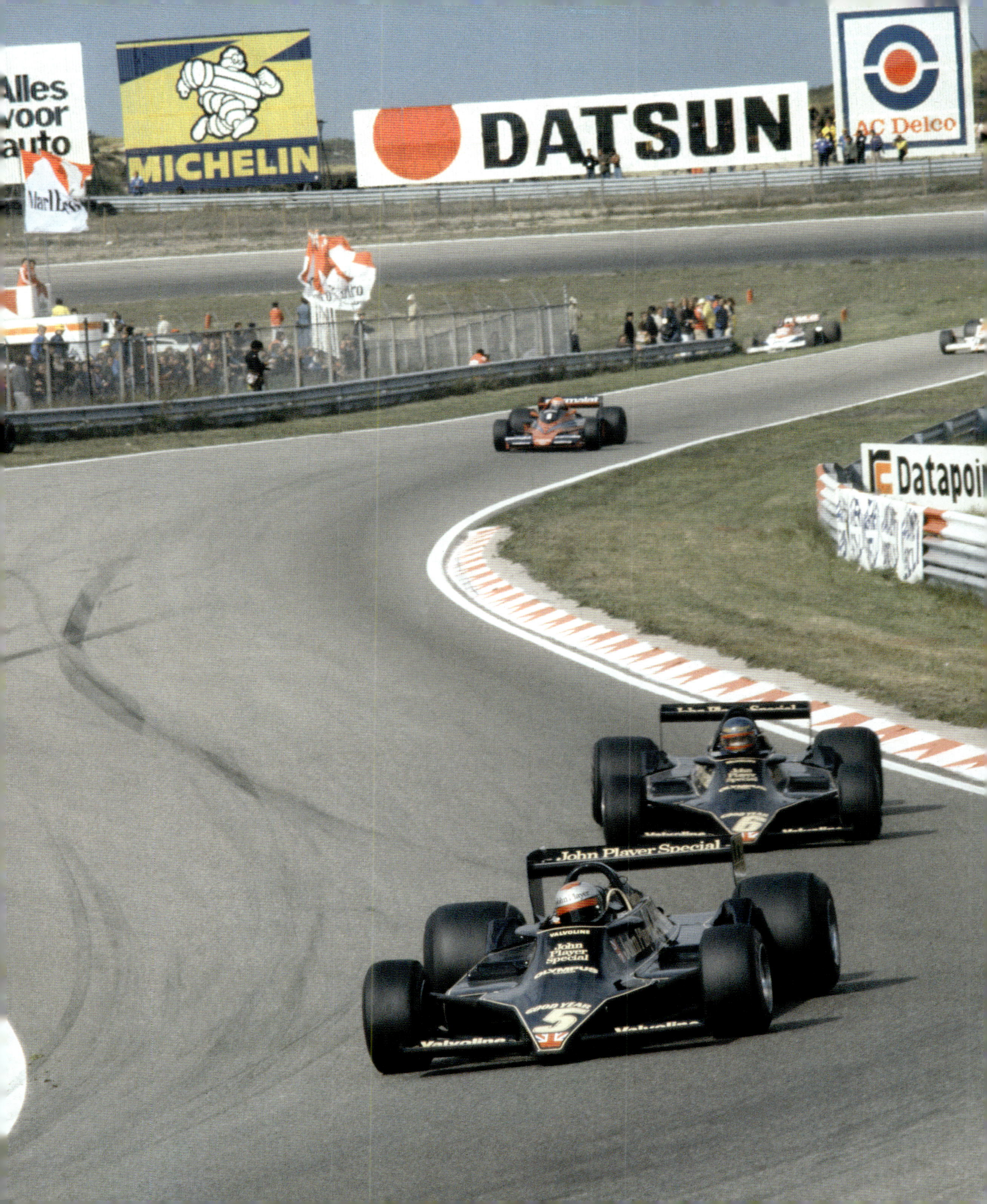
Alles
voor
auto
MICHELIN
DATSUN
AC Delco
Datapoi
John Player Special
5
6

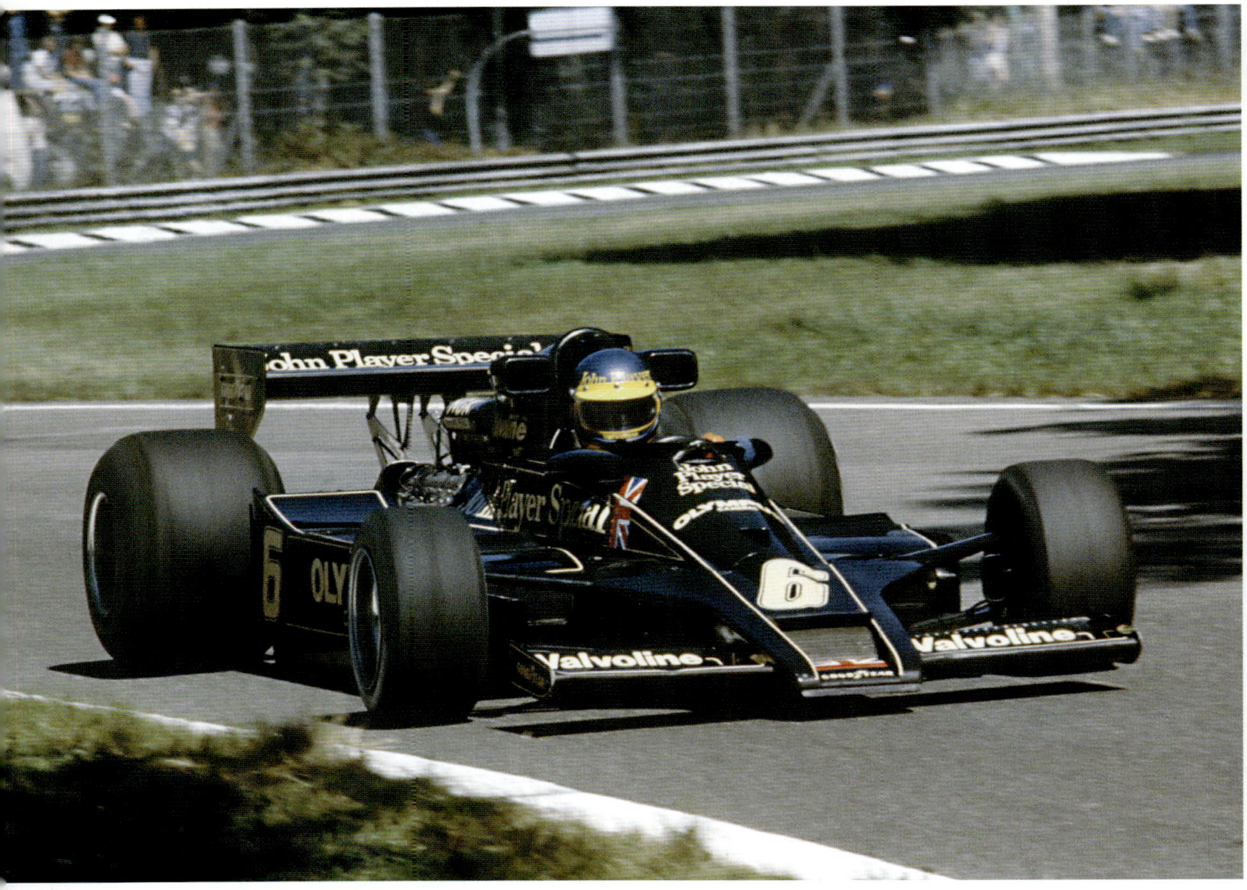

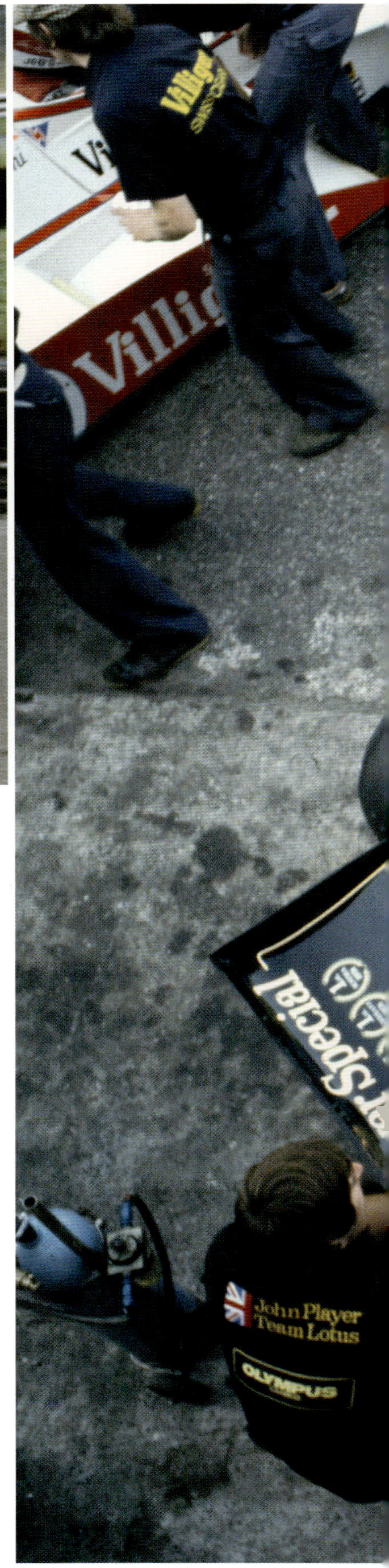

ABOVE Ronnie went second fastest behind Mario Andretti in the first Friday session on the Autodromo Nazionale di Monza, the scene of so many of his past successes, but then lost the engine in his Lotus 79. While his crew replaced it, he spent the afternoon setting up his older Lotus 78, with which he was more than 2sec slower. This car was the one used at the start of the season by Mario, and had won in Argentina. It was Ronnie's designated spare here, a third 79 being allocated to the team's number one driver.

RIGHT On the Saturday at Monza, with a new engine installed in his beautiful Lotus 79, Ronnie drove with the support of the world's fastest lizard, which accompanied him in the cockpit in the morning session. But then he lost a lot of track time while the crew dealt with a rear braking problem and a slipping clutch, and was unable to improve on his Friday lap-time. This was beaten by Gilles Villeneuve's Ferrari, Jean-Pierre Jabouille's turbo V6 Renault and Niki Lauda's Brabham-Alfa. Here Ronnie prepares for the race morning warm-up session, in which he violently encountered his next problem – a total rear brake failure on the fast entry to the first chicane. The 79 tore down four rows of catchfencing and was too badly damaged to be raced. However the rules allowed him to start the spare 78 from fifth on the grid.

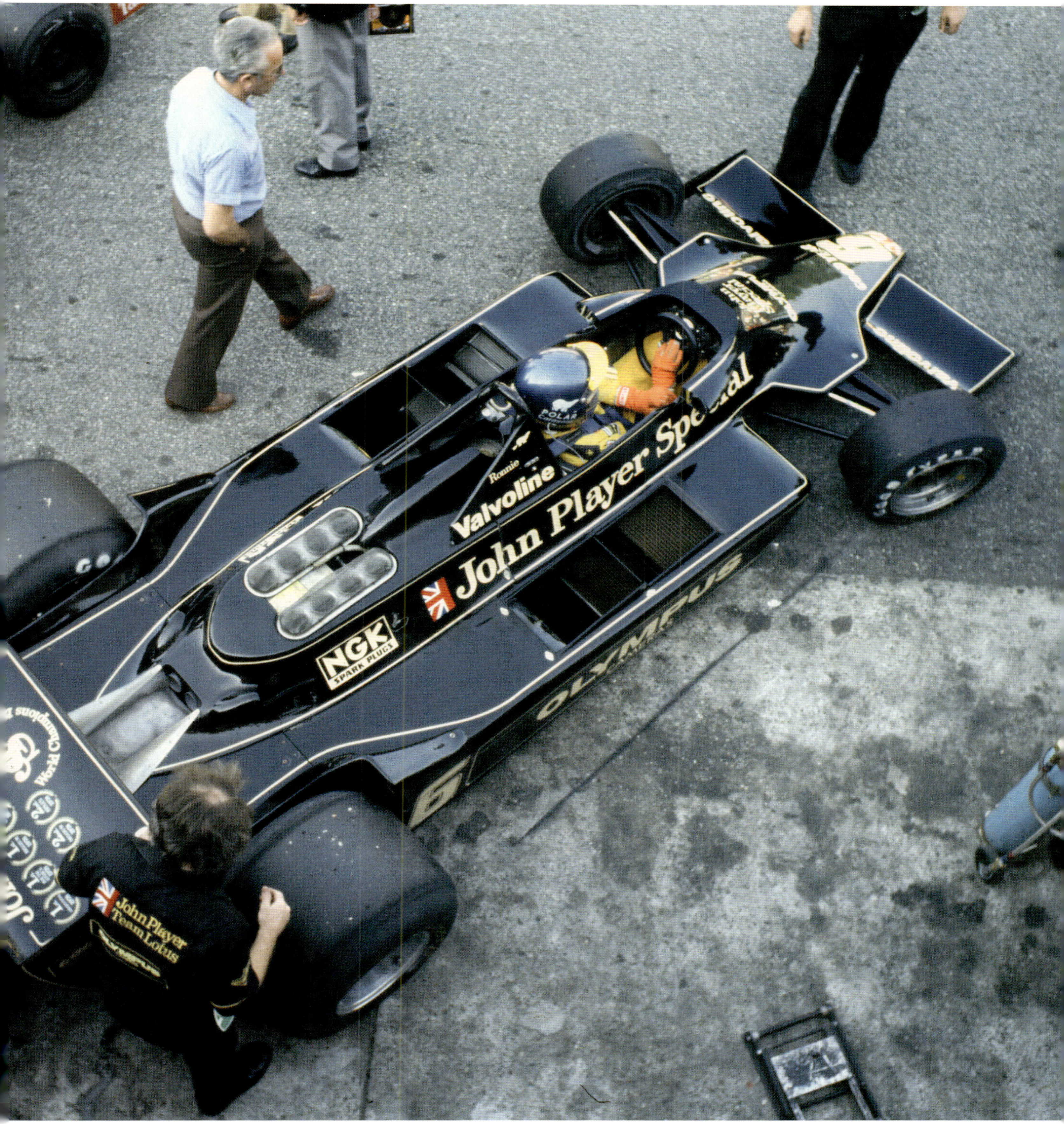
John Player Special
Valvoline
Ronnie
NGK
SPARK PLUGS
OLYMPUS
POLAR
John Player
Team Lotus

RIGHT The multiple accident at the start of the Italian Grand Prix was blamed on Formula 1 rookie Riccardo Patrese but, in reality, the start official was responsible. He released the field when only the cars on the front few rows of the grid were stationary, with the rest still to take up their positions and travelling between 10mph and more than 40mph. The result was a dramatic concertina effect as the field weaved towards the first corner, and an accident was virtually inevitable.

PAGES 232–33 As the rapidly contracting field of 24 cars jostled for position, those at the back moving the fastest, James Hunt's McLaren collided with Ronnie's Lotus, and eight other drivers – Vittorio Brambilla, Derek Daly, Patrick Depailler, Brett Lunger, Riccardo Patrese, Didier Pironi, Clay Regazzoni and Hans Stuck – all crashed in the ensuing mêlée. The Lotus was sent into a 120G impact with the barrier, and caught fire. Aided by a suited fire marshal, Hunt, Regazzoni and Depailler hauled Ronnie from the wreck before he received anything worse than minor burns. Here, as marshals at right attend to Brambilla, Ronnie has been laid out in the middle of the track, fully conscious. It is said to have taken 20 minutes for an ambulance to reach the scene. He was helicoptered to the Niguarda Hospital in Milan, where X-rays revealed that he had 17 fractures in one leg, three in the other. He had surgery to stabilise the broken bones but, overnight, bone marrow that had entered Ronnie's bloodstream from the fractures formed globules on his major organs. By dawn, he was in full renal failure, and was declared dead a few hours later, the cause being given as fat embolism.

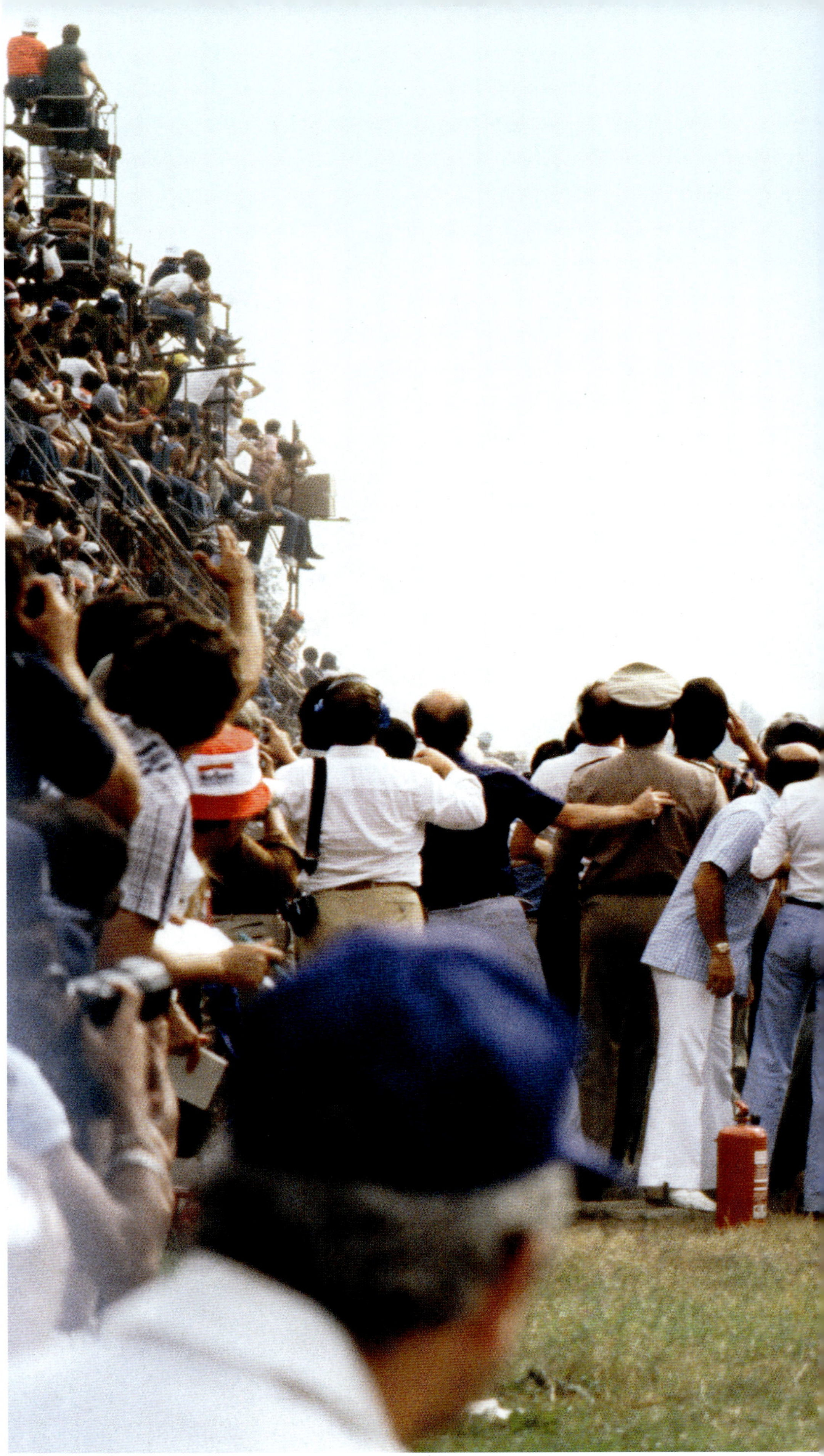

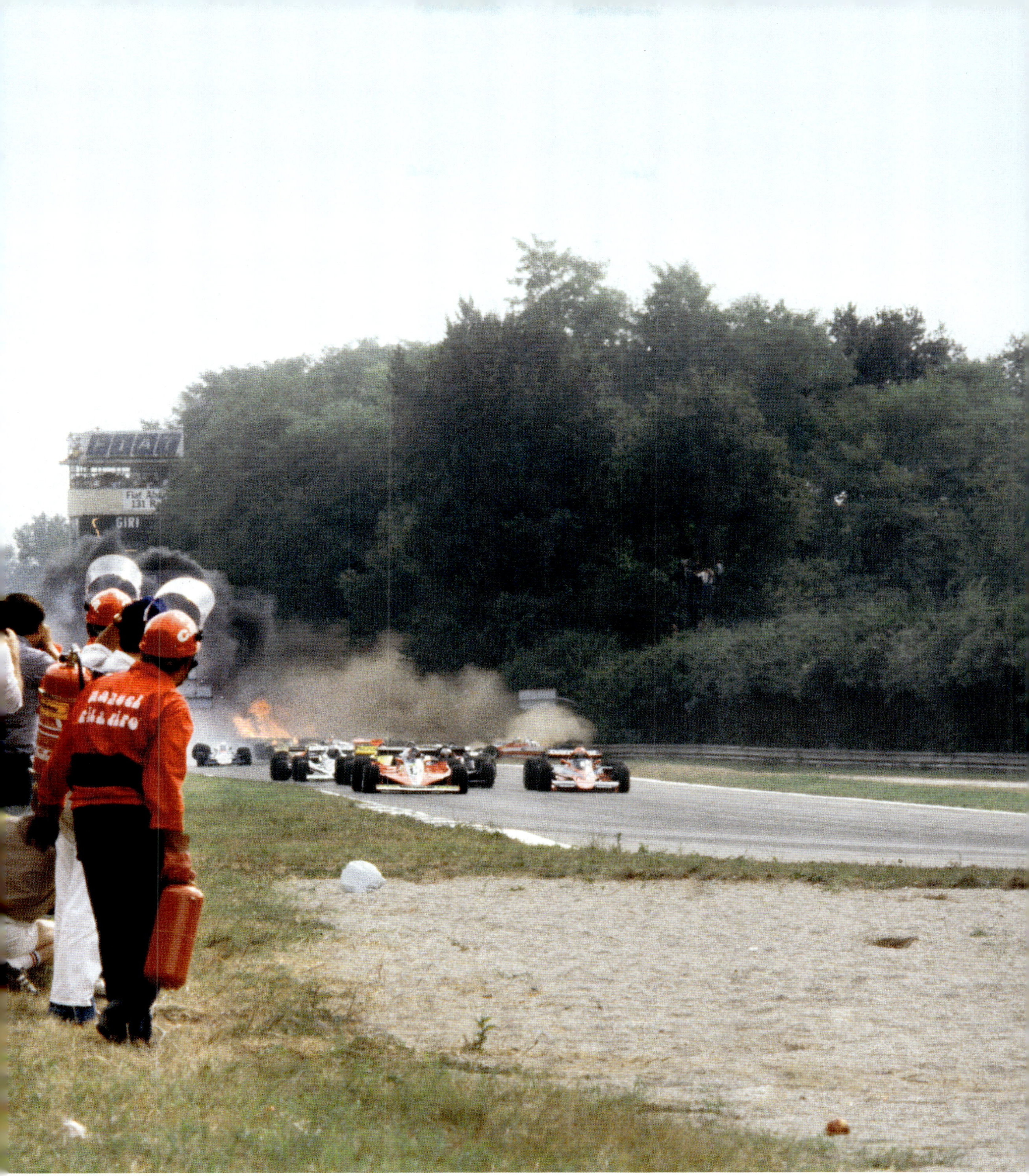
GIRI

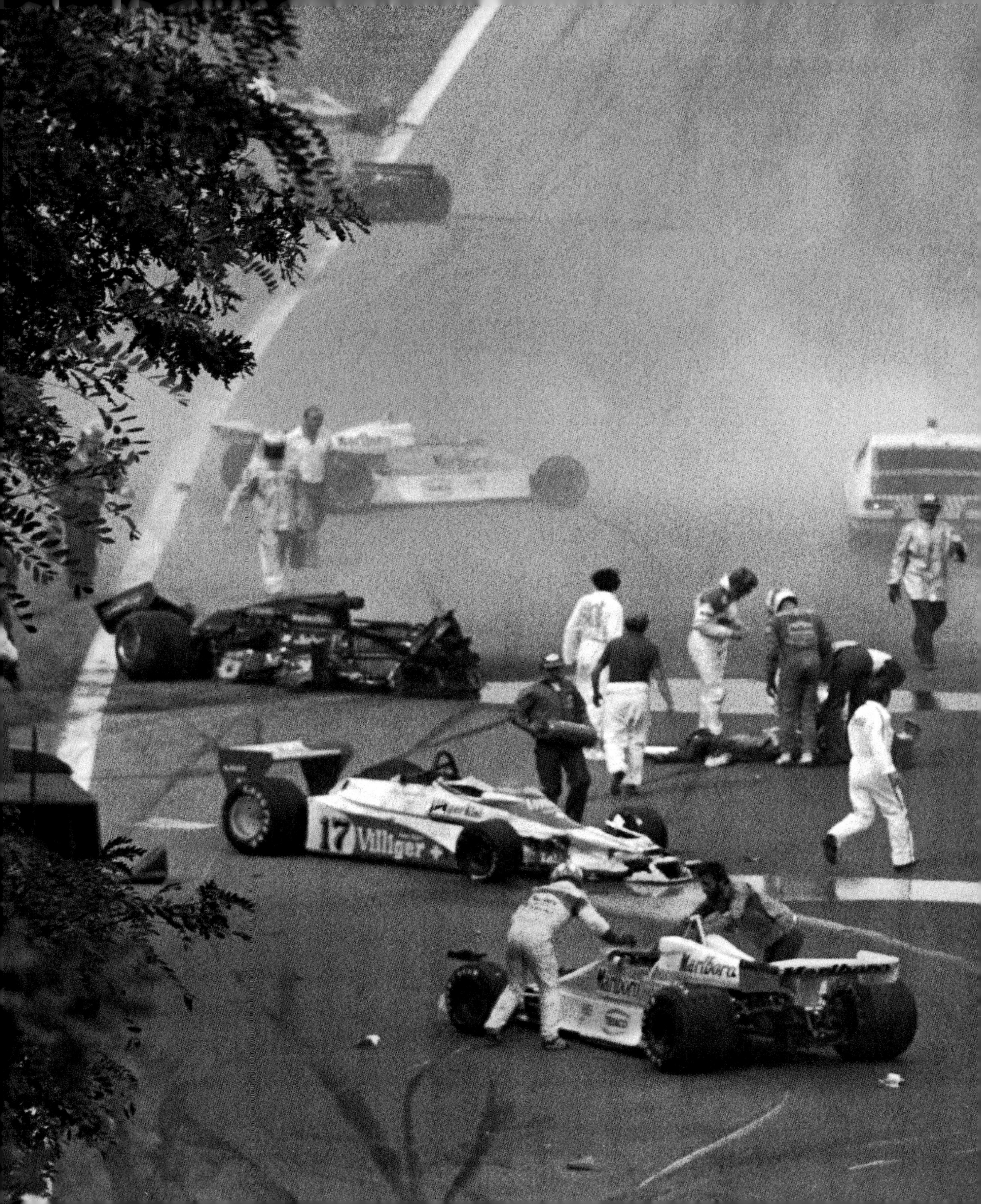
17
Villiger
Marlboro

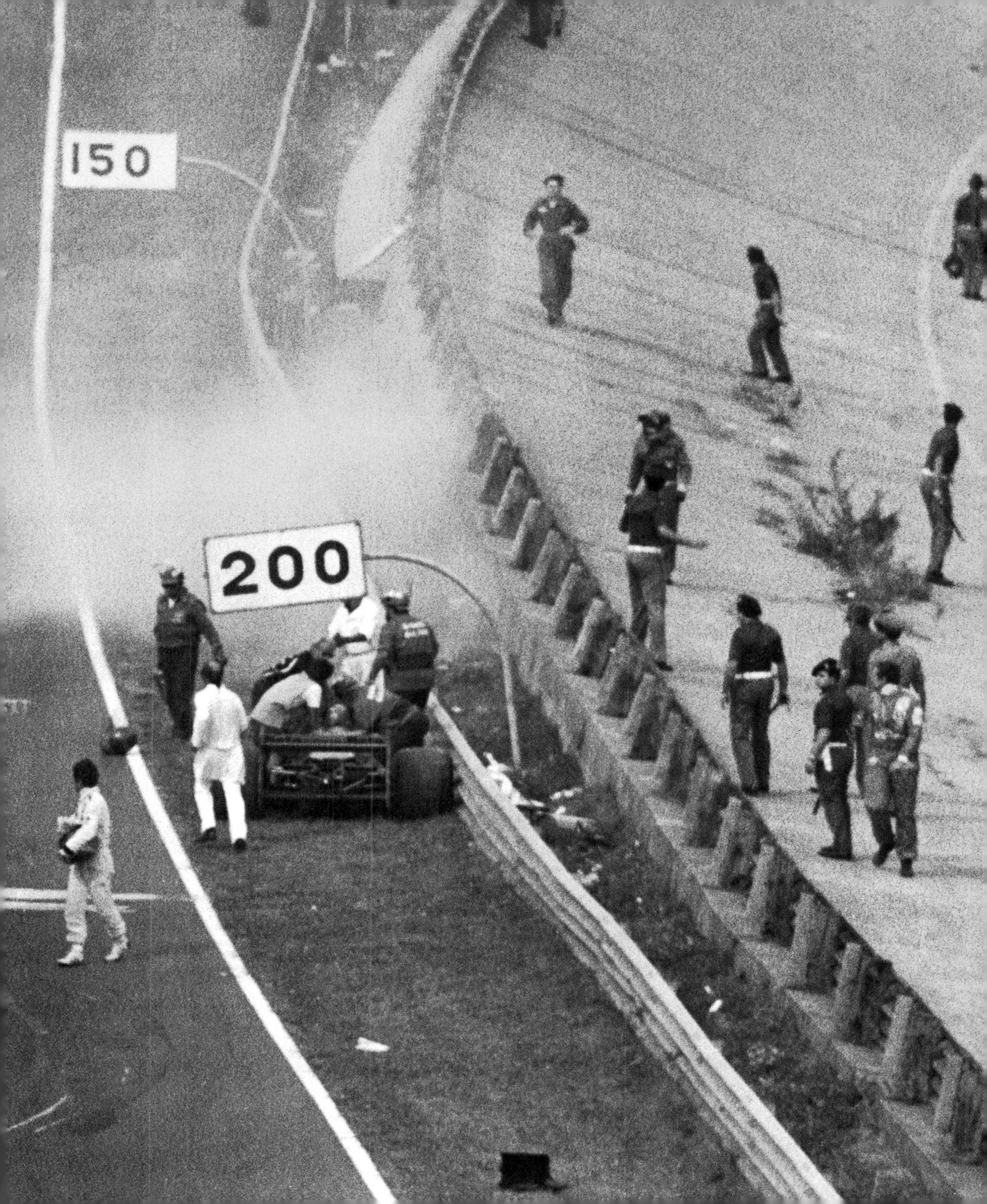
150
200

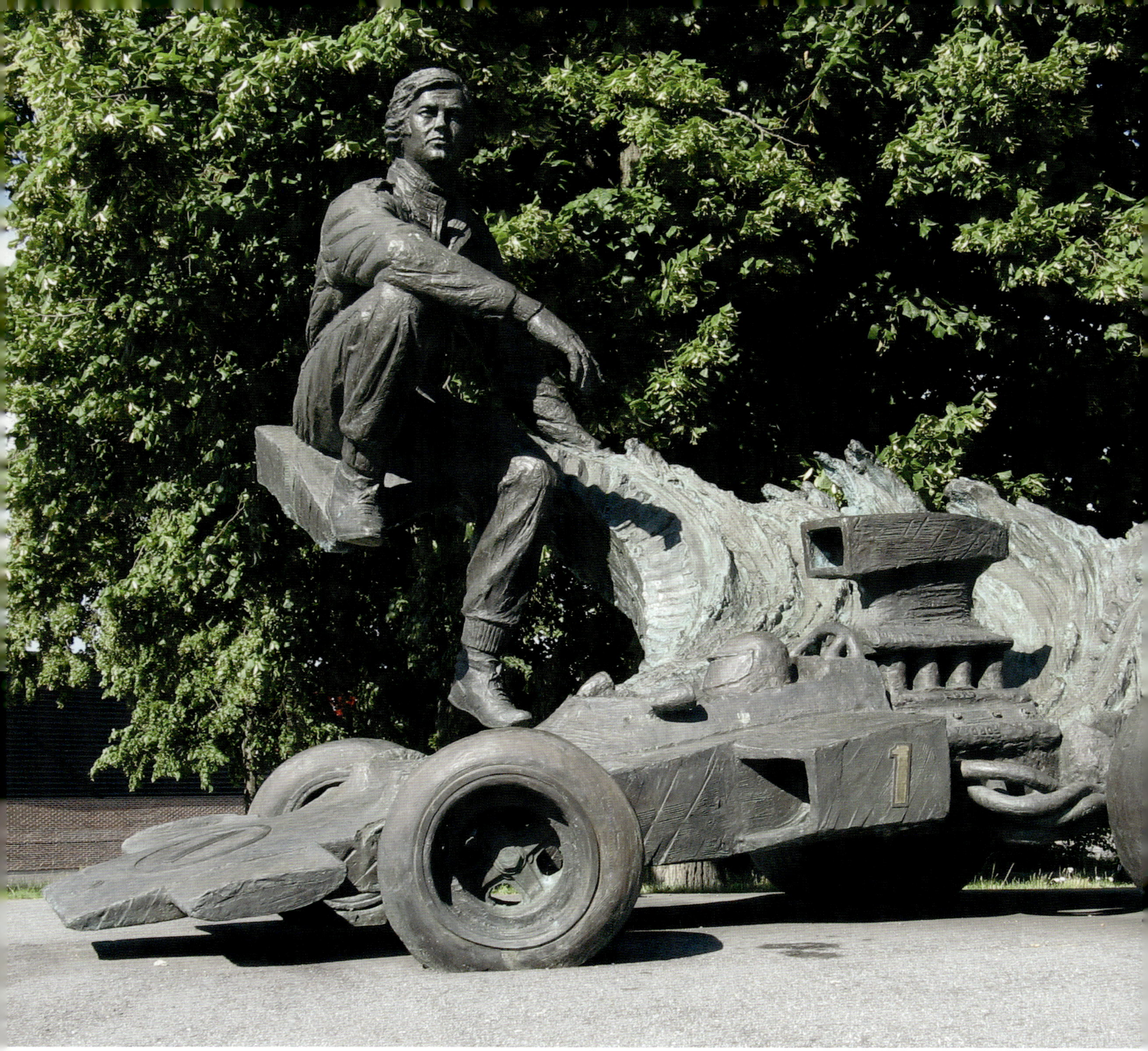

ABOVE This statue in Örebro, Ronnie's home town, was erected in his honour in 2003. It is by Richard Brixel, the same artist who was asked two years later to create a statue of Ayrton Senna in São Paulo. To mark the occasion when Ronnie's statue was unveiled, a commemorative exhibition was staged in the läns museum nearby. This led to a proposal to create a standalone museum dedicated to Ronnie's memory, which was finally opened in May 2008 – almost 30 years after his death. Ronnie's daughter, Nina, attended the opening but without her mother. Poor Barbro had never recovered from his loss and had committed suicide on 19 December 1987. Her body lies alongside Ronnie's in the Peterson family grave in Örebro.

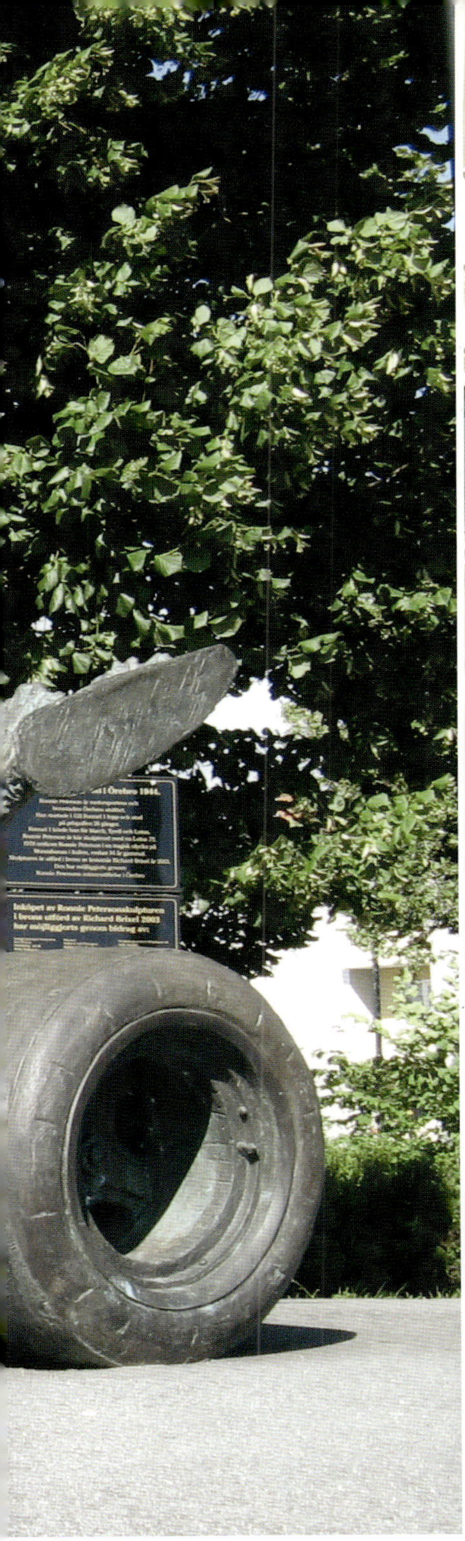

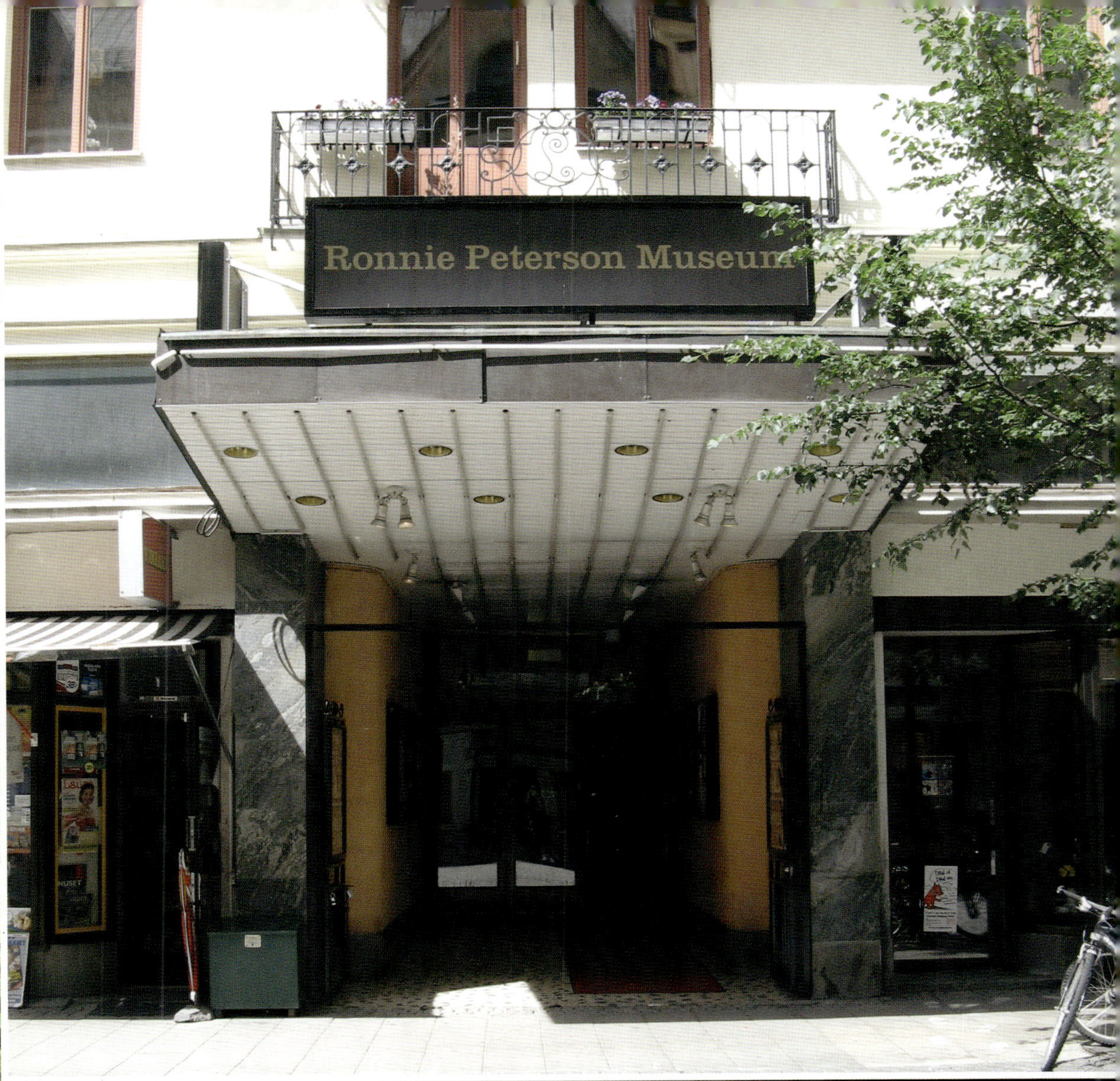
Ronnie Peterson Museum

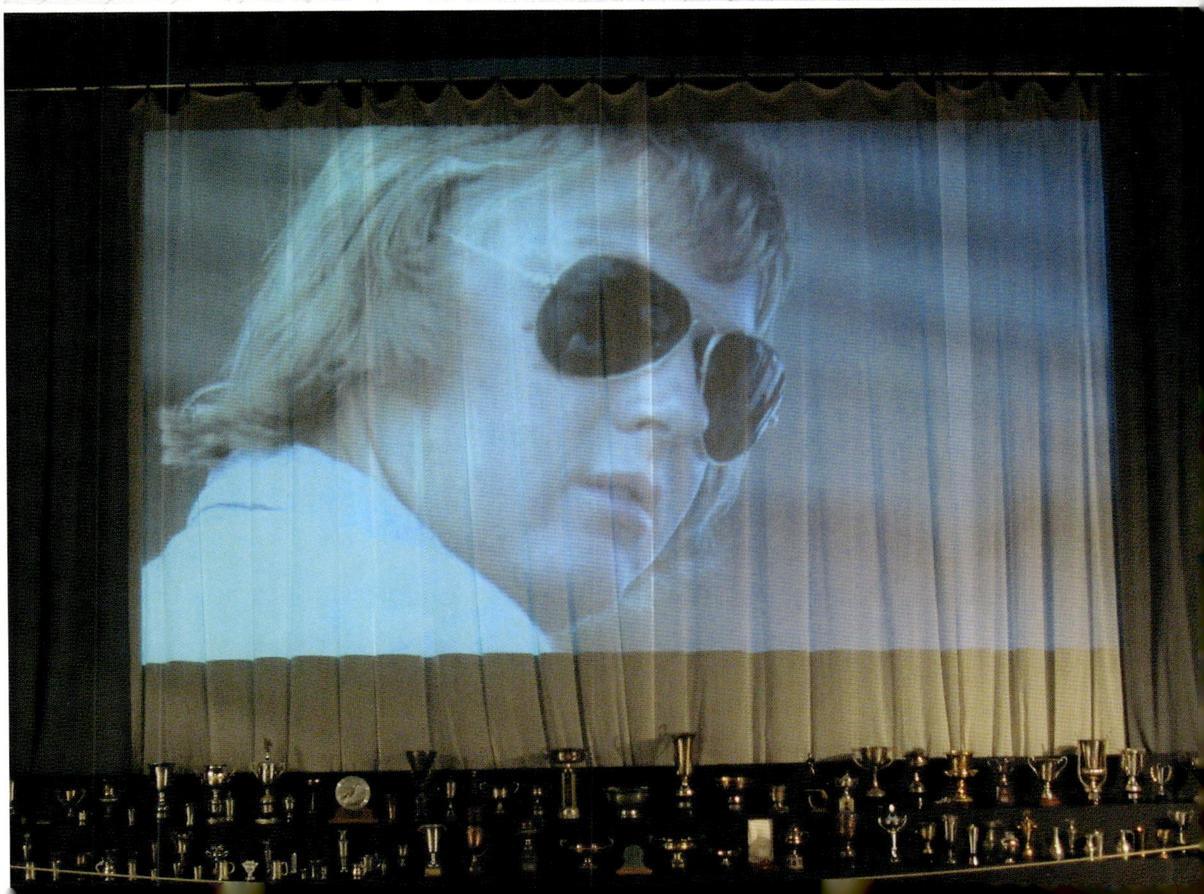

RACE RESULTS

Compiled by David Hayhoe

1966

Date	Country/event	Circuit	No	Car	Model	Engine	Configuration	Notes	Result
3-Jul	Bengtsforsloppet (non-ch F3)	Dalsland Ring, Sweden		Swebe		Ford			DNF
17-Jul	Kanonlöbet (non-ch F3)	Djursland Ring, Denmark		Swebe		Ford			7
14-Aug	Ford GP (non-ch F3)	Roskilde Ring, Denmark		Swebe		Ford			DNF
21-Aug	Kanonloppet (non-ch F3)	Karlskoga, Sweden	21	Swebe		Ford			15
16-Oct	SM-Finalen (Swed F3)	Karlskoga, Sweden	23	Brabham	BT18	Ford		accident	DNF

1967

Date	Country/event	Circuit	No	Car	Model	Engine	Configuration	Notes	Result
23-Apr	Åbningslöbet (non-ch F3)	Djursland Ring, Denmark	74	Brabham	BT18	Ford Cosworth	4	pole position	6
7-May	Skarpnäcksloppet (Swed F3)	Skarpnäck, Sweden	12	Brabham	BT18	Ford Cosworth	4		7
15-May	Dalsland Ring Cup (non-ch F3)	Dalsland Ring, Sweden	16	Brabham	BT18	Ford Cosworth	4		5
21-May	Velodromloppet F3 (Swed F3)	Karlskoga, Sweden	21	Brabham	BT18	Ford Cosworth	4		4
28-May	(non-ch F3)	Keimola Ring, Finland		Brabham	BT18	Ford Cosworth	4		2
23-Jun	Midnattsolsloppet (Swed F3)	Västerbotten, Sweden		Brabham	BT18	Ford Cosworth	4		4
2-Jul	Bengtsfors (Swed F3)	Dalsland Ring, Sweden	4	Brabham	BT18	Ford Cosworth	4		4
9-Jul	Circuito Intern. de Vila Real (non-ch F3)	Vila Real, Portugal	100	Brabham	BT18	Ford Cosworth	4	suspension	DNF
16-Jul	Grand Prix de la Ville de Nevers	Magny-Cours, France		Brabham	BT18	Ford Cosworth	4		NC
6-Aug	Västkustloppet (Swed F3)	Falkenberg, Sweden		Brabham	BT18	Ford Cosworth	4		3
20-Aug	Skarpnäcksloppet (Swed F3)	Skarpnäck, Sweden	36	Brabham	BT18	Ford Cosworth	4		DNF
27-Aug	Knutstorp Cup (non-ch F3)	Ring Knutstorp, Sweden	32	Brabham	BT18	Ford Cosworth	4	2 races (1st and 2nd)	2
3-Sep	Suomen GP (non-ch F3)	Keimola Ring, Finland	14	Brabham	BT18	Ford Cosworth	4	out of fuel	DNF
5-Sep	Hämeenlinna Ajot (non-ch F3)	Hämeenlinna, Finland	14	Brabham	BT18	Ford Cosworth	4		4
17-Sep	Sensommerlöbet (non-ch F3)	Roskilde Ring, Denmark		Brabham	BT18	Ford Cosworth	4		3
24-Sep	Stockholmsloppet (non-ch F3)	Skarpnäck, Sweden	12	Brabham	BT18	Ford Cosworth	4		3
1-Oct	European F3 Challenge (non-ch)	Hockenheim, Germany	45	Brabham	BT18	Ford Cosworth	4		13
8-Oct	Danmarksmesterskab (non-ch F3)	Jyllandsringen, Denmark	36	Brabham	BT18	Ford Cosworth	4		2
29-Oct	E.R. Hall Trophy (non-ch F3)	Brands Hatch, GB	23	Brabham	BT18	Ford Cosworth	4		DNQ
11-Nov	GP de España (non-ch F3)	Jarama, Spain		Brabham	BT18	Ford Cosworth	4		DNF

1968

Date	Country/event	Circuit	No	Car	Model	Engine	Configuration	Notes	Result
31-Mar	GP de Barcelona (non-ch F3)	Montjuïc, Spain	58	Tecno	68	Ford Cosworth	4	tyre/ accident	DNF
17-Apr	Trofeo B e F Vigorelli (non-ch F3)	Monza, Italy	41	Tecno	68	Ford Cosworth	4		4
21-Apr	Västkustloppet (non-ch F3)	Falkenberg, Sweden	24	Tecno	68	Ford Cosworth	4	fastest lap	1
28-Apr	Hyllinge M.S. (non-ch F3)	Ring Knutstorp, Sweden	2	Tecno	68	Ford Cosworth	4	pole position/ fastest lap	1
5-May	Velodromloppet (Swed F3)	Karlskoga, Sweden	2	Tecno	68	Ford Cosworth	4	2nd on grid/ice in carburettor	9
12-May	Skarpnäcksloppet (Swed F3)	Skarpnäck, Sweden	17	Tecno	68	Ford Cosworth	4	pole position/ fastest lap	1
19-May	(Swed F3)	Dalsland Ring, Sweden	1	Tecno	68	Ford Cosworth	4		1
25-May	GP de Monaco (non-ch F3)	Monte-Carlo, Monaco	86	Tecno	68	Ford Cosworth	4		3
2-Jun	Int. Hessenpreis (non-ch F3)	Hockenheim, Germany	40	Tecno	68	Ford Cosworth	4		1
7-Jun	(non-ch F3)	Hämeenlinna, Finland		Tecno	68	Ford Cosworth	4	pole position	2
9-Jun	(non-ch F3)	Keimola Ring, Finland		Tecno	68	Ford Cosworth	4	pole position/ battery	DNF
16-Jun	Anderstorps Premiärtävling (non-ch F3)	Anderstorp, Sweden	30	Tecno	68	Ford Cosworth	4	gearbox	DNF
7-Jul	GP de Vila Real (non-ch F3)	Vila Real, Portugal	40	Tecno	68	Ford Cosworth	4	2nd on grid/ crown wheel & pinion	DNF
14-Jul	Critérium de Nivernais (non-ch F3)	Magny-Cours, France		Tecno	68	Ford Cosworth	4	2nd on grid/ fastest lap	2
21-Jul	Solituderennen (non-ch F3)	Hockenheim, Germany	27	Tecno	68	Ford Cosworth	4		1
28-Jul	Petit Race (non-ch F3)	Djursland Ring, Denmark	10	Tecno	68	Ford Cosworth	4	fastest lap	1
4-Aug	Västkustloppet (Swed F3)	Falkenberg, Sweden	2	Tecno	68	Ford Cosworth	4	pole position/ fastest lap	1
11-Aug	Kanonloppet (non-ch F3)	Karlskoga, Sweden	25	Tecno	68	Ford Cosworth	4	pole position/ brakes	DNF
18-Aug	Hämeenlinna Ajot (non-ch F3)	Hämeenlinna, Finland	5	Tecno	68	Ford Cosworth	4		1
25-Aug	Knutstorp Cup (non-ch F3)	Ring Knutstorp, Sweden	16	Tecno	68	Ford Cosworth	4	camshaft	DNF
1-Sep	Stockholmsloppet (non-ch F3)	Skarpnäck, Sweden	3	Tecno	68	Ford Cosworth	4	pole position	1
8-Sep	Dalsland Ring Cup (non-ch F3)	Dalsland Ring, Sweden	2	Tecno	68	Ford Cosworth	4		3
15-Sep	(non-ch F3)	Hämeenlinna, Finland		Tecno	68	Ford Cosworth	4		1
22-Sep	Coppa dell'Autodromo (non-ch F3)	Monza, Italy	5	Tecno	68	Ford Cosworth	4	fastest lap	1
6-Oct	Coupe du Salon (non-ch F3)	Montlhéry, France	24	Tecno	68	Ford Cosworth	4		4
20-Oct	E.R. Hall Trophy (non-ch F3)	Brands Hatch, GB	74	Tecno	68	Ford Cosworth	4	gearbox	DNF

1969

Date	Country/event	Circuit	No	Car	Model	Engine	Configuration	Notes	Result
13-16/02	Swedish KAK Rally	Värmland	1	Volkswagen	1600TL	Volkswagen	F4	spin	DNF
7-Apr	Trofeo Nuvolari (Ital F3)	Monza, Italy	1	Tecno	69	Ford Cosworth	4		1
13-Apr	Coppa Ranieri Maria Pesci (Ital F3)	Vallelunga, Italy	14	Tecno	69	Ford Cosworth	4	pole position (heat 1)	1
20-Apr	Västkustloppet (non-ch F3)	Falkenberg, Sweden	7	Tecno	69	Ford Cosworth	4	pole position/ fastest lap	1
27-Apr	Hyllingeloppet (non-ch F3)	Ring Knutstorp, Sweden	20	Tecno	69	Ford Cosworth	4	pole position/ fastest lap	1
4-May	Velodromloppet (Swed F3)	Karlskoga, Sweden	2	Tecno	69	Ford Cosworth	4	pole position/ fastest lap	1
11-May	GP di Madunina (Ital F3)	Vallelunga, Italy		Tecno	69	Ford Cosworth	4	joint fastest lap	1
17-May	GP de Monaco (non-ch F3)	Monte-Carlo, Monaco	83	Tecno	69	Ford Cosworth	4	pole position (heat 1)	1
25-May	GP des Frontières (non-ch F3)	Chimay, Belgium	12	Tecno	69	Ford Cosworth	4		NC
26-May	Greater London Trophy (non-ch F3)	Crystal Palace, GB	67	Tecno	69	Ford Cosworth	4	pole position (heat 3)	2
8-Jun	Swederace (Swed F3)	Anderstorp, Sweden	1	Tecno	69	Ford Cosworth	4	pole position/ fastest lap	1
14-15/06	Le Mans 24-hours (Makes WC)	Le Mans, France	1	Chevrolet	Corvette	Chevrolet	V8	gearbox	DNF
22-Jun	GP della Lotteria (non-ch F2)	Monza, Italy	4	Tecno	68	Ford Cosworth	4	first F2 race	7
28-Jun	PR for Men Trophy (non-ch F3)	Anderstorp, Sweden	1	Tecno	69	Ford Cosworth	4	pole position/ joint fastest lap	1
14-Jul	Critérium de Magny-Cours (French F3)	Magny-Cours, France	46	Tecno	69	Ford Cosworth	4	pole position (heat 1)	2
14-Jul	Trois Jours de M-C (non-ch Sports)	Magny-Cours, France		Lola	T70 Mk3B	Chevrolet	V8		1
19-Jul	Plessey Trophy (non-ch F3)	Silverstone, GB	26	Tecno	69	Ford Cosworth	4		3
27-Jul	(non-ch Sports)	Österreichring, Austria		Lola	T70 Mk3B	Chevrolet	V8	accident	DNF
3-Aug	Västkustloppet (Swed F3)	Falkenberg, Sweden		Tecno	69	Ford Cosworth	4	pole position (heat 1)/ fastest lap	1
10-Aug	Premiärtävlingen (non-ch F3)	Kinnekulle, Sweden	2	Tecno	69	Ford Cosworth	4	fastest lap	1
17-Aug	Kanonloppet (Euro F3)	Karlskoga, Sweden	14	Tecno	69	Ford Cosworth	4	pole position (heat 1)	1
17-Aug	Swerige GP (non-ch Sports)	Karlskoga, Sweden	14	Lola	T70 Mk3B	Chevrolet	V8		3
24-Aug	Stockholmsloppet (non-ch F3)	Skarpnäck, Sweden	2	Tecno	69	Ford Cosworth	4	pole position/ fastest lap	1
31-Aug	Knutstorp Cup (non-ch F3)	Ring Knutstorp, Sweden	2	Tecno	69	Ford Cosworth	4		4
1-Sep	Guards Intern. Trophy (non-ch F3)	Brands Hatch, GB	24	Lotus	59	Ford Cosworth	4		13
7-Sep	SM-Finalen (Swed F3)	Dalsland Ring, Sweden	23	Tecno	69	Ford Cosworth	4	pole position	1
14-Sep	GP d'Albi (French F2)	Albi, France	40	Lotus	59B	Ford Cosworth	4		5
21-Sep	Coppa dell'Autodromo (Ital F3)	Monza, Italy	69	Tecno	69	Ford Cosworth	4		1
28-Sep	Lincolnshire Trophy (non-ch F3)	Cadwell Park, GB	2	March	693	Ford Cosworth	4		3
5-Oct	Coupe du Salon (French F3)	Montlhéry, France	17	March	693	Ford Cosworth	4	pole position/ accident/ injured	DNF

1970

Date	Country/event	Circuit	No	Car	Model	Engine	Configuration	Notes	Result
11-Jan	Temporada 1000km (non-ch Sports)	Buenos Aires, Argentina	20	Lola	T70B	Chevrolet	V8		7
11-15/02	Swedish KAK Rally	Värmland		Porsche	911L	Porsche	F6	with Sven-Olaf Svedberg/gearbox	DNF
12-Apr	Jim Clark Gedächtnisrennen (Euro F2)	Hockenheim, Germany	8	March	702	Ford Cosworth	4	first Euro F2 race, accident	DNF
26-Apr	GP de Barcelona (Euro F2)	Montjuïc, Spain	23	March	702	Ford Cosworth	4	clutch	DNF
3-May	Eifelrennen (non-ch F2)	Nürburgring, Germany	14	March	702	Ford Cosworth	4	accident in practice	DNS
10-May	MONACO GP	Monte-Carlo	23	March	701	Ford Cosworth	V8	first F1 WC Grand Prix	7
24-May	GP van Limbourg (non-ch F2)	Zolder, Belgium	29	March	702	Ford Cosworth	4	overheating	DNF
25-May	London Trophy (non-ch F2)	Crystal Palace, GB	36	March	702	Ford Cosworth	4	accident	DNF
7-Jun	BELGIAN GP	Spa-Francorchamps	14	March	701	Ford Cosworth	V8		NC
13-14/06	Le Mans 24-hours (Makes WC)	Le Mans, France	7	Ferrari	512S	Ferrari	V12	with Derek Bell/ valves	DNF
21-Jun	DUTCH GP	Zandvoort	22	March	701	Ford Cosworth	V8		9
28-Jun	GP de Rouen (Euro F2)	Rouen-les-Essarts, France	26	March	702	Ford Cosworth	4	NOT pole position	6
5-Jul	FRENCH GP	Clermont-Ferrand	18	March	701	Ford Cosworth	V8	crown wheel & pinion	DNF
18-Jul	BRITISH GP	Brands Hatch	27	March	701	Ford Cosworth	V8		9
26-Jul	(French F2)	Paul Ricard, France	15	March	702	Ford Cosworth	4		6
2-Aug	GERMAN GP	Hockenheim	22	March	701	Ford Cosworth	V8	engine	DNF
9-Aug	GP Sverige (non-ch Sports)	Karlskoga, Sweden	17	Porsche	908/2	Porsche	F8	drive shaft	DNF
23-Aug	Nordic Cup (Interserie)	Keimola Ring, Finland	14	Lola	T70 Mk3B	Chevrolet	V8		3
30-Aug	Mantorp Park Trophy (non-ch F2)	Mantorp Park, Sweden	6	March	702	Ford Cosworth	4	accident/ fuel pipe	DNF
6-Sep	ITALIAN GP	Monza	52	March	701	Ford Cosworth	V8	camshaft	DNF
13-Sep	Flugplatzrennen (Euro F2)	Tülln-Langenlebarn, Austria	16	March	702	Ford Cosworth	4		5
20-Sep	CANADIAN GP	Mont-Tremblant	26	March	701	Ford Cosworth	V8		NC
27-Sep	GP di Imola (Euro F2)	Imola, Italy	44	March	702	Ford Cosworth	4		4
4-Oct	USA GP	Watkins Glen	29	March	701	Ford Cosworth	V8		NC
11-Oct	Preis von Baden-W (Euro F2)	Hockenheim, Germany	16	March	702	Ford Cosworth	4	pole position	3
11-Oct	300 miles (Interserie)	Hockenheim, Germany		Lola	T210	Ford Cosworth	4		41

1971

Date	Country/event	Circuit	No	Car	Model	Engine	Configuration	Notes	Result
10-Jan	1000km (Makes WC)	Buenos Aires, Argentina	10	Lola	T212	Ford Cosworth	4	with Jorge Cupeiro/ accident	12/DNF
6-Mar	SOUTH AFRICAN GP	Kyalami	7	March	711	Ford Cosworth	V8		10
14-Mar	Speed Int. Trophy (non-ch F2)	Mallory Park, GB	30	March	712M	Ford Cosworth	4	pole/ joint fastest lap/ steering/ accident	DNF
21-Mar	Race of Champions (non-ch F1)	Brands Hatch, GB	12	March	711	Ford Cosworth	V8	brake shaft	DNF
28-Mar	Questor GP (non-ch F1)	Ontario, USA	21	March	711	Ford Cosworth	V8	2 races/ 16th in each	18
4-Apr	Jim Clark Gedächtnisrennen (Euro F2)	Hockenheim, Germany	30	March	712M	Ford Cosworth	4	pole/ 2 races/ engine in race 2/ fastest lap	2/DNF
12-Apr	J Rindt Memorial Trophy (Euro F2)	Thruxton, GB	36	March	712M	Ford Cosworth	4	pole position/ fastest lap	2
18-Apr	SPANISH GP	Montjuïc	18	March	711	Ford Cosworth	V8	ignition	DNF
25-Apr	GP de Pau (French F2)	Pau, France	20	March	712M	Ford Cosworth	4	2nd on grid/ rear wheel/ suspension	DNF
2-May	Eifelrennen (Euro F2)	Nürburgring, Germany	33	March	712M	Ford Cosworth	4	fastest lap/ accident	DNF
8-May	International Trophy (non-ch F1)	Silverstone, GB	11	March	711	Alfa Romeo	V8	2 heats/ accident	DNF
16-May	GP de Madrid (Euro F2)	Jarama, Spain	5	March	712M	Ford Cosworth	4	pole position/ engine	DNF
23-May	MONACO GP	Monte-Carlo	17	March	711	Ford Cosworth	V8		2/DNF
31-May	Hilton Transp Trophy (Euro F2)	Crystal Palace, GB	31	March	712M	Ford Cosworth	4	pole position/ joint fastest lap	3
5-Jun	Martini Trophy (RAC Sports Car)	Silverstone, GB	1	Lola	T212	Ford Cosworth	V8	2 races/ 4th and 1st	2
13-Jun	Jochen Rindt Memorial (non-ch F1)	Hockenheim, Germany	10	March	711	Ford Cosworth	V8		2
20-Jun	DUTCH GP	Zandvoort	16	March	711	Ford Cosworth	V8		4
27-Jun	GP de Rouen (Euro/French F2)	Rouen-les-Essarts, France	4	March	712M	Ford Cosworth	4	pole position	1
4-Jul	FRENCH GP	Paul Ricard	17	March	711	Alfa Romeo	V8	engine	DNF
17-Jul	BRITISH GP	Silverstone	18	March	711	Ford Cosworth	V8		2/DNF
24-Jul	6-hours (Makes WC)	Watkins Glen, USA	30	Alfa Romeo	T33/3	Alfa Romeo	V8	with Andrea de Adamich	1
1-Aug	GERMAN GP	Nürburgring	15	March	711	Ford Cosworth	V8		5
8-Aug	Mantorp Park Trophy (Euro F2)	Mantorp Park, Sweden	1	March	712M	Ford Cosworth	4	pole position/ fastest lap	1
15-Aug	AUSTRIAN GP	Österreichring	17	March	711	Ford Cosworth	V8		8
22-Aug	Swedish Gold Cup (non-ch F2)	Kinnekulle, Sweden	1	March	712M	Ford Cosworth	4	pole position/ fastest lap	1
30-Aug	Rothmans Int. Trophy (non-ch F2)	Brands Hatch, GB	16	March	712M	Ford Cosworth	4	pole position	1
5-Sep	ITALIAN GP	Monza	25	March	711	Ford Cosworth	V8		2
12-Sep	Flugplatzrennen (Euro F2)	Tülln-Langenlebarn, Austria	8	March	712M	Ford Cosworth	4	pole position	1
19-Sep	CANADIAN GP	Mosport Park	17	March	711	Ford Cosworth	V8		2
26-Sep	GP d'Albi (French F2)	Albi, France	10	March	712M	Ford Cosworth	4	2nd on grid	6
3-Oct	USA GP	Watkins Glen	25	March	711	Ford Cosworth	V8		3
10-Oct	GP di Roma (Euro F2)	Vallelunga, Italy	1	March	712M	Ford Cosworth	4	clinched European F2 title	1
11-Oct	1000km Barcelona (non-ch Sports)	Montjuic, Spain	16	Lola	T212	Ford Cosworth	V8	with Jo Bonnier	1
24-Oct	WC Victory Race (non-ch F1)	Brands Hatch, GB	4	March	711	Ford Cosworth	V8		16
31-Oct	(Brazil F2)	Interlagos, Brazil	8	March	712M	Ford Cosworth	4	joint fastest lap	2
7-Nov	(Brazil F2)	Interlagos, Brazil	8	March	712M	Ford Cosworth	4	fastest lap	10
14-Nov	(Brazil F2)	Porto Alegre, Brazil	8	March	712M	Ford Cosworth	4	ignition	DNF
21-Nov	(Brazil F2)	Cordoba, Brazil	8	March	712M	Ford Cosworth	4	pole position/ fuel pressure	DNF

1972

Date	Country/event	Circuit	No	Car	Model	Engine	Configuration	Notes	Result
9-Jan	Buenos Aires 1000km (Makes WC)	Buenos Aires, Argentina	30	Ferrari	312PB	Ferrari	F12	with Tim Schenken/ pole position	1
23-Jan	ARGENTINEAN GP	Buenos Aires No.9	14	March	721	Ford Cosworth	V8		6
6-Feb	Daytona 6-hours (Makes WC)	Daytona, USA	6	Ferrari	312PB	Ferrari	F12	with Tim Schenken	2
4-Mar	SOUTH AFRICAN GP	Kyalami	3	March	721	Ford Cosworth	V8		5
12-Mar	(Euro/Brit F2)	Mallory Park, GB	1	March	722	Ford Cosworth	4	pole position/ fastest lap/ accident	DNF
19-Mar	Race of Champions (non-ch F1)	Brands Hatch, GB	61	March	721X	Ford Cosworth	V8		12
25-Mar	Sebring 12-hours (Makes WC)	Sebring, USA	3	Ferrari	312PB	Ferrari	F12	with Tim Schenken/ fastest lap	2
30-Mar	Brazilian GP (non-ch F1)	Interlagos	10	March	721	Ford Cosworth	V8		2
3-Apr	J Rindt Memorial Trophy (Euro/Brit F2)	Thruxton, GB	22	March	722	Ford Cosworth	4	pole position/ fastest lap	1
16-Apr	BOAC 1000km (Makes WC)	Brands Hatch, GB	10	Ferrari	312PB	Ferrari	F12	with Tim Schenken/ joint fastest lap	2
25-Apr	Monza 1000km (Makes WC)	Monza, Italy	2	Ferrari	312PB	Ferrari	F12	with Tim Schenken/ fastest lap	3
1-May	SPANISH GP	Jarama	2	March	721X	Ford Cosworth	V8	accident/ fuel leak/ suspension	DNF
7-May	Spa 1000km (Makes WC)	Spa-Francorchamps, B	2	Ferrari	312PB	Ferrari	F12	with Tim Schenken	DNF
14-May	MONACO GP	Monte-Carlo	3	March	721X	Ford Cosworth	V8		11
28-May	Nürburgring 1000km (Makes WC)	Nürburgring, Germany	3	Ferrari	312PB	Ferrari	F12	with Tim Schenken/ pole position	1
29-May	International Gold Cup (non-ch F1)	Oulton Park, GB	48	March	721X	Ford Cosworth	V8	fastest lap/ accident	DNF
4-Jun	BELGIAN GP	Nivelles-Baulers	11	March	721X	Ford Cosworth	V8		9
11-Jun	Rhein-Pokalrennen (Euro F2)	Hockenheim, Germany	1	March	722	Ford Cosworth	4	2 heats (5th and 3rd)	3
25-Jun	Österreichring 1000km (Makes WC)	Österreichring, Austria	2	Ferrari	312PB	Ferrari	F12	with Tim Schenken	3
2-Jul	FRENCH GP	Clermont-Ferrand	12	March	721G	Ford Cosworth	V8		5
15-Jul	BRITISH GP	Brands Hatch	3	March	721G	Ford Cosworth	V8	engine/ accident	7/DNF
22-Jul	Watkins Glen 6-hours (Makes WC)	Watkins Glen, USA	86	Ferrari	312PB	Ferrari	F12	with Tim Schenken/ pole position	2
30-Jul	GERMAN GP	Nürburgring	10	March	721G	Ford Cosworth	V8		3
6-Aug	Mantorp GP (Euro F2)	Mantorp Park, Sweden	2	March	722	Ford Cosworth	4	head gasket/ flywheel	DNF
6-Aug	Touring cars	Mantorp Park, Sweden	31	Ford	Capri RS2600	Ford	V6		1
13-Aug	AUSTRIAN GP	Österreichring	5	March	721G	Ford Cosworth	V8		12
3-Sep	Festspielpreis/Festival Prize (Euro F2)	Salzburgring, Austria	2	March	722	Ford Cosworth	4	accident	DNF
10-Sep	ITALIAN GP	Monza	19	March	721G	Ford Cosworth	V8		9
16-Sep	(Brit F2)	Oulton Park, GB	4	March	722	Ford Cosworth	4	pole position/ joint fastest lap	1
24-Sep	CANADIAN GP	Mosport Park	25	March	721G	Ford Cosworth	V8	push start after accident	DSQ
1-Oct	Preis von Baden-W (Euro F2)	Hockenheim, Germany	8	March	722	Ford Cosworth	4		3
8-Oct	USA GP	Watkins Glen	4	March	721G	Ford Cosworth	V8		4
22-Oct	WC Victory Race (non-ch F1)	Brands Hatch, GB	12	March	721G	Ford Cosworth	V8	2nd on grid	8
29-Oct	(Brazil F2)	Interlagos, Brazil	14	Brabham	BT38	Ford Cosworth	4	accident	DNF
5-Nov	(Brazil F2)	Interlagos, Brazil	14	Brabham	BT38	Ford Cosworth	4	engine	DNF
12-Nov	(Brazil F2)	Interlagos, Brazil	14	Brabham	BT38	Ford Cosworth	4	engine	DNF

1973

Date	Country/event	Circuit	No	Car	Model	Engine	Configuration	Notes	Result
28-Jan	ARGENTINEAN GP	Buenos Aires No.9	4	JPS Lotus	72D	Ford Cosworth	V8	oil pressure	DNF
11-Feb	BRAZILIAN GP	Interlagos	2	JPS Lotus	72D	Ford Cosworth	V8	first F1 WC pole position/ rear wheel	DNF
15-18/02	Swedish KAK Rally	Värmland		Ford	Escort	Ford	4	with Torsten Palm/ accident	DNF
3-Mar	SOUTH AFRICAN GP	Kyalami	2	JPS Lotus	72D	Ford Cosworth	V8		11
18-Mar	Race of Champions (non-ch F1)	Brands Hatch, GB	65	JPS Lotus	72E	Ford Cosworth	V8	joint fastest lap/ gearbox	DNF
8-Apr	International Trophy (non-ch F1)	Silverstone, GB	2	JPS Lotus	72E	Ford Cosworth	V8	2nd on grid/ fastest lap	2
29-Apr	SPANISH GP	Montjuic	2	JPS Lotus	72E	Ford Cosworth	V8	fastest lap/ gearbox	DNF
20-May	BELGIAN GP	Zolder	2	JPS Lotus	72E	Ford Cosworth	V8	pole position/ accident	DNF
3-Jun	MONACO GP	Monte-Carlo	2	JPS Lotus	72E	Ford Cosworth	V8	2nd on grid	3
10-Jun	I G.B. GP (Euro F2)	Nivelles-Baulers, Belgium	2	Lotus	74	Lotus	4	oil pressure	DNF
17-Jun	SWEDISH GP	Anderstorp	2	JPS Lotus	72E	Ford Cosworth	V8	pole position	2
24-Jun	GP de Rouen (Euro F2)	Rouen-les-Essarts, France	2	Lotus	74	Lotus	4	fastest lap/ accident	DNF
1-Jul	FRENCH GP	Paul Ricard	2	JPS Lotus	72E	Ford Cosworth	V8	first WC F1 victory	1
14-Jul	BRITISH GP	Silverstone	2	JPS Lotus	72E	Ford Cosworth	V8	pole position	2
22-Jul	Coppa di Santamonica (non-ch F2)	Misano, Italy	2	Lotus	74	Lotus	4	engine	DNF
29-Jul	DUTCH GP	Zandvoort	2	JPS Lotus	72E	Ford Cosworth	V8	pole position/fastest lap/gearbox/engine	11DNF
5-Aug	GERMAN GP	Nürburgring	2	JPS Lotus	72E	Ford Cosworth	V8	2nd on grid/ distributor	DNF
12-Aug	Kanonloppet (Euro F2)	Karlskoga, Sweden	2	Lotus	74	Lotus	4		5
19-Aug	AUSTRIAN GP	Österreichring	2	JPS Lotus	72E	Ford Cosworth	V8	2nd on grid	1
26-Aug	GP del Mediterraneo (Euro F2)	Enna-Pergusa, Italy	19	Lotus	74	Lotus	4	2 races (8th and 7th)	7
2-Sep		Ring Knutstorp, Sweden		Ford	Escort	Ford	4	2 races	4 & DNF
9-Sep	ITALIAN GP	Monza	2	JPS Lotus	72E	Ford Cosworth	V8	pole position	1
16-Sep	GP d'Albi (Euro F2)	Albi, France	2	Lotus	74	Lotus	4	too many starters	DSQ
23-Sep	CANADIAN GP	Mosport Park	2	JPS Lotus	72E	Ford Cosworth	V8	pole position/ rear tyre/ accident	DNF
7-Oct	USA GP	Watkins Glen	2	JPS Lotus	72E	Ford Cosworth	V8	pole position	1
14-Oct	GP di Roma (Euro F2)	Vallelunga, Italy	2	Lotus	74	Lotus	4	engine	DNF

1974

Date	Country/event	Circuit	No	Car	Model	Engine	Configuration	Notes	Result
13-Jan	ARGENTINEAN GP	Buenos Aires No.15	1	JPS Lotus	72E	Ford Cosworth	V8	pole position	13
27-Jan	BRAZILIAN GP	Interlagos	1	JPS Lotus	72E	Ford Cosworth	V8		6
30-Mar	SOUTH AFRICAN GP	Kyalami	1	JPS Lotus	76	Ford Cosworth	V8	throttle/ accident	DNF
7-Apr	International Trophy (non-ch F1)	Silverstone, GB	1	JPS Lotus	76	Ford Cosworth	V8	2nd on grid/ engine/ tyres	DNF
28-Apr	SPANISH GP	Jarama	1	JPS Lotus	76	Ford Cosworth	V8	2nd on grid/ engine overheating	DNF
12-May	BELGIAN GP	Nivelles-Baulers	1	JPS Lotus	76	Ford Cosworth	V8	fuel tank leak	DNF
26-May	MONACO GP	Monte-Carlo	1	JPS Lotus	72E	Ford Cosworth	V8	fastest lap	1
9-Jun	SWEDISH GP	Anderstorp	1	JPS Lotus	72E	Ford Cosworth	V8	driveshaft	DNF
23-Jun	DUTCH GP	Zandvoort	1	JPS Lotus	72E	Ford Cosworth	V8	fastest lap	8
7-Jul	FRENCH GP	Dijon-Prenois	1	JPS Lotus	72E	Ford Cosworth	V8	2nd on grid	1
14-Jul	Nürburgring 6-hours (ETCC)	Nürburgring, Germany	1	BMW	3.0 CSL	BMW	6	with Hans-Joachim Stuck/ gearbox	DNF
20-Jul	BRITISH GP	Brands Hatch	1	JPS Lotus	72E	Ford Cosworth	V8	2nd on grid	10
4-Aug	GERMAN GP	Nürburgring	1	JPS Lotus	76	Ford Cosworth	V8		4
11-Aug	Kanonloppet (Euro F2)	Karlskoga, Sweden	2	March	742	BMW	4		1
18-Aug	AUSTRIAN GP	Österreichring	1	JPS Lotus	72E	Ford Cosworth	V8	universal joint	DNF
1-Sep		Ring Knutstorp, Sweden	1	BMW	3.0 CSL	BMW	6	2 races (heat 2 brakes/accident)	1 & DNF
8-Sep	ITALIAN GP	Monza	1	JPS Lotus	72E	Ford Cosworth	V8		1
14-Sep	IROC	Michigan, USA		Chevrolet	Camaro	Chevrolet	V8	pole position	7
22-Sep	CANADIAN GP	Mosport Park	1	JPS Lotus	72E	Ford Cosworth	V8		3
6-Oct	USA GP	Watkins Glen	1	JPS Lotus	72E	Ford Cosworth	V8	fuel line/ engine	DNF
26-27/10	IROC	Riverside, USA		Chevrolet	Camaro	Chevrolet	V8	2 races	7 & 8
9-Nov	Kyalami 6-hours (Makes WC)	Kyalami, South Africa	23	BMW	3.0 CSL	BMW	6	with Jody Scheckter/ accident	DNF

1975

Date	Country/event	Circuit	No	Car	Model	Engine	Configuration	Notes	Result
12-Jan	ARGENTINEAN GP	Buenos Aires No.15	5	JPS Lotus	72E	Ford Cosworth	V8	brakes/ gearbox	DNF
26-Jan	BRAZILIAN GP	Interlagos	5	JPS Lotus	72E	Ford Cosworth	V8		15
1/2/02	Daytona 24-hours (Makes WC/IMSA)	Daytona, USA	25	BMW	3.0 CSL	BMW	6	with Hans Stuck/ 2nd on grid/ conrod	DNF
14-Feb	IROC final	Daytona, USA	2	Chevrolet	Camaro	Chevrolet	V8	accident	DNF
1-Mar	SOUTH AFRICAN GP	Kyalami	5	JPS Lotus	72E	Ford Cosworth	V8		10
9-Mar	Gelleråsen Rallycross	Karlskoga, Sweden		Volkswagen	Beetle 2.2L	Porsche	F6	accident	DNF
16-Mar	Race of Champions (non-ch F1)	Brands Hatch, GB	5	Lotus	72E	Ford Cosworth	V8		3
31-Mar	J Rindt Memorial Trophy (Euro F2)	Thruxton, GB	1	March	752	BMW	4	accident	DNF
13-Apr	International Trophy (non-ch F1)	Silverstone, GB	5	JPS Lotus	72E	Ford Cosworth	V8	engine in free practice	ns
27-Apr	SPANISH GP	Montjuic	5	JPS Lotus	72E	Ford Cosworth	V8	accident	DNF
11-May	MONACO GP	Monte-Carlo	5	JPS Lotus	72E	Ford Cosworth	V8		4
25-May	BELGIAN GP	Zolder	5	JPS Lotus	72E	Ford Cosworth	V8	brakes/ accident	DNF
1-Jun	Gelleråsen Rallycross	Karlskoga, Sweden		Volkswagen	Beetle 2.2L	Porsche	F6		6
8-Jun	SWEDISH GP	Anderstorp	5	JPS Lotus	72E	Ford Cosworth	V8		9
22-Jun	DUTCH GP	Zandvoort	5	JPS Lotus	72E	Ford Cosworth	V8	out of fuel	15/DNF
29-Jun	(DRM)	Norisring, Germany	30	BMW	3.0 CSL	BMW	6	brakes	DNF
6-Jul	FRENCH GP	Paul Ricard	5	JPS Lotus	72E	Ford Cosworth	V8		10
12-Jul	Watkins Glen 6-hours (Makes WC)	Watkins Glen, USA	25	BMW	3.0 CSL	BMW	6	with Hans-Joachim Stuck/ fuel tank split	DNF
19-Jul	BRITISH GP	Silverstone	5	JPS Lotus	72E	Ford Cosworth	V8	engine	DNF
3-Aug	GERMAN GP	Nürburgring	5	JPS Lotus	72E	Ford Cosworth	V8	clutch	DNF
10-Aug	Gelleråsen (Euro Rallycross)	Karlskoga, Sweden		Volkswagen	Beetle 2.2 L	Porsche	F6		5
17-Aug	AUSTRIAN GP	Österreichring	5	JPS Lotus	72E	Ford Cosworth	V8		5
24-Aug	GP Suisse (non-ch F1)	Dijon-Prenois, France	5	JPS Lotus	72E	Ford Cosworth	V8		4
7-Sep	ITALIAN GP	Monza	5	JPS Lotus	72E	Ford Cosworth	V8	engine	DNF
5-Oct	USA GP	Watkins Glen	5	JPS Lotus	72E	Ford Cosworth	V8		5
1-Nov	Wynn's 1000km (Makes WC)	Kyalami, South Africa	25	BMW	3.0 CSL	BMW	6	with Hans-Joachim Stuck/ engine	DNF

1976

Date	Country/event	Circuit	No	Car	Model	Engine	Configuration	Notes	Result
25-Jan	BRAZILIAN GP	Interlagos	5	JPS Lotus	77	Ford Cosworth	V8	accident/ engine overheating	DNF
6-Mar	SOUTH AFRICAN GP	Kyalami	10	March	761	Ford Cosworth	V8	accident	DNF
28-Mar	USA West GP	Long Beach	10	March	761	Ford Cosworth	V8		10
11-Apr	Jim Clark Gedächtnisrennen (Euro F2)	Hockenheim, Germany	28	March	762	BMW	4	fuel pressure	DNF
2-May	SPANISH GP	Jarama	10	March	761	Ford Cosworth	V8	transmission	DNF
9-May	Silverstone 6-hours (Makes WC)	Silverstone, GB	1	BMW	3.0 CSL turbo	BMW	6	with Gunnar Nilsson/2nd on grid/ gearbox	DNF
16-May	BELGIAN GP	Zolder	10	March	761	Ford Cosworth	V8	accident	DNF
30-May	MONACO GP	Monte-Carlo	10	March	761	Ford Cosworth	V8	accident	DNF
13-Jun	SWEDISH GP	Anderstorp	10	March	761	Ford Cosworth	V8		7
27-Jun	Martha 6-hours (Makes WC)	Österreichring, Austria	15	BMW	3.0 CSL turbo	BMW	6	with Harald Grohs/ clutch	DNF
4-Jul	FRENCH GP	Paul Ricard	10	March	761	Ford Cosworth	V8	fuel metering unit	19DNF
10-Jul	Watkins Glen 6-hours (Makes WC)	Watkins Glen, USA	10	BMW	3.0 CSL turbo	BMW	6	with Dieter Quester	5
18-Jul	BRITISH GP	Brands Hatch	10	March	761	Ford Cosworth	V8	fuel pressure	DNF
1-Aug	GERMAN GP	Nürburgring	10	March	761	Ford Cosworth	V8	accident	DNF
15-Aug	AUSTRIAN GP	Österreichring	10	March	761	Ford Cosworth	V8		6
29-Aug	DUTCH GP	Zandvoort	10	March	761	Ford Cosworth	V8	pole position/ oil pressure	DNF
5-Sep	Dijon 6-hours (Makes WC)	Dijon-Prenois, France	21	BMW	3.0 CSL turbo	BMW	6	with Gunnar Nilsson/pole position/driveshaft	DNF
12-Sep	ITALIAN GP	Monza	10	March	761	Ford Cosworth	V8	fastest lap	1
3-Oct	CANADIAN GP	Mosport Park	10	March	761	Ford Cosworth	V8	2nd on grid	9
10-Oct	USA East GP	Watkins Glen	10	March	761	Ford Cosworth	V8	front suspension	DNF
24-Oct	JAPANESE GP	Fuji	10	March	761	Ford Cosworth	V8	engine	DNF
6-Nov	Kyalami 1000km (non-ch Sports)	Kyalami, South Africa		BMW	3.0 CSL turbo	BMW	6	with John Fitzpatrick/ fuel leak	DNF

1977

Date	Country/event	Circuit	No	Car	Model	Engine	Configuration	Notes	Result
9-Jan	ARGENTINEAN GP	Buenos Aires No.15	3	Tyrrell	P34	Ford Cosworth	V8	spin	DNF
23-Jan	BRAZILIAN GP	Interlagos	3	Tyrrell	P34	Ford Cosworth	V8	accident	DNF
5/6/02	Daytona 24-hours (Makes WC/IMSA)	Daytona, USA	2	BMW	320i	BMW	4	with David Hobbs & Sam Posey/ engine	DNF
5-Mar	SOUTH AFRICAN GP	Kyalami	3	Tyrrell	P34	Ford Cosworth	V8	fuel pressure	DNF
20-Mar	Race of Champions (non-ch F1)	Brands Hatch, GB	3	Tyrrell	P34	Ford Cosworth	V8	engine	10/DNF
27-Mar	300km Rennen (DRM)	Nürburgring, Germany	21	BMW	320i	BMW	4		3
3-Apr	USA West GP	Long Beach	3	Tyrrell	P34	Ford Cosworth	V8	fuel line	DNF
1-May	(DRM)	Nürburgring, Germany	21	BMW	320i	BMW	4		DNF
8-May	SPANISH GP	Jarama	3	Tyrrell	P34	Ford Cosworth	V8		8
15-May	Kosset 6-hours (Makes WC)	Silverstone, GB	51	BMW	320i	BMW	4	with Helmut Kelleners	4
22-May	MONACO GP	Monte-Carlo	3	Tyrrell	P34	Ford Cosworth	V8	brakes	DNF
5-Jun	BELGIAN GP	Zolder	3	Tyrrell	P34	Ford Cosworth	V8		3
19-Jun	SWEDISH GP	Anderstorp	3	Tyrrell	P34	Ford Cosworth	V8	ignition	DNF
3-Jul	FRENCH GP	Dijon-Prenois	3	Tyrrell	P34	Ford Cosworth	V8		12
9-Jul	Watkins Glen 6-hours (Makes WC)	Watkins Glen, USA	3	BMW	320i turbo	BMW	4	2nd on grid/ with David Hobbs/ accident	DNF
16-Jul	BRITISH GP	Silverstone	3	Tyrrell	P34	Ford Cosworth	V8	engine	DNF
31-Jul	GERMAN GP	Hockenheim	3	Tyrrell	P34	Ford Cosworth	V8	engine	9DNF
14-Aug	AUSTRIAN GP	Österreichring	3	Tyrrell	P34	Ford Cosworth	V8		5
20-Aug	6 hrs of Molson Diamond (Makes WC)	Mosport Park, Canada	2	BMW	320i turbo	BMW	4	with David Hobbs/ accident	DNF
28-Aug	DUTCH GP	Zandvoort	3	Tyrrell	P34	Ford Cosworth	V8	ignition	DNF
11-Sep	ITALIAN GP	Monza	3	Tyrrell	P34	Ford Cosworth	V8		6
25-Sep	Rivet Supply 6-hours (Makes WC)	Brands Hatch, GB	20	BMW	320i turbo	BMW	4	with Hans Stuck/ 2nd on grid/ accident	DNF
2-Oct	USA East GP	Watkins Glen	3	Tyrrell	P34	Ford Cosworth	V8	fastest lap	16
9-Oct	CANADIAN GP	Mosport Park	3	Tyrrell	P34	Ford Cosworth	V8	fuel leak	DNF
23-Oct	JAPANESE GP	Fuji	3	Tyrrell	P34	Ford Cosworth	V8	accident	DNF
5-Nov	Wynn's 1000km (non-ch Sports)	Kyalami, South Africa	11	BMW	320i turbo	BMW	4	with Hans Stuck/ gearbox in race 2	1 & DNF

1978

Date	Country/event	Circuit	No	Car	Model	Engine	Configuration	Notes	Result
15-Jan	ARGENTINEAN GP	Buenos Aires No.15	6	JPS Lotus	78	Ford Cosworth	V8		5
29-Jan	BRAZILIAN GP	Rio de Janeiro	6	JPS Lotus	78	Ford Cosworth	V8	pole position/ accident/ rear suspension	DNF
4/5/02	Daytona 24-hours (Makes WC/IMSA)	Daytona, USA	2	BMW	320i turbo	BMW	4	with David Hobbs/ piston	DNF
4-Mar	SOUTH AFRICAN GP	Kyalami	6	JPS Lotus	78	Ford Cosworth	V8		1
19-Mar	International Trophy (non-ch F1)	Silverstone, GB	6	JPS Lotus	78	Ford Cosworth	V8	pole position/ handling	DNF
2-Apr	USA West GP	Long Beach	6	JPS Lotus	78	Ford Cosworth	V8		4
30-Apr	Eifelrennen (DRM)	Nürburgring, Germany	17	BMW	320i turbo	BMW	4	accident in practice	DNS
7-May	MONACO GP	Monte-Carlo	6	JPS Lotus	78	Ford Cosworth	V8	gearbox	DNF
14-May	Silverstone 6-hours (Makes WC)	Silverstone, GB	38	BMW	320i turbo	BMW	4	with Hans-Joachim Stuck/ rear axle	DNF
21-May	BELGIAN GP	Zolder	6	JPS Lotus	78	Ford Cosworth	V8	fastest lap	2
28-May	Nürburgring 1000km (Makes WC)	Nürburgring, Germany	29	BMW	320i turbo	BMW	4	with Dieter Quester	7
4-Jun	SPANISH GP	Jarama	6	JPS Lotus	79	Ford Cosworth	V8	2nd on grid	2
17-Jun	SWEDISH GP	Anderstorp	6	JPS Lotus	79	Ford Cosworth	V8		3
2-Jul	FRENCH GP	Paul Ricard	6	JPS Lotus	79	Ford Cosworth	V8		2
8-Jul	Watkins Glen 6-hours (Makes WC)	Watkins Glen, USA	2	BMW	320i turbo	BMW	4	with David Hobbs/ valve	DNF
16-Jul	BRITISH GP	Brands Hatch	6	JPS Lotus	79	Ford Cosworth	V8	pole position/ fuel pump	DNF
30-Jul	GERMAN GP	Hockenheim	6	JPS Lotus	79	Ford Cosworth	V8	2nd on grid/ fastest lap/ gearbox	DNF
6-Aug	non-ch Sports)	Ring Knutstorp, Sweden	40	BMW	320i turbo	BMW	4	engine	DNF
13-Aug	AUSTRIAN GP	Österreichring	6	JPS Lotus	79	Ford Cosworth	V8	pole position/ fastest lap	1
27-Aug	DUTCH GP	Zandvoort	6	JPS Lotus	79	Ford Cosworth	V8	2nd on grid	2
3-Sep	Vallelunga 6-hours (Makes WC)	Vallelunga, Italy	2	BMW	320i turbo	BMW	4	with Hans-Joachim Stuck/ overheating	DNF
10-Sep	ITALIAN GP	Monza	6	JPS Lotus	78	Ford Cosworth	V8	fatal accident	DNF